REALISM, MEANING AND TRUTH

Second Edition

B

REALISM, MEANING AND TRUTH

Second Edition

Crispin Wright

BLACKWELL
Oxford UK & Cambridge USA

First edition first published 1987
Second edition first published 1993

Blackwell Publishers
108 Cowley Road
Oxford OX4 1JF
UK

238 Main Street
Suite 501
Cambridge, Massachusetts 02142
USA

British Library Cataloguing in Publication Data

A CIP catalogue record for this book is available from the British Library.

Library of Congress Cataloging-in-Publication Data
Wright, Crispin, 1942–
Realism, meaning, and truth / Crispin Wright. – 2nd ed.
p. cm.
Includes bibliographical references and index.
ISBN 0-631-17118-5 (pbk.)
1. Semantics (Philosophy) 2. Meaning (Philosophy) 3. Realism.
I. Title.
B840.W65 1993
121′.6 – dc20
92-19114
CIP

Typeset in 10/12pt Sabon by Best-set Typesetter Ltd., Hong Kong
Printed in Great Britain by TJ Press Ltd, Padstow, Cornwall

This book is printed on acid-free paper

For Michael Dummett

Contents

Preface to the Second Edition

I have added five further essays to the original collection. Two appear as new chapters 7 and 8 and are included in part I of the book concerning the 'negative programme'. 'Misconstruals Made Manifest' is a response to Simon Blackburn's 'Manifesting Realism' and first appeared alongside Blackburn's paper in volume 14 of *Midwest Studies in Philosophy*. It is devoted almost entirely to further elaboration of the 'Manifestation Challenge' in the light of Blackburn's criticisms of it, and forms a natural sequel to sections II and III of the Introduction. 'A Note on Two Realist Lines of Argument' responds to ideas concerning universal quantification and negation which have featured in the critique of semantic anti-realism developed in recent writings by Christopher Peacocke and dubbed 'manifestationism without verificationism' in chapter 1 of his *Thoughts*. It is here published for the first time.

Part II of the book contains the remaining three additions and offers something of an interlude, the essays concerning the 'positive programme' now being deferred to a new part III. Chapters 9 and 10 rework two recent papers on the Verification Principle: 'Scientific Realism, Observation and the Verification Principle', which first appeared in the festschrift edited by Graham Macdonald and myself for the half-centenary of the original publication of Freddie Ayer's *Language, Truth and Logic*, and 'The Verification Principle – Another Puncture, Another Patch', which appeared in *Mind* and responded to a difficulty found by David Lewis for the characterization of the Principle offered in the Ayer festschrift. These chapters do not contribute further to the 'negative programme' – the basic case against the realist conception of truth and meaning targeted by the kind of semantic anti-realism to which this book is devoted. But it is widely assumed both that semantic anti-realism is a version, or descendant, of the verificationism of the logical positivists, and that the association works to its discredit. So it seemed as well to include these essays, which serve to emphasize the differences between semantic anti-realism and logical positivism, as well as to show how the resources of Old Vienna are in any case greater than its critics have allowed, and to argue a new case for the importance of the Verification Principle to the debate about realism in natural science. Chapter 11, 'About "The Philosophical Significance of Gödel's Theorem": Some Issues', takes up an old controversy: the question whether Gödel's incompleteness theorems for arithmetic are at the service of a good argument against the idea that the cognitive capacities of the human mind are, in any interesting sense, mechanical and effects a connection between that debate and the attempt, challenged by Michael Dummett's 'The Philosophical Significance of Gödel's Theorem', to use the theorem to argue against the thesis that meaning must be exhaustively manifest in use.

I have tried to update the Bibliography to reflect some of the more interesting work on anti-realism published in the last six years. Considerations of manageability, however, have dictated that, apart from works actually referred to in the text, the new entries have been limited to writings bearing specifically on semantic (Dummettian) anti-realism, its relations to mathematical intuitionism and its bearing on classical logic. One cannot read everything and no doubt, even under this more restricted focus, some worthwhile contributions have been missed.

I have made no changes in the present edition to the original Introduction, although my perspective on the brief of the planned sequel, *Realism, Rules and Objectivity*, has altered in ways which supersede certain aspects of it. That project, as I now conceive it, will best be subdivided into a collection of papers on rule-following and 'objectivity of meaning' and a separate, self-contained treatment of a rather more variegated set of issues to do with 'objectivity of judgement' than anything I anticipated six years ago. Some of those issues were discussed in my Waynflete lectures given in Oxford in 1991 which have been published by Harvard University Press as *Truth and Objectivity*.

Among those to whom I would like to express my gratitude for discussion of and critical comment upon the new material are Ken Gemes, David Lewis, Bob Hale, John Foster, L. Jonathan Cohen, Stephen Yablo, Peter Mott and Christopher Peacocke. Thanks to Janet Kirk, Anne Cameron and Kyle Galloway for their usual efficient help in preparing the typescript and, once again, to Stig Rasmussen for invaluable work on the Index. The second edition has been completed during the invaluable opportunity for research and publication afforded by my tenure of a British Academy Research Readership.

St Andrews
March 1992

Preface and Acknowledgements to the First Edition

It is just over ten years since I wrote the first essay which appears in this book. At that time I had no intention of doing so much more work on the same topic, Michael Dummett's idea that a number of large and longstanding metaphysical disputes might best be treated by investigation of conflicting presuppositions about meaning. But one thing led to another, and this collection is one result. Because most of the essays were written as self-contained pieces, and none was written with its successors in mind, the organization of the whole is some distance from what I would impose if – were there but world enough and time – I was now attempting a new systematic treatment of the issues. One reason for including so extensive an Introduction was to try to explain, more sharply than would otherwise be likely to emerge, how I see the overall geography of the area, where on the map the concerns of the various essays should be located, and where further work is most needed.

The Introduction also attempts the more basic task of trying to explain what all the fuss has been about. I have tried to set down an outline of some of the causes of dissatisfaction with realist semantics which is both sufficiently straightforward to clarify them from scratch and sufficiently definite to persuade a sceptic that there is indeed a case to answer. This is not an easy task, and I do not know how well I have succeeded. For one thing the introductory ambition calls for over-simplifications which war with the justificatory one. But scepticism about the validity of the debate seems to have almost as many adherents as conviction of the correctness of realism. My book is aimed as much at such sceptics as at realism. Those who would believe that this kind of 'anti-realism' is merely a (British) eccentricity, fuelled by archaic epistemology, bad philosophy of mind and naive pre-Quinean thoughts about meaning, will be encouraged, I hope, to examine more fully than hitherto what basis there may be for thinking so.

It is one thing to believe, as I do, in the philosophical promise of investigating the connections between metaphysics and the philosophy of language. It is another to believe that metaphysical controversies in effect *are* controversies in the philosophy of language. And it is a third to hold what Dummett has urged, that to be a realist is to subscribe to the appropriateness of a certain sort of truth-conditional theory of meaning. My own belief is that the second and, as explained in the Introduction, the third are at most partial truths. But believing that is consistent, of course, with the view that the ideas which Dummett identifies with realism have the most wide-ranging philosophical significance in any case. It is this view which provides the focus and inspiration for this book. Other forms of connection between general metaphysics and the philosophy of language – the issues to do with rule-following and the objectivity of meaning which are so crucial to the philosophy of logic and the philosophy of mind, and the question of the general form of demarcation, if indeed there is one, between genuinely factual and 'projective' discourse – will assume centre stage in the sequel, *Realism, Rules and Objectivity*.

The Bibliography, compiled with Stig Rasmussen's help, mentions many works to which no reference occurs in the text. Our hope is that it provides a reasonably comprehensive and up-to-date compendium of the most interesting commentary on the issues. But the literature is now very extensive and it is more than likely that some useful contributions have been omitted. It will be unnecessary for me to disclaim the opinion that only those anti-anti-realists whose ideas I have attempted herein to address explicitly have said things worth trying to answer. But I especially regret that nothing is made in this volume of the thought of one of the most powerful allies of the cause. If this book were the systematic treatment which it is not, Hilary Putnam's work would take a very prominent place in it.

I cannot possibly acknowledge all those who, directly or indirectly, in conversation or by their writings, have influenced or assisted my thinking on these matters. A full list would certainly include James Hopkins, Samuel Guttenplan, Martin Davies, Dorothy Edgington, Roger Scruton, Brian Loar, Anthony Appiah, Peter Strawson, Bede Rundle, Simon Blackburn, Ian McFetridge, Elizabeth Fricker, Peter Hacker, Edward Craig, Graham McFee, Colin McGinn, Barry Smith, John Skorupski, Kit Fine, Stig Rasmussen, Andy Clark, Gordon Baker, Neil Tennant, Jens Ravnkilde, Jack Smart, Peter Carruthers, Donald Davidson, Charles Travis, Hilary Putnam, Catherine Wright, Hartry Field, Alan Weir, John Haldane and David Wiggins. I am indebted to them all. I took the opportunity to present much of the previously unpublished material herein to my graduate seminar at Princeton last autumn. It is not for me to say whether it has emerged stronger for the ordeal, but I am grateful to those who attended, and especially to Paul Benacerraf, Mark Johnston and David Lewis, for their vigorous criticisms. An older and very special debt is to the other members of a small discussion group, composed of Gareth Evans, John McDowell, Christopher Peacocke and me which met regularly in Oxford in 1976–8. We talked about nothing but realism and the theory of meaning. Evans insisted that detailed minutes were taken at every discussion. The result was an unusual continuity of focus and a sustained debate from which, I think, each of us learned far more about these questions than would have been likely otherwise. It is also a pleasure to acknowledge my more recent debt to my St Andrews colleagues, Stephen Read, Peter Clark and Leslie Stevenson, for many valuable criticisms and stimulating exchanges over the last few years.

The final typescript of the previously unpublished parts of the book was prepared at Princeton. I would like to thank Pearl Cavanaugh and her staff for their cheerful and efficient response to the additional demands which this work imposed on their heavily committed schedule. Let me here record my gratitude to Princeton for a most stimulating and enjoyable vist, to the Fulbright Commission for generous assistance with the costs entailed, and to St Andrews for allowing me Leave of Absence for the year.

My special thanks go to Stig Rasmussen for his work on the Index and Bibliography and to Kim Pickin and René Olivieri of Blackwell's for their unfailing patience, moral support and good will. It is a particular pleasure to produce a book for publishers with whom it is possible to deal as with friends.

It remains to record the greatest debt. When, as a third year undergraduate in Cambridge, it first occurred to me that postgraduate work in philosophy might not be a foolish notion, it was reading Michael Dummett's papers, 'Truth' and 'Wittgenstein's Philosophy of Mathematics', that convinced me of a line of research from which a thesis might eventually emerge. Subsequently he supervised me during the third and final year of my doctoral research, and we were, of course, colleagues at All Souls for nine years. It will hardly suffice to say that I have learned a great deal from him (indeed the extent of my heresies might provoke him to dispute it), or that my thinking about the questions with which this book is concerned is much influenced by his. The truth is simply that, but for his work, we would have hardly any conception of these fundamental questions. I do not know whether either 'realism' or 'anti-realism', in whatever form, can eventually expect to prevail. I do know that philosophical understanding is gained only by rising to philosophical challenges, and that Michael Dummett has invented some of the most fascinating challenges of twentieth-century analytical philosophy. My book is dedicated to him in admiration, gratitude and affection.

Origins of the Essays

'Truth-conditions and Criteria' was the second part of the symposium of that title which took place at the Joint Session of the Mind Association and the Aristotelian Society held at Warwick in 1976. Roger Scruton was the first symposiast. The essay originally appeared in *Proceedings of the Aristotelian Society*, Supplementary Volume L (1976). It is reprinted here by permission of the Aristotelian Society.

'Strawson on Anti-realism' was written in 1977, in response to the publication of the remarks of the Chairman at the 'Truth-conditions and Criteria' symposium. It originally appeared in *Synthese* 40 (1979), and in reprinted here by permission of D. Reidel Publishing Co.

'Realism, Truth-value Links, Other Minds and the Past' was written at the invitation of the organizers for the conference on the philosophy of language and logic held at Keele in April 1979. It was subsequently published in *Ratio* 22 (1980).

'Strict Finitism' was written in 1980 at Esa Saarinen's invitation for the special number of *Synthese* on realism (volume 51), which came out in 1982. It is reprinted here by permission of D. Reidel Publishing Co.

'Anti-realism, Timeless Truth and *Nineteen Eighty-Four*' was written in that year, and subsequently presented at the conference on the philosophy of language and logic held at Leicester in April 1985. It was first published in the original edition of this book.

'Theories of Meaning and Speakers' Knowledge' is a descendant of a paper written in 1981 at Edward Craig's invitation for a volume he planned to edit which never found a publisher. It was first published in the original edition of this book.

'Misconstruals Made Manifest' is a response to Simon Blackburn's 'Manifesting Realism' which he gave as a Nelson Lecture at the University of Michigan in 1988. It first appeared alongside Blackburn's paper in volume 14 of *Midwest Studies in Philosophy* in 1989 and is reprinted here, with slight emendations, by permission of the University of Notre Dame Press.

'A Note on Two Realist Lines of Argument' responds to two aspects of the critique of semantic anti-realism developed in recent writings of Christopher Peacocke. It is here published for the first time.

'Scientific Realism, Observation and Verificationism' reworks part of my 'Scientific Realism, Observation and the Verification Principle' which was published in 1987 in *Fact, Science and Morality*, the festschrift for the half-centenary of the first publication of A. J. Ayer's *Language, Truth and Logic*. It is here published for the first time in its present form.

'The Verification Principle' stitches together the remaining part of 'Scientific Realism, Observation and the Verification Principle' with the discussion of 'The Verification Principle – Another Puncture, Another Patch', which appeared in *Mind* in 1989. It is here published for the first time in its present form.

'About "The Philosophical Significance of Gödel's Theorem": Some Issues' was written for the conference on the philosophy of Michael Dummett held at Mussomeli in Sicily in September 1991. It is pledged to the volume that is to issue from that conference and is published here with the kind consent of the organizers.

'Anti-realist Semantics: The Role of Criteria' was written in 1978 for the Royal Institute of Philosophy's lecture series on 'Idealism: Past and Present'. It was subsequently published in the volume of that title brought out in a supplement to the journal *Philosophy* in 1982, and is here reprinted with the permission of Cambridge University Press.

'Second Thoughts about Criteria' was written in 1982 for a special number of *Synthese* (volume 58, 1984), edited by myself, on Wittgenstein's later philosophy. It is reprinted here by permission of D. Reidel Publishing Co.

'Can a Davidsonian Meaning-theory be Construed in Terms of Assertibility?' is a descendant of a paper written in 1983 in response to

Anthony Appiah's 'Anti-Realism Unrealized' which was published in the *Philosophical Quarterly* a year later.

'Anti-realism and Revisionism' is almost all of my critical study of Michael Dummett's *Truth and Other Enigmas* which appeared as 'Dummett and Revisionism' in the *Philosophical Quarterly* 31 (1981). It is reprinted here with the permission of the Editors.

'Realism, Bivalence and Classical Logic' was originally written in 1982 in response to Stig Rasmussen's and Jens Ravnkilde's 'Realism and Logic' which was published in *Synthese* 52 (1982). It was first published in the original edition of this book.

Introduction

I
Kinds of Realism

Philosophy in the Western tradition is an essentially critical discipline, so it is unsurprising that its historical record is one of sustained self-criticism. Philosophers of every period have selectively dismissed the methods and objectives of their predecessors. Hence none of us can prophesy with confidence how future philosophers will appraise the preoccupations and accomplishments of the analytical tradition in the middle-to-late twentieth century. Yet there is reason to anticipate that some at least of our preoccupations will find favour (whether or not our accomplishments are found wanting). A safe example is surely provided by the recent and contemporary debate about philosophical realism. If anything is distinctive of philosophical enquiry, it is the attempt to understand the relation between human thought and the world. The project is constitutive of metaphysics. While undergoing shifts of interpretation, it nevertheless supplies a dominant motif in the writings of all the great philosophers of the past. Realism simply supplies by far the most natural, pre-philosophically agreeable conclusion which this project could have. If our successors come to reject not the details but the very issue of the contemporary debate concerning realism, it will be because they have rejected philosophy itself.

Realism is a mixture of modesty and presumption. It modestly allows that humankind confronts an objective world, something almost entirely not of our making, possessing a host of occasional features which may pass altogether unnoticed by human consciousness and whose innermost nomological secrets may remain forever hidden from us. However, it presumes that we are, by and large and in favourable circumstances, capable of acquiring knowledge of the world and of understanding it. Two sorts of ability are thereby credited to us: the ability to form the right concepts for the classification of genuine, objective features of the world;

and the ability to come to know, or at least reasonably to believe, true statements about the world whose expression those concepts make possible. Even this much presumption tends, indeed, to be qualified. It is not a common theme in the writings of modern philosophical realists that the world can transcend our concept-forming powers, may exemplify features which human thought is essentially incapable of comprehending – though it is of course a prominent theme in theology. What is a common thought is that the range of states of affairs for whose description our concept-forming powers are adequate at best contingently coincides with, and may very well be more inclusive than the range which is subject to our knowledge-acquiring powers: in short, that some true statements which are fully intelligible to us may nevertheless be, as the point is widely expressed, evidence-transcendent.

The natural antagonists of realism, sketchily thus characterized, are scepticism and idealism. Scepticism represents a slide towards the pole of modesty. The sceptic agrees with the realist that our investigative efforts confront an autonomous world, that there are truths not of our making. But he disputes that there is ultimately any adequate warrant for regarding our routine investigative practices as apt to issue in knowledge of, or reasonable belief about the world. In more radical moments, indeed, the sceptic disputes that we have any reasonable basis for our confidence that we can so much as conceptualize the world as it really is. The distinguishing mark of the idealist, by contrast, is a more thoroughgoing presumption. In his view realism is founded on a misunderstanding of the nature of truth. It is an error to think of our investigations as confronting an objective array of states of affairs which are altogether independent of our modes of conceiving and investigative enterprises. No truth is altogether 'not of our making'. Rather reality is – on one version – a reification of our own conceptual and cognitive nature, with no more claim to autonomy than a mirror image. There is, accordingly, no possibility of states of affairs which outstrip our capacities for knowledge, still less transcend our understanding.

Anti-realism is simply opposition to realism. The foregoing suggests that any standpoint of appropriately sceptical or idealist persuasion could deserve the label 'anti-realist'. The fact that there is no tradition of so describing scepticism is owing entirely to Professor Dummett's introduction of 'anti-realism' into philosophical currency as denoting a kind of reservation about realism which would seem to belong, at least when viewed superficially, on the idealist wing. However, the depiction of Dummett's anti-realist as a kind of latter-day idealist oversimplifies in at least two important respects. First, the modern dispute is *many* disputes, each conducted with respect to a specific, restricted region of discourse. True, the best of the anti-realist arguments have a generality which makes it hard to see how they could succeed anywhere unless successful everywhere. But if it were decided that the anti-realist arguments were wanting in cogency when taken absolutely globally, that would not absolve the realist from the need to make the case for his preferred interpretation piecemeal. And it has to be anticipated that various regions of discourse may afford varying degrees of success to the attempt to do so. The traditional opposition between realism and idealism, on the other hand, is one, global dispute. Moreover, Dummett's anti-realist makes his complaint about the realist interpretation of certain statements by contrast with the situation of other statements – 'effectively decidable' statements – about which he has no quarrel with the realist view. For the traditional idealist, in contrast, the realist *totally* misconceives the nature of truth; there is no area of discourse – at least about public, external matters – of which a realist interpretation would be unobjectionable from an idealist point of view.

Second and more important, however, it is open to question whether modern anti-realism actually takes issue with realism on any point which marks a realist/idealist watershed. For the focal point of the debate, over the past 25 years or so, has been the realist's idea that our depictive powers may outstrip our cognitive capacities, that truth may intelligibly transcend evidence. Not that this is not an extremely important issue. Leading philosophical traditions in, for instance, the philosophies of mathematics and of mind, are founded on the conviction that truth may properly be so conceived. But, on the face of it at least, there is no immediate route from denying that conviction to denial of what seems essential to realism, as characterized above. What seems essential is the conception of truth as constituted by *fit* between our beliefs, or statements, and the features of an independent, determinate reality. One way of making this conception more concrete is indeed to hold that the world may be determinate in thinkable, describable, but unascertainable ways. But it is very far from obvious that such is the only way, that only by allowing that truth can transcend evidence can substance be given to the idea that truth is not in general of our creation but is constituted by correspondence with autonomous states of affairs. That opinion would have the consequence that, when restricted to the domain of states of affairs over which human cognitive powers *are* sovereign, the thesis of realism would have no content – yet that is precisely the domain where, intuitively, it ought to seem least problematic, and it is where Dummett's anti-realist, at least, proposes to leave it alone.

Any attempt to lay down what is essential to realism is liable to provoke opposition from at least some self-supposed realists. The fact is that realism, as implicitly characterized by the opinions of writers, in whatever area of philosophy, who regard themselves as realists, is a syndrome, a loose weave of separable presuppositions and attitudes. What have the mathematical platonist, the moral objectivist, and the scientific realist in common? In Dummett's writings, the cardinal realist thesis is that of the unrestricted acceptability of the principle of Bivalence, that every statement – so long as it is not too vague – is determinately either true or false. Undeniably this is an important element in the thought of many realists about pure mathematics. It is an expression of a certain conception of mathematical proof – that proof is, as it were, a mere cognitive auxiliary whereby finite, if ingenious, minds may sometimes gain access to infinitary states of affairs – coupled with the conviction that there is in our mathematical thinking no vagueness of the kind that can generate indeterminacy of truth-value elsewhere. Vagueness is, however, a pervasive and, arguably, an ineliminable feature of the greater part of our non-mathematical discourse. To suggest that Bivalence is, or should be the hallmark of realism everywhere is accordingly to be committed to claiming either that there is no such thing as realism about vague discourse, or that the vagueness of a statement, whatever exactly it is held to consist in, is a feature consistent with its possession of a determinate truth-value. Neither suggestion is remotely plausible. The obvious response would be to suggest that Bivalence is merely the natural form for an acceptance of the possibility of evidence-transcendent truth to take when we are concerned with statements which are not vague; and that it is, accordingly, the status of such a conception of truth which Dummett's proposal, generalized, would make the crucial issue.

Certainly, as noted, much of the literature has proceeded on the assumption that this is the crucial issue. But must the scientific realist, for instance, allow the notion of truth appropriate to scientific theories to be, at least potentially, an evidence-transcendent one? A definitive answer is far from easy. Scientific realism is best characterized as the view that the physical world has depths and dimensions for whose description the methods of concept-formation distinctive of theoretical science are indispensable, and for whose cognition we are reliant upon scientific method. This is a characterization which ought to be acceptable in advance of resolving problems concerning the demarcation of theoretical concepts and the proper characterization of rational scientific method. Its aim is merely to catch the conviction that the whole truth about the material world cannot be captured in language which could defensibly be regarded as 'observational', but may nevertheless be approached by optimum scientific methodology. To abandon the first claim is to move in the direction of instrumentalism or reductionism, while to reject the second is to embrace an extensive scepticism. Now, the question whether a scientific realist must accept the possibility of evidence-transcendent scientific truth is just the question whether he ought to allow that even the most refined experimental techniques and methodology may yet be too coarse to discern all the articulation and variety which our world possesses. There is of course a famous thesis, that of the Underdetermination of Theory by Empirical Data, which has been much discussed in connection with Quine's arguments for the indeterminacy of translation and which, if sustained, might drive a scientific realist in this direction. But it is controversial whether it should be sustained, at least in full generality. Here is not the place to attempt to review the issues. I merely record the opinion that it is a philosophical problem whether the scientific realist is compelled, by the Underdetermination Thesis or by some other considerations, to allow that certain truths about the physical world may resist the most refined scientific investigation. Accordingly, it cannot be satisfactory to characterize the issue between scientific realism and its opponents as concerning *ab initio* the possibility of evidence-transcendent truth. As for the issue between moral objectivists and others, I doubt if the idea that moral reality might somehow transcend our moral sensitivities would be at all congenial to most of the former.

Anyone who wants to generalize about realist/anti-realist disputes will do well to recognize three distinct species of objectivity. To hold that a class of statements may be fully intelligible to us although resolving their truth-values may defeat our cognitive powers (even when idealized), may naturally be described as believing in the *objectivity of truth*. For such statements, truth is not 'of our making' precisely because it may defy our powers of rational appraisal. However, truth-values cannot be settled unilaterally, as it were, by the world alone but are a function simultaneously of the meanings of the statements to which they attach. So much is a platitude, partially constitutive of the notion of meaning. But it is easy and widely customary to read into this platitude a certain conception of the *objectivity of meaning*: the notion that the meaning of a statement is a real constraint, to which we are bound, as it were, by contract, and to which verdicts about its truth-value may objectively conform, or fail to conform, quite independently of our considered opinion on the matter. The objectivity of meaning is a manifest implication of the objectivity of truth. If statements of certain sorts can be undetectably true, then we have no alternative but to think of their meanings as, so to speak, reaching into regions where we cannot follow: there is *already* a verdict about the truth-value of such a statement which – if it is intelligible to suppose that our cognitive powers could be appropriately extended – our present understanding of its constituents and syntax would oblige us to give once we had investigated matters properly. The converse implication, on the other hand, is by no means immediate. The objectivity of meaning, even characterized thus far, is something which we naturally endorse for decidable statements. Presented, for instance, with an elementary computational problem in arithmetic, we think there is already an answer which fidelity to our understanding of the concepts involved in its formulation obliges us to give. I have suggested elsewhere[1] that some at least of the usual grounds for suspicion of evidence-transcendent truth ought to generate qualms about the objectivity of meaning also. If that is correct, then there may be no stable philosophical position which, while accepting the objectivity of meaning generally, disavows the objectivity of truth. But, however that may be, the concepts are distinct, since the objectivity of meaning raises a philosophical question in the case of decidable but so far undecided statements, whereas the objectivity of truth does not.

These remarks, I am well aware, leave a good deal to be desired in point of precision, and a great many issues to be explored. Can the notion of meaning survive at all if the objectivity of meaning is rejected? If so, what is the proper construal of the normativity of meaning? Is the 'contractual' picture utterly misguided? Again, though, this is not the place to attempt to pursue such matters. The issues arising are those which take centre stage in Wittgenstein's recurrent discussions of the topic of following a rule in his later philosophy and in much recent commentary on his work. They are issues of great delicacy and philosophical importance. Here I wish only to suggest that, however exactly its content should be characterized, there is such a thing as belief in the objectivity of meaning which should be distinguished from belief in the objectivity of truth, and which is a yet more pervasive and perhaps more important element in realist habits of thought about various regions of discourse.

The third notion of objectivity is (what I propose to call) the *objectivity of judgement*: the kind of objectivity which statements have when they are apt to record, or misrecord features of the real world – features which would be appreciable by any creature possessed of appropriate cognitive powers, whatever its emotional capacities or affective dispositions. Objective judgements are those with a 'genuinely factual' subject matter. Once again, this is a largely unhelpful characterization, notoriously difficult to improve on. But all over philosophy there has been a repeated urge to attempt to draw some such distinction and to counsel against the unwitting assumption that every kind of discourse – moral, mathematical, scientific-theoretical, etc. – which seems to harbour the making of genuine statements, and so to call for a corresponding species of worldly states of affairs, has to be regarded as doing so. Hume famously denied that statements about causation are objective in this sense. Kripke has recently interpreted Wittgenstein's discussion of rule-following as arguing against the objectivity of judgement of discourse concerning meaning and cognate concepts.

1 See my *Wittgenstein on the Foundations of Mathematics*, chapter XI, section 7, and chapter XII, section 1.

Emotivism and its more sophisticated, contemporary Humean descendants dispute the objectivity of moral judgement. Instrumentalists dispute the objectivity of theoretical judgements in science. And the motivating spirit behind the formalism which Frege attacked was, presumably, an inchoate mistrust of the attribution of objectivity of judgement to pure mathematical statements.

Once again, there is an evident implication from objectivity of truth to objectivity of judgement: no one can coherently believe that the world is apt to confer potentially evidence-transcendent truth-values upon statements of a certain genre who does not believe that the world contains states of affairs of a kind appropriate to that genre. And once again the converse implication, at least in full generality, would seem to be at least unobvious. There is no reason evident in advance why the best analysis of what it is for statements to have a 'genuinely factual' subject-matter would have to involve the possibility of their being undetectably true or false. Such a result would be surprising and unwelcome, entailing that decidable statements could not qualify for objectivity of judgement. Admittedly, the question remains whether an anti-realist account can be given of what it is to accept objectivity of judgement for kinds of statements which are not effectively decidable and for which our working notion of truth does appear to be (potentially) verification-transcendent. I believe such an account can be given, but I must defer defence of that claim to another occasion.

The objectivity of truth, then, incorporates both the objectivity of meaning and the objectivity of judgement, but apparently exceeds their union. So the notions may be arrayed in order of strength if objectivity of meaning implies objectivity of judgement but not conversely. The first condition might seem a triviality. A believer in the objectivity of meaning of a certain class of statements will hold that their meanings, in conjunction with appropriate states of the world, can determine their truth-values independently and in advance of any opinions we may form. So the kind of contribution from the world which the objectivity of judgement requires is built into the account of what, roughly, a believer in the objectivity of meaning believes. However, matters are probably not so straightforward. Those who have held, for instance, that certain sorts of aesthetic judgement have no genuinely factual subject-matter have not meant to suggest that the statements which express them have no meaning or, equivalently, that there are no constraints on their proper use. So, on the surface anyway, there ought to be scope for a position which views those constraints after the fashion of a believer in the objectivity of meaning generally, but disputes that they are constraints on the truth-values assumed by genuine statements, expressing objective judgements. More generally: one would expect the issue of objectivity of meaning to arise with respect to utterances of every illocutionary force, not just assertion.

Conversely, it is unclear that someone who globally rejected the objectivity of meaning would have to regard any dispute about the factual character of some region of discourse as empty. Rejection of the objectivity of meaning might take a variety of forms: at one pole, no more might be involved than re-explanation of the normativity of meaning and some distancing from the contractual picture; at the other pole, no less might be involved than the utter rejection of the notion of meaning which followers of Quine have sometimes urged. It is notable that Quine himself has displayed no sense of a tension between this recommendation and a staunchly realist outlook towards scientific theory. Dubiously consistent as that position may be, the clarification of the relations between objectivity of meaning and objectivity of judgement must await a much more refined account of both notions.

Our immediate purpose, however, is merely geographical. What sort of map of the controversies between realism and its opponents do these distinctions suggest? One fairly immediate reflection, prefigured above, is that in a very significant class of cases the primary locus of dispute has been not objectivity of truth but objectivity of judgement. Such has been the character of the debate in ethics, aesthetics, and – in part anyway – in the philosophy of science. Second, it is evident that what has been at issue in another important class of cases is not any kind of objectivity but rather the *irreducibility* of a class of statements (whose suitability for making objective judgements is accepted on both sides). Thus run the disputes between materialists and phenomenalists about the external world, between behaviourism about mental states and its very various opponents, and the (now defunct) issue between scientific realists and those philosophers who, like Carnap, hoped to see a reduction of theoretical terms to some more purely observational, epistemologically favoured vocabulary. Third, the objectivity of meaning has been perceived for the issue it is only comparatively recently, and in very different ways, by Wittgenstein and Quine. To Wittgenstein belongs credit for the original perception that the notion is pivotal in the philosophy of mathematics and in our philosophical understanding of proof, logical necessity and the a priori in general, and that the issues concerning it cannot be separated from the project of a proper philosophical account of the notion of intention and its cognates; so that fundamental issues in the philosophy of logic and the philosophy of mind and action have to be engaged simultaneously. Much of the *Philosophical Investigations*, as I read it, is an attempt to do that.

A criticism sometimes levelled against Dummett's interpretation of realism as endorsement of a truth-conditional conception of meaning, married to a bivalent or evidence-transcendent notion of truth, is that it gives us no purchase on the *ontological* disputes in which positions styled as 'realist' have traditionally figured. The obvious modern example is the dispute between platonists and nominalists concerning the reality of the abstract objects of pure mathematics. The substance of the complaint seems to me to be correct.[2] A platonist about the natural numbers, to take the simplest example, suffers no evident commitment to the view that the proper interpretation of number-theoretic statements is realist in Dummett's sense; conversely, someone who endorsed the latter view would have kept his hands free for, for instance, the sort of reductionist rummagings which suspicion of abstract objects has so frequently provoked. The reality of mathematical objects and the objectivity of mathematical truth are indeed quite separate issues. If Kreisel's often quoted remark is taken to imply that the issues are the same, or that the ontological issue is uninteresting, then I think it mistaken. The same is not true, however, if the objectivity it concerns is the objectivity of mathematical judgement. If we believe that number theory deals in objective judgements, there is a powerful case for saying that the question whether numbers 'really' exist is intelligible only as raising the pair of questions whether the syntax of at least some number-theoretic statements is such that they could not be true unless numbers existed, and whether some of these number theoretic statements are indeed, by ordinary criteria, true. The matter is one of delicacy. But if this proposal, argued for in my *Frege's Conception of Numbers as Objects*, is defensible, it will allow generalization. Realism about theoretical entities, for instance, will amount to the view that theoretical statements possess objectivity of judgement, that a sub-class of such statements involve devices functioning as quantifiers or singular terms in such a way that they cannot be true unless there are such entities, and that some members of the sub-class are indeed true. It is, of course, the second claim which is typically disputed, by reductionism and nominalism, in the philosophy of mathematics. In the philosophy of science, the even more pessimistic prospects of reductionism, and the inapplicability of any programme comparable to nominalism, have tended to mould scepticism about theoretical entities into a doubt about objectivity of judgement.

Dummett's interpretation of realism, and the kind of general anti-realist criticism of it which he presents, are put forward by way of a recommended *Übersicht* of a significant class of disputes in traditional and modern philosophy. Part of the interest of his ideas is precisely their promise of heightening our understanding of what is really at issue in these disputes, of how they should be conducted, and – most appealingly of all – of helping

2 For a recent response to it by Dummett himself, see chapter 20 of his *The Interpretation of Frege's Philosophy*.

us see who, if anyone, should win. But the map just sketched suggests that the apparatus necessary to describe the points of contact and analogy, as well as the differences, between the various realist/anti-realist issues in different parts of philosophy will have to be more complex. The debates do indeed often concern some notion of objectivity; but objectivity is a multi-faceted concept with no promise of analysis purely in terms of evidence-transcendent truth.

We should recognize, nevertheless, that issues are widespread in philosophy in which the objectivity of truth does provide a focal point. It is the crux of the debate between platonism and intuitionism in the philosophy of mathematics. For the intuitionist, the truth of a mathematical statement can only consist in the availability of a proof of it or, in a more radical version, in our actually possessing a proof. For the platonist, as noted, proof is typically an indirect method, as it were, whereby infinitary states of affairs can impinge on finite minds; there is no question of such states of affairs *consisting* in the possibility, or our actual possession, of a proof. It might seem that generalizing the intuitionistic attitude would now require that truth in general consists in the availability, or in our actual possession, of grounds for holding a statement true. But such an account of truth would overlook the defeasibility of many of our standard types of ground for making assertions. The essential point is rather that, for the platonist, it is perfectly coherent to entertain the idea of a mathematical statement's being undecidably true – true although no ground for asserting it can be devised. That is what should be generalized. To treat truth as evidence-transcendent is to hold that the bare supposition that a statement is true need not, in general, involve any commitment to what can be known or reasonably believed. The intuitionistic attitude, generalized, is that an ascription of truth to a statement – even if it is merely a hypothesis – entails the availability of grounds for believing it.

The extent of our investment, both philosophically and pre-philosophically, in objective truth is very great. It is a cornerstone of the Cartesian philosophy of mind, which still tends to pass for common sense in non-philosophical circles. On this view, the sensations, moods, emotions, beliefs, desires and intentions of a subject are available to others only via (linguistic or non-linguistic) behavioural proxies; the states themselves, though introspectible by the subject, are strictly inaccessible to everyone else. Accordingly, the kind of state of affairs which confers truth upon the description of some aspect of someone else's mental state and the kind of state of affairs which, as ordinarily conceived, would constitute evidence for that description are quite different, independent states of affairs. There can be no entailment from the existence of one to the existence of the other, any more than a viral infection of the liver could logically entail that the sufferer would display some characteristic set of symptoms. That is just to say that, from each person's point of view, the notion of truth appropriate to descriptions of others' mental states has to be objective, potentially evidence-transcendent truth.

The most immediate difference between platonism about pure mathematics and Cartesianism about minds is that a mathematical proof, even as conceived by the platonist, makes available to the subject the very state of affairs which makes a proved statement true whereas, on the Cartesian view, nothing can do that for the state of affairs which renders true a statement about another's mental state. The epistemology of other minds is thus represented as founded upon the assumption of certain correlations between event-types, detectable in one's own case but inscrutable in the case of everyone else. There is no corresponding assumption in the platonist epistemology of mathematics (which, admittedly, has other problems enough). This renders the Cartesian philosophy of mind open to a very direct form of sceptical attack; simply, what possible reason could anyone have for thinking that such correlations hold generally – that, in so far as they seem to be borne out in one's own experience, the latter is not utterly idiosyncratic?

Scepticism, not just about other minds but about the material world, the past, induction – indeed of all the traditional varieties – is another major area of philosophical concern on which an investigation into the propriety of objective truth can be expected to shed light. Certainly light is still wanted; the notion is not unusual, at least among contemporary British philosophers, that, since Wittgenstein, we have somehow gone past or seen through the traditional epistemological problems.[3] This seems to me to be quite untrue. There is, rightly, no consensus about how best the sceptic's challenges should be formulated or about the resources which we should deploy against them. We should beware, however, of assuming that a verdict for or against the objectivity of truth would bear on scepticism in any very straightforward way. Certainly the *conclusion* of the sceptic's argument is always that the truth of statements in a certain class, so far from entailing the availability of evidence for their truth, is absolutely inscrutable. So if a successful anti-realist challenge can be mounted against objective truth, it will be successful against the conclusions of such arguments too. That, however, would not represent very much progress, since the sceptic's conclusions are manifestly unacceptable anyway. We need to do a lot more than *refute* the sceptic (though it would be something). As with all philosophical paradoxes, what is needed is insight and diagnosis. In particular, we need to determine whether the sceptic's best arguments must somehow presuppose the objectivity of truth or whether they are, in effect, arguments for it. I am of the opinion that some

3 A corresponding notion, minus the nod to Wittgenstein, is not unusual in America.

challenging forms of sceptical argument neither presuppose Dummettian realism nor, if sustained, drive us towards it. But the point which is worth emphasis now is merely that a reasoned global verdict on the objectivity of truth, or a set of local verdicts should no global verdict prove defensible, is certainly going to be an indispensable part of the progress on traditional epistemological problems which we still need to make.

It is in these three areas, the philosophy of mathematics, the philosophy of mind and general epistemology, that a proper appraisal of the objectivity of truth seems to me to be of the most certain importance. However, there are further possibilities which are worth emphasis. First, although it was suggested above that a scientific realist is not *eo ipso* a believer in the objectivity of truth, a demonstration that the Underdetermination Thesis did indeed hold globally (in some suitably non-trivial form) would foreclose the other options. For then a true scientific theory could never be empirically distinguished, no matter how refined the methods employed, from some false theory which joined with it to make an underdetermined pair. The belief that the theoretical statements of science are objective judgements will not cohere with the Underdetermination Thesis unless the objectivity of truth is defensible for them.

One other area in which issues concerning the objectivity of truth are of possibly crucial importance is the philosophy of time, and especially the interpretation of statements concerning the past. What makes it true, if it is true, that James II suffered a migraine on the afternoon of his 32nd birthday? The answer could hardly be other than: the state of affairs which then obtained. But that such a state of affairs obtained then, in 1665, can hardly entail the existence of any recognizable causal traces of it now. And such traces, including memory and testimony, are all that can constitute grounds for asserting any of a very wide class of statements about the past. (The exceptions are either known a priori or are projections back from well-entrenched scientific theory.) The truth of statements about the past does not in general entail the availability of evidence for their truth; it is therefore objective truth.

The significance of this simple train of thought is qualified, however, by the realization that it gives the idea of evidence being *available* a distinctive gloss which someone who is suspicious of objective truth as it figures in mathematical platonism, Cartesianism, traditional scepticism and (perhaps) scientific realism, need not obviously endorse. The gloss, of course, is temporal: if our ordinary view of statements concerning the past implicitly subscribes to the objectivity of truth, then the contrary view is being interpreted as requiring that truth requires more than the *sometime* availability of evidence. It is another question, of course, whether the kind of arguments which anti-realists proffer for mistrust of objective truth can be assuaged by yoking the concept of truth to the sometime-availability of evidence. I myself doubt if they can. But that is a doubt that needs to be justified before our ordinary conception of the past can be put at stake with the objectivity of truth in general.

II
Acquisition and Manifestation

Why should exception be taken to dissociating the truth of a statement from the availability of evidence for it? Two arguments in particular have been prominent in recent literature. I shall comment briefly on each of them.

The first, the so-called 'acquisition argument', belongs to a familiarly empiricist tradition. How are we supposed to be able to *form* any understanding of what it is for a particular statement to be true if the kind of state of affairs which it would take to make it true is conceived, *ex hypothesi*, as something beyond our experience, something which we cannot confirm and which is insulated from any distinctive impact on our consciousness? Obviously such a conception cannot be bestowed ostensively. And the challenge is simply declined if the answer is offered, 'by description'. For it is of our ability to form an understanding of precisely such a description that an account is being demanded; there could be no better description of the relevant kind of state of affairs than the very statement in question.

This is a pleasantly simple line of argument. In response, there may be an inclination to press a distinction between statements whose very content seems to guarantee their undecidability and the much wider class of statements whose truth, as we ordinarily conceive it, is indeed not guaranteed to be testable but is nevertheless often so. The statement-types of which anti-realists find the realist interpretation problematic – contingent unrestricted generalizations, statements about remote regions of space and time, statements about the conscious states of others, certain sorts of subjunctive conditional, and so on – tend to come in the latter category. Examples of the former kind, on the other hand, seem to be harder to conjure; old campaigners like 'Everything is uniformly increasing in size' and the inverted spectrum suggest themselves for consideration, but perhaps not many more. I suspect that a good number of people would feel uneasy about the realist interpretation of such absolutely unconfirmable statements without seeing themselves pressured towards doubts on anything like the scale of modern anti-realism. And a possible motivation for this attitude would be the thought that, where the truth of a statement need not but nevertheless *may* be reflected in available evidence, such evidence can form the basis on which an understanding of the truth-condition of the statement can be formed; whereas when the statement is guaranteed unconfirmable, no such basis is provided.

This is not a very coherent train of thought. It requires, to begin with, some work on the distinction between *verifiability*, in a strict sense, and the mere availability of (defeasible) evidence. The former should consist in the availability to investigation of a state of affairs of the very kind which constitutes the truth-condition of a statement; the latter in the availability of a different state of affairs which is taken to be a dependable indication that the truth-condition obtains. I suggest that it should seem quite unclear now evidence of this latter sort could provide the basis for forming an understanding of the truth-condition itself – confrontation with camels is not a good route to grasp of the concept of an antelope. But, second, even in cases where it is the truth-conferring state of affairs itself which is sometimes open to view, it remains unclear how acquaintance with it is supposed to induce a conception of how the *very same* kind of state of affairs can obtain without any detectable indication. How can explanations which concentrate on the case where statements of a certain kind are verified contain the resources to communicate an understanding of the quite different kind of case when those very same statements would be undetectably true?[4]

It is in fact just an oversight to suppose that, on a realist view, examples of absolutely unconfirmable statements remain a fairly rarified class. Whenever S is a statement of a kind whose truth, as conceived by the realist, may sometimes but need not in general be determinable, 'S is undetectably true' will constitute such an example. And it is only if the truth conditions of *this* statement are understood that the contingent tie between S's truth and the availability of evidence, essential to the realist's interpretation of it, has been grasped. We should learn two simple lessons. First, the intuition which would give best to the acquisition argument as far as guaranteed unconfirmable statements are concerned but would dispute the issue for, if I may so describe them, maybe-confirmable statements is unstable. Second, and more general, the anti-realist ought to grant no significance whatever to that distinction: a realist interpretation of maybe-unconfirmable statements stands or falls with the realist interpretation of guaranteed unconfirmable statements.

How best should this acquisition argument be responded to? There are various further likely responses, of varying degrees of force. One would be a reminder of the problems which empiricist accounts of concept-formation have always encountered with ideas which involve an element of

4 This thought is the nerve of the response to John McDowell's 'On "The Reality of the Past"' given in Essay 3. Compare the transition from good-humoured faces to the idea of an 'invisible smile'.

idealization. For instance, probably none of us has ever encountered a perfect circle. Even if we have, there is certainly no experience distinctive of such an object; there is no discernible difference between a perfect circle and one which is merely almost so. The same holds for the distinction between globally Euclidean space and space which is merely locally Euclidean with respect to a very large locality. (That is one reason why phenomenal geometry is *not* Euclidean.)[5] Yet do we not understand well enough the notion of a perfect circle, or of Euclidean space? If a theory of concept-formation is presented which calls the good standing of these notions into question, would it not be better to query the credibility of the theory? Well, perhaps. But although the notion of idealization is undoubtedly something of a blunt instrument, there is nevertheless no obvious way of utilizing it to mount a defence of the realist conception of truth. Perfect circularity, and perfect Euclideanism, are states to which ordinary measurable objects may approximate. A diagram on paper may be more or less circular, the measured properties of a large region of space more or less Euclidean. The kind of idealization involved in the notion of perfect circularity, or perfect Euclideanism, corresponds to a movement to the limit of a scale, as it were, whose intermediate values are ordered by a comparative – 'is more circular than' and 'is more Euclidean than'. Now, whether this type of concept-formation should be admissible from an empiricist point of view is not the issue. What is more to our purpose is that this is evidently quite the wrong scenario to bring to bear upon the concept – if there is indeed any such concept – of truth as understood by the realist. There is no germane comparative: no being more or less undetectably true. Movement to this concept is not movement down a scale, in a direction which is grounded and given content by empirically detectable differences. Objective truth is not in that way a limit concept, and the movement to it, to the extent that it is illuminated by concentration on such examples, is shown up for a leap in the dark.

It seems to me open to doubt, though, whether, unsupplemented, these thoughts about concept-acquisition can show very much. Really they are better described as a 'challenge'. In order to be more than a challenge, they would need the backing of a proven theory of concept-formation of a broadly empiricist sort. The traditional theories of that kind have long been recognized to be inadequate, and not just because there are certain specific modes of concept-formation – like that involved in idealization to a limit, or the ability noticed by Hume to imagine a shade of colour missing from a series – which they cannot easily explain. Concepts formed by those two routes correspond to predicates. But the most glaring example of our

5 That is not to say that it is non-Euclidean. For elaboration of this thought, see James Hopkins, 'Visual Geometry'.

ability to work with concepts which transgress the limits of what we have actually experienced is provided by the understanding each of us has of no end of sentences in our language which we have never previously heard. The anti-realist can hardly deny that we have such an ability in general. Moreover his position will lose any credibility unless he can dissociate it from the old positivist dogma that untestable statements are meaningless. So he should grant that we are able to understand statements of the kind for which he finds the realist interpretation problematic; his quarrel is not with the supposition that we do have such understanding, but only with the realist account of it. But now the realist seems to have a very simple answer. Given that the understanding of statements in general is to be viewed as consisting in possession of a concept of their truth-conditions, acquiring a concept of an evidence-transcendent state of affairs is simply a matter of acquiring an understanding of a statement for which that state of affairs would constitute the truth-condition. And such an understanding is acquired, like the understanding of any previously unheard sentence in the language, by understanding the constituent words and the significance of their mode of combination.

The anti-realist will reply, naturally, that his doubts are not to be allayed so easily, since he does not accept the realist's account of what our understanding of such statements consists in. But now he seems to need independent reason for rejecting it, reason which it is not clear that the thoughts about concept-acquisition sketched above can supply. Mastery of a language just does enable us to form and communicate conceptions of states of affairs of kinds we have never encountered. What exactly is the special problem supposed to be if the states of affairs in question not merely have not but could not be encountered, or at least could not be recognized for what they are?

It is the burden of the second main anti-realist argument, the 'manifestation argument', to disclose such a special problem. The argument is directly that the realist misdescribes what understanding a statement of the relevant sort consists in; or, better, that he *overdescribes* it, finding it to involve more than there is any warrant to suppose. One point of the later Wittgenstein's emphasis on the identity of meaning and use is to recommend that we think of understanding on the model of a practical ability, or complex of abilities, rather than as some kind of interior state. To understand an expression is to know how to use it properly, and the proof of such knowledge is that one does actually so use it. The anti-realist challenge to the realist is now: explain how your conception of understanding can be made to harmonize with Wittgenstein's insight. The difficulty is not far to seek. According to the realist, understanding a statement of one of the controversial kinds consists in knowing that a certain sort of potentially evidence-transcendent state of affairs both suffices and is necessary for its truth. How can that account be viewed as a description of any *practical* ability of use? No doubt someone who understands such a statement can be expected to have many relevant practical abilities. He will be able to appraise evidence for or against it, should any be available, or to recognize that no information in his possession bears on it. He will be able to recognize at least some of its logical consequences, and to identify beliefs from which commitment to it would follow. And he will, presumably, show himself sensitive to conditions under which it is appropriate to ascribe propositional attitudes embedding the statement to himself and others, and sensitive to the explanatory significance of such ascriptions. In short: in these and perhaps other important respects, he will show himself competent to use the statement. But the headings under which his practical abilities fall so far involve no mention of grasp of evidence-transcendent truth-conditions. Is it the realist's view that such mention is somehow there implicitly? If so, let the implication be brought out. Or is it perhaps that the headings omit some important category of practical ability whose description will invoke the realist's preferred account? If so, what is it?

The argument may be sharpened by considering the corresponding situation with decidable statements. Imagine that you are seated before a table on which are placed a number of bowls, containing various substances. How might you manifest, in this context, your understanding of statements, like 'this one is salty', 'this one is bitter', 'this one is sweet', etc.? Well, each of the practical abilities mentioned above continues to be germane: the ability to appraise (inconclusive) evidence for or against such statements, or to recognize that one has so far no such evidence; the ability to recognize the validity of inferences from and to such statements; and the ability to utilize such statements in the ascriptions of propositional attitude and thereby to explain e.g. why Jones puts that substance in his tea rather than the other one – each of these is the kind of thing we should expect of someone who understood such a statement. But of course the list so far omits all mention of one terribly important kind of practical ability: the ability to recognize the taste of the samples by placing them in one's mouth, and thereby to verify or falsify descriptions of their taste. There would be some point in identifying this range of recognitional abilities with knowledge of the truth-conditions of the relevant statements; recognizing the taste of something by tasting it *is* recognizing that in virtue of which the true description of its taste is true. But nothing at all corresponds to abilities of this kind in the case of statements for which the anti-realist finds the realist's account of understanding problematical. Moreover with the taste examples it is imaginable, if not very likely, that somebody might demonstrably lack this kind of recognitional ability although his performance in the other three respects canvassed in no way set him apart from people who possessed it. For instance, someone who, for whatever reason, was unable to taste sweetness might nevertheless have a good grasp of a range of inferential grounds for ascribing sweetness to things, as well as a good knowledge of the inferential liaisons of such ascriptions; and he might be as adept as anyone else at recognizing propositional attitudes in others whose content involved the concept of sweetness and, more generally, in his use of statements concerning such propositional attitudes.

The conclusion is that in cases where 'knowledge of truth-conditions' does denote a distinctive ability with a plausible claim to be regarded as central, or even constitutive of understanding – for I take it that someone who manifested the unlikely combination of abilities just described would only questionably be regarded as (fully) understanding the statement that sugar is sweet, – it is a *different* ability to anything with a counterpart among the abilities which constitute knowledge of the use of statements of the anti-realistically problematical sort. That is a reason for not describing the use-abilities of those who understand such statements as if they involved 'knowledge of truth-conditions'. A realist who accepts the Wittgensteinian premise seems to have no general candidate for an ability, common to all cases of statement-understanding, of which 'knowledge of truth-conditions' is a well-motivated description.

A possible response would be that the identification of statement-understanding with knowledge of truth-conditions is actually no more than the immediate consequence of a series of platitudes. Understanding a statement is knowing what it states; what it states will be that a certain state of affairs obtains; so one who understands a statement will know this and, hence, know what kind of state of affairs that would be. Plainly the obtaining of such a state of affairs will be both necessary and sufficient for the truth of the statement – since that such a state of affairs obtains is, to repeat, precisely what it states. Hence one who understands a statement thereby has a concept of the state of affairs which is the truth-condition for it; and, presumably, conceives it as such.[6]

It seems, however, that there is nothing here to which the anti-realist ought to want to object. If it is indeed, for such reasons, a platitude that to understand a statement is to know its truth-conditions, what follows is not that the anti-realist doubts are platitudinously wrong but that realism, as a substantial theory of statement-content, exceeds the platitude. And so, independently, it does. Someone, for instance, who understands 'Jones is in pain' will be credited, by the platitudinous reasoning, with

6 This, or a very similar train of thought is offered by John McDowell in his 'Anti-Realism and the Epistemology of Understanding'. See especially pp. 229–31. Compare section 2 of his 'In Defence of Modesty'.

a conception of a specific kind of state of affairs – Jones' being in pain – whose obtaining he conceives as necessary and sufficient for the truth of that statement. How do we proceed from there to foist on him a conception of how such a state of affairs can obtain *undetectably*? The platitudes may be allowed to reinstate 'knowledge of truth-conditions' as a general description of the abilities which those who understand a statement thereby have; but they do nothing to justify the idea that the notion of truth which the reference therein to 'truth-conditions' invokes is the realist's *objective* truth.[7]

All this proceeds on the assumption that the Wittgensteinian premise is indeed an insight. What if the realist, granting the conditional force of the argument, chooses to dispute the premise, and contraposes? He will then be quite at liberty to allow that the abilities typical of those who understand statements in the anti-realistically disputed class do not *per se* warrant description as knowledge of conditions of (objective) truth. But there will be no awkwardness for him in this concession, since he will not agree that understanding is *constituted* by such abilities. So the most the manifestation argument can show, it may seem, is that Wittgenstein's later philosophy of language is implicitly anti-realist. That is not, so far, to disclose any failing in realism.

Fully to appraise such a bluff rejoinder would require detailed analysis of the pressures from which Wittgenstein's later philosophy of language emerges. But something can be said without undertaking an enquiry on that scale. With decidable statements there is, as noted, *both* a distinctive recognitional ability related to their truth-conditions and plausibly regarded as central to understanding them, *and* a range of other abilities which are typical of understanding. The latter abilities may be possessed, again as noted, in the absence of the former, and so provide at best a fallible inferential basis for the claim that somebody understands such a statement.

7 McDowell, 'Anti-Realism and the Epistemology of Understanding', p. 231, misses this. He writes, '...if a sentence lacks an effective decision procedure, then the condition which any competent speaker knows he would be asserting to obtain if he used the sentence in order to make an assertion – which is in fact a condition under which the sentence would be true, whether or not a theory of meaning explicitly calls it that – is *ex hypothesi* not a condition whose obtaining, if it does obtain, a competent speaker can be sure of being able to put himself in a position to recognise. Thus, without lapsing into psychologism, we seem to have equipped ourselves with a kind of realism...' Hardly. A statement's not being effectively decidable consists in there being no guaranteed procedure for making an adequate case for or against it. It is therefore quite consistent to hold that S is not effectively decidable, that we understand its assertoric content to be that conditions obtain which are necessary and sufficient for its truth, and that we do *not* understand what it would be for those conditions to obtain undetectably. (Indeed, the trio would still be consistent if 'effectively' were omitted.) Somehow McDowell has – perfectly question-beggingly – run together lack of effective decidability with the capacity to be undetectably true.

Fallibility can be lived with *provided* we can get some grip on the frequency of failures. But that is what the realist now denies himself. Who is to say whether it is *likely* that someone who has the relevant sorts of practical ability really understands 'Jones is in pain' if what consitutes such understanding is a state – a 'conception' of a potentially undetectable state of affairs – which is quite distinct from those abilities – though conceived, who knows why, to issue in them – and for which there is no independent test? With decidable statements there is such a test, provided the realist is content to identify knowledge of truth-conditions with the appropriate recognitional ability. But in the case of statements of the disputed kind, the inescapable price, it appears, of rejecting the Wittgensteinian premise is surrender of any possible reason to suppose that there is such a thing as mutual understanding.[8]

That is bad enough, but it is not the end of the difficulties. In addition, the realist seems to be in no position to say anything to illuminate the *kind* of state which understanding a statement, in his recommendation, should be viewed as being. A feeling of familiarity, of 'knowing one's way about', when it is entertained? A propensity to have certain sorts of imagery and associations excited by hearing it? These are bankrupt proposals, long since exposed as such, and now standard cannon-fodder in undergraduate philosophy curricula.

Thus, in outline anyway, proceeds the challenge to the realist conception of truth posed by considerations to do with the manifestation of understanding. Doubtless the outline could and should be amplified and improved upon, but the general tenor should be clear enough. The argument has had a mixed reception in the literature, and its proper appraisal is an unresolved question. Let me briefly outline two comparatively recent lines of critical response.

The premise for the argument is that more ought not to be read into someone's understanding of an expression than can be manifested in his behaviour. But manifested to whom? What can be made plain to an audience depends upon *their* conceptual powers and understanding. Advanced musicianship cannot be manifested to the musically untrained; grandmaster skills at chess cannot be manifested to those who barely know the rules. Accordingly, the challenge to the realist to explain how understanding, as he conceives it, can be manifest in behaviour, has to be accompanied by a specification of the powers of a suitable audience; otherwise no definite challenge is posed. But what powers is it appropriate to assign to the audience in this case? If only the musically trained can appreciate Bach's genius, perhaps only those already equipped with a realist

8 Some seem prepared to pay this price. See, for instance, Edward Craig's 'Meaning, Use and Privacy'.

understanding can discern manifestations of that understanding. And if that is so, we should have to decide independently whether anyone can be so equipped – the manifestation argument, of itself, could accomplish nothing.[9]

If this were so, it would follow that the route into realist understanding could not be via the example of those who had already accomplished it; it would be a path which each of us would have to follow without guidance. But we have already seen that the realist can offer a response to the acquisition argument which is consistent with this consequence: the response that each of us forms distinctively realist conceptions by understanding – after the fashion dictated by the meanings of their constituents and their syntactic structure – sentences in the problematic class. So now we seem to glimpse the shape of a possible realist response to both the challenges; the route into realist conceptions is to deploy the powers of synthesis involved in the understanding of novel utterances generally; and that one has arrived, as it were, will be manifestable in ways appreciable by, but only by, those who have themselves followed that route.

These thoughts, it seems to me, should carry no conviction at all. The general point about the audience-dependence of what can be manifested is unquestionable. But it is so because we can, for example, embark on an account in detail of what the special skills and talents of a chess grandmaster consist in, and of what you need to be able to do in order to appreciate them. If the realist is right, everyone, including those of anti-realist sympathy, understands statements of the problematic kind in a realist fashion. But we are, precisely, *not* getting any detailed account of what this understanding consists in, or of how that very species of understanding might enable one to recognize it in others. The proposal is, so far, just so much hand-waving: we are invited to contemplate the possibility that the signs of realist understanding might somehow be there for those who have the right powers to appreciate them – but nothing at all is on offer about what exactly those signs are, or how in detail their appreciation demands the very conceptions in question.

We should not leave matters there, however. Rather, the anti-realist should grant his opponent an audience of 'manifestees' who fully understand whatever statements form the focus of the dispute. On the realist view, though not of course on the anti-realist view, that is the same thing as the concession that the audience is fitted out with realist conceptions. So, the manifestation argument can proceed without fear of circularity provided what it has to say about what is, or is not, manifestable to such an audience appeals only to an intuitive conception of understanding

9 Compare Simon Blackburn, *Spreading the Word*, pp. 65–6.

and depends on no implicit prejudice against the realist account. That, I suggest, is how it is with the outline sketched above. Certainly, only an audience which already understands will do: I can hardly assess your abilities to appraise evidence for a certain statement, to recognize the validity of inferences to and from it, and to handle propositional attitude contexts involving it, unless I myself understand that statement and a good deal else besides. But the argument turned on the reflection that if the statement in question is decidable, there is a further ability which you, if you understand it, can be expected to have, viz. the ability to recognize as such a state of affairs which makes it true; and that this ability can necessarily have no counterpart in the case of evidence-transcendent statements. Again the ability is such that, at least if it is to be tested in standard ways, the tester must also possess it. But that there is this difference in the range of abilities associated with understanding is apparently incontrovertible and quite independent of any point of view about what understanding is. To be sure, the argument then proceeds via the assumption that such abilities are constitutive rather than merely associated with understanding. But we have already glimpsed the perils of overturning that assumption.

The second recent line of response to the manifestation argument tries to view its credibility as deriving from a false dilemma: *either* there is nothing in someone's understanding of an expression which cannot be fully and distinctively manifested in his use of it *or* his understanding is a mysterious state which can connect merely symptomatically with his use, and about which we therefore rapidly fall into sceptical doubt after the fashion sketched. But in fact the relation between understanding and use is neither of these. Rather use – linguistic behaviour – is one species of rational behaviour, and understanding is one parameter which combines holistically with others in its explanation. The point is now generally received that there is no behaviour, or syndrome of behaviour, which may be regarded a priori as distinctive of a subject's possession of any particular belief. Beliefs which typically lead to certain types of course of action may equally find expression in other, quite contrary courses of action if we imagine appropriate changes in others of the subject's background beliefs and in his framework of desires. I may manifest my belief that the sea is cold by refusing to bathe (if I don't like cold water bathing) or plunging in joyously (if I do, or want to present an example of British fortitude, etc.). In the same way, the linguistic behaviour which expresses someone's understanding of a particular statement will be a function not just of that understanding but also of other beliefs he has about the world and about his audience, as well as his background intentions and desires. Meaning thus cannot be 'exhaustively' manifest in use; to suppose that it can is to make the same error as those who, in the tradition of Gilbert Ryle, attempted to construe intentional states as dispositions.

These thoughts seem to me to be importantly correct, (and it may well be that some expositions of the anti-realist's arguments strongly suggest that they have been overlooked). They are, however, completely irrelevant in the present context since the identification of meaning and use to which the argument appeals, at least as outlined above, does not have the reductive implications which would offend against them. The proposal was that understanding should be seen as constituted by a complex set of practical abilities. It was not proposed nor does it follow that there is any behaviour which is a priori distinctive of possession of these abilities. The ability, for instance, properly to appraise the bearing of evidence on a particular statement is subject, since it is the ability to form certain sorts of belief, to all the varieties of behavioural expression to which any belief is subject. The same goes for the other kinds of ability which were singled out. Actually, I do not know if a reductive, dispositional account is possible of any ability at all; but the Wittgensteinian premise most certainly generates no such commitment in the cases which interest us. It is between the ability and its behavioural manifestation that the shadow of holism falls, if I may so put it. Whereas the issue between the realist and the anti-realist is at one remove: it concerns the relation between understanding and ability. In short: when the anti-realist challenges the realist to indicate a potential manifestation of realist understanding of a statement, he is asking for an account of the *abilities* which would manifest it, not the behaviour. And there is, so far as I can see, no way of massaging the logic of holistic explanation so as to come up with a direct answer: a practical ability which stands to understanding an evidence-transcendent truth-condition as recognitional skills stand to decidable truth-conditions. That such recognitional skills are not themselves 'conclusively' manifestable in behaviour – because further hypotheses have to be entertained about the intentional states of the subject before the behaviour counts as displaying the appropriate skills – is beside the point.[10]

III
Normativity and Rule-following

There is a third argument against the realist view of truth and meaning which is easily conflated with the second, the manifestation argument, and which has been somewhat ignored. But it is distinct and well worth separate study. It might be called the 'argument from normativity'.

10 A development of the thought of the preceding paragraph would be the right response, I believe, to the central anti-Dummettian argument of McDowell's 'In Defence of Modesty' (see footnote 7).

Meaning is normative. To know the meaning of an expression is to know, perhaps unreflectively, how to appraise uses of it; it is to know a set of constraints to which correct uses must conform. Accordingly, to give the meaning of a statement is to describe such constraints; nothing has a claim to be regarded as an account of a statement's meaning which does not succeed in doing so. The argument is now that the realist's truth-conditional conception has indeed no such claim.

Consider any statement, S, whose truth, the realist believes, may be but does not have to be associated with the availability of supporting evidence. According to the realist, the meaning of such a statement is determined by its truth-conditions; they are what is known by someone who understands it. Such understanding must accordingly involve grasp of a constraint on S's correct use which is potentially distinct from that exerted by favourable evidence. For someone who is disposed to appraise such evidence in an acceptable manner, but has not grasped that the statement may be true when no such evidence can be obtained, must, on the realist view, have failed fully to grasp its content. What more is required is precisely grasp of the possibility that S be true undetectably; that is, on the realist view, grasp of the truth-conditions of

(S*) S is true although no evidence in its favour is available.

But now, what constraints do the truth-conditions of this proposition embody? What is required of someone if he is to show that he understands these truth-conditions? An answer can at least be started: the truth-conditions associated with (S*) have the effect that it should be denied if there is either evidence for S's falsity, hence against its undetectable *truth*, or evidence for its truth, hence against its *undetectable* truth. But that answer, so far, does nothing to distinguish the content of (S*) from that of 'S is undetectably false', or from that of 'No evidence bearing on S's truth or falsity is available'. The realist will certainly want to regard these three statements as differing in content, and the differences as constituted by their being associated with quite different respective truth-conditions. But what do these different associations consist in, and how in particular can it be legitimate to regard them as meaning-constituting, if they do not impose *different* constraints on the practice of those whose understanding of such statements the realist believes he can correctly describe?

The anti-realist will not dispute that (S*) and the other two examples do indeed differ in content, in ways straightforwardly reflected in aspects of their use. (Reflect, for instance, on their logical relations.) The question is whether the realist can give a satisfactory account of these differences. When the association of particular truth-conditions with a statement succeeds in being meaning-constituting, it does so because truth is a regulative ideal: it is what our assertions are, other things being equal, aimed at, and its absence is a ground for their criticism. But how can undetectable truth discharge this role? What is it to *try* to record the truth by use of (S*) rather than of one of its two competitors?

Consider an analogy. Suppose I place before you two small, identical-seeming boxes. Each has been sealed and cannot easily be opened. I tell you that each contains a vacuum, and that enclosed in one of them, but not the other, is a beetle, fashioned of a highly volatile substance that will vaporize tracelessly if it comes into contact with air. There is no betraying rattle or other symptom – difference in weight e.g. – to suggest which box this might be. The other contains an identical quantity of the same material, used as a lining. In such circumstances, there is serious doubt whether you can so much as try to pick the right box. The grounds for saying so are familiar ones, original to Wittgenstein's treatment of intention and related concepts in the *Philosophical Investigations*. If you think you can aim at the right box, ask yourself what this aiming would consist in. You might, for instance, reach out and tap one of the boxes with your finger, but that will not distinguish your intention from that of picking the wrong box, or just picking a box. You might accompany your gesture with the words, thought or spoken, 'This is the box with the mysterious beetle.' But your having that thought is no guarantee of the requisite intention; you might have had it while picking one of the boxes quite aimlessly. We can make the thought carry such a guarantee, perhaps, if we construe it as, in effect, a performative: 'I hereby intend to pick the box with the mysterious beetle in it.' But this construal sheds no light on what, if anything, makes such an intention possible in these *outré* circumstances; the question merely becomes whether the performative thought can succeed. A similar fate will befall any other candidates for psychological processes or episodes which are putatively characteristic of the controversial intention.

To cut a long story very short, intention is not a mental process or state through which a subject may pass – like a sensation, or mood – independently of what else is true of him. Intentions are formed in the context of *projects*, determined by the details of and priorities among a subject's beliefs and desires. In order to have an intention – to aim – a subject must want the result of implementing it and this want must be intelligible in the context of the more generalized scheme of wants that partially determines his character. He must also have beliefs about *how* to aim at that particular result; leaving on one side whether languageless creatures may have intentions, the subject who would be credited with action upon a certain intention must be ready to offer an account of why he did just what he did, why he conceived *that* course of action to be likely to promote its fulfilment (if only 'doing that often produces the desired result'). Finally, there are internal relations between the content of an intention ascribed to a subject and his responses, of satisfaction or frustration, as the sequence of events unfolds. (These relations admittedly presuppose the relative stability of intentions over time; but the concept is in any case explanatorily useless if that presupposition is held in question.)

There, very sketchily, are three aspects of the background and surroundings of the significant ascription of intention. They are all absent in the analogy of the boxes. It is utterly unclear what motive you could have for wishing to pick the right box – (you might to wish to go through the motions, of course, to humour me, e.g., but that is not the same thing). Further you will, so long as you are rational, have absolutely no beliefs about how to go about it – and even if it is granted that you might somehow be irrationally smitten with some sort of *idée fixe*, it would be an odd strategy for the realist to try to make conceptual stock out of possibilities open exclusively to the irrational. Finally, there is no question of your responding with frustration or satisfaction to the outcome; there is not going to be, in that sense, any outcome.

It is just the same with verification-transcendent truth. Why should anyone value it? How can a rational subject have beliefs about how to secure it? How can the satisfactions and frustrations of the subject disclose that it was indeed his aim? We should conclude that truth, so conceived, cannot *be* aimed at: the surroundings necessary if the concept of intention is to grip, so to speak, are missing. There is thus a tension, when truth is realistically conceived, between the truth-conditional conception of meaning and the essential normativity of meaning. In effect, we should have given no meaning to an expression if the only 'constraints' on its correct use were such that, for the reasons sketched, no one could aim compliance with them. The assignment, could it but be effected, of evidence-transcendent truth-conditions would impose just such 'constraints'. In so far as there *are* operational constraints on the correct use of statements whose meanings the realist views as determined by their association with transcendent truth-conditions, they are accordingly misrepresented by his view.

The three arguments sketched so far claim, respectively, that no one could actually form an understanding of a statement if to do so required grasping transcendent truth-conditions; that no one who had somehow achieved such grasp could give sufficient reason to another to suppose that he had, no matter how extensive the survey of his linguistic behaviour; and that to suppose that understanding could consist in such grasp offends against the essential normativity of meaning, whereby meaning has to be determined by constraints by which one can aim to regulate one's linguistic practice. The conclusion of a fourth argument, derived from Wittgenstein's discussions of rule-following in the *Philosophical Investigations* and elsewhere, is, though equally antagonistic to realism, yet more radical.

It was noted above that the realist conception of truth contains an implicit commitment to the objectivity of meaning: to suppose that statements which we can formulate and understand may be true, or false, unknowably is to suppose that the contribution towards determining the truth-value of a statement which is made by its meaning is quite independent of any actual human judgement or response on the specific issue. The meaning *already* settles the verdict, as it were; if, perhaps *per impossible*, our cognitive abilities were appropriately extended, then there is a judgement about the truth-value of the statement which, provided we had made no other relevant mistake, we would be obliged to arrive at so long as it was our intention to keep faith with the meaning of the statement as already determined. It follows that any serious general objection to the objectivity of meaning must also call into question the realist conception of truth.

Such an objection can, I believe, be gleaned from Wittgenstein's discussions. The issue will be one preoccupation of the sequel volume to this one, and is little discussed in the chapters which follow. (It surfaces briefly in Essay 4.) Let me here give merely the briefest sketch of its overall character.

The question is whether the objectivity of meaning can be reconciled with any satisfactory account of what *determines* the meaning of a statement. (If the meaning of a statement is viewed as determined by the meanings of its constituent expressions and the significance of the way in which they are put together, the question becomes, of course: what determines the meanings of the constituents, and the significance of the mode of construction?) How, so to speak, do the contracts get finalized to which our linguistic behaviour is to be held accountable? One – though not the only – way of proceeding here is to reflect on something like the 'sceptical argument' brilliantly expounded by Kripke.[11] The argument urges on us the realization that nothing in our previous (finite) linguistic behaviour, nor in the previous total pageant of our mental lives – our thoughts, imaginings and experiences – suffices to determine, against the background of some fixed state of the world, what judgement about the truth value of S would accord with our contractual obligations. But there seems to be nowhere else to search for factors to determine the content of those obligations. Thus it appears that meaning is underdetermined by the only factors that could determine it: thought and behaviour.

The conclusion of the sceptical argument is very strong; in effect, that the notion of meaning as traditionally conceived is a superstition, that there is no such thing as the meaning of an expression since there is nothing to make an expression mean one thing rather than another. Such a view

11 Saul Kripke, *Wittgenstein on Rules and Private Language*.

would, of course, entail rejection of the objectivity of meaning, but goes far beyond what is necessary for such a rejection. Kripke's Wittgenstein responds to the sceptical argument by, in effect, conceding that there is no such thing as meaning; more specifically, it is conceded that there are no substantial facts about meaning – in particular, about what courses of conduct do, or do not, conform with particular meanings. It is then the aim of the 'sceptical solution' to reconstruct some legitimate non-fact-stating role for talk of meaning and understanding. (In the terminology above, the conclusion of the sceptical argument is that meaning-discourse lacks *objectivity of judgement*; the sceptical solution then attempts to establish that it may still have a legitimate function.) However Wittgenstein himself would seem to have responded differently. In *Philosophical Investigations* 201, immediately after the series of paragraphs which suggested the sceptical argument to Kripke, Wittgenstein writes that the solution consists in seeing 'that there is a way of grasping a rule which is *not* an *interpretation*, but which is exhibited in what we call "obeying the rule" and "going against it" in actual cases'. Naturally this needs detailed exegesis, which I am not going to attempt to supply here. But the general drift, I take it, is that the sceptical argument is wrong in the assumption that meaning is determinate only if rational extrapolation from a finite sample of uses and psychological episodes can warrant a unique interpretation. This mistakes the relation between meaning and the data which, on the sceptic's view, are insufficient to determine it; and it mistakes the epistemology of understanding. Understanding cannot always be achieved via uniquely rational extrapolation from sample uses and explanations; and is not usually. Rather the path to understanding exploits certain *natural* propensities which we have, propensities to react and judge in particular ways. The concepts which we 'exhibit' by what we count as correct, or incorrect, use of a term need not be salient to a witness who is, if I may so put it, merely rational; the manner in which they are exhibited might be better compared to the way in which a sample cut from a piece of wallpaper represents the whole pattern of which it is a part.

Objectivity of meaning requires that there is always, in any germane worldly situation, a verdict about the truth, or falsity, of a statement which is ordained by its content as determined by aspects of our previous practice. But the adjustment which Wittgenstein would seem to be recommending would seem to involve that there is no substance in the idea of such an obligation to our previous practice. This is, emphatically, not to say that there is no such thing as 'going on in the same way'. Rather, we have to recognize that our judgements about what counts as so doing are ceaselessly determined by features of our sub-rational natures; that no content can be given to the idea of an ulterior standard, constituted by meaning itself, to which these judgements may or may not conform.[12] This is a topic of the greatest difficulty. It constitutes perhaps the most major challenge facing twentieth-century philosophy. But maybe the foregoing is sufficient to suggest how the demands made on the notion of meaning by the realist's conception of truth may be deeply at variance with lessons we have to learn if we are to understand how determinate meaning is possible at all.

IV
The Negative Programme

The essays which follow were, with two exceptions – Essays 2 and 16 – originally written as self-contained pieces. I have divided them into two groups, in accordance with whether their principal concern is with the negative or positive aspects of the kind of anti-realism to which this book is devoted. The placing of some of the essays on one or the other side of this distinction has inevitably felt a little *ad hoc*. But it seemed desirable to emphasize the distinction itself in some such way as this, since it is of great importance in these matters. Specifically, it is vital to separate the anti-realist critique of the objectivity of truth, and of the classical semantical tradition built upon it, from the issues which arise when we contemplate the prospect of a philosophy of language, and a style of semantics, based on concepts to which the critique does not apply. A good proportion of recent realist commentary on these issues has concentrated on trying to find limitations and problems in the positive semantic proposals which sympathizers with the anti-realist critique have offered. This is, of course, a legitimate and potentially interesting focus. But it is not the way to defuse the negative critique. A demonstration, if one were possible, that only classical semantics, based on a notion of truth of just the kind the anti-realist objects to, has the resources to account satisfactorily for the workings of our language would provide reason to doubt the force of the anti-realist misgivings only if there is independent good cause to suppose that such a general account can and should be provided. That question is open.

Both the negative and positive aspects are associated with research programmes which are very far from worked through. The negative programme is concerned with the development and appraisal of the anti-realist's criticism of the realist conception of truth and of traditional semantics. It ought to culminate in canonical formulations of the main negative arguments; in a clear account of their presuppositions; in an elucidation of the implications of accepting them; and, if successful, in rebuttal of certain objections. The first group of essays which follow are

12 Compare section III of my 'Skolem and the Skeptic'.

primarily concerned with these issues. Essays 1, 2 and 3 are largely devoted to exposition of some of the basic negative arguments and to trying to clarify them by response to two influential sets of counter-criticisms published by Sir Peter Strawson and John McDowell.

With two main qualifications I would still endorse these three chapters, at least as a basis for further discussion. First, Essay 1 contains a train of thought – the 'tribe-chess' example – which fails to separate the manifestation argument and the argument from normativity. While I do not think that the result is a lessening of cogency, it seems to me better, as above, to keep the two arguments distinct. Second, and more serious, the manner in which Essay 2 responds to one of Strawson's complaints now strikes me as misconceived. Strawson had suggested, in effect, that anti-realists had done insufficient to demarcate those statements for which classical semantics is, in their view, objectionable from those for which, because their truth would be detectable, it would not. My reply was that the force of the anti-realist case could not depend upon the sharpness of this distinction so long as it was clear – as, it seemed to me, it was – that, whatever the precise characterization of the notion, certain kinds of statement, realistically interpreted, would be assigned transcendent truth-conditions. If it were to turn out that this class was more extensive than had been expected, or even was comprehensive, that would merely widen the area of dispute. But what this reply overlooks is the role played by the idea of detectable truth in the anti-realist's basic arguments. The acquisition argument, for instance, proceeds by way of contrast between states of affairs which can be presented to consciousness in their entirety, as it were, and states of affairs which cannot. And the manifestation argument, as expounded above, made essential play with the claim that, when we compare the kind of abilities which are distinctive of understanding in the two sorts of case, there is one – the ability to detect an obtaining truth-condition as such – which gives point to the truth-conditional conception of understanding in decidable cases but is missing elsewhere. In order to appraise the significance of each of these arguments, therefore, we do need some grip on the idea of what it is for a state of affairs to be fully recognizable, or – equivalently – on what it is for a statement (describing such a state of affairs) to be verifiable. This notion of verifiability will contrast with the availability of supporting but defeasible evidence. Intuitively, one feels there ought to be such a distinction, but drawing it is complicated by the plausible thought that virtually every statement we can make is defeasible if our subsequent experience takes an appropriately awkward turn. The issue is taken up briefly in Essay 12 and again in Essay 3. The most extended treatment of it is in Essay 4, and the principal feature of the approach adopted – a distinction between two different kinds of defeasibility – is prominent in the account of 'superassertibility' sketched in Essay 14. I do not exclude the possibility that what I have said about the issue may turn out to be on the right lines. But the question, how best to draw the contrast between statements which can allow of conclusive verification, properly so termed, and statements for which, at most, non-verifying support is possible – if indeed there is such a distinction – is still an open question. Its significance should not be over-estimated: it is not needed, so far as I can see, in the presentation either of the argument from normativity or of the argument from rule-following. But until we know how matters stand with it, it is impossible to be clear just which class of statements it is of which a realist interpretation should be uncontroversial, and which can serve as the reference class for the acquisition- and manifestation arguments.

Distinguishing strict verification from more modest cognitive achievements is one important basic issue in the negative programme. There is another equally fundamental question which is closely related. The thrust of the negative arguments is that the truth of a statement requires that evidence be available of its truth. But what is the relevant notion of 'availability' here? What is the proper way of formulating the epistemological conditions by which, in the anti-realist view, the intelligible ascription of truth of falsity to a statement is constrained? To whom must evidence be available? To us, here and now? Or merely to someone appropriately placed in a spatio-temporal situation which may not be accessible to us? And what counts as 'availability'? Must it be possible for an actual human being to gather the evidence? Or would it suffice for the evidence to be available merely 'in principle', accessible only to a human being with substantially idealized capacities?

If we regard the logic and mathematics of the intuitionists, in the fashion which Dummett has recommended, as flowing from a general mistrust of truth epistemologically unfettered, it would seem the constraint which they implicitly apply is indeed a highly idealized one. The law of excluded middle is accepted, for instance, for all decidable number-theoretic statements, no matter how difficult or time-consuming it would be actually to implement the procedure which would yield a decision. A being who could actually decide an arbitrary such problem would require either unlimited time in which to work or to be subject to no limit on his rate of work. (No doubt he would require many other unusual qualities of character.) The *strict finitist* wing of the anti-realist movement is opposed to such idealization. It contends, with a good deal of plausibility, that intuitionism is representative of an unstable middle position and that the kind of epistemological constraint on the notion of truth which the original negative arguments demand, while admitting some kinds of idealization – we may, for instance, prescind from consideration of purely accidental barriers to investigation, like power-cuts, or a damaged hearing-aid – should reflect more closely the practical capacities possessed by actual human beings.

There is an interesting and fundamental research project connected with these ideas, with considerable bearing on, inter alia, problems to do with the semantics of vagueness and with the proper understanding of the notion of infinity. These and related matters are the topics of Essay 4.

However this book contains, unfortunately, no comparably extended treatment of the question: when, where and to whom must evidence, for or against, be available if the ascription of truth or falsity to a statement is to be in good order? The question is one of great difficulty. On the one hand, it seems unlikely that the critical thrust of the best formulation of the basic negative arguments could be met by proposing no more exacting a constraint than that, in order for a statement to be true, it must be in principle, somewhere, sometime, confirmable; that, to every true statement, corresponds at least one region of space-time within which a being whose abilities were of the human range, though perhaps inordinately (though finitely) large, would be able to make an adequate case for believing the statement. This conceptions seems still too idealized; it fairs no better than the realist conception when it comes to explaining, for instance, what ability *of ours* corresponds to grasp of the truth-conditions of controversial examples, or how truth in general can be the proper object of intention. On the other hand, if we slide all the way down to the extreme constraint that in order for a statement to be true, it is necessary that we are actually and currently capable of making an adequate case for believing it, even the most committed anti-realist is likely to experience some degree of failure of nerve. Something like this, of course – perhaps with 'in principle' in place of 'actually' – has to underlie the anti-realism about the past which is a prominent element in Dummett's writings on this topic. If someone sympathizes with the basic negative case but does not wish to go so far, where should he stop and on what principle?

It is exceedingly difficult to see how the negative arguments themselves might be developed so as to yield such a (unique) principle. The extreme position remains of considerable dialectical interest, if only because a demonstration of its ability to handle certain sorts of objection would simultaneously be a demonstration that all the less extreme positions can do likewise. However the ultimate credibility of the negative programme, it seems to me, must depend on the possibility of a principled decision about the proper form of the epistemological constraint to which the classical conception of truth should be subjected.

The strategy of attempting to show how the extreme position can fend off an objection dominates the discussion of Essay 5. One form of realist response, at least to the manifestation- and acquisition arguments, is to attempt to exploit the links in truth-value between statements which contain indexicals – personal pronouns, adverbs of place and tenses, for instance. An example would be the coincidence in truth-conditions of

'I have a headache', said by you to me in a particular two-person conversation between us, and 'You have a headache' said by me in the same context; likewise 'It is raining here' was truly assertible at a particular place and time if and only if 'It was [at that time] raining' is truly assertible at the same place at a later time. Statements about other minds and the past are two of the species about which the realist account is controversial. The proposal would be that one may form a conception of the truth-conditions of such statements precisely by projecting from one's own case, or from the present, in the fashion indicated by the truth-value links. Thus, 'I have a headache' is a type of utterance whose truth-conditions are unproblematic for each of us; in order to arrive at an understanding of the allegedly problematic truth-conditions of 'You have a headache', one has only to follow the connection illustrated by the truth-value link between an utterance of this sentence and an utterance of its allegedly unproblematic first-person counterpart.

This line of thought has very evident deficiencies, and Essay 3 is devoted to John McDowell's sophisticated attempt to improve on it.[13] It should be sharply distinguished, however, from a different way in which the realist may attempt to make use of the truth-value links, whose purpose is less to address the anti-realist negative arguments directly than to disclose a purported incoherence in their conclusion. Consider, for instance, the link between the present truth of a present-tensed sentence and the future truth of its past-tensed transformation. How can the anti-realist endorse such a link quite generally when it is evidently possible, in a suitable case, to have evidence both that a present-tensed sentence is presently true *and* that there will be no evidence for the truth of its past-tensed transformation at some relevant future time? Is there not a manifest inconsistency between this particular truth-value link and any proposal to the effect that a statement is true only when evidence for its truth is available? This simple argument figures prominently in the debate which closes Dummett's important discussion of anti-realism about the past.[14] In Essay 5 I have attempted, inter alia, to sharpen the argument, to give grounds for dissatisfaction with the anti-realist response to it which Dummett describes, and to indicate an alternative response.

The gist of the arguments from acquisition, manifestation and normativity is that truth-conditions, as the realist would conceive them, cannot figure in any appropriate way in the thought of those who understand a language. It seems fair to say that this is an objection to a realist theory of *meaning* only if a theory of meaning ought to be nothing other than a theory of understanding, a theory of the concepts and

13 In 'On "The Reality of the Past"'.
14 'The Reality of the Past'.

knowledge which must be possessed by one who understands a (particular) language. There are two lines of thought which are prima facie inimical to this equation. One is the idea that certain real (usually causal) relations between our words and the world may make an essential contribution to the content of utterances without in any way figuring in the knowledge of those who utter them. Causal theories of the reference of singular terms and essentialist theories of the extensions of natural-kind words both advance such a claim. It is important to realize that, although some actual philosophers of anti-realist sympathy – most notably, Dummett himself – have been independently critical of these views, there is nothing in them to which a critic of the realist conception of truth ought, qua critic, to object. The explanation is simple: to suppose that the truth conditions of e.g. statements involving singular terms or natural-kind terms may be determined, in part, by factors of which someone who understands those statements need not thereby be aware is – if indeed true – quite different from supposing that the truth-conditions so determined may be realized undetectably. So far as I can see, the first supposition provides no motive whatever for the second. Qualification of the slogan that a theory of meaning must be a theory of understanding would indeed seem to be called for by such views. But the suggestion that, for instance, I may – by ordinary criteria – fully understand the sentence, 'This ring is fashioned from 16 carat gold' without thereby knowing what, essentially, has to be the case in order for it to be true, carries no implication that the essence of gold cannot be identified or that samples of gold cannot be recognized qua instances of that essence. If there were such an implication, the form of essentialism associated with the writings of Kripke and Putnam would be open to anti-realist objection. But since there is none, the arguments for such a view provide no weaponry appropriate to the needs of those who seek to reject the basic negative case against the realist conception of truth.

The second line of thought which clashes with the slogan is less easily addressed. A stone does not know the theory of gravitation to which its motion conforms. Why should a theory of meaning, whose aim after all is the description of linguistic practice, be restricted to the use of concepts which those who competently engage in the practice may be presumed to have grasped? The natural answer is that meanings are constituted not by natural law but by *convention*; that regularities which are conventional must, whatever the detail of the proper analysis of the notion, be upheld by grace of the intentions of those who sustain them; and that it must be possible to describe an intention, properly so regarded, in a fashion which represents the content it has for the intending subject. All that seems plausible enough – until one reflects on the level of complexity and technicality which it seems a theory of meaning adequate even for an interesting fragment of English would have to have. Can it really be supposed that ordinary English speakers have mastered concepts like that of *infinite sequence*, *satisfaction* or the *star functor*, let alone whatever additional devices might be necessary satisfactorily to extend the Tarski–Davidson approach to accommodate indexicals, adverbs, predicate modifiers, modality, intentional contexts and quantifiers like 'many' and 'most'? To be sure, this is just one style of systematic semantics. But it seems unlikely that the level of technicality which it enjoins is a vice peculiar to the particular approach.

The general issue raised here is of the cognitive relation, if any, which must obtain between speakers of a natural language and the content of a theory of meaning which is to be an adequate account of their linguistic practice. More specifically, it concerns the sense, if any, in which the axiomatic and recursive basis of such a theory should describe, or reflect, actual states of the speakers. Dummett, for one, tends to write on the assumption that the contents of such a theory are *implicitly* known by the speakers of the language; and he has tended to base his criticisms of the realist conception of truth on its specific unsuitability to feature as the content of such implicit knowledge. The nature of implicit knowledge is, indeed, of fundamental importance not just for the interpreter of the constructions of semanticists and theoretical linguists but for cognitive psychology generally. It is a notion which it is easy to be sceptical about. A sustained investigation of it is long overdue, and the primary goal of Essay 6 is to contribute towards such an investigation and to consider alternative ways of approaching the general question about the relations between speakers and theories of meaning. But a secondary objective of the chapter is to make plausible the contention that, in so far as scepticism about the notion of implicit knowledge is justified, it is justified for reasons which do *not* question the propriety of the notion absolutely generally; and that there is no cause to regard the anti-realist's basic negative case as making use of the idea of implicit knowledge in a way which seems to deserve mistrust.

V
The Positive Programme

(a) *Anti-realist semantics*

The negative programme is devoted to the critical analysis of concepts and theses presupposed by the basic arguments against the realist conception of truth and meaning. The positive programme, by contrast, is devoted to investigation of the consequences of accepting that the gist of the basic negative arguments is correct: that truth, as conceived by realism, is a metaphysical superstition, which can discharge no genuine explanatory function anywhere but serves only to encourage spurious conceptions of meaning, understanding, objectivity and knowledge.

Two broad issues loom large in the positive programme. First, there is the question of what, if any, positive theory of meaning should now be offered. The question arises at two levels. Can a general, informal account of (declarative) sentence meaning be offered of comparable (apparent) explanatory power to the claim that meaning is determined by truth-conditions? And can a systematic formal theory of meaning, a theory which details for each sentence in a language how its meaning is a function of its structure and the meanings of its constituents, be contemplated if it is not to be based on truth-conditions?

Actually, a very important question, prefigured earlier, is begged by this way of presenting the issues; namely, whether someone inclined to reject the realist conception of truth may no longer work with a truth-conditional conception of meaning in general. Does truth-conditional semantics have to be realist semantics? The assumption that this must be so – at least if wholesale distortion is to be avoided of the intuitive truth-conditions of many statements – is apt to seem highly plausible. What candidate is there, the thought will run, for a guaranteed *detectable* truth-condition for e.g. 'Jones has a headache' if we are to avoid both physicalism and behaviourism? One famous answer (for this particular kind of example) would be provided, if it could be worked through successfully, by the kind of philosophy of mind which Wittgenstein attempts in the *Philosophical Investigations*. The claim would be that Cartesianism, physicalism and behaviourism do not exhaust the possibilities. The drive to the first mistakes the significance of the falsity of the second and the third. That mental states are a sub-species neither of the physical nor the behavioural, and that they may be simulated or concealed, are data which are misinterpreted by Cartesianism and can be brought into harmony with the publicity of the mental. It would be nice should this prove to be so.

I shall return to the question of the availability of truth-conditional semantics to anti-realism shortly. For the moment, suppose on the contrary that a positive anti-realist account of meaning, both informal and formal, should proceed in terms of some other central notion(s). Verification and/or falsification are possibilities. But if those terms are used strictly, contrasting with the mere availability of favourable/unfavourable evidence, then not every statement to which we attach intuitively clear content allows, even under favourable circumstances, of verification or falsification. What, it seems, we *must* understand – if we understand a statement at all – is the distinction between being in position reasonably to believe the statement and not being so. Even statements associated with, on the realist view, guaranteed absolutely undetectable truth-conditions can at least be recognized not to admit of warranted belief. If one is seeking a notion of a degree of generality comparable with that of truth-conditions, realistically conceived – something which every well-understood statement must have – *conditions of warranted belief* (with, as it were, the empty set as a limiting case) are an obvious starting point. This is the attraction of the proposal that an anti-realist theory of meaning, whether informal or formal, should take *assertibility-conditions* as central. Naturally, there can be conversational or social reasons why a belief which one is warranted in holding had better not be expressed in a particular context. But if we are concerned only with *epistemic* justification, then each of one's warranted beliefs corresponds to a justified possible assertion and vice versa.

Where decidable statements are concerned, one kind of assertibility-condition will also be a truth-condition: the condition constituted by the detectable obtaining of a state of affairs which renders the statement true. Other kinds of assertibility-condition, however, will fall short of constituting the truth of the statement and so will be – as the matter is usually expressed – defeasible: additional information, not yet in, may compromise the justification which they provide. If it is assumed that there are statements which, if they are to be assigned truth-conditions at all, can only be assigned realist truth-conditions without manifest distortion of their intuitive content, it will follow that in such cases all the assertibility-conditions are defeasible. And if we now essay to regard the meanings of such statements as determined by their assertibility-conditions, we seem to have committed ourselves to upholding something like the notion of a *criterion* which many commentators have found in the *Philosophical Investigations*: a condition whose obtaining justifies the relevant statement only defeasibly (so is not a truth-condition) but nevertheless provides such justification necessarily and internally, as a function of the statement's content (so is not a mere *symptom*). Because the notion of criterion connects in this way with the foundations of anti-realism, and because of its independent epistemological interest, I have included the discussions presented here as Essays 12 and 13. Essay 12 is concerned mainly with how best to formulate the notion and with the reasons why anti-realism may have to take it seriously. Essay 13 raises, as it seems to me, serious difficulties about its utility in epistemology and, indeed, its very coherence; but argues that such doubts can be reconciled with an assertibility-conditional conception of meaning.

There is one bad reason for dissatisfaction with the assertibility-conditional conception as an informal account of meaning which is worth pausing over. Is not the conception bound to misconstrue the content of workaday propositional attitudes? The fear, for instance, that there is a bear outside the tent is quite distinct from the fear that it is justifiably assertible that there is – to allay the latter fear need not be to allay the former. Likewise, to hope that you will one day meet the lover of your dreams is not to hope that it is justifiably assertible that you will – that hope would be all too easily dashed. The content of such attitudes is thus to be explicated not in terms of the proposition that it is justifiably assertible that some state of affairs obtains; the relevant proposition is that (it is *true* that) the relevant state of affairs obtains. However, the anti-realist has the resources to acknowledge this distinction. To suppose that he does not is to suppose that the proposal to regard statement meaning as determined by assertibility-conditions is tantamount to the proposal to regard the meaning of each statement, S, as coinciding with that of the statement that S is assertible. That is a coincidence which the assertibility-conditions theorist need not and should not countenance. Rather, he may – must – recognize that any situation which justifies assertion of S, even if defeasibly so, realizes the *truth-conditions* of 'It is assertible that S' and hence provides a justification for the latter which is indefeasible (by additional information). This distinction is quite sufficient to motivate the sort of contrast which the objection calls for.

Still, a doubt may remain. It is one thing for the assertibility-conditions theorist to show that he has the means for resisting the equation of 'X ϕs that S' and 'X ϕs that it is assertible that S'. It is another for him further to characterize the content of the former. The issue arises because, as the parentheses used above indicate, the intuitive difference between the contents of X's two attitudes is just that between the assertibility of the claim that S and its truth. If the assertibility-conditions theorist has proscribed all use of the notion of truth, he appears to owe a different account of the difference. If, on the other hand, he can make out a notion of truth to which he has no objection, will there still be any motive for an assertibility-conditional account of meaning rather than an (appropriately purified) truth-conditional account?

Which course should the anti-realist take in response to this dilemma? I have come to think that the better direction is the second. The anti-realist should attempt to elucidate a notion of truth which is distinct from assertibility-in-a-particular-situation, which is immune to censure in terms of his own basic negative arguments, and which allows us to regard the meaning of any statement as constituted by its truth-conditions without distortion of the kind of content which we want it to have. The crisis facing anyone who feels both the tug of the anti-realist negative arguments and the 'strong realist undertow' of which Dummett speaks is, of course, that these three conditions are likely to seem jointly unsatisfiable. But the way forward may well be via the discovery that they are not. If that is so, it will be of secondary importance whether we describe the discovery as being that anti-realism has no need to dethrone the notion of truth from its central place in the theory of meaning, or that realism has no need of the epistemological insensitivities which open it to anti-realist attack.

How in any case might a systematic theory of meaning proceed which was based on assertibility rather than truth? The output of (the core of) such a theory ought to consist in theorems pairing each significant declarative sentence of the object-language with a description of its assertibility-conditions. It immediately appears that such a theory could not be homophonic, even in the case when the object-language was a fragment of the metalanguage. For if S possesses only defeasible assertibility-conditions, a complete description of them – if such a thing were indeed possible – would presumably have to proceed by the use of other statements, statements which, unlike S, would be *verified* by the obtaining of such conditions. So now it appears that a theory of this sort will have to be based on axioms for the sub-sentential expressions of the language, in particular the predicates, relations and quantifiers, with a content of such a kind that heterophonic theorems of the desired sort are generated by orthodox deductive moves. It would be very difficult to be confident how such axioms might best be formulated. Presumably each predicate e.g. would be associated with a catalogue of circumstances whose obtaining would justify the claim that an individual (or sequence of individuals) satisfied it. But the dominant problem is not that devising such a catalogue might overtax our analytical ingenuity. It is that, as noted earlier in discussion of the manifestation argument, justified assertion is a holistically conditioned notion. One and the same state of affairs may sometimes justify an assertion, and sometimes not, according to how other relevant background beliefs are varied. And so it looks as though the sought-for axioms would have to include, in each case, an exhaustive description of all possible relevant background beliefs together with an account of how their inclusion, or exclusion, from the state of information of the subject would affect his warrant for claiming, in specified circumstances, that a given individual (or sequence of individuals) satisfied the predicate in question. The same complication would naturally affect the attempt even to state, for the case when the object-language is included in the metalanguage, the desirable form to be taken by a meaning-delivering theorem for a given S. I venture to suggest that this project is hopeless.

Toward the end of Essay 1, it is suggested that this problem is avoidable. A homophonic theory of, say, the Davidsonian kind will bear interpretation as a theory of assertibility, it is claimed, provided the connectives and quantifiers of the metalanguage are interpreted in a (broadly) intuitionistic way. But subsequent reflection has persuaded me that this claim was premature: that, when the T-predicate is interpreted as assertibility, there are continuing problems, both with the construal of the standard clause for negation, 'not-S' is T if and only if it is not the case that 'S' is T,

and with the construal of any clauses for tenses adequate to yield theorems corresponding to the standard truth-value links between differently tensed assertions. The detail of these difficulties is described in Essay 14. The single most important factor in generating them is the state-of-information-relative character of assertibility which – in contrast to truth, as usually understood – allows statements, timelessly construed, to come to be and cease to be assertible. The main positive proposal of Essay 14 is that it is possible to synthesize an extension of the notion of assertibility – 'superassertability' – which may provide a trouble-free construal of the T-predicate and deserve no reproach from one who sympathizes with the basic negative arguments.

There is, in addition, an interesting convergence here with some of the results suggested by David Wiggins' researches into the constraints imposed on the notion of truth if a theory of meaning, based on truth-conditions, is to contribute in the most effective way to the overall project of interpreting the speech and behaviour of a group.[15] Wiggins elicits a set of 'marks' which such a truth-predicate had better have. They fall short of anything which would turn the notion into truth as conceived by the realist; but each is a feature of superassertibility. It is natural to expect that a truth-predicate which exactly fitted the constraints which Wiggins' project aims to descry would be bound to be anti-realistically acceptable; the basic negative case, after all, is to the effect that truth, as conceived by realism, is a non-regulative fiction, void of any distinctive display or effective role in a community's linguistic practice, and hence of no interest to the would-be interpreter of that practice. I believe that one of the two most important questions currently on the agenda for the positive programme is whether (something like) superassertibility can indeed provide an interpretation of the truth-predicate with which it would be so convenient for the anti-realist to be able to equip himself, but without compromise of his negative principles. Such are the topics canvassed in Essay 14.

(b) Revisionism

The other most important single issue for the positive programme is whether, as Dummett has always suggested, repudiating the realist conception of truth must lead to revisions of classical logic. Famously, the mathematical intuitionists take it that this is so, at least in the domain of pure mathematics. But certain assumptions underlie this view which go deep in the philosophy of logic and are well worth examination.

15 Cf. his 'Truth, Invention and the Meaning of Life', 'Truth and Interpretation' and 'What Would be a Substantial Theory of Truth?'

Classical logic, as is familiar, is standardly based on classical semantics, which is in turn based on the principle of Bivalence, that every statement is determinately true or false. Since only effectively decidable statements can be guaranteed to be *recognizably* true or false, endorsing Bivalence for all statements would appear to commit one to realist conceptions of truth and falsity. If so, it would follow that the anti-realist should not endorse Bivalence, and must therefore reject the classical semantics of the connectives and quantifiers on which classical logic is based. It would *not* follow directly that classical logic itself should be modified. That depends on, among other things, whether some suitable non-classical semantics is available which involves only concepts acceptable to the anti-realist but which still validates classical logic. In fact, there is no doubt that various such semantical treatments are to hand. The question is whether there are other reasons for discarding them, reasons independent of the basic negative anti-realist case.

Second, there is an important difference between revisionism of the kind which the intuitionists prosecute in mathematics and the kind of global logical revisionism which Dummett recommends. Modification of principles of inference is called for when they are *unsound*: i.e. cannot be guaranteed to transmit from premises to conclusion whatever property it is which we take it sound inference must transmit. The intuitionist has no quarrel with the claim of classical logic to be sound with respect to truth, realistically conceived. His point is rather that this is the wrong property (if he grants that it is an intelligible property at all) to aim to transmit. Rather, we should aim at the transmission of a certain kind of constructive provability: our system of inference should be such that when it permits us to infer a particular conclusion from a set of premises each of which admits of constructive demonstration, there should be a guarantee that the conclusion is also constructively demonstrable – in a fashion consistent with the general intuitionistic semantics for a statement of its particular logical structure – *independently* of the particular inference. In other words, intuitionistic logic is designed to be *conservative* with respect to constructive demonstrability. Generalizing the revisionism of the intuitionists therefore requires disclosure of some corresponding general property which there is reason to expect an anti-realist to want his logic to conserve. The obvious thought is that assertibility should be such a property. But the holistic character of assertibility once again presents a problem. Perhaps there is a class of statements – *observation* statements – which are assertible, or not, purely on the basis of a barrage of experience and independently of any other beliefs held by the subject. If so, they are at best exceptional. The assertibility of the great majority of ordinary contingent statements is irreducibly conditioned by *inferences* reflecting the requirements which others of one's beliefs impose. Accordingly, if our logical practice is *already* classical, then the assertibility conditions, and hence the meanings, of most of our statements are already conditioned by that fact; and assertibility cannot be a property with respect to which classical logic is unsound and which something like intuitionistic logic might better conserve.

These issues are raised in Essay 10. I had not when I wrote that chapter much inkling of the notion of superassertibility, and so did not consider the question whether a generalized revisionism might be motivated by the desire to have one's logic superassertibility-conservative. Certainly, classical semantics cannot be sustained if truth is interpreted as superassertibility, since the case against Bivalence, so interpreted, remains essentially the same. Nevertheless I do not think that invoking superassertibility would make it easier to generalize the intuitionistic case for revising classical logic. Without drawing on the detail of Essay 9, it is fair to caption superassertibility as assertibility which is stable through indefinitely many feasible improvements in our state of information. Accordingly, if assertibility-in-a-particular-state-of-information is a notion conditioned by classical patterns of inference among the beliefs constituting a particular state of information, then the superassertibility of a statement will likewise be a function of what can be achieved via classical modes of reasoning; hence, like assertibility, it will presumably not be a notion whose conservation might require a more restricted logic.

There is a more basic point. The revisionism of the intuitionists presupposes that our logical practice can somehow systematically misfit the correct account of the semantics of the language; which in turn presupposes that such an account may be correct, and be recognized to be so, without consideration of all the detail of our actual inferential behaviour. This is an extremely uncomfortable-feeling assumption but it is hard to see how the revisionist can avoid it. Grant that the basic negative arguments force us to discard any proof-transcendent idea of mathematical truth. And grant, too, that the intuitionist can explain (predicatively) a notion of constructive provability which, when the connectives and quantifiers are construed in terms of it, is not always preserved through classically valid inferences. Then the question is simply: with what right does the intuitionist take constructive provability to be the cardinal notion in our understanding of our mathematical statements rather than, e.g. a notion that coincides with constructive provability as far as atomic statements are concerned but is elsewhere moulded by our unrestricted acceptance of classical logic? It can hardly be denied that there could be such a concept of proof. How is it to be recognized that those who practise classical logic, rather than displaying their commitment to such a concept, are actually being unfaithful to the intuitionistic concept which, deep down, is theirs?

Essay 10 was originally published as a critical study of Dummett's collection *Truth and Other Enigmas*. It contains, in addition to discussion of such doubts as these about the connections between anti-realism and logical revisionism, some reservations about Dummett's proposal, (which he has since qualified), that an unrestricted endorsement of Bivalence is the essential doctrine of realism, or at least constitutes its debatable substance once the usual metaphors are pared away. Stig Rasmussen and Jens Ravnkilde subsequently published an extended examination of the relationship between realism and logic in which they criticized many of the claims of Essay 15 and reaffirmed Dummett's original view that the anti-realist must be a logical revisionist and that Bivalence constitutes the core of realism. In Essay 16 I have attempted to respond to their case for these former anti-realist orthodoxies.

The Appendix to Essay 4, outlining an approach to a semantics for strict finitist arithmetic, was published with the original article. The Appendices to Essays 5 and 14 are new. Each of the Appendices concerns a potentially crucial topic which I would have preferred to treat in much fuller fashion. The Appendix to Essay 5 outlines a potential inconsistency in any view which denies the timelessness of truth. The Appendix to Essay 14 displays, inter alia, how, unless the epistemic constraint imposed by anti-realism on truth is to be quite anodyne, a much wider class of intuitions than is usually supposed comes under threat about which statements are apt to record real states of affairs.

I

The Negative Programme

1

Truth-conditions and Criteria

I

The observation is now commonplace that to have mastered a language of expressive power comparable to that of most natural languages is to understand a (potential) infinity of sentences. What ought to be aimed at by a theory of meaning for such a language is a systematic account of this knowledge. So the least the theory must achieve is a lot. It must provide a model of a master's recognition of the sense of any significant declarative sentence in his language. This recognition, it seems certain, is based on knowledge of the meanings of the constituents of a sentence and an appreciation of the way in which they are therein strung together. We therefore seek a theory which for an arbitrary declarative sentence of the language:

- i provides a breakdown of it into atomic semantically relevant constituents, such that the sense of each such constituent is of a general type described by the theory;
- ii within the framework of these general types, characterizes the *specific* senses of the constituents of the sentence in such a way that:
- iii an account of the sense of the sentence issues in a manner determined by its being a combination in just that fashion of just those constituents of just those general types.

The idea is that a correct theory of this sort will codify part of the information implicit knowledge of which constitutes knowledge of the language; that is, explicit knowledge of the theory *would* suffice for knowledge of part of the language.[1] But only of part of it; nothing would yet have been said about commands, questions, etc.

1 For an attempt to be somewhat more sensitive to the problems generated by this conception of implicit knowledge, see Essay 6.

Such a theory would be empirical. It would be contingent whether it characterized correctly the sense of any particular sentence in the studied language. The *philosophical* task is to determine the exact form which the theory should take. What primitives may the theory allow itself? What syntactic categories of expression (*types* of sense, as above) ought it to admit? How in general is the sense of a declarative sentence to be characterized? These are questions which become programmatically urgent. But they raise longstanding philosophical issues concerning explanation, logical form and the nature of knowledge of meaning.

It is to this philosophical task that the leading ideas of Davidson, with which Mr Scruton[2] believes himself to have some sympathy, are intended as a contribution. Indeed, if like Davidson[3] we believe in 'the obvious connection between a definition of truth of the kind Tarski has shown how to construct and the concept of meaning', namely: 'to give truth-conditions is a way of giving the meaning of a sentence', then the general account of the project commended by Davidson is plausible.

In the first half of his paper Scruton is concerned with the charge that Davidson's blue-print – like any implicitly *realist* conception of meaning, in the sense characterized in Scruton's section 1 – leaves out of account essential epistemological aspects of the concept of meaning, somehow overlooks that a theory of meaning ought also to be a theory of understanding. It does so because it is an example of a 'purely "referential" theory of meaning, a theory which analyses meaning only in terms of such notions as reference, satisfaction and truth' and gives no work to 'verification or assertibility'. Scruton conceives this charge to issue from the 'anti-realist', or 'verificationist',[4] standpoint sketched in many of Dummett's writings. It is with exposition of this complaint that I shall primarily be occupied, for I do not think that Scruton has fully grasped its character – that is, the character which in my opinion it ought to have. It is true that he explicitly disavows any concern but with '*one* possible contrast between realism and verificationism', and that it is only, presumably, as understood in that way that 'the two theories may in fact be compatible'. But this is hardly interesting unless he believes that his interpretation of the 'verificationist' position may well do justice to its strengths and motivation. That is what I deny.

I take it that Scruton is recommending the following view of the matter. There are indeed epistemological questions concerning language-mastery

2 In 'Truth-conditions and Criteria'.

3 Davidson, 'Truth and Meaning', in his *Inquiries into Truth and Interpretation*, p. 24.

4 Neither title is particularly happy. Realism may be attacked from all sorts of standpoint; and verification need not be the central notion in an anti-realist theory of meaning. But it is hard to think of better ones; and we are stuck with 'anti-realism' now anyway.

to which a realist theory, e.g. as envisaged by Davidson, does not address itself. But in order to face these questions, it is not required, as is supposed by an anti-realist, that the central role in the theory be played by conditions other than those of (possibly verification-transcendent) truth. Davidson is right in thinking that we have a theory of meaning for a language when we have a systematic means for determining the truth-conditions of any of its declarative sentences, based on an account of the sentence's structure and the semantic roles of its structurally essential constituents. Unless the theory takes this form, it will be incapable of achieving one end which a theory of meaning certainly ought to achieve: that of explaining our judgements of logical validity. Otherwise, like the mathematical intuitionists, we shall wind up with a theory enjoining extensive *revision* in our conception of what principles of inference are valid. A theory which 'does so much violence to our ordinary way of thought' ought to be avoided. Rather, what truth-theory requires, if we are to achieve a full understanding of the workings of our language, is supplementation.

What sort of supplementation? Davidson distinguishes two tasks: 'uncovering the logical grammar or form of sentences (which is in the province of the theory of meaning as I construe it) and the analysis of individual words or expressions (which are treated as primitive by the theory).'[5] Scruton's suggestion is that it is in this supplementary work of analysis that justice can be done to the demand that the theory of meaning face certain epistemological issues: how the expressions treated as 'primitive' by the theory are understood, what e.g. it *is* to be in pain. Thus the latter part of his paper concentrates on the question how Wittgenstein's notion of a *criterion*, or refinements of it, may figure in such analyses. The outcome is to be that we may legitimately 'combine an epistemological account of the understanding of individual predicates with a realist account of the truth-conditions of the sentences in which those predicates occur'. For 'the criterion theory of analysis is inherently epistemological in character.'

My suspicion is that a large part of the motive for this suggestion originates in a confusion about the sense in which a truth-theory will treat certain of the object-language's predicates as primitive. Naturally, it will conceive of some of them as semantically unstructured. But it will not confine itself to a characterization of their semantic *type*. In a fully fledged such theory there will be, for each such predicate of the object-language, a base-clause specifying in the chosen metalanguage the exact conditions under which an *n*-tuple (or infinite sequence) of objects satisfies it. But the connection between satisfaction-conditions and predicate sense has every right to be thought as perspicuous as that between truth-conditions

5 Davidson, 'Truth and Meaning', footnote 3, p. 31.

and sentence sense; the connections, indeed, are interwoven. So why does an adequate truth-theory for a language not already characterize perfectly the senses of its primitive predicates? How is it that we do not have in the base-clauses of the theory a complete characterization of what it is that someone who understands the primitives *knows*, viz. their conditions of application?

It is, of course, perfectly true that, as Scruton emphasizes, the axioms in question give us no way of *explaining* the meaning of primitive predicates to someone who is not familiar with the metalanguage. In order to understand any theory, one has to understand the language in which it is couched. But why should a philosopher – and how is he competent to – be interested in how an understanding of these predicates can be imbued? (It might be possible to induce it biochemically.) His proper concern is in what understanding the expressions *consists*; and this a complete truth-theory will purportedly tell us. The anti-realist's charge will indeed be that a truth-theory, interpreted as realist, does not everywhere adequately answer this question. But his complaint is not that an *incomplete* account has been given of the predicates which the theory treats as semantically unstructured. In fact he will have no objection to the part of the theory dealing with such expressions unless they are assigned verification-transcendent satisfaction-conditions; when it will concern not what the theory leaves unsaid but what it purports to state.

To avoid misunderstanding, I am not here disputing that there is such a thing as semantic analysis, very possibly correctly conceived as concerned with the elucidation of criteria and capable of achieving results of importance.[6] (Actually, the methodology of such an investigation seems unclear.)[7] What I am suggesting is that a complete truth-theory for a language, if it is properly seen as a theory of meaning[8] at all, is a

6 One might have supposed that a central task of analysis would be to determine the class of sentences to which the theory of truth is applicable. It struck me as curious that Davidson should have been pleased to side-step e.g. questions to do with the character of evaluative discourse. A central point of controversy has always been exactly whether the notion of truth is properly *applicable* to 'Bardot is good'. It may be that Scruton's remarks in the last section of his paper show the naivete of this.

7 I do not share Scruton's confidence that it will be straightforward to draw the distinction between criteria and evidence from an observer's point of view. (A different problem is that the idea that we can know *reflectively* what criteria we use appears, when natural assumptions are made about how exactly this knowledge can be achieved, to lead to paradoxes which threaten the whole programme of a systematic description of language use. See Dummett, 'Wang's Paradox', Wright, 'On the Coherence of Vague Predicates' and Wright, 'Language-Mastery and the Sorites Paradox'.

8 As remarked, it remains to construct a theory of commands, wishes, etc. I am assuming the propriety of seeing this task as supplementary to that of constructing a theory of meaning in the sense sketched at the beginning.

complete theory of meaning too. Nothing further remains to be done by way of characterizing the essential knowledge of a master of the object-language. If the meaning of any declarative sentence is fixed by determining its truth-conditions, then knowledge of the meaning of any such expression is knowledge of its truth-conditions; so to give an account of the truth-conditions of all such expressions in the language, based on their structure and the semantic properties of their constituents, is exhaustively to characterize both what the master knows and how he may be conceived as knowing it. Semantic analysis cannot supplement the theory as a programme for answering *these questions*. But Scruton evidently intends the project of analysis of primitive predicates (why does he not explicitly envisage its extension to singular terms, functional expressions and, crucially, *quantifiers*?) to contribute towards the question, in what does an understanding of these expressions consist? What space is left for such a contribution, if we have a theory which computes the truth-conditions of every declarative sentence containing such a predicate as a function of the satisfaction-conditions which it explicitly associates with the predicate? The theory *states*, in a most economical fashion, what someone who understands the predicate knows.

What would foster the illusion that space remains for semantic analysis to make such a contribution is a muddle which has frustrated relevant criticism of Davidson's project from the outset: the idea that the base-clauses serve only to pair expressions in the object- and metalanguages, that they only prescribe coincidences in sense and do not make explicit *what* the object-language primitives mean. I hesitate to attribute exactly this muddle to Scruton; a hostile reader might think he detected it in the 'mimsy' 'borogove' passage.

Analysis, then, is not correctly conceived as completing an answer to questions to which a realist truth-theory, qua purported theory of meaning, addresses itself but answers only 'partially'. Precisely what sort of question it can answer if truth-theory bags 'What is known by anyone who understands L?' – how exactly it can enlarge our understanding of understanding of L – seems to me still to need an account. All I am suggesting now is the following. It may be right to repudiate truth-theory as the model of a genuine theory of meaning. But Scruton is reluctant to do so. Given this reluctance, his conception of the *nature* of semantic analysis (= that it proceeds by the elucidation of criteria) seems not to be in tension with his conception of its *place* (= that it tells us what someone who understands the analysed expression essentially knows) only if the claim of truth-theory to answer the latter question passes without due acknowledgement. Otherwise, this crucial issue has to be faced: what is the relation between grasp of such criteria and knowledge of satisfaction-conditions as characterized by the truth-theory? If the theory really is a theory of meaning, the latter knowledge is presumably constitutive of understanding; but the latter knowledge is not reducible to the former if the predicate in question is not decidable but is associated with (inconclusive) criteria – e.g. 'is in pain' as applied to others; what part, then, does the former knowledge play? (Or, better, what part does the *latter* play – what *is* it?) Exactly here is the point at which the anti-realist's concern about the adequacy of a satisfaction-conditions conception of predicate-meaning originates. But Scruton, having failed to appreciate that for a truth-theory to treat certain of the object-language predicates as primitive is not for it to keep (even partial) silence about their sense, fails to reach this point.

None of this detracts from the interest of what Scruton has to say about criteria. But I shall not have space to pursue his suggestions. Rather I want to try to explain what, as it seems to me, the anti-realist charge essentially is. And subsequently I want to touch on four assumptions which Scruton makes, if I interpret him correctly, in the course of his discussion:

1 that truth-theory 'despite its empiricist overtones, certainly ought to be considered a realist theory in Dummett's sense';
2 that truth-theory can provide an explanation of our 'intuitions' of logical validity; (especially, those intuitions which are called into question by the intuitionists(!) and which, Scruton thinks, will inevitably be so by a more generalized anti-realism also);
3 that a theory of meaning *ought* to sanctify inferential custom;
4 that a generalized anti-realism is bound to be revisionary of our standard logical practices.

II

What exactly *is* the connection between truth-conditions and declarative sentence meaning? Whatever it is, it has to be reconcilable with the fundamental insight that grasp of the sense of any expression resides in the capacity to use, and respond to its uses, correctly. Scruton sees no tension between this foundational element of Wittgenstein's later philosophy of language and an endorsement of realism: 'What is it to understand or know the meaning of a sentence? On one interpretation of Davidson's account we might say this: a man understands a sentence if he uses it as part of a language and in conformity with whatever constraints are imposed by the truth-theory for that language. Thus the rules of truth will also provide an account of the speaker's understanding.'

It is not implausible to suppose that knowledge of the use of a declarative sentence will generally involve knowledge of the circumstances under which it could be used to state something true; truth, we conceive, is in general a necessary condition for the correct assertoric use of these expressions. But, obviously, the role which we may here allowably assign to the concept of truth has to be a function of what may legitimately be counted *as* grasp of the circumstances under which a sentence would state something true. What is it to have such grasp, if it is to have the desired connection with knowledge of use? Evidently it is unnecessary that someone be able to produce an articulate formulation of the sentence's truth-conditions in some further way; still less does he have to possess articulate knowledge of a truth-theory for his language, or be able to supply any kind of analysis of his understanding in the particular case. More important, the ability to produce a correct account of the truth-conditions is also insufficient. Somebody might be able to do that while misunderstanding both the sentence and his account of its truth-conditions. What would show that such was the situation? Precisely his failure to use the sentence appropriately, in particular a tendency not to assent to its assertion in circumstances when its truth-conditions obtained and he was in a position to appreciate as much.

Knowledge of use is not essentially verbalizable knowledge. So if knowledge of declarative sentence meaning is to be knowledge of truth-conditions, we should not construe the latter as essentially articulate. Rather it must be a recognitional capacity: the ability to recognize, if appropriately placed, circumstances which do, or do not, fulfil the truth-conditions of a sentence and to be prepared accordingly to assent to, or withhold assent to, its assertion. There is no hiatus between this ability and knowledge of the sentence's meaning; to attribute to someone the ability to recognize as such circumstances which do, or do not, fulfil the truth-conditions of a sentence – however problematic the criteria for such an attribution – *is* to attribute to him understanding of the sentence.

So much connection between truth-conditions and meaning is, I imagine, acceptable to anyone. What is contentious is the converse connection: is it acceptable that if someone understands a declarative sentence, he must possess a *recognitional* grasp of the circumstances under which it would be true? The difficulty is immediate: what if our standard conception of the truth-conditions of the sentence is such that if actualized, they would not, or need not, be recognizably so? Multifarious types of sentence are in this situation: unrestricted spatial or temporal generalizations, many subjunctive conditions, descriptions of the remote past, hypotheses about the mental life of others or of animals. If it is to be insisted that knowledge of truth-conditions has to be a recognitional capacity, then in cases like these there is not, or need not, be anything in which this alleged knowledge can consist. We thus have a dilemma: we can retain in such cases the connection between understanding and knowledge of truth-conditions only at the cost of attributing to ourselves a capacity to know what certain circumstances would be like which reduces to no capacity of recognition; what, in that case, of the connection between understanding and knowledge of use? *Or* we can reject the suggestion that the concept of truth plays the central role in our knowledge of the meanings of sentences of these sorts.

The latter is the anti-realist course. Grasp of the sense of a sentence cannot be displayed in response to unrecognizable conditions; nor, if we take seriously the connection between meaning and use, can such grasp go any further than its capacity to be displayed. But it cannot be supposed a mere illusion that we understand sentences of this kind. For there is a communal capacity of discrimination between correct and incorrect assertoric uses of them. So the right account is rather that our understanding of sentences whose truth-conditions we picture to ourselves as (possibly) verification-transcendent – because their 'verification' would require an infinitistic extension of capacities we possess, or possession of capacities which we altogether lack – is to be dislocated from such pictures of the 'circumstances' under which they would be true; instead it must have to do with more mundane circumstances which we can actually (or at least in principle)[9] recognize to obtain.

What sort of circumstances will these be? In examples like those cited they will typically consist in the existence of what we customarily regard as good but inconclusive evidence of such sentences' truth. In other cases, where conclusive verification is possible, it will continue to be admissible to think of understanding as consisting in knowledge of truth-conditions; for this knowledge is here recognitional. But the concept of truth surrenders two traditional aspects of its objectivity: for something to be fact it will be both necessary (no transcendence) and sufficient (no scepticism) that we can achieve a verification, by ordinary criteria, that it is so. In pure mathematics, for example, we banish the notion that theses may be true in virtue of the characteristics of hard, infinitistic conceptual structures which we finite beings can determine, if at all, only indirectly, albeit conclusively, by proof. Proof will constitute such sentences' truth.

Scruton suggests a realist will argue that such a notion is not correctly interpreted as one of *truth* at all – that *all* objectivity is lost – and hints at Kantian reasons for thinking so, of which a more explicit account would have been welcome. As it stands, the contrast between 'world-oriented' and 'speaker-oriented' notions of truth is not what is in play. Anti-realism

9 By 'in principle' possibilities I intend, roughly: feats in practice possible for a being with the same range of abilities as we, but possessing them to greater though still finite degree. Whether anything turns on this distinction, from the point of view of a prospective anti-realist, is an unsolved, and fundamental, question.

is not a species of idealism. We do not ordinarily think of those aspects of reality which we are able conclusively to determine as any less *of* the world. All that is being suggested here is that such aspects constitute the world – or, at least, those of its features to which we can give intelligible expression.

In general, we have to distinguish at least four categories of sentences to which we should ordinarily apply the notion of truth: those which are effectively decidable; those whose truth-conditions we so conceive that, if true, they must (at least in principle) be recognizably true, though the corresponding connection between falsity and falsifiability fails; those whose truth we do not conceive as requiring their verifiability, though we are not in a position to rule out the possibility of verification, (Fermat's 'theorem', e.g., or any ascription of a dispositional property whose circumstances of revelation we cannot effectively bring about but can recognize if they occur); and those whose verification is always beyond us. For a realist, these differences are quite inconsequential for the notion of understanding; to know the meaning of a sentence of any of these sorts is to know that it is true under certain specified circumstances and false under any others. But take any example in the fourth category; what in such a case is supposed to *constitute* this alleged knowledge? The only apparent candidate is: a capacity to formulate a conventionally correct account of just those circumstances. But this capacity, as noted, is two-way independent of the ability to use the sentence correctly in response to one's experience. If the latter ability is essential to an understanding of the sentence, the fact remains that there can be no experience of the sentence's truth. If linguistic understanding, then, is conceived as essentially a practical skill, we have no alternative but to conclude in such cases either that there is nothing for knowledge of truth-conditions to be or that it resides in an ability which is neither necessary nor sufficient for grasp of the sense of the sentence in question. Either way, we let go the fixation that it is in terms of knowledge of truth-conditions that the theory of meaning should depict our understanding of declarative sentences.

If we seek a general account of what an understanding of any of these four types of sentence amounts to, the only plausible strategy is to have it conform to the slogan: grasp of the sense of a declarative sentence is an operational grasp of the distinction between states of information which justify its assertoric use and states of information which do not. The achievement of a verification is *one* state of the former kind. So where verification is possible, it is quite unexceptionable to think of knowledge of truth-conditions, of this non-transcendent sort, as playing an essential role in grasp of meaning. But such knowledge will not be the *whole* of understanding in any case where other kinds of informational state are conceived as criterial justification for the assertion of the sentence – where mastery of its use requires the ability to recognize the relevance of such states. And in cases of the fourth type, knowledge of truth-conditions has no part to play.

On Scruton's conception of the matter, it is true, a realist theory of meaning, in the form of a theory of truth, nowhere directly attributes to those whose linguistic practice it seeks to describe knowledge of truth-conditions as such. Rather, for the theory to be a theory of their actual language is for them to be disposed to use declarative sentences 'in conformity with whatever constraints are imposed' by the theory, i.e. by its T-theorems. So their practice is, as it were, described obliquely. Their understanding e.g. of sentences of the fourth type does indeed consist in knowledge of their use; but that they accept just the states of information as justifying the assertion of these sentences which they do accept is to be explained in terms of an underlying, verification-transcendent notion of truth.

It is important to see that this is a vacuous refinement. In order for the theory to be testable, *we* at least – its devisors – have to be able to recognize just what constraints on the correct assertoric use of a sentence *are* imposed by assigning to it such-and-such transcendent, truth-conditions, Scruton provides no clue what the nature of this 'constraint' might be, *how* such an assignment enjoins a certain pattern of use. But the main point is that unless we can credit *ourselves* with an independent grasp of the truth-conditions in question, there is no route *through* the assignment to an account of the circumstances under which we can expect users of the object-language to count the assertion of the sentence as justified. But then the problem remains of giving practical content to this alleged grasp; and practical content it must be given, distinct from that associated with grasp of the states of information justifying the assertion of the sentence – for this is what it is supposed to *explain*, to provide a unifying principle for – before it can meaningfully be claimed that only by appeal to such a notion can the use of the sentence be characterized. The fact is, however, that no account is in sight of what grasp of transcendent truth-conditions is which can play this explanatory role. So the suspicion remains that realist truth-theory passes for a theory of meaning only because we, as it were, ignore the reference to truth and regard the T-theorems simply as identifying what assertions the quoted expressions are used to effect, testing them by reference to our grasp of the states of information which warrant those assertions. And the charge remains unanswered that as an attempted theory of linguistic practice, the realist version proceeds in terms of the wrong central notion.

III

Part of the motivation for realism surely is the idea that unless we invoke the notion of truth, it will be impossible to explain the *variety* of states of information which may be taken to justify the assertion of a particular sentence. How is it that a variety of proofs may be possible of a mathatical conjecture, or that another may display his social unease in a variety of ways? Do we not require an account of the sense of a sentence which makes clear the relevance to it of each of varying sorts of state of information which are deemed to justify its assertion?

Consider any contingent generalization: for all x, Fx. It is natural to suppose that the sense of 'all' is invariant with respect to the size of the domain of quantification. But the 'assertibility-conditions' of such generalizations seem not to be so. If the domain is small, and we possess a criterion for its having been exhaustively examined, then the optimum state of information is that consequent on such an examination. If it is large, we shall probably rely on indirect, argumentative grounds, even if we possess such a criterion. If it is infinite, we have no recourse but to such grounds; likewise in any case, irrespective of size, if we have no way of knowing that the whole domain has been checked. How can we make intelligible to ourselves the continuity in sense of 'all' through this variety of cases unless there is a uniform explanation appropriate for each of them? And how can this be given by reference to assertibility-conditions when their character varies among the cases? To invoke a uniform notion of truth, it might be thought, will supply this continuity.

How, exactly? The picture, I think, would have to be this: we are able to recognize, inductively I suppose, that the indirect type of ground is a good guide to the truth or falsity of decidable cases. We then export an analogous notion of truth to all cases; and though it now becomes verification-transcendent in some of them, it is only because we have such an analogy in the background that we can make intelligible the full range of criteria which we actually employ.

The picture, and its motivation, are suspect on four counts. First, we have to face the possibility that our impression of continuity of sense may be a product of the absorption into our preconceptions about our language of inadmissible (realist) imagery; the impression is therefore liable to reassessment in the light of a better philosophical perspective on the nature of linguistic understanding. Second, and more important, it is far from clear that it is any part of the brief of a theorist of meaning to *make intelligible*, in the sense appealed to, a variety in the assertibility-conditions of a particular sort of sentence. His task is to characterize what a master of the object-language essentially knows. If there is a variety of this kind, a master will know of it; so the theory must characterize it. But it does not have to *explain* it, if that is to mean: provide a something in virtue of which the variety can be seen as unified in source. There is such a thing, I suppose, as our all recognizing the appropriateness of a hitherto unenvisaged sort of state of information as justification for a particular assertion – as opposed e.g. to our all being disposed to accept a certain analogical extension of its assertibility-conditions. (Probably the distinction is highly problematic.) So an adequate theory of meaning for our language will have to associate with that sentence such so far unexploited grounds of assertion. But there is no reason to think that only a realist theory will be able to cope with this sort of problem; if ever it seems needed, better to re-examine the idea that our admission of the new assertion-grounds is a matter of *recognition*. Third, what is it to export an *analogous* notion of truth from decidable cases to the others? It had better be more than an assimilation of their use – their proof-theoretic liaisons and assertibility-conditions; for it is this assimilation which it is invoked to 'make intelligible'. The analogy is somehow to *mediate* the assimilation. But it can only do so if we can get some independent purchase on the verification-transcendent analogue. This is what we lack. The truth is that the 'analogy' contains no explanation – it is a veiled stipulation: do not worry about the apparent disharmony between the assertion-grounds and classical proof-theoretic properties of e.g. infinitistic generalizations, but pretend you have an underlying concept from which both can be seen to flow. Fourth, the idea that 'all' is univocal through the various cases actually gets quite enough support from the preservation of certain absolutely central logical properties, e.g. the Instantiation rule, by an anti-realist view of its meaning.

This is only one example. But the first two points are general, and the third is generalizable.

IV

In the exposition which I am trying to develop, the case for anti-realism is independent of considerations about how knowledge of meaning can be acquired; it has to do rather with how it can be manifested – with the character of the data which it will be the task of the theory of meaning to codify. Consider an analogous task: that of devising a theory of a game in the same sense of 'theory'. That is, we want a systematic representation of the knowledge how to play the game. Suppose the case is that of a two-person board game, with different pieces associated with different powers, etc. Knowledge how to play involves knowledge – not necessarily explicit, propositional knowledge – of two sorts: knowledge of the initial configuration, of when one is entitled to move, and of what moves are admissable in any particular situation; and knowledge of when someone – and who – has won, and that the aim is to win. To be able to play the game is to have just these discriminative abilities and overriding intention; a theory of the game is exactly a complete, explicit specification of what anyone who can play the game implicitly knows.

Suppose we come across a tribe whose language we do not understand and who play a game much akin to chess. Our task is to construct a theory of their game, 'tribe-chess', purely from observation of their play. Our observations suggest that the theories of chess and tribe-chess should coincide with respect to the first category of information above. But winning is different. Games of tribe-chess are never played to a chess conclusion. Instead a system of arbitration seems to operate, each player apparently having the right on making a move to call on a referee – a revered class – to assess the resulting position. Sometimes the referee awards the game to the plaintiff; sometimes he bids play continue; sometimes he awards a draw (e.g. he holds both Kings aloft). All this is our interpretation, of course. Suppose it very well supported by the tribesmen's behaviour.

To win in tribe-chess, then, is to get the verdict on going to arbitration. But that statement is no good for the purpose of our theory. Just to know that, plus all the first-category information, is not yet to know how to *try* to win. The players have to know what *kind* of position can be expected to elicit a favourable verdict.

Suppose that matters seem straightforward. The referees award wins only when our experts agree that the plaintiff has indeed secured an advantage which, on best play, is likely to secure him a chess win. *Mutatis mutandis* for the verdicts, 'draw' and 'continue'. Then it might seem we should complete the section on winning thus: a player wins in tribe-chess just in case he achieves a position from which he can, by best play, win in chess.[10] Correspondingly for a draw. The role of the referees is just to assess configurations for these features.

The trouble with this account is that it attributes to tribe-chess a gratuitous theoretic flaw: to have won, as so characterized, does not entail that it can be recognized that one has.[11] So it cannot be excluded that people may play through tribe-chess wins without it being possible for them, or the referee to realize as much. In chess, in contrast, we may overlook that we *can* win from a particular position; but it is recognizable if we *have* won. But there is an obvious remedy: characterize the players as aiming at a position of which it *can be recognized* that best play will eventually secure them a chess win. This hypothesis explains the same facts while avoiding the flaw.

Its main advantage, however, is philosophical. If we are attempting to construct a systematic theory of a rule-structured, goal-directed activity, we have to ascribe *feasible* intentions to the participants – goals such that if achieved, the participants will be able to recognize it. The ground for

10 In a fully explicit theory, of course, we should explain away the reference to chess.

11 For example, it is not known, so far as I am aware, whether White cannot always win if he knows how.

saying so is simply that any recognition-transcendent residue in the attributed goals – the difference e.g. between the original and emended hypotheses about winning in tribe-chess – will be theoretical slack, void of observational warrant. None of our observations can possibly suggest that the tribe-chess players are aiming to win *irrespective* of whether anyone can see that they have. If our theory of their practice is to be an empirical theory, the only objectives which we have any business attributing to them must be such that their behaviour, as it unfolds in the practice of the game, can supply grounds for the attribution.

The point, then, has nothing to do with armchair speculation about how an understanding of the practice can be acquired. But there is no harm in putting it like this: a practice involving recognition-transcendent objectives is not as such a *communicable* practice; for it will not matter if someone misunderstands an objective of this sort providing he grasps aright the circumstances under which the claim that it is realized may legitimately be made. Thus it is not that we *can* only learn the nature of certain goals by experience of what it is like for them to have been achieved; rather, it is sense to think of someone as aiming at a particular goal only if it is sense to think that he has learned its nature *somehow* i.e. can provide evidence that he understands it.

The point of the example resides in an important analogy[12] between winning and truth. An understanding that one is to *aim* to win/make true assertions is fundamental to an understanding of the game/assertoric discourse. Scruton's emendation was: aim at asserting sentences in accordance with the constraints consequent upon a correct truth-definition for them. But truth-theory is to be an empirical theory; its construction is e.g. the end of a programme of radical translation. So if the emendation is not to introduce theoretical slack, the meeting of the constraints in question must in any particular case always be explained as a situation which, if actual, can be recognized to be so – by the theorists at least. It follows that it can never consist in the realization of verification-transcendent truth-conditions; more, that a picture of what it is for such conditions to obtain is no essential part of a language-master's equipment – for the evidence cannot require us to characterize his objectives in terms of a notion which it can afford us no grounds to suppose he possesses. Truth, then, is unsuited to serve as the central notion in an empirical theory of meaning. The central notion must register a non-transcendent objective, for whose possession by the object-language community there can be direct, observational evidence. So we must describe ourselves, and others, as aiming at 'warranted assertion', where this catchphrase signals our

12 Cf. Wittgenstein, *Remarks on the Foundations of Mathematics*, Appendix I, pp. 1–6; Dummett, 'Truth', p. 2 in his *Truth and Other Enigmas*.

ambition to construct a theory for whose lowest-level theorems – the analogues of the old T-theorems – there can be the most direct evidential support.

On this view, there is no alternative to the conclusion that we habitually misrepresent to ourselves the character of our understanding of certain sentences. For it cannot be other than as such a theory would characterize it. We conceive, for example, of infinitistic contingent generalizations as, if true, being so in virtue of a tailored infinitistic fact, essentially inaccessible to us and of which we can only detect the symptoms; when the truth is merely that we have so fixed the use of these sentences that the optimum state of information justifying their assertion always falls short of verification – that we are always prepared to envisage the enlargement of such a state into one which warrants their denial.

It is futile to refer the demand for evidence of our possession of a verification-transcendent notion of truth for such sentences back to our habitual application to them of principles of classical logic. Are we to surrender the view that the validity of such principles ought to be a function of the senses of the logical constants – that Excluded Middle, e.g., is valid, if at all, in virtue of the senses of 'or' and 'not' as characterized absolutely generally by a satisfactory theory of meaning (so one which does not employ a recognition-transcendent central notion) and the general form of explanation of declarative sentence meaning which it offers? If logic is to be so answerable, the behaviour in question is evidence not of the currency of a realist notion of truth, but that a lay-philosophical misconception has become more than a picture and has been enshrined in linguistic practice. If logic is not to be so answerable, the behaviour in question shows nothing about our understanding of the sentences to which it is applied. (More of this shortly.)

Such, then, is how I interpret the motivation for a globally anti-realist philosophy of language. Whatever is thought of it, it is clear that the complaint made against realism could not be appeased by any kind of supplement to a realist truth-theory. It is only in a facetious sense that we can say that there may be *more* information to be given about the meaning of a particular declarative sentence than is captured by its T-theorem in a 'correct' realist truth-theory; for unless the theorem associates the truth of the sentence with recognizable conditions, it supplies *no* constraints on its correct use, and so fails to characterize its sense altogether.

V

The scope of the foregoing considerations is no wider than the question, in what does an understanding of a particular declarative sentence consist.

We have been concerned only with the desirable *output* of a theory of meaning. Doubts remain concerning the mechanics of a theory which is to have such an output. How are we to treat sentences containing unasserted sentential parts? Surely the *fear* that P, for example, cannot in general be plausibly construed as the fear that P is justifiably assertible; what is feared is that P is *true*. Similarly, surely the antecedents of conditionals must be taken as hypotheses not of warranted assertibility but of truth. I may very well know that a conditional which I believe, e.g. about the events at Thermopylae, has an antecedent for which there is no evidence whatever. The irrelevance of this knowledge to my semantic intention in asserting it is attested by its provision of no motive for using the subjunctive mood.

The doubt is exactly whether a systematic anti-realist theory of meaning is possible. I could not allay it here, even if I knew how. But I want to scotch one source of it. It is inescapable that such a theory ought generally to construe the senses of declarative compounds as a function of the assertibility-conditions of their constituents. But this does not require that we treat the unasserted constituents as interchangeable with statements of their own warranted assertibility. We are not *allowed* in general to do so, for a simple reason: they are not the same statement. 'P is justifiably assertible (in the present state of information)' is, if true, always in principle decidably so; whereas there may be no notion of verification for P, and, if there is, the former may still be verified in circumstances falling short of it.

But how, in that case, are we to construe unasserted occurrences of P in compounds? In many cases, at least, by adapting the work of the intuitionists. Consider their account of mathematical conditionals:

> 'P→Q' is proved just in case we have a construction, C, of which we can recognize that, had we a proof of P, we could use C to transform it into a proof of Q.

A natural generalization is:

> A state of information justifies our assertion of 'if P, then Q' just in case we can recognize that its enlargement into a state justifying the assertion of P would *eo ipso* transform it into a state justifying the assertion of Q.

Such an account would provide a treatment of a large class of conditionals without either invoking a realist notion of truth or requiring us to identify their antecedents with hypotheses of warranted assertibility.

VI

Scruton writes: 'A theory of truth should be able to lead us to an account of validity. Only then will it have embraced all those aspects of linguistic behaviour which can provide evidence for a theory of meaning. But, as it happens, there seems to be no prospect of accounting for those inferences recognized by normal speakers as valid or invalid without assuming a transcendent conception of truth.' This idea has some plausibility; for we tend to think of our recognition of validity, and necessity in general, as an application of the very discriminations of structure and semantic role which it is the task of a theory of meaning to characterize. This is just an adaptation of the old idea, 'true purely in virtue of meaning'.

But how exactly is a truth-theory to *account* for validity? Presumably, if P expresses a necessary truth, we want to be able to prove a theorem, ⊢P is true, from the clauses of the theory. (For a valid principle of inference, 'P' will be a suitable corresponding conditional.) Obviously, however, whether or not we can do so depends on the proof-theory in which the theory of truth is embedded. Consider a simple example. We are to construct a truth-theory in English for a (fragment of a) language consisting of a finite number of semantically unstructured sentences whose role is to record the colour of presented patches, and any sentences accessible from these by finitely many applications of the unary connective, 'nee', and the binary connective, 'aurt'. Thus we have the base clauses:

> 'hab ruch' is true ≡ it is red,
> 'hab vereid' is true ≡ it is green, etc.,

and the recursive clauses:

> P⌢'aurt'⌢Q is true ≡ (P is true) ∨ (Q is true),
> 'nee'⌢P is true ≡ ~(P is true)

Suppose that speakers of this tongue accept a Double Negation Elimination rule for these sentences. Can we elucidate their 'intuition'? We are asking in effect, can we derive the theorem: ⊢ 'nee'⌢'nee'⌢P is true ⊃ P is true? The answer is, trivially, 'yes' if we have: ~ ~ P ⊢ P as a meta-linguistic rule of inference; otherwise, 'no'. So 'no' if we have only the apparatus necessary for deriving the Tarski biconditionals.

A pure truth-theory, then – one which contains only that apparatus – will in general be quite impotent to get to grips with questions of validity in the object language. Do we want to sanctify this aspect of the speakers' practice or fault it? It is a question to be decided by informal philosophical reflection on the semantics of vague expressions. Depending on the results of that reflection, we shall want to tailor our meta-linguistic rules so as to yield, or leave inaccessible, the theorem in question. But the resulting truth-theory will merely embody an insight achieved by quite different methods. There is no question of it leading us to that insight.

In one sense, naturally, we can 'account' for the speakers' habitual acceptance of any inferential pattern just by tailoring our theory so that it yields the relevant theorem. But this cannot be the sense which Scruton had in mind; for we could so account for our acceptance of classical logic without any appeal to a verification-transcendent notion of truth, but merely by mindlessly couching a truth-theory for our language in a classical proof-theory. A theory of meaning which is to meet Scruton's requirement must incorporate some informal philosophy. So there is a potential tension between that requirement and the idea that the formal truth-theoretic part must square with as wide a field of evidence as possible. There is no question of our having to give equal weight to *all* aspects of the speakers' regular inferential practice as evidence for or against the theory; rather, in proportion as our confidence in the theory grows, we shall take the capacity of their practice, so interpreted, to meet philosophical requirements as the test of *its* correctness. Scruton may be right in thinking that, at the informal level, it is only by appeal to a realist notion of truth that we can get a general exegesis of the validity of classical principles.[13] But in calling for a substantial account of validity, he puts the intelligibility of this notion beyond support by appeal to the character of our habitual practices. It stands or falls under philosophical scrutiny.

A pure truth-theory is thus not yet a realist truth-theory. Does it have to be interpreted as a theory of *truth* at all? Does anything that happens in such a theory prevent our taking it as a theory of warranted assertibility?

Scruton contests that we could so interpret the sort of straightforward negation clause illustrated. The point, if I interpret him right, is that we cannot suppose that 'not P' is justifiably assertible just in case it is not the case that P is; for the latter may be true in a state of information which does not warrant the *denial* of P.

Convention T requires that any sentence comprising the right-hand of a Tarski biconditional be a translation of the quoted sentence to the left. Evidently, therefore, to interpret a pure truth-theory meeting this constraint as a theory of assertibility requires that we take these biconditionals as something other than material equivalences. That is, in any correct biconditional,

$$\text{P is justifiably assertible} \equiv \phi,$$

ϕ cannot be synonymous with P in any case where 'P is justifiably assertible' may be verified in circumstances falling short of a verification of P. The obvious strategy is to adapt the generalized intuitionistic account of the conditional, sketched earlier. We read the Tarski biconditionals as pairs of conditionals whose assertibility-conditions are as then explained.

13 Actually, it is a very moot point whether this would be right. See Essays 15 and 16.

Thereby, I surmise, it will be possible to reconcile the output of a pure truth-theory, satisfying Convention T, with its interpretation as a theory of assertibility. For, plausibly, to be justified in asserting that P is justifiably assertible is to be justified in making an assertoric use of any sentence synonymous with P.

This does not yet make clear how we can interpret in terms of assertibility both occurrences of 'is T' in a straightforward negation clause:

$$\text{'not'}^\frown\text{P is T} \leftrightarrow \sim(\text{P is T}).$$

But this is only a schema for arriving at an account of the assertibility-conditions of 'not'⌢P, and not yet a final deliverance of them. The theory will, it is to be hoped, provide a T-theorem: P is T $\leftrightarrow \phi$. Assuming, then, that our proof-theory contains the meta-rule:

$$A \leftrightarrow B \vdash \sim A \leftrightarrow \sim B,$$

the final deliverance is:

$$\text{'not'}^\frown\text{P is T} \leftrightarrow \sim\phi,$$

i.e. any state of information justifying the assertion that 'not'⌢P is justifiably assertible justifies the denial of ϕ, and conversely. Which, if ϕ is a translation of P, comes to what we want.

Any pure truth-theory will contain the needed meta-rule. And it is easily seen to be justified in terms of the most natural generalization of the intuitionists' account of mathematical negation:

> The negation of a sentence is proved just in case we have reduced to absurdity the supposition that a construction constituting a proof of that sentence can be achieved.

Namely:

> A state of information justifies the assertion of the negation of a sentence just in case it justifies the assertion that an (overall) state of information justifying the assertion of that sentence cannot be achieved.

On this account, if P and Q have the same assertibility-conditions, so do their negations.

If an anti-realist cannot accept the straightforward recursions for the logical constants given in a pure truth-theory, reinterpreted along the lines illustrated, I have to confess that I have not been able to detect why not.[14] Indeed, the possibility suggests itself that he may simply take over the legacy of the approach to structural problems which those working within a

14 But see Essay 14.

truth-theoretic framework have bestowed, confident that their results – so long as not achieved by essential recourse to classical concepts and methods in regions where he will contest their legitimacy – will survive reinterpretation in his terms. Anyone who feels that there is much to be said for Davidson's approach, and something to be said for the earlier part of this paper, ought to hope that this is so.

It would, at any rate, be easier to understand the role of a programme of analysis of the kind which Scruton envisages. When a truth-theory is interpreted as a theory of assertibility, its T-theorem for any particular object-language sentence, P, characterizes the states of information which justify assertoric use of P as those which justify a particular assertion, metalinguistically expressed. Plausibly, this is to characterize what assertion is effected by P – which is what anyone who understands it essentially knows – and, as before, the mode of deliverance of the relevant T-theorem will suggest a model of how his mastery of the language bestows this knowledge. But there may still be such a thing as further articulating what in any particular case this knowledge consists in. The trouble with Scruton's account was precisely that it is impossible to see recognition-transcendent knowledge as *consisting* in knowledge of criteria. Now, however, there is room for analysis, conceived as the elucidation of criteria, to be *of* the very knowledge characterized by the formal theory. Its goal will be e.g. to explain the verification conditions of 'P is justifiably assertible in the present state of information'.

VII

I have tried to give reasons for thinking that it is not necessarily outrageous if a theory of meaning proves revisionary of inferential practice, if its formal part contains no acknowledgement of certain aspects of inferential custom in the described community. We cannot be required to count everything as evidence for or against the theory if we conceive that it is to be *deeply* explanatory of linguistic practice, in the sense invited by the idea that the theory should elucidate the 'flow' of validity, and necessity in general, from semantic features. But a quite different view is possible, far removed from realism. According to it, the substance to the notion that we recognize validity, and necessity in general, by apprehending semantic features is merely that we take an obdurate non-recognition as a criterion for a misapprehension. 'He *cannot* understand the sentence as we do.' But there need be no possibility of an illuminating explanation of *how* necessity is a product of semantic properties in any particular case. Some principles may simply be accepted as constitutive of the meanings of the expressions involved. It may simply not be possible to trace the validity of such principles back to a source in a general account, e.g. of the logical constants, which balances the ideals of accord with object-language practice and philosophical respectability. It may be, for example, that it would prove impossible for an anti-realist visitor from space, essaying a theory of meaning of English, to provide a general account of 'not' which explained (as e.g. the generalized intuitionistic account, above, explains the principle, $P \leftrightarrow Q \vdash {\sim}P \leftrightarrow {\sim}Q$) our general acceptance of Double Negation Elimination, save at the cost of not explaining other central principles. But it may also be that we take a failure to grasp Double Negation Elimination as a criterion of muddle about the effect of negating a sentence twice. In that case, rather than hold our acceptance of the principle to be suspect, our visitor should require his theory somehow to record that it is accepted.

On this view, a theory of meaning may afford grounds for attributing false empirical beliefs to speakers of the studied language, but it cannot convict them of inferential malpractice. For the logical principles which they accept are simply constitutive of the concepts involved; necessary statements *determine* the meanings which they are 'true purely in virtue of'.

There is not obviously any conflict of this idea with the general conception that an understanding of any declarative sentence is constituted by the ability to discriminate between states of information which justify its assertion and states of information which do not. Its conflict is rather with an assumption implicit in the idea that this conception is bound to prove revisionary of classical logic in a wide class of cases. Consider the key example of Excluded Middle. Why does this seem unassailable from a realist point of view? For a realist, the sense of any declarative sentence is determined by associating with it certain necessary and sufficient conditions of truth. In *any other* circumstances the claim that the sentence is not true (= what is expressed by its negation) will be correct. So Excluded Middle follows by an appeal to the distributivity of truth over disjunction, i.e. the requirement that it is both necessary and sufficient for the truth of a disjunction that one of the disjuncts be true. On a (generalized) intuitionistic account of the logical constants, the distributivity of the central notion is retained. Thus a state of information justifies the assertion of a disjunction just in case it justifies, or can be recognized to be capable of effective enlargement into a state which justifies the assertion of one of the disjuncts. A valid disjunction is one whose assertion is so justified in any state of information. So if negation is interpreted in the generalized intuitionistic way sketched above, it is apparent that many examples of Excluded Middle are not now valid. That is, for a wide variety of statements, S, states of information are conceivable which justify neither the assertion of S *nor* the assertion that a state of information justifying the assertion of S cannot be achieved, and such that no effective way is apparent of enlarging them into a state justifying one of those two assertions.

One assumption made here is that an anti-realist should go for such an account of negation. Another is the distributivity of the central notion over disjunction (whose rejection would seem to threaten other principles; e.g. Modus Tollendo Ponens).[15] But more fundamental, and common to both accounts, is the idea that the validity of Excluded Middle is to be assessed by application of general explanations of disjunction and negation. And this is just a reflection of our tendency to think of the necessity of many sentences as originating in, and to be explained in terms of, their structure and the pre-established semantic properties of their constituents.

The alternative view rejects this assumption. It is the position of the later Wittgenstein. It is evident that if there is to be a theory of meaning at all, all the sympathy of the Wittgenstein of the *Investigations* and *Remarks on the Foundations of Mathematics* would be with the anti-realist project. Yet he took an explicitly anti-revisionist view of the philosophy of language.[16] It is plausible that at least part of the explanation of this was his idea that logic and mathematics should be seen as 'antecedent' to questions of truth[17] (or justifiable assertibility). The principles of inference which we employ are not to be seen as *answerable* e.g. to the senses of the logical constants, and so in principle capable of revision in the light of a theory which correctly characterizes those senses. Rather they are antecedent to all such questions, themselves entering into the determination of the assertibility-conditions of the potential infinity of contingent sentences whose construction the language allows; for the assertion of any such sentence may be justified on the basis of inference. Principles of inference are among the rules of the 'language-game'; and a systematic description of the practice should record as much. Excluded Middle is not answerable to a general account of disjunction and negation; rather, if its acceptance is indeed deeply embedded in linguistic practice, that it is so should be *part* of such an account.

Quite how the anti-realist space visitor, radically translating our language, should implement this idea is another matter. If he just adds the axiom '"P or not P" is unrestrictedly justifiably assertible', how is he to avoid the transition, via the recursions of his theory, to something equivalent to $\vdash A \vee \sim A$, which is what he rejects? Perhaps he should regard the quoted part of the axiom as uninterpreted, as not subject to treatment in terms of the clauses for 'or' and 'not'; certainly its role is to supplement the information which those clauses give.

15 See, however, the discussion of Vel-Elimination in section III of Essay 15.

16 Cf. *Investigations*, I, 124; and *Remarks on the Foundations of Mathematics*, IV, 52.

17 Cf. *Remarks on the Foundations of Mathematics*, I, 155. See also Moore, 'Wittgenstein's Lectures of 1930–33'.

Our reluctance to accept these ideas needs little support from their programmatic obscurity; it is just our reluctance to accept the extreme conventionalism about necessity which Wittgenstein later came to hold. Two intuitive ideas militate against its acceptance: the idea that recognition of necessity generally *is* recognition in the light of understanding, that the necessity of a sentence – save in the case of an explicit convention – will be a *product* of its structure and the independently assigned semantic roles of its constituents; and the idea that principles of inference have a responsibility to the truth- (or assertibility-) status of the contingent sentences which they will enable us to link as premises and conclusions in practical inferential contexts. Wittgenstein disputed that necessity has an epistemology, and rejected the idea that we could *fail* in the latter responsibility.

I think it is fair to say that, if his reasons for doing so were bad, we have yet to earn the right to be sure of it. But if this extreme conventionalism were incorrect, that would not yet be for it to be evident that a fully anti-realist theory of meaning is bound to be revisionary of certain of our traditional logical habits. At any rate, someone who thinks it is so owes us an explanation of why, if the distinction can indeed be made good between explicit conventions and those sentences whose necessity is consequent upon pre-established semantic properties of their constituents, those generally accepted classical principles whose validity proves inaccessible in terms of the anti-realist account should not be regarded as falling within the former class.[18]

18 The ideas of this last section I have since elaborated in Essay 15 and in my *Wittgenstein on the Foundations of Mathematics*; see especially chapters II, IV, V, XIV, XVIII, XIX, XXII and XXIII. More recently, see my 'Inventing Logical Necessity'.

2

Strawson on Anti-realism

This paper is not self-contained but is a response to the remarks of the Chairman, Sir Peter Strawson,[1] at the Mind/Aristotelian Society symposium entitled 'Truth-conditions and Critera'.[2] Strawson seemed to me to misdescribe both what was essentially at issue between the symposiasts (Roger Scruton and myself) and, much more importantly, a broad range of features of the topography – motivation, points of vulnerability, and general implications – of anti-realism. And if that were not sufficient reason for a reply, the grateful reception of his remarks by an audience who seemed, by and large, to think that anti-realism could be nothing other than the positivism of the thirties, would provide one.

I

Strawson takes it that the main issue between Scruton and myself was whether a Davidson-style truth-theory, conceived as a theory of speakers' understanding, needed any kind of supplementation.[3] Scruton is represented as holding that some such supplementation is required in the case of predicates treated as primitive by the theory;[4] and that the supplement should take the form of supplying an analysis of the criteria – in something intended to be close to Wittgenstein's sense of that term – by reference to which correct application of such predicates would be assessed. Strawson represents me, on the other hand, first as complaining that, if such supplementary analysis is desirable at all, there seems no reason why it should be desirable only in the case of primitive predicates and not also

1 Strawson, 'Scruton and Wright on Anti-realism, etc.'.

2 The second paper of the symposium appears above as Essay 1.

3 Strawson, 'Scruton and Wright on Anti-realism, etc.', pp. 15–16.

4 That is, predicates for which, in case the object-language is a fragment of the language in which the theory is stated, a homophonic axiom will be employed.

e.g. in the case of quantifiers and singular terms; and, second, as doubting whether in fact such supplementation is required – whether, that is, a truth-theory, if both philosophically and empirically acceptable as far as it went, would not be in effect a complete account of speakers' understanding of the declarative part of the language.

Strawson rejects this doubt. Granted that understanding any declarative sentence is knowing its truth-conditions, it follows that a theory which correctly states the truth-conditions of every declarative sentence in the object-language *is* a complete account of what anyone who understands the declarative part of the language knows. But it is not so far any sort of account of what, in the case of any particular sentence, possession of the relevant piece of knowledge *consists in*; of what, in practice, the distinctive manifestation of that piece of knowledge would be.

Strawson seems to me quite right to press this distinction. But my principal objection to Scruton's proposals actually proceeded in terms of it. There are some declarative sentences which we should ordinarily take to be the possessors of truth-values but which are such that, even before we find out any facts which we should take to bear on what truth-value they have, we have to acknowledge that our investigations, while at best persuasive, will be in the nature of the case inconclusive. If our understanding even of such sentences is held to be a matter of knowledge of truth-conditions, then of course a truth-theory can aspire to state what, when we understand any particular such sentence, we thereby know. But my objection to Scruton was precisely that to endorse truth-theory that far precludes the belief that by a programme of analysis of criteria the question can then be answered whose legitimacy Strawson thought I had overlooked and which a truth-theory, unsupplemented, cannot answer.

The satisfaction of criteria for the justified assertion of a sentence is, both on Wittgenstein's and – I took it – on Scruton's conception of a criterion, a decidable matter: a situation which, if actual, can be recognized by speakers of the language to be so. Therefore to attribute to someone knowledge of criteria need involve no more than to credit him with a capacity to respond appropriately to the obtaining of certain detectable circumstances; and it would be with the detailed description of such capacities in particular cases that Scruton's supplementary programme would turn out to be concerned. But how can possession of such a capacity, or range of capacities, *constitute* grasp of what it is for a possibly verification-transcendent truth-condition to obtain? How can a conception of a possibly *transcendent* state of affairs be exhausted by a sensitivity to recognizable circumstances? I took it that it could not (and so, implicitly, did Strawson, for he speaks of the rational speaker's responses as being *governed* by the transcendent conception).[5] But in that case the knowledge which Scruton's supplementary work would be concerned with is not the same knowledge as the knowledge which the truth-theory, interpreted as realist, attributes to the object-language speakers.

Let us then sharply distinguish the questions:

What is known by anyone who understands S?

and

What sort of behaviour manifests an understanding of S?

Then my objection was not that a correct truth-theory, if such a thing were possible, would stand in no *need* of supplementation. It was that I could not see how it was possible to construe either Scruton's proposal, or any supplementary programme concerned with the description of responses to detectable circumstances, as an appropriate way to attempt to answer the second kind of question, if a realist truth-theory is regarded as an appropriate way to attempt to answer questions of the first type. And indeed one way of expressing the anti-realist challenge is as the demand for an explanation how a generalized realism can in the end satisfactorily address itself to the second type of question when (possibly) verification-transcendent sentences are involved.

Strawson, then, appears to have mistaken what essentially I was objecting to in Scruton's proposal. That, to be sure, may have been mainly my fault; but it is natural to wonder whether that misapprehension and the assurance that no serious challenge is posed to realism by the considerations which I tried to describe are wholly unrelated.

II

Before it can be clear what the issue between the anti-realist and his truth-theoretical opponent amounts to, Strawson holds,

> ...we need to know *at least* what is to count as falling within the range of 'recognisable situations'; what is to count as conclusive verification; *whose* capacity in fact or in principle to do the recognising is in question; what importance, if any, to attach to the disjunction: in fact or in principle; and what 'in principle' means.

These are relevant, and very difficult, questions. But if Strawson meant to suggest that until more progress on them has been made, it cannot be clear that there is any anti-realist challenge to answer, then he seems to

5 p. 16.

me mistaken. Certainly, answers are needed to these problems before it can be clear which, if any, are the sentences whose meaning, for realist and anti-realist alike, can be regarded as fixed in terms of truth-conditions. But we don't need to be clear about that issue in order to be clear whether there are any sentences in whose case the anti-realist is bound to be dissatisfied with the realist account. It is required only that there are some sentences whose conclusive verification is precluded in the nature of the case, whatever more specific account of the notion of conclusive verification may subsequently content us as correct; sentences for which the claim, 'I have conclusively verified S', will be taken *ceteris paribus*, to betray a misunderstanding of S. And that, surely, is the situation of the kinds of example on which discussion of these issues has tended to concentrate: unrestrictedly general hypotheses, many types of subjunctive conditional, many types of description of the remote past and future, many types of description of others' mental states, etc.

The notion of conclusive verification, in particular, may well prove ineluctably obscure – provided, at least, that we want there to be conclusively verifiable sentences. And this, no doubt, would be a serious objection to any version of anti-realism which proposed to cast the notion of verification in the role traditionally played by the notion of truth. But the kind of case against realism which I tried to describe in 'Truth-conditions and Criteria' needs recourse to the notion of verification only negatively, in that it requires, to repeat, that there be some sentences with, intuitively, a clear meaning but for which we simply have no use for the notion of verification: sentences such that, whatever the informational context, to claim 'I have conclusively verified S', will be regarded as inappropriate. The anti-realist grants, for the sake of argument, that we may legitimately be held to have understood the truth-conditions of all sentences of which we have understood the conditions of conclusive verification; and then challenges the realist to explain why that 'all' should not be strengthened to 'all and *only*'. If 'conclusive verification' were to turn out to be very restricted, or even chimerical, in application, the challenge would simply be generalized: we should have a very wide, or all-inclusive, class of sentences for which it was problematic what grasp of truth-conditions could consist in, how it might be distinctively displayed.

III

Strawson argues that there are at least two important kinds of sentence for which there can be no satisfactory anti-realist account of meaning: ascriptions of sensations to others, and sentences about the relatively remote past.

The orthodox conception of the meaning of 'John is in pain', said of John by someone else, involves that, if true, it is made so by the obtaining of a state of affairs which is, strictly, inaccessible to everyone save John – so for which the speaker can only have indirect *evidence*, including perhaps John's word. If this conception of the truth-conditions of such sentences and their relation to the sentences' content is to be rejected, Strawson asks, with what alternative account is it to be replaced?

There are, Strawson holds, just three possibilities open to the anti-realist.

A He can deny that such sentences have any conditions of truth at all. Their meaning is fixed, rather, simply by their being associated with certain determinate, empirical conditions of acceptance and rejection; and understanding them is the practical ability to recognize fulfilment of these conditions as such.

B He can seek to locate *publicly accessible* truth-conditions for such sentences. On this type of view, understanding such sentences will be a matter of possessing a practical grasp of their truth-conditions, of a kind to which the anti-realist has no objection.[6]

C He can grant that these sentences have truth-conditions, which however have nothing at all to do with their meaning – save, perhaps, for whoever is undergoing the sensation. For other people it is a possibility fully to understand such a sentence without knowing what its truth-conditions are.

Strawson reckons each of (A) to (C) to be decisively objectionable. Here, however, I propose to leave (B) out of account. For whether or not some behaviourist, or physicalist, analysis of ascriptions of sensation to others can be satisfactorily made out, it seems certain that the general policy which (B) illustrates, viz. looking for a communally accessible truth-condition to do duty for what on the realist view would be a transcendent one, will prove unworkable with other examples (e.g. scientific laws). Moreover, Strawson's criticisms of (A) and (C) in no way depend on the particular example.

Strawson attributes to (C) the consequence

> ...that someone could have a complete grasp of the meaning of what he said without knowing what he was saying, that is, asserting – an unappealing thought.

But there is a tacit assumption at work here. We get that conclusion only if we presuppose that *what is stated* by an assertoric use of 'John is in pain' *has* to be explained by reference to necessary and sufficient conditions

6 Strawson suggests in the relevant passage that the truth-conditions of these sentences on this second type of view will be identified with the disjunction of states of affairs regarded as conditions of their warranted acceptance by the first type of view. In fact, of course, accounts of this second type could take all sorts of other forms; for example, the sort of physicalism described by Hopkins in 'Wittgenstein and Physicalism'.

for that sentence's truth. And it is to be expected that a C-type anti-realist would dispute that the assertoric content of 'John is in pain' was tied in this way to the truth-condition which, for whatever reason, he is conceding it to have.

To (A), which he considers the least unattractive, Strawson imputes the

> ...unsatisfactory feature that it leaves one with no account of what the speaker in uttering the sentence is actually doing.

One might have supposed that, for an anti-realist as for the realist, the correct account of what the speaker who utters 'John is in pain' is standardly doing is: asserting that John is in pain. But this is no good, Strawson says,

> ...when it has just been denied that there is anything he actually asserts in uttering it...some alternative account of what the speaker is doing must be forthcoming if a sentence is denied a truth-value. And the truth is that no remotely plausible account is in this case available.

But why should (A) be thought to involve denial that there is anything one actually asserts by uttering this type of sentence? Evidently, Strawson is presupposing that only sentences which have been assigned determinate truth-conditions can be used to state anything. And this presupposition is a consequence of the assumption noted in the case of (C); for if what is stated by S has to be explained by reference to an assignment of truth-conditions, then there is no explaining what S states, *a fortiori* no using S to state anything, unless it is assigned truth-conditions. Strawson produces no argument for this assumption. And its correctness looks to be crucial for the prospects of a successful anti-realist account of declarative sentence meaning. We shall return to the matter shortly.

Strawson's discussion of the example involves two further assumptions, each of which seems to me arguably wrong. The first is that (A) to (C) exhaust the anti-realist options. An anti-realism, (D), is conceivable which differs from (A) in holding that 'John is in pain' has a truth-condition – it is true if and only if John is in pain; and from (B) in holding that no reductive account is possible, in terms of behaviour or physical states or whatever, which renders the obtaining of that truth-condition something publicly accessible; and from (C) in holding that an understanding of 'John is in pain' does involve possession of a conception of what it is for this truth-condition to obtain; and from realism in holding that a reductive account *is* possible, in terms of the practical skills regarded by (A) as constitutive of an understanding of that sentence, of what it is to possess a conception of what those truth-conditions are.

Given a version of (A) in which the notion of a criterion was central, it would be (D) which, it seems to me, most closely approximated to the position of the later Wittgenstein. Thus: there is no *harm* in speaking of the truth, or otherwise, of 'John is in pain'; and understanding the sentence is if you like, grasping its truth-conditions. But to say that is so far to say virtually nothing; in particular, it remains to be explained what grasping truth-conditions is supposed to amount to. Therefore, since an account of that can be given only in terms of the criteria by reference to which we should determine whether someone understood the sentence, we come round in a circle. Progress can be made only by specifying the criteria. These have to do solely with responses to aspects of John's behaviour and physical condition. 'Grasping the truth-conditions' is thus constituted by possession of a complex discriminatory skill exercised in response to public circumstances. And it is a dangerous error to think of it, as does the realist, as something ulterior, the formation of a conception of something inaccessible, a conception which informs and governs both exercise of the relevant skill and all other aspects of the use of the sentence, e.g. in inferences.[7]

The other assumption is expressed in this passage:

> It is part of what it is now regrettably fashionable to call our general theory of the world that we regard other people as subject to roughly the same range of sensations as we are painfully, or joyously, or indifferently aware of in ourselves. And it is in no way contrary to reason to regard ourselves, as in any case we cannot help doing, as justified in certain circumstances in ascribing to John a particular state of feeling which we cannot in the nature of the case experience ourselves and his being in which is therefore, if such is the standard invoked, necessarily verification-transcendent. The Seas of Argument may wash forever around these rocks of truth; but the rocks are not worn away.

The assumption is that to oppose realism is to seek to change these aspects of our 'general theory of the world'. But it is open to an anti-realist to seek instead to interpret them. Thus the susceptibility of others to the same range of sensations as we ourselves may be viewed as an expression of the existence of a communal vocabulary of sensation, any element of which is applicable to any of us on the basis of communally acknowledged criteria; and the inaccessibility of others' states of feeling may be viewed as an expression of the essential *defeasibility* of other-ascriptions of sensation, the fact that any state of information which warrants such an ascription can always coherently be envisaged as being added to in such a way that the resulting state of information no longer does so.[8] By

7 Cf. my *Wittgenstein on the Foundations of Mathematics*, chapter XII, section 1.

8 Evidence emerges, e.g. of the insincerity of an avowal; or of the subject's linguistic incompetence; or perhaps the wider context of his behaviour becomes clear in such a way as to require reinterpretation of it. *Whereas* there is only dubious sense in the idea of discovering of oneself that one was insincere on a particular occasion; and *only* the discovery of one's own linguistic incompetence might constitute the enlargement of a state of information which prompted a particular sincere self-ascription of sensation into one which prompted its retraction.

contrast, the 'privileged access' we are traditionally thought to have to our own sensations may be viewed as an expression of the fact that our grammar of sensation provides for the possibility of discovering that one did not know what one was saying in making a particular self-ascription, but *not* for the possibility that one understood it and was mistaken. So viewed, the 'rocks of truth' are not worn away not because they are the erosion-proof base of the true, realist, philosophy of mind, but because they are platitudinous reflections of features of our mental language – and are thus above the water-line.

Naturally, this is only the sketch of an approach, and I cannot claim to know that it would prove satisfactory in detail. What is justified is at least the suspicion that here, as in other areas, we rather too readily tend to assume that opposition to realism is bound to be radically revisionary of our ordinary theories and linguistic practices.

Strawson moves to examples concerning events in the past sufficiently remote to be inaccessible to living memory; sentences like:

Lord Anglesey had his leg shot off at Wellington's side

and

Charles Stuart walked bareheaded to his place of execution.

He is concerned with the contrast in available grounds for assertion between the situation of someone making such claims on the strength of an immediately prior, or remembered, observation – e.g. later on the same day, and the situation of we, who, born when we were, are 'debarred from having been in a position to make any such observation', but must rely on historical evidence. The ordinary realist view would be, again, that our assertion of such a sentence is made determinately true or false by a state of affairs to which we cannot now have access. If that view is rejected, then, Strawson asks again, with what is it to be replaced? Do such sentences have any truth-conditions now? And if so, what is the relation of those conditions to their meaning?

The same range of answers, (A) to (C), seems to Strawson to be available. I shall continue to leave (B) out of consideration. And (D), it seems to me, again arguably affords a fourth option.

Contrary to what one might have expected, Strawson does not reaffirm his previous objections against (A) and (C), but charges instead that

> ...whatever answer is chosen has the consequence that the sentence in our mouths has a different *meaning* from that which it has in the mouths of those who were in fact or in principle...in a position to recognize that condition as obtaining which the sentence appears to describe.

This outcome Strawson regards as totally unacceptable; in particular,

> it must be unacceptable to anyone who rightly cherishes the doctrine that the meaning of a sentence is determined by the meaning of its constituents and the way in which they are combined in the sentence. For he will surely be reluctant to locate an *ambiguity* anywhere either in the constituents or in the construction of these sentences.

It is unclear, however, that an A- or C-type anti-realist would be committed to such a consequence. Each, certainly, will interpret an understanding of such a sentence as essentially a matter of practical knowledge of how circumstances *now* accessible to us have to be if the assertion of the sentence is to be justified. But there is no immediate transition from that conception to the conclusion that each will be committed to construing any *change* in the range of accessible conditions, caused by the march of time, as a change in the sentence's meaning. What is clear is that the 'rightly cherished' doctrine would not be rightly cherished if we were dealing with examples of rather less historical notoriety, say 'Strawson once visited the University of Warwick'. Here just to understand the meaning of the constituents and the structure of the sentence is not yet enough to provide knowledge of what has to be the case in order for it to be true; we need to know in addition the time of its (envisaged) assertion. This variation of truth-conditions – of what has to be the case in order for the sentence to be true – as a function of temporal context would not ordinarily be thought to introduce any ambiguity into such a sentence. So why, from the point of view of an assertibility-conditions account of meaning, should a systematic variation in assertibility-conditions – of how things have to be if the sentence is to be justifiably assertible – as a function of temporal context be thought to do so?[9] An anti-realist of one of the appropriate kinds can be expected to argue, on the contrary, that grasping the meaning of past-tense sentences precisely involves grasping how their conditions of warranted assertion shift as one's own temporal location shifts.

I do not mean to claim by the foregoing that (A) and (C) can clearly avoid Strawson's unpalatable consequence, but merely that he gives no clear reason why they cannot. However the justice of Strawson's criticisms of (A) and (C) here would follow from his implicit assumption noted earlier, that only by reference to an assigned truth-condition can any explanation be given of what is stated by the assertoric use of a particular

9 It might seem to be important, and to introduce a disanalogy, that in one way the truth-conditions of such sentences are temporally invariant: thus, *whenever* it is uttered, the Strawson sentence is true if and only if a state of affairs of a kind sufficient for its truth is realized at a time prior to that of its utterance. But in *this* sense assertibility-conditions are temporally invariant too: for, whenever the sentence is uttered, it is warrantedly asserted if and only if a state of affairs obtains at the time of utterance of a kind appropriate to justify its assertoric use at that time. Invariance of truth-conditions in this way is rather uninteresting.

sentence, an explanation, that is, of its assertoric content. If that assumption were correct, then plainly no anti-realist account of meaning eschewing all use of the concept of truth could explain what it was for distinct utterances to effect the *same* statement; *a fortiori* it could not succeed in explaining how it was possible for his Lordship's valet and ourselves to have made the same statement by utterances of the relevant sentence separated by more than a century. So we are brought back to the question whether that assumption is correct:[10] can a A- or C-type anti-realist show that he is entitled to the ordinary ideas that *ceteris paribus* we make a statement about John by an utterance of 'John is in pain', and that an utterance of the Lord Anglesey sentence today effects *ceteris paribus* the same statement as it would have effected if uttered later on the afternoon of his Lordship's misfortune?

Here let me merely make a couple of preliminary points about the issue. First, Strawson proceeds as though it was obvious that the realist was entitled to the ordinary ideas in question. But the truth of the matter seems to be merely that he is in a position easily to label, or paraphrase, them. Thus e.g. for a sentence to have assertoric content is for its use standardly to effect a claim that an instance obtains of that type of state of affairs determined as sufficient for its truth; while for the Lord Anglesey sentence to effect the same statement now as it did in his valet's mouth is simply for its truth-conditions to have continued to be the same. But no sceptic about the substance to the intuitive notions would be satisfied by such replies. He would press now for an explanation of what it is for a sentence to be used to make a claim in that way, and of what it is for it to retain its truth-conditions through a large lapse of time. The only way to meet the demand would be to provide a description of the practical operations of these concepts: a general account is wanted of how our linguistic practice makes it manifest that any particular utterance has assertoric content, and, in terms of that account, of how its particular assertoric content may – if it may – be revealed. Thereby, in turn, it will be possible to describe what it is for a sentence to have retained the same assertoric content throughout a large period.

Now it is, of course, quite familiar that these are *enormously* difficult issues. But until they are solved, the fact ought to be faced that, whether we are realists or not, we are actually in no position to give the only sort of explanation of the relevant intuitive notions which counts: an explanation which reveals them as operative in linguistic practice, and so as falling within the province which it is the task of a theory of meaning

10 The importance of the question is, of course, qualified by the prima facie availability of (D), an advocate of which can presumably take over verbatim any 'account', as far as it goes, which the realist chooses to give of e.g. what makes it the case that we and Anglesey's valet effect the same statement by utterance of the relevant sentence.

to describe. On the other hand, could we but give an explanation of the desired sort, it would be bound to be, I think, the kind of thing which an anti-realist could use to meet the challenge implicit in Strawson's criticisms; for it would proceed purely in terms of discernible aspects of our use of language.

The other preliminary point concerns a train of thought[11] which I suspect captures the hunch of many philosophers who feel that wherever the anti-realist proposes to leave truth out of his account of the meaning of a particular declarative sentence, he won't be able to give a satisfactory explanation of what the sentence is used to state. Suppose we have a version of (A), or (C), in which the notion of a criterion is taken as central. Then the argument is directly to the effect that if all someone possesses is practical knowledge of criteria for the assertion and denial of a sentence, and knows of no truth-condition for it, then he cannot be said to know what, if anything, it states. For consider the situation of someone to whom all we give by way of explanation of the use of S is that its assertion is warranted *par excellence* when such-and-such conditions obtain – though they fall short of conclusive verification of it; and that its denial is warranted *par excellence* in such-and-such other conditions – which, however, fall short of conclusive falsification of it. Then surely he could justifiably protest that while he now knew well enough how to *use* the sentence in question both in atomic and in a wide range of compound contexts,[12] still in a certain sense he did not know what he was saying in asserting the sentence; or what, when its assertibility-conditions were satisfied, and it was thereby reasonable to believe it, he was supposed exactly to believe. Looking at the matter from a realist point of view, the trouble could be expressed as that all the man knows is that the sentence very *likely* states a truth under these circumstances and very *likely* states a falsehood under those; and until he knows under what precise circumstances it actually states a truth, or falsehood, he does not know what it says.

What is certainly right about the argument is this: just to know of *some* particular circumstances that they criterially warrant the assertion of S, and of some particular circumstances that they criterially warrant its rejection, certainly *need* not amount to knowledge of its content. But that is not to say that knowledge of its content is anything more than knowledge describable in just those terms. A sentence which admits neither of conclusive verification nor conclusive falsification must be interpreted by an anti-realist of the kinds in question as a sentence whose assertion or denial is always *defeasible*, however well justified in the current state of

11 Put to me in discussion by Gareth Evans.

12 All compound contexts, in fact, whose assertibility-conditions, he could correctly construe as a function of those of their constituent sentences.

information; whenever, that is, its assertion is warranted, the possibility is left open that subsequent developments may warrant its withdrawal; similarly with its denial.[13] So it is open to him to suggest that knowledge of content comes when the trainee understands not merely that the conditions of assertion, and denial, explained to him are inconclusive but also just how things have to develop in any state of information warranting the assertion, or denial of the sentence in order for that situation to cease to obtain.

Thus, for example, it seems perfectly correct to deny that someone knows the assertoric content of 'John is in pain' if *all* he knows is e.g. that it is right to assert it if John displays a certain syndrome of writhings and groans, and right to deny it if John is sitting relaxedly playing cards or watching television; and understands of both these sorts of circumstance that their obtaining gives no guarantee against the assertion, or denial, being nevertheless incorrect. But suppose he has this knowledge: of every state of affairs criterially warranting the assertion, or denial, of 'John is in pain', he knows in a practical sense both that it has that status and under what circumstances it would be brought out that its status was merely criterial; that is, he knows the 'overturn-conditions' of any situation criterially warranting the assertion, or denial, of 'John is in pain'. No doubt we could not know for sure that someone had this knowledge; but the stronger our grounds for thinking that he did, the more baffling would be the allegation that he did not grasp the assertoric content of 'John is in pain'.

In fact, of course, provided someone had practical knowledge of *all* the types of situation criterially warranting the assertion, or denial, of an S of the relevant kind, he would have to have practical knowledge of all the 'overturn-conditions' also. It seems to me, therefore, that the initial plausibility of the argument turned on implicitly interpreting the knowledge possessed by the trainee as not being of that extent. And, naturally, if all he understands are *some* of the criteria for the assertion and denial of S, he ought not to be credited with a full understanding of what S states.

13 Proof: for S not to be conclusively verifiable is just for it always to be a possibility that its assertion is wrong, however well justified; likewise for S not to be conclusively falsifiable is for it to be the case that its denial may always be wrong, however well justified. But the anti-realist will have to interpret this ineradicable twofold possibility of error *constructively*: the possibility of the assertion's, or denial's, being wrong must be interpreted as the possibility of our being in a position to assert, provided we know sufficiently many facts, that it is (was) wrong. Therefore he must construe the situation of S as suggested: whenever a state of information warrants the assertion of S, it cannot be ruled out that an enlarged state of information may develop which warrants its retraction; likewise for its denial.

IV

There is a need sharply to distinguish between

a questions and difficulties to do with the adequacy of the traditional realist conception of truth to play the central role in a defensible account of what it is to understand any declarative sentence, and
b the thesis that this role should be played by some other notion – verification, falsification, criteria or otherwise undifferentiated conditions of warranted assertion or whatever.

Naturally, if someone thinks that the questions and problems (a) cannot be satisfactorily answered, then he has a strong motive for seeking a satisfactory version of the thesis (b). But he would not be committed to the belief that the search can succeed. The possibility would remain that no satisfactory general account can be given of what it is to understand a declarative sentence; that we shall be able to find what strike us as serious flaws in *anything* we say here aspiring to the level of generality which the truth-conditional, verificationist and other conceptions try for. In that case there would be no broadly characterizable type of condition, ϕ, such that a viable general theory of meaning could be developed around the core assumption that the meaning of any declarative sentence is determined by its ϕ-conditions.

I am not suggesting that this is so. But that there is this gulf means that realism cannot acquire any strength by *default*; whatever problems an attempt to vindicate the thesis (b) may encounter, we shall have no better reason just on that account for supposing that realism must be correct, or for thinking that any difficulties which seem to attend it must be resoluble. Therefore if – whether or not he demonstrates as much – Strawson's two chosen types of example do indeed defeat all anti-realist account, no argument for realism can issue from that fact while the gulf just described remains open. And closing it is likely to require meeting the anti-realist challenge head on.[14]

The essential challenge is to explain how man might manifest in his use of sentences of a certain sort that it was governed by a verification-transcendent conception of their truth-conditions. In 'Truth-conditions and Criteria' I took it that one implication of taking seriously the connection between meaning and use is that there is nothing to a man's understanding of language which he will not, in appropriate circumstances, make manifest

14 Though we cannot, I suppose, exclude all possibility of, as it were, an Olympian demonstration that a theory of meaning *has* to be possible.

by the way he uses it.[15] So unless realism can explain how, when by its lights our use of a certain kind of sentence is governed by a verification-transcendent conception, that it is so *shows itself*, it ought to be abandoned by those who would wish to preserve Wittgenstein's insight.

But Strawson sees no difficulty here:

> A rational speaker's grasp of his language is manifested, *inter alia*, in his responding in certain ways to the recognisable situations with which he is, and has been, confronted...but Mr. Wright seems to take it as evident that the rational speaker's response to such situations can in no case be *governed* by a certain kind of conception, a conception of a state of affairs, or of a condition of truth, which for one reason or another, in fact or in principle, is not, or is no longer, or is not for the speaker, accessible to direct observation or memory. But this...is just the question at issue, and one has the impression that Mr. Wright quite handsomely begs it...it *is* obvious that, as Wright puts it, 'grasp of the sense of a sentence cannot be displayed in response to unrecognisable conditions'...

However

> it is enough for the truth-theorist that the grasp of the sense of a sentence can be displayed in response to recognisable conditions – of various sorts. There are those which conclusively establish the truth or falsity of the sentence; there are those which (given our general theory of the world) consitute evidence, more or less good, for or against the truth of the sentence; there are even those which point to the unavoidable absence of evidence either way. The appropriate response varies of course from case to case, in the last case being of the form 'we shall never know whether p or not'.

These remarks, it seems to me, are quite unsatisfactory. The anti-realist question was not: do we have any use for sentences for which there is no notion of conclusive verification?, or: how can we manifest our understanding of such sentences? It was: what in the use which we do make of those sentences for which there is no notion of conclusive verification manifests our alleged grasp of verification-transcendent truth-conditions for them? Given that grasp of the truth-conditions cannot be a recognitional ability, what in our use of such sentences reveals that our understanding of them is anything other, or more, than a grasp of what would be regarded, on the realist view, as the recognizable conditions of their evidential support and disconfirmation? For it is only grasp of that which is clearly manifest in the responses which Strawson describes.

15 This, of course, is the point of the concluding remarks of what I believe is Dummett's earliest published formulation, in 'Truth', of the case for a general anti-realism based on the philosophical theory of meaning.

The prima facie availability of (D) complicates the issue slightly. For according to (D), it will be remembered, grasping the central core of the assertibility-conditions of a verification-transcendent sentence, and its use in compound contexts, *is* grasping its truth-conditions. So the question, how is the latter grasp made manifest, is already answered. But the essence of the realist view is, as Strawson puts it, that the conception of truth-conditions *governs* the use, that from this conception both our view of what constitutes good evidence for a sentence and our use of it in compound contexts – in particular, the logic which we regard ourselves as validly applying to it – flow; it is something ulterior which informs and, in so far as we use language correctly, vindicates our use of such sentences in both atomic and compound contexts. In this way it is quite literally the core of our understanding of the sentence. Whereas, according to (D), that we e.g. accepted such-and-such as evidence for a particular sentence and that we also e.g. accepted Excluded Middle as valid in application to it, would be essentially independent aspects of our 'grasp of its truth-conditions'.

The challenge is to explain how a full-blooded realist conception of truth-conditions in this sense can be manifested in a person's use of his language; to explain, that is, what, if anything, he could do to distinguish himself from a man whose competence was completely described by saying that he had grasped the assertibility-conditions both of the sentence and of all, or enough, compound sentences in which it was a constituent. One finds in Strawson's remarks no clear indication of how he thinks this challenge ought to be met.

If Strawson does not meet this challenge, still less does he make out his claim that

> the conception of verification-transcendent truth-conditions, at least in one or another of the relatively stringent senses of 'verification-transcendent' which Wright's anti-realist seems to favour – this conception, and its link with that of meaning, is an essential part of a general view of the world which is no way contrary to reason and to which we are in any case inescapably committed.

It would undoubtedly have demanded excess of a chairman's licence to make *that* claim good! Let me conclude by recording the suspicion, rather than arguing, that the implicit epistemology of realism involves in all essential respects the same difficulties which Wittgenstein exposed in the old idea that a shared grasp of 'universals' *explains* our propensity to agree in our use of attributives.[16]

16 'Let's not imagine the meaning as an occult connection the mind makes between a word and a thing, and that this connection *contains* the whole usage of a word as a seed might be said to contain the tree.' *Blue Book*, penultimate paragraph.

3

Realism, Truth-value Links, Other Minds and the Past

I

Realism about a particular class of statements is, for the purpose of this paper, the view that we so understand those statements as to render intelligible to ourselves the possibility that any of them be true without our being able to recognize that it is so. If the statements in question are not effectively decidable, then, obviously, we commit ourselves to realism in this sense if we hold of each of them that either it, or its negation, is determinately true.[1] So one who endorses the Principle of Bivalence for non-effectively decidable statements of a particular kind commits himself – provided he intends a truth-distributive interpretation of disjunction – to realism about them.

The converse connection is less obvious and has been argued, indeed, by McDowell[2] to fail. Let a *classical realist* be one who endorses the principle of Bivalence for a particular class of non-effectively decidable statements; and let a *bare realist* be one who takes it that there is no important objection to the idea that we can understand what it is for these statements to be true in a manner transcending our capacities for knowledge. Then – putting considerations to do with vagueness on one side – it may be unclear what *objection* the bare realist might have to classical realism; but McDowell is surely on strong ground in claiming that it is unclear that the bare realist suffers any commitment to classical realism.

1 Later this ceased to seem obvious to me. See section I of Essay 15 and, especially, section I of Essay 16.
2 Section 6 of 'Truth-conditions, Bivalence and Verificationism'.

In his published writings,[3] Dummett has tended to equate realism with classical realism. But the anti-realist polemic which he has expounded aims in essentials as its bare-realist core. The polemic consists in a twofold challenge: first that the realist should explain how, when our training is necessarily restricted to confrontation with experienceable situations, we are supposed to be able to form a conception of what it is for an experience-transcendent situation to obtain; and, second, that the realist should explain what evidence there is that we actually possess any such conception – what in our use of any particular statement would distinctively manifest that we understood what it was for that statement to be true in a manner transcending our capacities for verification.

The second challenge is, in a clear sense, the more fundamental of the two. For *if* it could be clear that we did indeed possess a realist understanding of certain statements, the question, how that understanding had been acquired, while no doubt of some independent interest, would cease to be of any importance in the – then defunct – issue between realism and its opponents. Moreover *unless* the second challenge can be satisfactorily met, nothing can uncontroversially count as a description of a route whereby a conception of verification-transcendent truth-conditions can be acquired; for we shall lack any criterion for saying that precisely that is what is acquired by that route. Be that as it may, the kind of understanding of statements about, say, the past or other minds with which the bare realist wants to credit himself is very directly susceptible to both challenges.[4]

That the manifestation-challenge is in the way described more fundamental does not mean that the acquisition-challenge may as well be disregarded. For to give an account of how a concept can be acquired, that is, a model explanation of it, is itself a method *par excellence* both of distinctively displaying ones understanding of the concept and of bringing its content into sharp relief. In any case, any philosophical account of our understanding of a concept which contrives to make it mysterious how that concept could be acquired in a, broadly speaking, empirical way is objectionable just on that account – not because some form of empiricism about concept-formation is incontrovertible, but because we have no business legislating against empiricism a priori.[5]

3 See especially *Truth and Other Enigmas*, Duckworth 1978, essays 1, 10, 11, 13, 14 and 21; *Frege: Philosophy of Language*, Duckworth 1973, passim (see the Brief Subject Index, under 'Verificationism versus realism as theories of meaning'); and 'What is a Theory of Meaning? (II)'.

4 For a further exposition of the latter, see Essay 1, sections II–IV.

5 Cf. my *Frege's Conception of Numbers as Objects*, chapter 1, section i; and, for an attempt to respond to a specific application of the challenge to a concept other than truth, section vii.

The anti-realist who figures in Dummett's 'The Reality of the Past' is preoccupied with the acquisition-challenge. Dummett writes:

> We learn the use of the past tense by learning to recognise certain situations as justifying the assertion of certain statements expressed by means of that tense. These situations of course include those in which we remember the occurrence of some event which we witnessed, and our initial training in the use of the past tense consists in learning to use past-tense statements as the expression of such memories...on this anti-realist account, there is no way by which we could be thought to have passed from a grasp of the kind of situation which justifies the assertion of a statement about the past to a conception of what it would be for such a statement to be true independently of any such situation which would justify its being now, or subsequently, asserted. The only notion of truth for past-tense statements which we could have acquired from our training in their use is that which coincides with the justifiability of assertions of such statements, i.e. with the existence of situations which we are capable of recognising as obtaining and which justify such assertions.[6]

More generally,

> What we learn to do is to accept...the occurrence of certain conditions which we have been trained to recognise, as conclusively justifying the assertion of a given statement of the disputed class and...the occurrence of certain other conditions as conclusively justifying its denial. In the very nature of the case, we could not possibly have come to understand what it would be for the statement to be true independently of that which we have learned to treat as establishing its truth; there was simply no means by which we could be shown this.[7]

Dummett proceeds by having his realist about the past attempt to meet this challenge by appeal to the truth-value links among differently tensed assertions made at different times; for example, the principle that an appropriately dated past-tense statement, uttered at the present time, is true if and only if a suitably related present-tense statement, uttered at the appropriate past time, would have been true at that time; it is, his realist claims,

> from an understanding of the truth-value link, as exemplified in such a case, that we derive a grasp of what it is for a statement in the past tense, whenever made, for example one made now, to be true.[8]

6 Dummett, *Truth and Other Enigmas*, p. 363.
7 Ibid., p. 362.
8 Ibid., p. 363.

How, more specifically, an appeal to truth-value links is supposed to help the realist meet the acquisition-challenge is not further considered by Dummett. Instead, he switches attention to the question how the anti-realist can make out a title to retain such truth-value links.[9] But in 'On "The Reality of the Past"', McDowell argues that appeal to the truth-value links is actually quite impotent to meet the acquisition-challenge, and suggests quite another way of meeting it.

It is with these suggestions that the present paper is mainly concerned.

II

It is usually assumed that there will be a wide class of statements for which the anti-realist will find the truth-conditional account of meaning unproblematic – statements for which the notion of truth will not be interpreted in recognition-transcendent terms. (It is worth emphasis that this is an assumption, for it remains to be demonstrated both how best to generalize the notion of effective decidability in mathematics to ordinary statements, and that a truth-conditional account of the meaning of statements in the resulting general class will be acceptably non-transcendent.)[10] Let us characterize as a *truth-value link realist* anyone who holds that bare realism about a particular class of anti-realistically problematic statements can be protected against the acquisition-challenge by systematically linking their truth-values with those of statements in the assumed anti-realistically unproblematic class. Provided, then, that we can take it that the latter class includes a broad range of present-tense statements, truth-value link realism about an appropriately corresponding class of past-tense statements is certainly something which, via the orthodox liaisons between the past and present tenses, a would-be bare realist about the past might essay. The attraction of truth-value link realism is that it really does promise to meet the acquisition-challenge head on. For, by hypothesis, it will build only upon circumstances which can feature as the truth-conditions of statements of an anti-realistically unproblematic kind: circumstances which can be given as embraceable objects of ostension within a trainee's experience; and it will then seek to explain, via certain truth-value links, how a bare-realist conception can be formed, on that basis, of the truth-conditions of certain anti-realistically problematic statements. But to do that is to do precisely what the acquisition-challenge demands should be done: explain how an understanding of certain possibly

9 See also my *Wittgenstein on the Foundations of Mathematics*, chapter X and Essay 5 below.

10 A suggestion about the first question is made below. For some consideration of the second, see the concluding section of Essay 12.

verification-transcendent circumstances could be acquired from a training in which contact took place – naturally – only with non-transcendent ones.

Obviously, a similar ploy might be attempted in support of realism about the remote future – the future, that is, remote enough to transcend the capacities of verification of anyone now living. And, as McDowell observes,[11] a kind of truth-value link realism is implicit in that lay-philosophical conception of the content of ascriptions of sensation to others which Wittgenstein challenged in the *Philosophical Investigations*. The relevant link would be that an ascription of, for example, pain to someone else is true just in case a *self-ascription* of pain by him would be true; where it is taken that the content of a self-ascription of pain can be given unproblematically in terms of truth-conditions, since circumstances of the appropriate kind can indeed have been wholly embraced within the language-learner's consciousness – namely, on occasions when the self in question was himself. The described truth-value link thus enables the language learner to form a conception of another's pain – that which makes 'Y is in pain', said of another, true – which both makes it an instance of the very same kind of thing as that which he experienced in the course of his training, and makes it lie beyond Y's detectable behaviour. A kind of inchoate truth-value link realism is thus the kernel of the idea, which comes so easily to us, that each of us understands what pain is from his own case.

The foregoing characterization of truth-value link realism is non-specific in what may seem an important respect. Consider any universally quantified statement, $(x)Fx$, whose range is an effectively enumerable infinite series and whose predicate is effectively decidable of each element in that series. Traditional mathematical platonism would regard it as a perfectly satisfactory explanation of the truth-conditions of such a statement to stipulate that it is true if and only if each member of the infinite series of statements is true, whose *n*th member is to the effect that F is truly predicable of the *n*th element of a particular effective enumeration of the range of the quantifier. Now, this sort of stipulation certainly systematically links the truth-values of statements in an anti-realistically problematic class with those of statements of which, since effectively decidable, we can for present purposes take it that a truth-conditional account will be anti-realistically acceptable. So, in terms of our characterization anyway, a sort of truth-value link realism is possible with respect to this particular kind of infinitely quantified statement. The crucial respect in which it would differ, however, from the kind of move adumbrated in the cases of the past tense and ascriptions of sensations to others is just this: in those two cases, the truth-conditions were actually specified as being those of

11 'On "The Reality of the Past"', §§ 2 and 3.

particular statements which, when made in certain circumstances, would possess truth-conditions with which a trainee could uncontroversially be presumed – or so let us suppose – to be familiar. The truth-conditions of past-tense utterances were specified as being those of certain (possible) present-tense utterances; and the truth-conditions of other-ascriptions of pain were specified as being those of certain self-ascriptions. No such connection is effected by the proposed stipulation about infinite quantification; here, there is no utterance-type in whose use the trainee can be presumed familiar and whose truth-conditions, when uttered in a particular context, coincide with those of the kind of statement being explained. To be sure, we can presume the trainee to be familiar with the use of each of, 'F*a*', 'F*b*',...etc., where '*a*', '*b*',...etc., designate objects in the range of the quantifier. But to claim that the truth-conditions of the quantified statement are that *each* of these statements should be true is simply to explain the truth-conditions of one infinitely quantified statement in terms of another; no direct link is effected with a type of state of affairs with which the traineee can be presumed to be acquainted.

Truth-value link realism about infinite quantification would thus seem to be a more fragile affair than in the case of the past or other minds. It might be preferable, indeed, so to refine our characterization of truth-value link realism as to exclude the kind of move considered in the case of infinite quantification; for it seems clear that there the acquisition-challenge can be met, if at all, only by some quite different tactic. Certainly, there is some prospect at this point that realism about, say, number-theory, and the natural sciences, might be unjustifiable while realism about other minds, and the past and the future, might not. It depends on whether McDowell is right in thinking that truth-value link manoeuvres are unsuccessful against the acquisition-challenge in the latter cases also.

III

Why does McDowell believe that those manoeuvres are unsuccessful? He writes:

> According to a truth-value link realist, the state of affairs which consists in another person's being in pain is never itself accessible to consciousness. An anti-realist finds it unintelligible that a conception of such a state of affairs should be involved in linguistic competence. The realist's purported answer is, in effect, this: 'You can see how a person can have the idea of what it is for someone to be in pain – when the someone in question is himself. Well, a sentence like "He is in pain", uttered in a context which fixes a reference for the pronoun, is understood as saying of some

> appropriate other person that he is in that very same state.' But this, so far from solving the problem, simply ignores it. If someone cannot see how another person's being in pain – on an interpretation of the circumstance which makes it inaccessible – can possibly enter into the meaning one attaches to some form of words, one does not allay his worry by baldly re-asserting that it does.
>
> Similarly with the past...An anti-realist finds it unintelligible that a conception of the truth-conditions of a past-tensed utterance, thought of as something whose obtaining is, in itself, inaccessible, should be involved in linguistic competence. The realist's purported reply is on these lines: 'You can see how someone can know what it is for rain to be falling. Well, a sentence like "It was raining" is understood as saying that that very circumstance obtained at some past time.' Again, this does not meet the worry but simply restates the claim which gave rise to it. The problem was precisely an inability to see how the past obtaining of that circumstance – an instance of a kind of circumstance which the realism we are considering makes inaccessible – can possibly enter into any meaning one could succeed in attaching to a sentence.[12]

The point is: how exactly is the 'projection' via the truth-value links supposed to work? We have, for example, crudely,

> 'It was raining' is true iff 'It is raining' was true;

and,

> 'He is in pain', said by me, is true iff 'I am in pain', said by him, is true.

In both cases the quoted sentence on the right-hand side of the biconditional is, to be sure, one with whose truth-conditions, when it is uttered in a certain sort of context, an anti-realist may – or so we are supposing – assume a trainee to be familiar. But the contexts in question are precisely when 'It is raining' is – *at the present time* – true, and when 'I am in pain' is true of *the trainee*. The important projection is not that from right to left across the truth-value links; it is that involved in securing *ingress*, as it were, into the right-hand sides. The problem, after all, was to explain how it was that a trainee, familiar with what it is for it to be raining at the present time, could arrive at a conception of what it is for that very same sort of circumstance to have obtained, in a manner possibly transcending our present capacities of awareness, at a particular past time. In supposing that the biconditional in question can be of any use to him, the problem is tacitly assumed to have been solved. Likewise, by supposing

12 McDowell, 'On "The Reality of the Past"', pp. 132–3.

that the truth-conditions of 'I am in pain', said by *him*, are familiar to *me* – the trainee, it is assumed that I have already passed beyond the conception of my own, invariably detectable, pains to an understanding of what it is for someone else to suffer, albeit possibly undetectably, in the same way. It appears, then, that, notwithstanding their difference from the truth-value link manoeuvre with the type of infinite quantification described above, these two ploys proffer against the acquisition-challenge a response not one whit stronger.

This way of formulating McDowell's criticism, however, omits stress of one element in his own exposition quoted: the idea, namely, that truth-value link realism will treat the states of affairs constituting the truth of past-tense statements, or of other-ascriptions of sensation, as circumstances which not merely may be, but are *always* and *essentially* inaccessible to us. McDowell's thought here is that if circumstances which made ascription of a particular sensation to another true could ever *directly* impinge on a trainee's consciousness, there would simply be no need for an attempted projection from what it was like for him to have that sensation himself. Similarly, if it were ever possible directly to verify that a particular past-tense statement was true, there would be no need to suppose that a conception of what it was for such a statement to be true had to be acquired from the putatively unproblematic case of the present. For McDowell, then, the very idea that an appeal to the relevant truth-value links might be of help commits the realist to a conception of the past, or of other minds, as domains of in principle inaccessible truth of which we can only experience the present, or outward, symptoms.

For an anti-realist, in contrast, any respectably explained truth-condition for a statement will be such that if it obtains, it will always, at least in principle,[13] be possible for us to recognize that it does so. That is less than saying that truth has to be *effectively* recognizable truth: ingenuity, or just good luck, can play a part in our being in a position to recognize as such a state of affairs which makes a particular statement true. What, for the anti-realist, is of dubious intelligibility is the idea that a statement can be made true by the obtaining of a state of affairs which, however lucky or ingenious, we should be unable to apprehend as having that status. For, because of the familiar points about manifestation and acquisition, there is no way in which we could have succeeded in attaching such a content to the statement.

The leading idea of McDowell's paper is to attempt to occupy what now emerges as potential middle ground. For, as McDowell believes, there is possible, at any rate in the case of other minds and the past, an intermediate kind of realism – what I shall call *M-realism* – differing from

13 I hope I may here permissibly leave the lid on this particular Pandora's Box.

truth-value link realism in holding that satisfaction of the truth-conditions of past-tense statements, and statements about other minds, is, at least on occasion, accessible to us; and from anti-realism in being at least bare-realistic – that is, in holding us to understand the possibility that statements of the two relevant sorts can also, on occasion, be true in virtue of states of affairs which we cannot detect. According to McDowell, whatever impulsion there may seem to be in the direction of anti-realism comes only from the manifest inadequacy of truth-value link realism; in fact, however, both the manifestation- and the acquisition-challenge can be met from an M-realist standpoint.

Clearly, this would be a very substantial result. We must investigate, therefore, the powers and possible scope of M-realism. Will it, where available, be less revisionary of ordinary linguistic practice than, under natural assumptions,[14] anti-realism threatens to be? Is it genuinely available in the case of other minds and the past? Is its claim to be able to meet the anti-realist challenges really any stronger than that of truth-value link realism?

IV

Truth-value link realism suffers, as it seems to me, three injustices at McDowell's hands. To begin with, a truth-value link realist who did indeed accept, as McDowell believes he ought, that the truth-conditions of ascriptions of sensations to others were always constituted by the obtaining of inaccessible facts, would not thereby have committed himself to wanting

> to avoid mentioning, in his description of competence with the problematic sorts of sentence, circumstances which, when they manifest themselves to awareness, warrant assertions of the sentences.[15]

That is to say, there would be no clear commitment to the view that the accessible assertibility-conditions of a statement whose truth-conditions were always inaccessible would always be of merely symptomatic relevance to it, playing no part in determining its content. It wants an argument, and McDowell gives none, why the realist should not hold that our understanding of the relevant kind of statement involves *both* grasping what it is for their inaccessible conditions of truth to obtain *and* sensitivity to conditions, falling short of verification, which *criterially* justify the assertion of such statements; that is, ignorance of the relevance of which would be a matter of imperfect comprehension, rather than of factual

14 See the concluding section of Essay 1 and footnote 18 on p. 69.
15 McDowell, 'On "The Reality of the Past"', p. 135.

innocence. So far as I can see, there is no immediate reason why the idea that our conception of someone else's pain as of something essentially inaccessible to us, which we can grasp only by projection from our own case, should preclude that the relation between another's behaviour and his pain should on occasion be criterial rather than symptomatic. Indeed such would be the obvious strategy of defence for the truth-value link realist against the scepticism which, as McDowell suggests,[16] his view may otherwise so easily fall prey to. It may be that such a strategy would involve a kind of incoherent overdetermination of content; but the matter needs much fuller exploration.[17]

It is quite unfair, secondly, to lumber the truth-value link realist with the 'grotesque piece of philosophical mythology' which McDowell stigmatizes in the final section of his paper:

> The truth-value link realist's view of what it is, say, for something to have occurred is unintelligible. He conceals that from himself with a confused thought of a being with knowledge-acquiring powers different from ours. Thus the realist's view of the reality of the past can be described, with only the mildest caricature, as the idea of another place, in which past events are still occurring, watched, perhaps, by God.[18]

But to hold that our conception of the truth-conditions of past-tense assertions is achieved in the way supposed by the truth-value link realist is surely absolutely independent of the fantasy of the accessibility of such conditions at all times to some sort of superior cognitive faculty, with the associated image of the past as another 'place'. Truth-value link realism may, somehow, tempt an adherent to such a fantasy; but it ought not to do so. For if we could indeed form a conception of facts transcendent of our cognitive powers by appealing to truth-value links, then that would precisely be a way of forming such a conception *without* appeal to the idea of the cognitive powers of a superior being. Indeed whatever advantages M-realism might prove to have over truth-value link realism, that such fantasies are any less tempting is not among them. Rather, the temptation is there as soon as, in the role of M-realists, we ask ourselves the question: what is it for the *possibility* which we admit – that the truth-conditions of a past-tense statement should obtain undetectably – to be actualized? Is it not natural, here, to invoke the idea of a being for whom whatever stands between us and detection of the actualized truth-conditions is no barrier – so that for the truth-conditions to be actualized is for Him to know what they are? As natural as ever.

16 Ibid., p. 132, footnote 10.
17 For a change of heart on this, see Essay 13, section II, especially pp. 393–4.
18 'On "The Reality of the Past"', pp. 143–4.

The third injustice, however, is the most important. McDowell argued that there would be no point in a realist about the past, or about other minds, invoking truth-value links unless he thought that circumstances constituting the truth-conditions of past-tense assertions, or, say, ascriptions of sensation, were always strictly inaccessible to us. But *if* it is true that we really can, on occasion, non-inferentially see that so-and-so occurred, or that someone else is having such-and-such a sensation, there is surely absolutely no reason why a truth-value link realist should be embarrassed to acknowledge the fact. On the contrary; for even if such verifications are on occasion possible, the trainee, if he is to arrive at a *realist* understanding of the relevant sorts of statement, is still going to have to make a 'projection': he is going to have to advance from an understanding of what it is like to observe that such verifying conditions obtain to the formation of a conception of how the very same conditions which one then verifies to obtain can also obtain undetectably. Would not this be, for someone who believed in the efficacy of the truth-value link against the acquisition-challenge, precisely the place to invoke it? If we suppose that observation of certain sorts of behaviour, and perhaps overt physical condition – a grotesquely mutilated arm, say – *is* observation that another is in pain, is there not then a striking lacuna between coming to grasp that ascriptions of pain are true when such circumstances obtain and coming to grasp that stoicism is a possibility – that, indeed, in special circumstances a man's pain may go unreflected in anything he does or the overt state of his body? And is it not as plausible (or implausible) as before to say that we understand this possibility precisely because we know from our own case what it would be like to try to bottle a pain up, and, perhaps, to succeed?

It is thus incorrect, or so it seems to me, to hold that the belief that appeal to truth-value links might help meet the acquisition-challenge, either in the case of the past-tense or other-ascriptions of sensation, presupposes the view that the truth-conditions of both kinds of statement are *always* verification-transcendent. What it presupposes is only that there is no essential connection between the realization of those conditions and our ability to recognize the fact – exactly the characteristic belief of bare realism. If this is right, then the relation between realism and the truth-value links is closer than McDowell would have us suppose. And the mistake is important because, as I shall argue later, it leads him to credit M-realism with illusory advantages over truth-value link realism.

V

According to M-realism about other-ascriptions of sensation,

> ...what warrants the assertion that another person is in pain, on one of the relevant occasions, is the detectable obtaining of the circumstance of

> that person's being in pain: an instance of a kind of circumstance – another person's being in pain – which is available to awareness, in its own right and not merely through behavioural proxies, on some occasions, including this one, although, on other occasions the obtaining of other instances can be quite beyond detection.[19]

And, for an M-realist about the past,

> ...what warrants the assertion, on one of the relevant occasions, that, say, some event of a specified kind occurred in the past is the obtaining of a circumstance which consists simply in such an event's having occurred: an instance of a kind of circumstance which is available to awareness, in its own right and not merely through traces going proxy for it, on some occasions, including this one, although, on other occasions the obtaining of other instances can be quite outside our reach.[20]

The essential M-realist supposition is that if, and only if, a certain sort of non-effectively decidable truth condition can on occasion be realized detectably, we can form a genuinely bare-realistic conception of what it is for that condition to be satisfied. The 'only if' part is by way of concession to what the M-realist sees as the justice in the acquisition-challenge; and the 'if' part will exercise us in section VI below.

M-realism is a possibility, then, whenever we are concerned with a class of non-effectively decidable statements for which, however, conclusive verification cannot be ruled out. Mathematical proof, one would ordinarily suppose, is conclusive enough verification by any standards. So, unlike truth-value link realism, M-realism may be an option with respect to a large class of mathematical statements. Even granting the soundness of M-realism, however, that thought should be of only dubious comfort to the classical mathematician – unless McDowell is wrong in the belief that bare realism involves no commitment to classical realism. Otherwise, there is no very clear reason why M-realist number-theory, for example, should interestingly differ from, say, intuitionist number-theory. More generally, indeed, in any language containing the means of expression of no modal notions but otherwise as rich as you like, it is unclear whether M-realism as such would commit one to the legitimacy of any moves about which a generalized intuitionistic anti-realism would have cause to complain. And where no defensible notion of conclusive verification is available, as for example, presumably, with the general hypotheses of scientific theory, the M-realist's desire to respect that he sees as just in the acquisition-challenge will lead him to anti-realism; that is, he will reject as unintelligible the

19 McDowell, 'On "The Reality of the Past"', pp. 135–6.
20 Ibid., p. 136.

idea that truth-conditions for such statements can be realized in a manner transcending our capacities of awareness.

Obviously it becomes crucial at this point to determine just how wide the class of statements is whose truth can, under favourable circumstances, be wholly embraced by the human mind – whose conclusive verification is not ruled out. McDowell gives the matter little explicit attention. He talks, as we have seen of circumstances 'being available to awareness in their own right' and not merely through 'proxies'. Elsewhere his M-realist recommends the view that

> ...on those occasions which are paradigmatically suitable for training in the assertoric use of the relevant part of the language, one can literally perceive, in another person's facial expression or his behaviour, that he is in pain, and not just infer that he is in pain from what one perceives.
>
> The analogue, in the case of the past, would be insistence that knowledge of the past occurrence of an event of a specified kind (say) is something non-inferential.[21]

Well, that no inference, via 'proxies' or whatever, should be involved is quite consistent with what is actually perceived being not that someone is in pain, *tout court*, but that criteria – in what I take to be the *Philosophical Investigations* sense – that he is in pain are satisfied. Criteria are not proxies, and they do not form the bases of inferences, correctly so described. But, in contrast with truth-conditions, a claim made on the basis of satisfaction of its criteria can subsequently be jettisoned consistently with retention of the belief that criteria were indeed satisfied.[22] So the M-realist about a particular kind of statement has to hold not just that inference via proxies is not invariably involved when the assertoric use of those statements is justified, but more: that the occasions which are 'paradigmatically suitable' for training in their assertoric use involve not just satisfaction of criteria – otherwise experience of them will be experience of a situation whose obtaining is consistent with the falsity of the relevant statements – but realization of truth-conditions, properly so regarded.[23]

That might make it look as though the proper course for the M-realist would be to argue that circumstances can so arrange themselves as to endow a witness with an *indefeasible* warrant to make a particular claim about the past, or about someone else's mental state. But care is needed in formulation here. For it is doubtful whether indefeasible certainty can ever be legitimate about any contingent statement; one can always turn

21 Ibid.

22 This aspect of the notion of a criterion, or at least its importance here, may have escaped McDowell. See ibid., footnote 17.

23 I believe that the 'thin' notion of criterion surviving at the end of the discussion in Essay 13 will subserve the point of this paragraph.

out to be the victim of a misjudgement or misperception (or at least of a misunderstanding), even in the case of reports about one's immediate physical environment (or one's own mental states). Without arguing the matter in detail, it seems to me likely that we must either jettison altogether the notion that truth-conditions can obtain detectably or give an account of what it is for them to do so which does not require that to have experienced the obtaining of such a condition is to be entitled to have an indefeasible certainty about the truth of the corresponding statement.

How might such an account go? Well, some statements, including all (effectively) decidable mathematical statements, have the characteristic that they are associated with a possible course of action which it is within the power of finite beings to implement and which is such that, if an agent carries it through correctly and with full attention, then, provided he makes no perceptual error and correctly understands the statement in question, the opinion which he forms concerning the truth-value of that statement is bound to be correct. '23 is a prime' has this property; and so, in appropriate contexts, do 'The cat is on the mat in the sitting-room' and 'The curtains are blue'. It seems to me that this is a reasonable generalization of the notion of decidability in mathematics; that, for a statement to be decidably true or false is for there actually to be a procedure meeting the conditions described, (and for us to have recognized that we are in a position *effectively* to decide a particular statement is for us to have recognized, in advance of knowing what its truth-value is, that we actually possess such a procedure in its case). In the case of the latter two examples cited, for instance, and indeed the whole class of statements concerning present goings-on in bounded, smallish, nearby regions of space which they represent, the appropriate procedure is: position yourself suitably and observe. The certainty which we can, in general, secure about decidable statements falls short of indefeasibility not because we cannot fully embrace in consciousness the appropriate truth- or falsity-conferring circumstances – for carrying out the appropriate procedure in a way which meets the described conditions is doing just that – but because we cannot, in general, secure an indefeasible certainty that the procedure in question has been so implemented: that we have been sufficiently attentive, have made no perceptual or procedural error, and correctly understand the statement at issue.[24]

We can say, then, that for the truth-conditions of a statement to obtain detectably is for that statement to be associated with a procedure meeting the described conditions, and for it to be the case that the bound-to-be-correct opinion which an agent will form when all the constraints are met will be that the statement in question is true. A clear example of a class of

24 Essay 4, section 3, attempts to improve and enlarge on this proposal.

statements with, by this test, no detectable truth-conditions would be – as one would hope – the class of unrestrictedly generally quantified contingent statements. For no matter what investigative procedure we carry out into the truth or falsity of such a statement, it is consistent with our doing so correctly, and with full attention, and with our making no perceptual error and perfectly understanding the statement at issue, that we form an incorrect opinion about its truth-value – that, say, a falsifying instance is just around the corner, outside the purview of that particular procedure.

It seems to me, however, that statements about other minds and about the past also lie on this side of the distinction, the wrong side from the point of view of McDowell's M-realism. Consider the case of any particular ascription of pain to another. If the M-realist is right, then the truth-conditions of the claim that another is in pain can obtain detectably, can reside in aspects of his behaviour and overt physical condition. But surely it is part of our concept of another person's pain that, for any particular finite period of time at least, he can, say, behave as if he was in pain in a *completely convincing way* – he may even seem to have suffered extensive physical damage – without actually feeling any pain. The same applies, *mutatis mutandis*, for the case of suppression of a pain which *is* felt. And if this is right, then it follows that so long as our 'procedure' is confined to observation of someone's behaviour and the apparent surface of his body, then, no matter how attentive we are, and even allowing that we make no perceptual error and grasp perfectly what is at issue, we can still form an incorrect opinion about whether or not the subject is in pain. (Just this is the substance in 'grammar', if you like, of the dualist's idea that another's sensations are inaccessible to us.)

The same, I suggest, holds good of statements about the past; though, again, I have no argument for the point save to appeal to our intuitive preconceptions. The question is: can any plausible account be produced of the *province* – corresponding to behaviour and overt physical condition in the M-realist's account of others' pains – on which one who wished, supposing such a thing were ever possible, directly to verify a statement about the past would have to concentrate? Clearly it will not do merely to invite him to 'observe the past'. What is the species of presently accessible states of affairs such that an agent who in a sufficiently attentive, comprehending, and perceptual-error free way observes enough such states of affairs cannot arrive at a mistaken view about a putative state of affairs which antedated them all? McDowell does not tell us; the play with traces in the nervous system made in section 6 of his paper[25] serves only to make a plausible case for supposing that our propensity to assert past-tense statements cannot everywhere be seen as a propensity to make certain

25 McDowell, 'On "The Reality of the Past"', pp. 136–8.

sorts of inference. But that does not meet the issue; it merely serves to satisfy one necessary condition for meeting it. Examples in some detail are what is wanted here; we need to be told how, subject to all the relevant conditions, we can actually directly observe that it rained yesterday, for instance; failing such detail, that an M-realist view of the past might be feasible looks to be merely one more philosophical thesis whose falsity it might be illuminating fully to comprehend.

VI

Let us turn finally to consideration of the M-realist's response to the twin challenges of the anti-realist.

McDowell sees no difficulty with the manifestation-challenge:

> Certainly it seems reasonable to insist that a practical capacity, such as competence with a language, should be observable in its operations. But our realist

– the M-realist –

> can claim that linguistic competence, as he describes it, is indeed observable in linguistic behaviour. Competence with sentences of one of the problematic sorts involves a conception of the sort of circumstance that constitutes their truth-conditions: possession of the conception sometimes manifests itself in linguistic behaviour which – on our realist's view – can be observed as a response to the detectable obtaining of a truth-condition.
>
> A theory of meaning in the style of our realist ascribes to a competent speaker (among other things) dispositions to respond to the obtaining of truth-conditions – circumstances of sorts which need not be detectable – when they *are* detectable. Of course nothing could be observed to be a response to the undetectable obtaining of a truth-condition; but that was not the kind of response which a realistic theory credited the speaker with the ability to make.[26]

On the face of it, this line of thought simply misses the point of the manifestation-challenge. What, an anti-realist who is inclined to press that challenge will want to know, in the responses of speakers to the detectable obtaining of conditions warrants the attribution to them of a conception that the *very same* conditions can obtain undetectably? What could distinguish the performance of someone who had grasped that possibility from that of someone who had not but who was prepared to count the statements in question as verified in the appropriate detectable circumstances? There is no need for the anti-realist to dispute that if the

26 Ibid., pp. 138–9.

circumstances of a particular class of statements were meet for a species of M-realism, then it would be proper to attribute to speakers of the language grasp of truth-conditions for them. The question is: what would warrant the step of attributing to speakers such a conception of those truth-conditions as to allow that they could obtain undetectably?

But McDowell does not believe that he is missing the point:

> It is crucial to this realist rejection of the anti-realist argument that the conception which the realist claims the right to ascribe is a conception of a *kind* of circumstance. He claims the right to ascribe it on the basis of behaviour construable as a response to *some* instances of the kind, in spite of the admitted fact that *other* instances, on his view, are incapable of eliciting any response from the possessor of the conception.[27]

There is a sound point here. Whatever style of theory of meaning is favoured, it will not be reasonable to demand that *every* aspect of the competence with which it will credit a speaker of its object-language should be capable of being manifested in his behaviour. Sometimes it will be reasonable to credit a speaker with understanding of a particular sentence not because he has yet directly manifested competence with that sentence but because in other sentential constructions he has manifested competence with the semantic atoms which feature in it, and with the general mode of construction which it exemplifies. In such a case, as it happens, the actual conditions by reference to which we could test his putative competence directly – from a realist point of view, the truth-conditions of the sentence; from an anti-realist point of view, conditions, perhaps, of some other kind – may simply not be realized. And in that case, the demand that he manifest his understanding is unreasonable; at least, it is either unreasonable or it has been met by what he has done already with other sentences.[28]

This is obviously correct as far as it goes, but the manifestation-challenge is still being evaded rather than answered. Suppose that McDowell were right about the occasional direct observability that another is in pain; and consider a trainee, X, well-versed in the attribution of pain to other people in the relevant kind of circumstance. Now suppose that Y, who is known to X, is never actually going to suffer any pain in X's presence. Then X is never going to have the opportunity directly to manifest his understanding of the statement that Y is in pain. In spite of that, everyone can agree, to be sure, that it can be reasonable to attribute to him an understanding of that statement; in general, a man may possess a grasp of the truth-conditions of a particular statement although circumstances

27 Ibid., p. 139.
28 Or so I take to be the point of 'On "The Reality of the Past"', section 7.

contrive to prevent his being able to display that grasp in the most direct way – by sensitivity to the truth-conditions' realization. Now, that sounds close enough to what McDowell has in his mind to make it intelligible, perhaps, why he should have thought that the manifestation-challenge could be met along these lines; the idea is that to grasp possibly verification-transcendent truth-conditions is in essential respects comparable to any recognitional skill which there may be no chance to exercise. But this is surely a muddle. The understanding of what it is for Y to be in pain which, in the circumstances described, we have reason to attribute to X need be no more than a disposition to respond appropriately to Y's observably being in pain if such a situation were ever to arise – which, by hypothesis, it won't – within X's view. That type of attribution of, as it happens, non-directly manifestable understanding – an unexercised and, as it happens, never-to-be exercised propensity – is justified because the ability with which the speaker is credited is of a type which he has manifested elsewhere. But knowing what it is for a truth-condition to obtain *undetectably* is *not* knowledge which can straightforwardly be viewed as of a type with certain clear-cut recognitional skills. The M-realist wants to make two quite different attributions to X: he wants to credit him with recognitional abilities which, as it happens, he may not get the chance to display; and he wants to credit him with an understanding of what it is for certain truth-conditions to obtain undetectably. McDowell's answer to the manifestation-challenge is to claim, in effect, that these two attributions are exactly on a par. But the fact is that they are not. Grasping M-realist truth-conditions for a particular statement involves *both* possession of a recognitional skill, whose exercise may be pre-empted either by falsity or by undetectable truth, *and* an understanding of what it *is* for the statement to be undetectably true. No reason is so far apparent why the behaviour which McDowell's theorist discerns among object-language speakers entitles him to do any more than attribute the first; whereas the manifestation-challenge asks for an account of what would justify attribution of the second.

What of the acquisition-challenge? Someone who holds, as McDowell believes the truth-value link realist ought to hold, that another's pain is always essentially inaccessible to us obviously runs up against this wing of the anti-realist's attack as soon as he tries to explain how training in the behavioural conditions under which other-ascriptions of pain are warranted can induce an understanding of the real content of those ascriptions. All that can thereby be imparted, it seems, is something less than what needs to be grasped – the language learner has somehow to extract more from the training which he receives than is actually there explicitly in it. It is as if he was told: 'All these states are indeed evidence for the truth of what you say when you assert than another is in pain;

but *what* you are saying when you say that is something which you have to divine for yourself.' Now, if as McDowell convincingly argues, supplementation of that sort of training with an understanding of self-ascriptions of pain, when the self in question is oneself, and drill in the truth-value links, is still no help, how exactly is M-realism supposed to be any better off? Well, because now, McDowell writes,

> ...formation of the required conception needs no leap beyond the bounds of awareness: it can be drawn from actual confrontation with instances of the sort of circumstances involved.[29]

But, the anti-realist will, as we know, complain, there is still a blatant leap! It is precisely from grasp of certain verification-conditions for the statement in question to the conception that the very same sort of circumstance which a verification discerns, when it is open to view, can obtain undetectably. The anti-realist will want to take the M-realist to task here in exactly the way in which McDowell took the truth-value link realist to task in the passage which I quoted at the start of section 3. He will say, for example,

> The M-realist is saying, in effect, 'You can see how a person can have the idea of what it is for someone else to be in pain – when the pain is conclusively manifested in his behaviour. Well, a sentence like "He is in pain", uttered in a context which fixes a reference for the pronoun, is just to be understood always as saying of the appropriate person that he is in that very same state, whether or not there is any behavioural manifestation of it.' But so far from solving the problem, this simply ignores it. If someone cannot see how another person's being in pain – on an interpretation of that circumstance which allows it to hide from our view – can possibly enter into the meaning which we attach to the appropriate statement, if he cannot see, that is to say, how the putative M-realist truth-conditions can intelligently be received by a trainee as anything other than a certain sort of verification-conditions, one does not allay his worry by baldly insisting that they can.

Remember, there is to be no attempt, however confused it might be to try, to protect the required conception from one's own case. The M-realist is holding that we can form a realist conception of what it is for it to be true that someone else is in pain simply on the basis of confrontation with the alleged class of cases in which that subjects are in pain is observationally verifiable. But surely it *is* mysterious how the trick is to be pulled. Put yourself in the position of the trainee: you confront a series of cases in which there is a distinctive common pattern of behaviour, – facial expressions, grunts, groans, shrieks and so on; and in each of these cases

29 McDowell, 'On "The Reality of the Past"', p. 140.

it is true, or so you are told, that the subject is ϕ. But now you are told of people whose behaviour is totally different that, the difference notwithstanding, they too may be ϕ. Wouldn't there be a temptation to think that you had misunderstood the original examples, that the distinctive behaviour had nothing to do with being ϕ? And if you were reassured about that, would you not then be constrained to think that the concept of being ϕ had a breadth to it which the original examples had simply not made clear and about which you needed some further clarification?

McDowell recognizes that there may be an inclination to press the acquisition-challenge in this way. But:

> There is no real difficulty here. Acquisition of one of the problematic conceptions is acquisition of competence with the relevant part of language. Exercising the conception, then, is nothing but exercising the relevant linguistic competence, in speech of one's own or in understanding the speech of others. Puzzlement over how the relevant sort of circumstances can figure in a person's thoughts, if not by way of imagery, is misplaced. The possibility of its figuring in his thoughts is secured, without any need for speculation about a vehicle, by the possibility of its figuring *in his speech*. A competent speaker has words to express, if need be, what state of affairs it is about whose perhaps undetectable obtaining he is capable of, for instance, self-consciously speculating or understanding a fellow-speaker of his language to be speculating.[30]

What this manoeuvre comes to is a tacit appeal to the priority of the manifestation-challenge. McDowell is saying, in effect, 'Never mind how such an allegedly problematic conception is acquired. The fact is that it is presumably acquired somehow because it is manifest in exercise of the relevant aspects of linguistic competence.' But by which aspects, exactly – in, say, the case of pain? Not, at any rate, by simply recognizing the correctness, or incorrectness, of particular ascriptions of pain. But do we not, for example, perfectly well understand the *speculation* that somebody who is smiling and joking at a party is actually concealing a splitting headache? 'Jones, for all that he gives no sign of it, may be in great pain.'

Clearly, something has gone wrong here: for if this response to the manifestation-challenge were feasible, a classical realist about mathematics, for example, could meet that challenge simply by calling attention to the currency of classical logic. He could claim that we manifest our understanding of the possession of possibly proof-transcendent truth-conditions by Fermat's 'Last Theorem' simply in regarding the law of Excluded Middle as validly applicable to it.

The most immediate reason why this response will not do is because

30 'On "The Reality of the Past"', p. 141.

Excluded Middle, and the sort of example which the statement about Jones illustrates, are statements the correctness of our assent to which the anti-realist will want to review. Of course, there are ways of expressing realist convictions – or if not, that is a decisive objection to realism. But if we are realists and sincerely offer such expressions of our conviction, we can scarcely expect the mere fact that we can do so, intelligibly and correctly as it seems to us, to carry the day. For the fact is that it is possible to hold a mistaken philosophical theory about the character of our understanding of a particular class of statements, and for that theory to insinuate itself into our linguistic practices, motivating speculations and claims which we might otherwise not be prepared to make.

Against this, the realist can be expected to protest that he is scarcely likely to be able to meet the manifestation-challenge if, every time he calls attention to promising-looking aspects of our talk, the anti-realist reserves the right to place the legitimacy / intelligibility of those aspects under suspicion! But the point is that the failure of the realist to meet the acquisition-challenge squarely *does* place such aspects under prima facie justified suspicion. Perhaps to move straight to the standpoint of revisionism, like the mathematical intuitionists, is precipitate; but the anti-realist is at least entitled to know what makes the realist sure that (bare) realist conceptions receive expression in those controversial aspects of our linguistic practice. Why, for example, does the remark about Jones have to be interpreted as expressive of a bare realist conception of Jones' pain, rather than as merely one ordinary way of giving expression to the essential defeasibility of statements about others' mental states advanced on the basis of behavioural criteria? So interpreted, the truth expressed by that sentence would be – to repeat – an encapsulation of an aspect of the 'grammar' of our language of mind. Awareness-transcendence would have nothing to do with it.

It is similar with Excluded Middle. One explanation of the classical mathematician's acceptance of that principle might be that he grasped proof-transcendent truth-conditions for the statements in his field. But it might be, too, that Excluded Middle was a mere convention, motivated by certain arrogated analogies between the finite and infinite; or that disjunction possessed a complexity unsuspected in either classical or intuitionistic semantics; or even that Excluded Middle was accepted wholly unthinkingly. All of these would be possibilities which a Martian visitor, attempting radically to interpret our linguistic practice, would have to consider. And the manifestation-challenge will be met only when one of the two things is achieved: *either* we must call attention to features of our practice which would provide the Martian with a sound motive for preferring to attribute to us at least a bare realist understanding of statements of the relevant sorts, rather than advance any of the alternative accounts; *or* we must divine, a priori, pure philosophical considerations which constrain the former interpretation of behaviour which, of itself, fits the alternative accounts. My hunch is that victory for realism, if and when it comes, will be achieved by the second route. But we are presently a long way from the necessary insights.

This paper has been largely critical. Let me say in conclusion that anyone who, like myself, believes that there is no more fundamental philosophical task confronting us at the present time than to see our way clear to disposing of, or sustaining, the anti-realist challenge in different areas of discourse, ought to be grateful to McDowell for something that is still unusual: a sensitive and resourceful attempt by a philosopher of broad realist conviction to meet the anti-realist's arguments *en face*.

4

Strict Finitism

I

This paper is primarily concerned with the Modus Tollens inference adverted to by Dummett in 'Wang's Paradox', namely: arguments essentially analogous to those which the mathematical intuitionists, at least when their case is presented in the way which Dummett has recommended,[1] use to support their revisions of classical logic and mathematics lead to a yet more radical *strict finitist*[2] outlook; this outlook, however, is incapable of issuing in a coherent philosophy of mathematics; therefore there must be something amiss with the arguments which lead to it, and, by analogy, with the original intuitionistic arguments also.[3]

As is familiar, Dummett's presentation of the case for intuitionism is based on very general considerations to do with meaning and understanding applying not just in mathematics but to statements of all kinds. I shall assume that the reader is *au courant* with this way of presenting the intuitionistic case, and I shall not here attempt to expound

1 See especially *Truth and Other Enigmas*, Essays 1, 10, 11, 13, 14 and 21; *Frege: Philosophy of Language*, passim (see the Brief Subject Index, under 'Verification versus realism as theories of meaning'); also 'What is a Theory of Meaning? (II)', and Concluding Philosophical Remarks, in *Elements of Intuitionism*.

2 The term was introduced by Kreisel in 'Wittgenstein's *Remarks on the Foundations of Mathematics*' to denote what he took to be an aspect of Wittgenstein's later philosophy of mathematics; and taken over by Kielkopf (*Strict Finitism*) – misunderstanding, as it seems to me, both Kreisel and Wittgenstein – as a label for Wittgenstein's later philosophy of mathematics in its entirety. It is not a happy label for the ideas I am concerned with, since it is only from non-strict finitist points of view that the strict finitist can be straightforwardly seen as stressing the finitude of human capacities, countenancing only finite sets, etc. (See subsections 5 and 6 below). But we need a label; and Dummett in 'Wang's Paradox' has already followed Kreisel's lead. Anyway, a rose by any other name...

3 Dummett, 'Wang's Paradox', in *Truth and Other Enigmas*, p. 302.

it afresh in detail nor to elaborate the manner in which the more radical, strict finitist view grows out of it.[4] Suffice it to say that the strict finitist is unable to see how, if it is – as it must be – by reference to experiences which we can *actually* have that we learn all language, and by means of capacities which we *actually* have that we manifest our grasp of it, there is any way in which we can genuinely have acquired an understanding of what it is for a statement to be true which we could not, if so, actually recognize to be true; nor any way in which we could so use our language as to constrain an interpreter to attribute such an understanding to us. Thus, whereas the intuitionist is content to regard as determinately true or false any arithmetical statement whose truth value can be effectively computed, at least 'in principle', the strict finitist will insist that the principle of Bivalence is acceptable only for statements the verification or falsification of which can be guaranteed to be humanly feasible.

It is evident that the philosophical and mathematical exegesis of the strict finitist attitude will involve extensive commerce with a range of concepts of human intellectual capability; the actual cogency – or, following the terminology of the later Wittgenstein, *surveyability* – of proofs, the actual intelligibility of symbols, and so on. In 'Wang's Paradox' Dummett takes it that 'surveyable', 'intelligible', etc. are vague in just the same way as predicates of colour, predicates of human maturity – e.g. 'child', 'adult' – and old faithfuls like 'bald', 'tall' and 'heap', and that the vagueness of all these predicates renders them susceptible to the Sorites Paradox. A predicate is a prima facie susceptible to that paradox just in case it is *tolerant*; that is, sufficiently small variations in some associated parameter are apparently insufficient to affect the justice with which it can be applied to something, whereas sufficiently large variations are always so sufficient. For 'red' the appropriate parameter is of course, *colour* – provided we allow that colour can admit of indiscriminable variation.[5] For 'bald' the appropriate parameter is *number of hairs*. For 'intelligible', as applied to numerals, the appropriate parameter is *size of the denoted positive integer*; and for 'surveyable', as applied to proofs, the appropriate parameters are *length* and *complexity*.

Startlingly, Dummett adopts the view that these expressions are genuinely semantically incoherent:[6] the Sorites reasoning is valid for them, and the associated paradoxes admit of no solution – a flawless case can be made for simultaneously applying and withholding these predicates to/from any object in their range of significant application. Whether or

4 See my *Wittgenstein on the Foundations of Mathematics*, pp. 123–8; Dummett, 'Wang's Paradox', in *Truth and Other Enigmas*, pp. 301–2.

5 See my 'On the Coherence of Vague Predicates', pp. 333–43.

6 See 'Wang's Paradox', in *Truth and Other Enigmas*, pp. 319–20.

not Frege's reasons for it were altogether different, Dummett thus in effect endorses the Fregean view that vague expressions are defective; and his argument is that strict finitism is totally vitiated as a viable philosophy of mathematics by its recourse to them.

The programme for the present paper is as follows. Section II will centre around the major premise of the Modus Tollens. Our question will be whether the intuitionist can provide cogent reason for drawing the line where he does draw it, and for refusing to travel on down the constructivist road in the company of the strict finitist. The issues here demand, obviously, close attention to the notion of *decidability in principle*: in particular, we shall need to attend to the notion of *verification* – something which, at the time of writing, is somewhat overdue from those of anti-realist sympathies. In section III the focus of consideration will shift to the minor premise in the Modus Tollens; and we shall consider what the strict finitist can do by way of rebuttal of Dummett's view that he can proffer no coherent philosophy of mathematics. I shall argue that the answer to the leading question of section II ought to be negative, but that Dummett's objections against the coherence of strict finitism can be beaten off. If these conclusions are correct, then strict finitism ought to be a growth area for researches in the foundations of mathematics; it is with a view to taking a small step towards fomenting that state of affairs that I offer, in the Appendix to this essay, an outline of an approach to a strict finitist semantics for arithmetic.

II
Can the Intuitionist Rebut the Major Premise of the Modus Tollens?

1 *A defective tactic*

We had better begin by closing off one, admittedly unattractive, way for the intuitionist to cope with the Modus Tollens, based on accepting Dummett's conclusion about strict finitism. Compare the situation, on that assumption, with the old debate concerning impredicative forms of reasoning in mathematics: the association of such reasoning with the classic logical and semantic paradoxes led many philosophers to regard it as essentially spurious; but others felt that there was no reason to suspect certain at least of the classical proofs involving impredicativity (famously, the proofs of the power-set theorem and that every bounded class of real numbers has a least bound). To be sure, philosophers in the latter group typically conceded that they thereby incurred an obligation to give some other account of the source(s) of the paradoxes, but it is not clear that they needed to do so, nor that it would have been straightforwardly irrational to call such reasoning into doubt when and only when paradoxical consequences were evident. If such an approach found few adherents, it was doubtless because nothing could have been more natural than to suppose that the paradoxes were the result of seductive but specific *fallacies*, which it should have been possible clearly to expose as such. But it is clear, with the benefit of hindsight, how difficult it is convincingly to support that natural view. The attitude remains competitive to the present day that there is nothing identifiably *wrong* with any of the assumptions or methods of derivation involved in the paradoxes save that, in combination, they generate paradox; so that there is no call for suspicion of any of them in isolation, nor reason to doubt them, or forgo their use, when no paradox appears to be forthcoming. Likewise, the fact that arguments at least very much alkin to those of the intuitionist culminate in a philosophy of mathematics beset by incoherence and paradox cannot be taken, without further ado, as decisive for the unacceptability of the intuitionist's own arguments. Rather the intuitionist may appeal to the very incoherence of the strict finitist position to justify his refusal to give his arguments so extensive, or radical, an application; and may then refer the onus back on to the platonist to show that those arguments do not at least merit the less extensive application which the intuitionist proposes to give them.

The trouble with this approach is that it costs the intuitionist's original philosophical arguments their purported *cogency*. The result is eclecticism: intuitionism remains a possible philosophy of mathematics but one for preferring which no compelling considerations can be advanced; just as no *compelling* reason can be advanced for admitting the legitimacy of impredicative definitions and methods of inference in areas where they do not seem to lead to paradox. It is true that some philosophers, notably Kreisel, tend to take just such an eclectic view of the rivalry between platonist and constructivist approaches. But such was never the intuitionists' view; for them, the distinctive methods and assumptions of classical mathematics were demonstrably unacceptable. If the general anti-realist ideas which Dummett has sketched are to be a satisfactory exegesis of the intuitionist standpoint, (purified of its original mentalism), those ideas must be taken to require dissatisfaction with classical mathematics and to command acceptance. And they cannot be reasonably taken to do either if they, or arguments closely akin to them, can be made to issue in a more extreme, radically defective outlook.

This way with the Modus Tollens, then, will not do. It is *possible* for an intuitionist to take the view that his arguments show both that we cannot rest content with the platonist conception of mathematics, or, as he sees them, the spurious concepts and unsound methods which it inspires; *and* that the incoherence of strict finitism shows that we must not allow those arguments to be applied as fully as they might otherwise seem to warrant. The resulting position is not, at any rate, absurd. But it is parallel to the simultaneous claims both that the orthodox, impredicative proofs of certain classical theorems are cogent and that the paradoxes show that impredicative methods cannot be applied as widely as was supposed. So long as no auxiliary independently objectionable assumptions are discerned in the cases where paradox is forthcoming, no one can be held to be unreasonable who refuses to regard impredicative methods as cogent; and so long as no important disanalogy is disclosed between the intuitionist and strict finitist critiques, bringing to light independent and objectionable features of the latter, the untenability of strict finitism, if it is untenable, will mean that no one can be deemed unreasonable who refuses to regard the intuitionist critique as compelling. The situation would not inevitably be that there was doubt about the coherence of mathematical intuitionism; but the best it could aspire to would be the status of an *option*, – the traditional crusading spirit of the intuitionists would be quite out of place.

2 *Decidability in principle*

What, then, are the candidates for the extra, putatively objectionable, assumptions which the strict finitist needs to make? The choice is somewhat restricted. The intuitionist demands that the platonist should explain how an understanding could be conveyed to someone of what it is for a mathematical statement to be true in a way that transcends – or at least has no essential connection with – the possibility of proof; and he demands too an explanation of how someone who had grasped this ethereal notion could distinctively show that he had. The strict finitist agrees with the intuitionist both that these are explanations which the platonist needs to give, and that no satisfactory such explanations are possible; but he holds also that parallel explanatory obligations are incurred by anyone who accepts that lack of a guarantee of humanly feasible verification or falsification is no bar to regarding a particular class of statements as determinate in truth-value. The intuitionist, by granting that any effectively computable arithmetical statement, for example, is determinately either true or false, commits himself to attributing to us a grasp of truth – or falsity – conferring circumstances of a kind which are in practice inaccessible not just to ordinary humans but to calculating prodigies and even to the most advanced computers; how are we supposed to acquire such a grasp, and how should we test whether someone indeed does have it?

The restricted choice, mentioned above, available to the intuitionist in response to these pertinent questions is no more than twofold: he must either answer the strict finitist questions or dispute their legitimacy! – but without, in either case, implicitly supplying the platonist with the means to mete out similar treatment to the corresponding intuitionist questions. The extra, objectionable assumption of the strict finitist would then be respectively either the assumption that his versions of the acquisition – and manifestation – challenges cannot be met by the intuitionist, or the assumption that they need to be met. But, arguably, neither tactic can be successful unless the intuitionist can satisfactorily characterize the class of statements which are *in principle* effectively decidable; for it is precisely in the case of this class of statements that the acquisition – and manifestation – challenges have to be shown either to be ill-taken or to be capable of being met. If no satisfactory account of this class can be given, it appears that the intuitionist will find himself on very thin ice indeed. Lacking any principled account of the extent of his revisions to classical mathematics, he will be powerless to resist the major premise of the Modus Tollens; so powerless to confound the suggestion that, if any kind of constructivist philosophy of mathematics can be cogently motivated, it will not at any rate be intuitionist.

This may seem unfair. We could, after all, restrict our attention to arithmetic, where at least the extension of the intended notion may seem to be clear: an undecided arithmetical statement can be guaranteed to be decidable in principle just in case it is either quantifier- and variable-free or involves quantification only over some finite, decidable subset of the natural numbers. As it stands, of course, the explanation is circular; but there is no reason at this stage to think it irremediably so, and the strict finitist is anyway prepared to cite at least some examples which he regards the intuitionist as mishandling. So locally at least, for the purposes of the philosophy of arithmetic, the intuitionist can set about trying to meet the challenge of strict finitism without attempting a general account of decidability in principle. However, the facts remain: first, only a general account of the notion can serve to make plain exactly what intuitionistic mathematical practice is to be, and exactly where, intuitionistically, classical logic is to be acceptable and where it is not; second, that the generality of the intuitionist and strict finitist ideas obviously entails that the issues between them, and with the realist, arise not just over mathematical statements but everywhere, so that there is no way of explaining what a generalized intuitionistic attitude comes to, let alone demonstrating its cogency and stability, without a generalized account of which statements may be regarded as decidably true or false in principle. We shall therefore investigate what can be offered by way of a completely general such account. If, or when, the investigation founders, that will be the time for the intuitionist to resort to more local tactics.

Intuitionistically,

$$100^{100^{100}} + 1 \text{ is prime}$$

may be regarded as subject to classical logic while Fermat's 'Last Theorem', for example, may not. At first blush, it seems easy both to see the intended distinction and to generalize it. Human beings have certain practical limitations; of intellect, will, memory, eyesight, concentration, stamina and time, etc. But any task is *in principle* within our compass if some *finite* extension of these, or others, of our capacities would bring it within our compass in practice. The simple suggestion is therefore:

> P: An undecided statement, S is decidable in principle just in case an appropriately large but finite extension of our capacities would confer on us the ability to verify it or falsify it in practice.

Clearly, however, the explanatory power of this principle hinges on the status in this context of *decidability in practice* and *finitude*. Of the former, it is true, a committed strict finitist has no right to demand an account here; for it is a notion which he takes for granted in his own supportive arguments. But he is owed clarification of the latter, for there can be no assumption that the notion of finitude which (P) requires is common ground. And further explanation of practical decidability is needed in any case; for otherwise it cannot be clear which statements in general satisfy (P) and are therefore, according to the generalized intuitionist view, acceptably subjected to classical logic – nor, I suppose, whether the mathematical intuitionists are right to accept classical logic for just those arithmetical statements for which they do accept it. Nevertheless I propose, initially in what follows, to take actually computably true or false arithmetical statements as a paradigm of practical decidability; this notion will be the subject matter of the next subsection, and finitude that of subsections 5 and 6.

3 *Verifiability*

It is usually supposed that, for example, the hypotheses of theoretical science and certain sorts of statement about others' mental states – in particular, ascriptions of sensation – about which our natural view is realist, would be susceptible to a generalization of the intuitionist challenge. Certainly it seems intuitively correct that no finite extension of any of our capacities would put us in a position directly to verify or falsify such statements. But what is verification? If arithmetical computation is to be a paradigm of verification, then to be entitled to claim to have verified a statement, in contrast with merely having good evidence for it, cannot be to be entitled to claim a conclusive, *indefeasible* warrant for its assertion; for the most painstaking and careful execution of a computation confers no indefeasible guarantee that it is correct. The defeasibility of any grounds we might have for a particular assertion is thus not sufficient to classify it as, properly speaking, unverifiable; equally, the availability of such grounds is not, as we should ordinarily think, even in the absence of all conflicting evidence, generally sufficient to constitute verifiability. In the case of very many types of scientific hypotheses, for example, we *can* guarantee actually to be able to amass a body either of supportive or of conflicting evidence; the same is plausible for many types of statement about others' mental states. But that is no guarantee, or so we ordinarily suppose, that we can actually *verify* or *falsify* such statements. The problem is how to draw a distinction for ordinary contingent statements between possession of a verification, properly so regarded, and possession of supportive evidence; whether or not evidence of some sort is effectively available in a particular case is therefore irrelevant – if it is to be genuinely verifying, the evidence has to be, though defeasible, of a certain character. What character?

A natural thought is the following. Let us say that a type of ground for asserting a particular statement is *canonical* just in case it is a constraint on any admissible ground for asserting that statement that it simultaneously justify a belief in the existence of grounds of that type. For instance, computation supplies canonical grounds for the assertion or denial of any computationally decidable arithmetical statement. Is verification, therefore, constituted simply by possession of strong, *canonical* grounds for the statement at issue?

Certainly mathematical proof in the widest sense, is presumably verificatory; and we accept no grounds for the assertion of mathematical statements which are not simultaneously grounds for believing in the existence of proofs of them. (Reliable authority in mathematics is reliable authority for the existence of proofs.)

The thought, however, is stillborn. It is neither necessary nor sufficient for grounds to be verificatory that they be canonical. It is not necessary because a proof by higher mathematical means of a computationally decidable statement is verificatory but not canonical; and if it was our practice to accept quasi-inductive grounds for asserting mathematical statements – Fermat's 'Last Theorem', for example, might be regarded as probably true if a very extensive computer run turned up no counter-example – it would be consistent both to continue to regard the appropriate kinds of proof as verificatory and to refuse to regard such indirect evidence as evidence for the existence of proofs. It is not sufficient because, if that were our practice, quasi-inductive grounds for Fermat's 'Last Theorem' would be canonical for that statement but not verificatory.[7]

It is, indeed, not even sufficient for a certain type of statement to admit of verification that it has canonical grounds. The most obvious counter-example is the lowest-level sort of scientific generalization: one containing

7 It is controversial, of course, whether such a practice could be rational.

no theoretical terms and capable of direct experimental corroboration. Such a statement is grounded if it is corroborated by a careful, appropriately extensive series of trials. But *any* ground for believing it is a ground for believing that it will, or would, be so corroborated; so that kind of ground is canonical. It is not, however, verificatory for such statements; and there are, plausibly, no grounds which are verificatory for such statements.

Is it, finally, a necessary condition for a type of statement to admit of verification that it be associated with canonical grounds of some kind? Certainly we do not want to regard statements about the past, for example, as susceptible to verification; and if memory, documentation, presently accessible traces and general theoretical considerations are an exhaustive catalogue of the types of ground we have for such statements, then, plausibly, they have no canonical grounds either. For possession of any (sub-combination) of these grounds is no ground for supposing the existence of the others. The same, *pace* certain sorts of physicalist, may hold for other-ascriptions of mental states. But these examples do not establish a general connection. And the only clear general connection seems to be this trivial one: any actually effectively decidable statement has canonical grounds, for any grounds we may have for asserting, or denying, such a statement are *eo ipso* grounds for an opinion about what the outcome of the appropriate decision-procedure would be. The trivial connection is, admittedly, not totally toothless: if our generalized strict finitist (or intuitionist) holds that only actually (or in principle) effectively decidable statements are properly subjected to classical logic, the connection gives him a simple sufficiency condition for the inappropriateness of classical logic for statements of a certain kind, viz. if none of the assertion-grounds associated with those statements are canonical. But we are no nearer a general account of what it is actually to verify a statement; the canonical status of arithmetical computation has pointed the way only to a cul-de-sac.

A second prima facie promising aspect of the relation between a feasible computation and any arithmetical statement which it verifies or falsifies is this: that *if* someone

i comprehendingly carries out the computation correctly; and
ii correctly apprehends the outcome; and
iii possesses a correct understanding of the statement in question,

the opinion he forms concerning the truth-value of the statement is bound to be correct; there is no *further* scope for error. In contrast, our best investigative procedures for unrestrictedly general scientific hypotheses, for instance, do not bear this relation to those statements; one can fully comprehendingly and correctly execute such a procedure, correctly apprehend the result, perfectly understand the statement(s) at issue, yet be simply wrong – as subsequent investigation may show. It is tempting to think that this contrast may point the way to a general account of practical verifiability according with our preconceptions.[8] The defeasibility of our conclusions in any particular case would be a consequence of the fact that our belief that (i) to (iii) were satisfied would itself always be defeasible; but if those three conditions, or appropriate analogues for them for non-arithmetical examples, are indeed satisfied, then we shall have wholly 'embraced in consciousness' circumstances sufficient for the truth, or falsity, of the statement at issue – and what else is verification, or falsification, but that?

What, if any, types of non-mathematical statement would turn out to be actually verifiable under this proposal? Not, plausibly, any of those for whose meaning a truth-conditional account is usually thought to be anti-realistically problematic. But the prime candidates for counterparts to actually effectively decidable mathematical statements are the traditionally conceived *observation-statements*:[9] statements concerning the presently perceptible qualities of middle-sized objects in bounded, smallish, nearby and accessible regions of space – 'the litmus paper in this solution is turning red', 'the bus is empty', 'there are nine cigarettes left in this packet', 'there is an extra chair in the next room'. Is there any type of procedure associated with these statements such that if we comprehendingly and correctly implement it, correctly apprehend the outcome, and fully understand the statement at issue, our evaluation of it is guaranteed correct – no further possibility of error remains? It is natural to think so, and that such a procedure is: see that you position yourself correctly and carry out the appropriate observations. But there are at least two complications.

The first is that 'positioning oneself appropriately' will, in any case where one is not already so positioned, take time; time in which, by hypothesis of the initial inappropriateness of one's position, relevant but not yet observable changes may take place in the circumstances to be observed. So even if the relevant analogues of (i) to (iii) hold, the possibility of such a change engenders a further potential source of error in one's assessment of the relevant statement – assuming the assessment is to be of its status at the original time of consideration. It therefore appears that, to get the best out of the proposal, we must restrict our attention either to statements for whose assessment the observer is already appropriately positioned or to short-term predictions of the situation at a time by which an observer can have reached that position.

8 I, at any rate, was so tempted in Essays 3 and 12. See this volume pp. 97–9 and 378–9.
9 Cf. Dummett, 'What is Theory of Meaning? (II)', pp. 94–8.

The second complication, however, is much more serious. What is it correctly to apprehend 'the outcome'? In the case of an arithmetical computation, the outcome had better be literally that one has produced a certain numeral; so, at any rate, (ii) has to be understood if the original claim, that satisfaction of (i) to (iii) precludes any further possibility of error, is to be correct. For if 'the outcome' were construed merely as that one *seemed* to have produced a particular numeral, satisfaction of (i) to (iii) would not preclude an error resulting from a divergence between what seemed to have resulted and what really had.[10] For the same reason, then, we cannot construe the outcome of the putative perceptual verification procedures, currently entertained, to be merely that the observer suffers a particular sensory barrage; the outcome has to be rather that he *observes* certain circumstances and goings-on. But then the proposal is completely trivialized; the analogues of (i) to (iii) guarantee no further possibility of error precisely because the analogue of (ii) is tantamount to the stipulation that the agent perceptually *verifies* how things before him stand in relation to the statement being tested. Construed as it has to be construed in order to be adequate, therefore, the proposal presupposes something which it ought rather to justify, viz. that there *is* such a thing as perceptual verification of the type of statement illustrated, and – worse – makes implicit use of the very notion it is supposed to explain. (A corresponding triviality in the case of computational verification is avoided because there can be correct apprehension of an erroneously reached outcome.)

The proposal founders, then, on the following disanalogy. There is an equivalence between the truth of any actually decidable arithmetical statement and that of a corresponding conditional to the effect that if such-and-such a feasible procedure is correctly carried out, so-and-so will be the result. But with observation-statements of the kind illustrated, the only plausible candidates for such equivalent conditionals will involve interpreting the 'result' of the correctly implemented procedure as something tantamount to verification of the statement in question; otherwise equivalence will not be ensured. But then the parallel with decidable arithmetical statements is bought only at the cost of presupposing that which it was to have been the point of the parallel to support.

The feeling persists, however, that there is something right about the spirit of this second unsuccessful strategy. Surely there is a genuine sense in which circumstances conferring truth on statements concerning the past, the remote future, others' sensations, and the totality of space and time

10 At least, the point holds good for computations done out loud or on paper; and we can ignore any complication occasioned by the apparent indefeasibility of our assessment of the outcomes of computations done 'in our heads', since it is inessential to the verificatory status of computation that we can effectually work in our heads at all.

cannot, at least in their entirety, be accessible to us, whereas those conferring truth on at least some observational statements can be; and surely the distinction has to do somehow with the *scope* of sources of possible error in our investigations of such statements, even if it cannot illuminatingly be drawn directly in terms of a connection, lacking in the former cases but present in the latter, between carrying out our best investigative procedures correctly and getting a correct opinion about the investigated statement. Intuitively, if someone carries out a calculation and forms a false opinion on that basis about the truth-value of an arithmetical statement which that calculation decides, there must be something *else* wrong as well: a further mistake, or a misunderstanding, or some sort of misperception. With investigations into the past, other minds, and the domain of scientific law, in contrast, we can finish up, as it may later transpire, *barely* wrong; there need be no independent error in the investigation, or misunderstanding, or oversight, or illusion. Should not at least some observation-statements be ranked with decidable arithmetical statements in this regard? If I investigate the statement, 'there are exactly nine cigarettes left in this packet', in the most direct perceptual way, and come to a wrong conclusion, can this be the full extent of my error – or must I not hold other, *logically independent* beliefs which are also incorrect? The crucial thing is the combination of incorrectness and logical independence. If I investigate and come, as it happens mistakenly, to believe some general scientific hypothesis, I must, if I am rational, accept a commitment to two broad classes of belief: first, the set of beliefs constituted by the logical consequences of the hypothesis; and second, a set of beliefs pertaining, broadly speaking, to the conduct of my investigation, such that a doubt about any of them would *ceteris paribus* call into question my title to the conclusion which I drew, even in the absence of any counter-evidence against that conclusion. But none of the second class of beliefs to which I am committed need in this case be mistaken; it may be possible to give a full explanation why it was that I came to hold a mistaken belief without impugning the truth of any member of that class. However that is not the situation with the cigarette example: if I carry out a first-hand, perceptual investigation into that statement, and come mistakenly to believe it, the explanation of my error will, it seems, be bound to advert to some false belief about my state, or the conditions or conduct of the investigation, to which I have committed myself by coming to the view of the investigated statement which I now hold and which is logically independent of the belief. Take the case of a miscount: in coming to believe, falsely, that the cigarette example is true, I will, if I am rational, accept a commitment to the belief that I did not miscount the cigarettes; this belief may be false, and its falsity would explain my false conclusion; but it is a belief whose truth would be consistent with the falsity of my conclusion and whose falsity would be consistent with its truth.

A suggestion, then, is as follows. Let S be any statement for which there is an investigative procedure, I; and let the *I-class* of statements for S contain every and only statements R satisfying the following conditions:

a any rational agent who considers that the upshot of performing I is a justified belief in S commits himself to believing R;
b one admissible explanation of the agent's coming falsely to believe S on the basis of I would be the falsity of R; and
c S does not entail R nor vice versa.

Plausibly, any statement to which we attach a clear sense is such that we have a conception at least of what it would be to *try* to uncover grounds for believing or disbelieving it; and it is, in this way, as essentially an attempt to uncover such grounds that I is to be understood – there is to be no presupposition of effectiveness, no presupposition that such grounds, one way or the other, must emerge. So every statement to which we attach clear sense is potentially associated with a non-empty I-class. If I is an attempt to construct a mathematical proof, for example, the I-class will contain all statements, R, whose negations entail the existence of errors in a resulting construction, or any sort of oversight, illusion or misunderstanding. Oversight, illusion and misunderstanding, of course, are all-pervasive potential sources of error; so whenever it is considered that an investigation justifies us in believing some S, we are rationally committed to believing that nothing of those sorts has occurred, and the composition of the corresponding I-class will reflect the fact. The I-classes associated with specific historical and scientific investigations will embrace, in addition, statements concerning the authenticity of documents and putative traces, proper exercise of controls, due care in setting up apparatus, and so on.

We can now make the following proposal:

> S is capable of *actual verification* if and only if there is some investigative procedure, I, such that (i) we can actually implement I and, on that basis, achieve, if we are rational, what we will consider to be a grounded belief in S; but (ii) subsequent grounds sufficient to call S into question would, if we are rational, have to be allowed to call into question simultaneously the truth of at least one member of the original I-class. (An undecided S may thus be regarded as *decidable in practice* just in case we have recognized that either it or its negation is capable of actual verification.)

Roughly speaking, then, statements are actually verifiable if and only if a putative instance of the best type of ground we can have for believing them is defeasible only by calling into question its *pedigree*; if an actually verifiable S has to be jettisoned, there is at least one kind of I for S such that, if belief in S was originally based on implementation of that I, members of the corresponding I-class have to be jettisoned also. This is not, on the face of it at least, the situation of the generalizations of natural science, statements concerning the past, statements concerning the still remote future, must subjunctive conditionals, and most types of description of others' mental states; in each of these kinds of case, all admissible grounds for belief can be overturned simply by *enrichments* of our total state of information quite consistent with our rationally retaining belief in each R in an original I-class. But it does appear that mathematical statements asserted on the basis of proof, or computation, at least some observation-statements, (and, perhaps, at least some first-person ascriptions of mental state) fit the bill. If I look inside the packet and count the cigarettes, concluding that 'there are nine cigarettes left in this packet' is true, I am rationally committed to believing that I overlooked nothing, did not miscount, suffered no illusion and correctly understand that statement; for a doubt along any of those lines would invalidate the warrant for my conclusion. At the same time, if any of those beliefs is false, that could constitute an explanation of the falsity of my conclusion, if that is false; and the truth of each of those beliefs is logically independent of the truth of my conclusion. So an appropriate formulation of each of them is in the relevant I-class. But if it later transpires that my findings were incorrect, must not at least one of those beliefs also have been incorrect? Even if the answer is 'No', it is plausible that it will be so only because the relevant I-class has other members: it would be because there is another way I can *go wrong*, another consideration doubt about which I would have to regard as invalidating my investigation without entailing doubt about the truth of the investigated statement.

I claim for this third suggestion only that it sketches an approach worth investigating to an extremely tricky question. The prizes for a correct answer might include not just clarification of a notion which has featured prominently in the literature on these matters but some purchase, perhaps, on the distinction, currently in disrepute in the philosophy of science, between observation- and theoretical statements.

4 *The role of verifiability in Dummett's arguments for intuitionism*

We saw it as to the point to call for an account of actual verifiability because only in the light of such an account could the scope of the principle (P) be clear; and only if that is clear can the generalized intuitionist demarcate the lines which he wishes to defend against the realist and strict finitist respectively, let alone construct the defence. But it is arguable that the notion of verifiability has a yet more crucial role in the realist/anti-realist dialectic.

It is a feature of Dummett's exposition of the anti-realist standpoint that there is within mathematics, and perhaps outside it, a class of statements an understanding of which *can* legitimately be regarded as constituted by a grasp of truth-conditions. For Dummett's anti-realist, understanding a statement is essentially a practical, discriminatory skill; it cannot, therefore, be held to be constituted by possession of alleged conceptions of possibly undetectable states of affairs save in so far as such 'conceptions' *reduce* to, are equivalent to, practical discriminatory skills. But where the realization of the truth-conditions of a statement can be ascertained, if only by ingenuity or by good fortune. Dummett's anti-realist has no objection to giving grasp of truth-conditions a legitimate semantical role to play.[11] Now, is this an essential feature of Dummett's exposition? Is it *necessary* that there be a base-class of statements for which the notion of truth is anti-realistically unproblematic, if the anti-realist critique is to be coherent, or is it not?

Strawson, for one, implicitly takes it that it is.[12] But the anti-realist can be expected to reply that legitimate doubts about the extricability of the notion of verification ('in practice' or 'in principle') or about the applicability outside logic and mathematics of any worthwhile notion which we might extricate, would be liable simply to *generalize* his challenge; their effect would be merely that the class of statements of whose meaning a realist account is problematic would be more extensive that had been initially supposed.[13] If that reply is acceptable, clarification of the notion of verifiability in principle is needed by the generalized intuitionist only for the reason described: to determine the extent of his revisions of the linquistic practices inspired by classical realism, and as a prerequisite for a completely general riposte to the strict finitist.

There is, however, some question whether, unless such clarification can be given and the resulting notion proves to be non-empty, the anti-realist polemic expounded by Dummett can be fully intelligible. Consider the manifestation argument. The suggestion was that understanding is essentially knowledge which can be distinctively displayed in behaviour; it is a network of discriminatory and responsive skills. So there is no place, in an acceptable philosophical account of understanding, for imputation

11 Whether 'can be ascertained' here is taken to allude to possibility in practice or in principle will not affect our treatment of the main issue of this subsection.

12 Strawson, 'Scruton and Wright on Anti-realism, Etc.', p. 17.

13 Cf. Essay 2, pp. 72–3.

of conceptions of (potentially) 'transcendent' states of affairs; whatever ability corresponds to such a conception, it cannot *show* itself as different from the abilities constituting knowledge of the *use* of the statement of whose truth-conditions it supposedly constitutes grasp. Only as a complex of recognitional skills can understanding be distinctively manifest in behaviour; understanding a statement is manifest in the ability to recognize when circumstances warrant the assertion, or denial, of it and of compound statements containing it, and to recognize its logical consequences and ancestry; this is all anyone can overtly *do* with the statement, and for the description of these abilities it is otiose 'theoretical slack' to invoke the notion that the speaker possesses a conception of a (potentially) transcendent state of affairs. His abilities can be fully described in terms of states of affairs which he can recognize: conditions decidably justifying assertions and denials involving that statement, and decidable logical relations between it and other statements.

What is striking is that it is unclear how this argument could be developed without reliance upon the notion of a *recognitional skill*: what is allegedly wrong with 'grasp of truth-conditions' as a description of statement-understanding in general is precisely that it cannot (always) be, whereas understanding always is, a recognitional skill, or complex of such skills. If it proved to be a mistake to see statement-understanding as a complex recognitional ability, the sketched objection to the truth-conditional account would, or so it appears, totally collapse. That grasp of truth-conditions could not everywhere be construed as a recognitional ability would rightly provoke the response, 'so what?'. But can the notion of a recognitional ability be explained without recourse to that of *verification*? If I am to be able effectively to recognize whether a statement is warrantedly assertible in particular circumstances, must not this be interpreted as a capacity of verification rather than of something weaker? For if it is something weaker, then grasp of the assertion-conditions of a statement will, it appears, be no less a transcendent conception than the originally suspect grasp of its truth-conditions. The whole strategy of argument appears to demand the existence of a class of states of affairs which we can, over and above having evidence for their obtaining or not, *verify* to obtain or not. It is against this class of states of affairs that all our concepts have to measure – by reference to these states of affairs that they have to be given content. It is in our responses to states of affairs of this class that the content we have succeeded in assigning to any particular concept is fully manifest and determined. Only if the notion of verification is satisfactorily explicable can this picture be defensible.

It is similar with the argument from acquisition. Here the point is, crudely, that there is no way anyone could possibly derive a conception of what it is for a verification-transcendent state of affairs to obtain from any training in the use of the language; for his experience is necessarily only of states of affairs which are not of that kind. It is only by reference to *accessible* states of affairs that the rules of the language he is learning can have an intelligible meaning for him; only at the observation of rules correlating the use of expressions in the language with states of affairs of that kind that he can intelligently aim. Again, then, it is hard to see what force could be attached to these considerations by someone who did not believe that there *are* states of affairs which do not transcend human capacities for verification, and which are accessible to us. If there are such states of affairs, there is then no obvious objection if certain of them are designated sufficient for the truth of certain statements in the language; which statements will then be susceptible to verification.

There are thus grounds for thinking that both these forms of anti-realist argument rely on the legitimacy of viewing our language as containing a (potential) base-class of verifiable statements. But caution is necessary; in particular, it needs investigation whether the crucial ideas for the anti-realist, of a recognitional ability and an ostensively definable state of affairs, might be elucidated not in terms which presuppose the notion of verification but in terms of something akin to the (later Wittgenstein's?) concept of art, *criterion*. Here it would be essential to understand the first term of the criterial relation as lying on the worldly side of the language/reality distinction. Criteria would not themselves be statements but recognizable and ostensible aspects of reality. But for no statement would they constitute a sufficient condition of *truth*; the ground which they provided for accepting any statement would always be defeasible. On this view, the way in which language engaged with the world would not be truth-conditional at all but through-and-through criterial. Whether such a conception is ultimately intelligible depends, of course, on whether it can be satisfactorily explained how it is that criteria everywhere fall short of truth-conditions; how it is that there are no statements, no *possible* statements, on which they confer truth.[14]

To Dummett's anti-realist arguments, in any case, the realist now has a powerful initial counter-argument: 'Explicate the notion of verifiability which those arguments seem to need to employ, or show that they do not need to employ it.' To be sure, this counter-argument is not available to a realist who accepts that he owes an account of how a conception of the truth-conditions of the original anti-realistically problematic examples can be imparted to someone; and conceives that the proper path is via *analogy* with states of affairs of an ascertainable type. Such a realist too is committed to a defence of the notion of verifiability. The enigma remains: we know how to describe the workings of virtually no part of the statement-making sector of our language save by reference to the notion

14 Cf. Essay 12, pp. 381–2.

of truth, yet we have no convincing demonstration that a truth-conditional account is the proper form for a description of this sector of our language to take. If some statements are verifiable, then, for them, grasp of truth-conditions can be seen as a recognitional ability; but the anti-realist arguments against a truth-conditional account of the remainder are then, so it seems to me, formidable. If no statements are verifiable, the question remains to be decisively settled whether that intensifies the anti-realist arguments or defuses them.

5 *Finitude*

The principle (P) has various disquieting aspects. First, however successful or unsuccessful the suggestions made in subsection 3, 'decidable in practice', like 'surveyable' and 'intelligible' is, if Dummett is right, irremediably Sorites-susceptible. If, as Dummett contends, its recourse to such predicates defeats the claims of strict finitism to be taken seriously, how can it be admissible for the intuitionist to attempt to explain one of his key notions in terms of such a predicate? Second, (P) is gaining no special plausibility from the fact that it is concerned with decidability; any appeal it has belongs equally to the more general proposal that all our capacities 'in principle' should be construed as capacities which we would actually have if our powers were appropriately, but finitely, extended. It is easy to overlook how bizarre an idealization this involves: I am, apparently, to be in principle able to launch myself at escape velocity from the earth just by leaping; to long-jump to America; to read the totality of English language publications in an afternoon; and singlehandedly to irrigate the Sahara in an evening. These are all things which I could, presumably, actually do if I was finitely stronger, more agile, more heat resistant, etc. than I am. If it really is to be *we*, creatures of blood and bone, of whom it is to make sense to hypothesize arbitrarily large, though finite, increases in capacity, the hypothesis has simultaneously to be of radical alterations in our present conception of physical and biochemical law. But we have in advance no specific idea, at least if the hypothesized increases are sufficiently vast, of the kind of alterations that might be called for. Is it evident, then, that we really do understand, quite independently of prevailing physical theory, what it would be to undergo such increases in capacity? Put starkly, the point is simply this: any of our capacities in which it is to make anti-realistic sense to hypothesize arbitrarily large, though finite, increases – (or for which it is to make anti-realistic sense just to hypothesize other creatures, perhaps constitutionally very different to ourselves, whose powers greatly, though finitely, exceed our own) – has to be ascertainable quite independently of prevailing scientific theory. Otherwise, as soon as the hypothesized increase is sufficiently large, it may contribute towards confounding a theory which at least partially determines the criteria we should use for detecting it; lacking any account of what would justify the claim that such an increase had taken place (or that such was the capacity of the constitutionally different creatures), there would therefore be a doubt about its content from an anti-realist point of view. Is it certain, then, that each of the capacities involved in, for instance, arithmetical computation on paper is, in the relevant way, pre-theoretically determinable?

Third, it is not obviously sensible to speak of a finite extension of at least some of the particular capacities determining the scope of our overall practical powers. People can have better and worse memories, greater and lesser powers of concentration, more or less stamina; but what are the metric units by reference to which, in contrast with rate of work, time available, and, perhaps, intelligence, increases in these powers might significantly be classed as finite? The only purchase, it seems, which we have on the idea of a finite increase in such powers is via the finitude of the tasks that would then be within our compass; now, though, on pain of circularity, an independent explanation is required of the finitude of tasks – independent, that is, of any appeal to the finitude of the capacities of creatures who could actually perform them.

The fourth doubt, however, is the most serious. Even where measurement in terms of an appropriate unit is possible, what is it for an increase in some capacity to be *finite*? On our ordinary understanding, such an increase is finite just in case it is by no more than n units and any set with n members is finite. So the question becomes: what is a finite set? Obviously, (P) will stand up as an explanation of what it is for statements to be decidable 'in principle' only if the concepts which it uses can themselves be explained without recourse to the general notion of: ϕ-ability in principle. It is very doubtful, however, whether this constraint can be met.

According to one classic conception, a set is finite just in case its members can be one-to-one mapped onto an initial segment of the series of positive integers in order of magnitude. But the trouble with this is immediate: what is it for such a mapping to be *possible*? Intuitionistically, a set will count as finite by this proposal if and only if an *effective* one-to-one function, f, *can be located* such that for each member x of the set, $f(x)$ *can be recognized* to be a particular positive integer m, $\leqslant$ a fixed positive integer n. Each of the italicized notions in that statement involves possibility; but possibility in principle or possibility in practice? If the former, this explanation of finitude is going to infect the principle (P) with circularity. But if the latter, sufficiently large but intuitionistically finite sets are not going to pass the test, with the result that the domain of statements admitted to be in principle decidable by (P) will be very much more restricted than the intuitionist needs and intends. For with sufficiently large but intuitionistically finite sets, there will not be any *actually effective* appropriate *f* because we will not *actually* be able to handle sufficiently many distinct numerals; and because, in a certain range of cases, even if we do have enough actually intelligible numerals, there will still be no actually effective one-to-one mapping since a count of the set in question will not be humanly feasible.

Initially this seems no more than an awkwardness which a little bit of ingenuity ought to be able to circumvent. For example, whatever our practical limitations in handling the numerals of any particular primitive notion, we can, surely, always actually invent a more powerful notation than any presently employed. Simplifications are always feasible, if only in certain places; we could write 'm^j_k', for example, to indicate k reiterations of the exponent j. Now if, as it appears, there is actually no limit on the size of the integers which we can surveyably represent, provided we are licensed to introduce *ad hoc* novel notations for the task, can we not secure the intended force of P without circularity by saying: a set is finite just in case, even if only by the introduction of a novel notation, we can actually specify an integral upper bound on its size?

No progress is made. Clearly there is no single notation adequate for the actually intelligible expression of (intuitionist) integers of any arbitrary size. But, if the proposal is to capture the intended notion, the introduction of new, more powerful notations must not inevitably be cumulative. For if there are integers an actually intelligible expression for which can be attained only via construction first of one extension of extant systems, then an extension of that...and so on, then there are going to be practical limitations, if only of time, on our ability to do *that*; and certain integers are going to lie beyond all practical possibility of intelligible expression. What the proposal requires, therefore, is that there should be no limit on the size of the integers which, at any stage, we can bring within our practical compass by *someone* feasible extension of extant notation. That is

(n) there is some feasible extension, E, of extant numerical notations such that integers $\geqslant n$ are actually intelligibly representable in E.

But this requirement cannot be met. In order to construct an actually intelligible symbol for what we can actually recognize to be an integral upper bound on a particular set, we need already to possess an actually intelligible expression for at least the approximate order of magnitude of the set; and this will have to make reference to, if not actually use, the already existing notion. There are, however, in the intuitionist series of positive integers elements of such a size that no such indication of their order of magnitude can at present actually be given; so there are, from the intuitionist point of view, *finite* sets of such a size that we cannot, by any single extension of extant notation, bring integers within the compass of our actually intelligible means of expression which are big enough to denote upper bounds on the sizes of those sets. Thus the second proposal is false to the intended sense of finitude.

Can the intuitionist do better by fashioning a third proposal out of the other classic account of finitude due to Dedekind, viz. that a set is infinite just in case it can be one-to-one mapped onto a proper part of itself, and finite just in case it is not infinite? Interpreted intuitionistically, the Dedekind account involves that, in order to be justified in regarding a set as infinite, we have to have found, or know we can find, a method for pairing the elements of the set with those of a proper subset of it without omission of any of the former or repetition of any of the latter; and in order to be entitled to regard a set as finite, we have to be in a position to deny that any such method can be found. The most immediate worry is whether all intuitionistically infinite sets will be classified as infinite by this account if, as on pain of circularity it must, all implicit play with 'possibility in principle' is excised from it. For, evidently, no one-to-one mapping of the positive integers onto any effectively enumerable subset of them is *actually* effective, if only – (at the risk of sending the reader to sleep) – because we cannot devise actually intelligible means for referring to every element in the two sets. But that, on reflection, may seem to be no very serious matter. The crucial thing is that the set of intuitionist positive integers should not be classified as *finite*; otherwise it is hard to see how the conclusion could be avoided that a finite extension of our capacities would put us in a position actually to decide the truth-value of Fermat's 'Last Theorem' in a purely computational way, and no validation would be possible of the intuitionist reservations concerning the application of classical logic to such examples.[15] But the danger of this particular kind of misclassification can be avoided, it seems. All the intuitionist needs to do is to *strengthen* the notion of finitude: to insist that finitude requires that we have a method for locating omissions or repetitions in any putative one-to-one mapping.[16]

15 The conclusion follows directly, provided it is granted that the net effect of finitely many finite increases in capacity is itself a finite increase.

16 A set, A, is not Dedekind-infinite just in case

$$\sim(\exists f)(\exists B)[B \subset A \,\&\, (x)(x \in A \rightarrow (\exists y)(y \in B \,\&\, fx = y \,\&\, (z)((z \in A \,\&\, fz = y) \rightarrow z = x)))]$$

The proposed strengthening comes to this: A is *finite* if and only if

$$(f)(B)[B \subset A \rightarrow (\exists x)(x \in A \,\&\, (\sim(\exists y)(y \in B \,\&\, fx = y) \vee (\exists z)(z \in A \,\&\, fz \in B \,\&\, fz = fx \,\&\, z \neq x)))]$$

(The additional strength derives, of course, from the failure of intuitionistic implication of $(\exists x)(P \,\&\, \sim Q)$ by $\sim(x)(P \rightarrow Q)$.)

Now, though, the problem is the obverse: will every intuitionistically finite set be classified as finite? For there will, most often, be no other way of locating omissions or repetitions save to enumerate the set in question and run through the values of the appropriate function. Suppose, for example, it is claimed that the positive integers up to and including 100^{100} can be one-to-one mapped onto the prime numbers in the same range in order of magnitude. It may be that the only method we have for defeating the suggestion that this mapping is one-to-one will involve enumerating the relevant primes in order of magnitude; so that it is only *in principle* that we can force the putative one-to-one mapping to break down. Again, then, the threat is of circularity or of misclassification; and this time the misclassification is serious, for it is essential to the intuitionist's intentions that a 100^{100}-fold increase in some measurable capacity of ours should be positively classified as a finite increase.

So long, then, as it is interpreted so as to have no implicit recourse to our capacities 'in principle', the Dedekind account will misrepresent the intuitionist's intended notions of finitude and infinity in one of two ways. If finitude requires only that we recognize that there is no question of constructing an actually effective mapping of a set onto a proper part of itself, intuitionistically infinite sets will be classified as finite. But if finitude requires, more strongly, that we can actually counter-exemplify the claims of any alleged mapping, then certain intuitionistically finite sets will not be classified as finite. Either way, the demarcation which the principle P was intended to capture will be subverted.

6 *Dedekind-infinity and the vagueness of surveyability predicates*

The plot thickens if the Dedekind account is combined with acceptance that the application of predicates of practical intellectual possibility (*surveyability predicates*) tolerates sufficiently marginal increases in length, complexity, detail, etc. Suppose that the measure of some hypothetical increase in a capacity of ours is, intuitively, very large; as large as, or larger than the set of integers actually intelligibly representable in decimal notation, Σ. And consider the set, $\{\Sigma - 1\}$. Now if 'integer actually intelligibly representable in decimal notation' is genuinely tolerant in the way Dummett takes it to be, then every such integer has a successor which also satisfies that predicate. Σ can therefore be mapped one-to-one onto $\{\Sigma - 1\}$, a proper subset of it. Thus Σ turns out infinite, and so does the measure of the hypothesized increase in our capacity.

Now, then, worse than merely failing to classify them as finite, the Dedekind account threatens to rank certain intuitively finite sets as infinite. It would follow that any increase in capacity too large to be captured by means of an integer in Σ ranks as an infinite increase, so that, again, the intended sense of the principle (P) is hopelessly lost.

It might be wondered whether the implicit assumption of this thought, that any set with an infinite subset is itself infinite, is any longer clearly allowable under the present restrictions. Perhaps Σ turns out, unintendedly, to be infinite; but that may yet not frustrate the intention of the principle (P) too badly, since it is quite unclear what could justify us in claiming that the measure of the increase in some capacity, necessary if a particular task were to come to be within our practical scope, would be *precisely* the number of integers actually intelligibly representable in decimal notation. And if a bigger increase is involved, it remains to be shown that sets of that order can indeed be actually effectively mapped one-to-one onto a proper subset of themselves. Would, for example, a $1{,}000{,}000^{1{,}000{,}000}$-fold set now rank as infinite? If so, onto which of its proper subsets could it in practice effectively be one-to-one mapped?

Obviously the question needs care. Intuitively, $\{\hat{n}{:}n \leqslant 1000000^{1000000}\}$ contains some integers with no actually intelligible means of representation in any extant notation; and that fact alone is sufficient to guarantee that we cannot in practice effectively one-to-one map its members onto any of its proper subsets. But, as noted, that must not be allowed to be decisive against infinity, or a like consideration will be decisive against the infinity of the intuitionist set of all positive integers. Let us experiment instead within the framework of the supposition that $\{\hat{n}{:}n \leqslant 1000000^{1000000}\}$ contains all and only those integers of which we can actually intelligently receive an expression and which we can actually recognize to be members of that set on that basis. (This is, presumably, exactly the way in which a strict finitist will view that set.) Can we now construct an appropriate, actually effective mapping?

Here is an argument for thinking that we can. Let 'An' mean: n is actually intelligibly representable in some extant notation; and let $K = \{\hat{n}{:} An \& n \leqslant 1000000^{1000000}\}$. Our task is to map K onto a proper part of itself; and we succeed just in case we can specify an $L, \subset K$, and an R for which it can be shown:

i $(n)[n \in K \rightarrow [(\exists m)(m \in L \& Rnm \& \sim(\exists o)(o \in L \& Rno \& o \neq m))]]$

and

ii $(m)[m \in L \rightarrow [\exists n)(n \in K \& Rnm \& \sim(\exists o)(o \in K \& Rom \& o \neq n))]]$

Clearly we cannot employ with K the same simple tactics as with Σ, for $1000000^{1000000} + 1$ is not in K. But let 'Bn' mean: n is actually intelligibly representable in decimal notation; and let K be partitioned into $U_1 = \{\hat{n}{:}n \in K \& Bn\}$, and $U_2 = \{\hat{n}{:}n \in K \& \sim Bn\}$. Then if $L = \{K - \{1{,}000000^{1000000}\}\}$ and Rnm holds good just in case *either* $n \in U_1$ and m

is the successor of n *or* $n \in U_2$ and m is the immediate predecessor of n, then a case for the above clauses (i) and (ii) can be constructed as follows:

Re (i). Suppose we are presented with any n which we can actually recognize to be a member of K. If $n \in U_1$ then m will be its successor; and, assuming the tolerance of B in the relevant parameters, we shall be able to construct an actually intelligible expression for m in decimal notation. So we shall have found an appropriate m for n such that $m \in L$ and Rnm. If, on the other hand, $n \in U_2$, then the appropriate m will be its immediate predecessor; assuming, then, that A is tolerant in the relevant respects (i.e. that '... – 1' is actually intelligible whenever '...' is) we shall again be able actually to locate an appropriate m such that $m \in L$ and Rnm. In either case, then, all that can obstruct the acceptability of (i) is if we are also able to locate an o such that $o \in L$ and Rno actually recognizably holds good but o is actually recognizably distinct from m. But, by the definition of R, no n can bear R to two distinct elements unless it is simultaneously a member of U_1 and U_2. And that, by the definition of those sets, is impossible. We have therefore shown that given any n in K, we can actually specify an m which satisfies the first two conjuncts of the consequent of (i), and for which the clause of which the third conjunct is the negation will be actually demonstrably absurd; so (i) holds good.

Re (ii). Suppose we are presented with any m which we can actually recognize to be a member of L. If $m \in U_1$, then n will be its immediate predecessor; and, since B applies to the immediate predecessor of any positive integer to which it applies, we shall be able to construct an actually intelligible expression for n in decimal notation. So we shall have found an appropriate n for m such that $n \in K$ and Rnm. If, on the other hand, $m \in U_2$, then the appropriate n will be its successor; assuming, then, that A is tolerant in the relevant respect (i.e. that '... + 1' is actually intelligible whenever '...' is) we shall again be able actually to locate an appropriate n such that $n \in K$ and Rnm. In either case, all that can obstruct the acceptability of (ii) is if we are also able to locate an o such that $o \in K$ and Rom actually recognizably holds good but o is actually recognizably distinct from n. But, by the definition of R, no two distinct elements of K can bear R to m if both are members of U_1 or of U_2; and since R is defined only for elements of U_1 and U_2, it follows that one of n and o must be in U_1 and the other in U_2. Suppose that $n \in U_1$ and $o \in U_2$. Then Bn; so by the tolerance of B and two steps of Universal Instantiation and Modus Ponens, we have Bo, contrary to hypothesis; (and a similar contradiction is forthcoming from ~Bo and the contrapositive of the tolerance principle for B). We have therefore shown that, given any m in L, we can actually specify an n which satisfies the first two conjuncts of the consequent of (ii), and for which the clause of which the third conjunct is the negation will be actually demonstrably absurd; so (ii) holds good.

There are two protests about this reasoning which someone may immediately want to make. The first is that it achieves no more than an illustration of the kind of nonsense we are bound to confront if we try to work with semantically incoherent expressions. To this it is fair to reply that, *pace* Dummett, it has yet to be made out that the assumption which the reasoning needs, viz. the *tolerance* of predicates like A and B in various parameters, entails their semantic incoherence. We shall take up the question of this supposed entailment in section III.

The second protest concerns the assumption that the partition of K into U_1 and U_2 is actually effective; the assumption is necessary if, presented with an arbitrary element of K, it is to be actually possible to locate an R-correlate of it, but it is tantamount to the assumption that B is actually effectively decidable for elements of K – and that assumption is apt to seem highly questionable. Surely there must be a large class of integers for which the question whether or not they can be actually intelligibly represented in decimal notation defies solution: integers falling within a range where we cannot actually compute the decimal resolution of the expression by means of which they are given to us, but can see that they are not at any rate so big as to make an actually intelligible decimal representation out of the question. (A computer might supply us with one.)

Formulated like this, the objection makes a presumably illicit use of the notion that an integer can have an actually intelligible decimal representation which we cannot in practice identify as such; presumably illicit because, in the context of an overall attempt to rebut the strict finitist challenge, argumentation cannot be cogent if it in effect presupposes already that that challenge is mistaken, that truth can intelligibly outrun our practical capacities to ascertain it. We have therefore to think of the sets, U_1 and U_2, as constituted as follows: U_1 contains all and only the elements of K of which we can actually recognize that we can actually locate and identify as such an actually intelligible decimal representation of them; and U_2 must be thought of as containing all and only the elements of K of which we can actually recognize that we cannot actually locate and identify as such an actually intelligible decimal representation of them. The proper way of putting the objection is now: what ground is there for thinking that K is exhausted by the union of U_1 and U_2? Equivalently, if '$\sim$' is interpreted so that '$\sim Bn$' expresses the condition, as now interpreted, which those of K's elements which are in U_2 have to satisfy, is the disjunction, '$Bn \vee \sim Bn$', valid?

Dummett's talk of surveyability predicates as *vague* might encourage doubts. Certainly, if tolerant, they are vague in one way: they lack, as Frege put it, sharp boundaries. But the tolerance of an expression seems to have no immediately clear connection with whether or not it can be actually effectively decidable; the relevant question seems to be rather whether it is *borderline-case* vague. It is, for example, easy to imagine uniform patches of colour which could neither definitely correctly be described as 'green' nor definitely correctly be described as 'not-green'. Are there, comparably, integers *n* of which we could actually recognize that neither 'B*n*' nor '~B*n*' could definitely correctly be asserted? The trouble is the phrase 'of which we could actually recognize'. Intuitively, it might very well be true of certain integers both that they had no actually intelligible decimal representation and that we could not recognize the fact; but that would be in the nature of the case a situation which we could not recognize to obtain – and would anyway be a matter of ignorance rather than a genuine borderline case. In fact, '*a* is green' and 'B*n*' appear to be disanalogous in this respect: if *a* is a recognized borderline case of 'green', we have sufficient grounds for a claim that no adequate justification can be given for asserting '*a* is green' without thereby having grounds for asserting '*a* is not green'; to have sufficient grounds for the claim that no adequate justification can be found for the assertion of 'B*n*', in contrast, would appear to be, in virtue of the very meaning of the predicate, to have sufficient grounds for the assertion '~B*n*'. The point looks as though it will generalize to surveyability predicates as a class; if it is correct, they are not borderline-case vague – at least according to the paradigm of colour predicates – so that that particular ground for disputing the actual effectiveness of our putative one-to-one mapping is spurious.

Lack of borderline cases, however, is not the same thing as actual decidability; the question remains, can it be guaranteed that, presented with an arbitrary $n \in K$, we shall be able to decide in favour either of 'B*n*' or of '~ B *n*'? It is hard to be sure. A simple line of thought, favouring a positive answer, is as follows. Suppose we try to compute the decimal representation of *n*; will we not just straightforwardly find out either that we can convincingly and surveyably do the job or that we cannot? Is it not inevitable that we find out one of these two things? The computation, and its result, will be surveyable just in case we can all agree about the results, can see that our respective computations tally in detail, can easily spot and agree about errors in any that do not, etc. *Must* not our attempt to resolve the issue culminate either in a situation of this type or in one of obdurate uncertainty and confusion: and do we not, either way, have a verification either of 'B*n*' or of '~B*n*'?[17]

The situation, however, is not so simple. Any concept of practical possibility – not just the intellectual ones which we are presently concerned with – is vague in at least this respect: the conditions under which failure

17 This thought was put to me in correspondence by Christopher Peacocke.

indicates inability in the relevant respect are not sharply determined. There is always an open set of possible excuses, an open set of possible reasons why somebody who *can* do something could not manage it on this occasion. (In contrast, there need be no comparably indefinite range of ways of explaining away a success; success, at least in the case of concepts of physical possibility, will often be decisive for ability.)[18] But given that our conception of the range of possible excuses is open, and that we are willing to pass from failure to inability only if we believe we have grounds for supposing that here *no* persuasive such excuse can be adduced, the lesson for the present example is simply: even if the attempt surveyably to compute an actually intelligible decimal representation of *n* culminates in uncertainty and confusion, we shall not thereby be entitled as a matter of course to assert '$\sim$B*n*'; for we shall need in addition reason for thinking that we have no decent excuse for not succeeding, that there are no *more favourable circumstances* under which we might very well succeed.

Nevertheless, if we press the matter, *must* we not wind up either with success or with reason to doubt that there is any decent excuse for our persistent failure? And so with grounds either for asserting 'B*n*' or for denying it? For if, despite varying the conditions of our attempt – trying at different times of day, after a cold shower, etc. – we continually fail, we are surely rationally bound to begin to doubt that there *are* any 'favourable conditions'.

That thought illustrates, in effect, a quite general argument for thinking that predicates of practical possibility are all, at least when relativized to specified agents, actually *weakly* decidable; that is, there is always a humanly feasible programme of investigation whose implementation is bound to produce at least *grounds for asserting* either that X can ϕ x or that X cannot ϕ x – even if not a verification of either statement. And actual weak decidability would serve the purposes of the earlier reasoning well enough.

The argument, however, is relying on there being a clear operational distinction between success and failure, as indeed with high-jumping and weight-lifting, for instance, there is; unless it is clear at any particular point whether X has so far succeeded in ϕ-ing x or not, no ground has yet been provided for thinking that we must be able to get into a position where we can (weakly) decide between the alternatives. And the conditions which must be satisfied if this is to be clear in the case of 'a decimal representation of *n* is actually intelligible for X' are prima facie importantly different to those germane for 'X can high-jump a 3.5 metre bar'. For, evidently, *we* cannot test X's capacities in the first respect unless we know what the decimal representation of *n* is. Unless, therefore, we are saved by the

18 You cannot, for instance, fluke a 20 metre shot put.

contingency of the availability of computer technology, or of some other way of identifying the expression in question, the most the argument entitles us to assert is that 'a decimal representation of *n* is actually intelligible for X' is actually weakly decidable relative only to a state of information in which we are entitled to assert that *we* have the same capacity. But then no actually weakly effective procedure has really been indicated. *If* we have grounds for asserting one member of the class of statements at issue – when 'we' is substituted for 'X' – then we have an argument for thinking that the others are actually weakly decidable; but no actually effective method for getting grounds for asserting or denying *that* member has so far been described.

The thought of the argument for the actual weak decidability of B was simply this: all we have to do is to try persistently enough and one of two outcomes is assured – we either succeed or go on failing under a sufficient variety of circumstances to warrant the conclusion that we are unable. But if the issue is whether it is possible for us surveyably to compute and recognize as such a decimal representation of some integer given in some more powerful notation, how are we guaranteed to be able to recognize our success or failure? Part of any adequate answer must be that we shall deem ourselves to have succeeded only if we start getting a certain result *reliably*, are confident that we shall go on getting it, can generally find mistakes on occasions when we do not get it. These, however, are matters of *degree*. How reliable does a certain result have to be, *how* few unexplained divergences are tolerable, *how* confident do we have to be that we shall go on getting the result in question?

Surveyability predicates thus appear to differ from at least proto-typical, if not all, predicates of practical physical possibility in two respects. First, their application may be competently tested only by creatures to whom they apply; and, second, warranted self-ascription of them may depend on whether a certain constancy in performance is reliable. So there seems to be a loophole after all in the argument for the actual weak decidability of surveyability predicates. Suppose, for example, the issue is whether we can surveyably do some computation and ascertain its result; could not our efforts work out like this – on the one hand, nothing emerges which we feel to be, dependably, the right result; but, on the other hand, things do not go *so* badly, under so wide a variety of circumstances, that we feel justified in claiming that to identify the right result is beyond us? Perhaps one result figures often enough to make us suspect that it is the right one even though we cannot depend on getting it or actually being able to locate errors if we do not.

Against this, it could be urged again that if things were to stay that way long enough, we should be bound to accrue grounds for a negative verdict, bound to accrue grounds for thinking that we ought not to be credited with the capacity surveyably to perform the computation in question and determine its outcome. I shall not attempt to take the issue further here. It may be that different surveyability predicates fare somewhat differently; we have not, for instance, ventured to consider in any detail what being 'actually intelligible' ought to involve. What, I hope, *is* now clear is the need to distinguish, for any given predicate, the questions: whether it admits of borderline cases; whether it is a predicate of degree; whether it is tolerant; whether it is (weakly) decidable. We have reviewed some fairly immediate considerations concerning the status of surveyability predicates in these four respects; but nothing has been settled. And the prospect remains that, from a strict finitist point of view, every well-defined set of integers large enough to contain the extension of some tolerant surveyability predicate as a subset will rank as Dedekind-infinite. (We shall return to consideration of the tolerance and decidability of surveyability predicates in subsection 12).

7 *The prospects of a generalized intuitionism*

The upshot of the preceding two subsections is as follows. (P), a purported explanation of decidability in principle, makes use of a notion of finitude; our best efforts to explain the intended notion of finitude involve more or less explicit appeal to possibility in principle; but the general notion of possibility in principle can hardly be clear if the special case of decidability in principle is not; so (P) fails.

That, it might seem, is no very important matter unless it is clear that (P) is the very best that can be offered to serve the generalized intuitionist's needs. And that that is so has not been shown. What it is strictly necessary to show, however, is not so strong; it suffices if there is no explaining the class of statements for which the generalized intuitionist will regard classical logic as acceptable, that is, the class of statements which are decidable in principle, without at some point or other making use of the notion of finitude. It is, admittedly, unclear how this might be demonstrated conclusively; but just the reflection that all quantifier- and variable-free arithmetical statements are to go on one side of the distinction, while those which quantify unrestrictedly over all the positive integers go on the other, is surely very persuasive.

The suggestion, then, is that the notions of finitude, infinity, and ϕ-ability in principle, interlock in an impenetrable circle in much the same way in which, according to Quine's famous argument, analyticity, syntheticity and meaning interlock. If this suggestion is correct, then a scepticism, parallel to Quine's, may seem to be enjoined. The situation will be not merely that the intuitionist cannot get his cardinal notions across to a committed strict finitist; it will be that we lack any coherent model of how a grasp of those notions, as they are intended, can be acquired at all, so that scepticism about their full intelligibility will be the only rational attitude. In those circumstances, the problem for the generalized intuitionist will not be to locate a disanalogy between the strict finitist's arguments and his own, on the basis of which he can dispute the cogency of the former while continuing to press the latter; that will not be his problem, since it will then be dubious whether *any* argument for a generalized intuitionist stance is possible – whether a fully general version of the acquisition- and manifestation-challenges can be intelligibly formulated save in terms of what is actually humanly feasible. There will be no problem about preventing the slide of generalized intuitionist arguments into strict finitist ones, since there will be no intelligible formulation of the generalized intuitionist arguments in the first place. The arrow of the Modus Tollens will fail to strike the generalized intuitionist position only because there is no position to hit.

8 *A local argument for intuitionism*

The case for intuitionism must thus be made *locally*, for different areas of discourse, on the basis either of a syntactic demarcation of the classes of statement about which traditional realism and an anti-realism of practical possibility are respectively to be opposed – or at least of a demarcation based on some other notion than that of 'decidability in principle'. Even if 'decidability in principle' is rejected as mythical, any standpoint can still be reasonably seen as intuitionist which, like mathematical intuitionism, opposes a realist view of a certain type of statement while continuing to hold that the acceptability of the principle of Bivalence nowhere requires a guarantee of actual decidability. The result may be a certain heterogeneity in 'intuitionist' standpoints in different areas; that is the price which the considerations of the preceding two subsections, if correct, demand.

Let us concentrate on arithmetic and the question of the acceptability of the law of Excluded Middle, taking it that for the intuitionist the law is to be acceptable for a particular class of statements if and only if the principle of Bivalence holds good for that class. In this instance at least it is, as noted, straightforward to draw the broad outlines of the strict finitist/intuitionist/platonist dispute in syntactic terms: if we divide the arithmetical sentences with no free variables into those containing quantifiers and those containing none, and ask whether Excluded Middle is acceptable for those two classes of statement, the answers are respectively, 'for some only' and 'for some only', 'for some only' and 'for all' and 'for all' and 'for all'. It is true that the intuitionist and strict finitist conceptions of the constitution of the two classes so characterized will not coincide, since for the intuitionist each will contain denumerably infinitely many arithmetical sentences whose well-formedness we could not actually recognize. Just for that reason, however, they can play no part in our actual arithmetical practice; so, as far as the justification of intuitionist arithmetical practice is concerned, they require no attention. The local task for the intuitionist here is thus clear-cut and twofold: he must justify Bivalence for the second class of statements, and he must at least make it plausible that there is no justification of Bivalence for the first class of statements. What can he offer?

There is a natural approach to the first part of the task. For any particular arithmetical statement containing neither quantifiers nor free variables we can actually give a clear description of a procedure which, as we conceive, would result, if completely and correctly implemented, in a determination of the truth-value of the statement. This description has to be acknowledged as *definite* in two ways: first, it leaves no lacunae – whatever stage we reach in implementing the procedure, the general description determines what the next stage ought to be; but second, the *content* of the description does not wait on whatever our practical limitations may turn out to be. For the strict finitist thesis is not that *sense* cannot outrun human capacities for actual verification; it is that acceptable applications of Bivalence cannot do so. Even the strict finitist has to acknowledge that it is contingent where our practical limitations lie; that there is always such a thing as trying to implement the kind of procedure in question and finding out that one can, or cannot, surveyably do so. Of course, our limitations here are very familiar to us; we seldom, if ever, attempt a computation which proves to be just too lengthy or elaborate for us, or despair of attempting one which we could actually surveyably accomplish. Nevertheless it has to come originally by way of a discovery what these limitations are; and it is in general appropriate to think of ourselves as in a position to *discover* whether we can manufacture an instance of some concept only if the content of the concept is clear. So, the argument goes, we therefore have a clear understanding of what it would be to effect a verification or falsification of a statement of the kind in question; and we have it in virtue of having a clear understanding of what it would be, on trying fully to implement the described procedure, to succeed.

One train of thought which might provoke reservations about the foregoing was noted earlier in subsection 5: it comes as a straightforward empirical discovery where our practical limitations lie only if the criteria for determining them are appropriately pre-theoretical. But we do not need to engage that complication now; for it threatens disturbance only in the case of described decision-procedures whose implementation would require very substantially different computational capabilities to those which we have discovered that we actually possess, and the intuitionist argument which I wish to consider does not apply only to those examples. Let ϕ be, then, a full description (= set of instructions) for the decision procedure appropriate to a particular arithmetical statement S containing neither quantifiers nor free variables. And suppose the procedure described by ϕ is such that it really does come by way of a straightforward, pre-theoretical discovery that we cannot actually surveyably execute it in this case. In these circumstances the strict finitist ought to have no quarrel with the *significance* of a conditional of the form: if we ever come to be able surveyably to implement the procedure described in ϕ,...'; at least, he ought to have no such quarrel based merely on the identity of its antecedent. Consider therefore the conditional:

> C If we ever come to be able surveyably to implement the procedure described in ϕ, we shall be able to effect a verification either of S or of its negation.

Whether (C) would be acceptable to a strict finitist depends, of course, on the way in which he reads the conditional construction and the other logical connectives. Here we run into the difficulty that not merely do we lack any account of how the connectives should be read strict finitistically; in addition, the intuitionist accounts of the connectives have tended to cater only for their role in compound statements all of those constituents are candidates for resolution by mathematical construction. (C) however, is not of that character; its antecedent is the supposition of a contingency. So, although the validity of 'S $\vee$ ~S' in this instance is intuitionistically acceptable, and it is to be presumed that the intuitionist would have no quarrel with (C), we are not in a position to ground that assumption in the intuitionist explanations of the connectives; nor to be positive that (C) would be strict finitistically acceptable. It is, for all that, impossible to see what objection to (C) a strict finitist might have; for given the *effectiveness* of the procedure described in ϕ, we should, in the circumstances depicted by the antecedent of (C) – viz. being able *surveyably* to implement the procedure – be in a position actually to recognize either that S admitted of actual verification or that its negation did.[19]

We shall make, at any rate, two assumptions about a satisfactory generalized strict finitist semantics for the connectives: first, that it will be sufficient for the acceptability of a conditional to recognize that our achievement of an actual verification of its antecedent will/would put us in a position actually to verify its consequent: and second, that strict finitist

19 For one approach to informal generalization to ordinary statements of the orthodox intuitionist explanations of the connectives, see my *Wittgenstein on the Foundations of Mathematics*, pp. 210–15, and Essay 15 of this volume, passim.

acceptability will distribute over the logical connectives, so that, in particular, a disjunction will count as acceptable if and only if one of its disjuncts is. Given, now, that S is equivalent to: 'if we ever come to be able surveyably to implement the procedure described in ϕ, we shall be able to effect a verification of S', and that ~S is equivalent to: 'if we ever come to be able surveyably to implement the procedure described in ϕ, we shall be able to effect a falsification of S', the intuitionist belief in Bivalence for S is simply an affirmation of the disjunction:

D It is the case *either* that if we ever come to be able surveyably to implement the procedure described in ϕ, we shall be able to effect a verification of S *or* that if we ever come to be able surveyably to implement the procedure described in ϕ, we shall be able to effect a falsification of S.

As is familiar, the transition from $A \rightarrow (B \vee \sim B)$ to $(A \rightarrow B) \vee (A \rightarrow \sim B)$ is not in general acceptable inside intuitionist mathematics. But an intuitionist would, I am taking it, accept the present instance of the pattern, if only because (D) is acceptable to him in its own right. The crucial question is therefore whether an argument can be found to force a strict finitist to grant the transition from (C) to (D). For if he can be forced to grant it, the acceptability-distributive character of his interpretation of disjunction, assumed above, will force him to accept – and so to acknowledge his understanding of the circumstance that – either S, or its negation, holds good, even though human beings, limited as we are, have no cognitive access to which.

We have to recognize straight away that if the strict finitist chooses, as compatibly with distributivity he may, to adopt the intuitionist account of disjunction, generalized in a most obvious way so as to apply to ordinary statements and then refined so as to stress human practical possibility, viz.:

> 'A or B' is acceptable just in case we have recognized either that A is acceptable, or that B is acceptable, or that, without interfering with any relevant aspects of the world, we can actually get into a situation of having recognized either that A is acceptable or that B is acceptable,

then he will be constrained to reject the transition from (C) to (D). For by hypothesis we have grounds for neither disjunct nor for thinking that we can actually get grounds for one or the other. When disjunction is so interpreted, the transition is simply unsound; and the arithmetical intuitionist cannot dispute the right of a strict finitist to work within the constraints of that interpretation. The question is whether a more liberal conception of what it is for a statement to be acceptable can somehow be made to command the strict finitist's recognition; so that even if he were to refuse to interpret the logical constants in terms of if, he could not dispute the right of others to explain, in the obvious way, *a* concept of disjunction by reference to this notion; nor dispute that the transition from (C) to (D) would, so interpreted, be sound.

Let us for the moment put to one side speculation about intuitionist and strict finitist interpretation of the logical connectives of ordinary speech, and, following Dummett's example in 'The Philosophical Basis of Intuitionistic Logic', try to get clear why the transition from (C) to (D) is so compelling.[20] One superficially tempting line of reasoning, purporting to establish the validity of all transitions of the relevant pattern, is as follows. The premise gives the information that, under certain circumstances, a certain disjunction will hold good; if the disjunction will hold good, then one of the disjuncts will hold good; *whichever it is*, it can therefore correctly be asserted of it that it will hold good if those circumstances are realized; so one of the disjoint conditionals in the conclusion holds good, and the conclusion may therefore validly be drawn.

One, radical way in which this reasoning might be called into question is this. The notion of a 'correct assertion' which it uses is evidently not that of an assertion justified by the speaker's state of information at the time it is made. The latter is a temporal notion: it permits one and the same assertion to be correct at one time and not at another, or vice versa. But the former is timeless; in this sense, if an assertion is ever correct, it always is, though it may, of course, take appropriate transformations of mood, tense, pronoun and adverb in order that different speakers, at different times and places, should be able to effect it. Without assumption of a timeless notion of correct assertibility, the argument falls flat. For the possibility is opened up that (C) holds good only in virtue of the fact that, under the circumstances depicted by its antecedent, one of the disjuncts in its consequent will *become* correctly assertible; but that of neither of them can it *yet* correctly be asserted that it will be the one. The 'superficially tempting' argument will not therefore tempt any anti-realist who is persuaded that he has no title to a timeless notion of correct assertion;[21] nor any of those philosophers who, though not through global anti-realist sympathies, have assayed to regard the future as 'open'.

20 *Truth and Other Enigmas*, pp. 243–7; for discussion of whether the intuitionist's acceptance of Excluded Middle for effectively decidable arithmetical statements has to be interpreted as an acceptance of D-type statements, rather than C-type statements, see my *Wittgenstein on the Foundations of Mathematics*, pp. 204–15.

21 For discussion of anti-realism and timeless truth (correct assertibility) see, of course, Dummett 'The Reality of the Past', in *Truth and Other Enigmas*, pp. 358–75; also my *Wittgenstein on the Foundations of Mathematics*, chapter x, pp. 182–94, and Essay 5 of this volume.

So radical a stance is not, however, required in order to find fault with the suggestion that the general form of argument which the transition from (C) to (D) exemplifies is valid. Dummett considers a counter-factual example, but the two types of ground which, he suggests, we intuitively regard as exposing the pattern of reasoning as unsound in certain counter-factual cases are germane to indicative conditionals also. Broadly speaking, we will not be sold a transition of this form if we believe that the question, which disjunct of the consequent of the premise would be true under the circumstances depicted in its antecedent, is *indeterministic*; so we should find fault, for example, with appropriate examples concerning quantum jumps or, perhaps, absolutely arbitrary choices. Likewise, we shall fault the reasoning if we believe that the identity of the consequent's true disjunct would depend on what other circumstances accompanied those depicted in the antecedent; so, to adapt Dummett's own example, while 'if Castro meets Reagan, he will either insult him or be perfectly polite,' is acceptable, *which* he does may be a function e.g. of whether or not the meeting takes place in Cuba, so that neither 'if Castro meets Reagan, he will insult him' nor 'if Castro meets Reagan, he will be perfectly polite' is acceptable without qualification.

The simplest explanation of the failure of the ordinary conditional straightforwardly to distribute over disjunction would be if it had roughly the force of: P is singly sufficient for Q. But that cannot be its force in general, or we would not venture most of the conditionals which we are willing to assert. A better suggestion would construe the content of the conditional as a claim of the sufficiency of P for Q relative to other circumstances which we are entitled to expect. Confirmation that this suggestion is at least in the vicinity of the conditional of ordinary speech comes from the reflection that, in order justifiably to contradict a conditional, it is not usually considered necessary that one have grounds for asserting a contrary conditional; it is enough to be in a position to point out that P is not a sufficient condition for Q in the sense just sketched – 'no, it is perfectly possible, for all we have reason to expect, that P will be true but Q false'. We shall do well, however, to avoid getting tangled in this topic. The suggestion I want to carry forward is merely this: the conditional of ordinary speech is considered acceptable if, provided other circumstances are then as we are entitled to expect, a realization of P would *bring about* the truth of Q. We shall need nothing more refined in order to explicate our intuitive response to the inference from (C) to (D).

Dummett does not positively assert that, provided the example is not indeterministic or one where unspecified features might play a part in determining the outcome, the transition in question is, for ordinary counterfactual conditionals at least, valid. But he does see the fact that arithmetical examples of the (C)/(D) pattern are of neither of those two kinds as importantly contributive to our inclination to sympathize, on this point at least, with the intuitionists. An argument against strict finitism, however, will have to do better than diagnose our intuitive opposition. Is it or is it not the case that whenever an example is not of one of Dummett's two kinds, and its premise is acceptable by the standard just described, we cannot escape the admission that one of the disjuncts of the conclusion must be acceptable by the same standard, even if we cannot actually find out which?

Suppose that we are concerned with an example in the future indicative. We are given

i that P is in the relevant sense sufficient for the disjunction of Q with R;[22] that is, that a realization of P will bring about the truth of that disjunction provided other circumstances are in all respects as we are entitled to expect, = 'P rel/suff Q or R'. We also have

ii that, whatever the correct way of explicating the point might be, there is to be no *indeterminism* about whether Q, or R, will turn out to be true if P is realized; and

iii that there are no circumstances, T, whose accompaniment of a realization of P we are in no position to anticipate or discount, such that {P, T} rel/suff Q and {P, ~T} rel/suff R.[23]

Do these three conditions guarantee that either 'P rel/suff Q' or 'P rel/suff R' must hold good? The answer is 'No'. The third condition is too simple, permitting, in conjunction with the other two, the following state of affairs:

P ~~rel/suff~~ Q; P ~~rel/suff~~ R; {P, T} rel/suff Q;
{P, ~T} ~~rel/suff~~ R; {P, ~T, U} rel/suff R;
{P, ~T, ~U} ~~rel/suff~~ Q; {P, ~T, ~U, V} rel/suff Q;
{P, ~T, ~U, ~V} ~~rel/suff~~ R;....etc.[24]

Here T, U, V, etc., all describe conditions whose accompaniment of a realization of P we are in no position to anticipate or discount. The situation depicted is consistent with the truth of P being in the relevant sense sufficient for that of the disjunction of Q with R; and with it never being underdetermined *which* disjunct is true under circumstances P. So (i) and (ii) permit this situation; and there is no simple condition whose

22 Q incompatible with R.

23 Cf. Dummett, 'The Philosophical Basis of Intuitionistic Logic', in *Truth and Other Enigmas*, p. 245.

24 Thus, for instance, let P = Castro meets Reagan; Q = Castro insults Reagan; R = Castro is civil to Reagan; T = the meeting taken place in Cuba; U = Castro wants American trade sanctions to be lifted; V = Castro wishes to inflame anti-American feeling in Cuba...it is easy, without too much implausibility, to protect the example in the appropriate way *ad lib*. (The horizontal stroke, of course, negates 'rel/suff'.)

realization along with the realization of P will be jointly sufficient for Q but whose non-realization along with a realization of P will be jointly sufficient for R.

There may be more subtle responses, but let us simply replace (iii) by

iii* there are no circumstances, T, U, which we have no reason to think would accompany a realization of P, such that {P, T} rel/suff Q; and {P, U} rel/suff R.

Evidently however, it still does not follow that a realization of P would, provided the accompanying circumstances were as we should expect, bring about the truth of Q or bring about the truth of R. It is difficult to think of a plausible counter-example because condition (iii*) is so strong; but the form of the loophole left open is that either Q, or R, should possess sufficiency conditions among certain of the circumstances which we can anticipate accompanying realization of P only because we have reason to expect their realization in any event. In such a case it would be at best in a vacuous sense that we could claim that one of 'P rel/suff Q' and 'P rel/suff R' was acceptable

The simplest curative is

iv it is not the case that, whether or not P, there are grounds for expecting the truth of 'Q or R'.

And now we do appear to have captured conditions our acceptance of which in a particular case would constrain us to grant that one of 'P rel/suff Q' or 'P rel/suff R' must hold good, even if we do not know which. For consider: by (i) a realization of P will guarantee *ceteris paribus* that either Q or R is realized, and by (ii) *which* is realized will be, somehow, fully determined; but, by (iii*) it will not be determined by, so will not vary with, factors whose realization under P-circumstances we have no reason to anticipate; so it seems inescapable that the circumstances which we can expect to obtain if P is realized collectively embody either a sufficiency condition for Q or a sufficiency condition for R; by (iv), however, there is no reason to think circumstances sufficient for Q or sufficient for R will obtain if P is not realized; it follows that we have reason to think of a realization of P as *bringing about* a state of affairs determinately sufficient either for Q or for R which we have no reason to think would have otherwise obtained; and that is to say that, provided things are otherwise as we are entitled to expect, a realization of P will bring about the truth either of Q or of R.

What is striking is that not merely do arguments of the (C)/(D) type satisfy each of (i) to (iv) but that it is hard to think of any other examples which do. That (i) is satisfied is just the hypothesis of (C); and there is, or so we may suppose, no prospect of our getting into a position where we may actually verify S or may verify its negation unless we come to be able surveyably to implement the procedure described in ϕ; so (iv) is satisfied also. Yet it is our grounds for thinking that the example satisfies conditions (ii) and (iii*) which are its most striking feature: not merely, as we ordinarily think, is it not undetermined whether we should be able to effect a verification of S or of its negation if the antecedent of (C) were realized; *which* would be true is a function, we suppose, *purely and wholly* of the character of the procedure described in ϕ. It is for that reason that the result of a realization of (C)'s antecedent could not vary in accordance with other accompanying circumstances which we are not in a position to anticipate. The outcome of a computation, correctly executed, *cannot* vary; that is what most immediately distinguishes it from an experiment. There is thus, so we think, an *internal relation*, to use an old-fashioned terminology, between the character of correct implementation of the procedure described in ϕ and the outcome, whatever it might be, which correct implementation of that procedure would secure; the outcome is stored up in the procedure just as the maximum number of tricks Declarer can lose is stored up in the distribution of the cards. Which statement, S, or its negation, we should be in a position actually to verify if a surveyable implementation of the procedure described in ϕ came to be within our compass is thus predetermined by the character of that procedure; the truth of one disjunct of (D) and the falsity of the other, is thus likewise predeterminate.

This is a most seductive train of thought. We slip very easily into thinking that when it comes to computing the truth-value of a decidable arithmetical statement, we have, as it were, only a spectator's role to play; that we are capable of so conferring a meaning on the symbols involved in the statement as to decide the statement's truth, or falsity, ahead of ourselves, and independently of whatever verdict we reach on actually doing the computation if we are able to. To repeat: only one result *can* issue if all the constitutive steps are correctly taken; if the example is one where we can actually surveyably complete the computation, then, given the general level of competence which human beings can usually attain in these matters, that is probably the result which we shall get. But which result is correct in no sense awaits our judgement; when we do the computation, we merely trace out connections to which, by the meanings which we have given to the relevant signs – by the character of the concepts which thereby come to be involved in the statement's truth or falsity – we have already committed ourselves.

The idea of a predetermined internal relation between the procedure described in ϕ and the achievement, say, of a verification of S would not stand up for a minute if we supposed that ϕ, with its present meaning, could characterize a variety of procedures or that it was somehow not fully settled what would count as a realization of it. The seductive train of thought thus evinces an implicit belief in a strong *objectivity* of meaning: at its most general, the idea that a sign of any kind can be associated with a meaning – or, since 'reification' of meanings is quite inessential to the point, semantically qualified – in such a way that certain particular uses of it on particular occasions simply do not, whatever we come to think, cohere with its being so associated, or so qualified. (With the kind of example with which we are presently concerned, indeed, we can omit 'on particular occasions'.) But the crucial point is this: the idea that it is somehow stored up in the character of the procedure described in ϕ whether its implementation would culminate in a verification of S or of its negation is simply unintelligible unless we take it that the question whether an unfolding procedure complies, stage by stage, with ϕ is something taken care of wholly by the content of ϕ and the character of the stages – that no contribution from us is needed towards deciding the question.

This syndrome of thought, more than supporting the arithmetical intuitionist's opposition to strict finitism, is actually, so it seems to me, the cornerstone of arithmetical platonism. Take the simplest kind of example where the intuitionist quarrels with the platonist: a statement of the form, $(x)Fx$, 'x' ranging over zero and the positive integers and 'F' a general recursive predicate. For the intuitionist, thinking as just adumbrated, each statement 'Fn', however large the number denoted by 'n' and however complex the appropriate computation would be, will be determinate in truth-value. All the platonist does is take the additional step, perhaps not seeing it as such, of concluding that it must therefore be determinate whether $(x)Fx$ or $(\exists x) \sim Fx$ holds good; for if it is a determinate matter of each nth integer whether it is F or not, how can it not also be determinate whether all are F or at least one is not?

The essential doctrines of arithmetical platonism are thus two. First, any quantifier- and variable-free arithmetical statement is determinate in truth-value, its truth, or falsity, being constituted by a ratification-independent internal conceptual relation. Second, quantification over zero and the positive integers is legitimately seen as an operation which always preserves Bivalence; that is, the resulting quantified statement is bivalent provided each of the statements which instantiates it is. The intuitionists' objection to platonism, as far as arithmetic is concerned, has to do entirely with this second element; (though, if our earlier reflections are correct, it will not do to express the opposition by saying that quantification may legitimately be seen as Bivalence-preserving only when it preserves decidability in principle.) There is no intuitionistic opposition to the first element; on the contrary, it is the nerve of what is probably the arithmetical intuitionist's best argument for parting company with the strict finitist.

Let me conclude this subsection by summarizing that argument once again. It is assumed first, that it is contingent and, in a large class of cases, comes as a straightforward empirical discovery what our practical computational limitations are, so that we can make straightforward sense of the idea of extensions in the relevant capacities; 'a humanly surveyable implementation of the procedure described in ϕ' can thus be a description that we perfectly well understand but which is, quite contingently, true of nothing. Second, it is a feature of any computation that, if it is in all respects correct, it cannot but lead to one specific, uniquely determined outcome; the outcome achieved was, all along, the only outcome that it was possible to achieve provided no errors of any kind occurred. The first premise guarantees a straightforward sense for a large class of conditionals of the kind for which (C) was our prototype; and it was argued that a strict finitist ought to have no quarrel with their truth. So the first of four conditions is satisfied whose joint satisfaction was argued to guarantee that one disjunct in the corresponding (D)-type statement was determinately acceptable and the other determinately unacceptable. The second premise entails that the second and third conditions are satisfied. And the fourth condition is easily seen to be satisfied for these arithmetical examples.[25] So, assuming that the four conditions can jointly do enough to explain the appropriate notion of acceptability, the conclusion has to be that conditional statements of the relevant kind, and hence the arithmetical statements to which they are equivalent, may be acceptable even though we cannot actually recognize the fact. The stronger claim that Bivalence holds good for the arithmetical equivalents is merely a consequence of the composition of (D)-type disjunctions.

We noted that the two leading premises involve a larger assumption: the 'spectator' picture of our role in arithmetical computation, and a certain consequent autonomy in what constitutes correct use of our language. If we attempt surveyably to execute a particular specified computation but find that we cannot do so, the idea that there is still a unique predeterminate outcome of that computation – the only one at which we could possibly arrive if our powers were appropriately extended and we were correctly to carry the computation through – commits us to a plethora of unratified mutual determinations of correct use between various descriptions: the initial specification of the computation, descriptions of its character and results at various stages, and, of course a description of the final result. Just that, of course, is precisely the species of commitment which the argument aims to bring out: we are committed, it contends, by our conception of the character of correct computation in general, and our

25 We never have reason to think that *inactivity* will put us in a position to verify, or to falsify, a decidable arithmetical statement.

belief that we clearly understand what it would be to suffer at least some orders of enlargement in the range of computations which we can actually surveyably perform, to the view that the use of so-extended powers could not but lead us, provided we made no mistake, to certain predeterminate results; and in that case there must be something correct, if actually unverifiable, to be said *now* about what those results would be.

9 *A strict finitist reply*

The argument, if accepted, has at least some prospect of stabilizing the arithmetical intuitionist's position. For the arithmetical platonist can emulate it if, and only if, he can show that there is sense in the idea of a boundless extension of our capacities – if, and only if, he can provide a clear account of what it would be to discover that one had ceased to have *any* limitations of speed, or accuracy, of computation. If that could be successfully argued, then an argument parallel to the foregoing would be available for an arithmetical, though not global mathematical, platonism. (The parallel is not quite straightforward, since a connection needs to be made between the ability to complete Russell's two minute computational check on Goldbach's Conjecture and the ability to know whether or not a counter-example was encountered at any stage.) The possibility of 'supertasks' has of course been much discussed;[26] but discussion has tended to focus upon the question of the *consistency* of supposing certain sorts of infinite process to be merely contingently beyond us. And, apart from the fact that there is no evident reason why nonsense should be inconsistent, construction of a platonist parallel to the foregoing argument would require, beyond demonstrating consistency, to explain how, if in my sleep, say, a genie granted me appropriately boundless computational powers, it could be clear to me on waking that that was what he had done. I see grounds for nothing but scepticism that such an explanation can be given.

Be that as it may, the 'local' argument cannot, if indeed cogent, be conclusive against the strict finitist proposal that only actually decidable arithmetical statements may legitimately be regarded as subject to Bivalence. For the argument makes no attempt to meet the strict finitist challenges head-on, but attempts to show instead that the view that arithmetical truth outruns our capacities for actual decision is forced on us by certain background considerations; namely, that our computational

26 See in particular, Thomson, 'Tasks and Supertasks'; Benacerraf, 'Tasks, Supertasks, and the Modern Eleatics'; Chihara, 'On the possibility of Completing an Infinite Process'; Grünbaum, 'Can an Infinitude of Operations be Performed in a Finite Time?'

limitations might have been less, indeed might yet come to be less, and that our concepts can, and typically would, survive such changes in *integrity*; so that what we could then verify it to be correct to say is what it was *all along* correct to say (given that arithmetic deals in changeless truths). But articulation of these background considerations does nothing to show that the strict finitist's concern about the intelligibility of the problematic notion is groundless; it serves merely to indicate the depth of the roots of the problematic notion, the underlying beliefs on which our adherence to it is based. The arithmetical platonist could, comparably, in response to the intuitionist, simply call attention to the deep presupposition which largely motivates his position: the Bivalence-preserving conception of universal and existential quantification. For the conviction that the quantifiers may be clearly and fully intelligibly construed in that way underlies all our intuitive thinking about pure mathematics and the natural sciences. But to call attention to it is not to confront the intuitionist with an argument.

The difference is that the platonist conception of the quantifiers was under explicit intuitionist attack in any case; whereas the background ideas with which the strict finitist arguments now seem to be in collision were not the original explicit target. If he can find no way of blocking the reasoning of the preceding subsection,[27] it is, I suppose, open to a sufficiently committed strict finitist simply to contrapose on its premises; but his position will be the more credible if he is able to mount some sort of independent attack on them.

Such an attack is to be found, at least if Kripke, myself and others are right about the broad intent on those passages,[28] in Wittgenstein's discussion in the *Investigations* and *Remarks on the Foundations of Mathematics* of what it is to follow a rule. Wittgenstein's argument is not, of course, a finite, linearly ordered array of sentences, each of which is either an acceptable premise or a consequence of certain of its superiors by acceptable rules of inference. It is rather a loose weave of challenges, questions, platitudes and paradox. And the scope of the argument, of course, far exceeds our present concerns. Its target is, absolutely generally, what I have elsewhere called *investigation-independence*:[29] the idea that meaning can be so conferred upon at least some of the statements of our language that whether they are correct is something settled in advance and independently of any investigation we might make – more generally still,

27 Repudiation of the timelessness of arithmetical truth would be one, radical, tactic.
28 Kripke, 'Wittgenstein on Rules and Private Language'; my *Wittgenstein on the Foundations of Mathematics*, passim, but especially chapters II, XI, XX. See also my 'Rule Following, Objectivity and the Theory of Meaning', and 'Kripke's Account of the Argument against Private Language'.
29 *Wittgenstein on the Foundations of Mathematics*, pp. 204–7.

that what judgements are correct in particular circumstances is something determined quite independently of human reaction to those circumstances. The belief that any well-described computation has, whether it is ever performed or not, a unique, predeterminate outcome cannot survive a rejection of investigation-independence; and neither can the belief that we may speak straightforwardly of *extensions* of our cognitive powers – at least, not if such talk is to carry any more robust an implication than that we know what it would be to be able to decide to *our* satisfaction issues which we presently cannot decide.

Some of the salient points in Wittgenstein's thinking on the issue are the following. Judgement is essentially a linguistic activity; to judge truly is comprehendingly to endorse a true statement, so that only the linguistically competent can judge. (Wittgenstein is much less dogmatic than that makes him sound, but I read the Ballard discussion as advancing precisely this view at least for judgements of a certain level of sophistication; and it ought to be uncontroversial for the arithmetical examples which we are presently concerned with.) The investigation-independent truth of judgements therefore requires the investigation-independent truth of statements; and the investigation-independent truth of statements requires that their truth is settled, autonomously and without the need for human interference, by their meaning and the character of the relevant facts. For a complex set of reasons, however, no notion of meaning can be legitimized which will play this role. There are *ontological* difficulties: the meaning of a statement, if it is to make the relevant, autonomous contribution towards determining that statement's truth-value, cannot be thought of as fully determined by previous uses of that statement or, if it is a novel statement, by previous uses of its constituents and by its syntax; for those factors can always be reconciled with the statement's having any truth-value, no matter what the worldly facts are taken to be. The same goes for prior *phenomenological episodes* – imagery, models – in the minds of the linguistically competent. Nothing, therefore, in the previous use of the statement, or of its constituents, or in the prior streams of consciousness of competent speakers, is, if its meaning is in conjunction with the facts to determine its truth-value, sufficient to fix its meaning. So what does?

There are consequent epistemological difficulties: how are we supposed to know, even conditionally, what the meaning of a statement requires of us? The awkward points which we have to face are three. First, such knowledge cannot be persistently singlehanded; if someone cannot persuade the rest of us that he is using a statement correctly and we are not, then, so far from being in a position to credit himself with unilateral recognition of the constraints imposed by the meaning of that statement, he has to conclude that he does not know what it means. Second, or so the private language argument urges, there is no residual, privileged knowledge which each of us has of the dictates of his *idiolect*; the man out of step cannot take comfort in the thought that at least he knows what *he* means by the statement even if that it is not the communal understanding, and knows what use that meaning enjoins. For what is this first-person privileged knowledge of an idiolect? It is futile to look to the model of our knowledge of our own intentions; if previously intended use of a statement, or of its constituents, is to impose any real constraint, there has to be an intelligible contrast possible between the use which actually conforms to those intentions and the use which one takes to do so. Otherwise, keeping faith with one's prior intentions comes to no more, assuming one's present use of language to be sincere, than keeping faith with one's present inclinations; which is no more real a constraint than that of keeping pace with one's own shadow.[30] It is, however, wholly obscure how the needed contrast is to be made out. Third, it seems quite impossible to explain how, as members of an ongoing linguistic community of non-collusive assent (more or less), we can be in a position to recognize, a least conditionally, constraints imposed by the meaning of statements in our language which, if the first point above is correct, cannot be recognized in a persistently singlehanded way. What, over and above our broad disposition to concur in reaction, judgement and definition, *constitutes* the fact that our ongoing usage of language conforms, by and large, to antecedently determined meanings? The standpoint of investigation-independence sees our linguistic and cognitive competence as a disposition to suit our use of language to the requirements of a determinate underlying framework of semantic and syntactic rules; but if that is going to be our standpoint, so that there is always at best a contingent correspondence between what we take the requirements of those rules to be and what they really are, what *determines* the latter?[31]

If we despair of answering that question satisfactorily, we have, it appears, radically to revise our whole conception of meaning: there is no property of a statement which, irrespective of how we react or whether we ever get the chance to do so, combines with the character of the relevant non-linguistic facts to determine correct use of that statement. What constitutes correct use of the statement in particular circumstances always needs a contribution from *us*, from our dispositions to react and judge, in short from our nature. Where we cannot give that contribution, if only

30 I owe this image to James Hopkins ('Wittgenstein and Physicalism', p. 136).

31 This paragraph, in effect, summarizes the argument of the concluding section of chapter XI of my *Wittgenstein on the Foundations of Mathematics*. For a somewhat different and, as I conceive it now, improved formulation, see my 'Rule-following, Meaning and Constructivism'.

for external, trivial-seeming reasons like lack of facility or shortness of time, what constitutes correct use is therefore so far indeterminate.

These are extremely difficult issues. One's initial response is bewilderment and scepticism; one wants to sympathize with much of what Wittgenstein says, yet it seems incredible that so radical an anti-realism should issue from it. However that may be, my intention here has only been to locate an issue. The intuitionist attacks our pretensions to a certain kind of objectivity: that involved in the notion that we can form definite, clear ideas of specific states of affairs to which no being with limitations akin to our own need be capable of cognitive access. But the strict finitist is disputing our entitlement to a yet more entrenched idea of objectivity: the objectivity of meaning.

Let it be noted, finally, that the form of the strict finitist's reply has been an attempt to *undermine* the intuitionist's local argument. To attack the premises on which the intuitionist based his belief that the (C)/(D) transition satisfied the four conditions which were imposed on its soundness is to argue that the belief is groundless, not that it is incorrect. The attack thus commits the strict finitist to no more than agnosticism about the soundness of the (C)/(D) transition. It does not have to be taken as an argument for *denying* that the transition meets one of the specified conditions. Whether such a denial ought nevertheless to be made and, if so, how exactly it should be explained, I shall not here enquire.

III
Can the Strict Finitist Rebut the Minor Premise of the Modus Tollens?

10 *Under what assumptions would the semantic incoherence of surveyability predicates destroy the viability of strict finitism as a coherent philosophy of mathematics?*

In this and the next subsection we shall work under the assumption that 'intelligible', 'surveyable', 'actually decidable' and the like are, in appropriate respects, tolerant predicates. If, as Dummett suggest, they are as a class semantically incoherent in consequence, how exactly does that call into question the viability of strict finitism as a philosophy of mathematics?

Notice to begin with that if Dummett is right about these expressions, and about others, most particularly observation-predicates like those for colours, then one intuitively prepossessing reason for doubting the viability of any philosophical position involving essential play with semantically incoherent expressions comes to seem less so. That reason is the plausible thought that we do not *genuinely understand* any semantically incoherent expression. But it is merely aberrant to suppose that we do not understand colour predicates, and the others, when their use embodies a successful communicative practice. The Sorites paradox disturbs no intuitions about the correct use of the expressions which seem to be susceptible to it; we do not, for example, come to doubt the orangeness of the rightmost terminal patch in a suitable array of patches as a result of a Sorites proof that it is red; nor the adulthood of my parents as a result of the possibility of a Sorites proof that they are children. The institution of agreed *use* of these expressions survives the discovery of the Sorites paradoxes; and where there is an ongoing non-collusive institution of correct use, there surely is mutual understanding. If surveyability predicates are as a class semantically incoherent, it is open to the strict finitist to wonder why the involvement of his philosophy with such expressions any more calls its viability into question than its involvement with certain other such expressions calls into question the viability of art criticism.

In what ways, though, is strict finitism essentially involved with surveyability predicates? Dummett speculates in 'Wittgenstein's Philosophy of Mathematics' about whether the induction axiom would survive under a strict finitist reconstruction of arithmetic. For while every number actually intelligibly representable in a given notation will have a successor actually intelligibly representable in that notion, not every number will be so representable.[32] But the most immediate point to make about the example is that there is, presumably, no question of attempting to carry out an induction with respect to a surveyability predicate *within* strict finitist arithmetic, whose vocabulary will contain no such predicates but merely the standard logical and number-theoretic primitives. For this reason, there is no immediate prospect that the semantic incoherence of surveyability predicates might lead to an inconsistency in strict finitist arithmetic or some ulterior branch of strict finitist mathematics. I say 'no immediate prospect' because it is still a possibility that the use of semantically incoherent expressions in the strict finitist explanations of the logical constants and others of his mathematical primitives might somehow motivate inconsistent rules of proof or axioms. But again there is no obvious reason for suspecting that this would have to be so.

The strict finitist makes indispensable use of surveyability predicates only in two places: first, in making his informal philosophical case, in particular his formulation of the manifestation- and acquisition-challenges; and second, in the explanations which he will presumably try to give of the legimate content which we can attach to the logical constants and other mathematical primitives. If surveyability predicates are semantically

32 *Truth and Other Enigmas*, p. 182.

incoherent, that is no reason whatever, unless we assume that no such predicate is genuinely intelligible, to doubt their capacity to play the first of these roles. The correctness of the minor premise of the Modus Tollens thus requires that, for some reason other than one resting on that dubious thesis, they cannot play the second role. However that may be, it is worth stressing now that the coherence of the strict finitist *critique* of the classical and intuitionist approaches is not at this point in serious doubt. If no satisfactory motivation for a distinctive style of strict finitist logic and mathematics can be arrived at, that calls into question the cogency of the strict finitist opposition to fundamental presuppositions of classical and intuitionist semantics only if we have antecedent grounds for thinking that it *has* to be possible to secure the kind of harmony between mathematical practice and favoured semantic theory which both the classical and intuitionist approaches try for. In fact, three assumptions are needed: *if* we have antecedent grounds for that belief, and *if* surveyability predicates are as a class semantically incoherent, and *if* their being so somehow obstructs – for some reason other than the dubious claims that they are therefore unintelligible, or that a semantics which gives them a central place is bound to motivate inconsistent formal theories – the development of a well-founded strict finitist semantics for logic and the most central branches of pure mathematics, then Dummett is, plausibly, right to conclude that there can be no viable strict finitist philosophy of mathematics. But the status of none of the three hypotheses is exactly pellucid. I shall not discuss the first here.[33] The second involves the assumption that surveyability predicates are tolerant, which will be considered in subsection 12, and the assumption that tolerance cannot but lead to Sorites-susceptibility, which, along with the third hypothesis, we shall consider next.

11 *Would the tolerance of surveyability predicates have to prevent the strict finitist from constructing satisfactory semantics for his formal theories?*

For the strict finitist, only those first-order numerical expressions may be thought of as having sense, and therefore reference, which are actually capable of intelligible employment by the community; the positive integers no longer, therefore, outrun our means of actually intelligible representation of them. What sort of collective structure do they now exemplify? The *totality* of positive integers actually intelligibly representable in some notion or other promises to contain 'gaps' not just

33 For discussion of it, see this volume, Essay 15, and my *Wittgenstein and the Foundations of Mathematics*, chapter XIV.

from the traditional point of view but from that of the strict finitist also: we have, for example, an actual intelligible symbol for the difference between 17^{1000} and 2, but do not, presumably, actually understand anything like $17^{1000} - 2$ numerical expressions. If we try to work, then, with the totality of actually intelligible numerical expressions, it can no longer be guaranteed that each such expression '*n*' stands for an integer with *n* predecessors; and the intuitive meaning of elementary arithmetical operations like addition and subtraction appears to be in some jeopardy. The natural proposal is therefore that the strict finitist should waive the attempt to conceive of the positive integers *en bloc* as any kind of totality, and concentrate instead upon the development of a formal theory suitable to treat the positive integers which are actually intelligibly expressible in in a particular canonical notation, say the stroke, binary, or decimal notation.

What sort of structure will such a collection constitute? Consider, as an analogue, a series of metronomic clicks taking place against the background of an E-flat sounded on an organ which is then modulated so smoothly and gradually into an F-sharp that even the most refined musical ear can detect no difference in background pitch between any pair of adjacent clicks. Here it looks as though the predicate, 'click with E-flat as a background' determines what Dummett calls a *weakly finite*, but *weakly infinite* totality:[34] there is an integral upper bound on the number of its members but it has no last member. We can arrive at a suitable upper bound by counting the clicks until it is perfectly clear to everyone that the accompanying note is no longer E-flat; while that there is no last member issues from the apparent tolerance of the predicate in question with respect to the transition from one click to the next. Since the totality is well-ordered by 'occurs earlier than', we appear to have an intuitive model for the standard arithmetical axioms for zero and successor (and an intuitive demonstration of the non-categoricity of those axioms for the notion of infinity as it is classically and intuitionistically understood). If, then, 'has an actually intelligible representation in binary notation' is tolerant with respect to the kind of changes involved in passing from an integer to its successor, then the set of such integers is presumably a structure of the same kind; and we appear to be in a position to motivate acceptance of at least the first four of the standard first-order Peano Axioms.

The status of the fifth, the induction axiom, awaits clarification of the strict finitist interpretation of the quantifiers. If a proof of '$(x)Fx$' has to accomplish a demonstration that we can *actually get* a surveyable proof of 'Fa' for any object, *a*, in the range of the quantifier, then the standard

34 'Wang's Paradox', in Truth and Other Enigmas, p. 312.

induction axiom looks to be unacceptable even if restricted to orthodox number-theoretic predicates. For it may be true that 'F0' can be proved, and that we can surveyably prove that F holds of the successor of n whenever we can surveyably prove that Fn, yet the series of integers k, for which Fk *can* be surveyably proved be 'shorter' than the series of integers actually intelligibly representable in the canonical notion in which we are working. Likewise the recursions for '+' and '×' will not, presumably, be totally defined over the elements of such a series.

These seem to be straightforward prologomena to the determination of a strict finitist arithmetic. But the trouble is, and this is why Dummett doubts that the enterprise can be carried through, that the coherence of the notion of a weakly finite but weakly infinite totality obviously depends upon there being no conflict between the assignability of an upper bound and the weak infinity principle. And just such a conflict in what the Sorites paradox purports to elicit. The most immediate reply is that it remains to be shown that Sorites paradoxes continue to be generatable within the framework of strict finitism; for in order to derive such a paradox, other than by using an analogue of mathematical induction, twice as many lines will be needed (successive universal instantiation and Modus Ponens steps) as there are elements in the relevant series between the F starting point and the non-F terminus. Will any such derivations be surveyable? Is it ever actually possible surveyably to derive a Sorites paradox 'in the long', as it were?

Here is an argument for thinking that it is. It is plausible to suppose that there is some particular number, k, such that k successive pairwise steps of universal instantiation and Modus Ponens constitute a surveyable proof structure, while $2k$ such steps do not. Let us say that m is *small* just in case $m+k$ such pairwise steps constitute a surveyable structure. Then 0 is small; and it is plausible to suppose that if n is small, so is its successor; (at any rate, it is *as* plausible to maintain that one more step of the pattern:

$$\begin{array}{ll} \vdots & \\ Fn & \\ \hline Fn \rightarrow Fn' & \text{UI} \\ Fn' & \text{MPP} \\ \hline \vdots & \end{array}$$

cannot transform a surveyable proof structure into one that is not as it is to maintain that a decimal numeral consisting of an initial '1' followed by n '0's is actually intelligible whenever n '9's is actually intelligible.) Thus by k pairwise steps of universal instantiation and Modus Ponens we can prove that $k+k, = 2k$, is small, contrary to hypothesis.[35]

Two queries spring to mind about this. The first, somewhat in the strict finitist's favour, is: granting its plausibility, how can the above argument be *generalized*? For it is not good enough to show that *some* intuitive Sorites paradoxes are surveyably completable. If there are to be *no* weakly finite, but weakly infinite totalities, even from a strict finitist point of view, then *all* the relevant predicates of practical intellectual possibility must be strict-finitistically Sorites-susceptible. The argument, however, conveys no explicit suggestion about how to construct such derivations except in the case of predicates definable by reference to 'surveyable' as applied to formal proofs. The situation, in general, is that in order to be able to construct a surveyable Sorites paradox for a particular F, we require:

i non-inferential recognition that Fa and that $\sim$Fb;
ii that a can be transformed into something qualitatively indistinguishable from b by k steps of a certain kind such that whenever y results from x by such a step, then xRy holds good for a specified R;
iii that, plausibly, $(\mathrm{F}x \,\&\, x\mathrm{R}y) \rightarrow \mathrm{F}y$;
iv that k pairwise steps of universal instantiation and Modus Ponens is a surveyable proof structure.

Certain Sorites paradoxes, for example 'the heartbeats of my childhood',[36] are not going to satisfy these conditions. The question is whether, whenever a predicate is intuitively Sorites-susceptible, an R and a k can always be located for it which enable the paradox to be developed surveyably. (We might try taking the heartbeats in 100-fold packages!) It is not implausible that this might be so; but it seems impossible that it might be established a priori. That the notion of a weakly finite but weakly infinite totality is incoherent *per se* has not, therefore, been demonstrated in strict finitistically acceptable terms.

There is, indeed, on reflection, a plausible counter-example. Let us say that a system of notation for zero and the positive integers is *complete* just in case every integer actually intelligibly representable in that notation by a numeral n has n predecessors likewise so representable; and let us say that N *supersedes* M just in case both M and N are complete and an upper bound for the integers actually intelligibly representable in M can be actually intelligibly represented in N. Let L be a complete system of notation with no recognizable supersessor. Intuitively there must be such

35 For essentially this argument, see Dummett, 'Wang's Paradox', in *Truth and Other Enigmas*, pp. 306–7.

36 From Yessenin-Volpin's, 'Le Programme ultra-intuitioniste des fondements des mathématiques'.

systems of notation, since the price of relative brevity in the numerals in a system is relative richness of primitive symbolism, and our memories are limited. But if L has no recognizable supersessor, there is no question of surveyably developing a Sorites paradox with respect to the predicate, 'is actually intelligibly representable in L' since we shall have no notation in which to work. It will still be the case however that the totality of integers so representable can be assigned a specific integral upper bound; there are not so many as $10^{10^{10}}$ actually intelligible numerals, for example, in any complete system of notation. Granted, then, the possibility of such a system of notation, L, tolerance cannot everywhere surveyably be demonstrated to involve Sorites-susceptibility. An obvious ploy for the strict finitist would thus be to take the subject matter of arithmetic to be constituted by the integers actually intelligibly representable in a complete system of notation with no recognizable supersessor.

The second query provoked by the 'small' argument is less sympathetic to strict finitism: what argument does strict finitism have for insisting that we have a Sorites paradox only when the derivation can be surveyably formalized 'in the long'? For even where such a formalization could not be given, there is surely no doubt about our ability to recognize where we *would* get to if the appropriate number of universal instantiation and Modus Ponens steps were taken. Is there not a legitimate sense of surveyability of proof for which physical reproducibility is unnecessary?

The answer, I think, is that we have to distinguish two kinds of case. If we are actually able to say of a proof what, if it is carried out correctly, its every *n*th line will be, then even if the labour of writing it out correctly and convincing ourselves that that is what we had done would be beyond us, the proof is surely, in any relevant sense, a surveyable one, of whose every detail we are in command of a clear view. Nothing in the general arguments for strict finitism suggests that adherence to proofs which are surveyable in the narrower physical sense should be mandatory. What those arguments enjoin is repudiation of the idea that the extension of the concept of proof can outrun human capacity for ratification of proof; but ratification of a proof is not so much, though it typically occurs via, a meticulous check of a write-up of it as a matter of getting oneself fully to understand it, familiarizing oneself with all its stages, coming to know why it works. Until a proof is fully understood in this way, its status is comparable to that of, for instance, a complicated arithmetical calculation which we think is merely *probably* correct; so that disclosure of an error will lead us to doubt whether that proof, i.e. a proof that way of that result, exists at all. But when the proof is fully understood, fully accepted as such, disclosure of an error will, at least initially, be thought of as stigmatizing only that particular *performance* of the proof.

That is the first kind of case: proofs which, though we cannot actually *physically* perform them and reasonably convince ourselves that that is what we have done, are nevertheless fully understood. We fully understand them not merely in the sense that we can describe in detail the patterns of reasoning which they employ, but also can recognize and exactly locate the place in the proof of an arbitrarily selected step. Just such a proof would be the Sorites paradox of 'actually intelligibly representable in binary notation' developed for the integers actually intelligibly representable in decimal notation. Even if no version of that paradox can surveyably be given in longhand, it therefore appears that the strict finitist should respect it and that, pending some kind of solution to it, the concept 'actually intelligibly representable in binary notation' should be regarded not as determining a weakly finite but weakly infinite totality but as of *structurally indeterminate extension*.

To be sure, no absolutely compelling reason has been given why the strict finitist should accept this suggestion, why he should not simply dig in and insist on proofs which we can actually physically reproduce and surveyably check. It is merely that his motivating arguments do not seem to explain such a stance. In fact, however, he will lose nothing, at least in the present context, if he admits as legitimate proofs which are surveyable in the more liberal sense, for it is still not true that every intuitive Sorites paradox then becomes strict finitistically demonstrable. A proof counts as surveyable in the more liberal sense only if, even if it is not physically reproducible in a practically convincing way, we have a clear concept of its identity; and this requires more than possession of a general idea of the kind of steps that it takes – we need to know where it would take us *if* it was actually correctly performed, and to be able actually to recognize as such and know the location of any surveyable sub-proof within it. If we do not have these abilities, there is nothing we can actually do to distinguish our putative understanding of the proof from that of a great many other possible structures which are initially akin to it. The second kind of 'surveyable' but physically unperformable proof would not be associated with such practical capacities; it would be a case where, although we could describe its overall mechanics perfectly, and could convince ourselves of the general character of its eventual results, we might not be able to recognize as such an actual transcription of that result printed out by a computer, or to identify constituent sub-proofs, because of increasing notational complexity. A proof which is surveyable only in this yet weaker sense is not strict finitistically acceptable for the reason just mentioned: our concept of the proof is not sufficiently distinctive; we lack the practical recognitional skills which, if we were fortunate enough to look in the right places, would guarantee us the ability to expose certain putative physical instances of it as imposters.

The same example will serve as before: even in terms of the original liberalization of surveyability, a Sorites paradox will be surveyably developable for a predicate of the kind 'actually intelligibly representable in notation L' only if L has a recognizable supersessor. Otherwise we will not be able to identify a numerical expression, *m*, of which we are in a position to assert the following: that the *sentence*, '*m*' is actually intelligibly representable in L' expresses a falsehood, but would be reached by appropriately many steps of universal instantiation and Modus Ponens from an apparently acceptable major premise expressing the tolerance of the predicate and the minor premise that 0 is actually intelligibly representable in L. If L has no recognizable supersessor, the only expressions, *s*, for which '*s* is actually intelligibly representable in L' will express a recognizable falsehood will be expressions selected from *incomplete* notations; there will therefore be no chain of universal instantiation and Modus Ponens steps of the appropriate kind of which each constituent line is actually intelligible, whose starting point is a truth of the form, '*k* is actually intelligibly representable in L', whose terminus is '*s* is actually intelligibly representable in L', and whose major premise stipulates that 'actually intelligibly representable in L' tolerates the transition from an integer to its successor. There is therefore no strict finitistically acceptable demonstration of a Sorites paradox for 'actually intelligibly representable in L', even if the original liberalization of surveyability is accepted.[37]

Our governing assumption so far, to be reviewed in the next subsection, has been that surveyability predicates are indeed tolerant. Our question has been: how does that vindicate the minor premise of the Modus Tollens, how does it call the viability of a strict finitist philosophy of mathematics into question? Let us review our main conclusions. First, the consistency of strict finitist mathematics is not threatened in the most obvious way, since, even if semantically incoherent, the relevant predicates will not feature in the formal theories. They will feature essentially only in the statement of the philosophical *motif* for strict finitism, and in any strict finitist semantics for logical and mathematical languages. Second, even if surveyability predicates are semantically incoherent, the power of the philosophical case for strict finitist attitudes is not compromised unless it is assumed that semantic incoherence is sufficient for unintelligibility; but the proper conclusion for someone disposed to accept Sorites paradoxes for a large class of familiar expression ought to be exactly the opposite. Third, there is a question whether the strict finitist can satisfactorily motivate a choice of axioms for arithmetic. For if surveyability predicates

37 For a more detailed discussion of the surveyability of proofs, and Wittgenstein's use of the notion, see my *Wittgenstein on the Foundations of Mathematics* chapter VII.

are semantically incoherent, then, if it is proposed that arithmetic should deal with the integers actually intelligibly representable in some particular complete notation, it will deal with the extension of an incoherent predicate; and if it attempts to deal, instead, with all the integers actually intelligibly representable in some notation or other, then it will be dealing with a union of such extensions. Either way, how can there be anything coherent to say about the collective structure of the entities with which it will deal? We noted the assumption behind this question that any viable philosophy of mathematics must, within the framework of what it considers to be a satisfactory conception of meaning, at least informally elucidate intended models and interpretations for those branches of mathematics which it proposes to sanction. But the semantic incoherence of surveyability predicates as a class is, in any case, in doubt; for even if the tolerance of those predicates is accepted along with the underlying logic for the Sorites reasoning, there is the question of the surveyability of the derivations. It was argued that some, but not all, intuitive Sorites paradoxes would, under our governing assumption, be strict finitistically cogent under both a narrower and a more liberal interpretation of surveyability; but that, so long as we have not recognized a complete notation L to have a supersessor, we can have no grounds for thinking that a Sorites paradox can be surveyably derived, in either sense, for 'actually intelligibly representable in L'. Whatever we conclude about the tolerance of surveyability predicates, therefore, Dummett's conclusion, that the notion of a weakly finite, weakly infinite totality is incoherent, is premature. From a strict finitist point of view, we are not in a position to rule out the possibility of such totalities; the recognition of a positive instance will require both validation of the tolerance of the appropriate predicate and recognition that no surveyable demonstration of inconsistency can be given; if we could recognize a particular numerical notation, L, to be complete and without supersessor, and that the predicate 'actually intelligibly representable L' was tolerant with respect to the transition from an integer to its successor, we should have a specific instance. It is not absurd to suppose that we might have good grounds for supposing a notation to have each of these three features.

12 *Surveyability predicates, vagueness and tolerance*

If the preceding reasoning is correct, the tolerance of at least some predicates of practical intellectual possibility poses no threat, when the situation is viewed strict finitistically, to their semantic coherence. What is at stake in the question of the tolerance of surveyability predicates as a class is thus whether these predicates are semantically coherent from other than strict finitist points of view; and whether the arithmetic of the set of integers actually intelligibly representable in some complete notation can be the arithmetic of a weakly infinite totality.

As noted earlier, Dummett seems simply to take it for granted that surveyability predicates are vague; and, sometimes, that vagueness generates Sorites-susceptibility.[38] But it can seem equally plausible to suppose that surveyability predicates cannot be vague: that our intellectual capacities must be as sharply limited as our physical capacities, since, at bottom, it is physical capacities in which they consist – physical capacities of the brain. On this view, there can no more be an a priori objection to the idea of a sharp cut-off to, for example, the length of the formal proofs which a particular agent can survey than in the case of activities like weight-lifting, high-jumping and loading camels.

Provided the distinctions urged at the conclusion of subsection 6 are accepted, the lines of implication among vagueness (i.e. possession of borderline cases), Sorites-susceptibility, and lack of sharp boundaries, are by no means immediate. There is no evident reason why a vague predicate should be tolerant; borderline cases can result from a conflict of perfectly sharp criteria – the predicate 'is entitled to Israeli nationality' might be an example. And while tolerance guarantees lack of sharp boundaries, it is a muddle to pass in the opposite direction: the muddle involved in conflating the distinction between lacking instructions to 'draw the line' somewhere and possessing instructions that the line is nowhere to be drawn.

It is a mistake also, at least in the context of our present concerns, to pass from lack of borderline cases to possession of sharp boundaries. Earlier we had occasion to notice that, like all predicates of practical capacity, surveyability predicates seem to be vague in at least this respect: the conditions under which failure indicates inability are not sharply circumscribed – someone who can ϕ may fail to do so because the conditions are not suitable. But, it is natural to wonder, is this really a matter of *vagueness*? Plausibly, to say that someone is able to ϕ is to say that there is some complex of conditions, C, under which the agent will function at his best, and that if he tries to ϕ under C-conditions, then he will ϕ. And if this account is acceptable, then the apparent vagueness in the rejection conditions of 'X can ϕ' is merely *epistemic*. For either there is a condition C as described or there is not; the problem is merely that of fixing upon the evidence class for the latter disjunct.

One response to this thought would be to wonder whether the notion of conditions under which an agent 'functions at his best' is not itself vague – in particular, whether the distinction between conditions where

38 Dummett, 'Wittgenstein's Philosophy of Mathematics', in *Truth and Other Enigmas*, p. 182; 'Wang's Paradox', pp. 304, 316.

an agent *realizes his actual capacities* and conditions under which he *fulfils his potential capacities* is not shot through with indeterminacy. But the more important point is that, even if the mooted account of the truth-conditions of 'X is able to ϕ' warrants the belief that there are no borderline cases for the truth of that sentence, justification of a belief in sharp cut-offs for the application of surveyability predicates will require, for any anti-realist, that surveyability predicates be *decidable*. Not but what we tried to run an argument for the weak decidability of such predicates earlier; but the discussion was inconclusive, and there is no evident implication of the decidability of 'X can ϕ' by the proposed account of its truth-conditions.

We noted earlier that self-ascription of surveyability predicates may well involve consideration of parameters of degree, but the point is actually more general. For unlike predicates of practical capacity in the high jumping and weight-lifting bracket, the conditions of success, or the conditions under which success indicates application of the predicate, do not seem everywhere sharp in the case of surveyability predicates. In contrast with raising a bar above one's head, for example, there is no finite performance which conclusively shows that somebody finds a particular expression *intelligible*; and while genuine recognition of a reduplication of a proof shows that one found the original surveyable, there is no sharp behavioural distinction between an identification based on genuine recognition and one fluked on a guess. Here there is undoubtedly a parameter of degree involved in testing the application of a predicate: that of the reliability of certain sorts of performance over a series of trials. That does not immediately entail that the predicate can apply to greater and lesser degrees. But if we find we do not know how to answer the question: *how* well does somebody have to be able to handle an expression before it is clear that he finds it intelligible?, surely the explanation is not that we do not know sufficiently many *non-linguistic* facts.

The central point I should wish to urge, however, is, again, that there is a priori no clear reason why tolerant predicates should be either vague or predicates of degree; predicates of phenomenal position, or of phenomenal shade of colour, for instance, are obvious counter-examples. The intuition that surveyability predicates do indeed tolerate marginal alterations in length, complexity, etc., need have no connection with assumptions about their vagueness or their applicability to greater and lesser degrees; so there is, without further argument anyway, no point in trying to challenge it by challenging such assumptions.

For all its initial plausibility, however, an intuition is all that it remains; and the physicalist's simple denial of it should certainly give pause to anyone who feels its tug. What, if any, *argument* can be given for the tolerance of surveyability predicates? In 'On the Coherence of Vague

Predicates' and 'Language-Mastery and the Sorites Paradox', I called attention to several kinds of consideration which would serve, if accepted, to justify regarding certain predicates as tolerant. Predicates of casual observation – 'heap', 'tidy', 'tall', 'bald' – can be expected to tolerate changes too subtle to be determined by casual observation. Predicates whose conditions of correct application we have to be able to remember without external aids can be expected to tolerate changes too slight for our memories to detect; colour predicates, and many others, come into this category. Predicates associated with very substantial moral and explanatory distinctions – 'child', 'idiot', 'lunatic' – can be expected to tolerate very marginal changes in an agent to whom they apply. And predicates whose conditions of application are capable of purely ostensive explanation must, it appears, tolerate any changes which we cannot ostensively indicate. These are all direct, theoretical arguments for regarding it as implicit in the senses of the relevant expressions that they will tolerate certain sorts of possible change; and it is the possibility, and only the possibility, of such arguments which gives the Sorites paradox the status of more than a sophism. But none of them appears germane to the case of surveyability predicates. So why is Dummett's intuition plausible?

An uncharitable explanation would be that it is because we tend to concentrate on relatively short proofs, or relatively simple numerical expressions, which our competence to survey or understand goes well beyond. But I doubt if anyone will think the correct diagnosis so simple who gives due weight to the *intellectual* aspect of surveyability: the surveyability of a proof, or intelligibility of an expression, as the notion is relevant to strict finitism, is not just a matter of the practical reproducibility 'by mere copying'[39] of the symbolic structure involved but requires its *comprehension*. The issue is complex and there is no substitute, alas, for detailed consideration of a variety of surveyability predicates, for it cannot be assumed that like considerations apply in all cases. Let us briefly review some of the considerations which are germane to just one case: the predicate, F*n* = 'the decimal notation expression for *n*, [= *Dec.n*] is actually intelligible for X', '*n*' ranging over the positive integers and X a particular agent. (I shall describe the major premise of any purported Sorites-proof of the semantic incoherence of a surveyability predicate as, in deference to Dummett's belief in the tolerance of such predicates, an instance of *Dummett's Principle.*)

Points worth noting straight away are these two. First, assuming that the strict finitist, like the intuitionist, will interpret the existential quantifier *constructively*, it will be admissible to assert the classical negation of an instance of Dummett's Principle: $(\exists n)Fn \& \sim Fn'$, only if we can actually

39 Cf. Wittgenstein, *Remarks on the Foundations of Mathematics*, III, 41.

locate a particular *k* which we can actually recognize to satisfy that condition. (Nothing less than that will be required if the strict finitist treatment of zero and the positive integers should be as of a definite, finite totality.)[40] Second, if in contrast with 'red', 'child', 'bald', etc., predicates of surveyability are neither predicates of degree nor borderline-case vague, if indeed they are weakly effectively decidable, there is no obvious possibility of blocking the move from: $\sim(\exists n)\mathrm{F}n \,\&\, \sim\mathrm{F}n'$ to $(n)\mathrm{F}n \rightarrow \mathrm{F}n'$; in other words, recognition that we cannot actually locate a sharp cut-off point for F will be immediately transformable into recognition of the assertibility of the appropriate instance of Dummett's Principle. This is not the situation with 'red', 'child', and so on; there it is necessary to argue *directly* for the relevant instances of Dummett's Principle, but with surveyability predicates, if actually weakly decidable, it is enough to show that we are in no position to recognize a counter-example.

Can that now be argued? Certainly X cannot, singlehandedly, recognize a counter-example. For no value of *n* can it seem to him that he understands *Dec.n*, but does not understand *Dec.n'*; for in order to recognize that *Dec.n'* does not seem intelligible to him, he must first recognize some expression as *being Dec.n'* – and that he can do, singlehandedly, only if he can understand it. To this extent, a counter-example to the relevant instance of Dummett's Principle is unimaginable from X's first-person point of view. Of course, there is no argument here for the acceptability of the relevant instance of Dummett's Principle; a counter-example to the proposition that X's auditory range extended arbitrarily high would have, for X, just the same kind of unimaginability. The lesson is merely that, in order for X to recognize a smallest decimal numeral which he cannot understand, he will have to have some *independent* way of identifying it as denoting the successor of a number whose decimal numeral he does understand. And what goes for X goes for the community at large; so recognition of sharp boundaries to what we can survey, or understand, is going to require recourse to some kind of technology.

That is all quite unexciting and does not seem to locate the real motivation for Dummett's intuition, so let us try a different tack. Suppose we accept two plausible-seeming principles: first, that any *n*-fold sequence of single decimal numerals is neither easier nor harder to take in than any other *n*-fold such sequence differing from it in at most one place; second, that if *x* is ϕ-able by X, and *y* is no harder to ϕ than *x*, then *y* is ϕ-able by X. Then if a decimal numeral is actually intelligible for X, it can be

40 That is, the actual verifiability of $(\exists n)\mathrm{F}n \,\&\, \sim\mathrm{F}n'$ will be a necessary condition, from the strict finitist point of view, of the appropriateness of *denying* that the F-integers constitute a weakly finite, weakly infinite totality.

surveyably proved (if only in the liberalized sense) of any particular decimal numeral of equal length that it too is actually intelligible for X. All, therefore, it appears, that can obstruct the acceptability of the present example of Dummett's principle is if it does not hold for the case where *Dec.n* = a sequence of '9's. It has thus to be a possibility that X can understand some such *m*-fold numeral, *Dec.k*, so can recognize as such – by the above two principles – an *m*-fold sequence of zeros; yet cannot understand the result of prefixing the latter by a single '1'. We can suppose that he understands the description 'the result of prefixing an *m*-fold sequence of zeros by a single "1"', and knows that what satisfies it denotes k'. Given this, and the recognitional character of his understanding of '*m*-fold sequence of zero's', it is not perhaps *absurd* to suppose that he simply cannot recognize occurrences of *Dec.k'* as such; but it surely seems extremely odd. By hypothesis, he can recognize as such the constituent *m*-fold sequence of zero's; by hypothesis, he knows what *Dec.k'* is like, knows that all is needed is to tag a '1' appropriately closely onto the front of an *m*-fold sequence of zero's. So, once he has identified the *m*-fold constituent of the symbol we present to him, what on earth could be preventing him from seeing that the residue simply consists in a single prefixed '1' and so from identifying the whole as *Dec.k'* ?[41]

I offer these reflections as diagnostic of the appeal of Dummett's Principle in this instance, rather than as an argument. For a conclusive argument would have to be of a quite different character. The crucial issue is how 'molecular' a view it is defensible to take of our understanding of sub-sentential expressions which, like the numerals, form an indefinitely extensible recursive system. If ϕ-ing is jumping, or lifting, each statement of the form, 'x is ϕ-able by X' may be tested in isolation, irrespective of whether any *other* such statements, 'y is ϕ-able by X', has been tested. Of course, success at a particular height, say, is *eo ipso* success at any smaller height and failure at any particular height is *eo ipso* failure at any greater height, but we can assess success or failure at a particular height on the basis purely of trials in which the bar is set at that particular height. No analogue of this holds in the case of surveyability predicates: no one can provide the best kind of evidence that he understands a particular numeral, for example, if the tests are somehow confined to operations with that particular numeral and no other. Understanding a numeral is in some essential way a matter of understanding the system of which it is a constituent.

That much holism is uncontroversial: however favourable X's handling of a particular numeral, the claim that he understands it at a particular time is defeasible by reflection on anterior and subsequent operations by

41 An exactly parallel line of reasoning could be constructed for binary notation.

X with other numerals; nothing parallel holds for the claim that X can jump an *n* metre bar at a particular time. But the vital question is whether, more particularly, we have built it into our criteria of understanding any particular numeral that somebody can convincingly satisfy them only by correct handling both of it and of those in its vicinity *on both sides*. If not, then, however puzzling earlier considerations make it seem, there can be no convincing objection against the possibility of a sharp limit to X's capacity to comprehend decimal numerals; but if so, then incomprehending responses to *Dec.n'* on X's part are going to cast doubt on the value of his performance with *Dec.n*, so that, contrapositively, the best grounds for supposing that *Dec.n* is intelligible to him will be grounds for the same supposition of *Dec.n'* ; and the relevant instance of Dummett's Principle will be a consequence. The issue is thus one of some subtlety; and, so far as I am aware, it is quite undecided by existing commentary.

IV
Conclusion

Dummett's objections to the coherence of the strict finitist philosophy of mathematics are thus, at the present time at least, ill-taken. We have so far no definitive treatment of Sorites paradoxes; so no conclusive ground for dismissing Dummett's response – the response of simply writing off a large class of familiar, confidently handled expressions as semantically incoherent. I believe that cannot be the right response, if only because it threatens to open an unacceptable gulf between the insight into his own understanding available to a philosophically reflective speaker and the conclusions available to one confined to observing the former's linguistic practice; for an observer of our linguistic practice could never justifiably arrive at the conclusion that 'red', 'child', etc., are governed by inconsistent rules. But the Sorites is not the subject of this paper. The points I hope to have made plausible are: that a generalized intuitionist position cannot be so much as formulated and that even a most local intuitionism, argued for the special case of arithmetic, is hard pressed effectively to stabilize and defend itself; that strict finitism remains the natural outcome of the anti-realism which Dummett has propounded by way of support for the intuitionist philosophy of mathematics; that it is powerfully buttressed by the ideas of the latter Wittgenstein on rule-following; and that there is no extant compelling reason to suppose that its involvement with predicates of surveyability calls its coherence into question. The correct philosophical assessment of strict finitism, and its proper mathematical exegesis, remain absolutely open, almost virgin issues. This is not a situation which philosophers of mathematics should tolerate very much longer.

APPENDIX

Outline of a strict finitist semantics for first-order arithmetic

(i) The following fairly simple-minded approach will at least serve to indicate some of the issues and difficulties. We shall take the notion of an (actually intelligible) *numeral* for granted, along with the more general notion of an (actually intelligible) natural-number denoting expression (an *nde*). A *numerical notational scheme* for a first-order arithmetical language, L, is a set of actually intelligible signs comprising only numerals of L and other *nde*'s formed from them by means of the *nde*-forming resources of L.

(ii) An *elementary arithmetical accumulation*, A, is the union of the members of a quintuple, $\langle M_A, E_A, S_A, P_A, K_A, \rangle$, where M_A is a numerical notational scheme, and E_A, S_A, P_A and K_A are relations on the elements of M_A satisfying the following conditions:

a if $E_A\bar{m}\bar{n}$, then it is actually verifiable that *m* and *n* are identical.
b if $S_A\bar{m}\bar{n}$, then it is actually verifiable that *n* is the immediate successor of *m*.
c if $P_A\bar{k}\bar{m}\bar{n}$, then it is actually verifiable that the sum of *k* and *m* is *n*.
d if $K_A\bar{k}\bar{m}\bar{n}$, then it is actually verifiable that the product of *k* and *m* is *n*.

(iii) An elementary arithmetical accumulation thus represents the pool of a set of actually intelligible *nde*'s with a set of actually verifiable elementary arithmetical statements involving just those *nde*'s. Intuitively, any such accumulation represents (part of) a logically possible state of human information as far as elementary arithmetic is concerned. It is plausible, however, that we ought, strict finitistically, to restrict our attention to accumulations which could be aimed at, and be reasonably believed to have been attained, by a human team working in a co-ordinated way. The motive for the restriction, vaguely formulated as it is, is simply that a larger accumulation will not really represent the full increase in information over a smaller one which it includes unless it is *surveyable*; unless it is possible for us to know what, assuming all has gone well, the net gains have been, even though none of us could singly accomplish, or check out, those gains.

The restriction, be it noted, is stronger than the requirement that membership of an accumulation be an actually decidable question. Accumulations which satisfy it we shall call *manageable*, (reserving 'surveyable' for proof-structures). Henceforward we shall deal only in manageable accumulations. How more exactly the manageability-constraint should be formulated, and whether it is indeed strict finitistically inescapable, we cannot attempt to settle here.

(iv) Let A be any manageable accumulation, and let T_A contain any manageable accumulation B, $\supseteq$ A, which we can actually attain if we start with A. Consider a set whose members are all and only sequences, Σ, satisfying the following conditions:

> Σ contains only elements of T_A;
> Σ has A as initial element;
> Σ is well ordered by $\subset$;
> If C immediately succeeds B in Σ, C exceeds B by the addition of one and only one element to M_B, E_B, S_B, P_B or K_B;
> Σ is a humanly practicable sequence of information-gathering.

Such a set, T^*_A, is a *strict finitist tree* for A. Intuitively, it represents every feasible way of advancing our elementary arithmetical knowledge beyond A by single steps while preserving the manageability of the successive informational states at which we arrive.

(v) What sort of structure is T^*_A? Suppose that actual intelligibility tolerates the transition from any *nde*, $\bar{m}$, of the L for which A is a numerical notational scheme to an *nde* of L denoting the immediate successor of *m*; and suppose that the manageability of an accumulation, B, tolerates the addition of any single actually intelligible *nde*. Then there will be indefinitely many ways of moving on from B by adding a single element to M_B. Each accumulation, B, in a sequence in T^*_A will thus have indefinitely many sequences continue out of it, and each such sequence will be indefinitely long, irrespective of the number of ways of moving on from B by adding to E_B, S_B, P_B or K_B. It cannot be assumed, however, that any particular elementary arithmetical statement which is actually verifiable if we start out from A will determine an acceptable single addition to E_B, S_B, P_B, or K_B, if only because its verification may involve verification *en route* of *many* new statements. (A statement is verified, for example, at every line of a multiplication table).

The last consideration brings us to a point which threatens some very distinctive consequences for strict finitist logic and mathematics: we cannot assume that every elementary arithmetical statement which is actually verifiable if we start out from A will be represented in some accumulation, sooner or later, in every Σ, $\in T^*_A$. It may be that achieving a verification of P is a sufficiently protracted, elaborate business to ensure that while we can actually advance from A to a manageable accumulation in which P is represented, the same does not hold for every B, $\supset$ A, in some Σ in T^*_A – either because too many additions are involved in verifying P to preserve manageability or because, simply, too much work is involved. The effect is that the totality of actually verifiable statements is not stable but *shrinks* as our knowledge advances. So there is an obvious threat to, for example, the validity of conjunction-introduction: both P and Q may separately be actually verifiable if we start from A, but it may be that of no accumulation in which either is represented is there any manageable extension which contains a representation of the other.

Might this instability be avoided by a different approach? Well, clearly no single agent can actually collectively verify even most of the statements which are at any particular time individually within his verificatory powers; and what goes for a single agent goes for a team, no matter how big – just by devoting their effort to particular problems, whether individually or collectively, they will pass up the opportunity to work effectually on others. If, on the other hand, we see ourselves – perhaps more realistically – as a 'team' which is permitted to add indefinitely to its stock of workers, the question is whether our results are to be subjected to any sort of manageability constraint. If so, no advantage is gained. But if not, then, while no initially actually verifiable statement need ever cease to be so, it can no longer be guaranteed that progress down a sequence will represent a real increase in information, since we may lose track of what has previously been accomplished. But, whichever way we try to play the situation, no way is apparent for securing *both* a stable, unchanging stock of actually verifiable statements *and* a guarantee that that the more is actually verified, the more is known. By submitting to a manageability constraint we avail ourselves of the latter at the expense of the former.

(vi) Let L, now, be a language suitable for first-order arithmetic: and let A be an elementary arithmetical accumulation whose M_A is a numerical notational scheme for L. Then letting 'B', 'C', 'D', range over the elements of the constituent sequences of T^*_A, and 'Σ', 'Σ'', 'Σ''', range over those constitutent sequences, we recursively specify *verification-conditions* for the closed sentences, P, Q, R of L as follows:

P is verified at B if and only if

1 P is elementary and a representation of $P \in B$; or
2 P is Q & R and both Q and R are verified at B; or
3 P is $Q \vee R$ and either Q, or R, is verified at B; or
4 P is $\sim Q$ and there is no Σ such that, for some $C \in \Sigma$, Q is verified at C; or
5 P is $Q \rightarrow R$ and for any Σ, any $B \in \Sigma$, and any $C \in \Sigma$: if Q is verified at C, then there is a Σ', such that $B, C \in \Sigma'$ and, for some D in Σ', R is verified at D; or
6 P is $(\exists x)Fx$ and there is an *nde*, n, $\in M_B$, such that $F\bar{n}$ is verified at B; or
7 P is $(x)Fx$ and for any *nde*, $\bar{n}$, any Σ, $B \in \Sigma$, and any $C \in \Sigma$; if $\bar{n} \in M_C$, then there is a Σ', such that $B, C \in \Sigma'$ and, for some $D \in \Sigma'$, $F\bar{n}$ is verified at D.

Remarks

Each of these clauses is to be read as stating a condition our recognition of whose satisfaction constitutes a verification of the appropriate type of closed sentence. Thus verification of a conditional consists in recognition that, should we advance in any way to a verification of its antecedent, a verification will then be feasible – if not already attained – of its consequent; verification of a universal statement consists, roughly, in recognition that, for any *nde*, $\bar{n}$, which we have either already constructed or can manageably go on to construct, a verification will be feasible of the instantiation of the universal statement to $\bar{n}$; and verification of the negation of a statement consists in recognition that it is nowhere verified.

The clause for negation has what may seem the unwelcome consequence that we may deny a statement simply on the ground that we could not surveyably assess it. How the clause might be improved, or whether it might be made to seem acceptable that such 'unmathematical' considerations should enter into the verification-conditions of mathematical statements, are questions which here I must leave to the reader's judgement. Notice that (4) is at any rate better than:

4′ : P is $\sim$Q and there is no Σ, B $\in \Sigma$, such that for some C $\in \Sigma$, Q is verified at C.

The latter would have the effect that we might come to be in position to deny a statement just in virtue of recognizing that we could not *now* manageably achieve its verification, although at earlier, slimmer accumulations, a manageable accumulation incorporating the results of a test might have been attainable. The consistency of the definition of *assertibility* below would then be in jeopardy.

It would be natural now to attempt a proof that if P is verified at B $\in \Sigma$, it is verified at every C $\in \Sigma$ such that B $\subset$ C. But the strategy of proof by induction on the degree of syntactic complexity of P awaits validation of induction, which is in doubt. On the other hand it is by no means obvious how we might approach questions of validity in general without that particular lemma. I have no better proposal at this stage than that we simply help ourselves to it, with no justification whatever.

(vii) An open sentence, F*x*, may be considered as verified at an accumulation just in case its universal closure is.

A sentence is *assertible* just in case there is a B $\in$ some Σ in T^*_A at which it is verified.

A sentence is *valid* just in case it is verified at every B $\in$ some Σ in T^*_A.

Let us conclude by briefly reviewing any evident points of difference between intuitionist arithmetic and what appears well-motivated in the light of the foregoing.

Logic. Consider the following axiomatic formalization of intuitionist logic, IC:

Axioms:
(1) $P \to (P \vee Q)$ (2) $Q \to (P \vee Q)$
(3) $(P \& Q) \to P$ (4) $(P \& Q) \to Q$
(5) $P \to (Q \to P)$ (6) $P \to (\sim P \to Q)$
(7) $(P \to Q) \to ((P \to (Q \to R)) \to (P \to R))$ (8) $P \to (Q \to (P \& Q))$
(9) $(P \to Q) \to ((P \to \sim Q) \to \sim P)$ (10) $(P \vee Q) \to ((P \to R) \to ((Q \to R) \to R))$
(11) $(x)Fx \to Ft$ (12) $Ft \to (\exists x)Fx$

Rules: (i) Modus Ponens; and, subject to the usual restrictions,

(ii) $\dfrac{Fy \to P}{((\exists x)Fx) \to P}$ and (iii) $\dfrac{P \to Fy}{P \to (x)Fx}$

We have to ask whether (1) to (12) are valid under any uniform substitutions; and, I propose, whether a verification of the premise(s) of any of the rules guarantees at least the assertibility of the conclusion. With the aid of our pirated lemma, Modus Ponens clearly passes the test. What of (ii)?

Suppose $Fy \to P$ verified at some accumulation, B, in T^*_A. Can we guarantee that $((\exists x)Fx) \to P$ is verified somewhere? It might seem not, for could not the situation be as in figure 1?

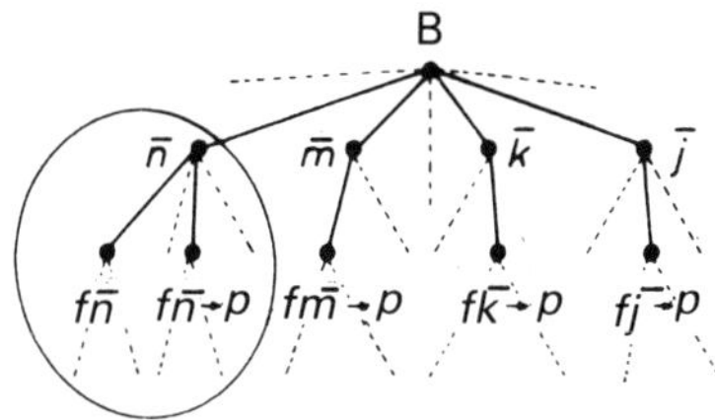

Figure 1

The fact that, for any *nde*, $\bar{n}$, in M_B, or which we can manageably add to it, we can advance to a verification of $F\bar{n} \to P$ is no guarantee that any path from B on which $(\exists x)Fx$ is verified can be extended to lead to a verification of P. It may be rather, as the ringed section of the diagram indicates, that, having constructed $\bar{n}$, we can either advance to a verification of $F\bar{n}$ or to one of $F\bar{n} \to P$ but cannot actually do both; so that the accumulations at which F$\bar{n}$ and F$\bar{n}$→P are respectively verified have no common descendants.

For all that it seems to advert to a genuine possibility, the counter-example is evidently spurious in the presence of our unproved lemma; for, by the lemma, if F*y*→P is verified at B it is also verified at the accumulation on the leftmost branch of the depicted structure at which F$\bar{n}$ is verified; so there has to be a path from that accumulation on which both F$\bar{n}$→P and, appealing again to the lemma, F$\bar{n}$ are verified. The worrying thing is the perspective in which the lemma is therefore placed: for clause (7) can be reconciled with the lemma only if verification of a universally quantified statement is constrained to involve our possession of a method for verifying its instances whose implementation is *always* manageability-preserving. So no construction will count as a verification of (*x*)F*x* if, for some particular $\bar{n}$ which we can manageably add to our present state of elementary arithmetic information, the practical possibility of using the construction to get a verification of F$\bar{n}$, though presently open, can lapse if we choose to give our arithmetical attention long enough to other matters. Thus: without the lemma, there seems no prospect of blocking the counter-example; but with the lemma, the conditions we are implicitly imposing on verification of universally quantified statements threaten to be impracticably severe.

How do things stand with (iii)? Suppose we have verified P→F*y* at some accumulation, B; can we now guarantee that P→(*x*)F*x* is verified somewhere? Clearly so, provided we are allowed appeal to the lemma. For let C be any accumulation at which P is verified lying on some path out of B. By the lemma, P→F*y* is also verified at C; which, by the appropriate clauses, intuitively means that, for every $\bar{n}$ in M_C or occurring at some accumulation on some path out of C, P→F$\bar{n}$ is verified at some accumulation on a path out of the accumulation at which $\bar{n}$ first occurs. So since, by hypothesis and the lemma, P is verified at each accumulation on each path out of C, every F$\bar{n}$, for each $\bar{n}$ in M_C or occurring at some accumulation on some path out of C, is likewise verified at some accumulation on a path out of the accumulation at which $\bar{n}$ first occurs. But that is just to say that (*x*)F*x* is verified at C: so that, by clause (5), P→F*x* is verified at B.

Again, however, unless we allow appeal to the lemma, no method of validating the rule is apparent within the purview of the proposed recursive clauses; I leave it to the reader to satisfy himself of the obstacles that then arise.

What of the axioms? There is no evident difficulty with any of (1) to (5), (11) and (12). (7) might seem intuitively suspect, since a verification of both P→Q and P→(Q→R) at some B would not, by (5) alone, guarantee that the situation was not of the type suggested by figure 2.

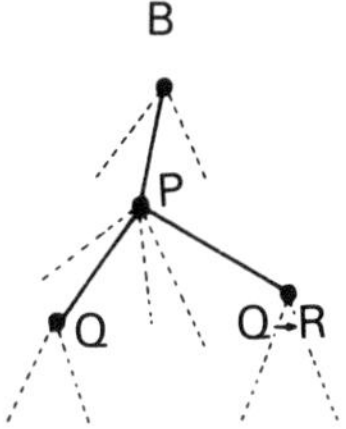

Figure 2

Here it cannot be assumed that R occurs anywhere below B, since there is no reason to suppose that Q and Q→R are, once P is verified, co-verifiable. But, again, trouble is nipped in the bud by the lemma; for P→Q, once verified at B, must be verified at every accumulation on every path out of B – so, in particular, at the accumulation at which Q→R is verified. Whence, since, by the lemma, P is also verified at that accumulation, both Q→R and Q must be co-verified at some accumulation below.

It is notable too, after our earlier misgivings about conjunction introduction, that (8) would seem to be valid. The misgivings were sound enough, of course; the assertibility of a conjunction cannot be guaranteed by the individual assertibility of its conjuncts. But, such is clause (5), (8) in no way vies with that. I leave it to the reader to satisfy himself on the point. As for (6), (9), and (10), there at least no obvious way of counter-exemplifying them; but this is not the place for a more decisive investigation.

What it appears fair to conclude is that, within the framework of the foregoing and – as it seems to me – natural interpretations of the logical constants on behalf of strict finitism, the prospect of validation of a logic close in strength to intuitionist logic is at least not closed; but it would seem to rest on the assumption incorporated in our lemma, the effect of which is to impose constraints of ominous severity on the verification-conditions of universal and conditional statements, far exceeding the overt requirements of clauses (7) and (5).

Arithmetic. To IC we can add the following standard first-order axioms to obtain intuitionist arithmetic, IA:

A	$(\exists x)x = 0$	Peano axioms
B	$(x)(\exists y)y = x'$	
C	$(x)0 \neq x'$	
D	$(x)(y)x' = y' \rightarrow x = y$	
E	$((x)(Fx \rightarrow Fx') \& F0) \rightarrow (x)Fx$	

F $(x)x = x$		Axioms for identity
G $(x)(y)x = y \rightarrow tx = ty$	('t' any term forming operator)	
H $(x)(y)x = y \rightarrow (Fx \rightarrow Fy)$		
I $(x)x + 0 = x$		Axioms for sum and product
J $(x)(y)x + y' = (x + y)'$		
K $(x)x \times 0 = 0$		
L $(x)(y)x \times y' = (x \times y) + x$		

We close with three observations about this group. First, the assertibility of the axioms for zero and successor, (A) to (D) will require that the manageability of an accumulation, B, always tolerates the addition to M_B of $\bar{n}'$ for any $\bar{n}$ in M_B and that such an addition is invariably actually possible.

Second, there may be a temptation to think that, despite the reservations expressed in subsection 11, the induction axiom (E) may be saved by the strength given by the lemma to our interpretations of the universal quantifier and the conditional. For suppose we have verified both F0 and $(x)Fx \rightarrow Fx'$ at some accumulation, B; then for any *nde*, $\bar{n}$, and any path through B, if $\bar{n}$ occurs on Σ at C, then a verification of $F\bar{n} \rightarrow F\bar{n}'$ occurs on some Σ' such that B, C $\in \Sigma'$. Hence a verification of $F0'$ occurs at some accumulation, D, on a path out of B. By the lemma, however, $(x)Fx \rightarrow Fx'$ is verified at that accumulation also; so, by the same reasoning as before, $F0''$ occurs at some accumulation F on a path out of D...and so on. Thus there is a path out of B on which each of F0, $F0'$, $F0''$,...etc. is verified; does it not follow *a fortiori* that $(x)Fx$ is verified at B?

It is, to be sure, especially uncomfortable to appeal to our unproved lemma in attempting to vindicate the assertibility of induction. But the reasoning fails anyway: we cannot advance to the conclusion that $(x)Fx$ is verified at B, or anywhere else, unless we can guarantee *either* that no *nde*'s feature anywhere in T^*_A which are not of the canonical form, $0'^{\cdots'}$ – a restriction already violated by (I) to (L) – *or* that any non-canonical *nde* has a verified canonical equivalent on any path on which it features. In the latter case not every actually intelligible *nde* could feature in T^*_A; (not to deny that such a price in terms of comprehensiveness might be worth paying if induction could thereby saved.)

Third, the axioms (J) and (L) expressing the recursions for sum and product threaten, on two natural assumptions, to be *deniable*. For suppose B were an accumulation at which (L) say, was verified. Then every path out of B is such that for every pair of *nde*'s, $\bar{n}$ and $\bar{m}$, on it, there is a verification of $\bar{n} \times \bar{m}' = (\bar{n} \times \bar{m}) + \bar{n}$ on some continuation of the path. But what is such verification? The first assumption is that if it first requires a computation of a canonical numeral $\bar{j}$, such that $\bar{n} \times \bar{m} = \bar{j}$; then a computation of a canonical numeral, $\bar{k}$, such that $\bar{n} \times \bar{m} = \bar{k}$; and then a verification that $\bar{k}+\bar{n}=\bar{j}$, then there will be a large class of actually intelligible (and indeed canonical) 'rogue' *nde*'s for which there is no question of our being able actually to verify the relevant equality. So B must be such that no such *nde*'s occur on any path out of it. But that cannot be so if – (the second assumption) – the manageability of any accumulation tolerates the addition of any single actually intelligible *nde*, and any such addition is always humanly feasible. For then the comprehensiveness of T_A^* requires that there are certain to be paths out of B on which 'rogue' *nde*'s feature. So there can be no such B, and, by clause (4), ~(L) is consequently verified everywhere. (The same holds for (J) provided, as seems plausible, there occur on paths out of each B actually intelligible *nde*'s whose addition cannot surveyably be performed.)

The particular approach which we have adopted looks as though it holds some prospect of support for Wang's suggestion, reported by Dummett in 'Wittgenstein's Philosophy of Mathematics' that strict finitist logic might coincide with intuitionist logic but that the arithmetic would be weaker. But there are many alternative ploys to explore within the type of strategy illustrated; and many alternative strategies to try as well – most notably, an investigation of ways of restricting the lemma, and their consequences. If strict finitist formal theories do prove rich and interesting in the end, well and good. But the real philosophical gain to be harvested from this line of research will be an understanding of the cost of combining the most powerful, general anti-realist polemic with the assumptions which led the intuitionists to revisionism.[42]

42 It is disappointing to have to report that, in the four years since the original publication of this paper, no further work on strict finitist semantics has come to my attention. The germ of the approach I have taken was sown by Kit Fine when he replied to a paper I read to the Ockham Society in Oxford in 1969. Needless to say, he takes no blame for the faults in the way I have developed it.

5

Anti-realism, Timeless Truth and *Nineteen Eighty-Four*

O'Brien was looking down at him speculatively. More than ever he had the air of a teacher taking pains with a wayward but promising child.

'There is a Party slogan dealing with the control of the past,' he said. 'Repeat it, if you please.'

'"Who controls the past controls the future: who controls the present controls the past,"' repeated Winston obediently.

'"Who controls the present controls the past,"' said O'Brien, nodding his head with slow approval. 'Is it your opinion, Winston, that the past has real existence?'

Again the feeling of helplessness descended upon Winston. His eyes flitted towards the dial. He not only did not know whether 'yes' or 'no' was the answer that would save him from pain; he did not even know which answer he believed to be the true one.

O'Brien smiled faintly. 'You are no metaphysician, Winston,' he said. 'Until this moment you had never considered what is meant by existence. I will put it more precisely. Does the past exist concretely, in space? Is there somewhere or other a place, a world of solid objects, where the past is still happening?'

'No.'

'Then where does the past exist, if at all?'

'In records. It is written down.'

'In records. And...?'

'In the mind. In human memories.'

'In memory. Very well, then. We, the Party, control all records, and we control all memories. Then we control the past, do we not?'

(from George Orwell's *Nineteen Eighty-Four*)

I
Timeless Truth and the Truth-value Links

The thesis of the timelessness of truth is here to be understood as the quite ordinary-seeming idea that what is ever true is always true. More specifically: whatever someone can truly state at a particular time can be truly stated by anyone, no matter when, where, and who; though to effect the same statement on a different occasion will frequently involve changes in mood, tense, pronoun and adverb. The truth-value links are specific biconditional principles which associate the truth-conditions of tensed utterances made on different occasions. An example is:

> 'It is raining' will be true at *t* if and only if 'It will be raining at *t*' is true (now)

The timelessness of truth is not meant to be a thesis about the expressive power of English, or any other particular language. It is a metaphysical thesis, one effect of which is that there can be such a thing as a language which, for any particular truth, enables any of its speakers, no matter who, where or when, to articulate that truth. The connection of the timelessness of truth with the truth-value links is merely that no language which fails to incorporate them, can, it appears, live up to the metaphysical thesis: either there will be truths which it cannot express at all or there will be truths the opportunity for whose expression will, for its speakers, be ephemeral.

The timelessness thesis has had its critics over the centuries. Aristotle, in particular, saw it as enjoining fatalism, and sought to deny it by way of escape.[1] One way of interpreting Aristotle's recommendation would indeed be to reject one of the truth-value links. We would debar the transition, for instance, from

> 'A sea fight is taking place or it is not' will be true [tomorrow],

to:

> 'A sea fight will [tomorrow] be taking place or it will not' is true [today].

The idea would be that the truth of the first is guaranteed by the reflection that the future, whatever form it takes, is logically constrained to be describable by means of one or the other of the present-tense disjuncts; whereas the truth of the second requires that there already be something in virtue of which one of the future-tense disjuncts is true – which is what,

1 *De Interpretatione* 9, sections 18a–19b.

according to the Aristotelian view, should cause us to regard the occurrence of a sea battle on the morrow, or its non-occurrence, as fated.

Whether or not there really is an entailment of fatalism by timeless truth, further argument is needed why denial of the truth-value link would be a felicitous way of expressing the diametrically opposed idea that the future is open, that the truth is subject to becoming. What the Aristotelian really wants to say, it seems, is that while the options open to the future are logically restricted, there is nothing true to say yet about the specific form which it will assume. But that idea seems as compatible with the second formulation above as with the first; what is barred is rather the transition to the claim that one of 'A sea fight will take place' and 'A sea fight will not take place' is already determinately true. Rather than tamper with the truth-value links, the Aristotelian would do better, it seems, to construe the truth-conditions of future-tense statements supervaluationally.[2] The truth of a statement about the future would e.g. be taken to consist in its holding in every sufficiently specific model of the course of future history which is compatible – in a sense the Aristotelian will explain – with what is already the case. Under such a construal, it is quite intelligible how 'A sea fight will be taking place tomorrow or it will not' might already be true even though neither of its disjuncts is. Perhaps the Aristotelian cannot in the end consistently acknowledge all the truth-value links;[3] but it is not initially clear that his best case should proceed via their denial.

II
The Prima Facie Clash of Anti-realism with both Timeless Truth and the Truth-value Links

Michael Dummett writes:

> Statements about the past form a class the application to which of an argument of the anti-realist type seems to be called for. That it has not often been so applied is doubtless due to certain obvious difficulties arising from applying it: namely, that an anti-realist interpretation of past tense statements appears incompatible with acknowledging the existence of a systematic link between the truth-values of differently tensed statements uttered at different times. This difficulty is central to the whole issue.[4]

The anti-realist challenges the realist satisfactorily to explain how we could come by, and distinctively display, an idea of what it would be for a

2 Cf. Dummett, 'The Reality of the Past', especially pp. 366–7 in *Truth and Other Enigmas*; and section III of Essay 15 in this volume.
3 See the Appendix to this essay.
4 Dummett, 'The Reality of the Past', in *Truth and Other Enigmas*, pp. 362–3.

statement to be true independently of the existence of any means for our determining its truth. One problem which the anti-realist encounters over the truth-value links is that they seem to provide the realist with a promising strategy for meeting this challenge head-on. To understand, for instance, that

> 'I have a headache on 12 October 1986' is true if and only if 'I had a headache on 12 October 1986' will be true (in 1989)

is, when coupled with the reflection that the truth of the left hand side of the biconditional entails nothing about the existence of symptoms of its truth at any future time, apparently to understand how a statement about the past may be unverifiably true.

Plainly the anti-realist will have succeeded in exposing some sort of lacuna in this simple train of though if he can demonstrate that he can consistently acknowledge the truth-value links. But that point does not exhaust the reasons why his acknowledgement of them would be desirable. The truth-value links are not to be compared to those features of, say, classical logic which undergo modification by the intuitionists. The intuitionistic modifications are deep-reaching; but they are relatively conservative with respect to our ordinary notion of valid inference. Wholesale rejection of the truth-value links, in contrast, would be bound to leave us, it seems, with no clear conception of how tensed language was supposed to work at all. What, for instance, is someone who asserts 'It will rain at noon tomorrow' to be taken as saying if the truth-conditions of his utterance are not held to coincide with that of any utterance of 'It is raining' at noon tomorrow? Maybe there could be a coherent revisionary programme for tensed discourse, pivoting around rejection of the truth-value links as the intuitionistic revisions of classical logic pivot around rejection of Bivalence; and perhaps we should be left with a surprising amount to say. But it does not seem likely.

However that may be, a simple train of thought makes it seem that anti-realism cannot accept the timelessness thesis. If the application of the predicate 'true' is to be constrained by our powers of verification – in an appropriately weak sense of the term[5] – how can what is true be eternally true when what is verifiable is unceasingly changing? The intuitionistic proposal to constrain the notion of mathematical truth by that of proof generates no problem of this sort precisely because the opportunity to construct any particular mathematical proof is, in the relevant sense, eternal. When it comes to making a case for or against ordinary tensed statements, in contrast, opportunity knocks. So much is obvious.

5 I do not mean to suggest that no distinction is to be drawn between the possibility of verification, properly so styled and the availability of favourable evidence; nor that it is the latter which the anti-realist should regard as limiting the applicability of 'true'. I mean merely – here at least – to leave these issues open.

It would seem, then, that the global anti-realist – one who seeks to generalize the intuitionists' ideas about the meaning of mathematical statements to all statements – has some rather clever boxing to do. He must explain how rejection of the truth-value links, and with them the timelessness thesis, could be a practicable proposition after all. Or he must show how, contrary to expectations, he is entitled to both. Or he must earn the right to retain the truth-value links while the timelessness thesis is discarded. None of these possibilities is well explored in the literature. Does any of them promise a viable path?

III
Varieties of Temporal Anti-realism

It should not be completely obvious that someone who respects Dummett's exegesis of the intuitionists' ideas and wishes to generalize them to ordinary statements must come into collision with the timelessness of truth. Any proposal to the effect that the application of the concept of truth be restricted to within the class of decidable statements can properly be regarded as anti-realist. Obviously, however, the force of such a proposal turns on the intended sense of 'decidable'. If we take it that what is intended is weak decision – so that a statement has been decided when an adequate but not necessarily conclusive case has been made for accepting it or for accepting its negation – a number of parameters still remain: decidable by whom, and when, and by what means? Varieties of anti-realism may be ranged on a scale according to the degree of idealization involved in the answers offered to these questions. The limiting case would be a kind of egocentricity of the present time and place: for each of us, the application of the concept of truth would be restricted at any particular time, to within the class of statements which we can in fact weakly decide at that time. (Of course the constitution of this class will be a function, inter alia, of who and where we are.) Those who have faith in the overall anti-realist motif do well to believe that there is some principled reason for stopping short of this view. Some distance from it on the spectrum is a standpoint which embraces a double idealization: decidable statements are taken to be those which we are capable *in principle* of deciding – that is, which a subject with the same range of cognitive powers as we, whose capacities exceeded our own only in finite degree, would be capable of deciding in practice – at *some time or other*. On this view, any statement of which we can recognize that world history has or will contain a point at which a rational subject whose powers exceeded ours only finitely could actually carry through an investigation which would have to terminate in justification for the statement or for its negation – any such statement may be regarded *at all times* as determinately either true or false.

The picture of the world appropriate to this idea would seem to be somewhat as follows. We in no sense create the world, it does not even come into being as we explore.[6] We journey through it, temporally speaking, as observers. But it is a world without properties other than those which we can in principle apprehend. Some of its properties are not always apprehensible; but for each of these an opportunity arises when it can, at least in principle, be apprehended – like the number of sheep in a field seen from a moving train. If the opportunity is not taken, still what could have been verified remains the case.

Clearly there is no tension between this liberal anti-realism – *I/S anti-realism*[7] – and the thesis of the timelessness of truth. The opportunity for verifying a statement may not yet have arisen, or it may have been lost; but the opportunity for truly making the statement can neither arise nor be lost. The facts, on this view, are always as they would have been determined to be if the opportunity to test them had been taken; they are eternal

If one were convinced of the correctness of I/S anti-realism on general grounds and were then to consider what philosophy of mathematics would be appropriate to it, the answer would be exactly the 'de-psychologized' form of intuitionism which Dummett has presented. So it cannot be assumed without further ado that the generalization of Dummett's argument to ordinary statements has to raise an issue about the timelessness of truth and the validity of the truth-value links. The question is whether I/S anti-realism is stable, or whether the best arguments in support of it support something stronger.

Dummett's discussions[8] implicitly assume that the latter is the correct viewpoint. It is easy to sympathize. When a past-tense statement is used appropriately, what *makes* its use appropriate are the conditions which obtain at the time of utterance, all of which therefore post-date the events or states of affairs which intuitively form its subject-matter. It is accordingly a distinction among possible situations obtaining *at the time of utterance* of a past-tense statement that a training in the use of the past tense has to get across; and the training will be deemed to have been successful when a child manifests his understanding of this distinction. This is all, it seems, that can be taught, all that can be manifestly understood. There can be no part to be played by conceptions relating not to the circumstances obtaining when the use of a past-tense statement is envisaged but to

6 Cf. the concluding remarks of the penultimate paragraph of Dummett's 'Truth', p. 18, and of the last paragraph of 'Wittgenstein's Philosophy of Mathematics', p. 185 in *Truth and Other Enigmas*.

7 In principle/Sometime.

8 In 'Truth' and 'The Reality of the Past'.

circumstances of a vanished breed, any connection of which with things that can now impinge on a trainee's consciousness has to be acknowledged as quite contingent.[9] However we rate this train of thought, it sufficiently resembles the prototypical anti-realist case to cause serious doubt whether the 'sometime' ingredient in I/S anti-realism should appeal to anyone who sympathizes with Dummett's case for mathematical intuitionism. (I shall continue to prescind from consideration of the 'in principle' ingredient in this essay – for reservations about its content, see Essay 4.)

A number of possibilities now open up. An Aristotelian standpoint would replace 'sometime' by 'now or in the past'. The resulting *I/NP anti-realism* would accordingly restrict the application of the concept of truth to within the class of statements which are currently in principle decidable or which we can recognize to have been in principle decidable at earlier times although the opportunity to assess them may now have lapsed. Alternatively, replacing 'sometime' by 'now or in the future', *I/NF anti-realism* would restrict the application of the concept of truth to within the class of statements which are currently decidable or which will subsequently come to be so. Obviously, I/NP anti-realism inherits just the dubious liberality of I/S anti-realism outlined above. But the situation with I/NF anti-realism is less clear cut. What is it for a statement to be decidable in the future? Any assessment of a statement is going to take time to complete; what is the objection to regarding a statement whose (weak) verification or falsification would not be possible for days, or even years, as *currently* in principle decidable but associated with a very lengthy decision procedure (perhaps 'wait and see')? The intuitionists place no finite upper bound on the length of respectable decision procedures in mathematics: provided a statement is associated with a finite decision procedure, however lengthy, they are content to regard it as in principle decidable. Would not I/NF anti-realism be the proper generalization of their standpoint?

The suggestion is, in effect, that there is no interesting distinction between I/NF anti-realism and the *I/N anti-realism* which would gloss 'decidable' as characterizing statements which we are in principle capable of deciding *now*. Taken one way, this might seem to essay an incoherent restriction: of no statement which we have not yet assessed can it be said that it is capable of decision 'now', for if we start now, we shall finish in the future. But the proposed restriction is not to *instantaneous* decidability. Intuitively, we can recognize at any time a threefold division among possible statements: those which it is too late to assess if they have not already been assessed; those which it is so far too early to assess; and those for which the opportunity for a relevant assessment is current. Typically, though not invariably, these will be, respectively, statements in

9 Cf. Dummett, 'The Reality of the Past', in *Truth and Other Enigmas*, pp. 363–4.

the past, future, and present tenses. What I/N anti-realism proposes is to restrict the application of the concepts of truth and falsity to statements which come into the third category. I/NF anti-realism, in contrast, extends the class of statements apt to be true or false to include the second category as well. Plainly there is a difference; the question is whether it is one which the anti-realist should regard as relevant.

My own view is that he should, but for reasons which would call into question the propriety of the 'in principle' ingredient as well. States of affairs lying in the distant future are not available to serve as paradigms for the application of concepts, nor as a backcloth against which someone may display mastery. But this is not a limitation of principle if everything which would be brought within our compass by a *finite* extension of our capacities – including longevity – is to be deemed possible 'in principle'. Should we so deem? It is notable that the idealization involved in the intuitionistic conception of effective mathematical decidability does not have to be of this sort: finite increases in intellectual dexterity instead would always suffice. Admittedly, I have no straightforward reason to offer why the one kind of idealization should be deemed satisfactory but the other not. But it is worth recognizing that to hold that there is no significant difference between I/NF anti-realism and I/N anti-realism is to take a position on the question, viz. that there is no such reason to find.

However our present purpose – that of assessing how matters stand, from an anti-realist point of view, with the truth-value links and the timelessness thesis – does not require commitment on the issue. I/N anti-realism will assume centre stage in the following discussion. But should it turn out that I/NF anti-realism constitutes 'best play' of the anti-realist position, that would not alter the main conclusions which I shall suggest.

IV
Forthright and Agnostic Anti-realism

It is natural enough to interpret the overall effect of I/N anti-realism as being that the sufficiently distant past and future are somehow diminished in point of reality: for there is much less that is currently decidably true of them than of the present. Certainly there can be no states of affairs in the past or future which only a simultaneous *observation* could reveal to us. In terms of the railway analogy, the picture would be that nothing true may be stated at any given time save as may in principle be verified by observation from the carriage window at that time; or may be verified non-observationally at any time. The totality of facts would thus appear to shift continuously: there is nothing ahead on the tracks save what we can see coming, and nothing behind save what we can see receding into the distance. Naturally, the appopriateness of this picture requires there to be an analogue of the *span* of time during which observations from the carriage window can be relevant to a particular question: currently in principle decidable statements, that is, must retain that status for a while – there has to be a period within which it can be true to say that though we could have tested such an S already, still it is not too late to do so for the facts relevant to S are still in view, so to speak. It would be a serious blow to I/N anti-realism if this idea could not be made good. But at least one obstacle is spurious: there is no reason why the relevant span of time should be a mysterious constant, invariant from statement to statement, and no force accordingly in the general challenge to say how long, for these purposes, the present continues.

The picture presents a vivid rejection of the timelessness thesis: it bids us to think of truth as coming to be and fading away. Is some such picture not inescapable for I/N anti-realism? For if truth is constrained by current decidability, the point will bear repetition that what we can verify in principle varies from time to time. But matters are not in fact quite so straightforward. We have been implicitly assuming that an anti-realist rejection of the realist's conception of truth has to involve accepting some such conditional as

i If S is true, then S is (weakly) verifiable.

The question has been, accordingly, what gloss the anti-realist should put on the notion of verifiability featuring in the consequent. However he answers, the conditional will commit him, contraposing, to denying that any statement is true which he has reason to regard as undecidable, ergo non-verifiable. Hence the apparent inescapability, for the I/N anti-realist, of the principle that if a statement is not currently decidable, it is not true. Now, there is precedent for the acceptability of (i), or at least for its contrapositive, in the intuitionistic semantics for negation, which yield that a proof that no proof can be given of a particular statement is to be counted as a proof of a negation of that statement. But there is another aspect of intuitionistic thinking which points in a different direction. This is the tradition of *agnosticism* with respect to classically valid principles, like Excluded Middle, whose unrestricted acceptance the intuitionists view as involving commitment to proof-transcendent mathematical truth. Whatever gloss the anti-realist puts on 'decidable', his realist opponent will see no objection to the supposition, for a large class of statements S, that S may be undecidably true. If the anti-realist *denies* this possibility, he must wind up committed to some version of (i). But a more cautious anti-realism may merely *refuse* to *endorse* the possibility. The result would be, in the present instance, a form of agnostic I/N anti-realism which would hold that only currently in principle decidable statements may *justifiably* be regarded as determinately either true or false; but would not accept the inference from a statement's current undecidability to its not being true. Such an anti-realist could consistently have exactly the qualms about the applicability of Bivalence to 'Jones was brave' which Dummett elaborates in his inaugural exposition. But by not accepting the contrapositive of (i), the agnostic I/N anti-realist seems to evade the immediate commitment to rejection of the timelessness thesis which the shifting character of what is currently decidable would appear to impose inescapably on his more forthright colleague.

It is, however, the latter with whom this section will be mainly concerned. The most pressing question is whether the forthright I/N standpoint can consistently acknowledge the truth-value links. Let S be an arbitrary present tensed sentence of English, and let '*Past*:S' and '*Fut*:S' denote, respectively, appropriate past- and future-tense transformations of it. Then, intuitively, each of e.g. the following equivalences hold:

A $(\forall t_2)$ [*Past*:S is true at t_2 iff $(\exists t_1)$ (S was true at t_1)]
B $(\forall t_1)$ [*Fut*:S is true at t_1 iff $(\exists t_2)$ (S will be true at t_2)]
C $(\forall t_2)$ [S is true at t_2 iff $(\forall t_1)$ (*Fut*:S was true at t_1)]
D $(\forall t_1)$ [S is true at t_1 iff $(\forall t_2)$ (*Past*:S will be true at t_2)]

.

.

.

and so on,

where t_1 is an appropriately earlier time than t_2. Now each of these equivalences, be it noted, has to be understood as providing for what may be truly asserted at any particular *present* time: t_2 in the case of (A) and (C), t_1 in the case of (B) and (D). So much is implicit in the occurrence within them of past- and future-tense inflections of the predicate 'is true'. Accordingly, if the forthright I/N anti-realist elects to regard the class of currently in principle decidable statements as closed under inferences yielded by (A) to (D) and their kin, why exactly should he get into trouble?

The answer may seem evident enough. Suppose the sentence, 'Dummett is at present, on the morning of 16 November 1986, working at the keyboard of his word processor' is now, as I write, true. Then, taking t_1 as the present, and t_2 as a year hence, equivalence (D) yields that 'Dummett was, on the morning of 16 November 1986, working at the keyboard of his word processor' will then be true. Suppose we now verify the present-tense version. It would be peculiar but not impossible simultaneously to have excellent reason to think that there will, in a year's time, be absolutely no basis for affirming the past-tense version; perhaps we are a band of conspirators who intend to destroy all evidence of Dummett's present whereabouts in order to frame him for a crime to be committed elsewhere in Oxford, and then to administer to ourselves a special amnesia-inducing drug in order to be able to resist any subsequent interrogation. The anti-realist must, presumably, at least understand the example. What it illustrates is not merely how it may happen that the truth of a past-tense statement transcends verification by currently available methods but – what an anti-realist would anyway demand, in order to be persuaded that the possibility is genuine – how we might have adequate reason to believe in the occurrence of such a thing. (D) is thus, the argument is, in collision with the I/N anti-realist restriction of truth to the domain of the currently in principle decidable. Indeed there is an explicit contradiction. For if our present beliefs about the character of the data available in a year's time are correct, the I/N anti-realist has simultaneously to recognize that the past-tense version will not then be true, since undecidable.

The agnostic I/N anti-realist would not, of course, be vulnerable to this argument, since he does not accept the contrapositive of (i), on which the argument depends. But his forthright colleague is in any case not bereft of a response. There is, he allows, an outright contradiction if he is so unwise as to commit himself to a *tenseless* version of (i):

i* $(\forall t)$ if S is true at t, then S is verifiable at t.

This, in conjunction with the special features of the example, does indeed entail that we – the conspirators – now have reason to believe that the past-tense version will not be true a year from now; and (D) yields precisely the opposite. But what follows, it may appear, is only that the I/N anti-realist should not endorse (i*). One who believes in a *species aeternitatis* is no doubt bound to interpret the anti-realist as endorsing such a principle. But the anti-realist himself should insist that what he is affirming is rather

i** If S is true, then S is verifiable at the present time.

This principle is to be understood as formulated in the present tense. It therefore entails nothing about what, if any, conclusions may be drawn from the undecidability of sentences at times other than the present. So nothing follows from it, plus our present beliefs about our state of information a year hence, which should contradict what we are entitled to affirm on the basis of our present state of information and (D). For the same reason there is nothing in the example to impose an understanding of how the truth of a past-tense statement may transcend its current decidability. What the example teaches is rather how, if the truth-value links are accepted, the truth of a past-tense statement at a time *other* than the present can transcend the means for deciding it at that time. But that is not at all the same thing.

The realist, of course, will want to protest that it *is* the same thing: since the present was once future, to understand how truth and decidability might come apart in the future is to understand how they might *already* have done so. But this natural thought is simply tantamount to the assumption that the passage of time should have no part to play in determining our conception of what states of affairs may coherently be conceived as possible, that what goes for what is presently future goes for any 'future' – including those which are no longer future. And this assumption, of course, is here at issue.

However, the realist has not yet exhausted his hand. For there is, he counters, a principle – a counterpart of what the anti-realist now affirms by (i**) – which he – the anti-realist – will affirm in a year's time. And the truth-value links contain, presumably, the means whereby we may express that principle *now*. Since the anti-realist will then, presumably, use the very same form of words displayed in (i**), the proper *present* expression of what he will then be saying is presumably something like

i^{fut} If S will be true a year hence, then S will then be verifiable.

Plainly the anti-realist cannot accept (i^{fut}) *now* or – on the assumptions of the example – he will be committed both to affirming that the past tense sentence about Professor Dummett will be true in a year's time and – contraposing on (i^{fut}) – to denying it. But if (i^{fut}) is not now to be endorsed, then – by truth-value link (B) – neither is the claim that 'If S is true, then S is verifiable at present' will be true in a year's time.

Note that the position is not merely that the anti-realist may not now endorse (i^{fut}). Because, in conjunction with the truth-value links and the hypothesized features of the example, it introduces inconsistency, he must, further, *deny* it – i.e. deny that it is presently true. But this denial must, by (B), commit him to the claim that when, in a year's time, he gives expression to the thesis presumably distinctive of his position, what he claims will not be true. That is not, admittedly, to disclose any inconsistency in the anti-realist's *present* beliefs. But ought he not to be disconcerted, to say the least, by the disclosure of a commitment to repudiating the viewpoint of his future self?

A comparison is worthwhile at this point with the final objection brought by the realist in Dummett's dialogue. The realist says:

> ...you must surely agree that if, in a year's time, you still maintain the same philosophical views, you will in fact say that, on the supposition we made, namely that all evidence for the truth of the past tense statement...is then lacking, and will always remain so, [that statement] is *not* true...and surely also you must maintain that, in saying that, you will be correct. And this establishes the sense in which you are forced to contradict the truth value link.[10]

10 Dummett, 'The Reality of the Past', in *Truth and Other Enigmas*, pp. 372–3.

Now, there is indeed a contradiction if the anti-realist's presumed willingness to admit that in a year's time he will *correctly* deny the truth of the past-tense statement is taken to entail, by our (B), that it is *now* true to say that that statement will not then be true. But this entailment cannot be allowed unless the anti-realist is *now* in a position to endorse the principle by whose lights his denial of the truth of the past-tense statement in a year's time will be correct. Otherwise 'correct' merely means: in accordance with a principle which the anti-realist will then hold; and that does not sustain the inference to truth. Dummett has his anti-realist respond to the objection by a manoeuvre which concedes the stability in sense of the predicate 'is true' across time (of which more later). But what we have seen is that his anti-realist is in fact forced to make a different reply. Since his adherence to the truth value links commits him to a denial of (i^{fut}), he is simply in no position to grant Dummett's realist the claim that the denial, in a year's time, of the truth of the past-tense statement will – on the assumptions of the example – be correct.

Naturally, it should be of absolutely no comfort to the anti-realist to be able to avoid in this fashion the objection formulated by Dummett's realist. Is it not absurd if his endeavours to conserve the truth-value links commit him, at any particular time, to denying the truth of sentences which – by those very links – serve to say the same as sentences which, at different times, he would affirm as constitutive of his position? A philosophical thesis worthy of respect should have an *enduring* claim to credibility. The present anti-realist seems committed, in contrast, to ceaseless repudiation of the views of his former and subsequent selves. For as soon as he acknowledges versions of (i) in other than the present tense, application of the truth-value links to a suitably constructed example will trap him into contradictory assignments of truth value.

What the anti-realist would *like* to do at this point is precisely to invoke the idea of truth as capable of *becoming*. He would like to be able to regard successive affirmations of instances of the sentence-type (i^{**}) as effecting statements which, while true at the time they are made, were formerly and will subsequently again come to be not true. And this is exactly what he has yet to entitle himself to. If the statement which I now affirm by an utterance of (i^{**}) has only just now, at t_2 say, become true, then it presumably was not true before, at t_1 say. So someone who expressed it at t_1 did not then speak the truth. Since the proper form for its expression was then, presumably, (i^{fut}), the result is in contradiction of truth-value link (C).

V
The Agnostic Confronts a Similar Difficulty

Since he endorses none of the conditionals, (i), (i^*), (i^{**}), and (i^{fut}), the agnostic I/N anti-realist is so far unscathed. Indeed his position may seem to deserve additional credibility in view of the difficulties encountered by his more forthright colleague. Whether that is really so depends, of course, upon whether agnosticism can be made out to be a proper expression of the critical thrust of the original arguments against the realist's conception of truth. However that may be, it may come as something of a surprise to realize that the agnostic I/N anti-realist is in fact prey to difficulties very similar to those with which we have just been concerned.

The agnostic endorses none of the (i)-group conditionals, but he does – of course – endorse

ii If S is currently in principle decidable, then S is determinately either true or false.

Now consider again Dummett's celebrated example of the untried Jones. The situation is that Jones is dead; that, in the course of his life, he gave evidence neither for nor against the hypothesis that he was a brave man (now construed as the counter-factual, 'if Jones had encountered danger, he would have acted bravely'); and that we know this to be the position. In these circumstances the agnostic I/N anti-realist will decline to endorse the claim that 'Jones was brave' is determinately either true or false; and accordingly – assuming, with Dummett, that the anti-realist account of disjunction is orthodox (rather than e.g. supervaluational) – he will decline to endorse the claim that the disjunction, 'Jones was brave or Jones was not brave' is true. The question is whether this combination of views – acceptance of (ii), acceptance of the truth-value links, but refusal to accept, in the circumstances described, the past-tense instance of the Law of Excluded Middle – is coherent.

Not so, if we may soundly reason as follows.

1 '"Jones is brave" is currently in principle decidable' was true at t_1
2 '"Jones is brave or Jones is not brave" is true' was true at t_1
3 '"Jones is brave or Jones is not brave" was true' is true at t_2
4 'Jones is brave or Jones is not brave' was true
5 'Jones was brave or Jones was not brave' is true

Jones, it is here supposed, was alive and in his prime at t_1 but is now, at t_2, dead. Line (1) affirms, what seems uncontestable, that 'Jones is brave' was among the class of sentences that could truly have been claimed at t_1 to be then in principle decidable. Line (5), on the other hand, is just what the agnostic I/N anti-realist wishes, in the circumstances of the example, to be entitled to refuse to endorse. So where does he find fault with the reasoning?

There seems to be no room for manoeuvre from line (2) onwards. The transition from line (2) to line (3) is a straightforward application of truth-value link (A), and that from line (3) to line (4) an application of the surely uncontestable principle that if a particular sentence is now true, we may now truly *use* that sentence to make an assertion. The final transition, from line (4) to line (5), might also be viewed as a straightforward application of truth-value link (A). But if someone was inclined to find it less than straightforward, it is not difficult to see how the case for its acceptability might be spelled out. Granted that the former truth of a disjunctive sentence requires the former truth of one of its disjuncts, we may move from line (4) to

4* 'Jones is brave' was true or 'Jones is not brave' was true

whence the reasoning can proceed in the pattern of a disjunction-elimination: we apply truth-value link (A) to each disjunct of line (4*) in turn, inferring line (5) in both cases by disjunction-introduction. (I do not mean to suggest, incidentally, that there could be no controversy about the transition from line (4) to line (4*). The point is only that *this* anti-realist will not take part in that controversy: his reservations about the present assertibility of 'Jones was brave or Jones was not brave' are based on the very principle – the distributivity of truth over disjunction – to which the transition from line (4) to line (4*) appeals.)

It would appear, then, that the agnostic I/N anti-realist must disclose some difficulty with the transition from line (1) to line (2). But how? Line (2) follows from

1* '"Jones is brave" is determinately either true or false' was true at t_1

by innocuous paraphrase of its single-quoted ingredient as

'Jones is brave' is true or 'Jones is not brave' is true

and application of the straightforward recursion for 'or'. So the problem must be with the move from line (1) to line (1*). But that move is, apparently, just an application of the principle (ii).

It is the last assertion, it seems, that the agnostic I/N anti-realist must disclaim. Clearly he would have absolutely no room for manoeuvre if he accepted

ii* 'If S is currently in principle decidable, then S is determinately either true or false' was true at t_1

– unless he rejected the suggestion that Modus Ponens held at t_1! So he has to disentangle his endorsement of (ii) from any commitment to (ii*). Now a direct application of truth-value link (A) to (ii*) yields

ii** 'If S was then in principle decidable, then S was [at t_1] determinately either true or false' is true at t_2

which, since t_2 is the present, may be disquoted to provide

ii^{past} If S was then in principle decidable, then S was [at t_1] determinately either true or false.

(Again, the direct application of a truth-value link to a compound statement may be defended by appropriate interposition of steps: (ii*) and (ii**) are easily shown to be equivalent by appropriate steps of Modus Ponens, Conditional Proof and applications of truth-value link (A) to their antecedents and consequents.) The agnostic I/N anti-realist must thus apparently take his stand on the distinction between endorsing (ii) and endorsing (ii^{past}).

Now an endorsement of (ii) is not, admittedly, definitive of the agnostic's position as endorsement of (i) was definitive of the standpoint of his more forthright colleague. Still the principle ought to be uncontentious for him: it describes the conditions under which he is willing to endorse Bivalence. And the predicament in which he now finds himself is essentially that which the forthright I/N anti-realist confronted. There was, we may suppose, such a principle which the agnostic was/would have been willing to endorse at t_1. He would, no doubt, have used the very form of words displayed in (ii). In response to the question, 'How do you *now* say that the principle which you then accepted should, at t_1, have been expressed?' he seems to have no better answer to offer than to allow that that very form of words was the appropriate mode of expression. Since, saddled as he is with the truth-value links, it is only by refusing to endorse (ii^{past}) that he can avoid contradictory attitudes to line (5), the fate of the agnostic is to be ceaselessly committed to refusing to grant the truth of principles which, on his own admission, he would at other times endorse as constitutive, in part, of his philosophical position. The I/N anti-realist who would accept the truth-value links would thus appear to be doomed, whether he is forthright or agnostic, to perpetual conflicts of principle with his former (and subsequent) selves – and doomed, it is essential to stress, to recognition that this is the situation.

VI
The Response of Dummett's Anti-realist

Both forms of I/N anti-realism are now very much on the defensive. I know of only two possible forms of response.

The first is briefly canvassed by Dummett and constitutes his anti-realist's last move in the debate described in 'The Reality of the Past'. Dummett has his anti-realist make this response by way of reply to the realist objection which I quoted earlier – an objection whose presuppositions, as then noted, the (forthright) anti-realist is anyway in no position to accept. Now, though, the time might seem right to play this particular card. What is involved is a rather unexpected form of rejection of the timelessness thesis. Our idea throughout has been that the anti-realist might wind up rejecting the timelessness thesis because committed to allowing that a statement may become true or cease to be so. But this form of rejection presupposes that statements, at least, *are* timeless: that what may be said by anyone at any particular time may at least *be said* by anyone else at any other time, even if sometimes true and sometimes not. And it is this which it is not clear that the anti-realist should accept, and which he may in any case deny. The analogy of the railway invites us to picture a constantly shifting totality of facts. But this involves thinking of a statement as capable of becoming and ceasing to be true only if the statement can itself survive through the shifts. Now, suppose it agreed on all hands that the content of any statement involves the concept of truth: the making of a statement *is* the claim that it is true. Then the effect of viewing the totality of facts are perpetually shifting is that the truth predicate acquires the status of an *indexical*, comparable e.g. to 'now'. When I claim that a statement is true, I claim that it is made true by the facts, where 'the facts' can only be regarded as denoting all the facts that *presently* exist. The result is that the content of a statement, whenever it is made, will, in so far as it involves a claim to truth, be a function of *when* it is made; just as the content of any claim made by the use of a temporal indexical is a function of the time of making it.

This way of presenting the point does not quite coincide with that of Dummett's anti-realist in 'The Reality of the Past'. There the thought is rather than as the totality of facts shifts, so the range of quantification in 'There is something in virtue of which S is true' changes; and as the range of the quantifier changes, so the content of the statement effected by a use of that sentence, and with it the content of the statement S itself, changes in tandem.[11] But I am uneasy about this way of putting the matter since I do not think that the connection which it presumes to obtain between change in the range of a quantifier and change in content is evident. Suppose I enter a lecture room and say 'Some member of this class has pink hair' – truly, as it happens. Intuitively, the statement which I make could have been false if the composition of the class had been different. But, of course, it is essential to that intuitive possibility that change in the range of the quantifier 'some member of the class' *not* be deemed to affect the identity of the statement made. Why should it be different with the anti-realist's ever-shifting range of quantification in 'There is something in virtue of which S is true'?

Suppose instead that I watch a long procession of students filing through the lecture room, during which I truly say 'One of the students now in the room has pink hair'. And suppose I am prevented, or forbidden, from making any but present tensed statements. Then – assuming there is only

11 Dummett, 'The Reality of the Past', in *Truth and Other Enigmas*, pp. 373–4.

one pink-haired student in the procession – the opportunity for truly making that particular statement survives only as long as she is in the room. Once she is gone, only recourse to the past tense – which, by hypothesis, I am unable, or forbidden, to have – would enable me to make *that* statement again. The analogy is this. The anti-realist would have us think of the facts as, so to speak, filing past – with the difference that they did not exist before they entered the room and cease to be as soon as they leave. And, in parallel, our opportunity for truly making the statement expressed by 'there is a fact in virtue of which S is true' will – so long as we are confined to the present tense – be restricted by the presence of the fact in question. The anti-realist move to which Dummett adverts is best viewed, I suggest, as the claim that the alleged indexical character of the truth predicate does, in effect, so confine us. Of course we may perfectly intelligibly form the past-tense transformation of S, or of 'There is a fact in virtue of which S is true', and use it to say something true. But the realist's error is to suppose that the use of tenses somehow transcends the boundaries of the lecture room. If I affirm 'It was the case that S', what I claim is that it is *now* true that it was the case that S. Any statement which I make, however tensed, cannot but be interpreted as intended to answer to the population of facts which now obtain – for they are the only facts which there are. There is accordingly no recovering the content of a statement which was, or will be intended to answer to a different population.

The advantage of this manoeuvre is apparently that it enables the I/N anti-realist to accept the truth-value links, and consequent commitment to the rejection of principles like (i^{fut}) and (ii^{past}), without admitting that he is thereby doomed to betray the constitutive principles of his later and earlier self. Rather, he will claim that there is no way in which he can *now* give expression to those principles. The forthright I/N anti-realist will, for instance, acknowledge that the conditions of our original example commit him to denying that the form of words used in (i**) will express a truth in a year's time; and he will acknowledge that he will, in a year's time, regard that very form of words as expressing a truth. But collision is avoided, he will contend, by the reflection that his present denial has to be understood as answerable to the states of affairs which presently obtain; it is a claim about what is, irreducibly, *now* the case. Whereas his endorsement of the relevant form of words in a year's time will be answerable to a so-far unborn population of states of affairs, and need in no way conflict with what he says now.

There has, admittedly, to be some question why the less forthright, agnostic anti-realist should wish to offer quite this form of reply, since no motive has emerged for endorsing the idea of a 'shifting' domain of facts save acceptance of (i) – which is just where the agnostic and the forthright I/N anti-realist part company. But there is, as it seems to me, a serious cause for dissatisfaction with the line of thought involved in any case. The trouble is that if it has any power at all, it seems far *too* powerful. Intuitively, there is no difficulty in the idea of a contradiction between statements made at widely different times – times sufficiently far apart, in particular, to determine, according to the proposal, substantially different fact populations. But the result of construing the truth predicate as, in effect, a now-oriented indexical is that it becomes quite unclear how such a contradiction can occur. The statement effected by an utterance of 'Someone in the room has pink hair' does not contradict that effected by an utterance of 'No one in the room has pink hair' if the population of the room changes between the times of utterance. The result is that if Dummett's anti-realist has indeed found a way to explain how he can avoid dismissing the views of his earlier and later self, the threatened cost is an unability to explain how there can be such a thing as conflicting views held by protagonists who are sufficiently separated in time.

Dummett's anti-realist is therefore open to a simple dilemma. Does his position permit the reconstruction of some sort of general notion of diachronic inconsistency, or does it not? If it does not, that merely furnishes the realist with a further powerful objection – what account are we now to give of the growth of human knowledge, the hard-won gradual defeat of superstition and error in which we are encouraged to believe, etc. etc.? But if some sort of notion of diachronic inconsistency can be saved, the task will still remain of showing that the kind of clash which an indexical conception of truth *does* allow to hold between statements widely separated in time does not obtain between his present and his later, and earlier, opinions. In short: if something can still be made of the notion of diachronic inconsistency, the original objection ought to be reformulable in terms of the revampted notion; and if nothing can now be made of it, that seems too high a price to pay.

VII
Double-indexing and Truth-value Links

The second reply is, I think, stronger. It involves an explicit rejection of the timelessness of truth; but it retains the timelessness of statements. The crucial move is a reinterpretation of the truth-value links. Precisely because, according to the classical conception of the matter, a statement bears whatever truth-value it has eternally, there is nothing to choose – as we should ordinarily suppose – between the way the truth-value links were expressed on p. 185 and the following mode of expression:

A* $(\forall t_2)$ [What *Past*:S expresses at t_2 is true iff $(\exists t_1)$ (what S expressed at t_1 is true)]

B* $(\forall t_1)$ [What *Fut*:S expresses at t_1 is true iff $(\exists t_2)$ (what S will express at t_2 is true)]

C* $(\forall t_2)$ [What S expresses at t_2 is true iff $(\forall t_1)$ (what *Fut*:S expressed at t_1 is true)]

D* $(\forall t_1)$ [What S expresses at t_1 is true iff $(\forall t_2)$ (what *Past*:S will express at t_2 is true)]

.

.

.

and so on,

in which the original tense-inflections of the truth predicate have been supplanted by corresponding tensing of the verb, 'to express'. Both (A) and (A*), for instance, serve to identify the respective statements effected by *Past*:S now and S at some appropriate earlier time. The reason, indeed, why the truth-value links enter so deeply into our understanding of tense, and why jettisoning them would be so desperate a step to contemplate, is because their role is, in this way, to identify the statement effected by the utterance of a tensed sentence at a particular time as a function of the time of utterance. Understanding a type-sentence is, after all, knowing what it could be used to say as a function of the context – when, where, and by whom – it is used to say it. Without the truth-value links it simply is not clear what the understanding of a type-tensed sentence should be conceived as consisting in. But what the anti-realist now contends is that the realist's objections have all depended upon a tendentious construal of the truth-value links. As the realist has been understanding truth-value link (B), for instance, it is equivalent both to (B*) above and to

B$^+$ $(\forall t_1)$ [What *Fut*:S expresses at t_1 is true iff $(\exists t_2)$ (what S will express at t_2 will be true)].

But (B$^+$) is not acceptable to the anti-realist precisely because it evinces a conviction of the stability of the truth predicate over time in a manner insensitive to variation in the domain of what is in principle decidable.

Thus the anti-realist now discerns two quite different sets of principles buried in the original formulations of which (A) to (D) are illustrative. There are principles which are indeed constitutive of our understanding of tense, serving to identify the statement made by a tensed sentence uttered at different times as a function of its tense and the envisaged times of utterance; and there are principles which serve *in addition* to express the stability of truth as a predicate of statements. The first set of principles can quite satisfactorily be expressed by formulations, as illustrated by

(A*) to (D*), in which all occurrences of the truth predicate are *present-tense*. The second set of principles, in contrast, demand stronger formulation, as illustrated by (B+), in which each occurrence of the truth predicate borrows its tense from that of the occurrence of the verb 'to express' in the noun phrase to which it is appended. The anti-realist accepts the first set of principles, and thereby, he claims, avails himself of what is valid and important in the truth-value links. But he disowns the second set as involving a (realist) conception of truth which he rejects.

The immediate question concerns the exact manner in which (A*) to (D*) fail to subserve the two arguments respectively brought to bear above against the forthright and agnostic anti-realists. The first argument involved a present tensed sentence S about which it was hypothesized to be correct to say

1 S is true at t_1;

and

2 *Past*:S will not be in principle verifiable at t_2.

From 1 and truth-value link (D) it was held to follow that

3 *Past*:S will be true at t_2

and hence that the anti-realist cannot consistently accept

4 If *Past*:S will be true at t_2, then *Past*:S will be in principle verifiable at t_2.

But the anti-realist knows now (at t_1) that he will at t_2 hold a conviction then expressible using the form of words

5 'If *Past*:S is true [at t_2], then *Past*:S is currently in principle verifiable'.

Does he or does he not affirm now that what he then accepts will be true? If he does, then he endorses

6 'If *Past*:S is true, then *Past*:S is currently in principle verifiable' will be true at t_2

and hence, by truth-value link (B), he is committed to

7 'If *Past*:S will be true at t_2, then *Past*:S will be in principle verifiable at t_2' is true at t_1

whose permissible disquotation saddles him with (4) and the resulting contradiction. But if, on the other hand, he denies that the endorsement, by his future self, of (5) will be correct, the result is the earlier-to-later schizophrenia on which the realist is trying to capitalize.

Now: how does the argument fare when it is (B*) and (D*) that are at its service, rather than (B) and (D)? First, after (1) is appropriately re-expressed, what follows from it and (D*) is

3* What *Past*:S will express at t_2 *is* true.

And (6), if it is to be something to which truth-value link (B*) can be applied, will have to be read as

6* What 'If *Past*:S is true, then *Past*:S is currently in principle decidable' will express at t_2 is true.

What follows from this by (B*) is that what the future-tense transform of the quoted sentence in (6*) now expresses, at t_1, is true. But it is evident that, since the occurrence of the truth predicate in (3*) is *present*-tense, there is no prospect of a contradiction from an endorsement of (6*) unless the future-tense transform of the conditional therein quoted leaves unaltered the present-tense occurrence of 'is true' in its antecedent. And that it cannot do. For suppose that, at t_2, someone asserts the quoted conditional in (6*); and ask, what sentence should we *then* have to endorse in order to set up a Modus Ponens step? The answer, framed in terms suitable for an application of (A*) to (D*), is

What *Past*:S now [at t_2] expresses is true.

Since this claims that something is true *at* t_2, its future-tense transform, appropriate to making the same claim at t_1, cannot leave the tense of 'is true' unaltered; for if it did, it would serve only to claim the truth of a statement at t_1, which – for the anti-realist anyway – may not be assumed to be the same thing. Accordingly, what the anti-realist should allow to follow from (6*) by (B*) is something like

7* What 'If what *Past*:S will express at t_2 will (then) be true, then *Past*:S will be in principle decidable at t_2' expresses at t_1 is true.

Disquoting, we then arrive at a conditional principle which, conjoined with (2) yields not the negation of (3*) but rather

8* What *Past*:S will express at t_2 *will not* be true.

and this is inconsistent with 3* only on the assumption that truth is timeless.

A possible response is that, in order to be fully reconciled with his future, t_2, self, what the anti-realist needs to be able consistently to endorse is not (6*) but

6+ What 'If *Past*:S is true, then *Past*: S is currently in principle decidable' will express at t_2 *will be* true (at t_2).

Naturally, the reformulated truth-value links, in which all occurrences of the truth predicate are present tensed, have no direct bearing on this. But that is no reason to treat (6^+) as though it was logically inert. Information about the truth-value at another time of what is then expressed by a compound sentence ought to engage in standard ways with information about the truth-values of what are then expressed by its constituents. Hence, given in particular

2^+ What '*Past*:S is currently in principle decidable' will express at t_2 will not be true (at t_2),

it ought to be legitimate to infer

8^+ What '*Past*:S is true' will express at t_2 will not be true (at t_2),

(by a projective Modus Tollens, as it were.)

Even so, no contradiction is salient. As before, no conclusion to the contrary seems to be entailed by (1), re-expressed in the appropriate mode, and (D^*). All that issues is

3^+ What '*Past*:S is true' will express at t_2 *is* true (at t_1)

– which clashes with (8^+) only assuming, once again, that whatever once is true, always is.

The upshot is that when the truth-value links are construed as the anti-realist now proposes, the kind of example envisaged commits him only to acknowledging something which, at least from a realist point of view, was implicit in his position anyway: that the truth predicate must, in the presence of any such principle as (i), itself acquire a significant tense. It is, admittedly somewhat surprising to find the anti-realist committed to this so nakedly; one might have anticipated some manoeuvre whereby commitment could have been avoided. If I have made no mistake, that is not to be.

What of the second argument – which of course cuts against both agnostic and forthright anti-realists alike? Consider line (1^*):

'"Jones is brave" is determinately either true or false' was true at t_1.

This is now ambiguous from the anti-realist's point of view. One interpretation is

1^*a What '"Jones is brave" is determinately either true or false' expressed at t_1 is true.

The other is

1^*b What '"Jones is brave" is determinately either true or false' expressed at t_1 was true at t_1.

Trying (1*a) first, the next move is to

2a What '"Jones is brave or Jones is not brave" is true' expressed at t_1 is true,

which seems unexceptionable as before. Link (A*) then provides

3a What '"Jones is brave or Jones is not brave" was true' expresses at t_2 is true,

and there is no evident objection to the disquotation to

4a 'Jones is brave or Jones is not brave' was true.

But how is this to be interpreted? The unacceptable result, for the agnostic anti-realist, would be a commitment to

5a′ What 'Jones was brave or Jones was not brave' expresses at t_2 is true,

which would have to come, via (A*), from

4a′ What 'Jones is brave or Jones is not brave' expressed at t_1 is true.

However (4a′) cannot be (4a). The single quoted ingredient in (2a) could as well have been written

What 'Jones is brave or Jones is not brave' expresses (at t_1) is true (at t_1).

So (3a), if it is to follow by (A*), becomes

What 'what "Jones is brave or Jones is not brave" expressed (at t_1) was true (at t_1),' expresses at t_2 is true,

whence, disquoting, we have, not (4a′) but

4a″ What 'Jones is brave or Jones is not brave' expressed at t_1 *was* true.

In the original argument, it seemed that the agnostic anti-realist had no recourse once (1*) was granted – that was what brought him into a (potential) difference of opinion with his former self. But now it apears that he has no cause to worry if endorsement of the opinions of his former self commits him to (1*a). He can happily let the argument run as far as (4a″), reserving his agnosticism for the conversion to (4a′).

Now, the argument for (1*a) would presumably be from

1a What '"Jones is brave" is currently in principle decidable' expressed at t_1 is true,

via

ii*a What 'If S is currently in principle decidable, the S is determinately either true or false' expressed at t_1 is true, and the compelling thought that if both what was expressed by a conditional sentence and by its antecedent at some former time are true, then so is what was then expressed by its consequent. But, again, it is plausible that endorsing the opinion of his former self ought – in the presence of agnosticism about the timelessness of truth – to involve the anti-realist's acceptance not of (ii*a) but of

ii*b What 'If S is currently in principle decidable, then S is determinately either true or false' expressed at t_1 *was* true (at t_1).

Presumably he will have no quarrel with

1b What '"Jones is brave" is currently in principle decidable' expressed at t_1 was true (at t_1),

and a retrospective counterpart of the 'compelling thought' above will then generate (1*b) (see p. 198).

How do things proceed from there? There should be no objection to moving from (1*b) to

2b What '"Jones is brave or Jones is not brave" is true' expressed at t_1 was true (at t_1).

But clearly (A*), being present-tense, is not at the service of any argument from (2b). Admittedly, it is not clear that the anti-realist should quarrel with any set of truth-value links in which occurrences of the truth predicate are *uniformly* tensed; and the past-tense counterpart of (A*) will at least provide

3b What '"Jones is brave or Jones is not brave" was true' expresses at t_2 was true (at t_1).

But now in any case the disquotational step fails. And, anyway, it is a claim about the *present* (t_2) truth of the relevant disjunction that the anti-realist wants to avoid. So no amount of play with truth-value links whose occurrences of the truth predicate are *not* present-tense can pitch him any curves.

Thus both the forthright and agnostic anti-realist can evade the charge, it would seem, that endorsing the truth-value links commits them to ceaselessly disclaiming the opinions which their philosophical views bid them hold at times other than the present. When endorsing the truth-value links is interpreted as endorsement of principles of the sort illustrated by (A*) to (D*), each anti-realist can allow that he is right to endorse at other times the principles which he endorses at present – right both in so far as what he thinks at other times is true at present and in so far as it is true when he thinks it. The cost he pays is an explicit rejection of the timelessness of truth, if he is forthright; the agnostic merely has this too to be agnostic about.

VIII
Conclusion

Our conclusion, then, – which, like any on these elusive matters, had better be suitably tentative – is that the I/N anti-realist may accept the truth-value links, appropriately interpreted, and the timelessness of statements, at the cost of surrender of, or agnosticism about, the timelessness of truth. The proposed reinterpretations of the truth-value links enable the forthright anti-realist, indeed, to speak quite freely of truth as capable of becoming and ceasing to be without fear of the sort of contradiction illustrated in the concluding paragraph of section IV. It would be idle to pretend that the resulting position is likely to strike many as comfortable. One effect of our conclusion is that, should (forthright) I/N anti-realism indeed prove to be the logical terminus of the anti-realist polemic, the prospect of rehabilitating something importantly akin to the classical notion of truth is, in effect, finally dashed. Another is that, if Winston Smith was no metaphysician, the same is not true of his author. *Nineteen Eighty-Four* has not (so far) proved socially or politically prophetic, at least in the West (I think). But if the Party's offical views on time are indeed the tissue of terrifying sophisms they at first appear, it is no trivial undertaking to show it.[12]

APPENDIX
A PUZZLE FOR ARISTOTLE AND O'BRIEN

Had the circumstances been less distracting, (and he more of a metaphysician), the following train of thought might have occurred to Winston. The problem arises for anyone who accepts the starred group (see p. 195) of truth-value links but denies the timelessness of truth. The following formulation is directed specifically against Aristotelian neutralism concerning the future.

The neutralist holds that it may happen that, where *Fut*:S is a sentence concerning events at some future time, t_2,

1 What *Fut*:S expresses at t_1 (now) is not true at t_1,

But

2 What S – its present tense transform – will express at t_2 will be true at t_2.

12 For one unresolved doubt about their coherence, see the Appendix to this essay. I am grateful to Christopher Peacocke for helpful comments on an earlier draft of this essay, and to the audience at Leicester for some perceptive questions.

Now since the time at which (2) is assumed to hold is t_1, there should be no objection to rendering that explicit:

3 What (2) expresses at t_1 is true at t_1.

Moreover (2) is uniformly future-tense. So link (B*) permits the inference from (3) to the conclusion that there is a future t such that what the present-tense transform of (2) will express at t is true at t_1. Explicitly

4 What 'What S expresses at t_2 is true at t_2' will express at t is true at t_1.

Notice that (4) defies construal unless $t = t_2$, since its quoted ingredient is uniformly present-tense. And now suppose

5 What *Fut*:S expresses at t_1 coincides with what S will express at t_2.

This is an example of the kind of supposition, identifying the content of appropriately differently tensed assertions made at different times, which retaining the starred truth-value links was aimed at conserving our right to make. It and (1) conjointly entail

6 What S will express at t_2 is not true at t_1.

Now intuitively the affirmation of a sentence at any time should have the same truth-value as the affirmation, at that time, that what that sentence then expresses is then true. So affirming S at t_2 should have the same truth-value as affirming 'What S expresses at t_2 is true at t_2'. Hence, it seems, it should be possible to substitute the latter for 'S' in (6) *salva veritate*. The result is

7 What 'What S expresses at t_2 is true at t_2' will express at t_2 is not true at t_1,

which, on the assumption that $t = t_2$, contradicts (4).

I do not know how this reasoning should best be responded to. It seems unlikely that the trouble can lie with the assumption that $t = t_2$. A better thought might seem to be that, when truth-values are temporally unstable, sameness of truth-value may be also; and hence that the material equivalence at t_2 of the contents,

What S will express at t_2, and
What 'What S expresses at t_2 is true at t_2' will express at t_2,

– which is indeed intuitively compelling – need carry no implication of their equivalence at t_1. But – granting, as is necessary, if this thought is to be coherent, that the two contents are distinct – which of them, in that case, has changed its truth-value between t_1 and t_2, and why?

Inserting indices in an intuitively obvious way, the challenge posed is to provide a well-motivated explanation of which values for n, given fixed m, will conserve the material equivalence of

'S'$_{t_m}$ is true$_{t_n}$

and

'"S"$_{t_m}$ is true$_{t_m}$'$_{t_m}$ is true$_{t_n}$.

Not all values of n can do so, it seems, once timelessness is rejected, so long as the starred truth-value links are retained.

In order to present a version of the argument better suited to O'Brien's views about the past, rather than to neutralism concerning the future, Winston could have proceeded from

1′ What S expresses at t_1 (now) is true at t_1,

and

2′ What *Past*:S will express at t_2 will not be true at t_2.

As the reader may verify, matters then proceed in much the same way; a small difference is that problems ensue not in the form of contradictory claims about the truth-value of some sentence at t_1 but in the form that contradictory sentences are both claimed to be true at t_1. (Whether Winston would have been wise to raise the matter is another question.)

6

Theories of Meaning and Speakers' Knowledge

This paper is concerned with recent – 1970s – trends and emphases in British philosophy of language, particularly as practised in Oxford. The question, what form should be assumed by a satisfactory theory of meaning for a natural language, quite suddenly came to seem absolutely fundamental, with the most comprehensive philosophical insights at stake. My concern here, however, is not to survey that issue, or to comment on the general significance it was (and still is) widely believed to have, but to explore certain assumptions which those who led opposite sides in the debate – principally Professors Davidson and Dummett – seem to have had in common: assumptions whose correctness is arguably not just essential for the philosophical significance – even a fairly local philosophical significance – of a 'theory of meaning' but is tacitly presupposed by the greater part of all philosophical semantic endeavour.

I

Davidson's proposal[1] that a theory of meaning for a natural language should take the form of a recursive truth definition in the style which Tarski devised for certain formal languages is opposed, or qualified, by Dummett in three principal respects. First, such a theory could be at best the core of a fully fledged theory of meaning; it would need to be embedded within a theory of *force*, a theory concerned with the difference between assertion, command, question, wish and other modes of illocution, and which made plain how these different types of speech act were signalled in the language

1 The *locus classicus* is his 'Truth and Meaning'. The paper is reprinted as Essay 2 in his *Inquiries into Truth and Interpretation*. His book, and especially the section consisting of the first five essays, is pervaded by the proposal.

under study.[2] Second, whereas Davidson seems content, in the case where the language in which the theory is formulated includes as a proper part the language theorized about, that the theory should be *homophonic* – that is, that the form taken by its meaning-delivering theorems should involve *use* of the very sentences whose meaning is being characterized – Dummett requires that the theory should be *full-blooded*, that it should, where possible, analyse and illuminate meanings.[3] Third, Dummett has disputed Davidson's choice of truth as the central notion in terms of which an account of meaning should be given: if what the theory says about any particular sentence aspires to be what anyone familiar with the meaning of that sentence knows, there are 'anti-realist' arguments, made familiar by Dummett, why it cannot in general suffice for the theory to assign truth-conditions to sentences.[4]

These are substantial differences. But they all concern what Dummett sees as deficiencies in the *output* of a theory of the projected kind – the first two being deficiencies of omission, while the third, though absolutely fundamental at the level of interpretation, may require no substantial alteration of the form of a Davidsonian theory. Dummett's criticism does not express any antagonism to Davidson's overall project; indeed, the points of agreement seem more striking than the disagreements. Davidson intends that a theory of truth is acceptable as a theory of meaning only if

i it is finitely axiomatizable and
ii it delivers a T-theorem for each declarative sentence of the object language in a manner that reflects the semantic structure discerned in that sentence.[5]

Why should the theory be finitely axiomatizable? Different passages in Davidson's writings suggest slightly different answers. Sometimes the thought is that understanding a language involves the capacity to make

2 See e.g. M. Dummett, 'What is a Theory of Meaning? (II)', pp. 72–6 and passim.

3 See M. Dummett, 'What is a Theory of Meaning?', pp. 102–6 and passim.

4 These arguments are widespread in Dummett's writings. See especially 'What is a Theory of Meaning? (II)' and Essays 1, 10, 11, 14 and 21 in his *Truth and Other Enigmas*. Note, however, page xxii of the latter's Preface where Dummett expresses dissatisfaction with the idea that the anti-realist arguments must call in question the propriety of truth-conditional theories of meaning, suggesting instead that their bearing is on the proper interpretation of *truth*. Cf. Essay 14 of this volume.

5 See the indexed references under *finiteness requirement* in *Inquiries into Truth and Interpretation*, and pp. 56–7 (of Essay 4, 'Semantics for Natural Languages') which the indexer missed. For those quite innocent of these matters, the 'T-theorems' take the form illustrated by

'Snow is white' is true if and only if snow is white,

whereby the quoted sentence is used to characterize its own truth-conditions and hence – controversially – its own meaning.

sense of no end of distinct expressions, and that this (potential) infinity contrasts sharply with the finitude of our capacities in general (most relevantly, presumably, the finitude of our capacities for information storage). A finitely based theory of meaning of the sort he is recommending will, Davidson believes, give us an insight into

> ...how an infinite aptitude can be encompassed by finite accomplishments.[6]

A neighbouring but distinct point is that if a language admits of characterization by a finitely based Davidsonian theory, then we have an insight into how the language can be learnable.[7] The point is distinct because creatures with infinite capacities for information storage but no other infinitary abilities could only learn finitely much in a finite time. Finally, not quite the same thought as either of these is the idea that:

> Speakers of a language can effectively determine the meaning or meanings of an arbitrary expression (if it has a meaning) and...it is the central task of a theory of meaning to show how this is possible.[8]

The theory of meaning is thus to contribute towards the explanation of how speakers can understand sentences which are novel to them. This thought is different because the question would arise – if it is a good question at all – for infinite creatures too, and for finite languages which, while semantically structured, possess no indefinitely iterable devices of the sort which generate a potential infinity of meaningful sentences.

However, the marginal distinctions among the questions, 'How can finite minds have infinite abilities?', 'How can languages be learnable?', 'How can speakers determine the meanings of novel utterances?', are not important. What is important is that the capacity of Davidsonian theory to assist in the provision of answers to any of them requires that it be admissible to think of actual speakers as equipped with the information codified in the axioms of a successful Davidsonian theory, and as prone to deploy that information in ways reflected by the derivations of meaning-delivering theorems afforded by the theory. Whether the theory aspires to cast light on *our* ability, finite as we are, to master a potentially infinite language, or *our* ability to complete the learning of the language, or on *our* ability to understand novel utterances, or on all three, success must depend, it seems, on its being permissible to suppose that it encodes information which *we* actually possess.

If Davidson is somewhat inexplicit about this, Dummett is not. A very definite commitment to the idea that the explanatory ambitions of a theory

6 *Inquiries into Truth and Interpretation*, Essay 1 ('Theories of Meaning and Learnable Languages'), p. 8.
7 See e.g. 'Truth and Meaning', opening paragraph.
8 *Inquiries into Truth and Interpretation*, Essay 2 ('Truth and Meaning'), p. 35.

of meaning depend upon recourse to some idea of speakers' *implicit knowledge* of its axiomatic contents is evinced in his writings on the topic. For instance:

> A theory of meaning will, then, represent the practical ability possessed by a speaker as consisting in his grasp of a set of propositions; since the speaker derives his understanding of a sentence from the meanings of its component words, these propositions will most naturally form a deductively connected system. The knowledge of these propositions that is attributed to a speaker can only be an implicit knowledge. In general, it cannot be demanded of someone who has any given practical ability that he have more than an implicit knowledge of those propositions by means of which we give a theoretical representation of that ability.[9]

In an earlier paper, Dummett refers to

> ...our intuitive conviction that a speaker derives his understanding of a sentence from his understanding of the words composing it and the way they are put together.[10]

and relates Davidsonian theory to this intuitive conviction by the remark that:

> What plays the role, within a theory of meaning of Davidson's kind, of a grasp of the meanings of the words is a knowledge of the axioms governing these words.[11]

Further:

> It is one of the merits of a theory of meaning which represents mastery of a language as the knowledge not of isolated, but of deductively interconnected propositions, that it makes due acknowledgement of the undoubted fact that a process of derivation of some kind is involved in the understanding of a sentence.[12]

For Dummett, the explanatory ambitions of a theory of meaning would seem to be entirely dependent upon the permissibility of thinking of speakers of its object language as knowing the propositions which its axioms codify and of their deriving their understanding of (novel) sentences in a manner mirrored by the derivation, in the theory, of the appropriate theorems.

There is accordingly a case for saying that, whatever their differences, Dummett and Davidson are in broad agreement about the interest of the project of a theory of meaning of this sort, and about the manner in which such a theory needs to be interpreted if it is to sustain that interest; and that they share a broad, underlying assumption about the nature of

9 'What is a Theory of Meaning? (II)', p. 70.
10 'What is a Theory of Meaning?', p. 109.
11 Ibid.
12 Ibid., p. 112.

linguistic competence, viz, that it is fruitfully to be compared – at least in its basics – to any open-ended computational ability which – like, say, the ability to do simple arithmetical multiplications – deploys finite information in rule-prescribed ways. The difference is just that the knowledge which constitues understanding of a language is gained, for the most part, not from an explicit statement – in contrast, e.g. with the multiplication tables, or the rules of chess – but by immersion in the practice of speaking the language in question.

That we understand novel utterances because we understand the words in them and significance of the way in which they are put together is apt to strike one as a platitude. But it is no platitude that the sort of project which Dummett, explicitly, and Davidson, implicitly, seem to have in view makes philosophical sense. If the gap is not immediately apparent, it ought to suffice to reflect that the platitude need only be regarded as describing a feature of the 'grammar' of *misunderstanding*: nobody may properly be described as misunderstanding a sentence unless guilty of some more specific misunderstanding, either of words deployed within it or of its syntax. Contraposing, we have the incontestable claim that if someone understands the vocabulary and syntax of a significant sentence, then they understand the (type) sentence. Platitude is left behind when the antecedent of this conditional is taken to describe an ulterior state of information which *enables* a subject to understand the sentence.

This paper is concerned with a number of interconnected questions. Let us say that a theory is *compositional* just in case it meets the two Davidsonian constraints, (i) and (ii), noted above. Section II is concerned with the question whether there can be any good motive for insisting on compositionality in theories of meaning which *avoids* recourse to the idea of actual speakers' implicit knowledge. Baker and Hacker[13] have recently described Davidson's comparative inexplicitness on the topic as 'artful' – their thought being, I imagine, that, for the sort of reason outlined above, the questions on which Davidson hopes for illumination cannot be answered by Davidsonian theorizing unless implicit knowledge is invoked, but that Davidson has preferred not to elaborate on the issue, perceiving it for the Pandora's Box which they believe it to be. However that may be, it is important to be clear whether, besides the three mentioned, there is any different question, not directly concerned with the capacities of actual speakers, which devising a compositional theory of meaning might help to answer. Only if there is not is there any danger, should it emerge that there is absolutely nothing to be made of the notion of implicit knowledge, that Davidson's project will prove to have been a waste of time. Section III then takes up the question, what, if any, defensible conception of

13 Baker and Hacker, *Language, Sense and Nonsense*, p. 324.

implicit knowledge may be attained? Is there cause for confidence that a notion can be made good which is apt to allow a compositional theory to be explanatory of actual speakers' capacities?

If no suitable notion of implicit knowledge can be extricated, it naturally occurs to one to wonder how that leaves matters with the realism/anti-realism dispute in the theory of meaning. For the essence of the most influential anti-realist critique of classical semantics is exactly that it cannot be a theory of speakers' understanding: that it places impossible demands on the range of what speakers may reasonably be regarded as (implicitly) knowing. The anti-realist charge is that if 'truth' is understood as the realist intends, there is, in an important class of cases, no such thing as knowing the truth-conditions of a sentence. If this is to be a criticism of realist semantics, it is essential that understanding may be regarded as a species of knowledge. And it is obvious that if it may, it cannot *everywhere* consist in *explicit* knowledge. The ability to paraphrase a sentence is a (defeasible) ground for crediting somebody with understanding it, but it is not an ability which we have for a large class of sentences which we think we understand, (and our language might, in any case, have been such as to contain the resources for no such paraphrase.) Accordingly, if understanding is knowledge at all, the kind of knowledge it *essentially* is must, it seems, be implicit. An important argument running through Dummett's writings[14] is exactly that only an anti-realist theory of meaning can sustain the demands made on the notion of implicit knowledge which, as we have seen, he believes that the theory of meaning must make. Section IV will contend that the anti-realist critique is not undermined by the worries about the notion of implicit knowledge whose well-foundedness there is most cause to suspect.

II

Doubts about the notion of implicit knowledge have surfaced frequently in the literature, even in the writings of those sympathetic to the spirit of the Davidsonian project. John Foster, for instance, writes

> ...having seen the generality of the theory required, we may wonder whether we should ascribe it to the speaker at all. The knowledge we would have to attribute to him is not, typically, what he would attribute to himself. His mastery of English equips him to interpret its expressions, but not to state the general principles to which these interpretations conform. Is it not

14 See footnote 4 above.

> unnatural, even incoherent, to ascribe states of knowledge to which the subject himself has no conscious access?[15]

But Foster believes that the issue can be side-stepped:

> ...we can capture all that matters to the philosophy of meaning by putting the original project the other way round. Rather than ask for a statement of the knowledge implicit in linguistic competence, let us ask for a statement of a theory whose knowledge would suffice for such competence. Instead of demanding a statement of those metalinguistic facts which the mastery of a language implicitly recognises, let us demand a statement of those facts explicit recognition of which gives mastery. What we are then demanding is still a theory of meaning, but without the questionable assumption that one who has mastered the language has, at some deep level, absorbed the information which it supplies. The theory reveals the semantic machinery which competence works, but leaves undetermined the psychological form in which competence exists.[16]

There are two thoughts here. First, there is the idea that the quest for a theory of meaning does not need to be motivated by the desire to understand the capacities of actual speakers of a given language. It is enough, in Foster's view, that we seek to describe knowledge which *would* generate those capacities, whether or not it is the source of actual speakers' possession of them. If it is wondered why we should seek to do that, Foster's answer seems to be, second, that what the theorist of meaning is interested in is primarily *the way the language works*. While we should not, perhaps despair of the possibility that the theory might illuminate the 'psychological form' of actual speakers' linguistic competence, the primary object is to describe the 'semantic machinery' which drives the language.

The trouble with this is that the demands which Foster is making of the notion of meaning – the demands implicit in the image of 'semantic machinery' – threaten no less conceptual strain than the demands on the notion of knowledge – those generated by its qualification as 'implicit' – which he is trying to avoid. The intuitive response to Foster's proposal would be that it generates an intolerable divide between the concepts of meaning and understanding: truths about meaning have to be, ultimately, constituted by facts about understanding, so to aspire to a theory which aims to describe 'semantic machinery' independently of any assumption about what speakers of the language know is to aspire to a theory with no proper subject matter.[17]

15 From his 'Meaning and Truth Theory', pp. 1–2.

16 Ibid., p. 2.

17 Compare the 'metaphysical perspective' of Elizabeth Fricker's, 'Semantic Structure and Speakers' Understanding', section I.

This response may involve over-simplification – depending on how 'ultimately' is understood – but it has great force, it seems to me, at the level of semantic primitives: expressions whose meanings are independent of the meanings of all other expressions of the language except those of which they are constituents, and to which a Davidsonian theory would devote its proper axioms. I do not think we can attach any content to the supposition that such an expression has a meaning except in so far as meaning is thought of as constituted, at least in part, by *convention*; and I do not think we can attain an account of the distinction between a convention and a corresponding regularity except by invoking the idea of practitioners' *intention*, qualified in various ways, to uphold that regularity. If both these, admittedly very vague, thoughts are correct, then the proper standing of the axioms of a theory of meaning must, it would seem, be grounded in speakers' intentions; and Foster's apparent belief that the theory can have an autonomous subject matter is of doubtful coherence.

There is another objection, perhaps less fundamental but more immediately clinically fatal. The fact is that there seems to be no necessary connection between Foster's recommendation that the theory should describe information which *would* suffice for mastery of a given, typical natural language and the constraints of compositionality. Or better: there seems to be no such connection in the case on which Davidsonians typically concentrate – the homophonic case. If one is aiming at construction of a heterophonic theory – whether because the object-language is quite different from that in which the theory is to be couched, or because one is aiming at a high degree of *full-bloodedness* in Dummett's sense – it may very well be that there is no way of completing Foster's task unless one aims for compositionality; that no other approach can effectively provide meaning-delivering theorems for every declarative sentence in the object-language. In the homophonic case matters stand differently. Provided we have a recursive specification of the syntax of the (declarative part of the) language, and provided we are content with the disquotational form of meaning-delivering theorem for which theories of truth are famous, Foster's project is well enough served by a semantic 'theory' which merely stipulates as an axiom every instance of the schema:

A is T if and only if P,

where 'P' may be replaced by any declarative sentence of the object language and 'A' by the quotational name of that sentence. This theory is not finitely axiomatized, but it is finitely *stated* and, in conjunction with the appropriate recursive syntax, it does yield the means for effectively arriving at a meaning-delivering theorem – assuming we have no independent reservations about truth theories on that score – for each declarative sentence in the object-language. It thus fits Foster's bill: it describes information whose possession would suffice for mastery of the (declarative part of the) object-language. At least, it does so provided a compositional Davidsonian theory whose T-theorematic output coincided with the axioms of this theory would do so. It is true, of course, that the non-compositional theory could not be used to *impart* this information to someone who did not already have it – but then no homophonic theory, whether compositional or not, fairs better in that regard. The moral is simple: the ambition to describe information which would suffice for mastery of a particular language may impose certain constraints on the form taken by the theorems of a theory of meaning, but it imposes no interesting constraints on the mechanics of the theory.

We are looking for a project whose execution would call for a compositional theory of meaning but which would not demand that actual speakers be deemed to know the full contents of that theory. Foster's thought, in effect, was to idealize the language with a view to a theory of how *it*, autonomously, works. A quite different thought would aim to see compositionality as called for by the ambition to describe not some body of knowledge which speakers putatively have but what they are typically able *to do*. Suppose we essay to regard each of the T-theorems of a Davidsonian theory as descriptive of a sub-competence which someone who fully understands the object language has: a sub-competence constituted by sensitivity, in using the relevant sentence, to the constraint which the appropriate T-theorem captures. Have we completely described the general competence in which mastery of the (declarative part of the) relevant language consists when we have a theory which correctly describes all these sub-competences? There is a prima facie persuasive reason why we should ask for more. No matter what ability we are concerned to describe, and however complete our characterization of its ingredient abilities, the description is incomplete if the ingredients have certain causal interrelations about which it keeps silence. Someone who has a strong tennis game may have a good drive, a good lob, and a good slice on his backhand wing; but a *full* description of his skills would not restrict itself to the statement that each of these strokes is dependable if, let us suppose, the lob and the drive – when, unusually, either is fragile – tend to break down together, although the slice tends to remain a strong shot even when the rest of his game is off-colour. So with the theory of meaning: a full description of the competence possessed by speakers should not merely characterize its ingredients but ought also to reflect their (causal inter-relations. This may inspire what Martin Davies[18] calls the *Mirror Constraint*. Suppose it is true of speakers (a) that once they know what

18 Martin Davies, *Meaning, Quantification, Necessity*, chapter III, p. 53 and following.

$S_1,\ldots,S_n$ mean, they are able to know what the distinct sentence, S, means without any further exposure to the use of the language; and (b) that if induced to revise their belief about what S means, they would need no further inducement to revise their beliefs about what some of $S_1,\ldots,S_n$ mean. Then the Mirror Constraint says simply that if, and only if, speakers' sub-competences with S, $S_1,\ldots,S_n$ are so interrelated, an adequate theory of meaning for their language should ensure that those of its resources which suffice for the derivation of meaning-delivering theorems for each of $S_1,\ldots,S_n$ should also suffice for the derivation of such a theorem for S.[19] A theory which satisfies the Mirror Constraint will thus be one whose deductive structure reflects the (causal) interrelations among speakers' sub-competences. When speakers are able to move to understanding of a novel utterance without special explanation, the theory will mirror their ability by supplying the means for deriving an appropriate theorem utilizing only axioms adequate for the specification of the meanings of sentences which they previously understood; and when speakers change their beliefs about the meaning of some sentence, appropriate modifications to the meaning-delivering theorem for that sentence will enjoin revisions in its axiomatic parentage which in turn entail shifts of meaning in exactly those sentences of which they consequentially change their understanding.

Davies himself raises various objections to the Mirror Constraint.[20] But he does not raise what I think is the most serious: that it provides no real reason for putting structure into a *semantic* theory. Let it be granted that the interrelations of competence whose reflection the Mirror Constraint seeks to ensure are worth describing. Still, why not describe them directly – why run the dogleg of having them 'reflected' in the deductive articulation of a theory of meaning? There is nothing to prevent a critic of the Mirror Constraint from taking over the syntax and catalogue of semantic primitives incorporated in a theory of meaning which satisfies it. He may then advance a theory of meaning of the infinitary sort canvassed above, adding only a rider to the effect that speakers are generally able to understand novel sentences, provided they involve only familiar semantic primitives, and that changes in their semantic beliefs about a sentence tend to be associated with changes in their semantic beliefs about *all* sentences – or at least all about which they have any such belief – containing some one or more of the semantic primitives figuring in that sentence. Admittedly, such a rider would not be a detailed, or

19 This does not coincide exactly with Davies' formulation, but differs, I believe, in no important respect.

20 For instance, that the constraint provides no guidance to the semantic theorist if the studied language has no actual speakers; and leaves no space for the idea that speakers might fail to know the meanings of sentences which are nevertheless determinate, fixed by syntactic constructions and semantic features familiar to them.

axiomatic, description of the interrelations which the Mirror Constraint would have a theory of meaning reflect. But there is every reason to think that the recursive *syntax* which the theorist adjoins to his infinitary semantic theory would supply the materials for the more specific descriptive task. He needs only to ensure that the syntax itself meets the Mirror Constraint: that when, and only when, speakers' understanding of $S_1,...,S_n$ and S are interrelated as described, those ingredients in the axiomatic bases and set of recursions for the syntax which suffice to characterize each of $S_1,...,S_n$ as well-formed suffice so to characterize S.

There is a different line of thought in Davies' discussion which seems more promising. It depends upon our being willing to entertain the idea that there is an admixture of rational inductive and deductive inference which can take a subject from knowledge of the meanings of a finite set of sentences to knowledge of the meaning of a sentence which is not in that set and is novel to him. It is, Davies writes,

> ...the possibility of self-conscious, reflective projection of meanings which encourages the attempt to provide a theory of meaning which not only delivers the correct meaning specifications but also reveals how the meanings of sentences depend upon the recurrence of particular syntactic constituents...[21]

Davies proceeds to propose what he calls the *Structural Constraint*: in effect, that if, but only if, it would be possible for someone who knew what $S_1,...,S_n$ each mean to proceed, by rational inductive and deductive methods and without further empirical investigation, to knowledge of what S means, the smallest set of axiomatic resources which suffice, in a theory of meaning for the language in question, to furnish meaning-delivering theorems for each of $S_1,...,S_n$ should also yield a meaning-delivering theorem for S. The effect of this constraint is that compositionality in a theory of meaning is demanded not by characteristics of actual speakers qua actual speakers but by the nature of an idealized epistemology of understanding. Whatever actual speakers do or do not know, it seems highly plausible that there is such a thing, in certain cases, as rational inference from knowledge of the meanings of the sentences in a particular set to knowledge of the meaning of a sentence outside that set: the cases in question are precisely those where, intuitively, the semantically contributive vocabulary and syntax of the new sentence are all variously on display among the sentences in the set. The effect of the Structural Constraint is that a satisfactory theory of meaning should mirror not the propensities for meaning-projection and revision of actual speakers but those of an ideal speaker, whose every semantic belief is informed by self-conscious rational inductive and deductive inference.

21 Davies, *Meaning, Quantification, Necessity*, p. 56.

In fact it seems reasonable to demand more. A satisfactory theory of meaning should not merely 'reflect' the path that will be taken by the ideal speaker, by discerning structure whenever he discerns structure, but should represent the inferences which he would – or could, qua rational – actually draw. Thus whenever he is able to advance to knowledge of the meaning of S from knowledge of the meanings of $S_1,\ldots,S_n$, the latter knowledge should constitute good evidence for the truth of those axioms in the theory needed to derive the meaning-delivering theorem for S; and the movement up, as it were, to the axioms and then down to that theorem ought to be the very movement which knowledge of the meanings of $S_1,\ldots,S_n$ is deemed to put a rational speaker in position to make. It is not completely clear whether Davies has this stronger interpretation of the Structural Constraint in mind. But it seems to be more satisfactory. The weaker interpretation is apt to make the constraint seem somewhat arbitrary: what question, exactly, would the theory of meaning have to be addressed to in order for it to be necessary that it discerns semantic structure in a group of sentences when and only when the ideal speaker would 'project' amongst them but not necessary that it represent inferential moves which he could, qua ideal, actually make? Under the stronger interpretation, however, the overriding question is clear. It is: granted that it is possible for a speaker to know, or at least to form rational beliefs, about the meanings of utterances whose use he has never witnessed, how in detail might this be possible?

This has to be a good question unless we are utterly sceptical about whether there is ever any *rational* route to an understanding of novel utterances. The project of trying to answer it has the interest that attaches to any programme of reconstructive analytic epistemology. Such projects have been a major current in the history of English-speaking philosophy: whether motivated by sceptical challenges or not, philosophers have repeatedly been drawn to the task of trying to explain how statements of some particular sort – about God, or the material world, or other minds, for instance – *could* be susceptible to rational cognition (even if our practice is to rely upon criteria of acceptability which fall far short of it). Admittedly, the sceptic about meaning is a somewhat recent entry on the philosophical scene; the project of constructing theories of meaning of the sort we are interested in did not originate as a response to sceptical pressure, and the various forms of scepticism about meaning which have comparatively recently come into prominence in any case concern more basic matters than knowledge of the meaning of novel utterances. Still, the possibility of such knowledge provides the material for a perfectly familiar species of analytical enquiry.

That is the principal of recommendation of this section. There *is* a recognizably *philosophical* project – at least it ought to be recognizable to anyone educated in the twentieth-century Anglo-American philosophical tradition – to which constructing a formal theory of meaning would be a contribution. This project has no immediate connections with the quest to explain the capacities of actual speakers of natural languages; the task to which a completed, adequate theory of meaning would contribute would rather be that of explaining how a complete knowledge of a particular natural language could be a rational achievement. We have no conception of how that might be so unless the rational subject is permitted to discern sub-sentential semantic structure. It follows that such a theory would have to comply with the second ingredient condition of compositionality, as characterized above, that the meaning-delivering theorems for sentences be derived within the theory in a manner which reflects the semantic contribution made by those sentences' constituents. The need for the first ingredient, that the axiomatic basis be finite, is less immediate: it is not evident that a rational being could not be in possession of infinitely many logically independent items of information. But it may be anticipated that if we are concerned with the powers of an ideally rational *human* speaker – so that the finitude of our capacities remains a constraint on the form which the theory should take – the *learnability* of the language – the possibility of a finite but rational creature coming to know the meaning of any particular sentence of it by way of exposure to and projection from the use of finitely many other sentences – will require that only a finitely axiomatized theory will fit the bill.[22]

Whatever we conclude, then, about the capacity of a formal theory of meaning to be yoked to the task of explaining actual speakers' abilities, there is an interpretation of the Davidson/Dummett project which promises to allow it to stand independently as legitimate a priori philosophy. This interpretation may or may not accord with part of the intentions of the leading protagonists in the field. But it does to contrive to supply, after all, some sense for Foster's notion that a natural language might have the sort of autonomy which would allow its theoretical description not to be directly a theory about actual speakers' semantic knowledge; and it suggests, in consequence, how the disinfection of the concept of implicit knowledge need not be a precondition for the philosophical health of the project of constructing theories of meaning.[23]

22 Davies shows, in fact, that on natural assumptions about what is requisite for the learnability of a language, the Structural Constraint enjoins that a theory satisfying it will indeed be finitely axiomatized. See *Meaning, Quantification, Necessity*, chapter III, section 2.

23 One important reservation about the proposal would concern whether knowledge of the meanings of an appropriate $S_1,\ldots,S_n$ could be enjoyed *independently* of knowledge of the meaning of an S to which, according to the sought-for theory, a rational projection from an understanding of $S_1,\ldots,S_n$ would be possible. The opposing thought, urged on me in discussion by Elizabeth Fricker and suggested by some of the argumentation in her 'Semantic

III

In order for a theory of meaning to be explanatory of the linguistic capacities of actual speakers, there has to be, it seems, a sense in which its axioms are true of them; or, at least, there have to be properties of the speakers for whose description the axioms are needed. It would be an error to suppose that the notion that speakers *implicitly know* the content of such a set of axioms is the only way of meeting this condition. It is evidently a tempting and natural suggestion – witness the widespread use of such ideas in the writings of theoretical linguists. But it is exceedingly difficult to be clear whether it is ultimately coherent.

The most immediate objection is based on the thought that the axioms of a theory of meaning ought to correspond to semantic *rules*. To amplify: such an axiom is supposed to describe the semantically relevant features of an expression; how could it do that if it failed to embody a condition on the correct use of that expression? For the meaning of an expression is essentially something normative; it is, crudely, only because expressions have meaning that there is such a thing as correct, or incorrect, use of them. This normativity does not *per se* conflict with the capacity of the theory to contribute towards the explanation of speakers' linguistic 'creativity' – their capacity to understand novel utterances; the proposal will be that the feature of a speaker which such an axiom can reflect is

---

Structure and Speakers' Meaning' (see in particular section IV), would be, in effect, that understanding any such S is a *criterion* for knowing the meanings of $S_1,\ldots,S_n$. Whereas the project of describing a basis for a rational inference to the meaning of S has content only if it is possible to be apprised of the basis and yet fail so to exploit it.

Clearly there is no objection of this kind where we are concerned with a *second* language: of course it is possible for an English speaker to know *what* each of finitely many French sentences means without having any idea *why*. The question is whether that distinction, between knowing what a sentence means and why it means it, has content for a first language – can there be such a thing as understanding a sentence of one's only language without understanding its semantic structure? It seems we would have to deny that there can if an explanation is to be possible of why – supposing it is so – sentence understanding has the sort of holistic character claimed by the objection. But notice, in that case, that we should then have a quite different form of response to the problem of motivating compositionality. A homphonic theory consisting of a recursive syntax plus an infinitary semantic axiom schema, or – for a finite language – a 'listiform' theory consisting simply of specifications of the meanings of all its sentences, would no longer have a claim to characterize what someone who understood the object-language thereby knew. At least, it would not do so with sufficient explicitness: a fully explicit account would have to contain the resources for describing, for each object-language sentence, not merely what it meant but why it meant it.

A fully satisfactory treatment of our topic would have to investigate this through to a conclusion. But I have felt justified in not attempting this here, because of the prospect that the objection, if sustained, would still conserve an a priori motive for compositionality.

precisely his knowledge of it. If we are given, for instance, a statement of the powers of the pieces in chess, there is no tension about supposing that it may serve both to articulate the norms determining what is and is not a legal move and to contribute towards the explanation of players' capacity to recognize the legality/illegality of moves which they have not previously encountered. The double function is secured by the bridging assumption that the players recognize exactly the rules which the statement describes. The salient point is therefore the need for a bridging assumption which hypothesizes practitioners' recognition of the set of norms which the axioms describe.

So what is the objection? Well, if something like a Davidsonian theory is indeed possible for English, it is a mighty iceberg about whose overall shape we have very little idea. We know that it would be a theory of great complexity which would impose a good deal of regimentation on the surface grammar of our language. The handling of tense, adverbs, predicate modifiers, modality, intentionality and even quantifiers are all controversial topics. The tendency, understandably, among researchers in the field has been to stay close to the Tarskian prototype and to the syntax of predicate calculus. But while interesting work has been done, even the most committed would have to allow that progress towards realization of the grand design has not been spectacular. Accordingly, someone who believes that English, or at least a good deal of it, does indeed admit of complete semantic description by means of a compositional formal theory would at present be hard pressed to justify a high degree of confidence that work has proceeded along the right sort of lines, or has been inspired by the most fruitful paradigms. In other words, apart from knowing that it will be difficult to design, will be complex of articulation and is likely to contain at present unforeseen devices, we have *very little* idea what a formal theory of meaning for a natural language of expressive power comparable to that of English would be like. Yet it is the axioms of such a theory which the implicit knowledge proposal would have us regard as *normative* with respect to our linguistic practice. Are there not manifest philosophical difficulties with the idea that our linguistic behaviour should be regarded as informed by our recognition of principles which we cannot state, which played no explicit part in our linguistic training, which will probably involve concepts of great sophistication and technicality, and which we might not recognize even if presented with a formulation? How can a principle function as a rule if those who engage in the practice which it is supposed to regulate have no consciousness of it?

Dummett writes:

> What plays the role, within a theory of meaning of Davidson's kind, of a grasp of the meanings of the words is a knowledge of the axioms governing

> those words: in our example [that of 'the earth moves'] these may be stated as '"the earth" denotes the earth' and 'it is true to say of something "it moves" if and only if that thing moves'. (This latter formulation of the axiom governing 'moves' is stated without appeal to the technical device of satisfaction by an infinite sequence, and is only an approximate indication of what is wanted: but, if we are intending a serious representation of what is known by anyone able to speak English, we cannot literally credit him with an understanding of that technical device.)[24]

We can sympathize with Dummett's reservations: it is a plausible enough constraint upon the significant attribution of belief, *a fortiori* of knowledge, that a subject possesses the concepts which figure in the content of the belief attributed to him, and it is utterly implausible that ordinary speakers of English should be credited with an understanding, at any level, of concepts like satisfaction, infinite sequence and the star functor. But Dummett's thought here is vulnerable to a simple dilemma. If this sort of technical apparatus is necessary for the development of a theory of meaning for a typical natural language, then speakers may not, on his own admission, be credited with a full implicit knowledge of that theory but only, perhaps, of a part of it; and the claims of the theory to provide a model of how speakers actually achieve an understanding of novel utterances must therefore be severely qualified. If, on the other hand, the technical apparatus is merely a convenience, an explanation is owing of how it may be dispensed with and the axiomatic and recursive basis of the theory developed purely in terms of concepts whose attribution to speakers is altogether more plausible. The promise of a thory of meaning to illuminate actual speakers' linguistic 'creativity' will then depend entirely on the success of this explanation – an explanation which we have, so far, not the slightest idea how to construct.

It will be apparent that there are two special and separate difficulties here which vindication of the notion of implicit knowledge in general would not necessarily resolve. There is the problem of explaining how a *rule* can be implicitly known, how, that is, it can function as a rule – exert a regulative influence – if practitioners are unaware of it. And there is the problem of how contents, putatively implicitly known, may involve concepts for their possessing which there is no direct evidence in practitioners' performance and which may, indeed, be sufficiently abstruse to be beyond their powers – at least their *apparent* powers – of comprehension. However I do not think that either problem is immediately fatal. It is true, of course, that a rule as a possible object of consultation has to be a possible object of consciousness. But it is perfectly obvious that the axioms of a homophonic theory of meaning are not meant to be rules in this

24 'What is a Theory of Meaning?', pp. 109–10.

sense since – because they use the expressions which they mention – only someone who already understood those expressions, and hence had no need to consult such 'rules', would be capable of consulting them. It does not follow that the axioms cannot be regarded as statements of rule at all, however. It would indeed be fatal to their claim to contain a theory of *meaning* if they could not. But the simple fact is that the characterization of a convention does not have to proceed in terms which could be used to explain the convention to someone previously ignorant of it. It is a convention of English that 'red' in its most basic, literal sense, is correctly predicated only of things which are red. Speakers of English who are credited with an understanding of 'red' in its most basic and literal sense are thereby credited, inter alia, with the intention to uphold this pattern of predication as a matter of convention. There is no better statement of the convention than the one I have given. And it is, at the same time, perfectly useless as an explanation of what the convention is to someone who doesn't already know it. The dilemma is therefore a false one: the axioms of a theory of meaning do not have to be explanatory, or 'objects of consultation', on pain of failing to concern meaning. It suffices that they describe linguistic conventions. And the question of speakers' implicit knowledge of them is thus, in effect, the question whether speakers may be regarded as implicitly recognizing the conventions which they state.

The proper analysis of the notion of convention is a subtle business.[25] It may be that the idea of a convention which is merely implicitly recognized would turn out to put the notion under great strain. But prima facie there seems no reason to expect so.[26] Whatever the details of a correct analysis, convention is going to turn out to supervene upon peoples' intentions, fundamentally the intention to uphold the regularity which the convention prescribes. The crucial question is therefore whether – whether or not they are, or can be brought to be, aware of it – the axioms and recursions of a theory of meaning might succeed in describing a set of linguistic constraints which competent speakers of English may be regarded as intending to uphold. If the answer is negative, the attempt to interpret the relation between speakers and an appropriate theory of meaning for their language as that of implicit knowledge must fail; but if affirmative, that interpretation has a chance of success. In any event it is to assail a man of straw to insist that the implicit knowledge theorist should explain how a principle can be actively regulative of a practice when none of the

25 The *locus classicus* is David Lewis's *Convention: a Philosophical Study*.

26 I intend no judgement, by this remark, about whether the very strong epistemic conditions involved in Lewis's original account *would* permit meaning-theoretic axioms of which subjects were unaware to encode conventions. But the crucial question is in any case that about intention to which the text now moves.

participants can profess to know it.[27] The issue rather concerns constraints on the ascription of intention. Does it make sense to ascribe intentions to people which they cannot articulate? Or intentions a correct description of which they cannot recognize when given it?

It is important to recognize that what is at issue here is not the propriety of *extending* the notion of intention so as to accommodate the implicit knowledge theorist's needs. If ordinary practice is to be the guide, it is clear that we *already* use intention, and cognate notions, in ways that can make his position seem quite natural. The attribution of intention is entailed whenever we credit a subject with agency; and we implicitly credit a subject with agency – the capacity for action, in the proper sense of the word – whenever we deem it appropriate to offer *rationalistic* explanations of its performance, explanations which proceed by the ascription of a system of beliefs and desires. Now the fact is – philosophically suspect, or not, as the practice may be – that we go in for simple rationalistic explanations of the behaviour of more intelligent animals. If a dog sets off from his home at roughly the same time each day, no one would think it outrageous to be offered the explanation that he expects his master to be returning home at about that time and wants to see him. Some philosophers (ironically enough, Davidson)[28] would argue that any rationalistic explanation of the behaviour of a languageless creature is misconceived. My point is only the descriptive one that such explanations are *commonplace*: in the above example, the dog is implicitly credited with the intention to intercept his master – an intention of which it can neither give nor recognize an adequate description.

Consider this case. It does not happen, but might, that small children could learn to play chess long before they could learn to understand speech – or at least to attain the level of understanding necessary to give or follow explicit descriptions of the rules of chess, or of points in the theory of the game, etc. They learn the moves, let us suppose, by just the sort of patient mixture of drill, demonstration and (inadvertent) reward by which any ordinary child learns the names for colours, or farmyard animals. And then, remarkably, some of them acquire the ability to play not merely legally but well, responding with subtlety and inventiveness to board configurations which they have never encountered before. It would be overwhelmingly natural to credit such children not merely with knowledge of the rules of chess but with the sort of insight into the potentialities of a situation which any good chess player possesses. It is, however, difficult to understand how such insight should be supposed to

27 One cause for complaint about Baker's and Hacker's *Language, Sense and Nonsense*, is their predilection for such opposition. There are other causes. See my review, 'Understanding Novel Utterances".

28 See 'Thought and Talk', Essay 11 of his *Inquiries into Truth and Interpretation.*

function if it is not essentially a faculty of *inference*: inference which goes to work on premises including, inter alia, the rules determining the powers of movement and capture of the various types of piece. It seems to me undeniable that, pre-philosophically as it were, we should be quite content to explain such childrens' performance by ascribing to them the knowledge and intentions constitutive of an understanding of, and the practice of playing by, the rules of chess; we would regard them as able to apprehend the implications of those rules for the potentialities of a particular state of play and thereby able to inform their selection of moves with the aim of winning, or at least avoiding defeat.

The parallel with the demands made by the implicit-knowledge interpretation of the theory of meaning, the speakers being credited with knowledge of the axioms and with the capacity to apprehend their more or less remote consequences, is obvious. Indeed the analogy may seem close enough to call the validity of what I have suggested would be our natural response to the hypothetical children into question. But to stress: my point is only that, whether or not the implicit-knowledge interpretation of the theory of meaning is ultimately coherent, the objection to it – for all we have so far seen, at least – ought not to be that it puts an impossible strain on our *ordinary* understanding of notions like knowledge, belief, intention, inference, etc. On the contrary, it is aspects of our ordinary understanding of those notions which make the implicit knowledge interpretation seem natural. If it is to be rejected, the prospect is thus not of excision of an unwarranted extension of our ordinary understanding but of revision of it.

The example of the dog is suggestive in a different way. Since Brentano, it has been the more or less received wisdom in the philosophy of mind that the truth-conditions of ascriptions of propositional attitude are indifferent to reference failure in the proposition in question, but sensitive to the intersubstitution of co-referential expressions. Whether or not these are genuinely semantic (contrast, pragmatic) phenomena, it is open to question whether either is a feature of the sorts of context in which we ascribe beliefs to, e.g. a dog. As far as indifference to existence is concerned, we go in for the ascription of propositional attitudes to animals only with a view to rationalizing, after a fashion, their modes of interaction with items which figure in their experience; since no non-existent items so figure, there is simply no explanatory role to be played by the ascription to them of attitudes to propositions which we can express only by recourse to empty singular terms.[29]

29 Any apparent counter-example to this claim is going to be controversial and marginal at best. One possibility: if humans, who share a magic mushroom, e.g., can co-hallucinate – 'Look at that little green man sitting by the window' – there might be circumstances in which a dog would best be described as e.g. barking at such a 'common object' of hallucination. But I can envisage no other circumstances in which we would have cause to use an empty singular term – rather than a quantifier – in ascribing an intentional state to an animal.

Inter-substitutivity is less straightforward. It is natural to report that the dog expects to see his master in the road, unnatural to report that he expects to see Joe Smith, or the high street newsagent. But the latter descriptions strike us as unacceptable only because we are unwilling to impute to the dog any conception of a personal proper name or the institution of newspaper selling. And the fact is that matters stand no better with the relevant concept *master*. A dog's master is, inter alia, ultimately responsible for its welfare and ultimately liable for its good conduct. He has the right to move it around (within, e.g. restrictions imposed by quarantine laws), and even to dispose of it. Does the dog know all that? There is a temptation to reply the dog has, as it were, a *thinner* conception of his master – one shorn of institutional trappings and based entirely on the history of interaction between them. I advise anyone who feels this temptation to attempt to specify this alleged conception, bearing in mind that the terms used must no way exceed the concepts which may plausibly be attributed to the dog. I do not anticipate success. The truth, I suggest, is that we have no definite idea what concept we are attributing to a dog in describing its behaviour in this sort of way; and that the (unsurprising) explanation of this unclarity is that we are not seriously attributing a *concept* at all. 'His master' is a term which we use for the convenience of ourselves or our audience; there is no constraint of fidelity to a mode of conceiving employed by the dog. If the man in question was known to most of those present as the high street newsagent, whose arrival was keenly awaited, and if the relation of the dog to this man were of no importance in context, it would not be unnatural to report that the dog had rushed off in the expectation of meeting the newsagent on the road.[30]

It is, of course, uncontentious that it is not *always* a paramount constraint on the satisfactory reportage of propositional attitudes that the content-specifying part involve only concepts attributable to the subject. So much has long been recognized. What I am now suggesting is something stronger: it is our practice, in certain cases, to ascribe propositional attitudes in such a way that not only do we not intend the form of words which we use to reflect the modes of conceiving pursued by the subject but, more, there *is* no form of words which, if it were important to us, would suit that purpose. One response would be that this, if true, displays

30 Indeed, why ascribe to a dog so much as a *sortal concept* of man, a conception of his master as a recurrent *particular*, rather than view it as operating a primitive feature-placing scheme of concepts? Note however that if the main claim of the text – that 'there is no constraint of fidelity to [the subject's] mode of conceiving' in such cases – is correct, it does not follow that co-extensive expressions will be unrestrictedly intersubstitutive in the relevant class of contexts. Whether that is so will depend on what *other* (audience- and reporter-related) constraints are in operation. Any purported counter-example to the main claim will therefore have to be shown not to be the effect of other such constraints.

a serious indeterminacy in the beliefs, etc., attributed and so calls into doubt the propriety of the attribution. But a different response is possible: that it may be perfectly proper to ascribe certain propositional attitudes to a subject even though there is no, as it were, *canonical* specification of the content of those attitudes, no specification of their content which exactly captures their content-for-the-subject. Despite the recent concentration of effort on 'folk psychology' and the intentional, I think we are some distance from the insights to motivate either response. But if the second is tenable, the likely abstruseness of the concepts necessary for the formulation of a full-blown theory of meaning need no longer constitute an objection to the implicit knowledge conception. Crudely: if a dog may have beliefs of which there is no formulation save by the use of concepts some of which should not be attributed to the dog, then perhaps speakers of a natural language may have intentions of which there is, again, no satisfactory account save by recourse to technicalities of which they have no concept. I do not know what it is right to think about this. I would urge only that those who would treat the objection from technicality as decisive against the implicit knowledge conception should recognize what they are doing: it is not so much a matter of siding with common sense as taking (to the best of my knowledge) an unargued stance on fundamental questions in the philosophy of mind concerning the proper limits of explanation by the postulation of intentional states and the proper constraints on the reportage of the content of such states.

There are, however, more subtle objections to the implicit knowledge conception. Let it be accepted that the prodigious children could properly be described as implicitly knowing the rules of chess and as possessing an appropriate range of intentions, and a measure of insight, which that knowledge served to inform. Still, the situation is not perfectly parallel to what is required in the case of a theory of meaning. The difference is that the axioms and recursions of a theory of meaning do not relate to correct linguistic practice as the 'axioms' of a theory of chess – i.e. the rules of the game – relate to correct play. Someone who intentionally and in good faith moves his Queen in the manner of a Knight shows that he doesn't know the rules prescribing the powers of movement of the Queen. There is no comparably simple and direct way of showing that you do not know the axiom governing the use, in English, of 'red' or 'elephant'. This is because only a use of a *sentence* makes, as Wittgenstein put it, a move in the language game. Thus an illicit move cannot violate a single axiom; rather, it has to violate a meaning-delivering theorem, and thereby all the axioms and recursive clauses involved in its derivation. Which among these you should then be deemed to be in ignorance of is a matter to be settled by reference to your use of other sentences in the derivation of whose meaning-delivering theorems those same clauses are involved, in the light of holistic constraints.

So much is obvious enough. Why does it constitute a problem? What it shows is that, even if the chess example is deemed to be entirely persuasive of the propriety *in general* of the ideas of implicit knowledge of rules, and of implicit inference, it cannot commit us to more, in the case of the theory of meaning, than the propriety of the notion that speakers implicitly know the meaning-delivering *theorems*, and can carry out (implicit) inferences from them. Whereas, of course, what needs to be legitimated is implicit knowledge of the axioms; and implicit inferences *to* the theorems (which, in any case, speakers are likely to know explicitly). The attraction of attributing implicit knowledge of the rules of chess to the fictional children is based on two things: first, their behaviour has all the trappings of intelligence, insight and purpose which would make it virtually impossible for us to regard it as anything but intentional; second, since they behave exactly as if they knew the rules of chess, the kind of rationalistic explanation which viewing their behaviour as intentional demands can hardly do better than ascribe such knowledge to them. The strength of the analogy is that both points apply to linguistic competence too: it manifestly has the richness which invites rationalistic explanation, and – if a theory of meaning is possible at all – the behaviour which would display knowledge of it would be exactly the behaviour constitutive of linguistic competence. But the weakness of the analogy is that behaving, in all respects short of explicit statement, as if one knew a theory of meaning cannot be distinguished from behaving as if one knew its meaning-delivering theorems; whereas there is no proper subset of the theorems of the 'theory' of chess whose knowledge would constitute the ability to play. The suggestion that speakers implicitly know a full theory of meaning for their language thus makes demands on the notion of implicit knowledge which have no counterpart in the chess example.

The additional demands, of course, are precisely what have to be made if the implicit knowledge conception is to provide an explanation of speakers' capacity to understand novel utterances. But is it not a welcome and foreseen effect of the attribution of implicit knowledge of the rules of chess to the children that we thereby secure the means to explain their recognition of the legality, or otherwise, of moves that they have never considered before? Surely. The difference is that the case for attributing implicit knowledge of the rules of chess to the children does not entirely consist in this phenomenon, but can be stated independently of it. The rules of chess comprise the *smallest* theory – (of this particular subject matter; we shall, of course, need to attribute a lot of other information to them, of different sorts) – which we need in order to give the envisaged sort of rationalistic explanation of their behaviour. Moreover, each item of knowledge which we thereby attribute to them has its own distinctive kind of behavioural display. If we seek a theory of meaning with these same two features, in contrast, we shall wind up with the sort of infinitary axiom schema which figured in the discussion of Foster above. The explanation of the children's ability to judge novel moves in point of legality may thus be viewed as a welcome by-product of an *independently* motivated attribution of implicit knowledge to them. That is not at all the situation with the implicit knowledge conception of the theory of meaning; linguistic 'creativity' here provides the entire *raison d'être*.

The response will be that it cannot be satisfactory just to credit speakers with knowledge of what is stated by perhaps indefinitely many meaning-delivering theorems, some of which concern sentences which they have never encountered, and leave it at that. The question must arise: what is the basis of this knowledge? My point, however, is not that we should discount this question but that the kind of play made with implicit knowledge in the fictional chess case – which was meant to epitomize the strength of the intuitions that underlie the implicit knowledge conception – provides no precedent for the supposition that this question should have a *psychological* answer. There has to be a perfectly respectable scientific question about the sources of our possession of the knowledge which the meaning-delivering theorems of a satisfactory theory of meaning would describe. But there is no a priori reason why the answer to this question should have to proceed via the postulation of further cognitive states. The sought-for finite basis may be better described in non-psychological terms.

There is an argument in Gareth Evans's discussion[31] which suggests that extending the notion of speakers' implicit knowledge to encompass the axioms and derivations within a theory of meaning would be a definite error. A rat may acquire the disposition to avoid a kind of foodstuff which is poisonous and has caused it sickness in the past. And we might casually ascribe its unwillingness to eat this material – or one that looked / smelt similar – to the belief that it was poisonous. But we should not, Evans urges, let casual language induce casual thought. Beliefs are essentially things which interact with desires and intentions in the production of behaviour. They are also essentially involved in the production of other beliefs. To ascribe a belief is significant only as part of the ascription of a *system* of beliefs. And what behaviour is expressive of a certain belief depends, in general, upon the other ingredients in this system and in the system of the subject's intentions and desires. Thus my belief that a certain substance is poisonous may manifest itself in a literally indefinite variety of ways. I may, like the rat, avoid the substance. But I may also take steps to ensure my family avoid it, or take steps to ensure they don't! I may take small but daily increasing quantities of the stuff in the belief that I can

31 Gareth Evans, 'Semantic Theory and Tacit Knowledge'. See especially section III. Compare Davies, *Meaning, Quantification, Necessity*, pp. 83–6.

thereby inure myself against its effects and that background circumstances are such that it may stand to my advantage to have done so. I may take a large quantity if I wish to commit suicide; and a smaller one if I wish to malinger my way out of some obligation. My belief that the substance is poisonous is thus, as Evans puts it, at the service of indefinitely many potential projects corresponding to indefinitely many transformations in my other beliefs and desires. With the rat, in contrast, concepts like the desire for suicide, or malign intent, can get no grip. The 'desires' which we are prepared to attribute to it are restricted, in the present context, to avoidance of distress; and its 'belief' that the substance is poisonous has consequently no other expression than in shunning it.

Evans's point, well made by this example, is that rationalistic explanations of behaviour are so much idle patter unless we are willing to credit the subject with the sophistication of a manifold system of interacting and evolving beliefs and desires, of a degree of organization sufficient to obstruct straightforward dispositional reductions of any particular belief ascription. There is no such obstruction in the case of the rat. Describing it as believing that the substance is poisonous adds nothing to the claim that it has suffered from it in the past and is now disposed to avoid it. If the rat were, e.g. to shift some of the substance to the habitual feeding place of an aggressor, to prevent her children from taking it, and to introduce some of it into the tea cup of the experimenter, on the other hand, we might begin to feel an incentive for serious rationalistic theorizing.

The force of this train of thought becomes apparent as soon as we ask how a defender of the implicit knowledge conception can distinguish those putatively intentional states, whose content he specifies using the axioms of a theory of meaning which he wishes to attribute to speakers, from the sort of dispositions whose behavioural expression is so inflexibly related to them as to disqualify them from the role of components in serious rationalistic theorizing. One of the chess-playing children will standardly manifest his knowledge of the rule governing the powers of movement and capture of the Queen by conforming to it. But other manifestations are possible: he may attempt to correct an opponent who breaks the rule, refuse to play with someone who makes a habit of doing so, or even deliberately break the rule himself as a somewhat unconventional mode of resignation, or by way of a pretended incompetence in the hope of short-circuiting a game he would rather not play. Likewise, someone who is credited with implicit knowledge of a meaning-delivering theorem may express his knowledge in an indefinite variety of ways, including, in appropriate contexts, lying, assent and silence. But the (implicit) knowledge of a meaning theoretic *axiom* would seem to be harnessed to the single project of forming beliefs about the content of sentences which contain the expression, or exemplify the mode of construction, which it concerns. Certainly, the precise beliefs which are formed will vary as a function of the content of the other relevant axioms of which a subject is also being supposed to have implicit knowledge. But what is supposed to be the role of *desire*? What is the (implicit?) desire which explains why the subject puts his semantic axiomatic beliefs to just this use, and what are the different uses to which they might be put if his desires were different?

The question draws a complete blank. The case is, in fact, worse than with the rat. We can begin to tell some sort of story – I did so above – of what sort of enrichment and complication of rodent behaviour might enable us to regard the belief that a substance was poisonous as manifested, via a particular kind of behaviour, along with something other than the desire to avoid discomfort. But what is the desire which, in conjunction with the knowledge represented by the meaning-theoretic axioms, is manifested in the formation of beliefs about the meanings of sentences? And what other manifestation might that knowledge have if this desire was different?[32] The truth is that the content of ascribing implicit knowledge of a meaning-theoretic axiom would appear to be no more than the ascription of a disposition to form beliefs about the meanings of sentences featuring the expression, or mode of construction, which it concerns: the disposition, precisely, to form beliefs which are appropriately constrained by the content of the axiom. Although Evans allows his discussion to proceed in terms of what he calls 'tacit knowledge', his own response to this train of thought is to abjure any form of intentionalistic construal of the relation between speakers and the axiomatic content of a theory of meaning. Rather, the axioms should indeed be seen precisely as describing certain dispositions which competent speakers have.[33]

32 Matters stand quite difficultly, of course, once the knowledge becomes *explicit*: lying, assent, silence, sarcastic denial, etc. all provide differing modes of expressing it, *modulo* variable contexts and desires. This, I think, is the correct form of reply to John Campbell's point in 'Knowledge and Understanding' about the relative paucity of projects which knowledge, e.g. of the plot structure of *Bleak House*, might be 'at the service of'. In the relevant sense – that of explaining covarying behaviour as other beliefs and desires are varied – such knowledge is indeed at the service of many projects.

33 It is notable that Evans's argument is explicitly directed only against the supposition that speakers *believe* what the axioms state. Earlier we had cause to take seriously the suggestion that *intention* might be the best candidate, from the point of view of the implicit knowledge conception, for the psychological bond between speakers and the contents of the axioms. The proposal was, roughly, that speakers should be credited with whatever (implicit) intentions would suffice to confer the status of conventions on the axioms. Might this make a difference? For there does not seem to be the same kind of holistic flexibility in what counts as manifesting a particular intention which obtains in the case of belief. If the belief that a substance is poisonous may be manifested in any number of ways, among which avoiding eating it is only one – though a usual – case, the intention to avoid eating it, for instance, is manifested by doing just that.

The reader must form his own judgement about whether the point really is fatal to the prospects of any sort of intentionalistic construal of the relation between speakers and axioms. Let me, though, attempt to ensure that he does so in awareness of some limitations of Evans's own positive proposals. I shall pursue Evans's example of a simple language containing just ten singular terms, *a*,*b*,*c*,..., and ten one-place predicates, F,G,H,..., together with the single sentence-forming operation of singular term-predicate concatenation. The language thus has 100 possible sentences, and allows of a finite but non-compositional truth-theoretic axiomatization consisting of 100 corresponding instances of the T-schema. Call this axiomatization T_1; and contrast it with the compositional axiomatization, T_2 which has 21 axioms: ten assigning denotations to the singular terms; ten stipulating satisfaction-conditions for the predicates; and a compositional axiom to the effect that a sentence coupling a name with a predicate is true if and only if the object denoted by the name satisfies the predicate. Evans's negative proposal is that T_2 should not be seen as describing the contents of any sort of intentional states of speakers of the object language. His positive proposal is that it should be seen as describing dispositions which they have; and, crucially, that even when so interpreted, it may be preferable to T_1.

The immediate question is: *what* dispositions, exactly, does T_2 describe? Evans's own account proceeds in terms of a notion of 'tacit

---

The suggestion is difficult to appraise in the absence of a detailed proposal. But there is some cause for pessimism. It is, to begin with, an error to suppose that there is a simple analytic connection between the content of an intention and the behaviour which manifests it. There is such a connection, but it is with whatever behaviour *implements* the intention; whereas the intention may be manifested by unsuccessful efforts to implement it, and indeed by any behaviour which the subject believes may (help to) carry it through. Intention, properly so regarded, will accordingly sustain a similar variety of possible modes of expression to that which characterizes belief. Evans's challenge ought therefore still to be good: how is the attribution of implicit intentions to be distinguished from, and justified in preference to, the attribution of dispositions to speak, and interpret the speech of others, in accordance with the meaning-theoretic axioms? Intention is distinguished from a mere disposition by the possibility of misguided attempts at fulfilment and by the subject's adaptability: his capacity to envisage a variety of ways in which it might be fulfilled and to modify his path accordingly. How can these ideas be made to grip in the present case?

In any case, intention cannot be the *whole* story. To be party to a convention is to have both intentions of a certain sort *and* beliefs – beliefs about just what regularities upholding the convention will require to be sustained. In David Lewis's study, for instance, it is necessary, if a regularity is to be conventional, that each of the participants expects the others to sustain it and that everyone prefers to sustain it if the others do (since a solution to a 'co-ordination problem' is thereby achieved.) So the challenge is immediate: how is the putative *belief* that everyone else will conform to the axioms of a theory of meaning to be distinguished from the *disposition* to form beliefs, as one successfully encounters novel utterances, that their behaviour will, *ceteris paribus*, conform to the requirements of the meaning-delivering theorems for those utterances?

knowledge' – (by way of deference, no doubt, to the free-wheeling use made of intentional terminology by so many psychologists and psycholinguists) – which, in contrast with what the considerations above might prompt us to regard as *genuinely* intentional states, does admit of an apparently straightforward dispositional account. His suggestion is that a speaker U tacitly knows that, for instance, the denotation of *a* is John if and only if he has a disposition such that:

> $(\Pi\phi)$ $(\Pi\psi)$ [if U tacitly knows that an object satisfies ϕ if and only if it is ψ; and U hears an utterance having the form ϕa; then U will judge that: the utterance is true if and only if John is ψ].

Likewise a speaker U tacitly knows that, for instance, an object satisfies F if and only if it is bald, if and only if he has a disposition such that:

> (Πx) $(\Pi\alpha)$ [if U tacitly knows that the denotation of α is x, and U hears an utterance having the form $F\alpha$, then U will judge that: the utterance is true if and only if x is bald.[34]

These proposals seem more or less inevitable. 'Tacit knowledge' ought to be a disposition which constitutes understanding; and what is it to understand a sub-sentential expression of Evans's simple language except to be disposed to make the right judgements about the truth-conditions of sentences containing it provided one understands the accompanying name or predicate? But there are a number of difficulties.

The first is, once again, that it is not clear how this interpretation of the relation between speakers and the axioms can provide a reason for preferring T_2 to T_1. The dispositions which T_2 assigns to speakers are dispositions of judgement concerning whole sentences; so why not simply describe them directly by using T_1? Evans's answer is that he intends the notion of disposition to which he is appealing to be understood in a 'full-blooded sense': the ascription of a disposition is to be interpreted as the ascription of an underlying state from which the relevant patterns of behaviour, described in the conditional which articulates what the disposition is a disposition to do, (causally) flow. Thus the difference between T_1 and T_2 is that the former ascribes 100 distinct such states to competent speakers of the object language whereas

> tacit knowledge of T_2 requires that there should be 20 such states of the subject – one corresponding to each expression of the language which the theory treats separately – such that the causal explanation

34 'π' is here a universal substitutional quantifier; and the variables ϕ,α,ψ, and x, have, respectively, the substitution classes of names of predicate expressions of the object-language, names of names of the object-language, predicate expressions of the metalanguage (English) and proper names of the metalanguage (English). Cf. Evans, 'Semantic Theory and Tacit Knowledge', pp. 124–5.

> of why the subject reacts in the way that he does to any sentence of the language involves two of these states, and any one of these states is involved in the explanation of the way he reacts to 10 sentences containing a common element.[35]

In Evans's view the claims of T_1 and T_2 to describe speakers competence may thus, under favourable circumstances, be empirically adjudicated. A satisfactory neurophysiological account of competence would be decisive;[36] but even in advance of attaining that, strong evidence for the superiority of T_2 would be afforded by the empirical findings (a) that speakers acquire the capacity to understand so far unencountered specimens from among the 100 possible sentences on the basis of exposure to utterances which contain the relevant constituents; and (b) that when speakers *lose* competence with any of the sentences – owing to forgetfulness, or disease, or damage – they tend simultaneously to lose competence with all the sentences which feature one, or both of its constituents.

Now, although I think Evans's deference to neurophysiology is mistaken – since it is evidence of types (a) and (b) which would determine our conception of what kind of neurophysiological theory to settle for – and although it is not clear exactly what account of identity and distinctness among (neurophysiological) *states* should provide the backcloth to his suggestions, the kind of data which he envisages would obviously be highly significant. But the question, of course, is why such data would properly motivate the adoption of T_2, rather than T_1 supplemented with some appropriate hypotheses, of a non-semantical sort, about the presumed causal substructure of the dispositions which T_1 describes. This is essentially the objection which featured in the discussion of the 'Mirror Constraint' earlier, and Evans's discussion contains, so far as I can see, no answer to it. The requirement that a theory of meaning should both describe the dispositions which the competent display in their handling of whole sentences and reflect the underlying causal structure of those dispositions – as witnessed by the details of their acquisition and loss and, perhaps, by their neurophysiology – provides absolutely no basis for preferring a theory of meaning to a description, or list, of the meaning-delivering theorems, supplemented by claims like

> Some single neurophysiological state is involved in the causal explanation of a speaker's competence with any sentence which features the expression *a*.

Why adopt T_2, or any theory whose axioms have a *semantical* subject matter, if the task is to reflect the *causal* structure of the dispositions which correspond to the meaning-delivering theorems?

35 'Semantic Theory and Tacit Knowledge', p. 125.
36 Ibid., p. 127.

There is a connection between this point and a peculiarity in Evans's exposition which the alert reader will already have noticed. Why does Evans speak of tacit knowledge of T_2 as involving 20 states of the subject when the axioms of T_2 are 21? The answer is obvious enough. The account which Evans offers of the dispositions which constitute tacit knowledge of the denotations of singular terms and the satisfaction conditions of predicates have the effect that a speaker who possesses them is thereby disposed to attach the proper significance to name-predicate coupling – since he is thereby disposed to attach the proper significance to sentences formed by coupling names and predicates. But this leaves Evans's proposal open to a simple objection. T_2 would be crippled without the compositional axiom, but if the brief of its axioms were *merely* the description of the dispositions which, on Evans's account, constitute tacit knowledge of them, the compositional axiom ought to be redundant. However there is in view no plausible modification of Evans's proposals concerning the dispositions relevant to singular terms and predicates which would need to be supplemented by a separate dispositional account concerning the compositional axiom. So the conclusion has to be that Evans's proposals misdescribe the content of the axioms of T_2. The conclusion of the preceding argument is therefore reinforced. We can grant that Evans has provided reason why a theory which concerned itself with a description of the dispositions which constituted a speakers' competence might wish to construe some of these dispositions as concerned with sub-sentential expressions. But since any compositional theory of meaning for a typical natural language will incorporate something like T_2, and since T_2 will not sustain that interpretation of its brief, Evans has provided no reason why we should seek a compositional theory of meaning.

Evans's proposal is apt to seem dissatisfying in a further respect. His account of what tacit knowledge of the denotation of a singular term disposes a subject to do appeals to a prior understanding of what it is to have tacit knowledge of the satisfaction conditions of a predicate; and vice versa. The two sets of dispositions are thus, as Evans acknowledges, 'interdefined'. Why is that not a recipe for vicious circularity? No one can follow Evans's characterization of what it is for U tacitly to know that the denotation of *a* is John unless he already understands what it is for U to have tacit knowledge of the satisfaction conditions of predicates in the language in question. If he doesn't understand that, Evans's account will plainly be of no avail to him, since it demands a prior understanding of what it is for U tacitly to know – of some arbitrarily selected singular term, which might be *a* – that its denotation is so-and-so.

This circularity may seem harmless for two reasons. First, it reflects an undoubted feature of our intuitive conception of what it is to understand sub-sentential expressions: to understand a name *is* to have the capacity to understand utterances in which it figures, provided one understands the remaining constituents and the mode of construction; and to understand the remaining constituents and the mode of construction *is* to have the capacity to understand utterances in which they feature provided one understands the rest of the sentence, which, in the basic case, takes us back to proper names. Second, circularity of this sort need in any case be no objection if the task is not to provide an *introductory* explanation of the concepts in question but to offer some measure of characterization of them.

Both of these points are fair. But the worry is not that the 'inter-definability' of Evans's axiomatic dispositions reflects no feature of our intuitive conception of what it is to understand the constituents of a sentence, but that, naively perhaps, one wants something better in the characterization of a *disposition.* To characterize a disposition ought to be to characterize both what it is a disposition to do and the circumstances under which it will be manifest. Often we settle for very imperfectly precise characterizations of both. But the complaint here is not of imprecision. If, for instance, I characterize the ductility of a metal by reference to certain observable phenomena which occur under background circumstances *including* the possession by the substance of certain further dispositions; and if it then turns out that a characterization of the distinctive manifestations of some of these further dispositions is possible only by reference to background circumstances in which the substances are assumed to be ductile – if that is the best that can be done, the reproach does not seem foolish that I have so far simply *failed to say* what ductility is. Evans's proposals would seem to leave the dispositions which they aim to characterize in this uncomfortable-seeming position. However, I offer the point more as something which someone who wished to advance Evans's account should say something about than as an objection. Perhaps a more sophisticated account of the notion of a disposition would remove the worry; my own suggestion would be that Evans's proposal should have proceeded by reference to states of a different sort – his real interest, after all, is in the underlying 'categorical' bases. But I anticipate.

One final point about Evans's treatment is worth emphasis. He writes

> ...it is implicit in what has gone before that the notion of tacit knowledge of a [compositional] theory of meaning, explained as I have explained it, cannot be used to explain the capacity to understand new sentences.[37]

This is because the dispositions which, on Evans's account, constitute tacit knowledge of the axioms of T_2, e.g., precisely *are* the dispositions to judge correctly the truth-conditions of novel sentences in the language in

37 Evans, 'Semantic Theory and Tacit Knowledge', p. 134.

question. Evans's claim on behalf of a compositional theory of meaning is that it is likely to give the empirically best attested description of what these dispositions are. I think he is right that, even there is no force whatever in the foregoing objections, this is the most that, on his account of the matter, could be claimed. Accordingly, an *explanation* of speakers' 'creativity' would have to consist, for Evans, in an account of how it is that speakers are prone to acquire just these dispositions on the basis of the incomplete and imperfect sampling in which a typical training in the use of a natural language consists.

This still leaves a theorist of meaning with a contribution to make to the explanatory project. Before an account can be given of the aetiology of the relevant dispositions, we need to know what they are. The ability of a learner to understand a novel utterance can, presumably, be made to seem non-miraculous only if the sample of uses which induced in him the dispositions which he thereby exercises themselves involved exercise of corresponding dispositions on the part of those whose speech he witnessed.

> Consequently, when a capacity to understand novel sentences is observed, the theorist of meaning has an indispensable role to play in its explanation, since he must exhibit the regularity between the old and the new.[38]

What is striking about this suggestion is the width of the gulf which it opens between what, on Evans's account, the theorist of meaning should be about and what in practice those philosophers who have taken an interest – none more than Evans – in the project of a theory of meaning have been content to do. One clear implication of Evans's account, for instance, is that the construction of a useful theory of meaning does demand elevation from the armchair. Data are needed about trainees' learning patterns – about just what 'projections' they tend to be able to make on the basis of exposure to just what sorts of sample – and about patterns of loss, before we can so much as form a best guess at the syntactic categories in terms of which Evans's basic dispositions should be described. This is not what has happened. The relevant syntactic categories have been persistently supposed to be, more or less, those which Frege invented; 'regimentation' of the surface grammar of natural language is acknowledged to be inevitable in the construction of a theory of the sought-for kind. I submit that if Evans's account of the project is the right one, this a priori indifference to the *overt form* of many of the utterances which the novice speaker is able 'creatively' to understand is rather strange methodology. Not that the surface/depth grammar distinction may not be amenable to excellent empirical motivation. My point is that philosophical

38 Ibid., pp. 135–6.

theorists of meaning seem to have assumed its propriety without reliance on the kind of data which, if Evans's account of their project were correct, it ought to depend on.

I do not mean to suggest that those philosophers who have set about the Davidsonian project with respect to (fragments of) English have relied on no data which could properly be viewed as empirical. They have relied, of course, on a rich set of intuitions about particular meanings, and the significance of particular constructions, which competent speakers of English tend to share. The point is rather that they have, by and large, relied on no data concerning language acquisition and loss. Admittedly, this may be taken as showing not that Evans's account of how we should conceive the relation between actual speakers and the target theory is altogether misconceived but only that the right account has not greatly impinged upon the consciousness of workers in the field. So it is worth noting, to conclude this section, that there is a proposal, similar in spirit to Evans's but different in detail, which harmonizes rather better with the relatively a prioristic approach that theorists have followed.

As is familiar, certain species of bird display what appears to be a remarkable ability to find their way home from distant and unfamiliar locations. The ability appears remarkable because unless we were allowed to rely on special equipment and knowledge – compasses, charts, the disposition of the stars and so on – we could not emulate it. How do they do it? There are, of course, a number of differences between this problem and that of linguistic creativity. For one thing, there is no analogue of compositionality; no platitudinous answer, like 'By understanding the words and the way in which they are put together', is in the offing to constrain a satisfactory answer. For another, part of what has to be resolved is the range of sensory cues to which the birds should be thought of as responding – whereas it is taken to be a *datum* that speakers respond to the overt visible or audible structure of a sentence. But what is importantly parallel is that we do not know how to approach the question about, in particular, pigeons unless we are allowed to construct a theory which, like a theory of meaning, serves to articulate possible modes of information processing. We would seek, that is to say, a theory which, if conjoined with supplementary information about features of its novel location which would, according to our best account of a pigeon's sensory apparatus, be discernible by the bird, would serve to issue in theorems whose content would be an instruction about what (sensed object) to fly towards. Of course, the suggestion that actual birds might *know* the content of such a theory would be vulnerable to the principal objection raised above. But it is in any case a suggestion to which we are not tempted; we do not, in setting about devising such a theory, regard ourselves as committed to viewing pigeons as intentional agents. On the contrary: the idea is to make them intelligible as a sophisticated sort of *mechanism*.

In a way, it is incidental that there are any such creatures. Even if there were not, the question could be posed whether a device could be designed which would 'home' in the way that pigeons actually do. A positive answer to the question would require a demonstration how a mechanism sensitive to certain features of its environment could process the data thereby accumulated so as to be disposed to relocate itself in the appropriate way. At the first stage, this is *entirely* an information-processing problem: it calls, in effect, for the devising of an appropriate computer program. At the second state, the problem would be that of explaining how this program, plus the relevant capacities of sensitivity and movement, might be incorporated into a physically possible device. The sort of understanding of the actual capacities of pigeons which is called for would be achieved exactly when enough was known about them to enable us to understand how in detail they embody such a device. And, of course, there can be no such understanding before we have formed the appropriate theoretical conception of the powers which the device must have. Doing that requires writing the computer program.

Three points are notable. First, devising such a program is not an *empirical* problem. What is sought is an axiomatic theory which, fed with (successive) appropriately formulated descriptions of environments distinct from 'home', will generate (successive) theorems encoding a successful homing strategy. This is a kind of problem which, when sufficiently precisely formulated, can be cracked in the armchair. The corresponding armchair problem for the theorist of meaning is to devise a theory which will take us from a description of relevant features of an arbitrary utterance to a theorem which characterizes its meaning. Second, the theorist will not best serve the next stage of the explanatory project – that of making good the claim that actual human beings embody, as it were, the relevant program – if he produces a theory with an infinitary axiom base. We do not understand what it would be to build a computer which incorporated infinitely many logically independent items of information in its program but no finite axiomatization of them. Simply to postulate that biological evolution can do what we cannot would be to reformulate rather than solve the original problem. And it is in any case unclear what could constitute neurophysiological reason for thinking that a pigeon, or human being, was the living embodiment of such a theory. A finiteness constraint at least thus appears to flow naturally from consideration of the overall character of the explanation which we are seeking. Finally, the connection between the axioms of the theory and speakers' (or pigeons') dispositions is less direct than on Evans's account. A completed explanation along the lines envisaged will of course involve the identification of (presumably neurophysiological) states which embody the various items of information corresponding to the axioms of the program. But these states need not be individuated, so far as I can see, as (categorical bases for) distinct dispositions; nor, in general, does there appear to be any a priori reason why the correspondence between the axioms and their neurophysiological realizations should be one-to-one.

I claim for this approach only that it may indicate the shape of a better account of the relevance of a theory of meaning to explaining the capacities of actual speakers than can be provided by play with the notion of 'implicit' intentional states, or by Evans's dispositionalist account. No doubt it will encounter problems of its own. It is obvious, above all, that clarification is needed of what it is for a system to 'embody' information – clarification which only a philosopher who is unusually well-informed in computational, psychological and neurophysiological science is likely to be able to achieve – and that there has to be, at least initially, a legitimate doubt in any case about the extension of this sort of notion to natural systems. I have wanted to indicate only that the horizon is not empty of all prospect of satisfactorily yoking together the philosophical project of a theory of meaning and the explanation of actual speakers' linguistic 'creativity'.

IV

It remains to draw some conclusions about how our discussion bears on the realism/anti-realism debate, when it is conceived in Dummett's way. The answer, it should now be clear, is: not at all. The anti-realist claim is that nobody may reasonably be credited with knowledge of the truth-conditions of any of a very substantial class of statements. (Precisely what class will depend upon the degree of anti-realism espoused.) The conclusion is then drawn that truth may not play the central role in a comprehensive theory of (statement) meaning – at least not when understood *à la mode réalistique*. The justification for this conclusion is that the theory is supposed to represent the knowledge in which understanding of the sentences of a language consists, which it must be failing to do if it cannot do better than articulate that knowledge in terms of concepts which they cannot have. Now if the discussion of implicit knowledge above had yielded the result that a theory of meaning simply cannot be concerned with the description of speakers' knowledge at all, then the anti-realist critique of (realist) truth-conditional semantics could not take exactly this form. But two points need emphasis. First, what emerged as problematic was the idea of speakers' implicit knowledge of the content of the *axioms* of a theory of meaning – no reason emerged to doubt the propriety of crediting them with implicit knowledge of the content of the meaning-delivering *theorems*; and I anticipate that no such reason could be produced which did not demand rejection of the idea of implicit knowledge altogether. Second, if the more radical anti-realist claims about the dubiety of a conception of verification-transcendent truth are correct, we – the theorists – have no business involving that 'notion' in any sort of theory, whether conceived as descriptive of the content of object-language speakers' understanding or not. There has been some curious muddle about this simple point in recent realist commentary.[39] So perhaps it is worth emphasizing the obvious: whether or not the theory of meaning is conceived – as Dummett always urges it must be – as a theory of speakers' understanding, the project is, trivially, constrained by the demand that the concepts which it uses be in good order. Criticism of that particular ingredient in Dummett's philosophy of language, or highlighting of the non-sequitur involved in the transition from the claims 1) that the meaning of a sentence is what someone who understands it knows, and 2) that the meaning of a sentence is determined by its truth-conditions, to 3) one who understands a sentence knows its truth-conditions,[40] is therefore entirely futile if what one is trying to do is to protect realist semantics from anti-realist attack. Indeed the anti-realist case has no less bearing on the desirable form for a theory of meaning to take if the project is conceived as having nothing directly to do with the concepts of actual speakers but is concerned entirely with the idealized epistemology of language acquisition, after the fashion of the proposal extracted earlier from Davies' discussion.[41]

39 An example is Michael Devitt's chapter 12, 'Dummett's Anti-Realism', of his *Realism and Truth*.

40 Cf. ibid., pp. 207–8.

41 I would like to thank Martin Davies and Elizabeth Fricker for detailed and very helpful comments on an earlier draft of this essay.

7

Misconstruals Made Manifest

A Reply to Simon Blackburn

In 'Manifesting Realism', Simon Blackburn offers an extended response to the case made by Dummett, myself and others for semantical anti-realism. The paper advances three principal claims:

First, that the semantical anti-realist polemic suffers for want of a realist opponent – Blackburn canvasses no fewer than six possible varieties of realist – who is both vulnerable to the arguments developed and philosophically substantial.

Second, that Dummett's overarching hope, to use (the resolution of) issues in the theory of meaning to illuminate traditional metaphysical controversies concerning realism, is misconceived – both in the assumption that an underlying unity in such controversies is to be expected across different subject matters and in the cardinal role he assigns to the philosophy of language. Rather the issues between realists and anti-realists vary with the regions of discourse – science, mathematics, modality, probability theory, morals etc., – about which they are in dispute. There is no overriding debate in the philosophy of language, and no talisman is provided thereby for use in the debates which there are, nor, Blackburn concludes,

> even a set of arguments playing any useful role in their solution.[1]

On the contrary, the debates

> ...are many, although they each require their own geography, for the shoe may pinch in different places, in the theory of morals, of possibility, probability, cause, or mind.[2]

1 'Manifesting Realism', p. 46.
2 'Manifesting Realism', p. 45.

Third – and somewhat surprising in company with the second claim – Blackburn does wish to commend a certain overview of these debates: it is one in which the realist is someone who believes that

> ...reference to a genuine order of objective facts is necessary to explain some aspect of our practice,[3]

and thus stands opposed to a character, Blackburn's *quasi-realist*, who holds that all aspects of the discourse in question can be conservatively explained without invocation of the idea of such a 'genuine order of objective facts' over which we should think of its assertions as having their truth-conditions defined.

I have some qualified sympathy with Blackburn's second claim. In the Preface[4] I express reservations both about Dummett's global identification of realism with belief in the appropriateness of a certain sort of truth-conditional theory of meaning and about the weaker thesis that these traditional metaphysical issues are generally amenable to relocation in a meaning-theoretic setting. But, as urged in the Introduction, it is unquestionable – or seems so to me – that, in an important class of cases, the metaphysical realist must offer up hostages to be redeemed by meaning-theoretic fortune. Not every realist, about whatever subject matter, is happily identified with Dummett's realist; but many kinds of realist that there actually are, about discourses as various as mathematics, science, history and intentional psychology, should have the keenest interest in the debate about Dummett's realist – for their philosophical survival may depend on its outcome.

In saying that, I am insisting, of course, that there *is* a debate about Dummett's realist, whose outcome is still uncertain – Blackburn's parade of notional strawmen and putative hardmen notwithstanding. A further attempt to clarify its main lines will be the primary business of this chapter,[5] and there are many interesting things in Blackburn's paper with which I will not engage. But I cannot resist a few, very general questions and comments about the quasi-realist alternative – 'queasy-realist' as he sometimes self-mockingly styles it – which he champions. So I will begin with those.

3 'Manifesting Realism', p. 45.

4 This volume, p. xi.

5 I am, in a way, rather regretful to have another occasion to do so. I had hoped that the Introduction to the first edition of the present work might have set the issues, especially those about manifestation, in a somewhat clearer light than Blackburn's discussion reflects.

I
'Queasy-realism', Projectivism and Pluralism

What exactly is the recommended format for a demonstration that it *is* possible to explain the functioning of a discourse without invoking the idea of a 'genuine order of objective facts' to which its apparent assertions (mis)correspond? In particular, is it necessary to provide an account of the discourse by whose lights its apparent assertions are portrayed as *only* apparent? This seemed to be so in chapter 6 of *Spreading the Word*. There, the quasi-realist programme for moral discourse explicitly undertakes an expressive, *ergo* non-assertoric, construal of moral 'assertions' in general, including forms of construction, such as the conditional, which are regarded as problematical precisely because they seem to demand that (some of) their constituents be apt for assertion. But if this is the way that matters are supposed to go, then we are owed a satisfactory resolution of a clutch of difficulties to which Blackburn has, so far as I am aware, no published effective response. For instance, we have yet to be shown a satisfactory quasi-realist treatment of the validity of moral Modus Ponens: patterns of inference, like

Stealing is wrong;
If stealing is wrong, so is encouraging others to steal;

Encouraging others to steal is wrong.

The *Spreading the Word* proposal about such matters has the effect that someone who accepts the premises but rejects the conclusion of the above inference is guilty only of a *moral* shortcoming,[6] while the modified account in 'Attitudes and Contents'[7] implicitly surrenders, as Hale has demonstrated,[8] the expressive construal of moral 'assertions'. In the absence of any account of so simple an inference pattern, there is simply not the slightest reason to believe that the quasi-realist has the resources for a satisfactory construal of moral argument.

There is, in any case, a very familiar kind of methodological bind about this particular version of the quasi-realist proposal. Success could only consist, it seems, in establishing rules of transformation between ordinary, apparently assertoric moral discourse – to stay with

6 See p. 33 and n. 19 of my 'Realism, Anti-realism, Irrealism, Quasi-realism'. Other problems besetting the *Spreading the Word* proposals for an expressive construal of moral discourse are raised by Bob Hale in 'The Compleat Projectivist', and by G. F. Schueler in 'Modus Ponens and Moral Realism'.
7 Blackburn, 'Attitudes and Contents'.
8 Hale, 'Can There Be a Logic of Attitudes?'.

this particular battleground – and a discourse in which no genuine assertions were made. So a simple dilemma arises: are the rules of transformation somehow guaranteed to be content-preserving? If not, nothing will have been shown. If so, how is it supposed to be clear that no genuine assertions are made in the *reductive* discourse? If apparently assertoric syntax can mislead, so can apparently non-assertoric syntax. So in which direction does the significance of the transformations run? The question could only be answered in the light of an *independent* account of genuine assertoric function. But if we had one, why couldn't we apply it directly to moral discourse – what possible purpose is served by labouring for a putatively expressive reconstrual, no matter how ingeniously, if its significance must remain in doubt until an independent demonstration is to hand that moral discourse has no genuinely assertoric function?

This is only an adaptation of a difficulty which a large class of reductionist proposals have to meet. It is most familiar, of course, in the context of ontological reduction.[9] So far as I am aware, Blackburn nowhere explicitly addresses it. But at least it is clear that a response which conserved the *Spreading the Word* conception of the quasi-realist programme would have to establish a robust distinction between the overt assertoric syntax of a class of sentences – their susceptibility to embedding within negation, the conditional construction, and operators of propositional attitude, etc., – and *genuine assertoric content*. What reason is there to think that that any such distinction can be drawn which is suitable for Blackburn's purpose?[10]

The broad alternative is to drop the *Spreading the Word* conception, and to allow that any discourse which possesses the right kind of overt syntax and whose use exhibits sufficient discipline – minimally, there have to be recognized standards of proper and improper use of its ingredient sentences – is genuinely assertoric, and hence truth-value bearing.[11] To grant this need not be to surrender all vestige of the quasi-realist motif – the programme would remain, for instance, of trying

9 See Alston, 'Ontological Commitments'; and my *Frege's Conception of Numbers as Objects*, ch. 1, sect. v.

10 Pessimism about such a distinction is well-motivated by the first part of Huw Price's *Facts and the Function of Truth*. One possible but, for Blackburn's purposes, unsuitable distinction is proposed in the concluding section of the present paper – unsuitable because it engages only 'assertions' which are apparently apt for undetectable truth and so has no bearing, presumably, on moral assertions. For further misgivings about the kind of distinction Blackburn needs, see my 'Realism, Anti-realism, Irrealism, Quasi-realism'; also my 'Anti-realism: The Contemporary Debate – W(h)ither Now?', forthcoming in Haldane and Wright (eds), *Reality, Representation and Projection*.

11 Since it is by way of a platitude that to assert a sentence is to present it as true.

to make out a distinction between truth-value-bearing discourses in philosophizing about which we need to invoke the idea of 'a genuine order of objective facts' and truth-value-bearing discourses for which that is not so. Blackburn himself has recently shown some sympathy for this redirection[12] and it is one of which I myself am a supporter. But it needs to be recognized that the major part of the work is to supply definite content for the type of phrase, like that just quoted, which too often is treated as helping to define what is in dispute in particular cases but is evidently incapable of really doing so. Until that is done, it is simply underdetermined what is really at issue about morals, or any of the other problematical discourses, or how it might competently be debated. Not the least merit of Dummett's overall interpretation of realist/anti-realist disputes is its very clear response to this need. One may question whether his proposal is appropriate in every such dispute. But it is no easy matter to do better – nor to elicit from 'Manifesting Realism' any proposal approaching the same degree of clarity.

One distinction which Blackburn's phrase might conjure, and which I believe is at least part of his meaning, is that between discourses which respectively pass and fail the Best Explanation constraint.[13] A discourse passes the Best Explanation constraint if mention of states of affairs of the sort which it putatively describes features ineliminably in the best explanations of our forming the beliefs attested to by our assertions within it. This idea has, of course, been extensively discussed, particularly in the context of its apparent bearing on science and morals.[14] My own view, which I cannot attempt to substantiate here, is that it is doubtful whether the requisite notion of *best* explanation can easily be clarified – at least if the target comparison is to be to the disadvantage of morals; and that the important consideration in the vicinity is not whether e.g. moral facts need to be adverted to in the best explanation of moral belief but whether they enjoy a sufficiently *wide cosmological role* – whether they have enough of a part to play in the explanation of things *besides* our moral beliefs – to give substance to the idea that our moral beliefs *respond* to them.[15] However that may be, the fact is that if such are to be the issues between the realist and the quasi-realist, Blackburn ought not to write as though he is offering a new perspective.

12 In Nelson lectures at the University of Michigan in September 1988.

13 Cf. 'Realism, Anti-realism, Irrealism, Quasi-realism', pp. 40–2, and 'Anti-realism: The Contemporary Debate – W(h)ither Now?', sect. IV.

14 See, for instance, Harman, *The Nature of Morality: An Introduction to Ethics*, ch. 1; Wiggins, *Needs, Values, Truth*, Essay IV, 'Truth as Predicated of Moral Judgements', sects 9 and 10; Sturgeon, 'Moral Explanations'.

15 For more on this, see, again, 'Anti-realism: The Contemporary Debate – W(h)ither Now?', sect. IV.

That there is a crux, on this point, for our intuitions about objectivity is already generally presupposed.

The suggestion that aptitude for truth-value need not be at stake in realist/anti-realist debates, if that is indeed the direction in which Blackburn is now moving, seems to me to be important and correct. So too does the emphasis on the diversity of issues at stake in such debates. But Blackburn errs, in my opinion, when he writes – with dubious consistency, as noted – as if this diversity precluded any useful overall perspective. The right picture, it seems to me, is rather along the following lines. Sometimes truth-aptitude is at stake, and anti-realism takes the form of *irrealism*. When that is so, the issue concerns whether the discourse in question can be established in such a way as to conform to the somewhat minimal constraints of syntax and discipline which the applicability of a truth-predicate calls for. This is, to give a single instance, precisely what is at issue over the possibility of 'private language'. More often, however, truth-aptitude is not – or ought not to be – at stake. It is not the issue, in particular, in any of the cases which Blackburn cites as prospective material for quasi-realist treatment (whatever exactly such a treatment would now consist in). What has been or may be at issue in such cases is indeed diverse: the prospects for convergence of opinion, the question whether divergence of opinion has to be attributable to something worth describing as cognitive shortcoming,[16] the questions to do with Best Explanation and Wide Cosmological Role, issues concerning whether the relation between *best* opinion – opinion formed by cognitively ideal subjects in cognitively ideal circumstances – and truth is, broadly, a relation of *constitution* or of *tracking*, and indeed the question whether truth for the discourse in question is correctly taken to be evidentially unconstrained – any of these five issues and, no doubt, others can provide a relevant focus of debate. But they provide a *relevant* focus because, in each case, should the decision go in favour of the realist, the truth-predicate takes on characteristics which go beyond anything demanded merely by its role in assertoric discourse – characteristics which are related in germane ways to the basic realist intuition of truth as a matter of a substantial correspondence between our thought and a domain of independent truth-conferring states of affairs.

It is clear enough, for instance, that we are committed so to regarding the truth-predicate in the case of any discourse which, we suppose, satisfies the Best Explanation constraint. If the situations which confer truth on certain of our beliefs also feature in the best explanation of our

16 The question of *Rational Command*, as it is styled in 'Realism, Anti-realism, Irrealism, Quasi-realism'.

holding those beliefs in the first place, there can be no question of regarding them merely as a grammatical *reflection*, as it were, of the truth of those beliefs – states of affairs to whose existence we are committed only and purely by holding the beliefs in question and which play no other role in the world. Similarly, should best opinion in a particular discourse turn out to stand in a tracking relation to the truth, rather than in a constitutive or partially determinative relation, we are thereby obliged to think of truth for that discourse in a way which contrasts it with ideal assertibility, and of our most refined standards of acceptability as means of *access* to truth, which is constituted independently. By contrast, there is nothing in the truth-aptitude of a discourse as such – before any of these matters are investigated – to frustrate the construal of its truth-predicate in terms of assertibility.[17]

Inevitably, these remarks are very compressed. I am under no illusion that they provide an argument for the overview I am recommending. But maybe they serve to suggest a strategy of some promise. What is very immediate is that the issue of the evidence-transcendence of truth fits in perfectly. There is no clearer way of giving content to the realist image of thought in confrontation with an independent world: that *has* to be the way to conceive of the truth-conferrers if truth can clash with, or float free from, the deliverances of all accessible evidence. Not that to demonstrate that our understanding of a particular discourse is informed by such a conception of truth would be to show that what, in so understanding it, we take to be possible really *is* possible. It is too seldom recognized that Dummett's realist cannot *win* by meeting his opponent's 'manifestation challenge' – he merely deflects an assault. But a demonstration that the challenge cannot be met is another matter. For it would be absurd to suppose that the world might undetectably confer truth and falsity upon certain of our beliefs, if nothing in our understanding of them involved any conception of how that might be so. Take it, then, that any such conception must be manifestable, and the dialectical point of the 'manifestation challenge' should be evident enough.

To be sure, the overall picture I have outlined would not allow us immediately to write off realism about a discourse for which the Manifestation Challenge proved unanswerable. The possibility may remain of giving substance to and justifying a realist view of it in one of the other ways briefly canvassed. Equally, it may not – evidence-transcendent truth may be too central a commitment of the realism in question to allow of retrenchment to a view which dispenses with it

17 Or, more specifically, in terms of *superassertibility*. See this volume, Essay 12, and 'Anti-realism: The Contemporary Debate – W(h)ither Now?', sect. II.

yet remains realist in the same spirit. That is the situation of the kind of mathematical platonism which stands opposed to Mathematical Intuitionism as Dummett has interpreted it. And it is also, I would surmise, the situation of scientific realism if some appropriately non-trivial version of the thesis of the Underdetermination of Empirical Theory by Data does indeed hold globally. In any case, the rightful place in the overall agenda belonging to the issue between Dummett's realist and his anti-realist is, *pace* Blackburn, incontrovertible.

II
The Manifestation Challenge

A head-on response to Blackburn's paper would identify one of his characters – the Teller, Surveyor, Theorist, Anti-reductionist, Insulationist or Non-guarantor – with the Real Realist, and proceed to explain why that character was indeed both philosophically substantial and vulnerable to anti-realist criticism. However, the impression that an adequate response would have to assume that form ignores, it seems to me, the extent to which the space of relevant alternatives is defined by the very arguments which figure in the anti-realist 'negative programme'. That is the point of calling those various lines of thought 'challenges'. A philosophical challenge consists in an argument that a number of beliefs, which are held individually to be attractive, are, if not outright inconsistent, at any rate in tension with each other. In the cases with which we are concerned, 'anti-realism' is the label associated with certain specific responses to such a putative tension. But the ingredients in the tension are multiple, and it is therefore to be expected that someone to whom the recommended responses are unattractive will have options; at the least, there will be the option of trying to make out that there is in reality no tension. The character whom the semantical anti-realist is 'anti' can thus be anyone who, for whatever reason, either disputes the reality of the tension, or favours a non-recommended response to it. There need be no well-defined, historically distinguished view, already thought of as 'realist', which neatly corresponds to one in particular of these reactions.

That said, it is, actually, easier to characterize the realist – for the purposes of this debate – than Blackburn manages to make it seem, and I will do so below. But the substantive questions are whether the tensions felt by the anti-realist are genuine, and whether, if so, there are defensible responses besides those 'recommended'.

What in these terms are the beliefs which combine to set up the 'manifestation challenge'? Essentially, they are three. The first is the broadly Wittgensteinian conception of meaning and understanding according to which understanding an expression is knowing its proper use, and such knowledge consists in a complex of practical abilities. The Wittgensteinian idea is familiar (and vague) enough to strike most people now as a harmless platitude. But it has definite and substantial implications. One is its repudiation of the idea of understanding as a kind of *interior informational state*, the source and explanation of competent use. Another is that *practical* abilities, in the spirit of the Wittgensteinian conception, are essentially abilities to perform appropriately in public: to perform in ways which may be publicly appraised as coming up to scratch, in the prevailing circumstances, or not. Now, possession of a publicly appraisable ability need not, in the general case, imply any capacity of self-appraisal, nor any capacity to recognize if, or how, prevailing circumstances are apt for its exercise. It is possible to be a performer without having the concepts of the critic – indeed, without having any concept of the circumstances to which the performance is a response. But it is different with understanding: the ability to appraise one's own and others' uses is here an essential ingredient in the original ability. The performance abilities that constitute an understanding of an expression count for nothing unless associated with the ability to *evaluate* one's own and others' performance with that expression. So understanding, if it is to be viewed as a practical ability at all, has to be seen as a complex of *discriminatory* capacities: an overall ability intentionally to suit one's use of the expression to the obtaining of factors which can be appreciated by oneself and others to render one's use apt.

A normal understanding of a declarative sentence, in particular, will involve a wide range of performance abilities: the ability to discriminate, *modulo* other germane beliefs, between what constitutes favourable, unfavourable and neutral evidence with respect to it; the ability to recognize its inferential ancestry and progeny; the ability to construct explanations which use it, or bear on why it might be true or false; the ability appropriately to deploy ascriptions of propositional attitude which embed it; and so on. But each of these is essentially an appreciable – that is, *manifestable* – ability, which is also – since such appreciation is part of understanding – a *recognitional* ability, an ability to recognize whether, and if so by what, a particular use of the sentence is rendered appropriate in a prevailing context. Thus the slogan: knowing the content of a statement is a complex of manifestable, recognitional skills.

Call this first, Wittgensteinian ingredient the *Manifestability Principle.* The second ingredient is the *Truth-Conditional Conception* of understanding: the thesis that what constitutes an understanding of any declarative sentence is a knowledge of its truth-conditions, a knowledge of how matters have to stand in order for it to be, respectively, either true or false. The Manifestability Principle and the Truth-Conditional Conception are not in overt tension exactly, although someone who wishes to endorse both at least has some explaining to do. The Manifestability Principle bids us view the understanding of a declarative sentence as a complex of abilities, and the Truth-Conditional Conception seems to superimpose a unifying frame, to postulate a thread which runs through the evidence-sifting, inferential and other abilities involved in understanding the sentence and somehow binds them together. Knowing the truth-conditions of the sentence has to be a state which somehow guarantees possession of these various abilities, and the question must therefore be acknowledged how the guarantee is sustained.

It is when the third ingredient – the thesis that truth is unconstrained by the availability of evidence (evidence-transcendence) – is introduced that a real tension is generated. For if truth in general is evidentially unconstrained, then – depending on its subject matter – knowing the truth-conditions of a sentence may require an understanding of how it could be undetectably true. And how could that knowledge consist – as the Manifestability Principle requires it must – in any ability whose proper exercise is tied to *appreciable* situations? How can knowing what it is for an unappreciable situation to obtain be constituted by capacities of discrimination exercised in response to appreciable ones?

I take it as obvious only that this is a good question, not that it doesn't have a good answer. But suppose it does not have a good answer. Then we ought to reject one or more of the ingredients that lead to the problem. What is characteristic of any anti-realist response to the situation is the belief that the tension is genuine and that the first of the three component theses which generate it should be inviolable. There is, in the anti-realist view, simply nothing for understanding to *be* if it is not as conceived by the Manifestability Principle. Now, there is, of course, logical space for a denial of that – Blackburn's Surveyor, for instance, occupies this space. But occupancy of the space is not the adversarial target of the challenge. On the contrary, the whole argument *presupposes* that nobody ought to want to be there.[18] In any case,

18 That is not to say that only men of straw are to be found there: cf. the passage from Sir Peter Strawson quoted below. If it seems to us obvious nowadays that there is nothing to be made of understanding if it is conceived contrary to the Manifestability Principle – for instance, as an interior representation of correct use – it is largely owing to the assimilation into the general philosophical consciousness of the critique of such ideas in the *Philosophical Investigations*. And the target of this critique was not the views of some imaginary Aunt Sally (or Fodorian Auntie), but an extremely natural and influential lay-philosophical misconception.

Blackburn never suggests that this is a space which he personally would favour occupying, or that it is a response to the challenge worth taking seriously.

The anti-realist, then, at least as far as the Manifestation Challenge is concerned, is someone who is persuaded that there is an irreconcilable tension between the three ingredients, and maintains that no satisfactory response to it can proceed via rejection of the Manifestability Principle. The options are therefore two: rejection of the Truth-Conditional Conception of statement understanding, or its retention subject to the constraint that the 'truth' in 'truth-conditions' denote an evidentially constrained notion. Many of Dummett's and my own earlier discussions of these matters proceeded on the assumption that truth is nothing if not classical (evidence-transcendent) and hence that the Truth-Conditional Conception has to be supplanted by something in which warranted assertion, or perhaps verification, plays the central role. It is therefore understandable that Blackburn's discussion should proceed on the same assumption – more specifically, on the assumption that anti-realist semantics has to be assertibility-conditional.[19] But, if understandable, it is an assumption which he should nevertheless have avoided. For the bifurcation in the anti-realist's options was explicit in the Introduction to the first edition of *Realism, Meaning and Truth*[20] – one of the sources to which Blackburn is responding – and the prospects for a truth-conditional version of anti-realist semantics are the centre of attention in Essay 12, in which the play is made with the notion of superassertibility to which Blackburn refers.[21]

When the issue is set up in the way I have been describing, it is clear that Blackburn has heavy-weathered the question, Who is the realist?

19 It is still, of course, an egregious error to attempt to make critical capital out of the supposed consequence of the assertibility-conditional approach that statements – like the 'old campaigners' – which are a priori insulated from all rational assessment, and hence have no conditions of warranted assertion, are therefore *meaningless*. Meaningless sentences, to be sure, do not – in the sense of ever being warrantedly assertible – have conditions of warranted assertion. But Blackburn argues as if the converse were evident. (See e.g. 'Manifesting Realism', p. 41.) And the fact is that the anti-realist has as much title as anyone else to treat it as a criterion for understanding one of the old campaigners – for instance, if it indeed comes into that category, 'Everything is uniformly increasing in size' – that someone be able, e.g., to explain why, in view of the meanings of its constituent expressions and their manner of combination, nothing could count as evidence for its truth. It is one thing for a sentence to lack assertibility-conditions; another for it to determine, by virtue of its semantic structure, assertibility-conditions which necessarily go uninstantiated. (A parallel argument to Blackburn's would conclude that, if meaning is determined by truth-conditions, contradictions are meaningless because they lack truth-conditions.)

20 This volume, p. 36.

21 'Manifesting Realism', p. 40.

Realism about a given discourse, for the purposes of the Manifestation Challenge, is simply the combination of views (a) that the proper account of our understanding of its statements is evidence-unconstrained truth-conditional, and (b) that the world on occasion exploits, so to speak, this understanding – does on occasion deliver up undetectable truth-conferrers for those statements.[22] And, to repeat, it is worth describing such a view as 'realism' because of the sharp separation which it imposes between the statements' being true on the one hand and their meeting our most refined criteria of acceptability on the other. None of the characters in Blackburn's parade is described as holding exactly this realism, though – if (b) is assumed – the Insulationist and the Non-guarantor will presumably do so.

Blackburn's claim, to be fair, was that it is difficult to find a *vulnerable* target for the Manifestation Challenge. Since there simply is no challenge if the Manifestability Principle is rejected, and since Blackburn himself shows no inclination to reject it, his thought has accordingly to be that there is no real tension: that it is consistent with accepting the Manifestability Principle to hold (a). So one real target is the realist as *Compatibilist*: a realist who aspires to a portfolio which contains (a), (b) and the Manifestability Principle. Is this a vulnerable target, or can such a combination be made coherent?

III
Compatibilism

I have no general, conclusive proof that it cannot. But Blackburn, for his part, simply fails to confront the issue squarely. In order to see what confronting it squarely would involve, consider the example, discussed in the Introduction,[23] of applications of simple predicates of taste – 'sweet', 'salty', 'bitter', 'sour', 'spicy' and so on. What is it to understand statements of the form, 'This is F', in which 'F' is one of these adjectives of taste and the demonstrated object is one of a number of food and drink samples placed in easy reach? What abilities are associated with such understanding? Well, there will typically be a number of 'neighbourhood abilities', in Blackburn's useful phrase: the abilities, for instance, to reason to and from such statements on the

22 Strictly, it might be enough if, even if the world never actually so delivered, its failure to do so was merely contingent. Note that Dummett's original formulations of realism, in which the view is characterized as essentially the endorsement of a bivalent truth-conditional semantics, thereby involve, for suitable discourses, a rolled-into-one version of the semantic and worldly aspects which I have separated as (a) and (b).
23 pp. 17ff.

basis of collateral information, and successfully to handle more complex sentences, for instance ascriptions of propositional attitude, in which descriptions of taste occur as embedded clauses. But in this instance, at least, there is an ingredient ability which is plausibly regarded as fundamental: the ability to recognize the tastes of the various samples by tasting them, and to report such recognition by using the statements in question.

That 'This is salty' expresses a truth is a state of affairs which, in appropriate circumstances, may be verified to obtain by tasting the demonstrated substance. So much is uncontentious (and quite neutral on matters like the defeasibility of simple descriptions of taste or the question whether they somehow typify a class of judgements which might play a foundational role in some semantic or epistemological project). Simply: there is such as thing as the ability to discriminate tastes by tasting, and it is an appreciable, recognitional ability. Since to exercise it is to recognize whether or not the truth-conditions of sentences of the sort in question are satisfied, it is perfectly appropriate to regard it as amounting to a knowledge of their truth-conditions.

This ability unquestionably constitutes one aspect of our understanding of the sentences in question. Is it just one aspect, though? It is tempting to say more: viz. that this recognitional grasp of the truth-conditions of such judgements constitutes the *core* of understanding them, so that if someone does indeed have this grasp, but apparently lacks some of the neighbourhood abilities, we are obliged to locate the deficiency in understanding – if that is what it is – elsewhere. Conversely, we are strongly inclined to say that someone who proved unable to acquire the core recognitional abilities could have no real understanding of the content of such statements, even if that person was rather successful at acquiring the neighbourhood abilities – rather as someone whose vision was monochromatic might acquire grasp of a good stock of proxy-grounds for claims about colour.

Plausibly, then, in the case of such judgements, the Manifestability Principle and the Truth-Conditional Conception can be made to cohere perfectly. Grasp of such judgements' truth-conditions will be a manifestable, recognitional skill, and there will be a case for regarding it as constitutive of an understanding of them. But what is here conspicuously lacking of course, is any place for the third ingredient in the original tension: the evidence-transcendence of truth. It is possible – if it is possible – to bring the Manifestability Principle and the Truth-Conditional Conception together in the fashion sketched only because 'grasp of truth-conditions' can here be *identified* with a recognitional ability; and it can be so only because we conceive of the states of affairs which confer truth and falsity on these judgements as, by their very nature, detectable. It would be different if we were concerned with a type of judgement whose truth-conferrers we conceived as merely sometimes detectable, but on other occasions inaccessible to us. For to grasp the truth-conditions of such judgements could not be *identified* merely with the ability to recognize that they were satisfied in the favourable kind of case; it would be necessary, in addition, to understand what it would be for them to be satisfied unrecognizably. And the problem would then be to construe *that* understanding as the Manifestability Principle requires.

Blackburn's patter about 'men of straw' and 'cracked instruments' notwithstanding, I believe that most people would be instinctually drawn on the idea that the role played by grasp of truth-conditions in the taste-example is in no way special – that what is special is only that here we can find a distinctive practical ability for grasp of truth-conditions to be. That is: when, as in the example – statements about the remote past, counterfactual conditionals, putative general laws and so on – on which the debate has tended to concentrate, the 'neighbourhood abilities' are all the practical abilities that there are, our instinct remains that there is something more: precisely, the old 'interior informational state', serving to inform the exercise of the neighbourhood abilities and to bind them together. Understanding a statement, the thought is, is *always* like that in essentials; what distinguishes the taste-example is just that, quite unusually, the core of understanding here steps forward to show itself on the surface. As I say, I believe that this is our instinctual view. But it does occasionally surface in professional philosophy. A clear contemporary expression is due not to a strawman but to Strawson:

> A rational speaker's grasp of his language is *manifested* in, *inter alia*, his responding in certain ways to the recognisable situations with which he is and has been confronted...Wright seems to take it as evident that the rational speaker's response to such situations can in *no* case be *governed* by a certain kind of conception – a conception of a state of affairs, of a condition of truth, which, for one reason or another, in fact or in principle, is not, or is no longer, or is not for the speaker, accessible to direct observation or memory...[But] this question – whether the rational speaker's response can be so governed – is just the question at issue.[24]

How can we interpret the emphasis on 'governed' if it is not that Strawson intends that the understanding should be thought of as something detached from the neighbourhood abilities, from which they flow?

24 Strawson, 'Scruton and Wright on Anti-realism, Etc.', p. 16.

However that may be, Blackburn is, as noted, agreed that this non-compatibilist direction is not the way to go. But then, what is the way to go? So far as I can see, there is only one: the compatibilist line has to be that the connection between understanding and grasp of truth-conditions is *platitudinous*.[25] And such is, in effect, Blackburn's proposal. One could spell the thought out like this. To understand a statement is to know what it says, which will be that a certain state of affairs obtains. But it is a priori, and common knowledge, that when S says that P, it follows that S is true if and only if P. So the obtaining of the relevant state of affairs has to be conceived, by one who understands the statement, as necessary and sufficient for its truth. Hence, whatever abilities constitute the understanding of a statement, we cannot but acquiesce in its description as 'grasp of truth-conditions'. In particular, if only 'neighbourhood abilities' are available, then *they* constitute a knowledge of the statement's truth-conditions.

The anti-realist who favours responding to the Manifestation Challenge by '...dethroning truth and falsity from their central place in...the theory of meaning'[26] presumably has some work to do in response to this line of thought. Not so, though, the anti-realist who favours retention of the Truth-Conditional Conception, *modulo* an evidentially constrained conception of truth. And the staring fact is that the line of thought does absolutely nothing to dissipate the tension to which this anti-realist is responding. *Identifying* grasp of a statement's truth-conditions with possession of a network of practical, discriminatory abilities – the 'neighbourhood abilities' – simply makes it the more puzzling how, in grasping those truth-conditions, we are somehow guaranteed to understand the possibility, in the case of a suitable example, that those conditions be satisfied undetectably. There is absolutely no progress. The question remains: how, specifically, is the idea that statements of a certain kind can be unrecognizably true or false on display in our ordinary evidential, inferential, explanatory and other practices with them? The 'neighbourhood abilities' are all appreciable, recognitional abilities. Let it be a platitude, or a consequence of platitudes, that they compose a knowledge of truth-conditions; the question is, how do they compose a knowledge of (potentially) *evidence-transcendent* truth-conditions – how would they differ if, for whatever reason, we thought of truth as essentially evidence-constrained?

25 This is the line pursued by John McDowell in 'Anti-realism and the Epistemology of Understanding'; see esp. pp. 229–31. For further references and discussion, see the Introduction to the present volume, pp. 18ff.

26 Dummett, concluding paragraph of 'Truth'.

Blackburn resurrects the charge, first made in *Spreading the Word*,[27] that the demand for manifestability is ill-conceived until we have specified the powers of the intended audience. I discussed this thought in the Introduction, but although Blackburn refers to that discussion, I do not seem to have succeeded in making its point clear. Summarily: there is *no problem at all* about specifying the powers of the intended audience – to manifest my understanding of a statement, I need an audience who *understand* that statement. This whole debate is taking place with respect to regions of discourse which all the protagonists are presumed fully to understand. The question is: what can someone do, in using a particular statement, to rightly convince an audience, who understand that statement, that the proper description of his/her understanding combines all three elements in the original tension? Blackburn's reply then comes to this: maybe nothing can be done unless the *audience's* understanding already combines those elements. But this offers no assurance whatever in a context in which their combinability is already *sub judice*. Besides, if Blackburn is right, the chances are that his anti-realist opponent provides a 'suitable audience', *malgré soi*. So why not just answer the question? Let us have a description – appreciable by anyone who understands whatever kind of statement is giving rise to the problem – of what specifically, in the exercise of an understanding of such statements, manifests the fact that it consists in grasping a potentially evidence-transcendent truth-condition.

It is important not to mistake what is being requested. The question is not – at least in the first instance – how one might manifest the *belief* that one's own understanding was realist. Presumably it would be allowable to *say* that it was. The issue rather concerns what in one's use of the relevant class of statements would manifest the fact that this belief was *true*.[28] In the nature of the case, then, one is looking for evidence in linguistic practice apart from the mere protestation of realism. Someone could *profess* a conception, for instance, which allowed that the comic quality of a situation could be evidence-transcendent. 'For the humour of a situation to be inaccessible to us', they might claim, 'is only and purely for the situation relevantly to resemble situations whose comic quality is apparent to us, but without the resemblance being apparent.' Compare: for someone to be unbreakably stoically in

27 *Spreading the Word*, pp. 65–6.

28 The situation is dialectically somewhat subtle, however. Suppose we recoil from the idea that a subject's possession of a belief could be manifest only in its avowal; then it might be a condition of so much as believing – genuinely believing – that one's understanding of a class of statements was realist that one behave in ways which would supply the materials for a direct response to the Manifestation Challenge, and thereby establish the belief as true.

pain – a Putnam X-worlder[29] – is just for it to be with them as it is with others who are in pain and, one way or another, can be brought to show it; it is just that this subject cannot be brought to show it. Such a possibility strikes us (doesn't it?) as an absurd misrepresentation of our understanding of discourse about the comic; we have no conception, surely, of what comic quality could consist in if it is allowed to transcend any elicitable human response. But *showing* that that is so would require, precisely, a demonstration that the best account of our understanding of statements about the comic, as manifested in our use of them, left no space for the alleged possibility.

So too for any philosophy of mind which would allow inscrutable stoicism to be a possibility: the prior question is whether we actually understand ascriptions of sensation, and of mental states in general, in such a way that evidence-transcendent truth-conferral makes sense. And that is a question which can be settled only by reference to the verdict on the matter of the best account of our use of discourse concerning the mental. Making good the compatibilist response, when understanding is regarded as platitudinously truth-conditional, has to consist in finding something in the overt nature of the 'neighbourhood abilities' – apart from mere professions of realism – which is best explained by viewing the 'truth' that is thereby platitudinously linked with understanding as (potentially) evidence-transcendent. The story could concern, perhaps, our acceptance of a particular kind of evidence, or inference pattern; or it might be that the use of certain embedding contexts was hard to explain otherwise.[30] I am far less confident than I was ten years ago that such a story can never be told. But to meet the Manifestation Challenge is to tell such a story, and Blackburn's paper contains no clear response to this simple and utterly legitimate demand. Indeed, except in his discussion of what he perceives as the shortcomings of the assertibility-conditions approach to our understanding of undecided mathematical statements, he never so much as gets down to cases.

Let me stress again that the manifestation question only concerns the character of our understanding. The question is: have we assigned meaning to the statements in a certain discourse in such a way that there is space for the world to deliver up evidence-transcendent truth-conferrers for them? So an affirmative answer is not yet a commitment to realism.[31] Someone might give an affirmative answer and hold that,

29 Putnam, 'Brains and Behavior', in his *Philosophical Papers 2: Mind, Language and Reality*, pp. 325–41.

30 Relevant problems here are posed by Fitch's Paradox – sometimes called the Paradox of Knowability; see Essay 13 below. See also the appendix to Essay 12.

31 This distinction is well emphasized in Luntley's *Language, Logic and Experience.*

for independent reasons, there is no reality to which the discourse answers at all. What we are exploring, in the issue about manifestation, is whether a *necessary* condition is satisfied for the appropriateness of a certain kind of realist view: the view that holds that, in the discourse in question, truth and optimal justification extensionally diverge, and hence that we have to think of the domain of states of affairs in which the truth-conferrers are to be found as constituted independently of our cognitive activity.

IV
Revisionism and Holism

If the whole semantical anti-realist polemic were provided by the Manifestation Challenge, as described, it might seem very unclear how there could be any support for the revisionist philosophy of logic which some sympathizers with it, most especially Dummett, have famously advocated. For surely one cannot sensibly urge both that it is moot whether anything in one's practice of a discourse of a certain kind manifests understanding of a certain character and, in the same breath, urge revision of aspects of the practice which, it is claimed, would only be appropriate *if* the understanding were of that character. Either, it seems, the case for revision must be inconclusive – because the relevant aspects of the practice could as well be sanctioned in other ways – or else it is ill-founded, those very aspects providing the requisite distinctive manifestation that one's understanding of the discourse has the character in question.

One answer would be that no difficulty need arise if the Dummettian revisionist can provide an *independent* argument that understanding cannot be evidence-transcendent truth-conditional – perhaps from considerations to do with concept-acquisition. But in that case there would be no purpose to the argument about manifestation. The ground for saying that the problematical understanding could not be manifest in practice would be that it could not in any case be *possessed*; and that would directly provide motive enough for revision of aspects of practice which seemed to depend upon it. So the question remains: how can the Manifestation Challenge contribute, as Dummett evidently intends that it should, to a revisionary philosophy of logic?

The answer is that revisionism, if it is to be based on the Manifestation Challenge, needs *molecularism*: it needs the claim that the dubious kind of understanding, if it were not to be dubious, would have to be manifest in our practice within a *fragment* of the discourse where it is, at least prima facie, not manifest. Only then can it coherently be argued that aspects of the discourse outside that fragment, in whose practice the dubious conception *is* reflected, involve malpractice.[32] Dummett, I hasten to say, has never been under any illusions about this, and has always taken an explicitly molecular view, believing that anything else will lead to an incoherent form of holism.

I myself am far from persuaded whether that is so; and somewhat sceptical also about the possibility of making good the presupposition that our understanding of the statements in a discourse may be fully on display in advance of any consideration of the way we use certain contexts which embed them.[33] But the point I want to emphasize is that it is in this context that the issues to do with holism arise. Blackburn represents Dummett as invoking the spectre of meaning-holism in response to the extension of 'grasp of truth-conditions' to cover all the 'neighbourhood abilities'.[34] I should expect Dummett, rightly in my view, to offer no objection to so using 'grasp of truth-conditions'. In any case, the issues to do with holism are properly located elsewhere on the map.

V
The Arguments from Rule-following and from Normativity

I have here concentrated on considerations to do with the manifestation of understanding, because Blackburn concentrates on them. Understandably, since the suggestion was not developed in the first edition of *Realism, Meaning and Truth*, he makes nothing of the fourth anti-realist argument which I briefly canvassed in the Introduction – that which ties the issues concerning evidence-transcendent truth-conditions to what have come to be known as 'the rule-following considerations'. The key thought here is that, since the relation which obtains between a statement and its truth-conferrer is an *internal* relation – it being an essential characteristic of that statement to be rendered true by that state of affairs and an essential characteristic of that state of affairs to render true any statement with that content – belief in evidence-transcendent truths is a commitment to belief in unratifiable internal relations. And that belief can be sustained only on the picture of rules and rule-following which embodies the 'myth of super-rigid machinery' on which

32 For a valuably detailed discussion of the issues here, see Tennant's *Anti-realism and Logic*, sects 6–10. See also Edwards's 'Atomic Realism, Intuitionist Logic and Tarskian Truth'.

33 See Essay 14 below for elaboration of these misgivings.

34 'Manifesting Realism', p. 35.

Wittgenstein targets his discussions. My own belief is that this is probably the most powerful of the weapons in the anti-realist's armoury, although I cannot of course go into its details here. But note that it bites in a rather different place to the Manifestation Challenge. The target of the latter is whether anything in our understanding of a discourse prepares for the possibility that the world might confer truth-values upon its statements undetectably; but the conclusion of the argument from rule-following is to the effect that, even if our understanding of a discourse is so prepared, the world cannot ever actually *bring about* a determinate undetectable truth. For a statement's being undetectably true could only consist, to repeat, in the obtaining of an unratifiable internal relation.

Blackburn does, however, have some things to say about what, in the Introduction, I called the Argument from Normativity. In rough outline, the argument runs like this. Only sentences with assertoric content are apt to be true. And, trivially, for a sentence to have assertoric content is for its content to equip it for use in accordance with whatever constraints assertions distinctively have to conform to. Accordingly, since truth is normative of proper assertion – is that at which assertion is, properly, essentially aimed – it is a condition of a sentence's having assertoric content that it may in certain circumstances be used as an *attempt* at the truth. But, for reasons to do with the nature of intention which were outlined in the Introduction,[35] there is no aiming at the truth by the use of a sentence whose truth, it is known – if it could be true – would transcend all possible evidence.

As Blackburn in effect argues, the argument bears directly only on his realist as Insulationist – a realist who believes that, in the nature of the case, the truth-values of the statements in a certain region of discourse are beyond human ken. For in that case, whatever is regulating proper practice in the discourse in question, it cannot be the aim of truth so conceived; and the 'grasp of truth-conditions' which platitudinously constitutes understanding of those statements cannot be grasp of conditions of insulated truth. Blackburn does not quarrel with the point about intention, and acknowledges that 'insulationism is tempting and worth fighting against'. Nevertheless, he finds the argument unconvincing:

> Truth may indeed be a norm governing assertoric discourse, but...this may not be its only role. The concept appears to figure in thoughts like 'there may be truths about which we shall never be able to reason', or 'there may be truths accessible only to minds alien to ours' and a

35 pp. 24–6 above.

> proponent of the normativity argument will need to wrestle with the stubborn appearance of intelligibility in such thoughts.[36]

Well, but are the allegedly possible truths to which these putatively intelligible thoughts advert at least to be expressible in our language? They had better be: it would be a stupendous *ignoratio elenchi* to reproach an argument which – like all the arguments for semantic anti-realism – is concerned with the proper account of truth and truth-conditions for assertoric discourses *which we understand* on the ground that it fails to dispose of realist sentiment which takes refuge in the ineffable. Assume, therefore, that Blackburn is not doing that, and that the 'stubbornly intelligible-seeming' thoughts refer to possible truths which we would have the means to convey by intelligible assertion. In that case, the argument was that it is a constraint on the means of conveyance that it be possible to use the relevant sentences to aim at the truth. The question is therefore: can we so aim in the putative cases in question? Not, according to the considerations about intention, if we *know* that the sentences in question, if they express truths at all, express truths which we cannot reason about and which cannot be accessible to minds like ours. But if our knowing that is not part of the scenario, then the supporter of the intelligibility of the thoughts in question cannot be Blackburn's Insulationist. The position calls, rather, for the realist as Non-Guarantor.

The Non-Guarantor holds not that truth and falsity within a given discourse are a priori inaccessible to us, but only that they may be. Is this position engaged by the Argument from Normativity? Blackburn fails to see that it can be, arguing that if truth for the statements of the discourse is merely potentially evidence-transcendent, then we can surely try for it, even if – de facto – we cannot actually succeed. But if I seemed to suggest anything to the contrary, I shouldn't have. The argument, as against the Non-Guarantor, is not that we cannot aim at truth in regions of discourse where we are prone to conceive of truth as potentially inaccessible, but rather that it is not *that* notion of truth at which we should be regarded as aiming. One case for saying so, sketched in 'Truth-conditions and Criteria',[37] is to the effect that there is simply no difference between aiming at a potentially evidence-transcendent objective and aiming at the realization of a situation in which there is evidence that the objective has after all been attained. This argument brings the issue back into the area of manifestability: the claim is that, as far as the pattern assumed by my linguistic practice is

36 'Manifesting Realism', p. 41.
37 This volume, Essay 1, pp. 58–61.

concerned, it is all the same whether I am aiming at a species of truth which may be associated with favourable evidence but may also be inaccessible in any particular case, or at a species of truth which, I conceive, must issue in the availability of favourable evidence whenever it applies. Either way, the constraints on proper assertion will be the same.

In the Introduction, however, I tried to tackle the Non-Guarantor somewhat differently.[38] To understand a statement as associated with potentially evidence-transcendent truth-conditions would have to be – assuming sufficient expressive resources in the language – to understand what it would be for a statement which averred that the former *was* undetectably true to be itself true, a fortiori undetectably so. But the possible truth of such a statement requires its possession of assertoric content, and therefore – it was supposed – its serviceability under certain circumstances for an *attempt* to speak the truth. And, so it was argued, there is no attempting anything if one has no beliefs about how to succeed, no intelligible motive for success, and if success will have no discernible consequences. So we cannot attempt the truth by the use of any statement which, like 'S is undetectably true', can only be true by being so undetectably. The consequence is that such a statement lacks genuine assertoric content, and hence is not itself in the market for truth; it follows that our understanding of the original S was misrepresented when portrayed as involving its association with potentially evidence-transcendent truth-conditions.

One difference between this argument against the Non-Guarantor and the original directed against the Insulationist is that the point about intention may now seem slightly less secure, on the ground that failure – in the form of S's turning out *detectably* true or false – *can* have discernible consequences. But I don't think that this is an important difference. At most, it can reinstate the *avoidance of detectable failure* as an attemptable objective; and avoiding detectable failure is not, in the examples we are concerned with, the same thing as success. In any case, the obligations of an opponent of these arguments are quite clear: reason must be found to reject either the proposed constraint on assertoric content, or the considerations about intention. Again, there is obviously much more to say, and I am by no means confident that it will go the anti-realist's way. For instance: can statements of, by the lights of the argument, dubious assertoric content ('S is undetectably true') sustain determinate logical relations with statements ('S is detectably true') for which the argument occasions no difficulty?

38 p. 24 above.

But I shall not pursue these issues further here. My purpose in this section has been only to clarify the normativity argument somewhat and to scotch the impression given by Blackburn that I had made no distinction between the Insulationist and Non-Guarantor as far as the bearing of the argument was concerned, believing that the de facto unavailability of evidence for the truth of a statement would be as much an obstacle to the possibility of using it with the aim of truth as would the knowledge a priori that no such evidence could be available.

8

A Note on Two Realist Lines of Argument

Christopher Peacocke on Classical Universal Quantification and Classical Negation

None of the writings of supporters of semantical realism surpasses the detail and rigour of the proposals which Christopher Peacocke has recently been developing, particularly the defence outlined in his *Thoughts* of a globally anti-verificationist account of propositional content, and the defence of a classical construal of the logical constants in his 1987 British Academy lecture.[1] Unlike most critics of anti-realism, Peacocke accepts many of the constraints which the anti-realist charges an account of meaning and understanding to respect, including in particular the crucial constraint of the manifestability of understanding, and tries to show that a best defence of realism can muster the resources to comply with them. If his proposals are correct in detail, an especially satisfying resolution of the issues is therefore in prospect.

A properly worked out anti-realist response to Peacocke's ideas would be a large project. In this brief note I shall be concerned merely to point out the insufficiency of two lines of thought which have, I believe, been formative in the recent development of his realist views.

I
Universal Quantification

In the terminology of *Thoughts*, a *canonical ground* for a content, P, is a condition, C, such that a thinker who judges that C is satisfied is thereby rationally committed to the judgement that P. Likewise a

1 C. Peacocke, *Thoughts: An Essay on Content*, and 'Understanding Logical Constants: A Realist's Account'. See also his 'The Limits of Intelligibility: A Post-Verificationist Proposal' and 'Proof and Truth'. Chs 2 and 3 of *Thoughts*, on observational contents and universal quantification, are prefigured in 'What Determines Truth-Conditions?'

canonical commitment is any condition, C, such that a thinker who judges that P is thereby rationally committed to judging that C is satisfied. Let the *acceptance-conditions* of a content, P, embrace all and only its canonical commitments and canonical grounds (either or both of these categories may, of course, be empty in particular cases). Then the guiding thesis of *Thoughts* is that there is a basic but wide class of contents whose truth-conditions are directly determined by certain of their acceptance conditions; while the truth-conditions of contents outside this class are fixed by certain of their relations to contents within it. This thesis is defended in connection with observational contents, certain contents whose principal operator is a universal or existential quantifier, contents whose principal operator is negation, and contents concerning inaccessible regions of space and time.

Peacocke's discussion of universally quantified statements in *Thoughts* centres on a subtle and complex treatment of examples where the range of quantification comprises currently existing material objects. But as far as the proposed treatment of the issues to do with manifestability is concerned, it will make no difference if we focus on universal quantification over the natural numbers. In both kinds of case Peacocke proposes what he calls a *commitment model* of the way in which truth-conditions are determined: that is, for universal quantifications of both these kinds, his contention is that there is a certain spectrum of canonical commitments such that the quantified statement is true if and only if each of those canonical commitments is fulfilled. Accounting for the form of such canonical commitments in the case of quantifications over contemporary material objects and defending the commitment model in the light of that account is what gives Peacocke most work. Matters are, by contrast, straightforward in the case of natural numbers:

> ...one who judges 'all natural numbers are G' is [canonically] committed to all instances of 'If n is sss...s0, then n is G', where the number of applications of the successor functor 's' is any natural number; any other commitments of the judgement are derivative from this family of commitments...

and 'All natural numbers are G' is true just in case each of these commitments is fulfilled. This account of the content of such judgements, Peacocke continues,

> does not make knowledge of what would constitute [their] proof a prerequisite for grasp of such contents...we take at face value the situation of someone who understands quantifiers over natural numbers, but who does not know how such contents would be proved – the situation of all of us before we discovered or learned inductive proofs. What we learn

> when this method of proof is taught is that certain premises guarantee the truth of a content previously grasped....Nor is knowledge of truth-conditions required for understanding, or for establishing, complex contents in which universal quantifications are embedded. If the truth-condition really is determined by the canonical commitments, a thinker who knows nothing of proof-conditions in the arithmetical case may be able to appreciate that if his commitments in judging 'all F's are G' and 'Fa' are fulfilled so too will be the commitments he incurs in judging 'Ga'. This can establish for him the complex content 'If all F's are G, and a is F, then a is G' without his knowing any proof-conditions for the universal quantification.[2]

The line of thought here gets its putative anti-anti-realist sting from two claims: first, that – so Peacocke contends – the truth-conditions determined for universally quantified contents in accordance with the commitment model are *classical*, evidentially unconstrained ones; second, that the manner in which such contents' truth-conditions are determined by their acceptance conditions provides the resources for a direct response to the anti-realist's 'manifestation challenge'. For a thinker may manifest the fact that he grasps a content with such a classical truth-condition in a way which need involve no displayed understanding of inductive or other proof-conditions of universally quantified number-theoretic statements, nor, more generally, any capacity for recognizing when the truth-conditions of such a content are realized. It is, Peacocke contends, simply a mistake to suppose that a grasp of truth-conditions can be manifest, if at all, only in a capacity to recognize when they are met:

> ...a classical truth-condition is manifested not by a thinker's actions when he recognises the truth-condition to obtain, but rather by his commitments when he judges the universal quantification: for all those commitments to be fulfilled, the classical truth-condition has to obtain, albeit that it is not conclusively knowable that it does so. For each one of these commitments, the thinker can manifest that it is one of his commitments: that a thinker judges a content with a particular family of commitments is not unmanifestable.[3]

There is a very good reason for sympathy with the general direction of these remarks: it is that the propriety of inductive proof in number theory might dawn on someone by way of a *discovery* – that a bright schoolboy, for instance, set the problem of devising a general strategy

2 *Thoughts*, p. 39.
3 *Thoughts*, pp. 40–1.

for establishing universally quantified conclusions over infinite or unsurveyable domains which can be arrayed in the form of a linear progression, might hit on induction as exactly such a strategy. Induction is an apt method of proof in the light of a *background* understanding we have of the sense of quantification over natural numbers, and any account which ties the understanding of such quantifications too tightly to their proof-conditions will have great difficulty in duly acknowledging the fact.

What is not clear is why it should be supposed that a *realist* account is necessary if that fact is to be duly acknowledged – and indeed, why exactly the commitment model should be supposed to import realism. I think Peacocke is simply mistaken about the matter, and that the mistake arises from overlooking that classical truth-conditional and constructivist proof-conditional accounts of universal quantification do not exhaust the field. The semantical anti-realist has absolutely no reason to – and had better not – contest the claim that to judge that all natural numbers are G is to be committed to each claim of the form

If n is sss...s0, then n is G,

nor to contest that the original judgement is true just in case each of these commitments is fulfilled. What he must, of course, contest is that our understanding of the original judgement is informed by a conception of what it is for the truth-condition in question to obtain *undetectably*; a conception, that is, of what it is for each of the commitments to be satisfied although we have in principle no way of recognizing the fact. But it is of course perfectly consistent to hold *both* that the spectrum of canonical commitments of ‘all natural numbers are G’ is exactly as Peacocke describes, with that judgement being true just in case each of the commitments is realized, *and* that the satisfaction of that truth-condition – which is to say: the realization of each of those commitments – is a state of affairs that may not coherently be conceived as evidence-transcendent.

The fact is that the commitment account of the content of universal quantifications over natural numbers is simply *neutral* as between realist and anti-realist conceptions of such contents’ truth-conditions. Consider how exactly someone might manifest an understanding of a universal quantification of which the commitment model supplied a correct account – how exactly, without displaying any capacity to recognize the satisfaction of such a content’s truth-conditions, a thinker might display the understanding which such an account is designed to describe. Peacocke’s discussion is surprisingly inexplicit on this crucial question. The germane idea in the last-quoted passage appears to be merely that for any particular one of the spectrum of canonical commitments associated with a universal quantification over natural numbers, a thinker can manifest that that is indeed one of his commitments; and *hence* his judging a content with that particular family of commitments is not unmanifestable. But how, precisely, does the conclusion follow? Suppose a thinker – Jones – manifests his acceptance of a large class of judgements of the form

If n is sss...s0, then n is G,

and in no known instance manifestly rejects any judgement of that form. Then it would be, in normal circumstances, a well-founded inductive step to

1 Jones would (manifestly) accept any statement of the form, 'If n is sss...s0, then n is G'.[4]

This would be to credit Jones with a certain general disposition. But it would be the merest 'operator-shift' fallacy to advance from that to

2 Jones accepts that any statement of the form 'if n is sss...s0, then n is G', is true

– the fallacy involved in the transition from

Of each statement of a certain type, Jones is disposed to accept that statement as true

to

Jones is disposed to accept that each statement of a certain type is true.

The latter formulation embeds, whereas the former does not embed, a universal quantifier in the content of a belief ascribed to Jones. And Jones might have the general disposition described in (1) without having the concept of universal quantification at all. Clearly, in the light of this very familiar distinction, acceptance of a universally quantified judgement, a fortiori acceptance of a universally quantified judgement with a

4 Strictly, of course, this claim is justified only if restricted to statements of the relevant form which the thinker in question could survey and understand; but we can prescind from that complication.

classical truth-condition, cannot be manifest *merely* in a (putative) acceptance of each of its canonical commitments.

What is required to close the gap is, naturally, some manifestation in the thinker's behaviour both that he understands and accepts the universally quantified judgement and that it is *in virtue of* that acceptance that he is disposed to accept each of a spectrum of canonical commitments. So Peacocke ought to have provided an account of how these additional factors could indeed be manifest in the thinker's behaviour. To be sure, that is presumably a remediable omission. But the fundamental lacuna will remain: it will be one thing to manifest, by the way one treats the canonical commitments and by manifesting the fact that one so treats them *because* one accepts the universally quantified judgement, that one assigns a content to that judgement such that it is true if and only if each of the spectrum of canonical commitments is realized; but it will be quite another to manifest that one has a well-founded conception of how that truth-condition might obtain *undetectably*. And it is the latter which is the crucial consideration if the commitment model is indeed to import a realist conception of universal quantification.

In sum: I think it should be granted that the commitment model of the content of universal quantifications over the natural numbers, and of other kinds of universal quantification to which it is appropriate, does justice to an important intuition which might have seemed to be grist to the realist's mill – the intuition that for this range of cases our conception of the appropriate assertibility-conditions (proof-conditions) is *informed by* a background conception of the content of such claims which cannot in consequence be *reduced to* a grasp of the assertibility-conditions. But it is precisely because the commitment model accommodates this intuition, yet is not, as we have seen, implicitly realistic, that it is a mistake to conclude without further ado that this background conception of the content of universal quantifications demands a realist explanation. It is true that in a number of Dummett's, and others', expositions of the manifestation challenge, the barrier to a manifestation of grasp of realist truth-conditions is supposed to depend on the consideration that such grasp could be, if anything, only a recognitional ability.[5] Peacocke's discussion goes a long way towards dislodging that assumption. But it is, after his discussion, no clearer than it was before how grasp of a distinctively *realist* – evidence-transcendent – truth-condition for a universal quantification is supposed to be manifest.

5 See for example the passage from Dummett's *Elements of Intuitionism* quoted on p. 40 of *Thoughts*.

II
Classical Negation

It is hardly controversial that nothing can rank as the negation of A unless its truth is incompatible with that of A. But in his British Academy lecture, Peacocke makes two interestingly stronger claims: first, that any ordinary thinker who grasps the concept of negation has the resources to recognize that the negation of A is identified, more specifically, as *the weakest proposition* incompatible with A; and second, that it follows from this identification that negation sustains its normal *classical* proof theory, in particular the rules of *reductio ad absurdum* (RAA) and double negation elimination (DNE).[6]

The second claim is obviously of great importance to the debate about semantical anti-realism. Peacocke himself stops short of the conclusion that his argument *enforces* a classical treatment of negation by showing any alternative to be simply unfaithful to the concept. I shall look briefly at the way he motivates this reserve. But, notwithstanding Peacocke's own concessive remarks, it would seem that, if his argument is good, there can be no avoiding the verdict that logics, like that of the Intuitionists, in which DNE is discarded, can only be ill-motivated. Someone who grants the argument must therefore conclude that either the connection, insisted on by Dummett, between semantical anti-realism and revision of classical logic, is misconceived, or that semantical anti-realism itself cannot do justice to the conceptual constitution of the logical constants.

Now, someone who wishes to resist Peacocke's argument had better find fault with the transition from the claim (IC), that the negation of P is the weakest proposition incompatible with P, to the conclusion that DNE is an unrestrictedly valid pattern of inference. For there is – or so it seems to me – no room for dispute of (IC) itself – once a modest but necessary reformulation is effected. Reflect that talk of *the* weakest statement with such-and-such features is infelicitous in any case where there need be no unique such statement but only a number of logical equivalents, all with the features in question. So in the present case: we have no a priori reason to exclude the possibility that there may be a variety of statements – different propositional contents – each incompatible with A, each entailed by any statement incompatible with A. (IC), properly formulated, affirms that ~A is true when, but only when *some* statement is true which is incompatible with A.

6 The Law of Excluded Middle will be, of course, an immediate corollary, in view of the straightforward provability of its double negation in any system of sentential logic containing RAA and vel-Intro.

Peacocke canvasses a number of 'essentially equivalent' ways to reach (IC).[7] But the heart of the matter, I think, concerns the equivalence

(N) $\sim$A is true $\dashv\not\models$ A is not true.

When reformulated as indicated, it is clear that (IC) is an immediate consequence of (N). For what is certainly true when any statement incompatible with A is true is that *A is not true* – so much is merely enjoined by such statements' incompatibility with A. But then (N) ensures that $\sim$A is true in the same range of cases, just as reformulated (IC) affirms.

The question, then, is, what if anything imposes (N)? And the answer is that it is a very direct consequence of the familiar equivalence

(T) A $\dashv\models$ A is true,

and the basic and incontrovertible property of negation that the negations of logical equivalents are equivalent. For then we have that

$\sim$A $\dashv\models$ $\sim$|A is true|.

Reflecting that substitution of '$\sim$A' for 'A' in (T) yields

$\sim$A $\dashv\models$ $\sim$A is true,

we arrive, by transitivity of '$\dashv\models$', at

$\sim$A is true $\dashv\models$ $\sim$|A is true|.

Since we may take the right-hand side of that as a harmless rewrite of 'A is not true', the result is effectively (N).

As, effectively, a consequence of that feature of the truth-predicate articulated in (T), (IC) must therefore be regarded as uncontroversial by

7 Three, in fact ('Understanding Logical Constants', p. 163). One is to reflect that RAA would not otherwise be valid, since A's generation (on certain assumptions) of incompatible consequences can only require that (on those assumptions) matters stand *somehow* incompatibly with A – there could be no valid inference to $\sim$A if $\sim$A's truth is merely one determinate (contrast: determinable) way for matters so to stand. A second is to realize that 'if $\sim$A were not the weakest such condition, then there would be a consistent content whose truth requires neither that of A nor that of this supposedly stronger negation of A'. A third is 'by starting from the realization that $\sim$A is true in any case in which A is not'. I am not sure what argumentative force attaches to the second. The third is closest to what is crucial, though it needs, I think, the elaboration which follows above.

anyone disinclined to dispute (T).[8] The issue, therefore, concerns the transition from (IC) to DNE.

Why does Peacocke regard (IC) as enjoining DNE? In his British Academy lecture, he writes, merely, that

> Anything incompatible with ~A, i.e. [by (IC)] something which entails ~~A, must also entail A too, – on pain of ~A not being the weakest condition incompatible with A.[9]

This is somewhat inexplicit. But one concern about it is salient anyway: the strategy of the train of thought, whatever its detail, would appear to proceed by a *reductio* of the pool of suppositions:

that P entails ~~A;
that P does not entail A;
that (IC) holds.

The most that is immediately in prospect, therefore, would seem to be a demonstration of the *negation* of the second supposition on the assumption of the other two. But if so, it is going to take a DNE step to get the intended result, that – granted (IC) – P entails A whenever it entails ~~A. So however it is supposed to run in detail, isn't the argument going to be circular at best?

True, the needed presupposition is not of the validity of DNE quite generally, but only of its validity as applied to statements of the form

~~|P entails A|.

Still, an argument would be owing why that limited case should have some prior claim to acceptability.[10]

8 In order to pre-empt one such line of dispute, I have deliberately registered (T) in the form of a claim of mutual logical consequence, rather than the more usual biconditional,

A is true ↔ A.

The biconditional is, of course, going to be suspect, on natural readings of '↔', for anyone who is working with truth-values besides truth and falsity, or with truth-value gaps – and who, as is natural, takes 'A is true' as *false* when A has a third, or no truth-value. The claim of mutual logical consequence, by contrast, is answerable only to what valuation is required, as a matter of logical necessity, whenever either ingredient takes the value, *true*.

9 'Understanding Logical Constants', p. 164.

10 Intuitionistically, DNE is, of course, uncontroversial when applied to sequents whose conclusions are effectively decidable. But of course entailment statements are not so, even if we restrict our attention to those whose ingredients are expressible entirely in first-order terms. In general, it is obscure what motive there might be to accept DNE for entailment statements as a class which was not a motive to accept it without restriction.

This misgiving is reinforced when we consider a second, much more explicit presentation which Peacocke offers in his 'Proof and Truth'. Let 'A/B' express that A is incompatible with B. Peacocke writes:

> If O is the weakest operator for which P/OP holds generally, the classical introduction and elimination rules are valid for it...suppose we had a case in which this inference fails
>
> $$\frac{\text{OOA}}{\text{A}}$$
>
> In this case we would have that OOA is true and A not true. Since OOA is incompatible with OA, OA must be not true in the given case. But if A and OA are both not true, OA is not the weakest proposition incompatible with A, for being the weakest entails that OA is true in any case in which A is not. Since by hypothesis OA is the weakest such proposition, there can be no case in which the analogue of classical negation elimination fails.[11]

A reaction to this corresponding to the reservation just expressed would be that no cogent argument for the validity of the classical negation rules as applied to the operator, O, can proceed by *reductio* on the premise-set {OOA, A is not true} – at least, not if RAA is taken in the form

$$\frac{\begin{matrix}\Gamma & \Gamma \\ \vdots & \vdots \\ B & \sim B\end{matrix}}{\sim\{\Gamma\}}$$

For all that will follow from a proof that not all the members of {OOA, A is not true} are true is the conditional,

$$\text{OOA} \rightarrow \sim(\text{A is not true}),$$

rather than the sought-after

$$\text{OOA} \rightarrow \text{A};$$

and it needs DNE to get us from the former to the latter.

11 'Proof and Truth'.

Now, this reaction is not quite technically fair, since Peacocke's argument does not (quite) put up {OOA, A is not true} for *reductio*, but rather something of which the possible truth of that premise-set is an immediate consequence, namely the supposition of a failure of the inference pattern,

$$\frac{\text{OOA}}{\text{A.}}$$

But the basic difficulty remains. All that can follow from a *reductio* of that supposition via the RAA rule schematized is that there is no A for which OOA does not entail A. Write 'ΦA' to indicate that there is an entailment from OOA to A. Then the conclusion of the argument will be a claim of the form, $\sim(\exists \text{A}) \sim \Phi\text{A}$. We can certainly advance from that to a claim of the form, $(\forall \text{A}) \sim\sim \Phi\text{A}$. But the sought-after claim is the DNE is unrestrictedly valid, i.e., $(\forall \text{A})\Phi\text{A}$. And to get to that, we need, once again, that DNE hold good, if not unrestrictedly, then at least for entailment-statements.

There would not he this difficulty, of course, if, rather than the version schematized above, we had RAA in the classical form

$$\frac{\begin{array}{cc} \sim\{\Gamma\} & \sim\{\Gamma\} \\ \cdot & \cdot \\ \cdot & \cdot \\ \cdot & \cdot \\ \text{B} & \sim\text{B} \end{array}}{\Gamma}$$

when Γ could be taken as {OOA entails A} and the reasoning could proceed, via ^{TM}{OOA, A is not true}, exactly as Peacocke describes. But this version of RAA is just a convenient way of packaging standard RAA plus DNE into one rule – we can hardly suppose that there is a motivation for it based on (IC) or other uncontroversial properties of negation if we have yet to descry a clear motive for DNE itself.

Putting on one side, for a moment, these reservations about its cogency, there is a puzzling aspect to Peacocke's commentary on his argument. He writes:

> It may be objected that an intuitionist will equally agree that it is primitively obvious that ~A is incompatible with A. Indeed he may also agree that there is nothing weaker than ~A which is incompatible with A. But if this is so, how can these two points determine classical rather than intuitionistic negation?

> The answer is that it is not the same points which hold for the intuitionist as for the classicist. When the intuitionist agrees that it is primitively obvious that ~A is incompatible with A, what he means by 'incompatible' is not what the classicist means. What the intuitionist means by the incompatibility of A with B is that the supposition that A and B are both verified leads to absurdity. In the intuitionist's sense, A is incompatible with 'It is not verified that A'. That is congenial to him, but there is no incompatibility on the classicist's realistic notion. Since different notions of incompatibility are being used, there is no sound objection to the claim that the semantic value of classical negation is determined.[12]

The puzzle emerges if we refer back to the quoted argument from 'Proof and Truth' and ask the simple question: at what point is it assumed, tacitly or otherwise, that the notion of incompatibility is being taken in a realist (non-constructive) sense? The answer, so far as I can see, is: nowhere. To simplify matters, let the supposition for *reductio* be the negation not of an entailment claim but of the corresponding conditional,

OOA is true → A is true.

The intuitionist ought – in this particular case[13] – to have no objection to the transition from the negation of that to

OOA is true & A is not true.

And when all relevant notions are interpreted constructively, 'OOA is true' and 'A is not true' are contradictory for the intuitionist no less than for the classicist. Their intuitionistic conjunction affirms that each can be proved. And to prove that A is not true is to prove that no constructive verification of A can be achieved – that any such verification could be used to generate a proof of a contradiction. Since that is exactly what is affirmed by the intuitionistic negation of A, as standardly interpreted, the intuitionist will have no objection to the equivalence (N) nor, in consequence, to the *reductio* Peacocke outlines in the second

12 'Understanding Logical Constants', p. 165.

13 Of course, an intuitionist will not accept the transition from ~(A → B) to A & ~B in general. But the material character of intuitionistic '→' ensures that the intuitionist will be content with the transition from ~(A → B) to ~~A & ~B. So – bearing in mind that *triple* negation does collapse, intuitionistically, into single negation – it follows that the stronger transition does go through if A is already a double negation, or equivalent to such, as in the present case.

half of the passage quoted. What the intuitionist *will* object to is taking that reasoning as a proof, on the assumptions of (N) and that **O**OA is true, of the truth of A, rather than of the untruth of 'A is not true'. That objection, however, has nothing to do with a constructive interpretation of incompatibility.

It is true that Peacocke's last-quoted remarks refer to the terse statement in the British Academy lecture. But we are in no position to contrast the argument to which that statement refers with the 'Proof and Truth' version. And a similar invocation of the contrast between the classical and intuitionist notions of incompatibility also occurs in 'Proof and Truth'.[14]

Reverting to the purported argument from (IC) to DNE, we noted, in effect, that no convincing version can proceed by *reductio* if the standard version of RAA is all we may assume; for then the reasoning will need in addition to rely on a DNE step. Since it does not seem as if the classical version of RAA could be motivated independently of some explicit argument for DNE, it would seem that a convincing version of Peacocke's thought cannot proceed by *reductio* at all.

How else might it proceed? Well, there is, I think, another line which may be read into the terse statement in the British Academy lecture. Write **W**(A, B) for

B is a weakest statement incompatible with A.

Plainly, if **W**(A, B), then any statement which entails that A is not true, and thereby via (IC) entails ~A, entails B. So in particular, ~A itself entails B. Now suppose the relation, **W**(A, B), is symmetric. Then whenever **W**(A, B) holds, so does **W**(B, A), and hence, by the reflection just mooted, ~B entails A. Since (IC) ensures that **W**(A, ~A), it follows – taking ~A for 'B' – that ~~A entails A. QED.

Valid reasoning from (IC) to DNE may avoid all use of *reductio*, then, if we may assume the symmetry of '**W**' – assume that whenever B is a weakest statement incompatible with A, A must likewise be a weakest statement incompatible with B. And such an assumption may seem quite intuitive – at least to a classical outlook which reasons as follows. If B is a weakest statement incompatible with A, it is true in *all* cases when A fails of truth – so if B fails of truth, it cannot be one of *those* cases with which we are concerned. But the only other kind of case are ones where A is true: so any statement which entails that B fails of truth must entail A.

14 'Proof and Truth'.

However, a less than classical outlook will find cause for concern, of course, in the implicit transition from the thought that the hypothesized case is not one in which A fails of truth to the thought that it must be a case in which A is true! In fact, the supposition that '**W**' is symmetric is quite trivially equivalent to the supposition that DNE holds good. Perhaps the simplest way to see the point is to reflect that **W**(A, B) is tantamount to the claim that B mutually entails ~A.[15] So the symmetry of '**W**' is just the thesis of the equivalence of ~A ⫤⊨ B with ~B ⫤⊨ A. And that equivalence entails and, in the company of otherwise uncontroversial rules, is entailed by DNE.[16]

That does not yet show that to argue from the symmetry of '**W**' to the validity of DNE is merely to skirmish in a circle. The question is whether *independent* motive can be supplied for the claim of the symmetry of it '**W**' – motive independent, that is, of classical sympathies. But there is every reason to doubt it. Reflect that the question, which statements are incompatible with a given statement and, a fortiori, which statements are weakest such statements, has a certain relativity – it depends on the universe of statements presupposed. And the fact is that the classicist and the constructivist (intuitionist) are not in general agreement about what statements – intelligible thought-contents – there are. For the intuitionist, for instance, the universe of intelligible mathematical thoughts consists – very crudely – in nothing but contents for which there is no difference between the claim that P and the claim that it is intuitionistically provable (I-provable) that P. What, in such a universe, is a weakest statement incompatible with P? Well, it is a weakest statement incompatible with the I-provability of P, so it is equivalent to the claim that P is not I-provable, i.e. to the claim that it is I-provable that it is not I-provable that P. So a weakest statement incompatible with that in turn will be equivalent to the claim that it is not I-provable that it is not I-provable that P, i.e. to the claim that it is I-provable that it is not I-provable that it is not I-provable that P. But the latter, in any case where P is not effectively decidable, is a potentially weaker statement than the claim that it is I-provable that P, i.e. the claim that P. For it may be that we can establish (I-prove) that there is

15 **W**(A, B) says two things: that B is incompatible with A, and that any statement incompatible with A entails B. The first is equivalent to the claim that B entails ~A; the second to the claim that ~A entails B (since P entails Q just in case any R which entails P entails Q).

16 That A ⊨ ~B can be inferred from ~A ⫤⊨ B using standard RAA; and that ~B ⊨ A can be inferred from ~A ⫤⊨ B if we can eliminate the double negation in ~B ⊨ ~~A. Conversely, if we are given the equivalence of ~A ⫤⊨ B with ~B ⫤⊨ A, we may easily pass from ~~A to ~B via the first, and then from ~B to A via the second.

no establishing that P cannot be I-proved without thereby accomplishing an I-proof of P. It follows that '**W**' cannot be guaranteed symmetric in the universe of intuitionistic thoughts.

The point is good for any domain of thoughts where three conditions are met:

i truth within the domain is conceived as biconditionally dependent on the satisfaction of some epistemic constraint – call it 'verifiability';
ii the domain is closed under negation; and
iii we cannot guarantee that for any thought, P, in the domain, either P or its negation is verifiable.

'**W**' cannot be guaranteed symmetric across such a domain of thoughts. For since, by (iii), we lack reason to suppose of an arbitrary P in the domain that either it or its negation is verifiable, it cannot in general be that to verify that the negation of P is not verifiable is verify P. But (i) and (ii) ensure that to verify that the negation of P is not verifiable is to effectively verify the double negation of P – a weakest proposition incompatible with not-P. So P cannot also be a weakest proposition incompatible with not-P, even though not-P is a weakest proposition incompatible with *it*.

I conclude that provided that a domain of thoughts may indeed meet the three conditions stated, Peacocke is mistaken in supposing that our most basic understanding of negation, as incorporated in (IC), provides any push in the direction of the distinctively classical conception of that connective.

II

Interlude

9

Scientific Realism, Observation and Verificationism

I

It is quite widely supposed, especially by those who have little admiration for either, that the spirit of Logical Positivism survives in the kind of semantical anti-realism with which these essays are concerned. To be sure, when 'spirit' is taken in a sufficiently general sense, the claim is hardly contestable. But more careful scrutiny reveals differences great enough both to discourage any attempt at a systematic understanding of the verificationism of half a century ago purely on the basis of the tenets of the modern trend and to scotch the lazy criticism that the latter must be vulnerable to the criticisms which eventually saw the demise of the former. Modern verificationists propose what they see as a constraint on the concept of truth rather than a criterion of meaningfulness;[1] no foundational place is generally assigned in modern verificationist semantics to corroboration by observation, or to 'observation-statements'; modern semantical anti-realism is not a reductionist doctrine; and logical positivism was never connected with revisionism in the philosophy of logic and mathematics.[2]

My purpose in this paper is to try to describe a somewhat different route into sympathy with the old-style Verification Principle – along with its luggage of observation-statements, the analytic/synthetic distinction, and all – for at least the class of statements, namely those of empirical science, whose status as 'literally significant' it was primarily meant to safeguard. If I am right about the logic of this route, and if, as I fear, the Principle cannot actually deliver the intended verdict for scientific statements generally, then certain costs have to be faced in the

1 But see p. 285 below.
2 Though it is controversial whether semantic anti-realism should indeed be revisionary. See this volume, Essays 15 and 16.

philosophy of science – costs whose severity has not, I think, been often appreciated.

II

As a familiar, and despite its author's best efforts, *Language, Truth and Logic* left the proper formulation – indeed the very formulability – of the Verification Principle completely up in the air. In the first edition, Ayer had proposed that a statement is verifiable, and consequently meaningful, if some experiential propositions can be deduced from it in conjunction with certain other premises, without being deducible from those other premises alone.[3] This has the consequence that any non-analytic statement, S, passes the test; for 'if S then O' is always an appropriate further premise, where O is an 'experiential proposition', i.e. an observation-statement. In response to the difficulty, Ayer proposed, in the Preface to the second edition, a more sophisticated, recursive account. S is to be accounted *directly verifiable* iff[4]

1 it is an observation-statement,

or

2 it entails, in conjunction with certain observation-statements, some observation-statement which does not follow from them alone.

And S is said to be *indirectly verifiable* iff[5]

3 it entails, in conjunction with certain other premises, some directly verifiable statement which does not follow from those other premises alone;

and

4 these supplementary premises include none which are not either analytic or directly verifiable, or (independently establishable as) indirectly verifiable.

3 *Language, Truth and Logic*, p. 39. All references to this text are to the 2nd edn (1946).
4 Actually, the text (p. 13) has 'if', but this is clearly a slip.
5 See note 4.

The Verification Principle is then the requirement that (all and) only statements which are directly or indirectly verifiable count as 'literally meaningful'.

Unfortunately, this emendation still admits every non-analytic statement. Let N be any 'nonsensical' statement, and O_1 and O_2 any pair of observation-statements which are logically independent of each other. Then consider the statement

A: Either O_1 or (not-N and not-O_2)

Conjoined with O_2, A entails O_1. But O_2 alone does not entail O_1 (by hypothesis). So A is directly verifiable. Therefore, since N, conjoined with A, entails O_1, which is not entailed by A alone (assuming that not-N and not-O_2 do not collectively entail O_1), N also passes as indirectly verifiable.

There are various ways in which a repair could be attempted. (We will investigate the matter in the next chapter.) Certainly the possibility of a successful repair should not be despaired of, since Ayer's proposals appear to have been informed by what seems a perfectly coherent intention. The notion of an observation-statement plays no indispensable part in generating the difficulty. The problem is purely a *structural* one: that of characterizing what it is for a hypothesis, in virtue of its content, potentially to have something to say, relative to some antecedent partial assignment of truth-values to the statements in some restricted class, about which other members of that class can be expected to be true. Ayer's interest was in the special case when the restricted class comprises exactly all possible observation-statements – whatever, exactly, they are taken to be. But structurally parallel issues arise concerning the characterization of statements with some measure of *moral* content, for instance, or of *historical* content, or *religious* content. It is highly implausible that these distinctions are merely empty, and so, presumably, do not admit of any account which neither incorporates ad hoc restrictions nor – as in the case of Ayer's two attempts – obliterates them altogether.

It is easy to be distracted by the rhetoric of meaninglessness with which Ayer's text is peppered and to forget the purpose for which the Verification Principle was originally specifically introduced.[6] A proposition which passes the test is thereby 'a genuine factual proposition', apt to make 'a significant statement of fact'. The demarcation aimed at is that between genuine statements, apt to record 'hard' facts, on the one hand, and – in more recent terminologies – 'quasi-assertions' or 'projections' on the other. The idea that the latter are, one and all,

6 See *Language, Truth and Logic*, pp. 39ff.

'nonsensical' was merely hyperbole – or if it was not, its implications were not pursued. It was no part of the emotive theory of value, for instance, that moral discourse was merely aberrant. The distinctive claim concerned, rather, the *kind* of content it could rightly be supposed to have. In contrast, to strip 'metaphysics' of its pretensions to factuality would be to divest of it its *raison d'être*: the uncovering of truths of a special, sublime sort, accessible only to the flights of speculative reason. 'Metaphysics' fails because, once disclosed as non-factual, the assertions of its practitioners – unlike, e.g., our ordinary moral and aesthetic judgements – fail of any socially valid role.

Now, when this aspect of the Verification Principle is kept in view, the shape taken by Ayer's second-edition emendation generates a puzzle. The positivists, for all the esteem they professed for the empirical scientific enterprise and its accomplishments, and notwithstanding their assignment of philosophy to a relatively auxiliary role, were no friends of scientific *realism* on the whole. Their extreme empiricism was always likely to generate difficulties when it came to construal of the specifically theoretical vocabulary of the natural sciences. Such empiricism is bound to hope that theoretical terms may prove amenable to reductive translation in terms of relatively unproblematic – observational – vocabulary. When it emerges that such translation is and must be impossible, some form of instrumentalist conception of the role of theoretical statements would seem to be enjoined. But this was not the perception of the matter in *Language, Truth and Logic*. The second-edition version of the Verification Principle is evidently designed, in the light of the then dominant perception of the architectonic of scientific theories, with the aim of vindicating the 'literal significance' of any hypothesis of a reputable scientific theory. Thus the lowest-level hypotheses, couched in observational vocabulary, will qualify – it is the intention – as directly verifiable; while the theory's high-level hypotheses, formulated purely in theoretical terms or else in a mixture of observational and theoretical language, will qualify as indirectly verifiable because, in conjunction with certain analytic statements which serve as (partial) definitions of the theoretical terms which they contain, they will entail directly verifiable hypotheses.

To endorse the Principle, as so intended, is not yet to forswear reductionism. All depends on the requirements placed on the bridging definitions which mediate the transitions from theoretical to observational hypotheses. If these are required to provide the means for a content-preserving *paraphrase* of any theoretical statement in purely observational vocabulary, whether term by term or contextually, then the intention is still reductionist. If they are not so required, but may permissibly have the status of 'implicitly definitional' analytic postulates, then it is not: theoretical statements can pass the test even though no correct finite – or even infinite – paraphrase of their content in purely observational vocabulary exists.

Which was Ayer's intention? Well, the textual evidence might seem quite definite. Immediately after introducing the emended version of the Verification Principle, he writes:

> in giving my account of the conditions in which a statement is to be considered indirectly verifiable, I have explicitly put in the proviso that the 'other premises' may include analytic statements; and my reason for doing this is that I intend in this way to allow for the case of scientific theories which are expressed in terms that do not themselves designate anything observable. For while the statements that contain these terms may not appear to describe anything that anyone could ever observe, a 'dictionary' may be provided by means by which they can be transformed into statements that are verifiable; and the statements which constitute the dictionary can be regarded as analytic. Were this not so, there would be nothing to chose between such scientific theories and those that I should dismiss as metaphysical; but I take it to be characteristic of the metaphysician...not only that his statements do not describe anything that is capable, even in principle, of being observed, but also that no dictionary is provided by means of which they can be transformed into statements that are directly or indirectly verifiable.[7]

Ayer proceeds to contrast the Verification Principle, so understood, with the 'older empiricist principle' (which he finds in Russell) which requires all meaningful terms to stand for things with which we can be acquainted, i.e. can observe. This is his point of departure from positivist instrumentalists such as Mach who

> hold that all symbols, other than logical constants, must either themselves stand for sense contents or else be explicitly definable in terms of symbols which stand for sense contents. It is plain that such physical symbols as 'atom' or 'molecule' or 'electron' fail to satisfy this condition.[8]

Those who, like Mach, have been prepared on that account to call the content of such expressions into question

> would not have been so ruthless if they had realized that they ought also, if they were consistent in the application of their criterion, to have condemned, the use of symbols which stand for material things...such familiar symbols as 'table' or 'chair' or 'coat' cannot be defined explicitly

7 *Language, Truth and Logic*, p. 13.
8 *Language, Truth and Logic*, p. 136.

> in terms of symbols which stand for sense contents but only in use...we must allow that the employment of a symbol is legitimate if it is possible, any rate in principle, *to give a rule for translating the sentences in which it occurs into sentences which refer to sense contents.*[9]

Surely, then, Ayer is espousing a globally reductionist view of scientific theory. His occasional recourse to instrumentalist-sounding language notwithstanding,[10] his belief is that reputable scientific hypotheses do, one and all, turn out to be directly or indirectly verifiable on his account because their content invariably can – as that account demands – be captured in purely observational terms. Towards the conclusion of the book he writes:

> there is a sense in which we ourselves desire to uphold the unity of science. For we maintain that it is a mistake to conceive of the various 'special sciences' as protraying different 'aspects of reality.' We have shown that all empirical hypotheses refer ultimately to our sense contents. They all function alike as 'rules for the anticipation of future experience';...What chiefly prevents this unity from being recognized at present is the unnecessary multiplicity of current scientific terminologies.[11]

There seems, then, to be no mistaking Ayer's official view. It is both anti-instrumentalist and anti-scientific-realist. Theoretical statements do qualify for 'factuality'. But the reason they do so is not that the world contains objective states of affairs for whose description something other than language of observation is required.

Hence the puzzle. For if this is a complete account of Ayer's intention, we seem to have no good explanation why Ayer couches the Verification Principle in the way he does. Why not something more explicitly reductionist? For instance,

> A statement is verifiable just in case it may be shown – by correct explicit and/or contextual definitions – to be equivalent to some truth-function (finite or infinite) of observation-statements.

Would this not be a more understandable direction, at least for a first approximation? It is, indeed, the direction taken by John Foster's impressive exegesis,[12] with ample textual justification, as we have seen. But the fact remains that the intuitive notion of 'having some bearing

9 *Language, Truth and Logic*, p. 136.
10 See, for instance, *Language, Truth and Logic*, pp. 97ff.
11 *Language, Truth and Logic*, p. 151.
12 Foster, *A. J. Ayer*. See pp. 20ff.

on' the truth and falsity of statements couched in a certain distinguished vocabulary – observational, moral, religious, etc. – would not naturally be taken to involve such a definability claim. And it is this notion which Ayer's formulations are most naturally viewed as attempting to make precise, as we noted earlier.

I am inclined to suggest, very tentatively, that some part of the author of *Language, Truth and Logic* may have wanted to provide for a kind of verificationist *realism*. Such a realism would hold that statements are apt for the depiction of genuine fact only provided their truth would have a bearing on which observation-statements could be expected to be true, but would eschew the demand that factually significant statements have a content which may be paraphrased, in whatever precise sense, in purely observational terms.

III

Someone steeped in the modern debate might wonder how there can be a *verificationist* realism. For according to the currently widespread terminology,[13] realism just is, in essentials, an anti-verificationist view about statement-meaning: to hold a realist view of statements of a certain sort is to hold that understanding them consists in knowing their truth-conditions, it being understood that the truth of a statement is something which may, even in principle, *elude our capacities for detection.*

Well, three ideas – the truth-conditional conception of meaning, belief in the general validity (prescinding from vagueness) of the Principle of Bivalence, and acceptance of the possibility of evidence-transcendent truth – undoubtedly form an intellectual syndrome – call it *semantic realism* – to which our thinking in many areas of discourse is prone. But it is another question whether they inform all the various realist positions in the multitude of local realist/anti-realist disputes which philosophers have engaged in. The phenomenalist about statements concerning material objects, the behaviourist about statements concerning mental states, and the (or one kind of) nominalist about abstract objects, for example, all believe that their realist opponents hold mistaken views about the meanings of the statements which form the *loci* of their respective disputes. But what each of these anti-realists – if we may so describe them – really wants to maintain is that his opponent is under a misapprehension about the kinds of states of affairs which the relevant statements describe; and there is no evident reason why the

13 Deriving from Dummett's writings.

cure for that misapprehension should exclude a semantic-realist attitude towards those statements. The behaviourist, for instance, does not inadvertently commit himself to a dualist view of the mental if he allows that Bivalence and the truth-conditional conception of understanding are appropriate to statements about mind, construed as he understands them, and grants that the truth of such a statement may yet be something beyond our power to know. Elsewhere, of course, the admissibility of semantic realism seems to be precisely what is at issue: the salient examples are disputes involving the mathematical intuitionists, anti-realists concerning the past, proponents of the 'open' future, and some of those who have disputed the admissibility of classical logic for counterfactual conditionals. An immediate question is therefore: are the disputes between *scientific realists* and their various types of opponents of this sort; or are they more akin to the earlier type of case illustrated by behaviourism, phenomenalism and nominalism?

The answer, with a qualification, is: neither. The qualification is that semantic realism with respect to theoretical statements is, of course, a live issue in the philosophy of science: it is precisely the issue raised by the thesis of the essential underdetermination of theory by empirical data. Suppose, for instance, that Special Relativity and the Lorentzian Theory of Corresponding States do indeed have precisely the same testable consequences.[14] Then the question whether one of those theories might be true at the expense of the other is, prima facie, precisely the question whether theoretical statements can be true in a way that transcends all evidence. But the acceptability of the underdetermination thesis – however it ought precisely to be formulated – is surely not a precondition of the *possibility* of scientific realism; and a scientific realist who rejects underdetermination is surely not committed to holding that the (uniquely) true theory of some class of phenomena can be evidence-transcendent. What, I suggest, scientific realism *essentially* maintains is, rather, just that (successful) scientific theories deal in aspects of *reality*: that there are aspects of the natural world for whose correct description the techniques of concept-formation used by theoretical scientists are indispensable. In short, the statements of scientific theories are candidates for literal (not merely disquotational) *truth*; and the aspects of reality which confer truth on them, if they are true, are completely describable only by the use of scientific theoretical vocabulary.[15]

So conceived, the scientific-realist position is open to the familiar – reductionist and instrumentalist – forms of opposition. But on this construal it is not – or not yet – susceptible to attack from the stand-

14 See Zahar, 'Why Did Einstein's Programme Supersede Lorentz's?'
15 Cf. van Fraassen, *The Scientific Image*, pp. 6–9.

point of semantic *anti*-realism. For although scientific realism, so understood, will presumably accept that our understanding of theoretical statements consists in grasp of their truth-conditions, there is so far no evident commitment to holding that the relevant notion of truth is one which may be evidence-transcendent, or that Bivalence is unrestrictedly acceptable for these statements.

Naturally, the position may not be stable. One way in which it could destabilize is if the underdetermination thesis were sustained in an appropriately general form. For a scientific realist who does not wish to leave open the possibility of evidence-transcendent truth will have to maintain, presumably, that we are capable of coming to know – or reasonably to believe – the truth of any true theoretical statement by scientific means: that is, I suppose, notoriously difficult though it may be to characterize the matter precisely, by the construction of a *recognizably successful* theory in which that statement features *essentially*. Now, whatever flesh is put on the bones, it is clear that this picture provides no room for reasonable belief that a particular theoretical statement is true if it so happens that its negation figures in an *alternative* theory which we can recognize, a priori, has the same testable results.

Suppose we were persuaded of the following thesis (*Maximal Underdetermination*):

> For any theoretical statement S and acceptable theory T essentially containing S, there is an acceptable theory T′ with the same testable consequences as T but which contains, essentially, the negation of S.

Then the belief that theoretical statements are capable of truth would indeed commit us to the evidence-transcendence of the relevant species of truth. But there is, as far as I am aware, absolutely no evidence for Maximal Underdetermination. It is obvious enough that we can cobble up incompatible theories with the same testable consequences by locating, for a given acceptable theory T, a set of otiose hypotheses such that the addition neither of them nor of their negations to T results in a theory whose testable consequences differ from those of T. But all that follows is that the evidence for T provides no grounds for believing any of the otiose hypotheses or their negations. No conclusion is warranted about the believability of the hypotheses of T itself, nor about whether some of the relevant hypotheses, otiose when added to T, might not yet figure essentially in some other acceptable theory.

Underdetermination of this 'cobbled up' sort does, admittedly, present an argument against the acceptability of Bivalence for theoretical statements in general. The argument is that if the truth of theoretical statements is not to be evidence-transcendent, then we cannot guarantee that every theoretical statement is determinately either true or false since we cannot guarantee that every such statement can be made to figure essentially in a theory of a recognizably acceptable or unacceptable sort. But it provides no argument for supposing that, unless it is to be evidence-transcendent, truth cannot justifiably be applied to theoretical statements at all. The view remains in play that it is entirely justified to claim the truth of any essential hypothesis of an acceptable theory. If an alternative, equally acceptable theory were developed in which something incompatible with that hypothesis figured essentially, that would merely defeat one's claim to be reasonably persuaded of the truth of the hypothesis. Thus if Special Relativity and its Lorentzian counterpart are indeed observationally equivalent, there can be no justified belief and hence, unless it is to be evidence-transcendent, no truth in either of the relevant sets of mutually incompatible hypotheses. But that such a situation sometimes occurs, if indeed it does, is not reason for believing in Maximal Underdetermination; nor, therefore, for thinking that semantic anti-realism must forgo all applications of the notion of truth to theoretical hypotheses, non-reductively construed.

IV

Two of scientific realism's antagonists, reductionism and instrumentalism, have an assumption in common. They suppose that there is a class of statements of an epistemologically basic, non-theoretical sort, whose truth-values can be decided by observation. It is this class which provides, respectively, the base class into which our theoretical conjectures are to be translated and the domain of statements among which it is their 'instrumetal' role to mediate inferences. If no such class exists, the reductionist has no vocabulary in terms of which to analyse out what he sees as epistemologically problematic theoretical concepts; and the instrumentalist cannot so much as formulate his preferred account of what it is that scientific theories enable us to do, viz. systematically to characterize and to anticipate observational phenomena. However the point generally seems to have won the day that there are *no* observation-statements in the sense required, that observation is *theory-laden*, as the matter is (quite unilluminatingly) usually expressed. There has been a good deal of discussion of Necker Cubes and Duck Rabbits in this connection, but the crux is not (primarily) whether the actual *phenomenology* of a subject's perceivings is invariably a function of his prior conceptual equipment and theoretical commitments. Rather, it is whether what one ought to *believe it correct to report* in response to particular observations is invariably a function of one's background beliefs; whether other people who did not share those beliefs, could quite properly not be disposed to endorse one's report, even if presented with the same observations (whatever it means to regard them as the same).

The widespread acceptance of the doctrine that observation is everywhere theory-laden is probably owing to confusion, at least in some measure, about the precise fashion in which the 'loading' or 'interpenetration' is supposed to take place. Bill Newton-Smith, for instance, attempts to illustrate the theory-ladenness of observational vocabulary by calling attention to aspects of the theory which, he believes, a full understanding of the meaning of colour words involves.[16] A mastery, for example, of 'yellow' involves knowledge, he claims, of such generalizations as:

i anything which is yellow is coloured;
ii yellow things retain their colour when unperceived;
iii yellow things tend to look the same colour under standard conditions to different persons.

But generalizations such as these, though they are indeed, plausibly, part of the standard luggage of those who are competent in the use of 'yellow', are not to the purpose unless it can be shown that someone who did not assent to them would thereby be disposed to use 'yellow' differently in *observational* reports. If theory-ladenness is to be an embarrassment to the reductionist and instrumentalist, it must not take a form which allows the correct assertibility of observation-statements to be independent of theoretical beliefs. For since, as Duhem made us realize, theoretical beliefs themselves hunt in packs for confirmation and disconfirmation, that would already be a quite sufficient basis for the distinction of the base class of statements which the reductionist and instrumentalist need.

Viewed in this light, Newton-Smith's generalizations, (i)–(iii), do not seem to be of the right sort. It is not clear what it would be to know (i) if one had no word meaning 'coloured' and a subject might anyway be smitten with neurotic doubts about whether objects change their colours in a darkened room,[17] and about whether other people could see colours as he did, without, it appears, any compromise of his mastery of standard colour vocabulary to describe the objects in his visual field.

16 Newton-Smith, *The Rationality of Science*, pp. 17–18.

17 Grasping that 'yellow' expresses a characteristic of material things rather than sensations does not, arguably, require knowledge of (ii), contrary to what Newton-Smith asserts (*The Rationality of Science*, p. 27). It would suffice to know that (ii) expresses a *possibility*. Such knowledge, like that of (i), and of (iii) (appropriately qualified) is a priori.

Theory-ladenness, in the sense which should interest us, demands that what is considered competence in the theory-laden vocabulary requires empirical theoretical beliefs which a subject cannot discharge, or lack, without repercussions on his use of that vocabulary in descriptions of his observations.

A similar qualification is necessary of the following thought:

> 'Here is a glass of water' cannot be verified by any observational experience. The reason is that the *universal terms* which occur in this statement ('glass', 'water') are dispositional: they denote physical bodies which exhibit certain *law like behaviour.*[18]

What the presence of dispositional terms entails is that such examples are always going to be in principle defeasible by a subsequent untoward train of events. But why should an observation-statement – whether or not the particular example ought to so qualify – have to be *conclusively* verifiable by observation? Some of the positivists wanted a rock-solid empirical basis for science; and hence they believed not merely that the statements at the base of the scientific 'pyramid' should be assessable by means free of theoretical prejudice but that individual perceptual experiences could be *decisive* for or against their truth.[19] But to suppose that there are no statements which meet the second requirement does not obviously entail there is none which meets the first. Observation-statements ought, presumably, to be statements apt for the description of states of affairs that can be publicly observed. Since our powers of observation are fallible and since objects can be presented in misleading ways, it is only to be expected that such statements will be defeasible. But that is not to say that their conditions of correct assertibility/justified belief have everywhere to be a function of our empirical theoretical beliefs.

My suggestion is that the purposes of the instrumentalist and theoretical reductionist would be well enough served if it turned out that (enough) observation-statements are theory-laden only in these two respects: first, that mastery of the concepts involved in their expression typically requires acceptance of certain a priori principles and, second, that assent to them, however well justified, may always be mistaken. If that is the full extent of the involvement of 'theory', such statements are indeed interestingly set apart from theoretical statements proper: it would seem reasonable to regard them as relatively epistemically secure,

18 Popper, *Conjectures and Refutations*, p. 387.

19 Carnap, Schlick and Neurath are examples. See *Language, Truth and Logic*, pp. 90–1.

and – crucially – their conditions of justified belief will not be a function of background *empirical* theory.

In fact, though, many of those who have wanted to deny that there is any worthwhile category of observation-statements have wanted to affirm precisely the involvement of empirical theory in all our judgements, even those which pre-philosophically impress us as most basic and free of presupposition. And it is fair to say, I think, that the dominant opinion among philosophers of science is both that this is so, and that its being so constitutes something of a decisive coup on behalf of the scientific realist's cause.[20] A principal thesis of this essay is that this is incorrect: a would-be scientific realist who welcomes the demise of the species, *observation-statement*, is like a man who delights in following a fire engine, not realizing that the house that is burning is his own.[21]

V

The immense intuitive attractions of scientific realism are very immediate. Science, as the realist wants to regard it, enables us to take intellectual wing, to transcend the mundane limitations of our ordinary

20 See Newton-Smith, *The Rationality of Science*, pp. 28–34.

21 It is important to recognize that the health of the species need not depend on the possibility of a basic, theoretically unconditioned *vocabulary*. Van Fraassen grants, 'All our language is thoroughly theory-infected If we could cleanse our language of theory-laden terms...we would end up with nothing useful. The way we talk, and scientists talk, is guided by the pictures provided by previously accepted theories...' But 'that we let our language be guided by a given picture, at some point, does not show how much we believe about that picture. When we speak of the sun coming up in the morning and setting at night, we are guided by a picture now explicitly disavowed' (*The Scientific Image*, p. 14). Surely this is right: we do not, in using a particular word or phrase in a particular context, necessarily saddle ourselves with commitment to the theory, if there is one, which originally motivated its use in that context, or in which it was first introduced. Observation-statements, in the sense which interests us, may make use of vocabulary of theoretical origin, and may retain idioms whose theoretical motivation has disappeared. The crucial question is: is the justifiability of what is affirmed in a particular context by the making of such a statement a function, inter alia, of background empirical beliefs? If not, then we may have an observation-statement, no matter how formulated.

Van Fraassen does not express himself in these terms, but it seems he would sympathize. Certainly he is explicit that he regards 'what is observable as a theory-independent question' (p. 57); though this wording is ambiguous. (More decisive, perhaps, is the thought that if there are no observation-statements, then whether a theory is *empirically adequate* will depend on background theoretical beliefs which it will not be possible – so far as I can see – to construe, in turn, as beliefs in empirical adequacy. If that were accepted, van Fraassen's 'constructive empiricism' would have no prospect of global application.)

perceivings and gain glimpses of aspects of reality that are usually inaccessible. (The attractions are rather like those of space travel.) Instrumentalism and reductionism emerge, by contrast, as belittling killjoys. Such attractions, however, are not purely the property of scientific *realism* (at least as characterized earlier). We are, in addition, tacitly assuming something more: that best scientific method may justifiably and correctly be viewed as affording an extension of our cognitive powers: that worldly states of affairs can thereby be bought with the domain of knowledge, or at least reasonable belief, which would otherwise elude us. Contrast a gloomy *absolute realism* which retains the belief that scientific theoretical statements are apt to be non-reductively true or false (in appropriately substantial, more-than-disquotational ways), but drops the epistemological optimism with which scientific realism is usually associated. The absolute realist denies that there is any cause to believe that the pursuit of 'best method' enhances the likelihood of truth. (His would be, precisely, the only position available to realism about science if Maximal Underdetermination were demonstrated to hold.)

Now, absolute realism is undoubtedly a bankrupt philosophy of science. An absolute notion of scientific theoretical truth, whose connection, if any, with the deliverances of best method is inscrutable, is thereby unfitted for any regulative role. It cannot be aimed at. The history of the hard-won methodological and inferential sophistication which we like to think modern science has attained becomes, under absolute realism, the history of a charade. Or if it is not, it is because the purposes served by meticulous preparation of apparatus, scrupulous measurement, the most careful monitoring of possible sources of interference, etc., etc., can be best described – if absolute truth is the only notion of truth to hand – in other terms, without recourse to the idea of truth at all. Indeed, the absolute realist is, arguably, somewhat soft on himself. If it is as likely as not, for all anyone can have cause to believe, that prosecution of best method leads to false theories as to true ones, what is the basis for believing that we can even so much as get lucky? Why suppose that human minds are capable even of forming the right sort of concepts – those suitable for the formulation of what are in fact absolutely true theoretical statements? Why should the truth not be that the world, as it really (microphysically) is, is largely inconceivable to us? Absolute realism has no resources to exclude the suggestion. The result is a realism which has no bearing on scientific practice. The best it can offer is the disjunction: *either* best scientific practice has no coherent rationale or its rationale is one in whose explication the idea of what it is for a scientific theoretical statement to be literally true has no part to play.

Why is this obvious difficulty not more generally acknowledged? Well, some of those who have been tempted to allow, whether in response to sceptical pressure or for whatever other reason, that the concept of truth appropriate to scientific theories must be an absolute one, have, I think, largely concealed from themselves the gloomy consequences of the view by some such (Popperian) thought as that best method at least has the rationale of minimizing the risk of *falsity*.[22] That is: while a theory which withstands the most severe testing may or may not be true, one which breaks down is most certainly false. If best method is method which, if the falsity of a theory can be detected, makes it most likely that it will be detected, then pursuit of best method is our best chance of avoiding falsity, so our best chance of hitting the truth, even if there is no knowing if we have done so.[23]

But this is confused. *Absolute* truth and falsity still have no regulative role to play. Best method, so rationalized, is our best chance of avoiding *detectable* falsity. It is true that if theories may be either absolutely or detectably false, and if there are no practical steps that we can take to minimize the chances of the first, then our best bet for avoiding falsity *tout court* is to minimize the chances of the second. But it remains that our practice is rationalized by the 'absolute' objectives only in so far as, and for precisely the same reason as, it is rationalized by the objective of avoiding empirical inadequacy.[24]

These are familiar reservations, which it would be naive to expect to move the committed. The question I want to raise concerns, rather, the non-absolute, optimistic form of scientific realism which tries to maintain the original promise of a genuine extension of our cognitive horizons. What is required, therefore, is a concept of scientific theoretical truth which is both recognizably realist, and for which evidence of empirical adequacy is unconditionally evidence. It is not to be, in other words, that – as happens under absolute realism – to have evidence for the empirical adequacy of a theory is merely to have evidence that it avoids one kind of failure, viz. detectable falsity. But nor, for the optimistic form of realism, is truth to collapse into empirical adequacy. In neither case is the original promise, that science can justifiably be taken to extend both our descriptive and our cognitive powers, fulfilled.

What is called for here is, in fact, a kind of scientific realism which has important parallels with (one reading of) the intuitionist philosophy

22 See, for instance, Worrall's 'Scientific Realism and Scientific Change'.

23 Worrall, 'Scientific Realism and Scientific Change', pp. 229–30.

24 I am happy to have the notions of empirical adequacy and inadequacy understood along van Fraassen's lines, in so far as I am clear about them.

of mathematics. It is analogous also to the philosophy of mind which Wittgenstein tantalizingly adumbrates in *Philosophical Investigations*, according to which the proper conception of the truth-conditions of the description, e.g., of another's sensations is neither dualist (absolute realist) nor behaviourist (truth as empirical adequacy). The middle ground is notoriously difficult to characterize and harder still to hold. But it is the ground, both for mind and for science, we would like to occupy. We do not know if the attempt is hopeless. But my suspicion is that we will indeed have to grant that it is hopeless, in the case of science, if all observation is theory-laden in the sense distinguished.

The problem is easily seen. Theories can have a variety of virtues, but none has any if it is not borne out by observation. Our practice recognizes the distinction between the theory on the basis of which a prediction is made and the report which confirms or fails to confirm that prediction. (No one disputes that there are 'observation-statements' in this minimal sense; the question concerns the role of empirical theory in their conditions of reasonable belief.) Now, the optimistic realist wants to take it that for a theory to be borne out by observation is for there to be evidence of its truth, where truth is neither absolute nor tantamount to empirical adequacy. But what basis can there be for that view unless he has reason to regard his reports of observation as true in their turn? The notion of scientific-theoretic truth which he needs has to have some kind of essential engagement with the capacity of a theory to explain and predict what observation can disclose to us. So there have to be *true* reports of observation, which we can be justifiably confident in, and against which we can measure the theory. But now, if the conditions under which it is reasonable to accept a report of observation are – as the suggestion is – *invariably* a function of background theoretical beliefs, then one is entitled to confidence in the truth of that report only to the extent that one is entitled to confidence in the truth of the background beliefs. And if the report is favourable to a theory being tested, there is likewise ground for seeing that as a reason for thinking the theory true only if there is antecedent reason to think the same about the background beliefs. In fact, the background beliefs must, obviously, be *more* secure than the theory being tested, if any conflict between the latter and observation is not to be an impasse. Obvious question: how did the background beliefs attain that status – how did we get into a position reasonably to believe *them* to be true?

To elaborate a little. Scientific realism requires realism about the data which, in seeking a theory, we seek to explain. A realist might, no doubt, turn agnostic about our capacity to detect the truth of observation-statements – but in that case, he in effect extends the sway of absolute realism to include not just theory but data also, and his position becomes complete scepticism. The optimistic realist has to be prepared to apply to observation-statements the conception of truth which he proposes to apply to theory; so their truth or falsity has to be thought of as a literal, objective but often enough (defeasibly) decidable matter. Clearly, once the truth or falsity of observation-statements is so conceived, there has to be adequate reason to believe in the truth of any background theory, conditioning our assent to a particular observation report, before we can have good reason to accept that report, let alone accept a theory for whose truth it would provide a test. Either, therefore, some such background theory can be confirmed by *theoretically unconditioned* observation, or the realist has to admit that the credibility of any particular group of theoretical statements depends upon the prior credibility of another. Three possibilities then yawn: circularity, infinite regress or a confirmational structure which terminates in theoretical assumptions for which there is no evidence and which could be false. In any case, the realist seems to have abrogated the resources which he needs to ward off the depredations of scepticism; inevitably, he can retain his realism only at the cost of absolutism.

The difficulty is no less for the Popperian brand of absolute realism, since it presupposes we have some kind of cognitive domain over the 'data' by which the falsity of theories can sometimes be detected. For 'detecting the falsity' of a theory has to mean: recognizing its discord with observation-statements which there is good reason to believe to be true. Since such good reason requires good reason to believe the background theories which, by hypothesis, condition our assent to those observation-statements, and since the relevant notion of truth is – presumably – absolute, the Popperian realist is in poor position to explain, what is crucial to his position, the possibility of reasonable confidence that a theory has been shown to be false.[25]

No such problem need arise for the view that truth in science comes to no more than empirical adequacy. For 'empirical adequacy' need not mean: concord with *true* reports of observation, 'true' interpreted in a realist sense. It need require only concord with *acceptable* reports of observation, it being recognized that acceptability need not presuppose any basis for our believing that those background theories which, in part, determine our conception of when such a statement is acceptable

25 This is not the familiar 'Duhem point', which concerns the selection of hypotheses for blame from among a set of hypotheses which collectively generate conflict with observation. It is rather that the Popperian who believes that the credibility of an observation-statement is always a function of background theory has abrogated the resources to explain what it is reasonably to believe that there is a conflict with observation at all, prior to any such selection.

are themselves true in any sense grateful to realism.[26] Such a view of scientific truth comes, in effect, to the thoroughgoing pragmatism associated with the last two sections of Quine's 'Two Dogmas of Empiricism'. Success in science, on this view, consists not in the attainment of (realistically) true theories, nor even the formulation of theories which correctly codify true observation-statements, but in the achievement of a network of theories whose collective practice minimizes the occurrence of situations in which there is inconsistency between the consequences of one theory and the environmental descriptions which, guided by others of our theories and the stimulations of the (now noumenal) world, we are motivated to accept. Whatever the attractions or horrors of this famous picture, it is not optimistic scientific realism.

The dilemma for the would-be scientific realist who accepts that all observation is theory-conditioned would seem to be the choice between absolute scepticism and a Quinean holistic pragmatism. The considerations which set the dilemma are simple. So why is it not more generally perceived? The answer, I suspect, is the illusory comfort afforded to a would-be realist by some such thought as that confirmation can suffuse *simultaneously* across both a theory being tested by reference to certain observations and a theory which conditions the way those observations are described. If what we are disposed to accept as correct reports of observation is a function of some theory – call it the *conditioning* theory – which we hold (perhaps half unconsciously), and if what strike us as correct observations in that light are nicely explained by a distinct theory, then that is good cause – is it not? – to hold both theories.

But that this is so is not denied by the reasoning which sets the dilemma. The difficulty for this thought is to distinguish itself from Quine's. A genuine scientific realism surely requires that there are data which a true scientific theory can *explain* in a full-blooded sense, i.e. of which it can account for the ulterior causes. Reason to think a theory to be true is, for realism, reason to think that it best explains certain objective data. But what, precisely, may we regard as being explained when a pair of theories combine in such a way that, according to the proposal, the sequence of events spreads confirmation across them both, notwithstanding the fact that the role of one of them is to determine the proper description of the data? The point is not that there is nothing worth calling 'confirmation' in such a case; it is that the *kind* of confirmation involved is not, as the realist ought to require, the converse of explanation. A conditioning theory can play no explanatory role, if without it, or an alternative, there would be nothing to explain.

26 This now, of course, is not 'empirical adequacy' in the theoretically unconditioned sense earlier associated with van Fraassen.

If its role were explanatory, it would have to be possible to know of, *ergo* to describe, the things which it explains without having any inkling of the conditioning theory. Success may make it reasonable to accept such a theory; but it does not provide it with the kind of explanatory role which the scientific realist must demand.

These ideas are somewhat abstract, so it's worth relating them to a tried example, often invoked by proponents of the theory-ladenness of observation. One might suppose that simple descriptions of colour are purely observational if any statements are. Yet even such statements turn out to be defeasible by highly theoretical considerations. 'That is yellow', said of what is in fact a distant, very rapidly receding star, expresses a judgement which is defeasible by highly sophisticated theory concerning optics and the physics of light, whose effect is that light, like sound, is subject to a Doppler effect. One's readiness to assent to such a statement is accordingly going to depend on what, if anything, one knows of such theory and what one knows about the star in question. And if even colour is vulnerable to such considerations, which concepts can be safe?[27]

My purpose now is not to consider what plausibility the example lends to the general thesis of theory-ladenness – very little, one would imagine – but to confront the thought it may inspire that, in contrast to what was suggested above, the conditioning theory involved here seems to be anything but unexplanatory. For notice that what it explains is how, under the circumstances described, something can *look* to be yellow without actually being so, even though none of the usual explanations – abnormal lighting, abnormal vision, tinted spectacles, etc. – obtains. The explanatory power of the conditioning theory is saved, in other words, only because there is a *subordinate datum* which it does not condition: the star looks yellow. There may be a temptation to respond that if 'yellow' is a theoretically conditioned term, so must be 'looks yellow'. But that is just a further example of the fuzziness that infects the notion of 'theory-ladenness'. The presence of theoretical vocabulary in a judgement need not 'load' the judgement with theory if that is to imply its defeasibility by empirical theoretical considerations.[28] No case has been made for thinking that 'that looks yellow' is conditioned by theory in the sense with which we are concerned, and which the example attempts to illustrate for 'that is yellow'.

Generally speaking, conditioning theories explain why something which it would have seemed reasonable or natural to accept in certain circumstances need nevertheless not be correct, or why something which

27 The example is used by Newton-Smith, *The Rationality of Science*, pp. 27–8.
28 Cf. note 21.

we might be reluctant to accept in certain circumstances may nevertheless be true. But if they are to play this part, then they cannot simultaneously, it seems, condition the proper description of what those circumstances are. What the circumstances are, and whether – prescinding from consideration of the conditioning theory – they would or would not justify assent to a particular judgement, are *data* for any particular application of such a theory – states of affairs whose proper description is taken for granted. The role of a conditioning theory is to condition what *further* description of them may be appropriate. It would seem, accordingly, that in order for a conditioning theory to play an explanatory role at all, it has to be applied to data whose proper description it does not condition. And where, for whatever reason, there are no such data, the theory can play no explanatory role. So whatever cause there is then for accepting it is not a reason for regarding the theory as *true* in a sense germane to scientific realism.

VI

What is the relation between optimistic realism and the verificationist realism canvassed in section III? Not necessarily identity. They are united in their rejection of absolute realism. Absolute realism holds that there is no essential connection between the harvest of best scientific method and truth. Left to right, the ingredients of the harvest may still be absolutely (undetectably) false. Right to left, true theories may be uncertifiable by best method. Optimistic realism, by contrast, wants to claim that pursuit of best scientific method puts us in position reasonably and (often) correctly to claim to have uncovered and to understand more of what is true of this world. So it needs to hold that the harvest of best method is likely to be truth and may, *qua* so harvested, be reasonably so regarded. Verificationist realism holds, in addition and conversely, that truth is essentially certifiable by best method: that for any true theory, sufficiently extensive researches must disclose an adequate, enduring case for taking it to be so.

One group of reasons why the optimistic realist might embrace verificationist realism are familiar from modern semantic anti-realist writings. But he has reason to sympathize in any case. For his optimism is not merely about the *efficacy* of his methodology, but about the *extent* of the domain of its competence. Undetectable truth, for the optimistic realist, can only arise in one of two ways. Either best method can make no case for any view on a particular question or it makes only partial, mutually balanced cases for conflicting views. But optimism requires the conviction that such examples are exceptional. And any tendency to regard the present stock of accepted scientific theories as a corpus of discovery requires the conviction that they at least come into neither category. If the evidence-transcendent truth of scientific theories is to be a possibility, the intuitive realistic belief in the power and promise of science requires it to be a marginal possibility; and the intuitive realistic belief in the achievement of science requires that it has not so far proved obtrusive – so *extant* accepted theory should be deemed, by the optimist, to satisfy whatever epistemic constraint the verificationist realist should impose.

Granted the contention of section V, that optimistic realism must defend the possibility of theoretically unladen observation, a chain of platitudes now leads to the thought that the relevant constraint, for empirical science, should be nothing other than complicance with the Verification Principle. Best method, whatever its details, is inter alia method which makes for rigorous and fair testing. Testing must consist, ultimately, in confronting hypotheses with true reports of observation. Such a confrontation is a test only if the hypotheses tested have something to say, if only conditionally, about which such reports can be expected to be true. But the Verification Principle is just the attempt to characterize which hypotheses meet that condition, are apt to be so tested. It would apparently follow that the belief that a particular theory is part of the true harvest of best method is a commitment to holding that each of its hypotheses passes the test which the Verification Principle aims to impose (or is entailed by others which do). The optimistic realist's conviction of the vast cognitive achievements of modern science requires a correspondingly vast extension within its theories for the concept of 'verifiability'. Yet it can hardly be clear that the requirement is met – for the Verification Principle itself was never satisfactorily formulated. That is a matter for the sequel.

10

The Verification Principle

I
Punctures and Patches[1]

Let us review something of the Principle's chequered history. I shall assume we are working in a language whose syntax is first-order and whose logic is classical. The language is to contain a decidable subset of sentences, $[O_1 \ldots O_n \ldots]$, expressing all the observation-statements we could want to make. (A background assumption for the significance – if any – of our findings is that such a language could be an adequate vehicle for science). The proposal of the second edition of *Language, Truth and Logic*, recall, was

1 S is *directly verifiable* iff
   i $(\exists O_i)\ S = O_i$; or
   ii $(\exists O_1)(\exists O_j \ldots O_m)(\{S\} \cup \{O_j \ldots O_m\} \models O_i \ \& \ \{O_j \ldots O_m\} \not\models O_i)$.
2 S is *indirectly verifiable* iff
   iii $(\exists T)(\exists T_j \ldots T_m)$(T is directly verifiable & $\{S\} \cup \{T_j \ldots T_m\} \models T$ & $\{T_j \ldots T_m\} \not\models T$); and
   iv each T_i, $\in \{T_j \ldots T_m\}$, is either analytic, or directly verifiable, or (independently establishable as) indirectly verifiable.
3 S is 'literally significant' (or whatever) iff S is directly or indirectly verifiable.

Hempel[2] and Church[3] led the fusillade. Hempel observed that if S passes as directly or indirectly verifiable, so must 'S & N' for arbitrary ('nonsensical') N, since augmentation of the premises of the entailments

1 David Lewis's 'Statements Partly About Observation' jibes at the 'punctures and patches' industry that has descended from Ayer's original defective formulations.
2 Hempel, 'Problems and Changes in the Empiricist Criterion of Meaning'.
3 Church, review of *Language, Truth and Logic*, 2nd edn.

specified in (1(ii)) and (2(iii)) will change nothing. It does not follow directly that N itself will qualify as directly or indirectly verifiable, since there is no immediate guarantee of an $\{O_j...O_m\}$ or $\{T_j...T_m\}$ with the appropriate properties. (The union of {S} with the original $\{O_j...O_m\}$, or with the original $\{T_j...O_m\}$, or with the original $\{T_j...T_m\}$, will not satisfy the restrictions, given the original choices of O_i and T.) But one would suppose that Ayer would want literal significance to be transmitted to (contingent) logical consequences. And Church constructed a simple example establishing the indirect verifiability of any non-analytic N. Let O_1, O_2, O_3, be any logically independent observation-statements, and let $S = (\sim O_1 \,\&\, O_2) \vee (\sim N \,\&\, O_3)$. S is directly verifiable. (Proof: Let $O_i = O_3$, $\{O_j...O_m\} = \{O_1\}$.) So N is indirectly verifiable. (Proof: Let $T = O_2$, $\{T_j...T_m\} = \{S\}$.)

Nidditch[4] responded by proposing a tightening of (2(iv)): let *each sentential component* of each T_i in $\{T_j...T_m\}$ be either analytic, or directly verifiable, or (independently establishable as) indirectly verifiable. That rules out taking Church's S as $\{T_j...T_m\}$. But it does nothing to offset Hempel's criticism. And the restriction can anyway easily be got around. Scheffler[5] for instance took $S = (N \,\&\, O_1) \vee \sim O_2$. S is directly verifiable. (Proof: Let $O_i = O_1$, $\{O_j...O_m\} = O_2$, where O_1 and O_2 are independent.) So N is indirectly verifiable, even after Nidditch's restriction. (Proof: Let T = S, and let $\{T_j...T_m\} = \{O_1\}$, and assume that $\{O_1, O_2\} \nvDash N$.) Ullian got the same effect with $S = N \,\&\, (O_1 \vee -O_2)$.[6] (Proof: identical, except that we need assume only that $O_1 \nvDash N$.[7])

Actually, Brown and Watling[8] had earlier proposed an extra condition which would have excluded the Ullian–Scheffler examples:

> If S is molecular, S contains no component whose deletion – *modulo* rebracketing – would produce an S′ with verifiable consequences differing from those of S.

4 Nidditch, 'A Defence of Ayer's Verifiability Principle against Church's Criticisms'. Nidditch, somewhat implausibly, presented his proposal as an interpretation of Ayer's original words, rather than as a restriction.

5 Sheffler, *The Anatomy of Inquiry*.

6 J. Ullian, 'A Note on Sheffler on Nidditch'.

7 Ullian's point was a modest strengthening of Sheffler's. If S is Sheffler's sentence, then if $\{0_1, 0_2\} \vDash N$, then $\{0_1, 0_2\} \vDash S$, $= (N \,\&\, 0_1) \vee \sim 0_2$, $= 0_2 \rightarrow (N \,\&\, 0_1)$. Hence $0_1 \vDash 0_2 \rightarrow (0_2 \rightarrow (N \,\&\, 0_1))$, $= 0_2 \rightarrow (N \,\&\, 0_1)$, = S. So clause (2(iii)) of Ayer's definition is violated. Thus, whereas Sheffler showed only that Nidditch's proposal allows any statement whatever to be indirectly verifiable unless it is entailed by some pair of independent observation-statements, Ullian shows that any statement whatever is accounted verifiable by Nidditch's proposal unless it is entailed by *some* observation-statement.

8 Brown and Watling, 'Amending the Verification Principle'.

Their condition was to apply to both direct and indirect verifiability. But it seems entirely ad hoc, and would anyway be far too restrictive, excluding not only the Church, Ullian and Scheffler examples but, e.g., any simple conjunction or disjunction of observation statements.

The debate lay dormant through the late 1960s and 1970s. Then Jonathan Cohen took it onto a new level of sophistication (and of 'ad hoc-ery').[9] Let 'C_nS' say that S is verifiable at level n. Then Cohen's proposal, somewhat reworded, is:

1 C_oS iff $(\exists O_i)\ S = O_i$.
2 C_1S iff
   a S is contingent, *and*
   b S is directly verifiable in Ayer's sense, *and*
   c from no irreducible conjunctive equivalent of S, none of whose conjuncts contains more occurrences of any non-logical term than are contained in S, is it possible to select some, but only some, of the conjuncts so as to generate a conjunction which passes (2(b)) for the same choices of O_i and $\{O_j...O_m\}$ as S.
3 $C_{n+1}S$ iff
   a S is contingent, *and*
   b $(\exists T_i)(\exists T_j...T_m)$(each of T_i, $T_j...T_m$ is verifiable at level n, and $\{S\} \cup \{T_j...T_m\} \models T_i$, and $\{T_j...T_m\} \not\models T_i$), *and*
   c from no irreducible conjunctive equivalent of S, none of whose conjuncts contains more occurrences of any non-logical term than are contained in S, is it possible to select some, but only some, of the conjuncts so as to generate a conjunction which passes (3(b)) for the same choices of T_i and $\{T_j...T_m\}$ as S.

(A *conjunctive equivalent* of S is any statement, S_1 &...& S_n, $\dashv\models$ S; such an equivalent is *irreducible* if any omission of conjuncts destroys its equivalence to S.)

4 S is *verifiable* iff $(\exists n)\ C_nS$ or C_nS', where S′ is an equivalent of S, or of the negation of S.

This copes with all the problem cases so far considered. Hempel's 'S & N' itself violates (2(c)) with respect to its first conjunct. Church's example factorizes into '$((\sim O_1 \& O_2) \vee \sim N) \& ((\sim O_1 \& O_2) \vee O_3)$' which violates (2(c)) with respect to its second conjunct. Scheffler's example factorizes into '$(\sim O_2 \vee O_1) \& (\sim O_2 \vee N)$' which violates

9 L. J. Cohen, 'Is a Criterion of Verifiability Possible?'

(2(c)) with respect to its first conjunct. Ullian's example comes ready factorized.

But Cohen's account has serious shortcomings. For one thing, clauses (2(c)) and (3(c)) hardly seem clearly motivated, and their implications are not evident. What is the point of the clause, '...none of whose conjuncts contains more occurrences of any non-logical term than are contained in S'? Cohen's explanation is that, without this condition, any generalization, $(\forall x)(Rx \rightarrow Sx)$ would fail of n + 1-verifiability since equivalent to (C):

$$[(\forall x)(Rx \rightarrow Sx) \lor ((\exists y)Ry \rightarrow (\forall y)Sy)] \ \& \\ [(\forall x)(Rx \rightarrow Sx) \lor \sim((\exists y)Ry \rightarrow (\forall y)Sy)],$$

whose first conjunct – his thought must be – will have the same n-verifiable consequences as the original generalization. Pokriefka claims that $(\forall x)$ $(Rx \ \& \ Rx \rightarrow Sx \ \& \ Sx)$ is still ruled out by Cohen's conditions.[10] But this is to overlook Cohen's clause (4). And both Cohen and Pokriefka appear to have overlooked that the first conjunct of (C) is equivalent to $(\forall x)$ $(Rx \rightarrow Sx)$ in any case: what we have here is not an *irreducible* conjunctive equivalent. So far as I can see, this is just an oversight; so Cohen in fact had no good motive for the extra complication.

It is not merely unmotivated. Intuitively, Cohen's thought was to exclude, at each level of the recursion >0, content superfluous to the deduction of consequences at the previous level. But can such content always be squeezed, on analysis, into a proper part of a conjunctive equivalent in a way that complies with his conditions? Foster gives an example which suggests not.[11] Let 'a' and 'b' be terms standing for observable individuals. Then a = b would seem to be Cohen-verifiable at level 1. (Proof: let 'Fx' be an observational predicate, take O_i = Fb, $\{O_j...O_m\}$ = {Fa}; no conjunctive equivalent violating (2(c)) is available.) Now let Mx be a 'metaphysical' predicate. Let S = Ma & ~Mb. Why is S not verifiable at level 2? (Take $T_i = a \neq b$, and $\{T_j...T_m\} = \Lambda$.) To rule it out, Cohen needs an irreducible conjunctive equivalent some proper part of which $\models a \neq b$ but none of whose conjuncts contains more occurrences of 'M', 'a' or 'b' than S (assuming that the consequences of $a \neq b$ exhaust the level 1-verifiable consequences of S). Can he construct one? Take $a \neq b$ itself as the first conjunct. Ma has to be a consequence of the result, so take it as the second conjunct. We cannot just select ~Mb as a third conjunct without violating

10 Pokriefka, 'Ayer's Definition of Empirical Significance Revisited'.
11 Foster, *A. J. Ayer*, pp. 19–20.

irreducibility, but the third selection must entail $\sim Mb \vee a = b$ and $\sim Mb \vee \sim Ma$. But the former contains one occurrence of 'b' too many, and the latter, conjoined with the second conjunct, entails S and so violates irreducibility.

Cohen's complication, then, more than being apparently ungrounded, would seem to obstruct his own intention. How does his account fare if, accordingly, we delete 'none of whose conjuncts contains more occurrences of any non-logical term than are contained in S' from both (2(c)) and (3(c))? Foster's example can then be handled. But a fundamental weakness is left unchanged: no adequate provision is made for *theoretical* vocabulary to participate in verifiable statements. It is true that e.g. $O_1 \,\&\, (T \vee \sim T)$ passes Cohen's test for verifiability at level 1. (Proof: let $O_i = O_1$, and $\{O_j \ldots O_m\} = \Lambda$. Notice that the unrevised test would have allowed this also.) But, for instance, if Fx and Gx are observational predicates, then even a hypothesis which places observational controls on a theoretically described state of affairs in the most direct and simple way, for instance

$$(\forall x)((Tx \rightarrow Fx) \,\&\, (\sim Tx \rightarrow Gx)),$$

is going to fail the test, since equivalent to

$$(\forall x)(\sim Fx \rightarrow (Gx \rightarrow \sim Tx)) \,\&\, (\forall x)(\sim Tx \rightarrow Gx) \,\&\, (\forall x)(\sim Fx \rightarrow Gx),$$

which is irreducibly equivalent to the original but whose third conjunct exhausts its observational content.

Cohen was under no illusions about this. He writes

> You cannot exclude observationally superfluous content, on the ground that it may be metaphysical, without also excluding any implications about nature that are superfluous to the observational content.[12]

But this is a philosophy of despair from the point of view of optimistic or verificationist realism. And why, in that case, not go for the simple type of proposal canvassed above (p. 284) and taken up in Foster's discussion?[13]

12 Cohen, 'Is a Criterion of Verifiability Possible?', p. 351.
13 Cohen's reply (p. 352) is that it need be neither sufficient nor necessary for a statement to count as observational that it be couched in a certain distinguished vocabulary. This is true, and important (cf. note 20). But the fact remains that, even if there is no distinguished vocabulary of observation, some (most?) theoretical terms are, presumably, not apt to contribute to the expression of observation-statements; and Cohen's recursion does nothing to explain how statements featuring such terms can nevertheless be 'empirically significant'.

Pokriefka proposed a recursion to overcome the limitations he found in Cohen's proposal (principally, that it failed to exclude sentences with 'nonsensical' components, like O_I & $(N \vee \sim N)$, as we noted; and that it excluded harmless generalizations like $(\forall x)(Fx \& Fx \rightarrow Gx \& Gx)$ – which, as remarked, was a confusion).[14] Essentially his offering was

S is *directly verifiable* iff
 i S is an atomic observation sentence, *or*
 ii S is a truth-function or quantification of directly verifiable sentences.
S is *indirectly verifiable* iff
 iii $(\exists T_i)(\exists T_j \ldots T_m)$ $(\{S\} \cup \{T_j \ldots T_m\}$ is consistent and $\{S\} \cup \{T_j \ldots T_m\} \not\models T_i$, $\{T_j \ldots T_m\} \not\models T_i$, and each member of $\{T_j \ldots T_m\}$ is directly or indirectly verifiable, and T_i is directly verifiable,) *or*
 iv S is a truth-function or quantification of indirectly verifiable sentences.

Pokriefka intended that theoretical statements should count as indirectly verifiable. But in fact he subsequently realized that no non-logical vocabulary which does not feature among the atomic observation-statements can ever feature in a statement classified as verifiable by his clauses.[15]

II
Towards a Permanent Repair

Is it possible to do better? Angels would fear to tread in this region – but I think it is. Notice, first, that the kind of 'superfluous content' which Cohen designed his account to exclude depends only on *syntax*. The problem cases are all specified formally – nothing turns on the particular interpretation of 'N' or 'Mx'. This is possible, of course, only because each of the problem cases exhibits a formal pattern of occurrences of non-logical vocabulary any instance of which would combine with the same supplementary premises $(\{O_j \ldots O_m\}$ or $\{T_j \ldots T_m\})$ to generate the same entailments. Why not explicitly rule that out?

We need here the idea of an entailment which is fully sensitive to the

14 Pokriefka, 'Ayer's Definition of Empirical Significance Revisited'.
15 Pokriefka, 'More on Empirical Significance'. Compare Dale, 'Hempel Revisited' in the same volume. Both work within the conception of a distinction between observational and theoretical vocabulary; and both their proofs make the unstated assumption of the two vocabularies' *analytical independence*. (See footnote 21 below.)

content of *all* the constituents in its premises in just the way in which any entailment is sensitive to the content of the *logical* vocabulary occurring in its premises. A fully content-sensitive entailment is thus sustained by contributions from the content of each of its premises' non-logical constituents – there is, as it were, no semantic passengers. Let us say that an entailment is *compact* just in case it is liable to disruption by uniform substitution for the occurrences of any non-logical constituent in its premises (while leaving unchanged any occurrences of that constituent in its conclusion). And let an entailment,

$$\{A_1 \ldots A_n, S\} \nvDash B,$$

be *S-compact* if and only if it is subject to disruption by uniform substitution for any non-logical constituent in S.

Compact entailment, so characterized, is not the obverse of formally valid entailment. Indeed, the distinctions, between compact and non-compact entailments and between formally valid entailments and entailments which are valid but not formally so, cut across each other. There are valid compact entailments which are not formally valid, for instance

Victoria has auburn fur;

Victoria has coloured fur.

But there are also formally valid compact entailments, for instance

Victoria is a vixen;

Provided that, if Victoria is a vixen, she is fierce, then Victoria is fierce.

Likewise, there are both non-compact entailments which are formally valid, for instance

Victoria is a vixen; all vixens are female foxes;

Victoria is a fox

– whose validity is indifferent to uniform substitutions for 'vixen' in its premises – and valid non-compact entailments which are not formally valid, for instance

Victoria is smaller than Reynard; Reynard is smaller than Mr Tod;

Victoria is smaller than Mr Tod,

whose validity is indifferent to uniform substitutions for 'Reynard', but depends upon the transitivity of 'is smaller than'.

With the idea of compact entailment to hand, we can now very simply refashion Ayer's second edition definition of verifiability. Thus

1 S is *directly verifiable* iff
  i $(\exists O_i)S = O_i$; or
  ii $(\exists O_i)(\exists O_j...O_m)(\{S\} \cup \{O_j...O_m\}$ S-compactly entails $O_i)$.

(There is, in view of the definition of S-compact entailment, no need to stipulate in addition, as originally, that $\{O_j...O_m\}$ should not entail O_i.) Likewise,

2 S is *indirectly verifiable* iff
  iii $(\exists T)(\exists T_j...T_m)$ (T is directly verifiable & $\{S\} \cup \{T_j...T_m\}$ S-compactly entails T); and
  iv each T_i, $\in \{T_j...T_m\}$, is either analytic, or directly verifiable, or (independently establishable as) indirectly verifiable.

This straightforward adjustment immediately blocks all the puncture-inducing examples so far reviewed. Consider again the Church and Foster cases. Church's example

Ch.: $(\sim O_1 \& O_2) \vee (\sim N \& O_3)$

was classed as directly verifiable on Ayer's original account since, in conjunction with O_1, it entails O_3. But it is not so classed by the revised proposal, since the entailment of O_3 goes through no matter what we substitute for either 'O_2' or 'N', and thus fails to be S-compact with respect to the relevant S. Since Ch. no longer ranks as directly verifiable, the argument for the indirect verifiability of N collapses in its turn. Likewise John Foster's problem case for Cohen's proposal involved first establishing the verifiability of $a = b$, and then that of Ma & ~Mb via its entailment of $a \neq b$. However this last entailment is indifferent to uniform substitutions for 'M' throughout its (sole) premise and is thus not compact. The reader can easily review the other examples.

There is, however, an obvious resultant awkwardness: how are we now to establish the verifiability of sentences which share the *form* of a problem case but contain, in place of 'N' or 'Mx', occurrences only of *empirically* respectable vocabulary? The best response, I think, is just to stipulate additionally that any truth-function or quantification of verifiable statements is to count as verifiable. That complicates the account, but we can get a compensating simplification by dispensing with the (pointless) distinction between direct and indirect verifiability, and dropping the mention of analytic supplementary premises (in clause 2 (iv)).[16] The following proposal is therefore suggested: S is verifiable if and only if S is contingent and

i S is an atomic observation statement, or
ii S is (equivalent to) a negation, disjunction or existential generalization of verifiable statements, or
iii Some verifiable T is S-compactly entailed by the union of S with some set, $(T_1 \ldots T_n)$, of verifiable statements, or...

Do we need anything further? Well, clause (ii) has the effect of guaranteeing that verifiability is closed with respect to statements compounded by means of the statement-forming operations of classical logic. It is not clear, however, that the clauses as formulated guarantee closure with respect to consequences which are logically *simpler* than their verifiable parentage. It therefore seems prudent to add:

iv S is entailed by some verifiable statement, and contains only vocabulary occurring in statements which may be proved verifiable by appeal only to (i)–(iii).[17]

It is worth observing that so invoking the idea of compact entailment is entirely in keeping with the original Positivists' intuitive thinking. Their contention was not – could not have been – that the statements which they wished to stigmatize as 'metaphysical' were just so much noise (or

16 Which we may do since, when A is analytic, $\{S\} \cup \{A\}$ entails B just in case S entails B, and the former entailment is S-compact just in case the latter is compact.
17 Clause (iv) also excludes a kind of example which bothered Pokriefka, typified by $(O \,\&\, (N \vee \sim N))$, in which metaphysical baggage is tacked on to bona fide verifiable statements.

It may occur to the alert reader that, as it stands, clause (iii) might make trouble when it comes to establishing the verifiability of statements containing singular terms; for now it will not suffice, in order to establish, for instance, the verifiability of Fa, to locate an appropriate T_i, $T_j \ldots T_m$ such that $\{Fa\} \cup \{T_j \ldots T_m\} \nvDash T_i$ etc., unless some Fb fails to have the same entailments. I would expect that, on the contrary, when no such Fb is available – so that we have, in effect, a proof of the verifiability of $(\exists x)Fx$, – then, *either* there will be a suitable set of substitutions possible throughout this proof which will generate a T_i', $T_j' \ldots T_m'$ appropriately specific to a proof of the verifiability of Fa, *or* there will indeed be a real question about the suitability of 'a' to figure in verifiable statements. Consider, for instance, $\{Fa, (\forall x)(Fx \rightarrow Gx)\} \nvDash (\exists x)Gx$. Any Fb replacing Fa will serve the entailment just as well. But replace 'Fx' by 'Fx & x = a', and 'Gx' by 'Gx & x = a'. Then Fb will not serve as well in

$$\{Fa, (\forall x)(Fx \,\&\, x = a \rightarrow Gx \,\&\, x = a)\} \vDash (\exists x)(Gx \,\&\, x = a).$$

scribble). Rather, the 'metaphysical' or factually insignificant character of certain kinds of discourse was to come by way of a *discovery* in the light of a proper account of 'literal significance'. Such a discovery could be possible only in the context of our apprehension of *some* kind of content in such statements: a kind of content which unfitted them to chime or clash with observation in determinate ways. It should have been evident from the start that, if chiming or clashing with observation was to be explained as a matter of entailment of observationally decidable consequences, some content-sensitive constraints had to be imposed on the kinds of entailment allowed. The proposal above is simply one natural outcome of the conviction, likely to be shared by anyone who surveys the literature, over half a century, of successive punctures and patches, that – provided verifiability is to satisfy other plausible closure conditions, for instance, closure with respect to truth-functional composition and quantification – there will always be *some* way of exploiting the presence of passengers – sentential or subsentential – in premises entailing observationally decidable statements, if any less exigent condition is imposed.

III
Lewis's Puncture

The proposal must now be refashioned, however, to seal off a puncture caused by David Lewis.[18] To see the problem, note first that clause (iii) is equivalent to the stipulation that verifiability is closed under converse compact entailment *simpliciter*. For if S, conjoined with verifiable $\{T_1 \ldots T_n\}$, entails a verifiable T, then – in the presence of clause (ii) – there will be a verifiable statement which it entails *sua sponte*, namely the conditional whose consequent is T and whose antecedent is a conjunction in which $T_1 \ldots T_n$ are the ingredient conjuncts. And this entailment will be compact if the entailment of T by $\{S, T_1 \ldots T_n\}$ is S-compact. (Conversely, of course, if S compactly entails T, then S entails T S-compactly.)

Now Lewis argues that, provided A and B are statements in a definitionally sufficiently rich language, it will always hold that, if A entails B, A will *ancestrally* compactly entail B. So any statement which entails, whether compactly or not, some verifiable T, is going to pass as verifiable by clause (iii), the play with compact entailment notwithstanding. He writes:

18 See his 'Statements Partly About Observation'.

> The proposal avoids collapse, sure enough, in a sufficiently impoverished language...But in a sufficiently rich language, the limitation to compact entailment accomplishes nothing. Take a language in which, for any P and Q, we have an atomic sentence, S, that does not occur in P or Q and that is equivalent to 'P & Q'...Then if P entails Q, whether compactly or not, it follows that P compactly entails S and S compactly entails Q. (Compact entailment is not transitive.) Closure under converse compact entailment has the same effect as closure under converse entailment simpliciter, except that sometimes we need two steps instead of one. Collapse ensues.[19]

So formulated, Lewis's objection is suggestive rather than cogent, since he errs in seeming to claim generally that, when S meets the conditions he describes, the entailment of S by P will be compact. Suppose, for instance, we were to formulate the first entailment exploited in Church's example as

$$(O_1 \,\&\, ((\sim O_1 \,\&\, O_2) \vee (\sim N \,\&\, O_3))) \not\models O_3.$$

A mechanical application of Lewis' quoted claim would involve taking P as

$$O_1 \,\&\, ((\sim O_1 \,\&\, O_2) \vee (\sim N \,\&\, O_3)),$$

Q as O_3, and S, accordingly, as an abbreviation of

$$(O_1 \,\&\, ((\sim O_1 \,\&\, O_2) \vee (\sim N \,\&\, O_3))) \,\&\, O_3.$$

Naturally, any entailment with S as sole premise will be compact – provided, of course, that the conclusion is not a logical truth – since S has no internal logical structure. But that, naturally, does not guarantee the compactness of any entailment of S as conclusion. And in fact the entailment of S by P above is *not* compact – substitute whatever you want for O_2 in P and the entailment survives.

Unfortunately, that does not show that Church's example cannot be reinstated by the ploy Lewis describes. Suppose instead that we reduce the first entailment in Church's example to a one-premise entailment in the fashion noted at the start of this section, so that O_1 is taken out of the set of premises to form the antecedent of a conditional conclusion. Then P now becomes

$$(\sim O_1 \,\&\, O_2) \vee (\sim N \,\&\, O_3),$$

19 Lewis, 'Statements Partly About Observation', p. 30, n. 12. I have replaced his pejorative 'idiosyncratic' by 'compact'.

and Q is $O_1 \rightarrow O_3$. So S, accordingly, now abbreviates

$$((\sim O_1 \& O_2) \vee (\sim N \& O_1)) \& (O_1 \rightarrow O_3).$$

Here the entailment of S by P *is* compact. The difference is that the entailment of P by *itself* is compact.

At least, it is natural to suppose so. But actually, even that is too quick. Consider the situation, in relation to Lewis's ploy, of the second ingredient entailment in Church's example. Now we have that P is N, Q becomes

$$((\sim O_1 \& O_2) \vee (\sim N \& O_3)) \rightarrow O_2,$$

and S abbreviates

$$N \& (((\sim O_1 \& O_2) \vee (\sim N \& O_3)) \rightarrow O_2).$$

And it is natural to suppose, without further ado, that here the entailment of S by P is compact – until one realizes that that is to assume, quite unwarrantedly in the general case, that N lacks any significant internal logical structure which might render its entailment of itself non-compact. For if it entails itself non-compactly, it will so entail S. And the same point applies, of course, to the first entailment also.

It is similar with Foster's example. Now we have that P is Ma & ~Mb, Q is a ≠ b and S is an abbreviation of (Ma & ~Mb) & a ≠ b. Here the entailment of S by P is compact provided Mx is atomic. But we cannot affirm its compactness in general. If Mx is non-atomic, it may happen that the entailment of S by P is not liable to disruption by substitution for certain selected constituents in Ma and ~Mb.

What, then, is the status of Lewis's objection? Well, his thought as quoted above is correct provided we restrict attention to statements, P, which are compactly self-entailing. For if P entails itself compactly, it will so entail P & Q for any Q which it also entails. Hence it will compactly entail any abbreviation of P & Q. So all compact self-entailers which entail, compactly or otherwise, any verifiable statement, will indeed be admitted by clause (iii), if Lewis's ploy is allowed. A wide range of unwelcome cases will therefore be admitted.

And in fact matters are likely to be worse. It is a plausible conjecture that any first-order statement which is not compactly self-entailing will have a compactly self-entailing equivalent.[20] If that is so, then whenever

20 After I had drafted this, Lewis sent me a proof of this claim for the language of classical sentential logic with the constants [t] and [f].

the Lewis ploy is unsuccessful in establishing the verifiability of a statement via clause (iii) – because that statement entails itself non-compactly – we can be sure that there will be a statement with the same truth-conditions which the Lewis ploy *does* get past clause (iii). It may not be true that every (non-analytic) statement which entails, compactly or otherwise, some verifiable statement will also ancestrally compactly entail it; but if it does not, some truth-conditional equivalent will. And that is effectively just as bad.

So, not so much a blow-out as a slow puncture. But the end result is deflation just the same.[21]

IV
A Further Patch

Might we simply outlaw Lewis's ploy – insist that the Verification Principle be applied to a language only when it is in, as it were, basic form, and all definitional abbreviations have been unpacked? It is not clear that the idea is coherent. In its primary class of uses, 'brother'

21 Readers of the original version of 'Scientific Realism, Observation and the Verification Principle' in *Fact, Morality and Science* may recall that on pp. 268–9 I offered a demonstration that problems of this kind would not afflict the proposed account. What was wrong with it? Nothing. Let me explain.

The reasoning made use of the idea of one vocabulary's being *analytically independent* of another. A pair of vocabularies are analytically independent just in case any analytically true statement involving elements from both vocabularies remains analytically true under uniform substitution, using materials from within or outwith the vocabularies in question, for any of its non-logical constituents. Conversely, two vocabularies are analytically dependent on each other just in case *some* analytic truths involving occurrences of elements of each may be disrupted by such substitution. What was demonstrated in the *Fact, Science and Morality* draft was that only statements whose non-logical constituents constitute a vocabulary which is ancestrally analytically dependent on the vocabulary of the base class of verifiable statements – whatever exactly that is – would be admitted by clause (iii).

This conclusion was perfectly sound. The error consisted in construing it as a ground for peace of mind. When it seemed to be such a ground, there was a tacit assumption in play that ancestral analytical dependence between vocabularies would guarantee the existence of interesting conceptual connections, necessarily absent in the sorts of problem case which we are trying to outlaw. But what Lewis's ploy with abbreviative definition brings out is that this assumption is false. For when the ploy works – that is, when some P, non-compactly entailing a verifiable Q, compactly entails the appropriate abbreviative S, then both 'If P, then S' and 'If S, then Q' will be analytically true but disruptible by uniform substitution for the non-logical vocabulary in their antecedents. So the non-logical vocabulary of P *will* be ancestrally analytically dependent on the non-logical vocabulary of Q, the absence – if they are absent – of 'interesting conceptual connections' notwithstanding.

abbreviates 'male sibling'. But we could also, plausibly, define 'x is a sibling' as:

x is a brother or x is a sister

and 'x is male' as:

x is a brother or if x were to be a sibling, x would be a brother.

We don't typically give either of these definitions, of course. But then, we don't typically explain 'brother' as short for 'male sibling'. The fact is that the definitions allowed by a typical natural language are not guaranteed to conform to any order of priority, built pyramid-style upon a base class of indefinables. And, for its inventors' purposes, the Verification Principle has to be applicable to natural languages.

Suppose that N non-compactly entails O and that we stipulate that S is to be an abbreviative equivalent of N & O. And suppose, as Lewis's ploy requires, that the result is that N compactly entails S, it being assured, of course, that S compactly entails O. A second thought is that we might try to bar S's entailment of O from counting, for the purposes of verifiability, on grounds of its possession of an equivalent, namely N & O, which entails O non-compactly.

Unfortunately, there is no mileage in that either. For whenever A entails B, compactly or otherwise, there will be some C, equivalent to A, which entails B non-compactly; C could be, for instance, (A & Q) ∨ (A & ~Q). So the effect would just be to bar *all* entailments from counting.

However a better thought is close at hand. The distinctive thing about Lewis's ploy – when it works, that is, when the self-entailment of the first conjunct in the abbreviated sentence is compact – is that it constructs not merely an equivalent but a *compact equivalent* of that conjunct.[22] In any example of the above structure, for instance, N and S will be compact equivalents. So the most natural way of barring monsters riding in on the backs of the compact entailments sustained by abbreviations is to insist that the compact entailment of some verifiable T by S qualifies S as verifiable only if S has no compact equivalent, S*, which entails T non-compactly. More specifically, we may add to clause (iii), as formulated above, a clause to the following effect:

...and S has no compact equivalent, S*, such that the entailment of T by $\{T_1 \ldots T_n, S^*\}$ is non-S*-compact, or...

22 Where a compact equivalence is, naturally, one in which both ingredient entailments are compact.

So patched, clause (iii) will allow an entailment of a particular T to admit S as verifiable only if unpatched clause (iii) would allow their entailment of T to admit each of S's compact equivalents. And that would appear to dispose of the problem.

V

Is this an objectionably ad hoc response? Well, let me attempt to explain in what precise sense it is ad hoc and then leave it to the reader to judge whether it is objectionably so, in the light of a mitigating consideration.

Compact entailment was invoked in an attempt to characterize, by reference to its 'survival-conditions', what it is for an entailment to be *fully content-sensitive* – to depend as fully as possible upon the extra-logical content of its premises. Our proposal was that there is such a full dependence if and only if any way of varying the premises' content – generated by uniform substitution for any of their non-logical constituents – has instances for which the entailment fails. But Lewis's objection brings out a simple problem with this proposal that can be appreciated quite independently of any concern with the formulation of the Verification Principle. Reflect that it will presumably be a feature of fully content-sensitive entailment that if A so entails B, and coincides in content with C – a narrower notion, of course, than logical equivalence – then C will so entail B. Compact entailment, however, lacks this feature. For definitional abbreviation conserves content; yet, when A abbreviates B, A may compactly entail C while B does not. So assuming, as seems reasonable, that all fully content-sensitive entailments are compact, it follows that compact entailments are a wider class than fully content-sensitive ones, and we need to include some further condition in a satisfactory characterization.

Now, had we been tackling the problem under this perspective, we could scarcely have failed to be struck by the following thought. Precisely because it will be a feature of the 'manufactured' cases that premises of the same content – since definition conserves content – do not sustain the same compact entailments, why not lay it down as the needed further condition that they *should* – that an entailment, $\{A_1 \ldots A_n\} \models B$, is fully content-sensitive if and only if it is compact and there is no non-compact entailment of B by premises of the same content as $\{A_1 \ldots A_n\}$? Well, someone might question whether the resulting characterization – call it the Intuitive Account – does not proceed *ad oscurum per oscurius*; whether the notion of *same content* is in good enough shape to be at the service of explaining anything. Replacing it by the relatively clear notion of compact equivalence naturally commends itself; which, in effect, is just what we did.

That brings out the sense in which what has been offered is ad hoc. The original intention was to devise clauses to ensure that verifiability would be closed under converse fully content-sensitive entailment. But we have not actually come up with a competitive general proposal about what fully content-sensitive entailment is except the Intuitive Account, which depends on the notion of sameness of content. And compact equivalence, for its part, is no account of sameness of content; for there are statements which are not compactly equivalent to themselves and, conversely, compactly equivalent statements whose contents intuitively diverge (for example, 'X is a closed plane figure with exactly three sides' and 'X is a closed plane figure whose interior angles sum to 180°'). We are therefore apparently open to the charge that we have abandoned the project of characterizing the notion of fully content-sensitive entailment, with a view to enlisting it in the formulation of the Verification Principle, and have merely grabbed at a convenient restriction – easily formulated by means of the materials to hand – to shore up original clause (iii).

But the charge is unfair. Here is the mitigating consideration. *Only* compactly self-entailing statements can get past original clause (iii). For statements which do not compactly entail themselves do not compactly entail anything.[23] Hence we are entitled, in the context of our problem, to restrict our attention to compactly self-entailing statements. And *among these* compact equivalence is at least a necessary condition of sameness of content.[24] So the restriction embodied in the response to Lewis does *not* betray the project of characterizing fully content-sensitive entailment. Rather it amounts – for the compactly self-entailing statements in which we are interested – to a step in the direction of the Intuitive Account; a step which does not take us all the way, but compensates by its relative clarity – and perhaps takes us as far as we need to go.

23 Proof: Suppose A is not compactly self-entailing but compactly entails B. Let t be an expression in A which is *slack* with respect to A's self-entailment; i.e., no matter how t is interpreted, the resulting sentence entails A. Then there is an interpretation, I, of t such that the resulting sentence, A^I, entails A but not B. A^I cannot be inconsistent, or it would entail B. So there are possible circumstances under which A^I is true and B is not. But these are all circumstances under which A is true. So A does not entail B, contrary to hypothesis.

24 Proof: Suppose A and B have the same content, entail themselves compactly, but that A non-compactly entails B. Let t be an expression in A which is slack (see note 23) with respect to A's entailment of B. Then there is an interpretation, I, of t such that the resulting sentence A^I entails B but not A. But that contradicts the hypothesis of the sameness of content, and hence logical equivalence of A and B.

VI
Too Tight a Seal?

Have we now excluded statements that should be admitted? Suppose, for instance, that 'x is female' counts as verifiable by observation. (Of course, it is not an observation statement in the Positivists' original sense; but then, nothing is.) Then the entailment of 'x is female' by 'x is a vixen' will not enable 'x is a vixen' to pass as verifiable via patched clause (iii), since 'x is female & x is a fox' is a compact equivalent of 'x is a vixen', whose entailment of 'x is female' survives uniform replacement of the occurrence of 'fox'. But that does not show that 'x is a vixen' cannot now qualify as verifiable at all. It could, for instance, still qualify via patched clause (iii) if we can find a better T – one whose entailment by 'x is a vixen' depends on both the foxy and the female aspects. Apart from that possibility, we ought now in any case to modify the proposed clause (iv) to read:

iv S is entailed by verifiable statements, and contains only vocabulary which features either in statements which may be established as verifiable by appeal to (i)–(iii), or in correct definitions of vocabulary which so features.

And now 'x is a vixen' can in any case qualify as verifiable via original clause (ii) and new clause (iv), if 'x is female' and 'x is a fox' can qualify independently. Any definiens of a verifiable statement can qualify via new clause (iv).

In general, of course, all this manoeuvring is pointless unless it leaves space for statements to qualify as verifiable some of whose constituent non-logical vocabulary neither features in any statement in the original base class – the 'atomic observation statements' – nor may be defined in terms of vocabulary which does so feature. It is essential to be able to capture statements as verifiable – *par excellence* scientific-theoretical statements – whose content cannot be analysed in terms which are apt for the reporting of observations. Naturally, one may be pessimistic whether that can be done. But the proposal in the *Fact, Science and Morality* discussion did leave space for the possibility, and so, as far as I can see, does the present proposal.

The original proposal left space like this. Suppose $T_1 \ldots T_n$ have already qualified as verifiable, and that their union with S entails a verifiable T. S therefore qualifies, by the original account, as verifiable, provided that this entailment is S-compact. How might this be so, if S contains non-logical vocabulary which neither features in nor can be defined in terms of vocabulary which features in $T_1 \ldots T_n$, T? Like this.

Suppose there are certain *analytically true* principles, $A_1...A_n$, expressive of certain analytical dependencies[25] between the two vocabularies, but falling short of providing the resources for definition of the relevant vocabulary in S. And suppose these principles mediate the derivation of T from $\{S, T_1...T_n\}$. Since they are analytically true, it is in order to suppress them and affirm that $\{S, T_1...T_n\}$ entails T. But that entailment can now be S-compact precisely because, when certain substitutions are made for the non-logical vocabulary in S, the results of making the same substitutions in $A_1...A_n$ may be principles which no longer hold analytically true and so are no longer suppressible premises in the entailment.

In order to construct plausible examples, we should need, of course, to come up with instances of analytic bridge principles connecting observational with theoretical vocabulary. But suppose, just for the sake of an example, that it is regarded as partly constitutive of the concept of an acid that litmus paper reddens when soaked in acidic substances; and as partly constitutive of the concept of chemical dissolution that there be a temperature increase in the dissolving medium. And suppose we regard the reddening of litmus paper and increase of temperature as verifiable matters. Then reflect that, letting

S = all acids dissolve iron,
A_1 = if litmus paper reddens when soaked in x, then x is acid,
A_2 = if x chemically dissolves y, then x increases in temperature,

and formalizing along obvious lines, we could formally derive – I shall not trouble to do so – that

T = if litmus paper reddens in this solution, then placing iron filings in it will result in its warming.

And now if A_1 and A_2 are regarded as analytic, in view of their concept-determining role, and so as suppressible in the derivation, we wind up with what is plausibly a compact entailment of T by S.

Two points are noteworthy. First, there seems no reason why a statement which qualified as verifiable via the indicated route would have to hit trouble once patched clause (iii) replaced original clause (iii); no reason to think, that is, that any such statement would have to have a compact equivalent, S*, such that the entailment of T by $\{S^*, T_1...T_n\}$ would not be S*-compact. Sure, there may be cause for pessimism

25 See note 21.

whether the route is actually frequently travelled; but the modification elicited by Lewis's difficulty should not occasion *additional* pessimism.

Second, the resources needed if theoretical statements are to qualify in this way – a base-class of observation statements, a firm analytic/synthetic distinction, and analytically true bridge principles linking increasingly higher levels of theoretical vocabulary with lower levels, and ultimately with the vocabulary of the base class – all these were central elements of the equipment which the Positivists believed was at their service. I tentatively conclude that if they *had* indeed had these resources, the formulation of the Verification Principle would not have had to be the additional problem it historically proved to be; and that an account of verifiability is possible which would have been suitable for the purposes both of Ayer's (official) reductionism and his (crypto) verificationist-realist self.

VII

The immediate question, of course, is whether the requirements even of Ayer's less demanding verificationist-realist self could possibly be sustained throughout reputable empirical science. Let me go over the grounds for retaining an interest, even in the 1990s, in the Verification Principle. The project for the verificationist-realist about science is to uphold a notion of truth for theoretical statements which is both non-reductive and epistemically constrained. And the optimistic (but non-verificationist) realist will want to hold that the verificationist-realist's project is feasible for the most part, and realized by the greater portion of contemporary science. Both will hold that corroboration by observation, under the most severe testing, is to be *eo ipso* good ground for believing theoretical statements whose content cannot be fully analysed in (whatever they regard as) observational vocabulary. But unless reputable theoretical vocabulary has an ancestral analytical dependence on observational vocabulary, it is very difficult to see why belief in the empirical adequacy of a theory and belief in its truth should not everywhere float free of each other, in the fashion emphasized by van Fraassen.[26] Why should concord with observation be taken to be a ground for regarding a theory as true *unless* the observational consequences of a theory are somehow *peculiar* to it under the intended interpretation of its theoretical terms? And how can they be so, if every observational consequence of a theory would survive under arbitrary uniform reinterpretation of its theoretical part? Yet the only way, it

26 Van Fraassen, *The Scientific Image*, *passim* but esp. chs 1 and 2.

appears, in which this situation may be avoided is if statements expressive of analytical dependencies so mediate the connections between hypotheses and their consequences that such reinterpretation (uniform substitution) changes what those consequences are – i.e., if the original entailments of those consequences are compact with respect to the theoretical vocabulary of the hypotheses under test. But that is just to say that only hypotheses whose observational content is secured by their *verifiability*, in the light of the Verification Principle as we now have it, can provide the would-be optimistic realist with the materials to resist van Fraassen's challenge.[27]

Someone who rejects analyticity altogether will have lost patience with these manoeuvres a while back, of course. But even someone who believes that the kind of analytical dependence called for can occur is bound to feel disquiet at the *multiplicity* of such connections which the optimistic or verificationist-realist would seem to need if they are to conserve the bulk of empirical science for their realism. *Every* theoretical term in a fully verifiable theory must ancestrally analytically depend on observational vocabulary. Surely this is a hostage to fortune which is unlikely to be redeemed. It just is not plausible to suppose that theoretical terms generally are explained by recourse to 'hypotheses' whose true role is recognized to be the articulation of such analytical dependencies. It is not clear that *any* is. And the prospects of making a convincing case for thinking that enough hypotheses do (unrecognized) play such a role are, familiarly, remote.

Let me summarize the principal points I have wished to suggest in this and the preceding essay.

First, the unquestioned attractions of scientific realism depend on its optimistic interpretation: there have to be grounds for confidence not merely that there is such a thing as the truth of a theory, non-reductively construed, but that it is often something we can have well-founded opinions about. So theoretical truth has often to make a detectable difference, whose detection provides the foundation for such opinion.

Second, this position needs to rely upon two currently unfashionable props: *observation-statements*, whose conditions of reasonable belief are not a function of the background empirical-theoretical beliefs of the believer; and the distinction between *analytic* and *synthetic* statements. Without the first, there seems no prospect of defeating a sceptic about our right to be sure of the data which a successful scientific theory seeks

27 I am not suggesting that the challenge would be easily met, even then. But some such connection of content across explanation is surely essential if there is to be any hope of meeting it.

to explain, save by retreat into the holistic pragmatism which surrenders all claim to a theory's literal descriptive adequacy (or retains it as only a vacuous ideal). Without the second, there seems no prospect of securing the kind of connection between theories and their observational content necessary if there is to be a link between truth and empirical adequacy which is sufficiently intimate for the realist's needs.

Third, I have tried to place the Verification Principle in a setting which should give it an attraction for someone excited by the seemingly great strides made by empirical science in this century, someone attracted to intellectual 'space travel'. Strictly, I ought to claim only that the Principle has a natural part to play in one possible exegesis of the theoretical commitments of this frame of mind. Other ways of explaining and defending the optimist's commitments may be tried, and may succeed. But I must confess to the sneaking conviction that the failure – supposing it does fail – of that conception of the meaning of theoretical terms to which the Verification Principle is committed marks the vanishing of the middle channel between the Scylla of 'Two Dogmas' and the Charybdis of *The Scientific Image*. Optimistic realism, if it is the most intuitive and attractive philosophy of science, is also the least easy to defend.[28]

28 I would like to thank John Foster and Jonathan Cohen for helpful discussion of a prototype of my proposed Verification Principle. The ideas about realism and observation-statements first figured in a lecture I gave to the British Society for the Philosophy of Science at University College, London, in 1982 and in a paper read to the conference on Scientific Realism at Dalhousie University in August 1983. I am grateful to those who took part in these discussions, especially George Pappas and Paul Churchland, for a number of useful comments. I am also grateful to Ken Gemes, Bob Hale, David Lewis, Larry Sklar and Stephen Yablo for more recent helpful discussion and correspondence.

11

About 'The Philosophical Significance of Gödel's Theorem': Some Issues

I
Dummett's Problem

It is a very natural supposition that, for any particular consistent formal system of arithmetic, one of the pair consisting of the Gödel sentence and its negation must be true. This was rejected by Wittgenstein in the notorious appendix on Gödel's Theorem in the *Remarks on the Foundations of Mathematics*.[1] Wittgenstein there implicitly repudiated not merely any Platonist conception of mathematics, as usually conceived, but the much more deeply rooted idea that arithmetic is in the business of *description* of a proper subject matter of any kind. His view, it seems, was that there simply is no defensible conception of truth for the sentences of a formal arithmetic which might coherently – whether or not justifiably – be thought to outrun derivability within it.

Wittgenstein's stance here goes right against the grain. Whatever the situation in other areas of pure mathematics, formal number theory, we intuitively feel, has to answer to a very definite pre-formal conception of the natural numbers, their structure and basic properties. We don't come by our basic arithmetical concepts by doing formal number theory; and the informal understanding which we acquire of those concepts suffices not merely to give the Peano axioms a cogency which would be quite missing if they had anything of the character of stipulations, but also to supply, we feel, a definite interpretation, at least in principle, for any arithmetical sentence. Thus it is hard not to accept that there is a subject matter to which the Peano axioms answer, and which, since no material vagueness intrudes, must confer determinate truth-values on a Gödel sentence and its negation.

1 *Remarks on the Foundations of Mathematics*, 3rd edn (Oxford, 1978), part I, Appendix III, pp. 116–23.

This view of the matter, however, sets up a prima facie difficulty – the difficulty to which Michael Dummett's well-known discussion responds.[2] As soon as it is granted that any intuitively sound system of arithmetic merely *partially* describes the subject matter to which it answers, an explanation is owing of *how* the subject matter in question can possess a determinacy transcending complete description. No doubt there are species of Platonism for which this demand would pose no special embarrassment. On such *rampant* Platonist views (John McDowell's term), description-transcendent determinacy should be no more puzzling, in the case of the subject matter of arithmetic, than it is in the case of the subject matter of physics, say, or astronomy – or in any case where a domain of reality is constituted in full independence of the conceptualizations and investigations performed by human beings. But any attractive form of Platonism will have to take a more moderate, 'conceptualist' line: the subject matter of arithmetic, and mathematics generally, whatever autonomy it may go on to acquire, will be conceived as originally constituted in the *arithmetical understanding* – so that the special concern of the arithmetician is with the implications of our arithmetical concepts as properly understood.

It is this saner Platonism which seems open to the advertised difficulty. The problem, simply, is that to allow that the subject matter of arithmetic is determinate beyond any systematic description is apparently, for the moderate Platonist, to admit that our understanding of arithmetical concepts transcends any systematic description of correct arithmetical practice: that no matter what we offer as a characterization of what is non-contingently true of the natural numbers, we will leave the status of certain such truths indeterminate. And that, it seems, is exactly for meaning to transcend use, just as Dummett says. The subject matter of arithmetic, on this view, is constituted by a definite conception which we hold 'in mind'; but any attempt at a systematic characterization of that conception will fail to determine the truth-values of statements on which the conception itself is not neutral.

Outlined in this way, the problem depends on an intuitive realism about arithmetic, with a bivalent conception of arithmetical truth as the principal ingredient. And there are alternatives to this realism besides the radical anti-descriptivism of Wittgenstein's Appendix. Surely it is possible to think of arithmetic as having a proper subject matter, which differing formal systems might portray with varying degrees of completeness, without being railroaded into an acceptance of the principle of Bivalence for arithmetical statements generally? Indeed, just that is

2 Michael Dummett, 'The Philosophical Significance of Gödel's Theorem', in his *Truth and Other Enigmas*, pp. 186–201.

the characteristic attitude of Mathematical Intuitionism. Might not the problem be avoided altogether on such a view? Once we discard the notion that every well-formed arithmetical sentence must be determinately true or false, there is no longer any reason to suppose that any particular arithmetical system must, by omitting a Gödel sentence and its negation, omit a determinate arithmetical truth.

As Dummett sets up the problem, however, discarding Bivalence would be of no avail. This is because:

> By Gödel's theorem there exists, for any intuitively correct formal system for elementary arithmetic, a statement U expressible in the system but not provable in it, which not only is true but can be recognised by us to be true.[3]

That is Dummett's opening statement of Gödel's 'result'. Like most such statements in the literature, it adds something on which Gödel's mathematical work is strictly neutral: not an endorsement of a bivalent conception of arithmetical truth, but the contention that *we are able to recognize the truth* of the universally quantified Gödel sentence. The idea is, indeed, quite orthodox that to follow Gödel's reasoning is, in the light of an ordinary understanding of arithmetical notions, to see that U – the universally quantified undecidable sentence – although unprovable in the system in question if the latter is consistent, is nevertheless an arithmetical truth. This thought involves no commitment to the principle of Bivalence, and could at the same time, I suppose, be repudiated by one who accepted Bivalence for arithmetic. But it apparently sets up just the same problem. If it is right, then, as before, it seems that no matter what systematic characterization we give of the range of statements which we understand to be true of the natural numbers, that characterization will be neutral on cases on which the understanding itself is not – cases which, following Gödel, we may informally recognize to be true.

Dummett offers a solution to the problem which exploits an extremely important idea he has called *indefinite extensibility*. A concept is indefinitely extensible if, roughly, any attempt at a comprehensive characterization of its extension immediately subserves the specification of new instances of the concept which that characterization demonstrably omits. A case can be made for regarding each of *class*, *ordinal number* and *real number* as indefinitely extensible in this way. And the real significance of Gödel's result, Dummett contends, is that it shows that the concepts, *statement true of all the natural numbers*, and

3 'The Philosophical Significance', p. 186.

ground for affirming that all natural numbers have a certain property are in like case. A solution to the problem is then to be accomplished, if I have not misunderstood, by the reflection that indefinite extensibility is a kind of *vagueness*, so that accepting the statement U as a further arithmetical truth need not be a fully determinate obligation of the arithmetical understanding – an understanding which, since the Gödelian construction may be iterated indefinitely, we would otherwise have to regard as transcending any systematic description of the obligations it imposed.

I have some misgivings, not about the idea of indefinite extensibility in general, but about its application in this context and its construal as a kind of vagueness. I will briefly return to Dummett's solution to his problem at the end of the paper.

II
Lucas and Penrose Against Mechanism

The problem concerning meaning and use is one of two major general philosophical concerns on which Gödel's theorem has been thought to bear. But the other has attracted a much greater volume of commentary. Writers such as J. R. Lucas[4] and, more recently, Roger Penrose[5] have argued that Gödel's theorem provides as clear a demonstration as philosophy could reasonably hope for that our arithmetical capacities in particular, and hence the powers of the human intellect in general, cannot in principle be simulated by a machine. Here is an expression of the idea by Penrose:

> ...*whatever*...algorithm a mathematician might use to establish mathematical truth...there will always be mathematical propositions, such as the explicit Gödel proposition [for the formal system associated with that algorithm], that his algorithm cannot provide an answer for. If the workings of the mathematician's mind are entirely algorithmic, then the algorithm...that he actually uses to form his judgements is not capable of dealing with the [Gödelian] proposition...constructed from his personal algorithm. Nevertheless *we* can (in principle) see that [that proposition] is *true*. That would seem to provide *him* with a contradiction, since *he* ought to be able to see that also. Perhaps this indicates that the mathematician was *not* using an algorithm at all![6]

4 Lucas, 'Minds, Machines and Gödel'.

5 Penrose, *The Emperor's New Mind*. See esp. the section entitled 'The Non-algorithmic Nature of Mathematical Insight' in ch. 10, pp. 538–41. See also the sections, 'Gödel's Theorem' and 'Mathematical Insight' in ch. 4, pp. 138–46.

6 *The Emperor's New Mind*, pp. 538–9.

The central thought here is very simple: Gödel's theorem teaches us that the class of arithmetical truths ratifiable by the human mind does not coincide with those deliverable by any particular programme for proof construction – any particular algorithm. Yet anything worth regarding as a *machine* has to be slave to such an algorithm. It follows that our arithmetical powers are not exhaustively mechanical.

A very distinguished tradition of disbelief has grown up in response to this line of argument. One common objection[7] is that our ability to construct a Gödel sentence for a particular formal system, and hence to recognize the truth of that sentence, is of course hostage to our capacity intelligently to receive a specification of the formal system – algorithm – in question. The Lucas/Penrose argument, the objection goes, simply overlooks the possibility that human arithmetical capacity is indeed encoded in a particular formal system of which, however, we are unable to comprehend any formal specification suitable for an application of the Gödelian construction. It need not be questioned that we can produce a Gödel sentence for any arithmetical system which we can take in. But even granting that we can recognize such a sentence to be true, what follows is merely a disjunction: *either* no such system encodes all human arithmetical capacity – the Lucas/Penrose thought – *or* any system which does has no axiomatic specification which human beings can comprehend.

Gödel himself seems to have proposed essentially this conclusion. He writes

> For if the human mind were equivalent to a finite machine,...there would exist *absolutely* unsolvable Diophantine problems of the type described above, where the epithet 'absolutely' means that they would be undecidable, not just within some particular axiomatic system, but by *any* mathematical proof the human mind can conceive. So the following disjunctive conclusion is inevitable: ...*the human mind (even within the realm of pure mathematics) infinitely surpasses the powers of any finite machine, or else there exist absolutely unsolvable Diophantine problems of the type specified.* [Godel's own emphasis][8]

But is this conservative – disjunctive – conclusion the most that is justified? It is never very clear what is meant by talk of the powers of

7 See for instance Paul Benacerraf's 'God, the Devil and Gödel'.

8 From MS p. 13 of Gödel's 1951 Josiah Willard Gibbs Lecture, delivered to the American Mathematical Society. See Kurt Gödel, *Collected Works*, vol. 3, forthcoming 1993. (The volume will indicate the page numbers of Gödel's original typescripts in the margins.) For discussion of Gödel's view, see George Boolos's 'Introductory Note to *#1951*' in the same volume.

the 'human mind'. But in this context the unclarity is urgent. If we are talking about actual human minds, constrained as they are by the volume and powers of actual human brains, then it can hardly be doubted that the range of arithmetical sentences whose truth we are capable, by whatever means, of ratifying, is finite. So there are, of course, algorithms which capture all those sentences and more. Since Lucas and Penrose are presumably in no doubt about that, we should conclude that the anti-mechanist thesis concerns the character of mathematical thought as reflected in what *in principle* we have the power to accomplish in mathematics. The comparison has to be not between *actual* human arithmetical capacities, even those of the most gifted and prodigious mathematicians, and *actual* theorem-proving machines, even the most powerful and sophisticated that technology will ever accomplish, but between what we can do in principle and what in principle can be accomplished by a machine, where a 'machine' is constrained only to the extent that its theorem-proving capacities correspond to the output of an effectively axiomatized system.

But what ought 'in principle' to mean for the purposes of such a comparison? I propose we should count any feat as within our compass in principle just in case some *finite* extension of powers we actually have would enable us to accomplish it *in practice*. Correspondingly for the powers in principle of a theorem-proving machine. So each first-order deductive consequence of the axioms which it encodes can in principle be proved by such a machine. Likewise, any arithmetical statement is ratifiable in principle by the human mind just in case, under some finite extension of capacities we actually possess, we could ratify it in practice.

Well plainly, if these are the terms of the intended comparison, then the mooted reservation about the Lucas/Penrose line lapses. There is no need for the second disjunct in the Gödelian statement. For any effectively axiomatized system of arithmetic is, in the relevant sense, *in principle surveyable* by human beings, who may consequently, in principle, carry out the Gödelian construction upon it. Even if in practice, limited as we actually are, our actual arithmetical capacities can be captured by a formal system whose specification we can neither comprehend nor, therefore, Gödelize, it remains that we have in principle the resources – a finite extension of our capacities would enable us – to do so. The qualification marked by the second disjunct in Gödel's statement is called for only if the words 'can conceive' concern human abilities in practice.

This is likely, I imagine, to provoke the following complaint. Let it be, for the sake of argument, that, in the sense of 'in principle' stipulated, what the human mind can do in principle and what is in principle possible for a theorem-proving machine do indeed diverge. Still, the intention of the opponents of mechanism is surely to make good a claim which concerns not *semi-divine* creatures – creatures whose powers in practice coincide with ours in principle – but actual living human beings. We were supposed to learn something about how to regard *ourselves*, limited as we are, and not about supermen who differ from us by having no finite limits of memory, rate of working, concentration, intellectual fluency, and so on.

However, I believe it is just a mistake to think that if the claimed disanalogy in powers 'in principle' were sustained, we would still learn nothing about our actual limited selves. On the contrary, we would learn that, limited though we are, we work with a concept of arithmetical demonstration whose extension allows no effective enumeration. By contrast, the extension of the concept of demonstration encoded in any formal system that might serve as the program for a theorem-proving machine *is* effectively enumerable. A satisfactory description of our actual arithmetical powers would thus have to acknowledge that they are informed by a concept of a sort by which, if our arithmetical thought were purely the implementation, as it were, of an in principle specifiable formal system, they would not be informed. Hence, if a disanalogy has been pointed to at all, then it indeed is between human beings as we actually are and as we would be if our mathematical thought were entirely algorithmic. The concept of demonstration which actually informs our construction and ratification of proofs would have been shown to have a feature which it would lack if our powers in those respects were purely mechanical.

If this is right, then there is a connection, seldom remarked on, between the two most general philosophical debates on which Gödel's theorem has been thought to bear. Dummett's problem, the prima facie difficulty raised by the theorem for the idea that meaning is determined by use, only arises if we take it that the theorem impels us to recognize that the extension of the concept, 'true of all natural numbers', outruns any attempt formally to characterize the conditions under which it is properly applied. And unless we accept that arithmetical statements are unrestrictedly bivalent, we are so impelled only if, with Dummett, we think that an informal demonstration of U attends the Gödelian construction. But if that is true – if Godel's theorem teaches us that arithmetical truth outruns any systematic characterization of its extension precisely by providing the basis for an informal demonstration of the universally closed undecidable sentence – then we simultaneously learn that our concept of an intuitively correct arithmetical demonstration cannot be thought of as the concept of whatever is sanctioned by some in principle specifiable set of algorithmic procedures. And that, Lucas and Penrose should contend, is just what mechanism, if it is to aspire to any clarity, must deny. So unless we accept Bivalence, Dummett's problem arises only on a supposition whose correctness would seem to settle the other debate in favour of Lucas/Penrose.

But of course the most widely accepted line of criticism of the Lucas/Penrose thesis has been precisely directed at the supposition that we can 'see' the Gödel sentence to be true – that Gödel's construction somehow provides or underpins an informal demonstration of it. Lucas and Penrose, the charge is, conveniently forget that any ground which emerges from Gödel's reasoning for accepting the truth of the universally quantified undecidable sentence is *entirely dependent* on the hypothesis of the consistency of the object system. And for that hypothesis Gödel's reasoning produces, of course, no grounds whatever. It may be a hypothesis of whose truth we are confident, and perhaps have good grounds for being so. Whatever grounds those may be then transfer into grounds for believing the truth of the Gödel sentence. But that's a far cry from saying that something worth regarding as a mathematical *demonstration* of U is in the offing. Thus Hilary Putnam writes:

> Let T be the Turing machine which 'represents' me in the sense that T can prove just the mathematical statements I can prove. Then the argument...is that by using Gödel's technique I can discover a proposition that T cannot prove, and moreover *I* can prove this proposition. This refutes the assumption that T 'represents' me, hence I am not a Turing machine. The fallacy is a misapplication of Gödel's theorem, pure and simple. Given an arbitrary machine T, all I can do is find a proposition U such that I can prove:
>
> (3) If T is consistent, U is true,
>
> where U is undecidable by T if T is in fact consistent. However, T can perfectly well prove (3) too! And the statement U, which T *cannot* prove (assuming consistency), *I* cannot prove either (unless I can prove that T is consistent, which is unlikely if T is very complicated).[9]

On this view, Gödel's construction ought to be regarded as providing no reason to affirm that the concepts 'demonstration that all natural numbers have a certain property' or 'statement true of all the natural numbers' are indefinitely extensible. Critics of Lucas and Penrose who advance this line ought therefore to hold that Dummett's problem is likewise misconceived. But are they right?

9 Putnam, 'Minds and Machines', in *Philosophical Papers 2: Mind, Language and Reality*, pp. 362–85, quotation from p. 366.

III
Dummett's Modus Ponens

Why does Dummett accept that U 'can be recognized by us to be true'? He writes:

> The argument for the truth of [the Gödel sentence] proceeds under the hypothesis that the formal system in question is consistent.[10]

and then again:

> The argument to establish the truth of [the Gödel sentence] involves establishing the consistency of the formal system. The interest of Gödel's theorem lies in its applicability to *any* intuitively correct system for number theory. ...We have, therefore, to consider the consistency proof with which Gödel's reasoning must be supplemented if the truth of [the Gödel sentence] is to be established as one we know we can give for *any* formal system [emphasis added], provided only that it is assumed about that system that it is intuitively correct.[11]

These remarks make it clear that the general form of demonstration of the Gödel sentence envisaged by Dummett is in effect a Modus Ponens on Putnam's conditional (3) – a conditional which, as Putnam remarked, can be established *within* whatever formal system Gödel's construction is applied to. Dummett's idea seems merely to be that, provided only that an arithmetic-containing system is intuitively correct, we can always accomplish a proof that it is consistent and then detach the consequent of the appropriate instance of (3).

Taken in full generality, that claim may seem merely preposterous – surely we may have no idea how to establish the consistency of a complex but intuitively sound system of set-theory, for instance. But as Dummett enlarges on his claim, it is not controversial at all. Provided we are given that the axioms of the system are true, and that its rules of inference are truth-preserving, a routine induction on the length of proofs in the system will, as Dummett remarks, yield that all its theorems are true and hence, since no true statement has a true (syntactic) negation, that of no statement can it be the case that both it and its negation are theorems. Dummett acknowledges, of course, that a proof of this kind is hardly 'genuinely informative' (his phrase). A 'genuinely informative' consistency proof must (presumably) do more than elicit, in this trivial way, an implication of the presupposition that

10 'The Philosophical Significance', p. 192.
11 'The Philosophical Significance', p. 194.

the axioms of the system are true and its rules of inference sound. It is additionally required, I take it, to afford some positive reason for regarding the intuitive credibility of the axioms and rules as an indication that they *are* indeed respectively true and sound. Thus the sort of consistency proof we would ideally want for an intuitively satisfactory system of arithmetic would be one which, rather than merely drawing out the implications of the presupposition that the intuitive cogency of the axioms is an indication of their truth, provided persuasive reason for reposing confidence in arithmetical intuition in the first place.

The kind of consistency proof to which Dummett adverts is powerless to do that.[12] But it is only a proof of that uninformative sort that there is reason to think can be obtained in every case where we have an intuitively correct system of arithmetic.[13] So how should we appraise the claim that Dummett's Modus Ponens *demonstrates* U? Obviously, it depends on what, in this context, is required of a demonstration. Here is

12 Such a 'demonstration' of consistency would have been available for Naive Set Theory before it was known that the Naive Abstraction axiom was inconsistent.

13 It is a nice question whether Gödel's second incompleteness theorem, that no consistent system of arithmetic can contain the proof-theoretic resources for a demonstration of its own consistency, provides the basis of a case that nothing better than an uninformative consistency proof can be obtained for *any* system of arithmetic to which the first theorem applies. The question is, in particular, whether the non-arithmetical resources deployed in formal proofs of the consistency of arithmetical systems, for example the use made of transfinite induction up to ε_0 in the famous Gentzen proof, are essentially no more transparent – no more epistemically secure – than the proof-theory, and especially the full-fledged Induction schema, of first-order number-theory itself. Gentzen himself thought otherwise: '...I am inclined to believe that in terms of the fundamental distinction between disputable and indisputable methods of proof, the *proof of the finiteness* of the reduction procedure' – the part of his proof that uses transfinite induction – 'can still be considered indisputable, so that the consistency proof represents a *real vindication* of the disputable parts of elementary number theory' (from ch. 4, 'The Consistency of Elementary Number Theory', of *The Collected Papers of Gerhard Gentzen*, p. 197).

The issue is certainly subtle and deserves detailed discussion. But it is hard not to feel sceptical about Gentzen's view. To accept the Gentzen proof is to be persuaded of a mapping between the proofs constructible in elementary number theory and the series of ordinals up to ε_0. And to understand the structure of the ordinals up to ε_0 is to grasp a concept which embeds and *builds on* an ordinary understanding of the series of natural numbers. So to trust the Gentzen proof is implicitly to forgo any doubt about the coherence of the concept of natural number. Any residual doubt about the consistency of first-order number theory would have, therefore, to concern whether the (fully coherent) concept of number is faithfully reflected by the standard first-order axioms – specifically, by all admissible instances of the induction schema. Such a doubt would have to concern whether, even when we are restricted to first-order arithmetical vocabulary, 'tricksy' predicates might not somehow be formulated whose use in inductions could lead to contradiction. Could someone reasonably worry about that who was confident in the consistency of Gentzen's methods? How might such a doubt be further elaborated?

one natural notion: an intellectual routine counts as a demonstration of P just in case an agnostic about P could nevertheless perfectly reasonably place confidence in the methods and principles deployed in the routine, and could arrive, on the basis of following it through, at considerations which would rationally oblige him a priori to assent to P. Say that a proof is *suasive* if it meets those conditions. Now clearly, since it takes the truth of the axioms and the soundness of the underlying logic as a premise, the sort of consistency proof outlined can hardly be suasive (except perhaps for a rather dim thinker to whom it has not occurred that you cannot get contradictions in a system with true axioms and truth-preserving rules). So it furnishes no demonstration of U; in particular, it has nothing to offer someone who already accepts, as it were on faith, the consistency of the system in question but now wants a mathematical argument that he is right to do so – something which he could use, for instance, to respond to a critic. If, on the other hand, we drop the requirement of suasiveness, then the sort of non-suasive demonstration of the consistency of S outlined doesn't contribute to something worth describing as, in Dummett's words, an 'argument to establish the truth of U'. In particular, it has nothing to offer a thinker who is agnostic about U and accepts the consistency of S only as a working assumption. Accordingly no ground is provided by such a demonstration for the presupposition of Dummett's problem, that the class of statements which we can recognize to be true of the natural numbers outruns any systematic characterization.

The dilemma, then, is this: if a demonstration has to be suasive, the construction of the Dummettian Modus Ponens will not in general constitute a demonstration and nothing obstructs Putnam's claim that there is, as a general rule, no demonstrating the Gödel sentence; but if demonstration doesn't have to be suasive, then while a Dummettian Modus Ponens can in general constitute a demonstration, it provides no basis for Dummett's problem or, indeed, for the contention of Lucas and Penrose.

IV
Inductive Knowledge of Consistency?

There is, however, a disanalogy. The Lucas/Penrose line requires, of course, that there be a demonstration – a cogent *a priori* argument – for the truth of the Gödel sentence. Their case entirely depends on the putative contrast between the concept of proof operated by the human mathematician and the concept of proof that governs the operations of a Turing machine. By contrast, would it not suffice to set up Dummett's problem if there were, not a priori, but *empirical-inductive* grounds for the assertion of the Gödel sentence? In order for the concept, 'Statement which may justifiably be claimed to be true of all the natural numbers', to be disclosed as indefinitely extensible by Gödel's result, it ought to suffice that we can invariably in principle produce a Gödel sentence for a given formal arithmetic, and then produce grounds *of some sort* for accepting it as true. If we have empirical-inductive reason to believe in the consistency of a particular arithmetic, this will transfer to the Gödel sentence which, by the conditional (3), may then be inferred. And if we had reason to believe not merely in the consistency but in the *truth* of the original system, then we will thereby have reason to believe in the truth, and hence the consistency, of that system augmented by its Gödel sentence. So the process will iterate.

But *do* we have empirical-inductive reason to believe in the consistency of arithmetic, or in that of any other branch of mathematics where an 'informative' consistency proof is not to be had? Hartry Field writes:

> ...a large part of the *reason* most of us believe that modern set theory is consistent is the thought that if it weren't consistent someone would probably have discovered an inconsistency by now.[14]

Likewise:

> ...much of our knowledge of possibility is to some extent inductive. For instance, our knowledge that [von Neumann–Bernays–Gödel set theory is consistent] seems to be based in part on the fact that we have been unable to find any inconsistency in [that system].[15]

Obviously enough, however, there cannot be a *strictly* inductive grounding for beliefs in consistency in such cases. Such grounding would beg an established correlation between the availability of the relevant kind of ground – viz. that no one has yet found any inconsistency – and the relevant system's actually *being* consistent. There would therefore have to be independent grounds for the latter – which is just what we do not have. Field's thought has to be, rather, that there is here an appropriate inference to the best explanation (or something of that sort). Roughly: things have reached a pass where the *most likely* explanation of the failure of any inconsistency to turn up is that there is none to turn up. But *why* is that the favoured explanation – what gives

14 Field, *Realism, Mathematics and Modality*, p. 232.
15 Field, *Realism, Mathematics and Modality*, p. 88.

us our grip on the probabilities? Why is it supposed to be relatively unlikely that, in at least some such cases, inconsistencies do exist to be unearthed, but by tricks and turns more subtle than any that have occurred to us? In particular, if we say that it is *improbable* that that is the situation of ordinary arithmetic, then again: on what basis are the probabilities established?

If someone claims that, for reasons such as these, Field's idea is simply a mistake, I do not think it is at all clear how to refute them. And unless the claim can be refuted, it may begin to seem not merely that the Modus Ponens route to the truth of the Gödel sentence founders for want of any real ground, a priori or empirical-inductive, for its minor premise, but more: that our faith in the consistency of the arithmetical part of our mathematical thinking, and hence in all that builds upon it, is without any justification whatever.[16]

However, it is not obvious that any demonstration of the Gödel sentence lurking in the vicinity *has* to be a Dummettian Modus Ponens. I shall outline two further trains of thought which attempt to proceed differently.

16 The status of this faith is an extremely interesting epistemological issue, well worth detailed investigation. Unfortunately, that must lie beyond the scope of this discussion. But one immediate consideration about the sceptical turn just bruited is that it wholly ignores the epistemological territory which was the centre of attention in Wittgenstein's notes *On Certainty*. Very crudely: beliefs for which one has no *earned* justification need not be beliefs for which one has no justification *tout court*. All justification, Wittgenstein argues, takes place within some system of beliefs: a system in which an unexamined heritage of belief will be a major component, but in which there will also be certain very general empirical-seeming beliefs whose logical role places them *beneath* evidential support (cf. my 'Facts and Certainty'), as well as fundamental principles of inference – principles of inference which we find intuitively completely compelling but of which no suasive demonstration can be constructed. A leading theme in *On Certainty* is that in cases of each of these kinds the justifiability of a belief need not depend on any cognitive *accomplishment* specific to the proposition concerned.

It is an open question whether or in what directions a compelling development of this idea may be made explicit. But it may be thought to strike an intuitive chord as far as the consistency of elementary arithmetic is concerned. Many would feel, that is to say, that the soundness of our arithmetical thought is something which we are entitled to assume on no other basis than its intuitive cogency, and that a demonstration which presupposes it as a premise is no more precarious on that account than any intuitively cogent demonstration. At the very least, it should be granted that the unavailability of both suasive a priori demonstration and empirical confirmation of the consistency of suitable systems of arithmetic does at least not *immediately* write off the Dummettian Modus Ponens as a suasive demonstration of U. The strategy remains of trying to make out that the belief in the consistency of intuitively sound systems of arithmetic is one in which we are *groundlessly* justified. But I will not pursue the issue further here.

V
A Simple Argument

The first is, at first blush, quite straightforward. Let S be an intuitively acceptable system of arithmetic – say, standard first-order Peano arithmetic – and U the universally closed Gödel sentence for S. Then we have a demonstration of

3 If S is consistent, then U,

and hence of

3′ If S is sound, then U,

where the soundness of S requires the truth of its axioms and the validity of its principles of inference. Now consider any formal derivation, D, of a sentence, P, carried out in S. S is as an intuitively acceptable system of arithmetic, and so we would ordinarily regard D as entitling us to affirm P unconditionally. But there are, of course, implicit conditions. Someone who regards the derivability of a particular sentence within a particular formal system as justifying the assertion of that sentence under some customary interpretation presupposes that the system in question is *faithful* to that interpretation: that the inference rules involved are valid, and that the axioms express truths when so interpreted. Thus, the contention of the Simple Argument is, what is immediately justified by D is only the *conditional* claim that provided S is sound (under the intended interpretation), then P is true.

The claim, then, is that *any* proof carried out within S strictly entitles one to no more than the conclusion:

If S is sound, then P,

and that in regarding such a proof as a demonstration of P *tout court*, we merely – justifiably enough – suppress the standard assumption of soundness. If that is right, then the thought may be encouraged that the conditional (3′), which it is agreed on all hands is established by Gödel's reasoning, differs in no interesting way from the form of what, strictly, is established by *any* derivation within an intuitively acceptable formal arithmetic. Mere consistency of policy thus demands, so says the argument, that we recognize Gödel's reasoning as a proof of U. True, all that is explicitly proved is the conditional (3), and hence (3′). But the warrant to affirm a sentence as demonstrated in arithmetic is *always* conditional on an assumption of soundness. That warrant can hardly be weakened if such an assumption, rather than playing its customary implicit role, actually figures explicitly, as in (3′).

This train of thought needs one immediate qualification. The claim of any proof within a formal arithmetic to rank as a demonstration of its conclusion need not depend upon the supposition of the soundness of the system as a whole. It will suffice if the *particular* axioms and rules of inference deployed in the proof are sound, and these need not of course comprise all the axioms and rules which the system involves. In this way, then, the standing of a proof within S as a demonstration may turn on less than the supposition that S is sound overall. So the strongest conclusion in prospect, if this line of thought is sustained, will be that the status of U in point of credibility, after we have the demonstration of (3) and hence (3′), is comparable to that of any sentence P, of which we have a syntactically correct proof within S, which appeals to *all* the axioms and deductive resources of S.[17] Since we might have more confidence in some aspects of S than others, the credibility given to U by the demonstration of (3) may not be as great as that afforded by some formal proofs within S. But this seems no very damaging a limitation.

The idea of the Simple Argument, then, is that, by contrast with the Dummettian Modus Ponens, a demonstration of U is effectively provided just by the formal proof of (3). There is no need to make a special case for the antecedent, viz. the consistency of S, since when S is an intuitively acceptable system of arithmetic – the only case which interests us – the assumption of the soundness of S is anyway implicit in the whole practice of receiving its formal proofs as demonstrations. Either, then, we should accept the proof of (3), hence (3′), as a demonstration of U, or we should cease to regard formal proofs constructible within S – or at least those which make maximal use of its resources – as demonstrations in the first place.

This line can seem quite arresting. But can it really work? Grant that the soundness of the principles employed is presupposed when we treat a formal proof as a demonstration, and remains as an implicit proviso when we proceed to affirm its conclusion. The question is whether it follows that something of the form

4 If (the relevant part of) S is sound, then P

is the strongest claim we are ever 'strictly' entitled to. Why, for instance, stop there? Will not the verification of such a conditional itself be the result of a substantial cognitive process? And does not our confidence in

17 Cf. Dummett, 'The Philosophical Significance', pp. 192–3.

its truth implicitly assume, therefore, the soundness of any principles appealed to in that process and the proper functioning of all relevant faculties? So are we not 'strictly' entitled merely to something of the form

> If [those principles are sound, and all relevant faculties functioned properly, etc.], then if (the relevant part of) S is sound, then P?

If so, where does this attenuation of strict entitlement stop? How are we ever 'strictly' entitled to anything? If not, what justifies the initial claim that (4) exhausts our strict entitlement? The moral suggests itself: granted that we implicitly presuppose soundness whenever we treat a formal proof as establishing a conclusion, P, it is nevertheless simply *incoherent to equate the role played by that presupposition with that of the tacitly discharged antecedent of a conditional whose consequent is P.*

That is one objection. But there is a strong suspicion that another, independent confusion is at work in the Simple Argument. If S is sound, then a formal proof in S of P really does demonstrate that P is true, and by running through the proof we really do *recognize* its truth. (Compare: if I am not now dreaming, then my visual experiences really do constitute a perception of my hand in front of my face and, by having those experiences, I really do recognize that my hand is there.) Presented with such a proof, therefore, we should be at least entitled to

> 4′ If (the relevant part of) S is sound, then P is demonstrated,

which of course entails but is not entailed by (4). Given (4′), the soundness of the relevant part of S is all we need to ensure that our running through a certain intellectual routine constitutes our verifying the truth of P. But what routine constitutes such a verification if all we are given is (4)? The only candidate is the proof of (4) itself, along with the thought that the truth of its antecedent is a presupposition of a kind we make in treating any proof in S as a demonstration. But *that* thought only makes the case so long as it is supposed to follow that conditionals like (4) are all we ever strictly get. And even if it is granted that all we ever 'strictly' get are conditionals with such antecedents, it remains that they are, in the arguably crucial respect illustrated by (4′), always stronger than those epitomized by (4). That a routine's claim to demonstrate P always rests on certain presuppositions is one thing; it does not follow that we cannot ask more of a demonstration of P than to be supplied with a proof that, if those presuppositions are true, then so is P.

It does not follow, but perhaps it might independently be argued. I do not claim that either of these lines of objection is decisive, only that the Simple Argument is not so simple as it seems. But a proponent of the view that the proof of (3) is, in effect, a demonstration of U, clearly has some work to do.

VI
An Intuitionistic Demonstration?

Dummett's Modus Ponens and something like the Simple Argument have each, I suspect, been at work, though with various degrees of explicitness, in the thought of many who have been inclined to regard U as effectively demonstrated. But there is also a, so far as I am aware, unremarked case for saying that a specifically *intuitionistic* demonstration of U arises directly out of Gödel's own reasoning. This demonstration does not proceed, like Dummett's Modus Ponens, by discharging a hypothesis of the consistency of S; but nor, like the Simple Argument, is it content to allow that the conditional (3) is the most that can strictly be demonstrated. The key ingredients are the intuitionists' official account of negation and the reflection that Gödel provides the resources for finding a contradiction in an intuitively satisfactory arithmetic if there were a counterexample to the appropriate U. The claim is that these considerations, suitably deployed, provide intuitionistic grounds for the affirmation of U which involve neither an inference from the presumed consistency of S nor any claim that a proof of (3) is somehow tantamount to a demonstration of U. Too good to be true?

In order to set matters up, we need to review a little of the general detail of Gödel's construction. As is familiar, the groundwork for his result is the assignment to each primitive symbol in the vocabulary of S, and thereby to each well-formed formula and sequence of such formulae, of a number – its *Gödel-number*. This assignment is two-way effective: i.e., given an arbitrary formula, or sequence of formulae of S, we can in principle effectively compute its Gödel-number; and given an arbitrary number, we can effectively determine whether it is the Gödel-number either of a formula or a sequence of formulae of S and if so, to which formula or sequence of formulae it belongs. Crucially, as Gödel shows, such an assignment may be done in such a way that a certain primitive recursive relation, *P*xy, holds between the numbers x and y just in case x is the Gödel-number of a sequence of formulae which constitutes a formal proof in S of a formula whose Gödel-number is y. That is, for all x and y,

> *Lemma*
> *P*xy iff y is the Gödel-number of a wff, B, of S and x is the Gödel-number of a sequence of wffs of S which constitute a proof in S of B.

The proof now proceeds by showing how the operation,

> substitution for each occurrence of the free variable with Gödel-number m in the formula whose Gödel-number is k by the numeral for n,

may be arithmetically represented; that is, how an effective function in three arguments, *Sub*<k,m,n>, may be arithmetically defined in such a way that, when k is the Gödel-number of a formula containing free occurrences of the variable with Gödel-number m, the value of *Sub*<k,m,n> will precisely be the Gödel-number of the formula that results from substituting the numeral for n for each free occurrence of that variable. We then consider the open sentence

> U* (∀x) ~(*P*x, *Sub*<y,m,y>),

where m is the Gödel-number assigned to the variable, 'y'. This will have a Gödel-number – say, g. So '*Sub*<g,m,g>' will denote the Gödel-number of the formula that results from substitution for each occurrence of the free variable with Gödel-number m in the formula whose Gödel-number is g, viz. (U*), by the numeral for g; i.e., '*Sub*<g,m,g>' will denote the Gödel-number of the formula

> U (∀x) ~(*P*x, *Sub*<g,m,g>),

– the undecidable sentence itself.

Now recall the standard informal explanation of intuitionistic negation:

> *Negation*:
> The negation of A is demonstrated by any construction which demonstrates that a contradiction could be demonstrated if we had a demonstration of A.[18]

18 Thus Heyting in his *Intuitionism: An Introduction*: '¬ P can be asserted if and only if we possess a construction which from the supposition that a construction [proving] P were carried out, leads to a contradiction' (p. 102). Compare Dummett in his *Elements of Intuitionism*: 'A proof of ¬ A is usually characterised as a construction of which we can recognise that, applied to any proof of A, it will yeild proof of a contradiction' (p. 13).

The focus of what follows will be on the consequences of the supposition that an intuitively correct arithmetical system S contains a proof of '*P*kg' for some particular choice of k. But to get any mileage, we now need to specify some assumptions about S. S is to be any formal arithmetic with a standard intuitionist logic which is strong enough to be within the scope of Gödel's theorems and such that:

1 S is *intuitionistically endorsed*, i.e. all the methods and assumptions of S are intuitionistically acceptable, so that every proof in S corresponds to an intuitionistic demonstration (I-demonstration). (Note that this is not to assume the consistency of S; what is entailed is merely that if S is inconsistent, then so are the principles and assumptions incorporated in the informal notion of I-demonstrability); and
2 S is *computationally adequate* – all arithmetical computations can be done in S. In particular, for each primitive recursive 'Axy', and arbitrary 'k' and 'n', either 'Akn' or '~Akn' is computationally decidable in S. Again, reflect that S can, of course, be inconsistent while having this feature.

(1) and (2) will be true of any formal arithmetic in which the intuitionist mathematician will be interested.

Now suppose that

i '*P*kg' is computationally verifiable. Then
ii '*P*kg' is provable in S – by (2). But
iii U is provable in S – from (i) by Gödel's *Lemma* above. So
iv '~*P*kg' is provable in S – since S has a standard intuitionist logic. So
v '*P*kg & ~*P*kg' is provable in S – by (ii) and (iv).

It has thus been shown that, had we a computational verification of '*P*kg', we could accomplish a proof in S, and hence, by (1), an I-demonstration, of a contradiction. But any I-demonstration of '*P*kg' will be, in view of the primitive recursiveness of the predicate, a demonstration of its computational verifiability, i.e., of (i). By the foregoing, it will therefore constitute a demonstration of (v), so by (1) a demonstration that a contradiction is demonstrable. So, in the light of *Negation*, (i)–(v) constitute an I-demonstration of '~*P*kg'.

If that is right, it may seem that nothing obstructs advancing to a demonstration of U itself – indeed that, as Dummett in effect remarks,[19]

19 'The Philosophical Significance', p. 192.

the further step is merely trivial. Intuitionistically a demonstration of arithmetical '$\forall x(Ax)$' is any construction which we can recognize may be used, for an arbitrary natural number k, to accomplish a demonstration of 'Ak'.[20] (Call this principle *Generality*). Well, the reasoning from (i) to (v) will evidently go through, if at all, then for an arbitrary choice of 'k'. So it ought to be acknowledged to constitute, by *Generality*, an I-demonstration of U. QED.

It appears, then, that the reasoning from (i) to (v) constitutes, on the assumptions made, the basis of an intuitionistically cogent inference to U. That will constitute no advance on what we have already, of course, if those assumptions somehow smuggle in a presupposition of consistency, either of the system S or, more generally, of the informal collection of principles and axioms which are sanctioned by the intuitionistic notion of demonstration. But crucially, as noted, this seems not to be so.

Why present this as a distinctively intuitionistic demonstration – what happens if we try to transpose the reasoning to provide for a *classical* demonstration of U? The crux is the part played by the intuitionistic account of negation – that which licenses the claim that you have demonstrated '~A' as soon as you have shown how, given any demonstration of 'A', a demonstration could then be given that a contradiction was demonstrable. Naturally, this account will not be acceptable to the classicist in all cases; classically, truth is one thing and demonstrability quite another and there is no general reason why a true sentence should not merely be absolutely unprovable but even such that if we could prove it, we could derive inconsistencies. However, might the intuitionistic account be classically acceptable in the relevant case, where A is '*P*kg' and therefore effectively decidable?

Well, the difference the effective decidability of '*P*kg' makes is that either it or its negation is thereby guaranteed to be classically demonstrable. A proof that either cannot be demonstrated is therefore a proof that the other can be. Now, we have in (i)–(v) a classically acceptable proof that, had we a demonstration of '*P*kg', we could demonstrate the obtainability of a contradiction. *If* that amounted to a proof that no demonstration of '*P*kg' can be given, then a classical demonstration that each '~*P*kg' is demonstrable, hence one of U, would be in prospect. But the problem is clear: no such conclusion follows unless we assume that it is classically impossible to demonstrate the classical obtainability of a contradiction. And that is tantamount to the forbidden assumption that the methods and principles incorporated in the classical notion of

20 Cf. Heyting, *Intuitionism*, p. 106, and Dummett *Elements of Intuitionism*, p. 12.

demonstration are consistent – a stronger assumption, indeed, than the antecedent of the conditional (3).

There appears, then, to be an asymmetry between the intuitionistic and classical cases. Intuitionistic demonstrations with no classical analogue are always interesting – more than interesting when the conclusion is arithmetical. Can it *really* be that we have one here?

There is one and, so far as I can see, only one serious doubt. It arises once we reflect that the intuitionist ought not to be satisfied with *Generality* as formulated above. For that formulation puts no specific controls on demonstrations of 'Ak'. What is required is, rather, something along the lines:

> A demonstration of arithmetical '∀x(Ax)' is any construction which we can recognize may be used, for an arbitrary numeral 'k', to accomplish a *constructive* demonstration of 'Ak'.

But what is a constructive demonstration in the case where 'Ak' is decidable by computation if not (a guarantee of the possibility of) the appropriate computation? Since '~*P*kg' is such a case, the reasoning in the intuitionistic demonstration, while admittedly applicable to an arbitrary numeral 'k', ought to be reckoned as providing a basis for the UI step to U only if it ensures that each '~*P*kg' is *computable*. Does it?

Well, suppose the wider notion of I-demonstrability *is*, alas, inconsistent, although the fragment consisting of arithmetical computation is consistent. Let S be inconsistent, and '*P*kg' actually computationally verifiable. Then the informal demonstration of '~*P*kg' still goes through, but now provides no assurance of computational verifiability. Hence, to treat it as providing such an assurance is implicitly to assume that our supposition does not obtain – i.e. that I-demonstrability is consistent. Either, then, the UI step is unjustified, since we have no assurance that each '~*P*kg' is constructively verifiable; or, in taking it that we have such an assurance, we implicitly assume the consistency of I-demonstrability – and the forbidden assumption is implicitly there after all.

This is a good objection as far as it goes. It rests, however, on the proposal that, where A is effectively decidable by computation, a constructive proof of A must consist in, or anyway establish the possibility of, the appropriate computation. And other proposals are possible. Not all computationally decidable statements are atomic. So one possible proposal would be to grant that, in the atomic case, a constructive demonstration must consist in (proving the possibility of) the appropriate computation; but to allow, for certain non-atomic forms of computationally decidable statement, that certain kinds of proof besides the relevant kind of computation may count as constructive. In the crucial case, in particular, of the negations of atomic statements, it might be held to be sufficient for constructivity that (one prove that) *effective* means exist for arriving at a contradiction should a computational verification be provided of the statement negated. Since the decoding of '*P*kg' and consequent location of a proof in S of U is an effective procedure, this more relaxed account would sanction the constructivity of the mode of demonstration outlined for each '~*P*kg', and would – apparently without the need for the forbidden assumption – thus reinstate the intuitionistic demonstration of U under the aegis of the tightened version of *Generality*.

The status of the intuitionistic demonstration turns, then, on the vexed question of the proper interpretation of the notion of constructive proof – specifically on whether the intuitionist ought or ought not to allow that the more relaxed notion of constructivity outlined is what is relevant to '~*P*kg'. But I cannot pursue the matter further here; clearly both proponent and opponent of the intuitionistic demonstration each have some considerable work to do.[21]

Let us take stock. I have now canvassed three ways whereby it might be contended that Gödel's theorem contributes to an informal demonstration, with respect to an appropriate system of arithmetic S, of the corresponding undecidable sentence U. But none has emerged as clearly

21 By way of a couple of opening shots, here are two considerations whereby the proponent might at least begin to try to motivate the more relaxed notion of constructivity which the intuitionistic demonstration requires.

(i) Don't we need the more relaxed notion to make sense of the very problem case described? For that is a case where there is, by hypothesis, an I-demonstration – *ergo* a *constructive* demonstration – of U which can be given in S; and whatever else that is, it is required – by tightened *Generality* – to involve a construction which enables us to provide a *constructive* demonstration of '~*P*kg', for arbitrary k. Yet the problem case is supposed to be one where no computational verification of '~*P*kg' is possible. So either the problem case makes no intuitionistic sense, or the notion of constructive demonstration cannot be restricted in the way required to make a problem in the first place!

(ii) It will not in general be sensible to rate proofs of truth-functional compounds of recursively decidable atomic statements as constructive only if they are constituted by the execution of the same class of recursive procedures. Such a proposal would restrict constructive proofs of, for instance, conditionals composed out of such statements to computational verifications of the consequent or falsifications of the antecedent – in no other case could such a conditional be regarded as constructively proved. But that would be to take all the conditionality out of the conditional, as it were – to abrogate the right to conditional claims in cases where one had no proof or disproof of either antecedent or consequent. The right account should allow such a conditional to have been constructively proved just in case we have shown how, given any computational verification of the antecedent, we could effectively get a computational verification of the consequent. If such a relaxation of the notion of constructive proof is appropriate for the conditional, why not for negation too?

successful. Unless some quite different approach has been overlooked, it would therefore appear that the widely accepted idea that, as Lucas expresses it, we are able to 'see' that U is true, has so far just not been made out.

Why *is* that idea so widely accepted? It certainly isn't because people accept the intuitionistic demonstration! I suspect the real reason is actually rather unflattering: that we succumb to a simple conflation, confusing the discovery of a *commitment* with the discovery of a *truth*. The proof of the conditional (3) for an intuitively correct S is a deeply impressive result which teaches us, on pain of accepting the inconsistency of our arithmetical thought, that we are *committed* to regarding each instance of U as computationally verifiable. Since we want to believe that our arithmetical thought is consistent – since, indeed, it is doubtful if agnosticism on the matter could be a practical option – there can therefore be no sitting on the fence as far as U is concerned. But it is quite another thing to view this commitment to U as something we incur on the basis of a *demonstration* of its truth. We are, as a rough parallel, similarly committed by everything we ordinarily think and do to the existence of the material world; no agnosticism on the point is practical. It would be very much easier than it is to dispose of material-world scepticism if this commitment could immediately be taken as the reflection of a cognitive achievement.

On this account, no informal demonstration of the undecidable sentence attends Gödel's proof, and nothing takes place worthy of dignification as 'recognition' of its truth. We are merely brought to see that our standing commitment to the consistency of our arithmetical thought embraces a plethora of unsuspected, specifically arithmetical commitments, each associated with a Gödelian undecidable sentence. That is enormously interesting. But it provides no basis for claims about the indefinite extensibility of the concept of arithmetical proof, and no support whatever for Lucas and Penrose.

VII
On a New Argument that Gödel's Theorem Supports Realism

Here is an appropriate point to make contact with a recent discussion of Christopher Peacocke's.[22] Peacocke argues that Gödel's construction does indeed subserve a simple, intuitively convincing train of thought which should be regarded as demonstrating the truth of U. But the

22 In section 4, 'Gödel's Theorem: A Problem for Constructivism', of his essay 'Proof and Truth' in Haldane and Wright, eds, *Reality, Representation and Projection*.

argument, he contends, can go through only in the context of a *realist* semantics and is inaccessible on any constructivist (proof-conditional) conception of the meaning of quantification over the natural numbers. In Peacocke's view, then, Gödel's theorem, so far from underpinning anything like the specifically intuitionistic demonstration which we have just reviewed, presents instead a special problem for constructivism and is testimony to the superiority of semantical realism. However, his argument contrasts with the attempt, targeted by Dummett's discussion, to use Gödel's theorem to confound the thesis that meaning is given by use, a central plank of semantical anti-realism. It is important to Peacocke that the specific form of semantic realism which, he believes, is necessary for his simple informal demonstration is, in the form he favours, quite compatible with an insistence that meaning cannot transcend use but must be fully manifest in linguistic practice.

It is worth separating three main issues raised by Peacocke's discussion: first, the issue whether the argument he describes is, as he claims, properly taken as a demonstration that U, though unprovable in S, is true; second, whether the argument does indeed call for a realist understanding of the dominant quantifier in U; and third, whether the constructivist has no prospect of finding an analogue. I do not think Peacocke makes a convincing case for his view on any of these issues. I'll begin by briefly reviewing the third.

Peacocke reasonably insists that any constructivistic attempt at a informal demonstration of U must be sanctioned by an explicit account of the proof-conditions of universally quantified arithmetical statements. He proceeds to indicate various ways in which such an account might stumble. Suppose, for instance, we are offered the following (where 'A' is a quantifier-free predicate):

> '∀x(Ax)' is proved just in case we have a (constructive) proof that each statement of the form 'Ak', 'k' a numeral, is provable in primitive recursive arithmetic.

This is viciously circular – or, if not quite circular, close enough to circularity to be nugatory.[23] This complaint does not presuppose that any account falls into circularity merely by using the concept of universal quantification in an account of the proof-conditions of statements of the form '∀x(Ax)'. No correct account could avoid circularity by that test. Rather, the point here concerns the *way* the above explanans involves the concept of universal quantification: it *embeds* an

23 Peacocke does not use this actual example, preferring a (so it seemed to me, rather unnatural) formulation in which a strict circularity is involved.

occurrence of the universal quantifier within a that-clause serving to specify the content of the kind of proof it requires us to have if we are to count as having proved '∀x(Ax)'. Since the totality quantified over, viz. statements of the form 'Ak', 'k' a numeral, is isomorphic to that of the natural numbers, the explanans presupposes a prior grasp of the proof-conditions of a species of universally quantified statement which is in no way interestingly different to the kind of statement whose proof-conditions it is supposed to explain.

That is one kind of abortive proposal. But of course it does not represent the constructivist's best shot. A better suggestion would run along the lines of the revised version of *Generality* mooted towards the end of the preceding section:

> A demonstration of arithmetical '∀x(Ax)' is any construction which we can recognize may be used, for an arbitrary numeral 'k', to accomplish a constructive demonstration of 'Ak'.

Here no grasp is presupposed, by the explanans, of what constitutes a proof of the universally quantified conclusion: the kinds of proof of which a grasp is presupposed are proofs of *singular* propositions of the form 'Ak'. Against this account – at least by the rules which Peacocke imposes on his own discussion – there is no legitimate complaint of circularity. What other complaint might be made?

Well, that nothing has so far been said about what, for the purposes of the explanans, should rank as a *constructive* demonstration. Peacocke writes:

> We presume, when issues in the theory of meaning are not at stake, that what distinguishes a constructivist is the semantical clauses he accepts for various constructions. Our hold on the idea of constructivism begins to slip if these semantical clauses themselves contain the notion of constructive proof *ineliminably*. [emphasis added]

This is perfectly fair: you have to say (predicatively) what a constructive proof *is*. But Peacocke offers no clear reason for his apparent view that this is a demand which the constructivist cannot be expected to meet. And the fact is that when our interest is in the intuitionistic demonstration already reviewed, there is no great problem about saying what a constructive proof is – no good reason to suppose that *for the purposes of that specific demonstration*, an ineliminable play with the notion of constructive proof cannot be avoided. On the contrary, we reviewed two accounts of what should count as a constructive proof of '~*P*kg'.

On one, there was indeed a problem for the ambition of the intuitionistic demonstration to avoid any assumption of consistency. But on the other we found no such problem. Admittedly, the second made use of the arguably vague notion of an *effective* means for locating a contradiction; but there is no doubt that the means supplied by Gödel's own construction rank as effective under any reasonable meaning of the term. I conclude that Peacocke's claim, that no genuinely constructivistic demonstration of U is in prospect – that the constructivist who thinks he has such a demonstration is either neglecting his explanatory responsibilities or has surreptitiously gone realist – is overtaken by our discussion above.[24]

Now to the train of thought on which Peacocke bases his contention that Gödel's construction does subserve an informal demonstration of the undecidable sentence, but one which demands a classical understanding of universal quantification. Peacocke draws here on the 'commitment account' of universal quantification developed in his *Thoughts*.[25] For the purposes of 'Proof and Truth' he offers the following simple outline:

> [The commitment account]...claims (a) that what makes it the case that someone is judging a content of the form 'All natural numbers are F' is that he thereby incurs this infinite family of commitments: to F0, to F1, to F2,... That someone has incurred this family rather than some other will be evidenced by the circumstances in which he is prepared to withdraw his judgement. The commitment account also claims (b) that a content of the form 'All natural numbers have property F' is true just in case all those commitments are fulfilled.

He adds:

> The commitment account makes it relatively unproblematic that a first-order quantification should, though true, be unprovable from a particular recursive set of axioms. On the commitment account, what gives the

24 Peacocke frames his critical discussion around a candidate intuitionistic demonstration which he calls the 'Wright demonstration'. This is based on conversations and correspondence with myself. But I have to warn the reader that, though similar in certain respects, this argument is *not* that with which we have been concerned. By contrast with the latter, Peacocke's 'Wright demonstration' features the soundness, and hence consistency, of the object system as an explicit and undischarged assumption. Any such demonstration can have, of course, absolutely no advantage over a straightforward Dummettian Modus Ponens, and any play it makes with specifically intuitionistic understandings of negation and the universal quantifier will therefore be window-dressing. However Peacocke's discussion is not weakened by its focus on the Wright demonstration, since his misgivings about it, as a purportedly constructivistic argument, are entirely focused on its final Universal Introduction step; and this it has in common with the more interesting intuitionistic demonstration with which we have been concerned.

25 Peacocke, *Thoughts: An Essay on Content*. See esp. chs 2 and 3.

> universal quantification its truth-condition is not the set of ways it can be proved, but the commitments incurred in judging it. The commitments of a first-order quantification may all be fulfilled, and hence the quantification may be true, even though it is not provable from the first-order axioms a subject is employing.[26]

I have expressed reservations elsewhere[27] about Peacocke's claim that the commitment account is inherently *realist*, or makes realism 'relatively unproblematic'. It seems to me that someone could quite consistently accept the account – accept that the content of a universal quantification over natural numbers is individuated by the commitments incurred by someone who judges it true, and that such a quantification may be understood on just that basis by someone innocent of any conception of what should count as a proof of it – yet still dispute that we have any conception of what it is for the infinite family of commitments associated with such a quantification to be fulfilled *undetectably*. But it is important to see that this line of objection can be correct without subtracting all the interest of Peacocke's application of the commitment account in the present context. For, whether or not it implicitly involves a realist (epistemically unconstrained) idea of truth, the commitment account certainly is at odds with *constructivism*: if someone can distinctively manifest his acceptance and hence grasp of a universally quantified arithmetical content just by appropriate patterns of behaviour in relation to its (effectively decidable) commitments, then such understanding does not depend on grasp of proof-conditions, nor require any conception of what should count as a proof of such a content. Were Peacocke's line of argument for the truth of U to depend on the commitment model, it would indeed be unavailable to constructivists even if not to all forms of anti-realist.

The line of argument is very simple and runs as follows. Reflect that Gödel's argument ensures that that if an arithmetical system is consistent, then for any natural number, k, the sentence '$\sim P$kg' is provable in that system. And suppose that the particular system, S, we are concerned with is sound – has true axioms and truth-preserving rules of inference. In that case, Peacocke writes,

> ...if for any k the sentence '$\sim P$kg' is provable [in S], then for any k the sentence '$\sim P$kg' is true. So all the commitments of the sentence '$(\forall x)\sim P$xg' are fulfilled. But according to the second part of the commitment account,...a universal numerical quantification is true if and only if all its commitments are fulfilled. So on the commitment account, '$(\forall x) \sim P$xg' is a true sentence.

26 Ibid.
27 See Essay 8 in this volume.

However,

> The reasoning in this straightforward answer is unavailable to the constructivist. The reasoning relies in the commitment account which allows for the possibility, incompatible with any constructivism deserving of the name, that a universally quantified arithmetical sentence be true though unestablishable.

But the reasoning *doesn't* properly rely on the commitment account – rather, as Peacocke himself remarks, it depends only on the second ingredient claim – claim (b) in the passage quoted. True, that claim refers to 'F0', 'F1', 'F2', etc., as 'commitments' of contents of the form, 'All natural numbers have property F'. But that is inessential: as far as its role in the reasoning is concerned, claim (b) comes to no more than – has no implications which are not shared by – the straightforward clause:

> 'All natural numbers have property F' is true if and only if for each number n, 'Fn' is true.

And this clause has no intrinsic anti-constructivist consequences, but may readily be endorsed not just on non-epistemic conceptions of truth but on conceptions of truth, like that of the intuitionists usually understood, whereby truth is held to consist in a kind of constructive provability and when the force of the biconditional is to claim that a constructive proof of either side is, or may be, transformed into a constructive proof of the other. Since Gödel effectively establishes, by intuitionistically acceptable means, the intuitionistic provability of each '~*P*kg', an intuitionist who accepts the straightforward clause, so interpreted, need have no difficulty in keeping company with Peacocke's simple demonstration.

It remains to observe, finally, that since Peacocke's 'demonstration' makes undischarged use of the assumption of the soundness, and hence consistency, of the system of arithmetic concerned, its claim to *demonstrate* the undecidable sentence – to provide cogent a priori reason for supposing that sentence to be true – is no more impressive than that of the Dummettian Modus Ponens. (And since the conditional which provides the major premise for Dummettian Modus Ponens:

> If I is consistent, then U,

may be established by intuitionistically acceptable means for intuitionistically acceptable systems, I, Peacocke should never have been in doubt that an intuitionist who is prepared to take on the assumptions of Peacocke's own demonstration can construct a simple proof of the undecidable sentence.)

VIII
The Lucas/Penrose Argument: Concluding Reflections

Let me finish by offering some very summary suggestions about how matters should be regarded *on the hypothesis that* a line of thought fit to be regarded as an informal demonstration of U, for an arbitrary intuitively acceptable arithmetical system, S, can after all be disclosed.

First on Lucas and Penrose. We have seen, in effect, that their argument has to be (i) that the concept of demonstration which governs human arithmetical practice is not the concept of demonstration which describes the operations of any Turing machine, and (ii) that the non-mechanical character of human mathematical thought is carried by this point. The claim will be that the former concept is shown, by the success of the hypothesized informal demonstration and the fact that such a demonstration is always available, to have an extension which admits of no effective enumeration. Given any effective enumeration (recursive axiomatization) of arithmetical truths, we have a method – contained in the technique for constructing the Gödel sentence and then proceeding, via the successful line of thought, to recognize its truth – for generating a new demonstration going beyond what can be accomplished, even in principle, by derivations from the axioms in question. In brief: the structure of the output-in-principle of the human mathematician and that of the output-in-principle of any Turing machine are different.

Two points seem to me worth logging concerning, respectively, the status of this disanalogy, and its capacity to carry an anti-mechanist conclusion. The first is a small but, in a context in which there has been much confusion about the role of suppositions of consistency, important qualification. Obviously, the disanalogy can be made out *only if* we take it that human arithmetical thought is consistent. Otherwise there is *of course* a Turing machine which generates all and only the arithmetical sentences of which we can in principle construct what, by our standards, rank as demonstrations. Even if the form of a demonstration of U can be disclosed in which the consistency of S does not feature as a premise, the claim to have shown thereby that, in general, the class of in principle humanly demonstrable arithmetical sentences is not effectively enumerable, will still depend on the assumption of the consistency of S and, indeed, of any intuitively acceptable arithmetic which strengthens S. The most that is in prospect, in other words, is still a *disjunctive* conclusion. But the disjunction is not the Gödelian disjunction cited in section II above. That disjunction featured as its second disjunct the proposition that the Turing machine which in fact encodes human arithmetical capacity is one whose formal specification no human being can comprehend. By contrast, the disjunction in prospect as the conclusion of the Lucas/Penrose line of thought supplants that disjunct by the (depressing) proposition that arithmetical demonstrability by arbitrary intuitively acceptable means is an inconsistent notion.

I said it was a small qualification. Clearly it is not a terribly damaging concession for Lucas and Penrose to have to make if their conclusion has to be not that

> Human arithmetical thought is non-mechanical,

but that

> Human arithmetical thought, if not inconsistent, is non-mechanical.

The latter would still be of considerable philosophical interest. There is, however – the second point – a question about the attainability of this conclusion on which our discussion has so far not impinged, and which seems to me very difficult. What we are assuming to be in prospect is a disanalogy, on the assumption of consistency, between the concept of demonstrability defined by the principles and methods which are intuitively acceptable to human mathematicians and any concept of demonstrability which governs the workings of a *Turing* machine. Since, as was stressed earlier, the feasible arithmetical output, so to speak, of even the most prodigious human mathematician can no doubt be matched and indeed surpassed by a suitable Turing machine, making the disanalogy good will require reflection on the *intensions* of the relevant concepts of demonstrability. A sufficiently explicit characterization will therefore be needed of the human notion, so to speak, to make it clear how, for any particular arithmetical Turing machine – still assuming consistency – an arithmetical demonstration lying beyond its scope might in principle effectively be found. Well, suppose that accomplished. Then the basis of the Lucas/Penrose thesis will have consisted in nothing other than the provision of an *effective* procedure for finding, for any particular recursive axiomatization of arithmetical demonstrations, an intuitively acceptable arithmetical demonstration not included within it.

Rather than striking a blow against mechanistic conceptions of the human intellect, there will therefore be an immediate question whether this whole trend of thought cannot at most disclose the inadequacy of the idea of a *Turing machine* as a stalking-horse for mechanism. What an argument against mechanism ought to show is that, for the area of human thought where the mechanist thesis is contested, insight, imagination and creativity have a role to play which cannot be simulated by mechanical model – which cannot be reduced to the implementation of any set of effective instructions. The great difficulty, always, is to render such ideas sufficiently precise to make them debatable, to make it clear what a defender or an opponent has to establish. But surely it is moot whether the debate as envisaged has succeeded in doing that. Whatever is shown by an argument which establishes that, for any particular recursive axiomatization of arithmetical truths, there exists – if human arithmetical thought is consistent – an *effective* procedure for constructing a demonstration of an arithmetical sentence not included in the list, it is *not* that human thought is essentially creative, gifted with a spark which transcends the merely mechanical implementation of any instructions which can be laid down in advance. Any consistent, recursively axiomatized system of arithmetic may be so specified that its Gödelization *is* an effective procedure. And to the sentence which results from that procedure may then, as it were mindlessly, be applied whatever is the general form of the informal demonstration we are assuming has been provided.

True, the sentences which result from indefinite iteration of this procedure on an intuitively acceptable base arithmetic – say standard first-order Peano arithmetic – will not be recursively axiomatizable – will not coincide with the output of any particular Turing machine. But a proponent of Lucas and Penrose needs to say something to disarm the conservative response that a device or organism may be lacking that which opponents of mechanism wish to claim for the human mind even though there is no recursive enumeration of specifications of all the tasks which it is able to perform.

IX
Dummett's Problem: Concluding Reflections

The same basic point shows, I think, that – retaining the hypothesis of the demonstrability of instances of U – there is no alternative but to view Michael Dummett's response to the problem about meaning and use as correct in its essentials. But I fear there may be some disagreement between Dummett and myself about what its essentials are. The problem only arises on three premises:

A that the meaning of an expression has to be fully capturable, as it were, by some substantial *description* of its proper use;
B that in the case of the expressions 'sentence true of all the natural numbers' and 'ground for affirming that all natural numbers have a certain property', such a description will have to consist in or provide for an effective axiomatization;
C that any intuitively correct arithmetical system may be Gödelized and the appropriate U informally demonstrated to be true.

No one is better aware than Dummett, of course, that much is unclear about premise (A). One would not expect, for instance, that it will always be possible substantially to characterize the proper use of an arbitrary expression *non-homophonically*; but homophonic characterization cannot be the rule, or constructing specifications of correct use will become a triviality, and premise (B), that an axiomatic specification is wanted in the case of arithmetical truth, will be overturned too easily. Still, if (A) is to be granted, at least for the two expressions cited, then, in whatever terms and format specifications of use ought generally to proceed, the solution to Dummett's problem must, on our hypothesis, consist in overturning (B). But now, if we are in a position to affirm (C) – if the needed general line of demonstration has been made out – then the terms in which (B) ought to be overturned are surely clear. True, there is no complete axiomatic characterization of the set of sentences which may be regarded as true of all the natural numbers, or of the set of acceptable arithmetical demonstrations. But we may lay it down as *part* of any characterization that, where S is standard first-order arithmetic,

i each axiom and theorem of S is true of all the natural numbers; and
ii any sentence formed by applying to an intuitively acceptable, recursively axiomatized set of arithmetical truths the following procedure...[and here we specify the construction of the sentence U for S] is to be regarded as true of all the natural numbers on the ground...[and here we apply to the sentence in question the general form of whatever we regard as the attendant informal demonstration].

This characterization may very well not be exhaustive. But there is no doubt that it is non-trivial, does speak to the immediate issue raised by Gödel's theorem and, above all, is, as Dummett describes his own proposal, 'as much in terms of *use* as any other'.[28]

28 'The Philosophical Significance', p. 198.

Since I claimed there is no alternative but to view Dummett's response to the problem as correct in essentials, it will be clear that what I am taking to be essential is just the thought that it is only in the light of a general characterization of the contours of the informal demonstration that we can be entitled to claim that such a demonstration is always available: i.e. that the justifiability of (C) presupposes that we have, for the predicates in question, what (A) demands. Now this omits, of course, any mention either of the idea of indefinite extensibility, or of the idea, which Dummett makes consequent upon it, that the notions, 'true of all the natural numbers' and 'ground for affirming that all natural numbers have a certain property', are *vague*. However, it seems to me questionable, in the light of Dummett's official formulations, whether, even assuming (C), the import of Gödel's result will be that the concepts in question *are* indefinitely extensible. And if that is right, we may here prescind from the question whether indefinite extensibility is best viewed as a kind of vagueness. A typical passage is this:

> ...It is precisely the concept of such a ground

– a ground for asserting that something is true of all the natural numbers –

> which is shown by Gödel's theorem to be indefinitely extensible; for any definite characterisation of a class of grounds for making an assertion about all natural numbers, there will be a natural extension of it. If we understand the word 'meaning'...so as to make the meaning of the expression 'natural number' involve not only the criterion for recognising a term as standing for a natural number, but also the criterion for asserting something about all natural numbers, then we have to recognise the meaning of 'natural number' as inherently vague.[29]

Allowing that a demonstration of the undecidable sentence attends the Gödelian construction, it seems to me still not to follow that 'for *any* definite characterization of a class of grounds for making an assertion about all natural numbers, there will be a natural extension of it'. The general type of ground for such an assertion, associated with the Gödel construction, will be definitely – or definitely enough – characterizable once and for all; for if it were not, there would be no basis for (C) and the problem would not arise. The 'natural extension' extends not *types* of ground, but particular *sets* of demonstrations captured by particular recursively axiomatized systems. What is always open to extension, that is to say, is not any definite characterization of a class of grounds, but

29 'The Philosophical Significance', p. 194.

any recursive enumeration of a class of proofs. That is quite consistent with the availability of a once-and-for-all characterization of the particular type of ground which attends Gödel's construction and of the particular class of arithmetical truths thereby demonstrated.

To avoid misunderstanding, I am not claiming that it is possible to give an illuminating yet absolutely general characterization of the extensions of the concept, 'true of all the natural numbers', or the concept, 'ground for affirming that all natural numbers have a certain property', nor ruling out that they may be vague in any respect. My point is merely the modest one that the situation generated by Gödel's theorem on the assumption of (C) is quite consistent with supposing that any characterization should at least contain components corresponding to (i) and (ii) above. If that is right, the immediate problem is, as it seems to me, disposed of.

III

The Positive Programme

12

Anti-realist Semantics: The Role of Criteria

I

Anti-realism of the sort which Michael Dummett has expounded[1] takes issue with the traditional idea that an understanding of any statement (here, declarative sentence) is philosophically correctly analysed as involving grasp of conditions necessary and sufficient for its truth. Many kinds of statement to which, as we ordinarily think, we attach a clear sense would have to be represented, according to this tradition, as possessing *verification-transcendent* truth-conditions; if true that is to say, they would be so in virtue of circumstances of a type transcending our range of possible awareness. Exactly where to draw the boundaries of our possible awareness might be controversial; but there is clearly no being aware, in the relevant sense, of the kind of state of affairs which would make true a generalization of theoretical physics, an assertion about James II's weight on his 32nd birthday, a claim about what would have happened if Edward Heath had not sought a fresh mandate during the miners' strike, or – from your point of view – the statement that my left ear aches. In each of these kinds of case the traditional view, while granting that we (or you) cannot experience the truth-conferring states of affairs as such, would nevertheless credit us with a clear conception of the type of thing they would be. To be sure, there is then no possibility of a straightforward construal of this conception as a recognitional capacity. But the traditional view tends to conceal from itself the problematic status which the alleged grasp of truth-conditions therefore assumes by working with the picture that the

1 I do not mean to imply that Dummett's exposition has remained uniform throughout his writings. The principal sources are the articles reprinted as chapters 1, 10, 11, 13, 14, 21 in *Truth and other Enigmas*, and 'What is a Theory of Meaning? (II)'. See also his *Frege: Philosophy of Language*, passim.

'conception' is *indirectly* recognitional, that it *issues in* a cluster of unproblematic recognitional capacities; in particular, the ability to recognize what is or is not good evidence for the relevant statement and the ability to recognize its logical relations to other statements.[2]

Now, what the anti-realist urges that we enquire is: what good reason is there to postulate any such ulterior 'conception' from which these abilities are supposed to flow – why, indeed, describe our understanding of these statements as involving knowledge of truth-conditions at all? His challenge to the realist is to make out a respectable notion of explanation in terms of which the truth-conditional account can be seen to be needed in order to explain these recognitional abilities. And his suspicion is that the challenge cannot be met.

If this suspicion is correct, the traditional truth-conditional account actually conveys, at least in the case of verification-transcendent statements, no substantial philosophical insight into what understanding essentially is. However, an account which, it seems, cannot possibly be open to objection in the same way would *identify* understanding with the cluster of abilities of which the truth-conditional view aimed to provide a unified explanation. Understanding a statement, on this view, would simply be a matter of practical mastery of all aspects of its *use*.

If a statement has truth-conditions whose actualization would be something which our experience can encompass, then part of this practical mastery will be the ability to recognize such an actualization, if one is appropriately placed to do so, and to respond accordingly; in such a case, knowledge of the truth-conditions will be a sub-species of knowledge of the conditions which warrant assertion of the statement – its *assertibility-conditions*. But it is now a grasp of assertibility-conditions which, for statements in general, will play the central role in the account of understanding. Such grasp can play this central role because, first, a practical knowledge of the logical relations of a statement is simply a knowledge of the role played in its assertibility-conditions by possible argumentation; and because, second, whether there is what the traditional account would regard merely as good evidence for a particular statement is something which – unlike whether or not it is true – a reasonable man can *always* recognize, which can never be transcendent. The thought is, in short, that understanding a statement is essentially a practical, discriminatory skill of which knowledge of assertibility-conditions is always, while knowledge of truth-conditions is at most sometimes, a satisfactory interpretation.

An endorsement of this assertibility-conditions conception of meaning is taken by Dummett to be part of the intent of the later Wittgenstein's

2 See, for example, Strawson, 'Scruton and Wright on Anti-realism, Etc.'.

identification of (knowledge of) meaning with (knowledge of) use. It is therefore natural to wonder what if any part ought to be played in a theory which elaborates the assertibility-conditions conception by the notion of a *criterion* deployed in Wittgenstein's later work. That is the main question which I want to consider: if we find ourselves in sympathy with the anti-realist's criticisms, and are led thereby to seek a philosophical account of meaning in which conditions of warranted assertion rather than of truth play the central role, ought we to try to substantiate and utilize something at least interestingly akin to Wittgenstein's notion?

II

In the *Blue Book*, as is familiar, Wittgenstein does not always sharply distinguish the concept of a criterion from that of a sufficient – or even a necessary and sufficient – condition of a statement's truth. (See, notoriously, the passage about angina on p. 25.) But the use which Wittgenstein makes of the notion both elsewhere in the *Blue Book* and in places in the *Investigations* makes it plain that he did not in general intend that satisfaction of the criteria of a statement should be the same thing as realization of truth-conditions. Consider for example *Investigations*, 377: 'What are the criteria for the redness of an image? For me, when it is someone else's image, what he says and does...'

But Wittgenstein explicitly disavows the behaviourism which would hold that the truth-conditions of 'X is experiencing a red image', said of another, are constituted by his verbal and non-verbal behaviour.[3] Compare 354:

> The fluctuation in grammar between criteria and symptoms makes it look as though there were nothing at all but symptoms. We say, for example: 'Experience teaches that there is rain when the barometer falls but it also teaches that there is rain when we have certain sensations of wet and cold or such-and-such visual impressions.' In defence of this one says that these sense-impressions can deceive us. But here one fails to reflect that the fact that the false appearance is precisely one of rain is founded on a definition.

The criteria of a statement, as Wittgenstein intends the notion, are, first and most importantly, in contrast with its symptoms, conditions which justify its assertion as a matter of 'definition' – as a function purely of its meaning – but which fall short of making it true. We can add that if the statement has a communally well-understood use, as Wittgenstein argued any genuine statement must, the conditions in question must, secondly,

3 For any agnostic about this claim, *Investigations* 393 should be explicit enough.

be *publicly accessible*. And Wittgenstein stresses, thirdly, that the criteria of a statement are generally *multiple*; see, for example, *Blue Book*, p. 51, on the multiplicity of criteria for statements about the perceivable world; *Brown Book*, 7, p. 144, on the multiplicity of criteria for someone's sincerity; *Investigations*, 164, for the case of reading, and many other passages.

Both Hacker[4] and Baker[5] take it to be an essential fourth feature of Wittgenstein's notion that the satisfaction of criteria confers *certainty*. Naturally, this cannot be so if we regard as certain only statements about which the possibility of error can be definitively excluded. But if certainty is taken to apply to all and only statements which may not reasonably be doubted, then – since what may reasonably be asserted cannot simultaneously be reasonably doubted[6] – the satisfaction of a statement's criteria will indeed pre-empt any reasonable doubt about it; for it will now be part of the *content* of the statement that it may reasonably be asserted in those circumstances. (Classical scepticism therefore presupposes something other than a criterial account of meaning; it requires an account which makes it coherent to call into question our warrant to assert a particular kind of statement in all the kinds of circumstances which we typically consider to justify its assertion without *eo ipso* calling into question the identity of the statement. The truth-conditional account will generally serve the sceptic's purpose admirably.)[7]

III

A natural thought is that the assertibility-conditions theorist will need to avail himself of something at least very close to Wittgenstein's distinction of criteria from conditions of warranted assertion in general if he is to give an account of what it is to *misunderstand* a statement. If somebody uses a statement in what seems to the rest of us a quite aberrant manner, factual misapprehension, prejudice and simple ignorance are among the most likely explanations. But another possibility, as we should ordinarily suppose, is that he doesn't understand the statement. The traditional view would mark this difference by drawing a distinction between aberrant uses

4 In *Insight and Illusion*, concluding chapter.

5 In 'Criteria: a New Foundation for Semantics'.

6 Actually, it is doubtful whether this is a sufficiently robust sense of 'certain' to give point to the Baker–Hacker claim. For, in this sense, any statement favoured, however marginally, by the balance of evidence will count as certain.

7 I stick to this as an account of the requirements of *classical* scepticism. But for some indication of the possibilities open to the sceptical temperament within the framework of criterial semantics, see Essay 13.

which respectively do and do not flow from a misconception of a statement's truth-conditions. But it looks to be unclear what account an anti-realist can give of the distinction so long as he is content to talk vaguely of understanding a statement as consisting in a practical knowledge of its assertibility-conditions; for the ignorant, mistaken or prejudiced man, after all, does in one way not know the assertibility-conditions of the statement of which his use is aberrant. If assertibility-conditions are divided into criteria and symptoms, on the other hand, then the anti-realist can propose that aberrant use betrays misunderstanding when and only when it is caused by misconceptions about, or ignorance of, the criteria for the statement in question.

Now, it is clear that, whatever else it may achieve, this proposal does not of itself convey a full account of misunderstanding. Saying that a misunderstanding consists in misconceptions about, or ignorance of, criteria is no more an account of the notion than saying that it consists in misconceptions about, or ignorance of, truth-conditions. In both cases we continue to await an explanation of how such a misconception is supposed to be manifest *as such* in a person's behaviour. Talk in terms of criteria, or truth-conditions, puts us in a position to *label* the notion of misunderstanding; and our desire to have such a label has whatever respectability the belief possesses that no satisfactory philosophy of language will be able to jettison the notion of misunderstanding altogether. But the fact is that to introduce the idea of aberrant usage which is attributable to misconceptions about, or ignorance of, criteria really makes it not one whit clearer how to provide a substantial account of misunderstanding: it merely serves to include provision of one on the (already packed) agenda.

This objection is reinforced if we look a little closer at the question how a substantial account might run. From whatever standpoint is emanated, it is clear that the account would have to respect the *holistically interlocking* character of the key concepts in the system whereby we explain a person's linguistic performance. In order to make his willingness to assent to, or dissent from, a particular statement in particular circumstances intelligible to us, we need to come up with hypotheses about his desires and beliefs and the manner in which he understands the statement. But his performance will be good evidence for any particular one of these hypotheses only against the background of the other two. (The same point applies, of course, to the simpler system of belief and desire in terms of which we interpret non-linguistic human behaviour. A person's behaviour will support a particular hypothesis about his desires only if we presuppose certain beliefs on his part about how he can achieve those desires and about the prevailing circumstances; conversely, we can support the claim that he has certain beliefs only if we are allowed to presuppose certain desires on his part.) We do not require a more refined account of this sort of holistic structure of explanation to appreciate the corollary that there is no behaviour which is absolutely distinctive, of and by itself, of a misunderstanding of a particular statement. Whatever someone does, he can be acquitted of the charge of misunderstanding if we are ready to plead his possession of suitably idiosyncratic desires or factual beliefs; in fact, there will be *no end* of available explanations of his behaviour none of which involves attribution of any misunderstanding. So a full account of the notion of misunderstanding must do no less than tackle the complex question: what makes an explanation in terms of misunderstanding preferable to one of another kind, given the freedom that the holistic character of this system of explanation in principle affords us?

One possibility, certainly, is that the assertibility-conditions theorist will have to invoke the notion of a criterion in order to answer that question; that, for example, responses to situations in which (arguable) criteria for a statement are realized are particularly important in determining our preferences concerning what sort of explanation to give of an aberrant use of it. But, in advance, there seems no very clear reason for expecting this to be so. It may be that wholly pragmatic considerations govern our preferences here; considerations, that is to say, which have to do solely with how powerful and manageable an overall theory of the individual's behaviour the contrasted explanations admit of integration into – our preference being, for example, to describe someone as misunderstanding only when a large *range* of aberrant usage can be elicited from him in which certain expressions recur, of which we can furnish an interpretation sanctioning a large part of the range.

Where that was the situation, we should expect, *ceteris paribus*, that patient re-explanation of the meanings of the relevant expressions, with perhaps a special eye towards ruling out the deviant interpretation in question, would bring our miscreant into line. And it will be, of course, in general a crucial element in our preferences about what kind of account to offer of aberrant use of a statement just what kind of 'further education' we anticipate will serve to eliminate it – explanations of meanings, or adduction of empirical fact, or neither. This reflection, however, provides a reason for supposing that the assertibility-conditions theorist will need to invoke criteria in order to account for the notion of misunderstanding only if it is already assumed that he will need to invoke criteria in order to make good the distinction between explaining meanings and calling attention to empirical facts. And that assumption is correct only if at least some explanations of meaning are distinguished as such precisely by serving to elucidate criteria for the correct use of certain statements. If *that* were clear, however, we should already have sufficient reason for supposing that an assertibility-conditions orientated philosophy of language ought to utilize Wittgenstein's notion; special consideration of misunderstanding would be a detour.

There is at any rate, as it seems to me, no easy path from the assumption that such a philosophy of language ought to provide an account of the notion of misunderstanding to the conclusion that it will need to distinguish among assertibility-conditions between those which are criterial and those which are merely symptomatic in status. That is not to say that there may not be a harder path.

IV

Let us experiment with the following *Criterial Schema*:

> If an agent has verified each of $\{D_1,\ldots,D_n\}$, and possesses no information telling against S and no information which would explain, without the need to suppose S, why $\{D_1,\ldots,D_n\}$ are true, then it is reasonable for him to believe S.

The Schema is satisifed for any particular statement S only by statements $\{D_1,\ldots,D_n\}$, which (collectively) describe conditions knowledge of whose realization is capable of justifying assertion of S. But as it stands, it embraces certain trivial cases: $\{D_1,\ldots,D_n\}$ may, for example, entail S; or they may include the statement that it is reasonable to believe S, or entail that statement independently of the additional conditions that no information telling against S, or equally good alternative explanations of the truth of $\{D_1,\ldots,D_n\}$, should be on hand. Let us therefore stipulate, first that $\{D_1,\ldots,D_n\}$ all be *decidable* statements; we thereby ensure that whenever S is verification-transcendent, knowledge of the truth of $\{D_1,\ldots,D_n\}$ will constitute at best a defeasible ground for asserting S, and will moreover be knowledge of an umproblematic recognitional sort (provided, of course, it is right to suppose that knowledge of the truth-conditions of decidable statements is correctly so regarded).[8] And let us also stipulate, second, that $\{D_1,\ldots,D_n\}$ are to be *S-predicative* statements: that is, statements which involve in particular no occurrences of S and, more generally, an understanding of which presupposes no understanding of S; we thereby ensure both that the second and, I believe also, the third trivial kinds of case are excluded, and, most importantly, that any $\{D_1,\ldots,D_n\}$ which satisfies the Schema for a particular S is suitable material for a non-circular explanation of the assertibility conditions of S – for, from the point of view of the assertibility-conditions theorist, it obviously has to be possible to explain S's assertibility-conditions without presupposing that the recipient already understands S.

8 A question to be aired in section VII of this paper.

To locate a set, $\{D_1,...,D_n\}$, which, for a particular S, satisfies the Schema, understood – as from here on we shall understand it – as so restricted, would not yet be fully to explain the use of S; full explanation would at least require, in addition, an S-predicative account of what it was to have no information telling against S, nor any competitive alternative explanation of the truth of $\{D_1,...,D_n\}$. Nevertheless it appears that we can now formulate our leading question in rather sharper terms: is the assertibility-conditions theorist committed to holding that, if S is a well-understood verification-transcendent statement, a set, $\{D_1,...,D_n\}$, can be located whose introduction with S into the Schema will result in a *non-contingent* truth? If so, then for each such S, he will be constrained to acknowledge a set of conditions which can be explained independently of an understanding of S and of which it is non-contingently true that their satisfaction defeasibly warrants S's assertion. That would surely be a commitment to something 'interestingly akin to' Wittgenstein's notion, even though the proposal does not speak directly to Wittgenstein's conditions concerning the publicity and variety of criterial support.

In order to try to clarify the matter, let us suppose the opposite: that there are verification-transcendent statements of whose assertibility-conditions we can, perhaps, give a general, though impredicative, description but of which no more specific, predicative description can be given generating a non-contingent instance of the Schema. For any such statement, S, we then confront two possibilities: either

i such S-predicative characterizations as can be given of S's assertibility-conditions yield contingent instances of the Schema; or
ii no S-predicative characterization can be given at all.

The question which it is now fruitful to consider is: how are the kind of circumstances which justify assertion of S to be conceived as initially communicable? On alternative (i), it appears that an explanation could at least begin by reference to an S-predicative description, C, of features, $E_1,...,E_k$, of certain such circumstances. But it would be *contingent* that the circumstances so described ever justified assertion of S – so before one could reasonably offer this sort of explanation, it would be necessary to have empirical grounds supporting it; empirical grounds for supposing that the appropriate instances of the Schema were (contingently) true. Evidently, in order to be in possession of such grounds, we should have to have had some anterior idea of *other* features, $F_1,...,F_k$, which would distinguish (at least some) circumstances justifying assertion of S. For unless we had some such idea, capable of elucidation in advance, it would be impossible to defend against the suggestion that we did *not* find empirical grounds for regarding C-type circumstances as justifying assertion of S but rather tacitly adopted a *convention* that they did so – contrary to (i). So the question now arises, in what manner is this anterior idea to be thought of as capable of explanation? Perhaps the relevant features, $F_1,\ldots,F_k$, can be S-predicatively characterized; but in that case, given (i), it will be contingent whether circumstances which exemplify them justify assertion of S, so the explanation given will in turn require empirical support. And, again, we shall be able to adduce such support only within the framework of yet other features, $G_1,\ldots,G_k$, regarded as distinguishing assertibility-conditions of S. Clearly, however, *these* features must not be those features, $E_1,\ldots,E_k$, originally specified in C – otherwise our putative empirical grounds for regarding C-circumstances as justifying assertion of S become circular. So we embark on a regress.

The position, in other words, is that if we are allowed recourse *only* to S-predicative descriptions of assertibility-conditions of S, then alternative (i) requires that in order to be entitled to regard our explanation as correct, we shall need to establish empirical support for infinitely many independent such descriptions – *per impossible*. That is, if it is possible to give an S-predicative characterization of assertibility-conditions of S which we are entitled to regard as correct, the case for saying so will have to advert to something other than an S-predicative characterization.

Notice, however, that for the assertibility-conditions theorist it must not be *unavoidable* for us to invoke an S-impredicative characterization at this point. For knowing S's assertibility-conditions is to involve more than grasping that certain types of circumstance justify its assertion – it is to involve attaining all the understanding of S which we, the trainers, enjoy. So, if C-type circumstances merely contingently justify assertion of S, one thing the trainee has to learn is *why* – by what principle – they are rightly judged to do so. But if we really cannot avoid bringing in reference to an S-impredicative characterization of S's assertibility-conditions in order to defend the correctness of C, then there cannot be any explanation of this principle intelligent receipt of which does not presuppose a prior understanding of S – and that is just to say that there is no full explanation of what it is for circumstances to justify the assertion of S save one which presupposes an understanding of S, an absurd situation from the point of view of the assertibility-conditions theorist.

The consequences of alternative (i) for the assertibility-conditions theorist are therefore as follows. In order to be entitled to regard any S-predicative description as characterizing a class of circumstances which justify S's assertion, we shall need to advert to features which we *cannot* capture by S-predicative description but which *can* be explained without recourse to S-impredicative description. Only someone who is apprised of these features and their role understands S; so no S-impredicative description of them is of any explanatory use. S's assertibility-conditions, alternative (i) therefore forces us to conclude, do not admit of a complete descriptive explanation.

If, on the other hand, as supposed on alternative (ii), it is somehow the case that no S-predicative characterization can be given at all of features distinctive of S's assertibility-conditions, the same conclusion swiftly follows. Now the only characterizations of S's assertibility-conditions which we will be entitled to regard as correct will all be S-impredicative; whereas if such a characterization is to be genuinely explanatory, it will have to be possible to presuppose on the part of its recipient a prior understanding of S, conferred in some other way than by a characterization of its assertibility-conditions. The truth-conditional conception has at least *scope* for such a presupposition; the requisite prior understanding of S will have been conferred by exactly an explanation of its *truth-conditions*, so there is no formal obstacle to an explanatory but S-impredicative characterization of its assertibility-conditions. But the assertibility-conditions theorist, obviously, has no such scope except in cases where he regards grasp of truth-conditions as unproblematic – contrary to the hypothesized situation of S. It therefore appears that in the case of any well-understood verification-transcendent statement he must either reject *both* alternatives, (i) and (ii), or else embrace their common consequence (for his point of view) that no description of the statement's assertibility-conditions can be given which is a full and adequate introductory explanation of them. To reject both alternatives, (i) and (ii), however, is just to postulate the existence of non-contingently true instances of the Schema – restricted as described – for the statement in question; that is, *criteria* for it. So we have an affirmative answer to our leading question as one disjunct of the conclusion of the foregoing argument.

V

The other option is that the theorist discard the idea that a full understanding of S can be imparted by description of its assertibility-conditions. Since, for him, an understanding of S *consists* in grasping its assertibility-conditions, this option immediately necessitates some other model of how a grasp of S's assertibility-conditions can be conferred. The only other form for a model to take is, of course – using the word in its broadest possible sense – *ostensive*: it has to be possible to make manifest what type of conditions justify the assertion of S by demonstration and example. Granted the soundness of the reasoning of the preceding section, the situation is therefore that an assertibility-conditions theorist is committed to elucidating criteria for any verification-transcendent statement, S, whose sense he considers to be well-determined but whose assertibility-conditions he considers could not be explained ostensively.

It might be thought that, bearing in mind that we learn the overwhelmingly greater part of our language by direct immersion, as it were, the demand on the assertibility-conditions theorist actually to spell out criteria is one which it will hardly ever be possible to make stick. Confidence in the correctness of that thought ought to await an investigation how it could be made apparent, *purely* by ostension, demonstration and example, under what circumstances past-tense, or unrestrictedly general, assertions – to take two potentially problematic-looking cases – were justifiably assertible. But even if the thought is correct, we still need to consider, before concluding that no reason is apparent for supposing that an assertibility-conditions theorist will have much work for criteria, whether even within the class of assertibility-conditions whose explanation does proceed, in the relevant broad sense, in purely ostensive terms, something 'interestingly akin to' the distinction between criteria and symptoms can still be explained.

It is natural to think that the answer must be negative. For the distinction as so far understood turns on whether a state of affairs of a particular type justifies assertion of a particular S contingently or non-contingently. And how can that issue so much as make sense if the type of state of affairs in question is associated with no particular description but is identified by ostensive means? All that can settle the question of contingency or non-contingency, it might be thought, is consideration of the meanings of S and of the description given of the type of state of affairs in question. So where, in the relevant sense, *no* description is given, the question cannot arise. Or if it does arise, some radically *de re* conception of contingency/non-contingency seems to be required to give it content.

Surely, though, of *any* explanation of assertibility-conditions of S, descriptive or ostensive, it has to make sense to enquire whether it admits of an empirical defence. If the community considers that a certain sort of state of affairs, of which they can give no better than an incompletely descriptive, largely ostensive characterization, justifies asserting S, it ought to be a reasonable enquiry what, if any, type of ground they have for thinking so. Three possibilities then open. The first is that they consider that they have empirical grounds; as when, for example, a particular behavioural syndrome, visually distinctive but difficult distinctively to describe, has been found to be associated with a particular kind of poisoning. Second, they may find that they are unable to adduce such grounds, and tend to treat that as calling into question the correctness of asserting S in that type of circumstance. Or, third, they may be disinclined to respond to their lack of empirical grounds in that way and, very likely, puzzled to know what to do to meet the demand for justification of this aspect of their practice. Obviously, it is this third possibility which is of interest in the present context. It is a possibility which it is certain would in actual practice be realized repeatedly. But the question is how to elicit a respectable notion of *convention* of such a sort that we can then regard communal responses of the third kind as possible indications that the association between the assertibility of the relevant statement and the obtaining of an instance of the ostensively explained species of circumstances is a conventional matter.

The obvious proposal is simply this: the connection between the occurrence of a particular ostensively explained type of state of affairs and a particular statement, S, is one of *conventional support* if and only if we would consider it acceptable in certain circumstances to assert S on the basis of knowledge of such a state of affairs; and we would not require, in order for someone to be credited with a full understanding both of S and of what type of state of affairs had been ostensively explained, that he know what it would be empirically to investigate whether occurrences of that type of state of affairs really did provide reason for believing S and to find that they did not.

In contrast, the connection is one of *contingent support* if and only if we would, once again, consider it acceptable in certain circumstances to assert S on the basis of knowledge of such a state of affairs; but would regard no one as fully understanding both the statement and what kind of state of affairs had been meant *unless* he grasped how it might be empirically investigated whether occurrences of the latter provided reason for believing the former and what it would be for it to turn out that they did not. If, for example, we give an ostensive demonstration of the syndrome of movements characteristic of mercuric poisoning, no one will be credited with a full understanding both of what kind of state of affairs we intended to demonstrate and of the statement, 'X is suffering from mercuric poisoning', unless he has some idea of what it would be empirically to investigate whether occurrences of that syndrome provided a reason for believing appropriate statements of that kind, and what it would be for it to turn out that they did not.

Let us say that a particular type of state of affairs is a **criterion* for a particular statement if and only if it affords that statement conventional support in the sense just described. Truth-conditions, clearly, where, if anywhere, they are capable of ostensive explanation, are a sub-class of **criteria* so characterized. Our question now is: will an assertibility-conditions theorist who is ready to grant that a particular class of verification-transcendent statements possess no criteria be committed to their possession of **criteria* instead?

Consider what sort of model the theorist is in a position to give of how an understanding of any one member of the class, S, is to be conferred if he tries to proceed without recourse to **criteria*. By hypothesis, he has abandoned the hope of elucidating criteria for S. So the materials at his disposal include only S-predicatively characterizable but symptomatic assertibility-conditions of S and ostensively explicable but merely contingently S-supportive states of affairs. The most immediate difficulty, as before, has to do with the defensibility of whatever explanation he chooses to advance. It has to do, that is to say, with how he can support the claim that his explanation enjoins *correct* use of S. For whatever type of explanation, ostensive or descriptive, which his model involves will connect only contingently with the justifiable use of S – will be such that competent members of his speech community will have a concept of how the adequacy of the explanation might be investigated empirically and of how it might turn out to be doubtful. If the explanation is ostensive, the point follows directly from the definition of contingent support; if the explanation is descriptive, it follows from the contingency, *ergo* possible falsity, of the appropriate instance of the Schema, the possibility interpreted – as an anti-realist must interpret it – constructively. So, either way, in order to provide a defence of the model explanation, the theorist will have to provide a reason for thinking that such an investigation would turn out favourably. In fact, though, it is clear that the most he will be able to provide will be reason for thinking that his explanation enjoins the same pattern of use as another, antecedently accepted as correct. And since this in turn can, by hypothesis, only be an ostension of contingently supportive circumstances or a predicative description of symptoms, the issue of *its* defensibility will immediately arise. Failing recourse to criteria or **criteria*, then, the theorist lands himself in the incoherent position of having to grant that there is an empirical question about the adequacy of any particular explanation of the use of S into which no *effective* (i.e. finite, non-circular and persuasive) investigation can be conducted.

To be sure, that is a predicament which the truth-conditions theorist might be prepared to tolerate. He might be prepared to accept that it is an empirical issue whether the grounds which we standardly accept for asserting a particular type of verification-transcendent statement are indeed a good indication that its transcendent conditions of truth are realized – it is just that the appropriate 'empirical investigation' is one which mere human beings cannot perform. But the only coherent stance of the anti-realist assertibility-conditions theorist is to postulate, for any communally well-understood verification-transcendent statement, S, the possibility of an explanation of its assertibility-conditions which, if ostensive, is associated with no communal conception of how its adequacy might be empirically investigated; or, if descriptive, results in a non-contingent instance of the Schema.

The same conclusion emerges another way if we draw on another of our earlier reflections and recall that, while the meaning of S is now viewed as being fully explained by fully explaining its assertibility-conditions, no one will count as fully understanding S whose responses to what we consider to be contingently S-supportive or S-symptomatic circumstances are more or less what we think of as the right ones but who has no conception of how it might be empirically investigated, and confirmed or disconfirmed, whether we are right. So the assertibility-conditions theorist must provide in his model a way of communicating such a conception; and it is clear that so long as his model makes play only with contingently supportive and symptomatic circumstances, the problem will be intractable. For no matter what lengths the model goes to, no matter how specification of assertibility-conditions is piled on specification, if, for each combination of the circumstances explained, the thesis that its realization would provide reason for believing S is in principle empirically defeasible, no one has fully grasped the meaning of S who has not grasped what it would be for that possibility to be realized – and that is something which the model itself cannot have made clear. A full understanding of S, therefore, if it is to be conferrable by an explanation of assertibility-conditions at all, has to be conceived as involving a knowledge of criteria, or **criteria*, or both.

It should be stressed that what has been established, assuming the soundness of these considerations, is the theorist's commitment to the existence of assertibility-conditions, for each statement for which he regards the truth-conditional account as problematic, of which there is no communal conception how they might be found *not* to provide a reason for believing the statement.[9] A full understanding of the statement, that is to say, while involving grasp of the role of these conditions, will not need to involve grasp that their status is susceptible to empirical investigation. Something *weaker* is therefore being said than that each such statement will be associated with assertibility-conditions for which there is a communal understanding that their status as such is *not* susceptible to empirical investigation. Critics of the Wittgensteinian notion[10] are usually realists holding, more or less consciously, the truth-conditional view; but they also tend to labour under the belief that the proponent of criteria is confronting them with some such strong notion. And the fact is that lots of prima facie examples of the weaker kind of thing tend not to be clear-cut examples of the stronger. I suggest, however, though I shall not attempt to argue the point here, that play with a notion of the weaker kind will subserve well enough the *Investigations* strategy with traditional

9 I now regard this as a slip; see section I, and the conclusion, of Essay 13. However, the sentence gives a fair report of the upshot of the argument if the 'not' is deleted.

10 See most notably Putnam, 'Brains and Behaviour'; also Chihara and Fodor, 'Operationalism and Ordinary Language; a Critique of Wittgenstein'.

forms of scepticism;[11] and that Wittgenstein's talk of the 'fluctuation between criteria and symptoms'[12] – an idea crucial to his diagnosis of the way in which the sceptic's ideas are able to take hold of us – is correctly interpreted as pointing in particular to the phenomenon whereby it can at one time be no part of understanding a certain statement to know what it would be empirically to investigate whether a particular kind of state of affairs, standardly taken to justify its assertion, really does so but at a later time essential to have a conception of just such an investigation. That some such thing has happened to, for example, statements identifying samples of the elements between the era of the alchemists and the present day seems clear enough; and that it reflects a change in concepts like 'gold' is also clear, since the requirements imposed on a full understanding of these concepts have changed. But whether the point is correctly interpreted as somehow compromising the continuity of the objects of scientific enquiry is quite another matter.

VI

A major area of enquiry opens up at this point. If the assertibility-conditions theorist is committed to finding either criteria or **criteria* for every communally well-understood statement for which he finds the truth-conditional account unacceptable, then if ever reason can be given for doubting that either criteria or **criteria* can be found in a relevant class of cases, that will tend to suggest that there is something amiss with the assertibility-conditions conception of statement meaning; and that in turn will pose the question whether anti-realism can succeed in proposing any defensible alternative to the truth-conditional view. How far, then, can the assertibility-conditions theorist meet this apparent commitment?

The question is too big for this essay. But let me at least make some rather cursory remarks about one central problematic case: that of statements about the past. An immediate reaction would be that the case looks promising for the anti-realist; for is it not most implausible to suppose that our apparent memories, or the possession of historical documentation, merely contingently provide reason for believing such statements? Is it not out of the question to suppose that a conditional like:

> If we all seem to recollect that S, and possess no countervailing evidence, nor any other explanation, equally as good as the

11 I would now regard with suspicion the suggestion that there is, in the *Investigations*, an epistemological strategy for which the notion of a criterion (or **criterion*) is of central importance.

12 In addition to the *Investigations* passage quoted on p. 243, see also *Zettel* 438.

> supposition that S, of our possession of such an apparent memory, then it is reasonable for us to believe that S,

although, as we should ordinarily suppose, true, could in principle turn out to be incorrect if certain contingencies were realized? No doubt an appropriate genre of *scepticism* would contest the truth of such a conditional; but it would do so on purely a priori grounds. And a philosopher who is not prepared to don the mantle of sceptic about the past, and who can adduce no plausible account of *what* contingent facts would have to change in order for such a conditional to cease to be true, seems to have no alternative to admitting that statements about the past are capable of defeasible but non-contingent support.

Even if the conditional is indeed a non-contingent truth, however, as a prospective indication of a source of criteria, in the sense in which we are interested, for statements about the past, it is, obviously, uselessly S-impredicative. It may well be true that apparent memory enters into some sort of non-contingent connection with the reasonableness of certain kinds of belief about the past; but there will be no milking criteria out of the connection unless an S-predicative characterization can be given of what it is to have an apparent memory that S, and a characterization, moreover, whose correctness in any particular state of affairs is a decidable matter. The prospect of doing so, however, looks very opaque: what distinctive but essential features *are* there of an apparent memory that S which could be captured by descriptions presupposing no understanding of S and whose collective realization would *constitute* an apparent memory that S? Nothing plausible comes into view; and the corresponding question about historical documentation looks, for its part, no less daunting.

Memory and documentation apart, our judgements concerning past events and states of affairs rely entirely upon more or less theoretically inspired beliefs concerning their presently accessible physical traces. That no such traces can enjoy the status of criteria seems to be settled by the simple reflection that their provision of a reason for believing a particular past-tense statement will always be contingent *either* on the outcome of a direct appeal to documentation or memory *or* on the degree of empirical support possessed by the theory which credits them with that status – itself a contingent matter. So the criteria, if there are any, for past-tense statements must, it seems, be sought in the areas of apparent memory and documentation. If, therefore, the suspicion is correct that none save S-impredicative characterizations of apparent memories and documentation will serve to generate non-contingent instances of the Schema for a past-tense statement, S, we must conclude that there are no criteria for statements about the past.

It appears, then, that the assertibility-conditions theorist must make a case for regarding apparent memory and/or documentation as possible sources of **criteria* for past-tense statements; and part of the case will have to be to argue that it is possible to explain ostensively, without presupposing an understanding of S, what it is for one to seem to remember that S or to have documentation that S.

In the case of documentation, it seems to be plain that little headway can be made. No doubt we could ostensively train someone to recognize written, or spoken, occurrences of the statement (that is to say, declarative sentence); but only a language-user could tell whether it was meant to be received as having been asserted or not – and, besides, the knowledge that others, dead or alive, assert the statement is next to useless as a clue to its content. Knowledge of the **criteria* of a statement ought to confer a *non-parasitic* knowledge of its correct assertoric use; so the kind of non-contingent connection with documentation, and hearsay in general, has with reasonable belief is of no help to the theorist here.

The crucial question is therefore, could we make intelligible to someone by, in the relevant broad sense, ostensive means, what it was for him to seem to remember that S without in any way presupposing a prior understanding of S on his part? One's first suspicion is: no. Obviously, it is possible for us to drill someone in a broadly ostensive way in the correct use of a particular statement only if we are in a position to know in what way, from situation to situation, he *ought* to use it. But, it is plausible to suppose, someone's apparent memories are a feature of his mental life of a kind of which, in contrast to many sensations and emotions, there is no distinctive behavioural manifestation *save* his report of them. So if, as is our hypothesis, someone is in no position to report his apparent memory that S, how can it be determined how the envisaged drill should proceed? How are we supposed to know what someone's apparent memories are, if he is not in a position to tell us? And how, therefore, could we drill him in their correct description?

If there are neither criteria nor **criteria* for past-tense statements, then, assuming the soundness of the reasoning of the preceding sections, it cannot be correct to view our understanding of such statements as consisting in knowledge of their assertibility-conditions. But we only have a prima facie case for that conclusion – and one to which the assertibility-conditions theorist is by no means bereft of a reply. He could point out, to begin with, that it is not as if a man's linguistically mature descriptions of his apparent memories are granted an absolutely unchallengeable authority. We often have a fairly definite idea when to expect someone to seem to remember something; and a fairly definite idea, too, of what it is to have a reasonable suspicion that someone is lying, or even sincerely mistaken, in claiming to seem to remember something. And if there are public standards for the correctness of apparent memory reports, ought it not to be possible to guide the envisaged ostensive training by these standards? After all, correct use of statements concerning one's own past is something in which most of us have been successfully trained simply by immersion within a linguistic community, something which we have learnt purely by example, prompting and correction. This training, somehow or other, gets across to us the distinction between making such statements on the basis of apparent memory and making them on other grounds. It may help to imagine our own practice changed in the following respect: suppose we never make, as it were, unguarded assertions about our past but always explicitly acknowledge the type of ground which we have for them: 'I am told that I was very angry', 'I seem to remember being very angry', 'I guess I must have been very angry', and so on. This new practice involves making no assertions in circumstances in which it would not have been correct to assert them before; so it could not be any more difficult to learn from scratch. Since its mastery, in contrast with mastery merely of the past tense, involves *explicit* knowledge of what it is to have apparent memories, surely there is no alternative to supposing that such knowledge is capable of ostensive communication.

This reply is more of a strong protest than a strong argument. I shall not try to take the matter any further here. The foregoing is at least a preliminary illustration of the way in which our leading question has a wider bearing than on the issue, interesting enough in itself, how Dummett's anti-realism connects with the ideas of the later Wittgenstein.

VII

We have so far been considering the role of criteria/**criteria* in an assertibility-conditions account of the meanings of verification-transcendent statements. In this final section I want briefly to consider the assumption that an anti-realist need have no quarrel with a truth-conditional view of the meanings of decidable ones.

If, as in Hacker and Baker,[13] the criterial relation is regarded as holding between statements, then an anti-realist who held that the meaning of *every* statement is determined by its association with criteria would commit himself to an impossible model of how an understanding of any statement could be acquired.[14] When the criterial

13 See works cited above.

14 Perhaps better: an impossible model, in the presence of the requirement of predicativity,

relation is so understood, therefore, a criterial theory of meaning cannot be a global theory of meaning; a base class of statements is required whose meaning is not determined by association with criteria, and the obvious strategy for finding it is to see whether, or how far, the truth-conditional conception can be regarded as unproblematic from an anti-realist point of view.

How should the idea of an (effectively) decidable mathematical statement best be generalized? The obvious proposal is simply to replace the notions of proof and disproof in the mathematical characterization by more general ones of verification and falsification. An (effectively) decidable statement would then be any statement for which (we can recognize in advance that) we have a finite procedure whose implementation will culminate in its verification or falsification.

In terms of this proposal, perhaps the most immediate contingent candidates for the status of effective decidability would be statements which concern presently observable characteristics of particulars which we can presently effectively find and identify; or, more generally, which concern finitely surveyable episodes or states of affairs in presently accessible regions of space and time. Thus 'My car is parked on the Scores', 'Tabitha is in her basket' and 'The sea is choppy today' would, making appropriate allowances for context and, where necessary, vagueness, turn out to be effectively decidable in these terms. The decision procedure appropriate in each case is: position yourself in the appropriate situation and observe.

Now, one might worry about what it is for a characteristic to be 'presently observable' or whether the idea of an 'effectively identifiable' particular has any legitimate place in a purported characterization of effective decidability. But the most major complication with the sort of example illustrated is that the role played by the idea of *position* has no counterpart in the mathematical cases from which we are trying to generalize. Anywhere is as good a place as anywhere else to determine whether or not 283 is a prime; and the same goes for time. But observation of the properties of spatio-temporal particulars, or of the goings-on within particular spatio-temporal regions, essentially requires getting oneself into an appropriate spatio-temporal position. Examples of this type, it might

---

of the language itself. For if the language contains the means of expression of S-predicative criteria for each of its statements, S, then it permits the construction of an infinite descending chain, $<S_0, S_1, S_2, S_3 \ldots>$, where each $S_{k,\geqslant 1}$, is a criterion for S_{k-1} and where the elements of each sub-chain, $<S_{k,\geqslant 1}, S_{k+1}, \ldots>$, can be understood independently of understanding the initial elements of $<S_0, S_1, S_2, S_3, \ldots>$, which that sub-chain omits. It follows that each S_k must display vocabulary and/or syntax which are displayed in no subsequent S_{k+m}, and hence that the language has no finite syntactico-semantic base.

be argued, are therefore properly regarded as effectively decidable only if where and when one is is itself an effectively decidable question; and it is proper to regard it as such only if we can rightly regard ourselves as having an effective finite procedure for determining where and when we are. But can it plausibly be claimed that we have any such procedure? Consider the case of spatial position on its own. Each of us finds his way around by relating the sequence of his experiences to a complex theoretic 'map' that he carries in his head of how the world is, by and large, disposed to affect his senses in different places. But the sense-affective dispositions of any particular place are, of course, in no way *essential* characteristics of it: how the world is at any particular place is something which we conceive to be capable of radical change. The theoretic map which we employ is thus a revisable empirical theory. Granting, then, that there is no effective procedure for settling the truth or falsity of such a theory, and that it is only within the framework which it supplies, that the sort of statement illustrated can be determined to be true or false, how can such statements be regarded as effectively decidable at all? After all, if any statement counts as effectively decidable of which we can recognize that its truth or falsity can be settled within the framework of what is merely a *well-supported* theory, there is likely to be no clear barrier against the effective decidability of many examples of the sort of statement for which the anti-realist finds the notion of truth unacceptably transcendent.

A more general doubt about the propriety of thinking of the sort of statement illustrated as capable of verification pivots on their essential *defeasibility*. For verification ought, or so it is natural to think, to be *conclusive* – otherwise there is no difference between data which verify a statement and data which merely support it. But no matter how sure a statement of the simple observational kind illustrated seems to be, developments are conceivable which may force us to retract it. For in addition to the complications generated by the role of spatio-temporal position, we have to acknowledge also possibilities like illusion and deception, possibilities which in any particular case may always suddenly open up on us.

The obvious thought at this point is that we may merely have picked the wrong type of example. But if there is to be a class of contingent statements on whose status as genuinely (effectively) decidable the above doubts do not bear, then the sources of defeasibility must not apply either. In the first instance, therefore, their verification must not presuppose that the agent verifies his own spatio-temporal position. So they will have to deal in what is happening *here* and *now*. Secondly, they will have to involve no modes of reference to or description of particulars whose appropriateness turns on presuppositions about their history or future; and this promises to proscribe all proper names, all definite descriptions involving sortal terms – 'man', 'tree', etc. (which always presuppose a certain sort of history); and all predicates, indeed, save ones which can be applied purely on the basis of present observation. But, thirdly, statements can meet these conditions, e.g. 'something here and now is red', but still be prone to a further source of defeasibility affecting every categorical assertion, however closely tied to present observation, which we venture about the external world: the possibility of developments which suggest that the conditions of observation are in some way radically *abnormal*. Any characteristic which we might easily take to be purely observational – characteristics, that is, which like colour, or the pitch of a note, or the texture of a surface, can be determined simply by looking, listening, feeling – will be such that a thing can *seem* to have it yet not do so because the conditions of observation somehow disqualify our findings.

It begins to look as though a retreat will be needed to statements concerning how things here and now *seem*. The statement, 'Something here and now seems to be red', for example, will not be compromised by the discovery, say, that it is subtly bathed in red light. But defeasibility is not to be shaken off so easily, provided such statements are construed as dealing in publicly accessible facts – provided, that is, the question of how things appear is sharply distinguished from the question of how they appear to any particular individual. For still the requirement of normality of the *observer* remains a source of defeasibility: something can here and now appear red to me, though not appear red *simpliciter*, because I am drugged, or colour-blind, or whatever. Indefeasible verifiability, it appears, is therefore going to require a retreat to description of how things seem to a single observer from his point of view – in short, to *privacy*; for each of us the statements in question will have to concern how things here and now seem to him, irrespective of his state, the conditions of observation, precisely what particulars of what kinds are within his experiental field, or where and when he is. But the price of taking statements of this kind to be indefeasibly certain will be that the anti-realist, following Wittgenstein's polemic in the *Investigations*, will be constrained to doubt whether we are concerned with a genuinely fact-stating type of statement at all.

It begins to look, at this point, to be only in a 'loose and popular sense', to borrow Butler's phrase,[15] that any contingent statement can be regarded as capable of verification. Strictly they are all verification-transcendent; capable of evidental confirmation but as little capable of verification, properly conceived, as Dummett's original examples: 'A city will never be built on this spot' and 'Jones was brave'.[16] And it would,

15 'The Analogy of Religion', in Perry, *Personal Identity*, p. 101.
16 In 'Truth'.

moreover, be a mistake, though one with a long history of attraction, to suppose that the situation is any different with decidable mathematical statements. For:

> ...one cannot contrast *mathematical* certainty with the relative uncertainty of empirical propositions. For the mathematical proposition has been obtained by a series of actions that are in no way different from the actions of the rest of our lives, and are in the same degree liable to forgetfulness, oversight and illusion. (*On Certainty*, 651)

If these considerations are correct, then we have to acknowledge that the contrast between any kind of statement which we can verify – whether as the result of implementation of an effective procedure, or by good fortune and/or ingenuity – and verification-transcendent statements is not to be explained, if indeed it can be made out at all, by the susceptibility of the former to indefeasible certainty. Moreover the strategy of trying to construe verifiability merely as a high-grade but defeasible kind of confirmability is certain not to produce a distinction between verifiable and verification-transcendent statements coinciding with what the anti-realist intuitively wants. There are, for example, lots of unrestrictedly general scientific hypotheses, and associated counter-factual conditionals, which have been confirmed to saturation point, so to speak; say, 'All men are mortal'. So is the class of verifiable contingent statements at best loosely so described and at worst mythical?

Well, a positive answer to that question would not compromise a genuine distinction drawn by refinement of the following idea. Some statements, including all decidable mathematical statements, have the feature of being associated with a procedure which it is within human power to implement and which is such that *if* it is implemented correctly and the agent correctly apprehends what goes on in the course of its implementation, he will thereby have determined whether the statement is true or not. *Effectively* decidable statements in general are those of which we can recognize that this is a correct characterization without yet knowing what their truth-value is. Both effectively decidable mathematical statements and the sort of contingent example which we started out considering come under this general rubric. It is just that in neither case can we conclusively, i.e. indefeasibly certainly, verify that the appropriate procedure has been implemented correctly and that we have correctly apprehended the course things took. Moreover, the rubric appears to put in the right place all the standard contingent examples for which the anti-realist urges that we should see problems in the truth-conditional account. There is, for example, no procedure within human compass such that if it is correctly implemented and its whole process correctly apprehended, the truth-value of an unrestricted generalization would *eo ipso* be among the information at one's disposal. The same, plausibly, applies to statements about the past, contingent counter-factual conditionals and statements about others' mental states: the best investigative procedures that we have for these statements are such that, no matter what good luck we enjoy or ingenuity we summon, if we carry them through correctly and correctly apprehend what we have done, we can *still* form an incorrect opinion. To put the matter in terms which an anti-realist would not accept: after implementation of any investigative procedure in these cases, the truth-value of the relevant statement may possibly be at our disposal in the sense that we have managed to form a correct opinion about it; but our investigations will have failed to *determine* the truth-value in the way they do when we are concerned with statements about which an incorrect opinion is possible after implementing the appropriate procedure only if the procedure was botched somehow or we misapprehended the course which things took.

If, however, it is only along these lines[17] that the contrast between decidable and verification-transcendent statements can be made out, the urgent question is whether it was right for the anti-realist to regard 'grasp of truth-conditions' as a problematic notion only in verification-transcendent cases. His original point was that 'grasp of truth-conditions', knowledge of the distinction between circumstances which make a particular statement true and circumstances which do not, ought to be an ability to *make* a distinction; i.e. to tell the difference. But it is so only when decidable statements are concerned; only then can someone show he has mastered the distinction in the way that fundamentally counts – by applying it directly to the two kinds of circumstances which it divides. For only in the case of decidable statements can truth-conditions be realized within the compass of our experience. But, now, if our best efforts at verification or falsification of decidable statements always remain in principle defeasible, then in just what sense *are* the truth-conditions of such statements realizable 'within the compass' of our experience? With what justification does the anti-realist credit us with a practical, discriminatory knowledge of truth-conditions in decidable cases, but not in verification-transcendent ones, if in *both* kinds of case only a defeasible purchase is possible on the facts by reference to which our putative knowledge is to be tested?

Provided defeasibility is, as it seems, absolutely pervasive and ineliminable, it does not in this context matter how (effectively) decidable statements are characterized. For it will remain unclear what the *special* problem about the truth-conditional view of verification-transcendent

17 For misgivings about this way of drawing the contrast, and an attempt to improve upon it, see section III of Essay 4.

statements is supposed to be. But it would not follow that the anti-realist ought to suspect error in his original doubts.[18] The logical conclusion for him to draw would be rather that truth-conditional semantics is a distortion right across the board; that everywhere it is at best a mere slogan to think of statement-understanding as consisting in knowledge of truth-conditions. Rather, what it fundamentally consists in, the ability in which it is fully manifest, is just the ability intelligibly to participate in the community's use of its language; the ability to join non-parasitically in a community of assent concerning the justifiability of asserting a particular statement. It is this ability which, whether it is verification-transcendent or decidable, provides the ultimate touchstone of understanding a statement. A recognitional grasp of truth-conditions ought to be testable; and it is testable only by assessment of the agent's responses to situations whereby the truth-conditions are, or are not, realized. But now it is unclear whether that is something which we can ever, strictly speaking, do. All we can do is test his responses to situations in which our best *but defeasible* opinion is that the truth-conditions are, or are not, realized. So his performance is assessed in relation not to how things are but to how we take them to be; and it is in the agent's ability to bear up favourably under this comparison that his understanding of the statement in question resides.

Lest there be any misunderstanding, I do not claim that it is clear that the anti-realist must follow this path, but only that it is at least understandable if he does. We are steering close now to a possible point of contact between anti-realism and the idealist tradition in philosophy which forms the subject matter of this series of lectures. The essential spirit of the realist philosophical outlook is captured by a three-term picture: whenever

a I form an opinion, there is
b the question whether others agree with me and
c the quite independent question whether I and/or they are right about the matter.

All idealists, whatever other differences there may have been between them, have agreed in holding either that there is no intelligible question (c) or, at least, that it cannot intelligibly be construed as 'quite independent', that how things are is *some* sort of conceptual function of how human beings take them to be. Now, so long as the anti-realist is content to allow that there is a base class of statements for which the truth-conditional account is appropriate, he has done nothing to cut himself off from realism about any subject matter debatable by the use solely of statements within that class. It will be open to him, that is to say, to endorse the three-term picture

18 Cf. Essay 2, section II. Again, however, see Essay 4, section III.

as appropriate to any opinion one forms on an issue within such a subject matter. If, in particular, he takes no issue with the truth-conditional view for all effectively decidable statements, then it is open to him – and perhaps required – to endorse the three-term picture for all effectively decidable questions. But if he takes the above considerations to heart and jettisons the idea of a truth-conditionally determined base class of statements, then his contention will have to be that the three-term picture everywhere encourages misdescription of the character of linguistic competence. The realist tries to see competence as a matter of the propensity to suit one's use of statements to correct answers to question (c); but the anti-realist is urging in effect that all that we can *display*, in any case where at most defeasible certainty is possible, is an ability for whose adequate description no acknowledgment of the legitimacy of question (c) is required. So he is within a whisker of idealism; and he can avoid an idealist stance only if he can somehow argue that question (c), although we do not have to acknowledge it in order to do justice to the character of statement-understanding, has to be acknowledged on other grounds. A leading corollary of the later Wittgenstein's recurrent discussion of rule-following is, I suspect, that the anti-realist cannot coherently develop such an argument. But I will not try to pursue that thought here.

We noted that anti-realism cannot coherently suppose that the meaning of every statement is determined by association with criteria. If it cannot coherently look, either, to a truth-conditionally determined base class of statements, there seem to be two remaining possibilities, one remaining within the walls of the assertibility-conditions conception and the other by way of a sortie. The first course would be to look to a base class of statements whose meaning was determined by their association with **criteria*. But of the realization of these **criteria* there would be provision for no other description save by the use of the very statements whose assertion they non-contingently supported. There would be, that is to say, no purer description of them whose assertion, over and above being non-contingently justified by them, they actually *made true*; for any attempt to formulate such a description would merely result in something defeasible, an understanding of whose truth-conditions would therefore be, for the anti-realist who has taken his path, an unproductive fiction. Certain passages in Wittgenstein's later work suggest that he may sometimes have had some such idea as this in mind; e.g. *Zettel* 114–16. But of course the idea cannot be so much as addressed unless we refuse Hacker's and Baker's proposed regimentation of Wittgenstein's equivocal pronouncements about the terms of the criterial relation, and are prepared to countenance the idea that a state of affairs can non-contingently justify a particular assertion in a way which is not parasitic on its description.

That is the first possibility, then: to look to a base class of statements whose meanings are fixed by ostensive training in the conditions which justify their assertion, of which conditions there is, however, no description save by the use of these or other statements for which they are less than truth-conditions. This would be to conceive of the nexus between language and reality as, so to speak, through and through *criterial.

The second alternative is to break with the assertibility-conditions conception of meaning and to look to a base class the correct use of whose members, while something on which any opinion is essentially defeasible, is thought of as founded not on the satisfaction of certain external conditions – even if not truth-conferring ones – but in human reaction alone; certain passages in Wittgenstein suggest this idea too (e.g. *On Certainty* 204). And its radical abnegation of the third term of the realist picture means that an anti-realist who takes it will have little justifiable complaint if he is regarded as a neo-idealist.

13

Second Thoughts about Criteria

This paper continues themes with which I was concerned in a lecture given at the invitation of the Royal Institute of Philosophy in 1978.[1] The main aims of that lecture were to sharpen the formulation of what I took to be the notion of a criterion introduced in the works of the later Wittgenstein, and to display its connections with anti-realist ideas on meaning. I am much less confident than formerly about the Wittgensteinian pedigree of the notion I was trying to sharpen, though the formulations of the lecture may still be of value in explicating the concept of a criterion that the philosophical community largely believes, rightly or wrongly, to have originated in Wittgenstein's work.[2] And I still hold that those philosophers of language who believe that assertion-conditions, rather than truth-conditions, should provide the basis for the philosophical theory of meaning are committed to explaining and utilizing some such concept. But it seems to me very much less clear now whether the concept can play the vigorous anti-sceptical role in the theory of knowledge that its advocates have confidently expected of it; or whether, indeed, as ordinarily interpreted, it is so much as coherent.

Orthodoxy in the interpretation of Wittgenstein attributes to criteria five cardinal features:[3]

1 that recognition of satisfaction of criteria for P can confer sceptic-proof knowledge that P;
2 that P's criteria determine *necessarily* good evidence for P, and thereby fix its content;

1 Essay 12 in this volume.

2 For some strong swimming against the tide, see John McDowell's 'Criteria, Defeasibility and Knowledge'.

3 See e.g. Hacker, *Insight and Illusion*, chapter X; McFee, 'On the Interpretation of Wittgenstein'; Baker, 'Defeasibility and Meaning'; and Baker, 'Criteria: A New Foundation for Semantics'.

3 that the criteria for P will typically be multiple;
4 that satisfaction of a criterion for P will always be a 'public' matter;
5 that to know of the satisfaction of criteria for P is always consistent with having, or discovering, further information whose effect is that the claim that P is not justified after all.

I shall canvass reasons for thinking that it is seriously unclear whether, with or without a realist background, the fifth feature – *Defeasibility* – can be made to harmonize either with the first – *the Knowledge Feature* – or with the second – *the Meaning Feature*. But criteria would not be interestingly different from (public) truth-conditions if defeasibility was waived; and jettison of the Meaning Feature would threaten the Knowledge Feature as well. While to forgo the Knowledge Feature would be to deprive the notion of what most advocates have seen as its principal point.

I
The Knowledge Feature, Defeasibility and Scepticism

It will be useful to consider what response a proponent of criteria ought to make to the following simple objection.[4] 'If I claim to know P, I will be understood to be claiming that my belief that P is guaranteed correct; so I must have a *conclusive* basis for that belief if my claim is to be true. But knowledge that criteria for P are satisfied is to be consistent' – by Defeasibility – 'with my obtaining further information as a result of which I no longer have a basis for the belief that P at all. Information that is genuinely conclusive for a certain belief, however, cannot lose that status as a result of being *added to*; so knowledge that criteria for P are satisfied cannot ever amount to knowledge that P – the two states have different essential characteristics.'

The technically correct response is that this misunderstands the sense in which recognition of the satisfaction of criteria is supposed to confer knowledge. To be sure, knowledge that criteria for P are satisfied will not, even in the most favourable circumstances, *constitute* knowledge that P is true. The point is rather that while recognition of the satisfaction of criteria for P will, other things being equal, *entitle one to claim* knowledge that P, this claim, like the assertion of P itself, may have to be withdrawn if certain sorts of development take place. It is, in other words, analytic of the concept of knowledge that whenever one is entitled to make a

4 The objection was put by John McDowell in his 'Anti-Realism, Truth-Value Links, and Other Minds'. Cf. McFee, 'On the Interpretation of Wittgenstein', p. 596. The initial development of the objection below owes a lot to the first section of McDowell's 'Criteria, Defeasibility and Knowledge'.

particular assertion on the basis of satisfaction of criteria for it, one is *eo ipso* entitled to make the corresponding knowledge-claim on the same basis. In this way the concepts of knowledge and of criterion are interlinked, and there can be no coherent sceptical doubt about our entitlement to advance knowledge-claims when appropriate criteria are satisfied. Our entitlement is simply a consequence of the content of those claims; the would-be sceptic is merely 'objecting to a convention'.[5]

No one ought to want to complain that this response leaves it unclear how the claim to know that P can differ in content from the claim that P. Their behaviour when embedded in more complex contexts is obviously quite different; for example, the circumstances that justify my denial that I know P need not, obviously, justify a denial of P. In any case, there is no suggestion that *every* type of ground for asserting P is to be a ground for claiming to know P, but only that the criteria for P are criteria for the knowledge-claim as well. But what the response *does* leave unclear is in what precise way the content of the two claims is supposed to differ; that is, in effect, what *knowledge* is being taken to be. If recognition that criteria for P are satisfied can justify a knowledge-claim that P without *constituting* knowledge that P, what *would* constitute it?

The question poses a prima facie awkward dilemma for a believer in the anti-sceptical powers of criteria. Suppose a subject does indeed know that P. Either the facts that constitute the truth of his claim lie within cognitive reach, so to speak, of the subject at the time he makes a justified claim to know that P – justified by his recognition of satisfaction of the appropriate criteria – or they do not. But neither alternative seems satisfactory. If the first is chosen, it immediately becomes unclear *why* criteria for P are treated as criteria for the claim to know that P as well: what is the point of this 'convention' when – provided the subject does indeed know that P – a further investigation will disclose a state of affairs which *constitutes* the fact? And how, in any case, can the first alternative cope with what seems certain to be a feature of any concrete example, viz., that the claim that P, and hence the claim to know that P, will always be open to 'defeat' by information not yet available? (It is intuitively evident, for example, that information serving to defeat the status of certain behaviour as a ground for the claim that another is in pain could emerge at any time after the behaviour episode.)

If, on the other hand, the state of affairs constituting the truth of the knowledge-claim lies beyond the cognitive reach of the subject at the stage when he, recognizing satisfaction of the appropriate criteria, advances the claim, then surely a gap now opens on which the sceptic can pounce. For

5 Cf. *Brown Book*, p. 57.

now it will be all the same to the subject at that stage whether the truth is that he knows that P or that he does not: his very best safeguards leave it open whether the knowledge-claim that they justify is actually true. The consequent sceptical query is this: how can our adoption of a *convention* that realization of one state of affairs, viz., satisfaction of criteria for the knowledge claim, provides a reason for claiming the existence of another, quite distinct, state of affairs, viz., that in which the truth of the knowledge-claim consists, be *reasonable*? There are, trivially, plenty of cases in which such a convention would be foolish. People might have the convention that snowdrops by the end of January justify the claim that March will be dry; but such a convention would hardly be distinguishable from a superstition, and open to objection in exactly the same way. So how is the needed distinction to be drawn? An inductive, or significant statistical correlation between the occurrence of instances of the two types of state of affairs might serve to repel the charge of superstition, but once the proponent of criteria has allowed things to go so far that *that* sort of answer seems appropriate, he will have to respond to the sort of sceptic – the sceptic about induction – whose stock-in-trade it is precisely to query that sort of answer. And no sort of deployment of the notion of criterion is going to help; on the contrary, the response is owed in order to prop the notion up.

The root of the problem on both horns is, obviously, the logical distinctness – the fact that either may be realized without the other – of the states of affairs respectively constituting satisfaction of the criteria for, and the truth of, the relevant knowledge-claim. To repeat, if the truth-conferring state of affairs is accessible independently to the claimant, why settle for recognition that the criteria are satisfied? And if it is inaccessible to him, how can it be a priori reasonable to rely on satisfaction of criteria as an indication of its existence? So the troublesome logical distinctness will have to be prevented. But how? For, to stress, recognition of satisfaction of criteria for P cannot, consistently with their defeasibility, be held to constitute knowledge that P without contravention of the truism that knowledge entails the truth of what is known.

A possible thought is that really there *is* no such truism; that belief in the truism only arises because of a mistaken interpretation of what seems to be its contrapositive. Undoubtedly it is a feature of the concept of knowledge that the claim to know P must be withdrawn if the balance of evidence turns against P. But other explanations of this fact are possible besides appeal to the alleged truism. It would, say, equally be explicable if knowledge-claims had an appropriate token-reflexivity. Suppose, for instance, that what constitutes the truth of a knowledge-claim that P is some feature of the state of information of the claimant at the time of the claim: then subsequent information telling, on balance, against P may be inconsistent with possession of that feature by the *later* state of information, so may require denial of the form of words formerly asserted. But the original knowledge-claim may no more be contradicted than would yesterday's claim, 'It is raining', by today's assertion of 'It is not raining'.

Accordingly, a proponent of criteria might seek to identify the content of the claim to know P with, e.g. that of the claim that one's present state of information includes awareness of satisfaction of criteria for P and of no consideration defeating the warrant for P which that supplies. Such a proposal slips past the dilemma. But, leaving on one side its handling of the disputed truism, it is surely false to the intuitive concept of knowledge in another important respect. A rational, perfectly recollective being could never *lose* any item of knowledge, as we ordinarily conceive it; whatever he came to know he would always know. This is why one cannot unparadoxically advance a claim of the form that one formerly knew some statement to be true which one knows no longer: any adequate grounds for the first part of the claim would be treated as adequate for the claim to know the statement at the present time. In terms of the proposal, however, there is nothing paradoxical about such a claim; the situation will be merely that one's previous state of information criterially supported the claim that P whereas one's present, enlarged state of information does not.

That the proposal is revisionary is of no great importance unless there are independent grounds for thinking that the changes it enjoins are worth avoiding. But it wants, to say the least, a deal of explaining how the promise to save the possibility of knowledge from the depredations of the sceptic can be redeemed by a *revisionary* proposal. For the sceptic precisely contests our entitlement to knowledge-claims if knowledge is to be a *stable, truth-entailing* state. The proposal, in effect, gives the sceptic the point and recommends that we work with a more modest concept. Those who have seen the notion of a criterion as epistemologically important surely did not mean that its role would be, in this way, one of retrenchment.

The reader may for some time have been anxious to urge the following thought. The foregoing difficulties arise only because, granting that to recognize satisfaction of criteria for P may warrant a defeasible knowledge-claim that P, we have continued to press for a further account of the *truth-conditions* of the latter claim. But if a criterial semantics is, as some proponents of criteria have suggested, something aimed to replace the classical truth-conditional line of goods, such a demand will be illegitimate. There will be *nothing* in which knowledge consists, if that requires the possibility of an explanation of the truth-conditions of knowledge-claims. Rather the content of such claims, as of any statements (except effectively decidable ones), will be given by explaining the criteria for making them and the conditions under which those criteria should be considered defeated and the statements withdrawn.

This can seem like a smart reply; and it is, in any case, inevitable for a theorist who has it in view that the meaning of all statements (save possibly the members of a base class of effectively decidable ones) is to be conceived as understood by reference to criteria. What is harder to see is that the sceptic is really in any way disarmed by the move. To appreciate the remaining difficulties, reflect on the simplest form of the problem of induction. Thus simply formulated, the problem is that of justifying belief in an unrestricted generalization that might yet be falsified by unobserved cases. What is striking is that there is no need to appeal to the notion of the *truth* of such a generalization in order to present the problem. Let us take it, simplistically no doubt, that such a generalization is assertible if an appropriate variety of cases has been examined and only positive instances have been encountered; and that it is deniable if one has reason to think that there is at least one negative instance. Now, if those conditions are regarded as fixing the meaning of such generalizations, it is apt to seem that there can be no coherent sceptical query whether such a statement *ought* to be asserted in the appropriate circumstances; and the same holds for the claim to know the generalization if it is held that the identical evidence criterially warrants its assertion as well.[6] But the sceptic is not to be shaken off so easily. For the fact is that we do not responsibly make such assertions with an open mind about subsequent defeat. If I assert such a generalization, believing myself fully justified, I will have determinate expectations about the way that future evidence-gathering will, or would, turn out. I shall be, and consider myself entitled to be, *surprised* if negative instances come to light. In this respect assertion is quite unlike the making of moves in, e.g., chess. I may, perfectly justifiably, advance a Bishop, say, although fully expecting a situation to arise in which it will be necessary to retreat again. But I cannot *justifiably* assert an unrestricted generalization, or indeed any statement, if I fully expect my present warrant to assert it to be overturned by subsequent developments – *or even merely consider that I am in no position to have a view on the likelihood of that eventuality.*

The classic form of the problem of induction trades, no doubt, on a distinction between the correct assertibility of H in a particular state of information and the truth of H; where the latter is taken to entail its correct assertibility in any state of information that can in principle be arrived at by enrichment of the original. Clearly *that* form of the problem cannot survive a successful attempt to describe the meaning of H without reference to any truth-conditions, properly so conceived. But, equally, some version of the problem is liable to survive so long as *any* notion of the correctness

6 This is something that formerly struck me as obvious; see p. 360 in Essay 12.

of H is in play distinct from its correct assertibility in an actual state of information. And such a distinction would appear to be implicit in the very notion of justified assertion. If the achievement of a total state of information in which the assertion of H is warranted is taken to entitle one to the expectation that subsequent states of information will *not* be of certain sorts, there cannot be any cogent objection to the introduction of a sense of *incorrectness* to go along with disappointment in that expectation. And the sceptic's question will then be, for instance: why does the warranted assertibility of H in our present state of information provide a reason for thinking that our state of information next Tuesday, say, will not show that our earlier assertion was, in just that sense, incorrect? And he can't be answered, of course, by insisting that it is merely part of the *content* of H that that is so, that to have reason for believing H *is* to have reason for believing in the H-favourable character of subsequent states of information. Such a response merely invites him to re-present his question as: how is it *reasonable* to associate a statement possessing those (ambitious) consequences with assertion-conditions of the relevant sort?

The example of induction, it will be seen, is merely one illustration of a form of sceptical difficulty that must remain even after the adoption of a thorough-going anti-realist semantics based upon criteria. The content of a claim cannot be *exhausted* by the statement that a criterial basis for its assertion exists. The best reason for saying so is not that it is otherwise inexplicable why it is *that* claim that has to be withdrawn if subsequent states of information are unfavourable – (various skirmishes to do with token-reflexivity would have to be fought through before that could be seen as a conclusive reason for the point). Rather, it is part of considering oneself fully justified in making a particular assertion – any assertion – that one anticipates that the sorts of development that would defeat that justification will not take place. To suppose that one had full reason for the assertion, yet no reason to discount such developments, would just be to pre-empt the ongoing practical consequences of the assertion; subsequently, it would be all the same whether the assertion had previously been justified or not. But it is of the essence of asserting that one seeks to transfer information which can be *acted on*. Hence if, for example, certain sorts of behaviour are taken to justify, defeasibly and as a matter of convention, certain sorts of ascription of mental states to others, that cannot squeeze out all scope for scepticism about statements concerning other minds. Certainly, the character of the sceptical problem changes. There is no longer a problem of explaining how it can be reasonable to take what is 'outer' as evidence for what is 'inner'; (no problem conceived as it has to be conceived in order to make argument from analogy a relevant, if very weak, response). The problem is rather to explain how it can be reasonable to suppose that a feature of one's present state of information – that it includes awareness of satisfaction of behavioural criteria for the claim that Jones is in pain and of no defeating circumstances – is going to survive into one's later states of information. Even now the temptation may remain to protest that it is precisely for the reasonableness of that supposition that the criteria are satisfied. But that is only bluster. The plain fact is that there is an inference from present to future – one among a range of alternative possible inferences, whose selection, the sceptic will insist, is therefore in need of defence.

The focus of the earlier part of this section was on the still popular claim that criteria provide a new and powerful weapon for the defence of knowledge-claims againt the sceptic. The truth is, however, that knowledge is something of a red herring in discussions of scepticism! It would not be too disturbing to have to cede the possibility of knowledge if we could at least defend the possibility of *reasonable belief* against sceptical assault. 'Perhaps we do not, strictly speaking, ever *know* what another is feeling or thinking, what the sun will do tomorrow, etc. ...but can merely have (highly) reasonable opinions on such matters.'[7] However, the nastiest forms of traditional scepticism call into question not merely our title to knowledge-claims of problematic subject matters but our right to any rationally supported opinions at all in those areas. These forms demand some sort of critical response; retrenchment is not an option. What (I am suggesting) must be recognized is that one such form of scepticism is endemic in the very practice of assertion: specifically, in the *consequential* character of assertion, whereby the justifiability of an assertion in a particular state of information is *eo ipso* taken to license expectations about the character, in relevant respects, of subsequent states of information. This guarantees a sceptically exploitable gulf whenever what is asserted does not admit of conclusive verification. And it is, to emphasize, an essential feature of asserting: it is impossible to see what it would be to put to practical use the 'assertions' of others if the convention was that no such expectations were licensed. So it is a feature that will be preserved by any worthwhile theory of meaning, including, if such a thing is possible, a criterial theory.

It is thus quite unclear how the promise of the Knowledge Feature can be fulfilled. On any account, the claim (to know) that Jones is in pain will be defeated by appropriately disconfirming, or equivocal, subsequent behaviour from Jones. It is part of being justified in making that claim about Jones that one also be justified in the belief that that possibility will not be realized. That the relationship between Jones's *present* behaviour and the justifiability of the claim, 'Jones is in pain' is one of convention

7 As Russell used to like to suppose.

cannot, from the sceptical viewpoint, make the possibility any more remote. No doubt there are indeed things seriously amiss with the sceptical viewpoint. But if what I have said is right, it is doubtful whether the proponent of criteria occupies a position in any way advantageous for their disclosure.

II
Defeasibility and the Meaning Feature

In the essay, I argued that an approach to meaning that sees conditions of warranted assertion rather than truth-conditions as central would be bound to find work for something 'interestingly akin to' Wittgenstein's notion of a criterion (as orthodoxy interprets it). The argument was, specifically, that at least some types of assertion-conditions for certain sorts of statements would have to be regarded both as having that status a priori and as defeasible. And it was suggested accordingly that difficulty in disclosing criteria for statements of the appropriate sort – in particular, statements about the past – would have to be regarded as calling into question the feasibility of a 'global' assertion-conditions conception of statement meaning. The doubt with which we are now concerned, however, is not whether criterial assertion-conditions can be found in *every* case where – according to this type of anti-realist conception of meaning – they ought to exist, but whether they *ever* can: whether the Meaning Feature and Defeasibility can be coherently combined at all. (If the doubt is sustained, it must, of course, if the argument of the essay was correct, immediately be put in question whether the meaning of statements can in general correctly be conceived as determined by conditions of warranted assertion.)

Let me recapitulate the essentials of that argument. The reason for thinking that the assertion-conditions theorist must, if he is to account for our understanding of enough of the statements which we want to regard as intelligible, regard some of them as associated with nothing but defeasible assertion-conditions, is straightforward enough. The most one can ask, if someone is to *show* that he understands a particular statement, is that he displays, as conclusively as merely finite samples of his behaviour can display, a practical grasp of the distinction between states of affairs that may reasonably be taken to warrant its assertion and states of affairs that may not. (Giving satisfactory verbal explanations of the content of a statement, and showing that he understands something of its deductive ancestry and offspring, supply grounds for attributing understanding only in so far as they are reliable indicators that someone possesses this type of practical grasp; and they are defeasible by behaviour that suggests that he does not.) The anti-realist, as is familiar, is impressed by the thought that a description of what understanding essentially *is* ought as little as possible to go beyond what someone is able to do who can supply the most one can reasonably demand by way of evidence for his understanding: there is to be in the notion of understanding as little theoretical residue as possible in excess of what is necessary for description of the essential skills of a language-master. But the classical truth-conditional conception of meaning breaks faith with this thought wherever it construes the kind of state of affairs that would render a particular statement true as something that can impinge only indirectly, or in part, on the faculties of one who understands the statement. Putative truth-conferring states of affairs which, for a particular agent, lie too far in the past for non-inferential recollection, or which lie in the remote future, or are spatially too distant from him to be visited, or are somehow infinite in extent, or are conceived to lie within the 'inaccessible confines of another's consciousness', can be the kind of states of affairs by reference to which his understanding of statements can be tested; testing must rather proceed by reference to conditions that we, the testers, can monitor and of whose obtaining our subject can be presumed to be perceptually aware. For any class of statements whose intelligibility he wishes to save the anti-realist has therefore no choices save *either* to describe truth-conditions for them of this 'unproblematic', accessible sort, *or* to deny that any of their assertion-conditions amount to truth-conditions.

The first response is, in effect, that of the mathematical intuitionist: proof, for the intuitionist, is to be seen as what *constitutes* truth in pure mathematics. But with most of the relevant sorts of contingent statements, the sort of reductionism involved – of the past and future to the present, of the mental to the behavioural and/or physical, of the spatio-temporally infinite to the finite – would be bound, it seems, massively to misdescribe our ordinary conception of their meaning. And that sits ill alongside the anti-realist's motivation to describe more accurately than the realist in what an understanding of these statements consists. So for these statements he is well advised to prefer the second response: their meaning will be explained by reference to conditions of warranted assertion whose obtaining is not sufficient for their truth.

That does not immediately entail that such conditions will provide at most defeasible grounds for the assertion of such statements. From a realist point of view there would be no absurdity in the idea, for some particular statement, that although our best evidence could not be conclusive for its truth, we could never amass additional, overriding evidence suggesting either that it was false, or at least that its truth should not be assumed. (An example of that sort of situation might be a scientific hypothesis which, although indirectly corroborated as part of a successful theory, could not be *specifically* tested because the laboratory conditions required to do so would require the acceleration of particles up to the speed of light.) But from an anti-realist point of view, the circumstance that standard assertion-conditions for a statement were not sufficient for its truth would have to be manifestable in the *use* of the statement; and the only way, it seems, in which that could be manifest is if the obtaining of those conditions were, under certain further circumstances, acknowledged as insufficient for the correct assertibility of the statement. Hence whenever the anti-realist takes the second option, his assertion-conditions will be, in just the sense that has informed our discussion so far, defeasible.

The reason for thinking that, for the assertion-conditions theorist, every contingent statement must be associated a priori with at least some of its assertion-conditions is probably best presented by Reductio. Let P be a contingent statement of definite content for which that is not the case; that is, for which it will betray no misunderstanding to demand, for *any* state of affairs presented – descriptively or ostensively – as warranting the assertion of P, *empirical* grounds for thinking that it does so. And let it be the case that P is indeed warrantedly assertible in certain actual circumstances, ϕ. How is the fact to be recognized? Only two forms of case seem possible. First, we may already possess empirical grounds for regarding the occurrence of ϕ-circumstances as a good indication of the occurrence of certain circumstances of *another* sort which we already have independent reason to regard as warranting the assertion of P. But plainly this model cannot be *generally* applicable, on pain of infinite regress. Second, ϕ-circumstances in general, or at any rate these ones, may have been noted to satisfy some condition F, which we again have an independent empirical reason to suppose characteristic of circumstances that justify the assertion of P. But since this is an *empirical* reason, it must consist, it would seem, *either* in grounds for regarding F-circumstances as symptomatic for the existence of another sort of circumstance already justifiably regarded as warranting the assertion of P – in which case we revert to the first model; *or* in grounds for regarding F as tending to be coinstantiated with some yet further condition, whose instances we already have reason to regard as justifying the assertion of P – which again, on pain of infinite regress, cannot *always* be the story. Either way, then, no *finite* model is to be had of how the warranted assertibility of P in ϕ-circumstances is to be apprehended. So it cannot be apprehended. Hence, generalizing on ϕ, we are not going to be able to make *any* application of the distinction between correct and incorrect assertion of P. So no one will be able to manifest an understanding of P in the sort of way the assertion-conditions theorist demands; wherefore P cannot rank, on his view, as a statement of definite content, contrary to hypothesis.

All this argument does is to elaborate somewhat, for the special case of statements and the assertion-conditions conception of their meaning, what follows from denying the plausible thought that, in order for an expression to have a determinate meaning at all, it must at some level be a matter of *convention* what its correct use consists in: that any significant empirical investigation into whether it is correctly used in a particular case presupposes such a convention.[8] The realist need not, of course, be hostile to that thought; but for him the relevant convention(s) for P will concern which states of affairs confer *truth* on P. It is therefore worth briefly pausing to inquire what the realist response should be to the argument sketched. Plainly he is at liberty simply to accept the argument if P happens to be *verifiable*; that is, is associated with truth-conditions whose realization we can recognize as such. But our interest is in the contrasting sort of case where the anti-realist finds the truth-conditional account problematic. If P is verification-transcendent, how should the realist view the status of the circumstances which we should reckon to warrant its assertion? If he accepts the argument, he will allow that certain of these circumstances have that status by convention. But what, in that case, is the function of the putative *further* conventional association with an (unrecognizable) truth-condition? What aspect of the use of P is the further convention needed to explain?[9] To reject the conclusion, on the other hand, that certain of the assertion-conditions of P have that status a priori, is just to accept that P fits the premise for the Reductio. So how, in that case, does the realist block the argument? Well, since for him the only conventions in the offing concern the assignment of verification-transcendent truth-conditions to P, he needs to show how these conventions render navigable either of the two sketched routes towards recognition that ϕ-circumstances warrant the assertion of P. So *either* he must explain how we could arrive at empirical grounds for supposing ϕ-circumstances – or any ascertainable circumstances – to be an indicator of a verification-transcendent state of affairs; *or* he must explain how we might gather empirical reason for supposing that circumstances satisfying F – or some other decidable condition – warrant a verification-transcendent claim. Either way, the evident problem is to make out how *experience* can teach us that the occurrence of certain factors within our experience reliably indicates the character of states of affairs beyond it.

Assuming its soundness, then, the argument does more than disclose a commitment to criteria on the part of the assertion-conditions theorist. In addition it brings into relief a dilemma for the realist. To recapitulate: what, in his view, is to be the relation between the assertion-conditions of verification-transcendent P and the truth-conditions he regards as

8 Cf. Essay 12, pp. 364–6, 368.

9 Essay 3, pp. 93–4, seems to me now somewhat over-sanguine about the availability of criteria to realism.

determining its content? If the former are regarded as merely contingent symptoms of the latter, the realist can expect to encounter grave difficulties when he comes to try to explain how we are to gather evidence that such indeed is the relationship in a particular case. But if certain of the assertion-conditions are regarded as having their status by convention, it is a very nice question why truth-conditions have any genuine semantic role to play at all. (And it is, independently, quite unclear with what right we could regard the occurrence of one type of state of affairs as a *conventional* indication of the occurrence of another, logically independent kind.)

So much, then, for rehearsal of the reasons why the assertion-conditions theorist has work for defeasible but conventional assertion-conditions, conditions apparently exemplifying the fifth and second features in our original list. What is the problem in combining these features supposed to be? The crucial consideration is again the *consequential* character of assertion, stressed above. When someone asserts P, even on grounds which are admitted to be inconclusive, he sets himself against the subsequent defeat of those grounds. In particular, the discovery of information, additional to his original grounds, which requires withdrawal, or even denial, of his original assertion must be a possibility which recipients of that assertion are, for practical purposes, intended to be entitled to ignore. Nevertheless, defeat always *is* a possibility where criteria are concerned. And it will be in the lap of the gods both whether it occurs in any particular case, and *how often* it happens that a particular type of criterial ground for P is subsequently overturned. It is to be expected, no doubt – if only for 'evolutionary' reasons – that we will in general have selected criteria so as to minimize the frequency of defeat. But that is not to say that it is certain that we have been successful in any particular case, or that success will last. So, in the absence of argument to the contrary for particular cases, it has to be a possibility that a type of criterion for a particular assertion be defeated often enough to shake our confidence in the propriety of that assertion when made solely on that ground. It would appear to follow that no type of ground, even one conventionally associated with P, can be *necessarily* 'good evidence' for P if it is regarded as a defeasible ground: for if it is defeasible, it may be defeated; and defeated, moreover, so frequently that, bearing in mind the consequential character of any assertion of P, one would rightly become reluctant to assert P on its basis.

This simple point is worth relating to two formulations suggested in Essay 12. The first, taking the criterial relation as obtaining between statements, was the following *Criterial Schema*:

> If an agent has verified each of $\{D_1,...,D_n\}$, *and* possesses no reason to doubt P and no information which would explain, without the need to suppose P, why $\{D_1,...,D_n\}$, are true, then it is reasonable for him to believe P.[10]

Here it is to be understood that $\{D_1,...,D_n\}$ are to be decidable statements – (whatever that means) – and P a verification-transcendent statement. Thus knowledge of the truth of $\{D_1,...,D_n\}$ will be at best an inconclusive ground for P. It is also to be the case that each of $\{D_1,...,D_n\}$ is *P-predicative*: that is, is a statement understanding which does not presuppose an understanding of P. (The intended effect of this restriction was to ensure that $\{D_1,...,D_n\}$ should not entail that it is reasonable to believe P *independently* of the provisos that the agent possesses no information telling against P and no information which would explain, without the need to suppose P, why those statements are true.)

Now, the thought was that $\{D_1,...,D_n\}$ will collectively constitute a criterion for a particular P just in case their introduction, with P, into the Schema results in a non-contingent truth. The fact is, however, that it is actually quite unclear whether that can ever be so. For, if upon nothing else, the truth of such an instance of the Schema has to be contingent at least upon the frequency with which verification of $\{D_1,...,D_n\}$ is subsequently associated with the development of considerations that overturn their evidential status. Any alleged example of the criterial relation is going to be controversial, but, to make the point vivid, let $\{D_1,...,D_n\}$ be as meticulous a description as you like of Jones's very typical behaviour and appearance as he sits miserably in the dentist's waiting room awaiting treatment for a (claimed) badly infected molar; and let P be 'Jones has toothache'. Then it is plausible that the Schema is at least true: that is, that someone who knows of the truth of the appropriate $\{D_1,...,D_n\}$ and has no reason to doubt that Jones has toothache, nor any better explanation of the facts recorded by $\{D_1,...,D_n\}$ than to suppose that Jones has toothache, is indeed in position reasonably to believe that Jones has toothache. But it is also plausible to suppose that it is contingent that this is so: that developments could have taken place as a result of which

10 Essay 12, p. 363. The original formulation was actually: '... and possesses no information telling against P and no information which would explain, without the need...'. The present reformulation is intended to resolve an ambiguity in 'no information telling against P'; viz., that between 'no reason to doubt P', i.e. no reason to believe not P, and 'no reason not to believe P', i.e. no reason *either* to doubt P *or*, more weakly, to suspend belief in P.

It may seem that the original Schema would not be vulnerable to the difficulty about to be adumbrated in the text (see also note 11), if the ambiguity were to be resolved in favour of the second, weaker interpretation instead. And that is so. For what threatens to be, however, as it seems to me, a decisive objection to the Schema under the weaker interpretation, keep reading.

$\{D_1,\ldots,D_n\}$ would not have had this power, even though both provisos – that the agent had no reason to doubt that Jones had toothache, nor a better explanation of his behaviour than to suppose that he did – were met. For it might have been, e.g., that – in order to avoid compulsory games, or whatever – there had been a very great deal of toothache simulation going on; but only sufficient to give cause for diffidence in drawing any firm conclusion about Jones – so, consistently with the provisos, not enough to provide a reason for doubting the veracity of his behaviour, or for accepting some alternative explanation of it.

There is, to be sure, scope for debate about whether toothache is a plausible candidate for possession of behavioural criteria. But it should be obvious that the point depends only upon the *structure* assigned by orthodoxy to the notion. If criterial grounds are always to be defeasible, then they must, if the world turns out sufficiently awkward, be defeasible in whole classes. The point is merely a consequence of the logical independence of the conditions for satisfaction and defeat respectively of a given (type of) criterion: if things can go badly at all, they can go badly often enough to put the utility of the very practice (of asserting P on the basis of that criterion) in doubt – which need not be to say, however, that P itself now becomes doubtful when that discredited (type of) criterion is satisfied.[11]

The second proposal, conceived for a view of the criterial relation which holds that its domain comprises not statements but worldly states of affairs, was this:

The occurrence of a particular (probably ostensively explained) type of state of affairs provides *conventional support* for a particular statement, P, if and only if it would standardly be considered acceptable in certain circumstances to assert P on the basis of knowledge of such a state of affairs; and we would not require, in order for someone to be credited with a full understanding both of P and of the type of state of affairs in point, that he knows what it would be *empirically* to investigate whether occurrences of that type of state of affairs really did provide, other

11 To amplify a little: it may not seem evident that the provisos really are met in the toothache case. Would not knowledge of all that attempted deceit have to provide *some* reason for doubting Jones? Perhaps; but if so, the fault lies with a rather weak example. For it is quite clear, in the abstract, that considerations serving to discredit a particular type of ground for an assertion do not *have* to take the form of reasons to doubt that assertion or to propose alternative explanations of the obtaining of the ground: it may just turn out that the ground is *unreliable* – and that it has proved so need provide no reason for *any* view about the status of the assertion this time, or about the correct explanation of this instance of the ground. Most discredited *symptoms* – early holly berries as a sign of a hard winter, premature baldness as a sign of virility, etc., etc. – are in this situation. The heart of the present difficulty for the Schema is that criteria for P must also, it appears, be liable to just this form of discredit as indicators of P's continuing assertibility.

things being equal, a reason for believing P and to find that they did not.[12]

The criteria for P, so conceived, will be states of affairs whose occurrence provides conventional support for P in this sense. (And the 'other things being equal' should be amplified in a manner appropriately corresponding to the provisos of the earlier Schema.) Again, though, it would seem that an empty notion has been characterized if criteria, so conceived, are to be defeasible. For anyone who understands both that a certain type of (ostensively characterizable) state of affairs conventionally supports P and that this support is defeasible by developments which, again, he understands and can recognize if they occur, *must* understand how experience could lead one to the conclusion that occurrences of that type of state of affairs did not, after all, provide an adequate reason for believing P, or asserting it. The possibility involved is, once again, just that of the world turning awkward, of too frequent accompaniment of states of affairs of the appropriate kind by subsequent defeating developments.

How should a proponent of criteria respond to these thoughts? A first response would quarrel with the supposition that, because it is possible for criterial support to be defeated in any particular case, it is possible for this to happen often enough to undermine confidence in the basis which the particular type of criterion supplies for the relevant sort of statement. The idea occurs frequently in discussions of scepticism. Concepts like pretence, or illusion, are themselves rooted, it is suggested, in behavioural, or perceptual, evidence. To suppose such phenomena sufficiently widespread is, in consequence, inevitably to weaken, or even to sever completely, those roots; and so to undermine the content of those very suppositions. The suggestion would be, accordingly, that when we get down to cases, the idea that a particular type of criterion for P might, if the world proved awkward, be defeated sufficiently frequently to make us hesitate to rely on it, would prove self-destructive in the same sort of way.

But this is surely a false hope. Matters might be different if defeat of a criterion for P had to take the form of the accumulation of additional information warranting the *denial* of P: then there might indeed be a tension between the supposition that such defeats might be common and the obtaining of conditions necessary for P to possess a sufficiently definite content to render such denials *intelligible*. But defeat of a criterion does not require that; it requires only development of a state of information in which the assertion of P should not be made, or, if previously made, should be withdrawn. So there is no prospect of a successful appeal to the conditions of intelligibility of P in order to impose an a priori restriction

12 Essay 12, p. 368.

on the frequency of the occasions in which criteria for P may be overturned: *worldly awkwardness may precisely take the form of an erosion of those conditions*.

A second response would be that nothing more serious is signalled than a need for further complication in the formulation of the notion of criterial support. We need, for example, it might be proposed, a further proviso in the antecedent of the Criterial Schema. Evidently it is necessary to hypothesize that the agent has no reason to think that the type of ground which $\{D_1,...,D_n\}$ affords for statements of the type of P has been so often defeated as to inhibit reasonable belief in P on the basis of $\{D_1,...,D_n\}$. On reflection, indeed, more is wanted: it is necessary to hypothesize that the agent should have no reason for remaining *agnostic* – keeping a perfectly open mind – about the likelihood of developments which defeat the support afforded by $\{D_1,...,D_n\}$ for P. No weaker proviso, it appears, will do. I may, for example, have verified an appropriate $\{D_1,...,D_n\}$ in the case of Jones's putative toothache, have no reason to doubt that Jones has a toothache, and be in possession of no information which I can use to explain Jones's behaviour without involving the supposition that he has a toothache and yet *still* have no reason to believe in his toothache *if* I am in possession of any sort of information whose effect is that it is reasonable to keep an open mind about the likelihood of developments which would subsequently force me to withdraw the assertion 'Jones has toothache' if I were to make it now. Such information would not have to concern a spate of unreliable toothache behaviour. I might merely have some special information about Jones which cautions circumspection, without giving me reason to doubt that he has toothache or to explain his behaviour in some independent way. So something like the following modified Schema would seem to be suggested:

If an agent

- i has verified $\{D_1,...,D_n\}$, and
- ii has no reason to doubt P, and
- iii is in possession of no information which would explain, without the need to suppose P, why $\{D_1,...,D_n\}$ are true, and
- iv has no reason for expecting, or even for retaining an open mind about the likelihood of, subsequent informational states which would force withdrawal of the assertion of P if he were now to make it,

then it is reasonable for him to believe P.

It is, however, unclear whether the Schema, so emended, can be satisfactory. The intended point is to capture, for a given verification-transcendent P, a threefold distinction among the possible substitutions for $\{D_1,...,D_n\}$: substitutions that would generate a non-contingent truth, substitutions which would generate a contingent truth, and substitutions that fail to satisfy the Schema. Otherwise we cannot effect the aimed-for distinction between information that criterially supports P, information that contingently (symptomatically) supports P, and information that has no bearing on the issue. In the presence of the new proviso, however, it now becomes unclear whether we can contrive any substitutions for $\{D_1,\ldots,D_n\}$ that will *fail* to satisfy the Schema. Suppose, as (iv) requires, that I have now, at *t*, no reason for expecting, or even for keeping an open mind about the likelihood of (*agnosticism* about), subsequent informational developments which would require me to withdraw a claim that P made at *t*. Suppose, too, that I have every reason to expect a lengthy, healthy, normally progressive cognitive future. Now clearly, if I subsequently arrive at a total state of information which, on balance, fails to justify the belief that P, I *will* then be in a position where I ought to withdraw any former claim that P. Accordingly, letting Q = 'some of my future total states of information will, on balance, fail to justify the belief that P', the suppositions entail:

1 I have at *t* no reason to believe Q.
2 I have at *t* no reason to be agnostic about Q.
3 I have at *t* every reason to expect to enjoy a lengthy series of, by and large, increasingly superior total states of information.

It is plausible, however, that, for any statement R of determinate content, reflection on my present total state of information must *either* provide reason to believe R, *or* provide reason to doubt R (= believe its negation), or – because my information is irrelevant, or equivocal – provide reason for agnosticism about R. Hence, given (1) and (2),

4 I have at *t* reason to believe the negation of Q = 'all my future total states of information will, on balance, not fail to justify the belief that P'.

In the presence of (3), and given that the relevant double negation elimination is unexceptionable, this is tantamount to

5 I have reason at *t* to anticipate enjoyment of a lengthy, largely progressive series of total states of information all of which will, on balance, justify the belief that P.

And if that is not for it to be reasonable for me to believe P *now*, at *t*, *why* is it not?

So (iv) threatens to guarantee the truth of the consequent of the Schema on its own; with the result that the Schema would fail to impose any interesting condition on the relation between $\{D_1,\ldots,D_n\}$ and P. I shall not here attempt the detailed consideration of the situation necessary to make it clear whether the difficulty is not merely one of formulation. What should be clear, at least, is that there *is* a difficulty. The proponent of criteria has to construct the Schema, or an analogue for ostensively given states of affairs, in such a way that (i) is supplemented with other provisos so that the three appropriate types of substitutions for $\{D_1,\ldots,D_n\}$ are possible for suitable cases of P. Clearly, then, the supplementary provisos must not, singly or in combination, guarantee the truth of the consequent; if they do, the Schema will have *only* non-contingent instances. Equally, however, satisfaction of all the provisos at *t* must not always be consistent with the agent's simultaneous possession of reason to expect, or at least to keep an open mind about the likelihood of, his subsequent informational states being such as to force withdrawal of an assertion of P made at *t*. Otherwise the Schema will have *no* non-contingent instances. The difficulty is that if we try to meet the second condition in the most natural and immediate way, we seem to spoil our prospects of meeting the first.

We arrive at a position, then, where there seem to be both good grounds for supposing that an assertion-conditions conception of meaning must have recourse to criteria and every possibility that the notion, standardly interpreted, is empty. If, as was suggested above, realism has no satisfactory response to the argument that seems to foist criteria on the assertion-conditions theorist, we are therefore on the brink of a paradox: neither truth-conditional nor assertion-conditional approaches hold out any prospect of a satisfactory account of the semantics of ordinary statements.

Let me briefly indicate how the paradox may perhaps be forestalled. The trouble, expressed somewhat simplistically, is that it is hard to see how defeasible grounds can be *necessarily* good grounds: there just is a tension, curiously unremarked in the literature, between the second and fifth features. But is it criteria in this sense to which the assertion-conditions theorist is committed (assuming the soundness of the earlier argument)? Certainly the argument commits him to holding that if P has communally acknowledged assertion-conditions at all, then some of them must have that status a priori. But is that the same thing? On reflection, it would seem that it is not. The force of the argument was that empirical support can be forthcoming for the claim that certain conditions justify the assertion of P only if P is associated with other assertion-conditions for which empirical support neither exists nor could intelligibly be sought. That is to say: it will be no part of understanding P to have any conception of how the status of these assertion-conditions might be empirically confirmed. But that claim is not, as the threatened Modus Tollens implicitly presupposes, the same as the claim that there will be no conception of how their status might be empirically *disconfirmed*: on the contrary, the argument has been that their very defeasibility must serve to supply such a conception. And it is the second claim which is needed if criteria are to supply 'necessarily good evidence'.

If the second claim cannot be made good, there is still, therefore, the possibility of a 'thinner' notion of criterion, apt for the needs of the assertion-conditions theorist. So that particular research programme may be able to survive even if criteria, as interpreted by orthodoxy, do not. The thin notion will retain that aspect of the Meaning Feature concerned with 'content fixing' while eschewing the bit about 'necessarily good evidence'. Orthodoxy overlooks that these are distinct.

It is another question whether the thin notion of criterion can assist in the exegesis of Wittgenstein's (steadfastly unselfconscious) employment of 'criterion' and its cognates in the *Investigations*; or whether it can yet have a useful part to play in combatting certain forms of scepticism. What is sure is that those who would have us believe that Wittgenstein discovered in criteria, as standardly interpreted, a tool of the greatest epistemological and semantic importance owe a treatment of the two difficulties with which this paper has been concerned.[13]

13 Some of these negative thoughts were caused by a re-reading of the Postscript to Albritton's 'On Wittgenstein's Use of the Term "Criterion" '. But I hesitate to attribute them to him; and he certainly takes no blame for any faults in my formulation. My thanks, and apologies, are owing to Gordon Baker, Peter Carruthers, Peter Hacker and Graham McFee, who all sent me extensive comments on an earlier draft attempting (unsuccessfully) to persuade me that First Thoughts had been best.

14

Can a Davidsonian Meaning-theory be Construed in Terms of Assertibility?

The question, specifically, is whether the T-predicate figuring in the content-specifying theorems of, say, a homophonic truth-theory for English, will sustain interpretation in terms of anti-realist assertibility rather than realist truth. The immediate obstacle is that if in

'P' is T ≡ A

'A' is, as intended, a correct translation of 'P', interpreting 'is T' as expressing warranted assertibility will put the biconditional in jeopardy in all cases where 'P' has assertibility-conditions falling short of conclusive verification. For then it may happen that the left-hand side (*lhs*) is true in circumstances when the right-hand side (*rhs*) is not. In 'Truth-Conditions and Criteria' it was suggested that the anti-realist could respond by replacing the material biconditional in the T-theorems with a connective of assertibility whose meaning would be characterized e.g. as follows:

BICON: 'C⟷B' is assertible in a state of information, I, just in case I warrants the assertion that any enlargement of it justifying the assertion of 'C' would justify the assertion of 'B', and vice versa.

The effect is that when '≡' is replaced by '⟷' in the general form of T-theorem above, reason to think that 'A' is indeed a correct translation of 'P' is once again reason to accept the biconditional: if you have reason to think that 'P' says that A, an enlarged state of information will put you in position to assert that A if and only if it puts you in position to claim that 'P' is assertible. Accordingly I canvassed the possibility that the assertibility theorist '... may simply take over the legacy of the approach to structural problems which those working within the truth-theoretic framework have bestowed, confident that their results...will survive reinterpretation in his terms'.[1]

It will be a matter of some importance if this should prove to be a mistaken hope. Considerable philosophical difficulties notoriously attend the overall interpretation of recursive truth-theoretic semantics. But the programme which it represents still constitutes the most refined extant response to the challenge of achieving understanding of what is often called (not entirely happily) our linguistic *creativity*: our ability to formulate and understand sentences which we have not previously encountered. If the conception of statement-meaning as determined by assertibility-conditions simply will not marry with the Davidsonian approach, that has to be cause for legitimate concern. Allaying that concern would require either the development of some other kind of recursive approach, based on assertibility, or the production of cogent reason to think that the project of understanding linguistic 'creativity' along such lines is altogether misconceived. At the moment, in my view, we have neither.

My proposal, generalized, was in effect that a truth-theory will sustain interpretation in terms of assertibility provided the proof theory which it utilizes involves only connectives and constants whose semantics are construed along the sort of generalized intuitionistic lines illustrated by BICON. But I have been forced to recognize prima facie serious difficulties with the idea.[2] Below I shall give two examples of the kind of problem which it encounters. We will then be in a position to see what is, I believe, the best form of anti-realist response – which in turn will teach us something about the proper interpretation of the anti-realist objections to realism. Whether the response is ultimately satisfactory is not something which I expect to be able to settle in this essay.

I
Tense

The treatment of tense, and indeed indexicals in general, is, rather surprisingly, one of the less developed facets of the truth-theoreticians' art. Basically, since truth is something which indexical sentences enjoy as a function of their context of utterance – when, where, by whom, to whom, etc. they are uttered – we require more, in particular, of a

1 Essay 1, this volume, pp. 65–6.

2 Largely by Anthony Appiah's work. See his 'Anti-realism Unrealized' and chapter 7 of his *For Truth in Semantics*.

satisfactory semantic theory of tense than merely delivery of theorems of the type

> 'It was raining' is T iff it was raining.

The additional requirement is an account of how the content of an utterance of 'It was raining', e.g., depends upon the context, here only the time, of utterance. It follows that, one way or another, a satisfactory truth-theoretic treatment of tense, even when couched in a metalanguage of which the object-language is a fragment, will have to break the strictly homophonic mould. For we want to characterize not just the conditions under which a contemporary utterance of 'P' is true, but also the conditions under which past and future utterances of tokens of that sentence type were or will be true at specific past or future times; which we manifestly cannot do by (contemporary) *uses* of 'P'.

The choices are two. We can appropriately convert the tense on the *rhs*; for example,

> 'It was raining' was T at t iff at t, it had been raining;
> 'It was raining' will be T at t iff at t, it will have been raining;

and so on. Or we can have recourse to formulations in a tenseless metalanguage; for example,

> 'It was raining' is (tenselessly) T at t iff it is (tenselessly) raining at some (contextually relevant) time prior to t.

The Tarskian tradition makes the latter a more natural approach. We might contrive a recursive definition of *satisfaction-at-a-time* for present-tense sentences in such a way, e.g. that

> *Sats* ('John is bald', S, t) iff at t, [John is bald]

is a theorem. We could then give a recursion for e.g. the past-tense (aorist) transformation of any such present-tense 'P' something like:

> PAST: $(\forall t)$ (*Sats* (*Past* 'P', S, t) iff $(\exists t')$ (Before t', t) & *Sats* ('P', S, t')))

The truth of a sentence at a time would then be identified with its satisfaction at that time by all sequences.[3]

The question is whether the output of such recursions would harmonize with the interpretation of 'T' in terms of assertibility. And the answer, it swiftly appears, is negative. Let t be *now*, and suppose that t' is before t and that, at t', 'John is bald' is T, i.e. is satisfied by all sequences. Then by the recursion, right-to-left, *Past* 'John is bald', (= 'John was bald')

3 Compare Woods, 'Existence and Tense', p. 253.

is satisfied by all sequences, and hence is T, now. So we have established that if, at a past t', 'John is bald' is (tenselessly) T, then 'John was bald' is now T. If we interpret 'T' in terms of assertibility, and construe the conditional in the generalized intuitionistic way suggested in BICON, this result seems evidently unacceptable. It is tantamount to the claim that any enlargement of our state of information which justified the assertion that 'John is bald' was assertible at t' would justify the assertion that 'John was bald' is assertible now. And that need not be so: suppose, for example, we have just learned that at t' John was hiding a full head of hair under an uncannily convincing flesh-tinted skull-cap....

It is important to realize that this sort of problem is independent of the detail of a satisfactory truth-theoretic treatment of tense. For it is reasonable to lay down in advance that any satisfactory treatment ought to sanction the *truth-value links*: the various biconditionals which like

i *Past* 'P' is T iff 'P' was T
ii 'P' is T iff *Past* 'P' will be T
iii *Fut* 'P' is T iff 'P' will be T
iv *Plup* 'P' is T iff *Past* 'P' was T[4]

serve to link the content of appropriately corresponding tensed sentences uttered at different times. There has been some – not enough – discussion of whether, or at what cost, anti-realism can sustain these links – for the issue, as Dummett has urged, is something of a watershed.[5] But it is certain that they cannot all be sustained if the biconditional is interpreted as in BICON and 'T' is interpreted as expressing assertibility at the time, or times, dictated by the tense of the relevant auxiliary verb. Each of (i) to (iv) so read, fails. The skull-cap case brings it out that (i) fails from right-to-left because we may (come to) wish to endorse the case, formally possessed, for making a certain claim without believing that we any longer have such a case; and there is failure also from left-to-right because we may (come to) consider that we have now a case for a certain claim about the past which was previously unavailable. Likewise (ii) fails from right-to-left because we may (come to) know that, in the future, all the evidence will be as if *Past* 'P' is then correct, but, as we know now, deceptively so; and fails from left-to-right because we may (come to) be in position to assert 'P' without being in position to assert that grounds will be available in the future for making the same claim, i.e. asserting *Past* 'P'. And so on.

The trouble, simply, is the diachronic variability of what is assertible. Statements come to be assertible as our knowledge advances; and may cease to be assertible as additional information undermines what was

4 For more refined formulations, see Essay 5, this volume, p. 185.
5 See 'The Reality of the Past' in Dummett, *Truth and Other Enigmas*, p. 364.

previously (taken to be) a satisfactory case. *Truth*, on the other hand, as ordinarily conceived, is timeless: if a statement is ever true, it always is. More accurately: if anyone, *x*, makes a statement at any time, then, no matter when, where, or who *y* may be, a sufficiently rich language will – by appropriate transformations, if necessary, of tense, pronoun, adverb, mood, etc. – enable *y* to say the same thing that *x* said, and the truth-values of the two utterances will be the same.

The timelessness of truth, so presented in full generality, is a strong doctrine, seemingly carrying an implication of the timelessness of thoughts and hence of concepts. Perhaps that implication can be sustained without uncomfortable idealization of the concept-forming powers of actual people. But this extra strength is in any case independent of the intuitive acceptability of the truth-value links for week-to-week purposes, as it were. What those equivalences collectively achieve is, *modulo* the assumption that the language is stable through appropriate periods of time, both to express the timelessness of truth and to indicate some of the 'appropriate transformations' alluded to by the general formulation. It would be natural to draw the conclusion that it is only if some correspondingly timeless notion of assertibility can be made out that there is any prospect either of saving the truth-value links under an assertibility-conditional interpretation or of wedding a satisfactory truth-theoretic treatment of tense, whatever exact form it takes, to such an interpretation.

What, though, if any, timeless, i.e. changeless, notion of assertibility is available? One immediate thought is that if a statement is ever assertible at a particular time, *t*, i.e. is justified by the state of information then obtaining, then it will be a timeless characteristic of that statement to be assertible-at-*t*. At first sight it seems obvious that this notion of assertibility will not sustain the truth-value links. Supposing, for example, that 'Jones is bald' was assertible at some prior *t*, we do not wish to conclude that 'Jones was bald' is *now* characterizable as assertible-at-*t* – as (i), right-to-left, would have us do – since that is as much as to say that someone could justifiably have used that very form of words at *t*; which need not be so. But this is a bad reason for writing off the candidature of assertibility-at-*t*. For truth itself is timeless only as a property of *statements*, not sentences. The truth-value links hold because what, for instance, *Past* 'P' now expresses is the same as what 'P' expressed at some appropriate past time. It would have been a perfectly adequate representation of the intended content of, say, (i) and (ii) if they had been formulated instead as, respectively,

i* What *Past* 'P' expresses is T iff what 'P' expressed is T
ii* What 'P' expresses is T iff what *Past* 'P' will express is T,

where the tense of the verb 'to express' appropriate in each constituent clause is taken from that of the predication of 'T' in the analogue of that clause in the original (i) and (ii), and the new predication of 'T' is taken tenselessly. So, in general for all the truth-value link equivalences. And now 'T' can be interpreted quite harmlessly as 'assertible-at-t', for any uniform selection of t, including 'is currently assertible' (if that is the notion which, for the anti-realist, should best supplant truth as the central notion in a systematic theory of meaning).

We can now see how the kind of recursion for the past tense, illustrated above, might yet be acceptable under interpretation in terms of assertibility. The troublesome output was achieved by construing '*Sats* ('P', S, t)' as: S satisfies 'P' at t, where 'at t' was understood to modify 'satisfies'. But now let us interpret 'satisfies' as 'currently satisfies' and 'at t' as giving the envisaged time of utterance of 'P'. And let a sentence's being T consist in its being currently satisfied by all sequences. Then the derivation of

If at t' 'John is bald' is T, then at t – [now] – 'John was bald' is T

proceeds exactly as before; but the result is no longer objectionable. It says, in effect, that the current assertibility of what 'John is bald' expressed at t' is sufficient for the current assertibility of what 'John was bald' expresses now.

I cannot pretend to know that there are no serious objections to this tactic for interpreting truth-theoretic treatments of tense, but we can satisfy ourselves that it at least escapes what would be the most serious objection: the objection that the theory, so interpreted, cannot achieve what a satisfactory semantic theory of tense must, above all, achieve, viz. a systematic description of how the content of tensed sentences varies as a function of their envisaged temporal context of utterance. Suppose that coincidence in (current) assertibility-conditions is taken to bear on sameness of content exactly as coincidence in truth-conditions is taken by the realist to do. Then the significance of the derivability, within an anti-realist T-theory, of

at t' 'John is bald' is T (currently assertible) $\leftrightarrow$
at t 'John was bald' is T (currently assertible)

(where t is *now*, and t' is earlier than t) is exactly the same as the significance attached by the realist to the derivability, within a T-theory under the standard interpretation, of

'John is bald' is T (true) at t' $\equiv$ 'John was bald' is T (true) at t;

namely, that when (as will be permissible since t is *now*) each *rhs* is biconditionally linked with the disquotation of 'John was bald', reason to think the theory satisfactory is reason to think that the content of the assertion of 'John is bald' at t' is what we can now express by the assertion that John was (then) bald. In short: the ploy of taking the temporal term in '*Sats* ('P', S, *t*)' as marking the time of utterance of 'P' rather than modifying the satisfaction relation, preserves the capacity of the theory to deliver an account of the content of the specified sentence uttered at variable times. So I conclude, tentatively, that if there were no independent reason for doubting whether a Davidsonian theory would permit construal as a theory of (current) assertibility, the form likely to be taken by a Davidsonian theory of tense would present no problem.

However, there are other reasons for doubt, to which I now turn.

II
Negation

Scruton[6] noted that the standard truth-theoretic clause for negation,

'Not'⁀'P' is T ≡ Not: 'P' is T

would be unacceptable under the interpretation of 'T' as 'assertible', since the *rhs* could then be true in states of information which had no tendency to warrant the assertion of 'Not'⁀'P'. Unfortunately, this difficulty seems to survive when '≡' is supplanted by '⟷', construed as in BICON, since a state of information which warrants the assertion that 'P' is not assertible need not, intuitively, warrant the assertion of the negation of 'P'. My response in Essay 1 above was to claim that, provided we have a satisfactory content-specifying theorem for 'P':

'P' is T⟷A,

and a proof theory strong enough to yield the inter-substitutivity of biconditional equivalents, a singularity in the clause for negation need be no very serious matter. For the final deliverance of the theory for 'Not'⁀'P' will then be

'Not'⁀'P' is T ↔ Not: A,

which, if A is a decent translation of 'P', is exactly what is wanted. And the final deliverance, my thought was, is what counts: only when all quotation has been eliminated from the *rhs* does the theory deliver its account of the meaning of an object-language sentence. In other words, since – provided the Davidsonian theory in which it is embedded is otherwise satisfactory – the straightforward clause for negation will ultimately yield acceptable results for the object-language sentences in

6 In his contribution to the symposium to which Essay 1 of this volume was mine. See p. 196 of Supplementary Volume of the *Proceedings of the Aristotelian Society* (1976).

which negation is the principal operator, it is no real cause to object to it that it is counter-intuitive.

A natural objection to this way with the difficulty is that the sort of instrumentalist outlook which it presupposes is at odds with the essential purposes of Davidsonian theories. The point, after all, in both the homophonic and heterophonic cases, is to display the syntactic and semantic features which co-determine the content of a particular object-language utterance. We can hardly claim to have done that – even if the theory correctly identifies that content – if the relevant theorem is derived from axioms which are intuitively quite incorrect. (Admittedly, this conception of the 'determination' of content may be objectionable in all sorts of ways; but it is unclear whether the Davidsonian project – and hence our title question – can have any point unless such objections can be met.)

This, though, is not in any case the full extent of the difficulty. The question is whether an anti-realist should or should not admit that if – as may easily happen – our state of information has no bearing on the assertibility either of 'P' or of 'Not'⌢'P', then, once apprised of the fact, we are justified in asserting both

Not: 'P' is assertible,

and

Not: 'Not'⌢'P' is assertible.

If he does, then, working from right-to-left across the recursion for 'Not':

'Not'⌢'P' is currently assertible⟷Not: 'P' is currently assertible,

we wind up in a position to assert that both 'Not'⌢'P' and 'Not'⌢'Not'⌢'P' are assertible – a contradiction. On the other hand, if the theorist is unwilling to accept that both those sentences are assertible in a neutral state of information, that seems dangerously close to an arbitrary insistence that the metalanguage should have no means for expressing such neutrality; which seems quite unsatisfactory.

This sort of difficulty is not restricted to negation. It would, for example, be an objectionable clause for disjunction which required that 'P'⌢'V'⌢'Q' may be regarded as currently assertible only if either 'P' or 'Q' may be so regarded: such a clause would require correct assertion of disjunctions to violate Grice's famous Co-operative Principle; and it would call into question the acceptance, deeply entrenched in intuitionistic mathematical practice, of the Law of Excluded Middle for decidable but so far undecided statements.

III
Superassertibility

The major obstacle to the interpretation of Davidsonian theory in terms of (current) assertibility is thus not the need to get a satisfactory treatment of tense but the problem of validating the straightforward clauses for the connectives. But it would be premature to conclude that the prospect of an assertibility-conditional interpretation has vanished altogether. Let us for a moment restrict our attention to pure mathematical statements, whose assertibility is constituted by proof. If 'T' is interpreted as 'proved', the problem with the recursion for 'Not' remains as just sketched: both 'Not: "P" is proved' and 'Not: "Not"$^\frown$"P" is proved' ought, it seems, to be assertible if 'P' is undecided. But matters are otherwise if 'T' is interpreted as 'provable'. Intuitionistically, the negation of a statement is proved just in case we have a construction which shows that no proof of that statement can in principle be achieved. Such a construction is exactly what would warrant the assertion of the *rhs* of the recursion cited for 'Not' when 'provable' replaces 'currently assertible'. If the negation of 'P' is then, in accordance with the intuitionistic account, to be counted as proved, *ergo* provable, the transition from right-to-left across the recursion becomes perfectly acceptable.

If we reflect that 'provable', unlike 'proved', is also intuitively a timeless property, we are pointed towards an obvious moral. The proposal has been to interpret 'T' in terms of current warranted assertibility. But what would suffice for a trouble-free construal of the recursions for the connectives is a notion of assertibility which stands to that notion as provability stands to 'is proved'.[7] If the analogy were exact, moreover, such a notion would be timeless and would thus supply a smooth interpretation for a truth-theoretic treatment of tense without the need for the interpretative manoeuvres sketched in the preceding section. Our question is therefore whether there is any general notion of assertibility

7 Interpreting the orthodox recursion for disjunction,

'P'$^\frown$'or'$^\frown$'Q' is T iff 'P' is T or 'Q' is T

in terms of provability does nothing, of course, to offset the two problems noted – avoiding violation of the Co-operative Principle, and validating Excluded Middle for undecided decidable statements – unless a claim of the form, '"P" is provable or "Q" is provable', can be based on a proof that one or the other statement is assertible which does not disclose which. For discussion of the intuitionists' entitlement to so liberalized a conception of disjunction, see Dummett, 'The Philosophical Basis of Intuitionistic Logic' in *Truth and Other Enigmas*, pp. 243–7; also Essay 4 in this volume section VIII. Cf. note 20 of Essay 4. For a further problem with this aspect of intuitionistic practice, see the Appendix to this essay.

of which the intuitionistic conception of provability is a special case: a notion which is timeless, which sustains the intuitive correctness of the standard recursions for the connectives, but which – unlike truth, classically conceived – is not open to anti-realist objection.

On the face of it, mathematical proof is a very special case. Besides being timelessly available, a good proof provides a ground for what it proves which is both conclusive and will withstand arbitrarily severe scrutiny. By contrast, the sort of grounds for which we have to settle in the case of most ordinary contingent statements seem to be a somewhat inferior kettle of fish: even if we manage to establish a *sound* case for a particular such statement,[8] it will typically fall short of anything that ought to be regarded as *conclusive* verification in all the examples where the anti-realist takes issue with the realist account – counter-factual conditionals, contingent generalizations, statements about other minds, statements about the remote past, etc. – and, besides, will very often be the product of our catching a relatively ephemeral opportunity to investigate. So it would be forgivable to suppose that there is no worthwhile generalization, apt for our purpose, of provability in mathematics. Forgivable but, I think, wrong.

In order to outline the form which the kind of notion we seek could take, it will be productive to consider a series of objections to the following natural generalization, intended to apply to all statements, of the intuitionistic conception of negation in mathematics:

NEG: a state of information justifies the assertion of 'Not' ⁀ 'P' just in case it justifies the assertion that no state of information justifying the assertion of 'P' can be achieved.

The first and immediate objection is: what is the proper interpretation of 'can'?[9] Not, presumably, mere *logical* possibility, or we shall not have much use for negation. For it is always logically possible, at least in the case of contingent statements, that a state of information could be achieved which justified their assertion. But if 'can' means: can *in practice*, then the existence of practical obstacles to conducting any relevant investigation will qualify us, quite counter-intuitively, to assert the negation of a statement.[10] The response has to be, clearly, that some element of idealization is involved in the relevant notion of possibility, though not so much that it deteriorates into mere logical possibility. The appropriate notion of possibility should transcend incidental obstacles to investigation

8 That is, a case with no feature whose disclosure would undermine its status as evidence for the statement.

9 Cf. Appiah, 'Anti-realism Unrealized', p. 97.

10 Cf. Essay 15 of this volume, section II.

but be constrained by other features of the actual world. What, in intention anyway, is being denied when 'Not'⌢'P' is asserted in accordance with NEG is that the actual world would allow the generation in rational subjects who were given the time, opportunity, and appropriate faculties, of a state of information which warranted the assertion of 'P'.

That is very vague, of course; but not so vague as to avoid a second objection. Asserting 'Not'⌢'P' would still be an exceedingly bold move. For rational subjects are no less subject, as a class, to brainwashing, hypnosis, etc. than others. The intention, obviously, is that the mode of generation of the relevant state of information be restricted to bona fide investigation, governed by an exercise of the subject's rationality and other appropriate faculties. But even that will not quite do, since rationality is not infallibility, and the most refined intellectual and perceptual capacities may still be prone to error. Clearly, the spirit of NEG does not intend that, before we can be in a position to assert the negation of a statement, we have to be able to foreclose on the possibility that rational subjects, carrying through a genuine investigation in the appropriate way, could *mistakenly* arrive at a state of information which justified the assertion of that statement.

The necessary refinement is, presumably, that by a 'state of information' we must understand something which can be defended as a *body of knowledge*, rather than merely a prima facie justified set of beliefs.[11] Of course the effect of this refinement is that it is no longer necessary to be so careful about the mode of generation of the state of information or the character of the investigating subject: the point of stipulating that the subject not be brainwashed but arrive at his beliefs by the rational exercise of bona fide investigative methods was just to try to ensure that knowledge was the product.

But there is still a third objection. Simply, it is not at all satisfactory to insist that warranted assertion of the negation of a statement requires us to be in a position to assert that *no* body of knowledge, warranting assertion of that statement, can be gleaned from the actual world. For the statement in question may admit of warranted assertion on grounds which fall short of conclusive verification; and it ought to be possible, in such a case, to get in position to deny the statement while recognizing that a body of knowledge warranting its assertion is indeed something that can actually be achieved, we ourselves, perhaps, having formally occupied a reduced state of information constituted by our possession of just such a body of knowledge. Clearly, the states of information falling

11 That the notion of knowledge undoubtedly has its problems should cause no nervousness about its invocation in the present context, unless its very content is thought to be in doubt or it is held somehow to presuppose realism.

in the range of the quantification on the *rhs* of NEG need to be restricted: states of information now superseded are not to be included. The obvious restriction would be to *enlargements* of our present body of knowledge. The drift of NEG would accordingly be that we are entitled to assert the negation of a statement just in case we are entitled to regard ourselves as possessing a body of knowledge with the feature that no matter how hard we were to try, nor how favourable the conditions for the attempt, we should never achieve an enlargement of it which warranted assertion of that statement.

No doubt further clarification is wanted, particularly of what it is for circumstances to be 'favourable' – i.e. as I intend the term, for both the subject and the background conditions to be optimal for the acquisition of knowledge. But what is striking is that at least the overall shape of the general notion of assertibility for which we were seeking can now be discerned. What we are claiming, when, in accordance with NEG as now interpreted, we assert the negation of a statement, is, in effect, that if it is possible to acquire a body of knowledge which warrants the assertion of that statement, some degree of enlargement of it is possible which will cause that feature to disappear.[12] *Superassertibility* – the generalization of mathematical provability which we seek – would be the opposite property: that which a statement possesses when it is both possible, under favourable circumstances, to achieve a body of knowledge which warrants its assertion and impossible, no matter how favourable the circumstances, to enlarge on that body of knowledge in such a way that the statement ceases to be warrantedly assertible. More specifically, 'P' is *superassertible* just in case the world will, in sufficiently favourable circumstances, permit the generation in an investigating subject, S, of a set of beliefs, $\{B_1,\ldots,B_n\}$ with the following characteristics:

a S has adequate grounds for regarding each of $\{B_1,\ldots,B_n\}$ as an item of knowledge.
b The status of each of $\{B_1,\ldots,B_n\}$ as an item of S's knowledge will survive arbitrarily close and extensive investigation.
c The state of information constituted by $\{B_1,\ldots,B_n\}$ warrants the assertion of 'P'.
d The case provided by $\{B_1,\ldots,B_n\}$ for 'P' is not, *in fact*, defeasible; i.e. no $\{B_1,\ldots,B_n,\ldots,B_z\}$ containing $\{B_1,\ldots,B_n\}$ and satisfying (a) and (b)

12 That degree of enlargement, namely, which adds to it as far as is necessary to incorporate our *present* state of information (which, by hypothesis, has no enlargement which would warrant assertion of the statement in question.)

for some S, yet *failing* to warrant 'P', can be achieved in this world, no matter now favourable the circumstances for the attempt.

The intended import of NEG can now be described simply as a proposal that the negation of a statement is assertible just in case we are warranted in denying that that statement is superassertible. The last of the three objections above, in particular, is met by the reflection that superseded states of information of the kind adverted to will fail to comply with condition (d). For a statement to be superassertible is, intuitively, for the actual world to contain the materials whereby not merely can a flawless case be made for asserting it but this case will survive no matter how much more thereafter we come to know. Superassertibility is assertibility which is stable under *both* rescrutiny of the pedigree of what we take to be our existing knowledge and further accretions to that knowledge. It generalizes mathematical provability in exactly those two respects; for a good proof precisely supplies a flawless case for a particular statement which, because conclusive, must stand unimpugned by the discovery of other proofs.

We have still explicitly to validate the orthodox recursion for negation,

'Not'⁀'P' is T ↔ Not: 'P' is T,

with 'T' expressing superassertibility. NEG prescribes that the assertion conditions for the negation of a statement coincide with those of the statement that it is not superassertible, and hence yields directly

Not: P⟷Not: 'P' is T.

So the interference from NEG to the recursion requires

'Not'⁀'P' is T ↔ Not: P,

which is just an instance of the general form of T-theorem.

However the claim that instances of the general form are acceptable when 'T' expresses superassertibility has yet to be made out. (Of course, the game is up if they are not!) Clearly, any reason to regard a statement as superassertible is equally a warrant for its assertoric use. So the question is whether possession of such a warrant has to entail reason to believe that the statement is superassertible; to believe, in effect, that the warrant possessed will be stable under arbitrary enlargements of the warrant-conferring state of information. The plausibility of an affirmative answer is enhanced by the reflection that warranted assertion is *eo ipso* justified belief; and that to believe a statement is, of course, to have expectations about the favourable character of information which could be but has yet to be gathered. But the claim that assertion is in general a commitment to superassertibility is, in effect, discussed more fully elsewhere in this volume, and I shall not add further to that discussion now.[13]

Interpreting the orthodox recursions for the other connectives in terms of superassertibility poses no special problems. Each connective takes on a content which is a natural generalization of its sense in intuitionistic mathematics. But we had two sets of difficulties in finding an assertibility-conditional construal of Davidsonian theory, one to do with the sentential connectives and the other to do with tense. Is superassertibility indeed a timeless property, and so apt for a straightforward interpretation of a successful truth-theoretic treatment of tense?

Intuitively, yes: if the world furnishes the relevant kind of flawless, stable case for a statement, then it was always true that it would and always will be true that it did. But the trouble is that this thought seems to appeal to the timelessness of truth to vindicate that of superassertibility as a special case. Accordingly, if there is any doubt whether the conception of truth as timeless is available to anti-realism, or certain forms of anti-realism,

13 See Essay 13, pp. 388–90 and 395. However it is worth adverting to two forms of purported counter-example to the claim that warrant for an assertion must involve reason to believe that it is superassertible, each put to me in seminar discussion by David Lewis. First, I warrantedly believe - or so I suppose - that cauliflower is nutritious. Yet I know there must be countless cases of illness, especially gastro-intestinal illness, whose onset but shortly postdated an episode of cauliflower-eating. So there is an enlargement of my present state of information which differs from it only by the addition of knowledge of the detail of a large number of these cases. Would not my confidence in cauliflower quite reasonably evaporate if I happened on this enlarged state of information? Second, I can warrantedly believe on the basis of standard sampling techniques that, say, the SDP/Liberal Alliance will poll better than one third of the votes cast at the next General Election in Britain; but at the same time know that it is possible (if unlikely) to proceed, by the use of those same techniques, to an enlarged state of information which suggests a quite different prognosis.

A statement is superassertible if there is *some* state of information (body of knowledge) which warrants believing it and will contrive to do so no matter how far enlarged by further items of knowledge. Strictly, then, neither example is to the purpose: each provides, at most, an illustration of how I can reasonably believe that a present state of information, which warrants a particular statement, can be misleadingly enlarged; but neither explains how my belief in their respective original statements can be reasonable if I am not merely to consider that my present state of information fails to instantiate the existential quantifier in the characterization of superassertibility but am to keep an open mind about whether there is *any* enlargement of it which fares any better. What needs to be shown is how it can be reasonable both to believe a statement and not to believe (not necessarily disbelieve) that it is superassertible. But my belief that cauliflower is nutritious involves, inter alia, the belief that there is a state of information which will explain the cases of post-cauliflower sickness away; and my belief about the Alliance's electoral prospects involves the belief that an enlarged state of information is possible from which the envisaged misleading sample would be disclosed as just that.

Even if we suppose that the present state of information (in each example respectively), has to be the one, if any, to instantiate the existential quantifier, both the examples have

then there is the ironic prospect that superassertibility might serve to interpret the T-predicate only on assumptions which only realism can consistently make.

Remember that the question may not be of decisive importance. For if superassertibility did turn out not to be timeless from an anti-realist point of view, there would still be the prospect that the tense problems could be overcome by an analogue of the interpretive manoeuvres described in section I. It is the (foreseeable) recursions for the tenses which, interpreted in the fashion those manoeuvres seek to sidestep, call for a timeless T-predicate. The recursions for the connectives, so far as I can see, do not, *per se*, do so. Accordingly the case outlined for supposing they will admit interpretation in terms of superassertibility holds out no hostage to fortune in this connection. But the matter is of considerable independent interest. Can sense be given to the possibility of a particular statement's being superassertible at one time but not at another? To claim superassertibility for a statement is to quantify over the totality of states of information which can, under favourable circumstances, be gleaned from the actual world. What sort of totality is that? The realist will view it, exactly as

---

their problems. The first example might as well have concerned any ascription of a disposition. Such an ascription may be supported by tried theory about the properties which underly the disposition ascribed; so with the cauliflower case. Or it may be based, generally with less security, on observation of a regular pattern of performance, so far unexplained. In the latter case, the belief that an enlargement of the present state of information is available which will differ just by the addition of detail concerning very many cases where the putative disposition is not manifest, is only dubiously consistent with the belief that the present state of information supports ascribing the disposition. In the former case, it simply is not clear why the enlarged state of information would no longer support ascribing the disposition. Sheer weight of numbers of cases where the disposition is not manifest counts for naught if the background theory enables us to attribute them to the presence of interfering factors. Reason to believe the theory ought to be reason to believe that will be so. And if it is built into the example that there is reason to believe that will not be so, it is, once again, only dubiously consistent to believe that the present state of information supports ascribing the disposition in the first place.

The election example meets a broadly similar dilemma. Statistical sampling provides no reason to believe anything unless there is reason to believe that the sample is representative. So the example does not engage the issue at all unless there is reason to think that there *will be* reason to think that the enlarged state of information includes a representative sample. Only then is it reasonable to suppose that, should we come to occupy that state of information, we could no longer reasonably believe the original statement. The question is therefore whether we *now* have reason to believe that the belief, reasonably held in the enlarged state of information, that the enlarged sample is representative, is mistaken. If so, we now have reason to deny that the enlarged state of information is a body of knowledge, so it ceases to be germane to issues concerning superassertibility. (Superassertibility, to stress, requires stable assertibility under accretions to our *knowledge*.) But if not, then we cannot have reason to believe that our present sample *is* representative; in which case we are not, after all, in position to believe the original statement about the Alliance's electoral prospects.

he views the totality of truth-conferring states of affairs, as a single stable totality *sub specie aeternitatis*. Some forms of anti-realism may concur. But the anti-realist who takes our station in time more seriously[14] will hold that there is no *species aeternitatis*; that the totality over which we succeed in quantifying when we make such a claim is, inescapably, a function of *when* we make the claim. If that is so, it is natural to conclude that it should be possible for the output of the 'function' to vary, and hence for the totality of 'gleanable' states of information to shift from time to time. And then there would of course be scope for 'is superassertible' to have a significant tense.

It wants some work to show that this natural conclusion is correct; that it does not tacitly depend upon the significance of comparisons which no one who is stationed in time can actually make – comparisons which would require us to straddle, as it were, distinct points in time simultaneously.[15] But my own present belief is that that sort of reservation about it is ultimately empty; that anti-realism of the relevant kind cannot comfortably view superassertibility as timeless. The case for saying so is that made with respect to truth in Essay 5 of the present volume. If superassertibility is to play the central role in a theory of meaning, the anti-realist must subject it to the epistemological constraints whose transgression by the classical conception of truth is the original cause of his dissatisfaction. And the form of constraint imposed by Dummett's anti-realist about the past, applied to superassertibility, will lead to exactly parallel conclusions to those outlined in Essay 5 concerning truth. I refer the reader to that discussion.[16]

IV
Content, Content-sense and Ingredient-sense

In *Frege: Philosophy of Language*, Dummett draws a distinction between what he calls the *content-sense* and the *ingredient-sense* of a sentence. The former is, roughly, what is known by someone who understands the use of the sentence in simple assertions; the latter is the contribution effected by that sentence to the sense of compound sentences in which it is embedded.[17] Under classical bivalent semantics, of course, the two types

14 Dummett's anti-realist in 'The Reality of the Past', for instance, or my I/N anti-realist of Essay 5.

15 Cf. section 2 of chapter X of my *Wittgenstein on the Foundations of Mathematics*, pp. 186–9.

16 See especially sections I, II, IV and VII.

17 Compare John Skorupski's distinction between *cognitive role* and *semantic content* in his 'Anti-realism: Cognitive Role and Semantic Content', *passim*.

of sense coincide: the truth-conditions of a sentence are both what is known by anyone who understands its assertoric use and what determines its semantic contribution under embedding. Not so, as Dummett points out, if we are e.g. working with a many-valued semantics, involving more than one distinct *undesignated* value. For then the possibility opens up that a pair of sentences should always take designated values together, yet take contrasting undesignated values in certain circumstances and so contribute differently to the determination of the truth-values of embedding contexts. The fact remains that in order to understand simple assertoric uses of the two sentences, it suffices to understand the conditions under which they take a designated, or undesignated, value; and here there is, by hypothesis, complete parity. In such a case, then, sentences may share content-sense while differing in ingredient-sense.[18]

In Essay 16 of this volume a doubt is raised whether

> ...once we consider utterances with assertion conditions which are at best defeasible, a generalized anti-realist semantics, based on the notion of warranted assertion, can have the systematic character displayed by classical truth conditional semantics...[19]

The ground for this doubt is just that sentences with the same conditions of warranted assertion may embed differently, *par excellence* within the scope of just the operations which we have been preoccupied with: negation and tense. Thus, whereas 'P' and 'It is currently assertible that P' are warranted in exactly the same circumstances, 'Not'⁀'P' and 'It is not currently assertible that P', or *Past* 'P' and 'It was currently assertible that P', are not. Accordingly, it seems, there can be no systematic semantics based on conditions of warranted assertion; for the essence of *systematic* semantics is that the various sentence-forming operators are construed as functions, so deliver uniform output for uniform input.

This conclusion stands. But it may occur to the reader to wonder whether Dummett's distinction, placed alongside the notion of superassertibility, does not suggest a way of pulling its teeth. Could not the anti-realist identify the content-sense of a statement with the conditions under which its assertion is warranted; and its ingredient sense with its conditions of *superassertibility*? For no obstacle has so far been presented against the possibility of systematic superassertibility-conditional semantics; on the contrary, that, in effect, is just what has been argued for. Is the pessimistic suggestion of Essay 16 concerning

18 The distinction is accepted and put to work in connection with the contingent a priori in Gareth Evans's 'Reference and Contingency'; see in particular section III. See also Martin Davies, *Meaning, Quantification, Necessity*, chapter X.
19 This volume, p. 469.

systematic anti-realist semantics (and its conventionalist corollary) premature?

If anti-realist semantics can indeed proceed systematically, in Davidsonian form, in terms of superassertibility, then yes. Even so, the specific proposal about content- and ingredient-senses seems unhappy. The proposal requires that 'P' and 'It is currently assertible that P' have different conditions of superassertibility. But any contemporary *reason* to think that either is superassertible is reason to think the other is: reason to regard 'P' as superassertible is certainly reason to regard it as currently assertible; and reason to regard 'P' as currently assertible is – if any belief is, in effect, a belief about superassertibility (see note 13) – reason to suppose that it is superassertible that it is currently assertible. The latter, conversely, is certainly reason to regard 'P' as currently assertible which is – currently – the best reason we can have for regarding 'P' as superassertible. If it seems obvious that the conditions of superassertibility are different, it is because we are thinking of the *statements* which contemporary assertoric uses of those sentences would respectively effect; where the statement made is something which different type-utterances by different speakers on different occasions can share. But once we so help ourselves to the notion of statement, the motive for introducing Dummett's distinction in the way described disappears. For there is no reason to identify the ordinary (non-super) assertibility-conditions of the *statements* effected by current uses of 'P' and 'It is currently assertible that P'. On the contrary, that there is such a thing as being in a position to assert one of those statements without being in a position to assert the other comes out precisely in the reflection that, for suitable 'P', either of the modifications of those two sentences apt for then expressing what we expressed by them today may, tomorrow, be assertible without the other being so.

That is: if we are concerned with the statements effected by current uses of those two sentences, the distinction between them may already be drawn in terms of their ordinary conditions of assertibility; one, but not the other, may be assertible tomorrow, and the invocation of superassertibility serves no purpose. If, on the other hand, we confine our attention to contemporary assertoric uses of the two *sentences*, we can currently have no reason to regard one as superassertible which is not reason so to regard the other, so that invoking superassertibility does not help to explain the semantic difference between them.

Rather than seek to exploit a version of the ingredient-sense/content-sense distinction, I believe that the anti-realist should respond to the matter as follows. Conditions of superassertibility, like truth-conditions in classical semantics, will in general determine *both* content-sense and ingredient-sense. The content of an assertion (= assertoric use of a sentence) should indeed be seen as being precisely that it is superassertible. So far as I can see, there is otherwise no natural way for the anti-realist to *explain* the fact that there can be such a thing as the overturn of a warrant for an assertion. Such an overturn has to take the form of a breach either of clause (b) or of clause (d) in the definition of superassertibility above. If the content of an assertion of 'P' coincided with that of 'It is currently assertible that P', it would be quite mysterious how anything could be a ground for criticism except evidence of a breach of clause (b). That stops being mysterious once something in the content of 'P' commits the assertor against subsequent breaches of clause (d). Taking 'P' to make a superassertibility claim effects just that: to be in a position to assert it is then to possess what seems to be a state of information with a legitimate promise to satisfy each of (a)...(d). Should it turn out not to do so, there will be no reason to think that any such state of information exists – hence no reason – according to the proposal – to continue to accept 'P'. So much is, perhaps, obvious. But perhaps it will serve to allay to some extent the misgivings of those[20] who complain that anti-realist semantics is bereft of the materials for any account of assertoric *content*.

In replying to some of Strawson's criticisms, I wrote that it would anyway be quite baffling to suggest, of someone who gave every indication of being able to tell the difference between states of information which warranted the assertion of 'John is in pain' and states of information which did not, that he nevertheless failed to understand the content of that sentence.[21] My thought was that this consideration accorded ill, moreover, with the realist account of its content, which would associate it with a transcendent truth-condition. For the inference from possession of such a practical discriminatory ability to possession of a conception of a transcendent truth-condition would have to be problematic. But does the present proposal, identifying assertoric content with a superassertibility claim, fare any better? The claim that it does will require that the practical ability to discriminate in general between situations in which the case for an assertion is good enough and situations in which it is not, or has ceased to be, involves knowing what it is for it to be superassertible. Properly understood, this requirement is, I think, satisfied. It suffices to reflect that someone who followed the policy of attempting to ensure that all his beliefs at any given time can be expressed by sentences warrantedly assertible at that time could not be distinguished from someone whose policy was continuously to refine his beliefs in accordance with the aim of superassertibility. Since the evidence that someone knows the assertion- and overturn-conditions for 'John is in pain' will naturally take the form of his regulating his pattern for assent to that sentence in accordance with

20 See most notably Strawson, 'Scruton and Wright on Anti-realism, Etc.' especially p. 19.
21 Essay 2, this volume, pp. 80–1.

the aim of assertibility, it will therefore be equally good evidence that he is aiming at superassertibility. The point has no tendency to suggest, of course, that the concepts are the same: their distinction is forced on us precisely by the asymmetries under negation and tense, e.g. with which we have been concerned. But they cannot be distinguished as *regulative ideals*: to stress, whatever grounds there are in a speakers' assertoric linguistic practice for interpreting it as governed by either goal are grounds for interpreting it as governed by the other.

V
Superassertibility and Truth

There is an objection which the reader may have wanted to make as soon as the notion of superassertibility was canvassed, and which will now seem extremely pressing. A central strand in the anti-realist polemic against realist semantics is exactly that, in a large class of examples, assertibility and *truth* stand in the relation just noted: that there is no practical distinction between them as regulative ideals. But in that case the anti-realist conclusion was – was it not? – that the residual content to which truth pretends is 'theoretical slack, void of observational warrant'.[22] If that was a fair conclusion, must not the same conclusion be drawn about superassertibility? Indeed, is it not, in many cases, a no less objectionably 'verification-transcendent' notion? For we shall typically have no way of verifying a claim of superassertibility, however promising the case.

If there is anything in the proposals sketched, this line of thought had better be a confusion. Fortunately it is. It is undeniable that superassertibility is not merely not an effectively decidable property but a property which, for all statements which do not admit of conclusive verification, has itself no conclusive verification-conditions. But it does not follow that it cannot serve as an intelligible objective. Anything can serve as an intelligible objective for a practice, i.e. can exert a regulative influence over our conduct, provided we possess *practical criteria* on which to base the claims that the objective has, or has not, been met in a particular case. It is a common misunderstanding of the thrust of the anti-realist's criticisms of the role assigned to truth in classical semantics that he believes that the central notion in the theory of meaning should be an effectively decidable one.[23] But there is, so far as I can see, no good motive for asking for so much. I can *try* to steer a certain course if, but only if, I know what will be a reason to think that I have gone off course and what

22 Essay 1, this volume, p. 60.
23 See, for instance, John McDowell's 'On "The Reality of the Past"', passim.

a reason to think I am continuing on it. The reasons don't have to be conclusive, but they do have to be such that I can actually recognizably have them. Superassertibility passes this test. But it does not follow that any distinction between it and assertibility must involve its infusion with 'theoretical slack'; to aim at one is, as we have seen, necessarily to aim at the other, but the distinction between the two is nevertheless *manifest* in our capacity to make, e.g. differential retrospective judgements about their achievement.

The anti-realist case may find better favour if he now admits that all this may, with a qualification, be said of the notion of truth. In so far as we have practical criteria for determining when the ascription of truth to a statement is justified, and when it is not, we can significantly *aim* at truth; in so far as contexts embedding ascriptions of truth and of assertibility to 'P' are used differently, we *have* attained a distinguishing grasp of the two concepts. It follows that anti-realism ought not to *deny* outright that truth is an appropriate notion to play the central role in a philosophical theory of meaning. It all depends on how the notion is understood, on whether the proviso – that we have the sort of practical criteria described – is guaranteed. The crux is that the classical realist conception of truth can in general offer no such guarantee. The distinctively realist thesis is precisely that our language affords the means for depicting no end of states of affairs whose obtaining connects only contingently, at best, with our capacity to accumulate grounds for claiming that they obtain. Among the various strands in the anti-realist polemic, none is more central than the reproach that as soon as this connection becomes one of contingency, the belief that truth is suitable to play the regulative role essential to the central notion of a theory of meaning is itself reduced to contingency.[24] What good reason can there be for a semantic theory to offer such a hostage to fortune – a hostage, moreover, which in some cases at least[25] it is certain will not be returned to us? In contrast, there is no such contingency in the case of superassertibility: if a state of information can indeed be arrived at satisfying each of (a) to (d) for a particular 'P', it *has* to be possible to gather reason to think that that is so: if the pedigree is faultless (condition (a)) and the case indefeasible by addition (condition (d)), patient scrutiny must disclose grounds for the first and further investigation must disclose (standard inductive) grounds for the second.

We do well to draw here on the important programme pursued by David Wiggins in his 'What Would be a Substantial Theory of Truth?' and

24 Compare the Introduction to this volume, pp. 23–6.

25 Namely, statements for whose truth it is guaranteed, on the contrary, that no evidence can be obtained. Compare the Introduction, pp. 13–17.

elsewhere.[26] Wiggins asks: supposing that we are seeking a theory of meaning, with the classic sort of biconditional output, as part of the overall project of achieving a satisfactory description-cum-explanation of the beliefs, attitudes, and life in general of a speech community – supposing this modest project, and taking that (what he dubs 'assertibility' but I shall designate) T is whatever notion is appropriate to play the disquotational role in the theorems, what can we learn about T from its suitability to play this role? What aspects ('marks', as Wiggins calls them) of the concept are thereby imposed on it? Wiggins arrives[27] at five:

i Speakers' willingness to assent to a sentence must, in general, be an indication of their belief that it is T; T is to be a property which assertions must normally be interpreted as aiming to possess.
ii A sentence's being T should, under favourable circumstances, lead to a tendency for opinions about the rightness of assent to it to converge.
iii A sentence's being T, or not, should be independent of any particular speaker's means of recognizing the fact.
iv When a sentence is T, there should be something in virtue of which it is T.
v When a pair of sentences are T, so is their conjunction.

Wiggins does not suggest that only these marks are imposed on the T-predicate by its role in the large-scale interpretative project described. But he does contend[28] that two further marks, dear to certain theorists of truth, are no features of the predicate implicitly defined by that project; namely

vi If a sentence is T, then it is fated to be agreed upon by all rational investigators (= a strengthening of (ii)). And
vii A sentence's being T is independent of the existence of any means of recognizing that it is so (= a strengthening of (iii)).

There is of course a great deal to be said about how best to formulate these 'marks' – the above are fairly liberal paraphrases of Wiggins's own formulations – and about Wiggins's contentions concerning them. What is notable in the present context is that each of (i) to (v) is a mark of superassertibility. Only, perhaps, in the case of (i) is the matter not immediately obvious, since the concept of superassertibility is naturally viewed as a philosophical invention, uncontemplated by ordinary speakers. Once again, it is good enough to reply, I think, that speakers will normally treat what is in fact (a lack of) evidence that a sentence is superassertible as a ground for (not) asserting it. On the other hand, (vii) is precisely

26 Cf. his 'Truth, Invention and the Meaning of Life', and 'Truth and Interpretation'.
27 See Wiggins, 'What Would be a Substantial Theory of Truth?', section V.
28 Ibid., note 26, pp. 218–19.

that mark of the realist conception of truth which is not shared by superassertibility.

What we can now see, though only in outline, is the prospect of a way of harmonizing the negative strictures of anti-realism with an approach to meaning which is, in effect, truth-conditional. If our earlier considerations are sound, and there is no reason to think that there are insuperable *technical* obstacles confronting the interpretation of Davidsonian theory as a theory of superassertibility; and if Wiggins is right and no further mark is enjoined by the large-scale interpretative project which would disqualify superassertibility as an interpretation of the predicate on which the marks are imposed – if both those (substantial) claims are true, then truth – or at least that notion of truth for which the equation of meaning with truth-conditions is defensible or even platitudinous[29] will turn out to *be* superassertibility.[30] And the reason why the anti-realist will be able to 'take over the legacy' of Davidsonian theory will not be because he can, against expectations as it were, come up with an alternative interpretation which squares with the mechanics of the theory, but because Davidsonian theory, when placed in the wider interpretational project in which Wiggins rightly locates it, cannot but be a theory of an anti-realistically acceptable notion.[31]

APPENDIX
COULD THATCHER BE A MASTER CRIMINAL?

Consider the following example, put to me in correspondence by John Skorupski. There are, presumably, good grounds for asserting a conditional like

A If Thatcher is a master criminal, she will have left no evidence that she is.

The more adept a crook is, the better at covering his tracks; and a master criminal is, plausibly, completely successful. But if the consequent of A

29 See John McDowell, 'Anti-realism and the Epistemology of Understanding', p. 229; and 'In Defence of Modesty', section 2. For discussion of the platitude, see this volume's Introduction, pp. 18–19.

30 There are obvious points of affinity between this suggestion and the 'internal realism' canvassed in Hilary Putnam's writings. See especially his 'Realism and Reason', and *Reason, Truth, and History*. Such convergence is encouraging.

31 I would like to thank Anthony Appiah, John Skorupski and Neil Tennant for helpful comments on an earlier draft of this paper. The main ideas were originally presented at an informal seminar held at Neil Tennant's home in Dunblane, Stirlingshire, in August 1983; my thanks to those staff and students of St Andrews and Stirling Universities who gave up a summer vacation afternoon to discuss such arcane matters.

holds, then no state of information can be achieved which warrants assertion of the antecedent; *a fortiori*, the antecedent is not *superassertible*. Assuming, then, for the purposes of a conditional proof, that Thatcher is a master criminal, and given that A itself is superassertible, NEG (see p. 412 above) puts us in a position to infer

B If Thatcher is a master criminal, Thatcher is not a master criminal,

and hence, on purely a priori grounds, that Thatcher is not a master criminal.

Skorupski's own response was to suggest that NEG is to blame; and therefore – since the inference to the denial that it is superassertible that Thatcher is a master criminal seems compelling – that the general proposal about assertoric content, made in section IV, (which would equate the claim that Thatcher is a master criminal with the claim that it is superassertible that she is) is unacceptable.

That, though, does not get to the heart of the matter. The distinctive anti-realist thesis (prescinding from consideration of the agnosticism discussed in Essay 5) is that truth must be epistemically constrained, cannot be evidence-transcendent. So some principle will be endorsed of the form

AR Evidence is available for my proposition which is true;

more formally,

1 $(\forall P)\ (P \rightarrow \Diamond KP)$.

But (A) and (AR) directly entail that it is not true that Thatcher is a master criminal, without appeal to NEG or the associated theory of assertoric content.

One thought is that both arguments overlook the evidence available to Thatcher. But it is incidental that the example concerns somebody living – let it be Benjamin Disraeli instead. If the erstwhile availability to him of the appropriate evidence, one way or the other, is to be enough to satisfy AR, we have dealt very summarily with anti-realism about the past.

The problem has affinities with one discussed by Dorothy Edgington.[32] Even if evidence is available for all truths, there are surely some for which no evidence has actually been gathered; formally

2 $(\exists P)\ (P \& \sim KP)$.

32 See her 'The Paradox of Knowability'. The argument she discusses seems to originate in Fitch, 'A Logical Analysis of Some Value Concepts'; and to have been rediscovered by Hart in 'The Epistemology of Abstract Objects', note 3, pp. 164–5. It is discussed by Timothy Williamson in 'Intuitionism Disproved?', *Analysis*, 42 (1982), pp. 203–7.

Let S be such a truth, so that

3 $S \& \sim KS$

Then, by (1) and (3),

4 $\Diamond K(S \& \sim KS)$.

If 'K' is taken to be truth-entailing and to distribute over conjunction, then contradiction follows. But (4) is in any case already absurd: it implies the possibility of a state of information in which one would be justified in claiming both the truth of a statement and the lack of any justification for it.

A natural response, not discussed by Edgington, would demur at (2), which is unacceptable if the quantifier is interpreted constructively. The proper way of expressing what (2) tries for, it would be contended, is

2′ $\sim(\forall P)\ (P \rightarrow KP)$,

which is classically but not intuitionistically equivalent to (2), and is intuitionistically consistent with (1), (even if 'K' is taken to be truth-entailing and transmissible across logical consequence).

Once again the complaint would be fair that we deal very summarily with a large issue – in this case the aspirations of non-revisionary anti-realism – if we take it that this is the right reply. But, perhaps more compelling, the problem – in essentials – can be presented, at the cost of a little more complexity, in what appears to be an intuitionistically acceptable form. Intuitionistically, a disjunction is known only if it is possible to know one or other of the disjuncts; formally,

5 $(\forall P)\ (\forall Q)\ [K(P \vee Q) \rightarrow (\Diamond KP \vee \Diamond KQ)]$

Conversely, whenever it can be guaranteed that one or other disjunct can be known – notably, when a statement has been recognized to be effectively decidable and the disjunction is the application to it of Excluded Middle – intuitionistic practice regards the disjunction as known, even if neither disjunct is known. For such a statement, S, then, we can know each of '$S \vee \sim S$', '$\sim KS$', and '$\sim K \sim S$'. Assuming transmissibility, we have

6 $K[(S \vee \sim S) \& \sim KS \& \sim K \sim S]$; equivalently, by DeMorgan,
7 $K[(S \& \sim KS \& \sim K \sim S) \vee (\sim S \& \sim KS \& \sim K \sim S)]$; hence
8 $K[(S \& \sim KS) \vee (\sim S \& \sim K \sim S)]$.

But this, via (5), provides

9 $\Diamond K(S \& \sim KS) \vee \Diamond K(\sim S \& \sim K \sim S)$,

each disjunct of which is absurd for the same reasons as (4). Since, to stress, there are intuitionistically acceptable examples of (6), the paradox is independent of the use of non-constructive assumptions like (3).

Edgington's solution to the original problem is to discern in its premises some suppressed occurrences of an indexical appropriate to secure rigid reference to how things *actually* are when occurring within modal and counter-factual contexts.[33] Thus AR becomes something like

AR* For any proposition which is actually true, evidence can be gathered that it is actually true,

where the second occurrence of 'actually' secures a reference to how matters actually stand, rather than to how they *would* stand if the evidence were gathered. Or, in a familiar style,

1* $(\forall P)$ $(P \text{ is true in } W_A \rightarrow (\exists W_1)\ (KW_1, P \text{ is true in } W_A))$

where 'KW_m, Q' says that Q is known in possible world W_m and 'W_A' denotes the actual world.[34] What now happens, of course, is that (4) becomes

4* $(\exists W_1)\ (KW_1,$ '$S\ \&\ {\sim}KW_AS$' is true in $W_A)$

which is unparadoxical. In effect, the state of affairs consisting of S's being true but unknown is something which it *is* possible to know, as the spirit of AR requires; but realization of that possibility would not put us in position to assert 'S is (actually) true but unknown', which perforce would refer to the circumstances *then* obtaining. The knowledge would have to be expressed some other way – whatever way would make the same claim that *we* can now make by use of that sentence.

The (5) to (9) paradox is easily handled along similar lines. The principle about disjunction becomes

5* $(\forall P)\ (\forall Q)$ [KW_A, '$P \vee Q$' is true in $W_A \rightarrow (\exists W_1)\ (\exists W_2)\ (KW_1$, P is true in $W_A \vee KW_2$, Q is true in $W_A)$],

and (9) becomes the unparadoxical

9* $(\exists W_1)\ (\exists W_2)\ ((KW_1,$ '$S\ \&\ {\sim}KW_AS$' is true in $W_A) \vee (KW_2,$ '${\sim}S\ \&\ {\sim}KW_A{\sim}S$' is true in $W_A))$.

What of Thatcher? Essentially the same strategy should suffice. (A) entails that W_A is void of evidence for Thatcher's master-criminality.

33 'I could have been taller than I actually am' does not advert to the possibility of circumstances in which 'I am taller than I actually am' would be true. Compare embedded uses of 'now'. To claim that '60 years ago the woman who is now Prime Minister had not been born' is not to claim that 60 years ago 'The woman who is now Prime Minister has not been born' was true.

34 As Edgington notes in 'The Paradox of Knowability', pp. 564–6, there are, strictly, awkwardnesses in yoking the apparatus of possible worlds to her purposes. But it will do no harm so to express her basic point.

(AR*) requires, if she is indeed a master criminal (in W_A), that there be a W_1 in which there is evidence both of Thatcher's criminal activities in W_A and of the absence in W_A of any symptom of them. There is no basis for a Modus Tollens here.

It may be that Edgington's ingenious proposal points out at least the shape of a satisfactory anti-realist response to these problems. But it also raises a number of difficult and, in some cases, crucial questions on which work will need to be expended before the situation can be clear. I conclude by mentioning three.

What would it be to have evidence for the proposition which would currently be expressed by 'Thatcher is a master criminal?' The proposal has it, presumably, that it would suffice to be in position to claim – in counter-factual circumstances – that if the circumstances then obtaining had been those which *actually* obtain, Thatcher's criminality would have been undetectable. Suppose, for instance, that Thatcher contracts a very high fever and blurts out the truth in a delirium. Then somebody might truly assert, 'If Thatcher had not fallen ill, her criminal activity would have been quite without trace.' And the state of affairs for which there is then evidence is – Edgington's proposal claims – the very same state of affairs as that which, if she does not fall ill, will make it true that Thatcher is a master criminal. Now, the proposal needs to make this claim because otherwise it fails to speak to the intention of (AR); if we are trying to explain how evidence is available for any true proposition, the proposition for which there is evidence in the counter-factual circumstances had better be the *same* proposition as that currently expressed by 'Thatcher is a master criminal'; *ergo*, the state of affairs described must be the same. But against this has to be set the perfectly natural thought that, in the sort of counter-factual circumstances envisaged, the state of affairs currently described by 'Thatcher is a master criminal' – to wit, her master criminality – simply would not exist. Compare this. Suppose that there is indeed going to be a surprise exam tomorrow. Then the thought that, if the news were to leak out, that would not be so, is not merely to the effect that the *sentence* would not be true; it is perfectly natural to say, more, that the depicted *state of affairs* – tomorrow's surprise exam – would not obtain. What follows is that the notion of *state of affairs* which Edgington's proposal needs is at best one aspect of a confused ordinary notion, and that theoretical explication is called for if it is to bear the load she is placing on it.[35]

35 A separate point is that it cannot be finally satisfactory, I believe, to represent the evidence which, purportedly, could be available for one of the problematic statements, as evidence for a counter-factual conditional. I do not mean (merely) the familiar contention that the truth of a counter-factual should be based in something expressible categorically. Rather the thought is that evidence which is irreducibly for how things *would be* in counter-factual circumstances is not evidence for how things *are* in the sense which (AR) intends.

Second, reflection on the paradox discussed by Edgington speedily discloses a separate difficulty, specifically related to the usual style of intuitionistic semantics for the conditional: 'if P, then Q' is accounted assertible (proved) just in case it is recognized that getting grounds for assertion (or a proof of) 'P' will put us in position to assert (construct a proof of) 'Q'. It would seem to follow that

$$(\forall P)\ (P \rightarrow KP)$$

should be unrestrictedly assertible for a number of interpretations of 'K', including 'is justified by the evidence' and 'is proved'. On such an account of the conditional, there is accordingly no question of endorsing

$$\sim(\forall P)\ (P \rightarrow KP)$$

as an expression of the existence of truths for which we have at present no evidence, in preference to

$$(\exists P)\ (P\ \&\ \sim KP)$$

as was entertained earlier. So the question becomes urgent, how in that case the plausible claim, that not all true (or assertible) statements are supported by presently possessed evidence, *is* to be expressed if such an account of the conditional is favoured.[36]

The third question is the most fundamental. Edgington's proposal has the anti-realist surrender the thought that evidence should *actually* be available for any actually true statement; it is to suffice that evidence be *possibly* available – that there be possible circumstances in which both the state of affairs which confers truth on the statement and appreciable evidence of it coexist. How liberal is this liberalization? Consider Dummett's Jones. The case Dummett made for refusing to accept that Jones was determinately either brave or not depended entirely on the circumstance, hypothesized in the example, that *as it happens* there is no evidence to be had one way or the other. But it follows therefrom that the disjunction about Jones is unacceptable only if the truth of either of its disjuncts is taken to require the *actual* availability of evidence of its truth. If that is not the requirement, it becomes unclear whether there is any compelling motive for Dummett's conclusion. Surely, there are *possible* circumstances in which Jones was tried and found, say, to be timid. If we take it that 'Jones is brave' was formerly an effectively decidable

36 The problem arises, of course, not just for those of intuitionistic sympathies but for anyone who is independently attracted to the relevant kind of account of the conditional. An example would be Anthony Appiah (see, e.g., his *Assertion and Conditionals*), certainly no friend in general of assertibility-conditional semantics.

statement, then there are possible circumstances in which we should now be in position to assert one of the past-tense disjuncts, *a fortiori* to assert their disjunction. So how could that assertion in the circumstances of the example violate the epistemic constraint intended by (AR) as interpreted by Edgington?

The matter goes further. Put on one side all statements with the characteristic that if evidence that they are true is unavailable in any possible circumstances, then it is unavailable in all possible circumstances. (If, as is normal, the availability of a cogent proof is conceived as contingent on nothing accidental, we hereby put aside all pure mathematical statements.) Then the question is whether among the remainder are to be found *any* statements where the kind of understanding with which realists wish to credit us would violate (AR) as now interpreted. Consider 'Everything is uniformly' – [by intention, therefore, undetectably] – 'increasing in size'. Until we know better what the constraints are on the survival of a state of affairs from one set of circumstances to another, what objection is there to the thought that even this might express a detectable truth – albeit detectable from the vantage point of counter-factual circumstances in which that *sentence* would no longer be the appropriate form of expression of the truth in question. It is the same for any example of the form, 'S is undetectably true'. If Edgington's implicit view of the real epistemic thrust of anti-realism's negative arguments is correct, it is unclear that to suppose we understand what it is for such a statement to be true is to suppose we understand what it is for truth to transcend evidence in any sense to which there ought to be an objection.

There are questions which need resolution before it can be clear to what extent traditional mathematical platonism would indeed emerge as a special case by Edgington's proposal. If, for instance, 'supertasks' are indeed the mere 'medical impossibilities' which Russell supposed, it would be a contingency that number-theoretic statements are not effectively decidable as a class, and (AR), as now interpreted, would pose no objection to classical number-theoretic practice. But it would be different with the classical theory of the continuum.[37] In any event, whereas some branches of classical mathematics would seem, when motivated by classical bivalent semantics, to go beyond what can be guaranteed sanitary even by the light of liberalized (AR), it is uncertain whether anything in ordinary non-mathematical linguistic practice or lay-semantics does so.

37 Because 'hypertasks' – the completion of uncountable processes – are necessarily unperformable. For proof, see Clark and Read, 'Hypertasks'.

The dilemma is therefore sharp. Either Edgington's proposal is only available to a 'soft' anti-realism, stopping far short of what is required by the basic negative case; or the requirements of that case have been badly misinterpreted by the greater part of the literature. But further pursuit of the matter must be postponed to another occasion.

15

Anti-realism and Revisionism

I want here to single out the idea, recurrent throughout Dummett's writings, that to abandon the realism with which we regard so many kinds of statement will involve abandoning the belief that classical logic holds valid for them.[1] There is no question that much of the interest which these writings have inspired is directly consequent on this notion: we are confronted by the prospect of being constrained by pure philosophical considerations to revise and modify not merely philosophical preconceptions which we hold, but substantial sections of our basic 'first-order' linguistic habits and practices. My concern here is thus not with the strengths or weaknesses of realism but with these putative revisionary implications of anti-realism: what, if any, outlets are open to someone who feels the force of the anti-realist arguments but who desires, for whatever reason, to conserve as much of our, apparently realism-inspired, linguistic practices as he can?

I

What exactly is the connection between those principles of classical logic which the mathematical intuitionists jettison, for example Excluded Middle and Double Negation Elimination, and realism? A superficial answer would be that the principle of Bivalence would appear, on certain natural assumptions, to entail the validity of both those examples. If every proposition, P, is determinately either true or false, and if the negation of P is true just in case P is false, then matters have to arrange themselves in such a way that, one way or the other, the disjunction of P with its negation is true; likewise, if the double negation of P is true, the negation

1 See, for example, *Truth and Other Enigmas*, pp. 18, 155, 167–8, 225–6, 288, 305 and 367.

of P will have to be false, so that P itself will be something other than false – and, by Bivalence, truth is the only remaining possibility.

Of course, for all that it may illustrate the frame of mind in which distinctively classical principles can seem unassailable, this reasoning tacitly appeals to various presuppositions: the orthodox Introduction and Elimination rules for disjunction, the convertibility of 'P is true' and 'P', Modus Tollendo Ponens, the principle that no proposition can simultaneously be true and false, and the transitivity of negation across the biconditional. But these presuppositions are not merely natural; they would all be acceptable to an intuitionist, so that the status of the reasoning as an explication of how Bivalence enjoins the validity of certain classical principles is in no way compromised by their part in it. The superficiality rather resides in the fact that no explanation has so far been given of why the realist should endorse Bivalence.

Often Dummett writes as though acceptance of Bivalence was absolutely constitutive of realism.[2] And it is true that if somebody accepts Bivalence for a class of statements for whose truth-values we cannot in every case guarantee means of decision, then he is at least committed to holding that we cannot guarantee that truth everywhere coincides with decidable truth. But unless he accepts the transition from 'we cannot guarantee that P' to 'it is a possibility that not-P', he has not thereby committed himself to the possibility of verification-transcendent truth. This transition is intuitionistically suspect: of any mathematical statement which is not effectively decidable it would be intuitionistically correct to say that we cannot guarantee the existence of means of verifying or falsifying it, but it is not, in view of the intuitionists' account of negation, acceptable as an intuitionistic possibility that there should simply *be* no means of verifying or falsifying the statement in question. There is therefore a doubt whether endorsement of Bivalence for other than effectively decidable statements is of itself an admission of the possibility of verification-transcendent truth.[3] Conversely, as McDowell has argued,[4] to allow that the truth or falsity of a certain class of statement may elude our capacities for detection would seem to carry no immediate commitment to Bivalence for them.

One reason why it could look as though Bivalence will be an important part of the realist's equipment is because we think of the truth-conditional conception of declarative-sentence meaning as involving not merely that each well-defined sentence is associated with determinate conditions of truth, but, more, that the information which an ideal explanation of its

2 For example, ibid., pp. xxxii, 146, 175, 228, 274, 315 and 358.

3 The reasoning of this paragraph is dissected in Rasmussen's and Ravnkilde's 'Realism and Logic'. For a reply to them, see Essay 16.

4 'Truth-conditions, Bivalence and Verificationism'.

meaning will get across, that is, the information which anyone who understands it grasps, is of this form: S is true if and only if conditions ϕ obtain, and is false in *any other circumstances*. For now it appears that the very mode whereby we confer a determinate sense upon a declarative sentence guarantees that the world must exemplify one of just two possible kinds of states of affairs: those which make that sentence true, and those which make it false. But the thought here is inconclusive. Bivalence requires a declarative sentence to be *determinately* true or false, so it fails for vague statements; but there is no reason why our understanding of a vague declarative sentence should not take the shape just described – it is just that the distinction between ϕ-circumstances and others will be vague. Thus 'X is bald' is true if circumstances obtain constituting X's baldness, and is false, *pace* Frege, Strawson et al., in circumstances of any other kind. If a realist is one who thinks that our understanding of all or most of the statements which we normally think we perfectly well understand is something that exemplifies the above truth-conditional schema, then he will commit himself to certain statements having truth-conditions which we cannot guarantee to be able to recognize when they obtain[5] and, in some cases perhaps, can guarantee not to be able to recognize when they obtain. But he will not have committed himself to Bivalence; nor, therefore, at any rate by the above route, to an endorsement of the unrestricted validity of classical logic.

We have, in fact, to distinguish at least four non-equivalent elements in realism as Dummett has described it:

i endorsement of Bivalence for statements which are not effectively decidable (henceforth 'non-ED statements');
ii admission of the possibility of verification-transcendent truth;
iii acceptance that our understanding of all statements fits the truth-conditional schema;
iv acceptance that for any true statement, there must be something in virtue of which it is true.

If the foregoing reflections are correct, then (i) and (ii) are two-way independent; and (iii), though it entails (ii),[6] does not entail (i). It would be interesting to explore the relations between the four strands further – but here we must be content to notice that an endorsement of (iv) would seem to be essential to the *revisionary* power of the thesis that pure mathematical

5 This seems unobvious to me now. An intuitionist, for instance, need not quarrel with the claim, for a non-effectively decidable mathematical statement A, that 'A is true in circumstances ϕ and false, i.e. its negation is true, in any other circumstances', provided all such 'circumstances' are thought of as constituted by the availability of constructive proofs.

6 See note 5.

truth cannot intelligibly transcend proof.[7] I shall from here on take it that (ii) is the cardinal doctrine of realism, simply because it is (ii) that Dummett's anti-realist arguments most directly attack.

II

Since the thesis to be considered is that to abandon realism involves abandoning classical logic for a large class of statements, it is arguable that what we ought to be enquiring is not whether realism sanctions classical logic but whether, conversely, to endorse classical logic for non-ED statements commits one to realism about them; if, and only if, that is so, is the thesis correct.

The natural argument here is parallel to the attempt, sketched above, to discern a commitment to verification-transcendent truth in an endorsement of Bivalence for non-ED statements. Suppose someone asserts of Dummett's now-dead, untried Jones that either he was brave or he was not. This is a disjunction, so, like any disjunction, if true, one of its disjuncts must be true. But the case is so constructed that there can be no question of evidence, let alone verification, for either disjunct; so surely the assertor has straightforwardly committed himself to the existence of a well-understood verification-transcendent truth.

The argument has fared better than its counterpart above merely because we have picked an example where the intuitionistically contentious transition, from 'we cannot guarantee to be able to verify or falsify P' to 'it is a possibility that we can neither verify nor falsify P', does not need to be negotiated; the context of the example has been specified to ensure that we can achieve neither verification nor falsification of it. But then, with Dummett, we have surreptitiously parted company with anything resembling the intuitionistic account of negation. Intuitionistically, the negation of P is counted as proved just in case we have a construction of which we can recognize that it would enable us, were we to obtain a proof of P, to construct a proof of a contradiction. Since, for the intuitionist, there is no question but that his mathematical thought is consistent, the account is tantamount to the stipulation that a proof of the negation of P is any construction which we can recognize to rule out the possibility of a proof of P. A natural generalization to ordinary, contingent statements, would therefore be:

(N) A total state of information (hereafter, a TSI) justifies the assertion of the negation of P just in case it justifies the assertion that a TSI

7 If statements may be true in contravention of (iv), so may disjunctions of such statements, including Excluded Middle.

> justifying the assertion of P cannot be achieved, no matter how thoroughgoing an investigation is conducted.[8]

But, on this account, there would be no question that a TSI might justify the assertion that no subsequent TSI could justify the assertion either of P *or* of its negation; rather, the description of the Jones example would entail that we were in a position to assert the negation of 'Jones is brave'. (So that, in general, it would no longer be possible to see the negation of a counter-factual conditional as another, contrary counter-factual.)

At this point it would appear that the crucial issue is whether (N), or something like it, is the appropriate form for a generalized anti-realist account of negation to take. If it is, there will be no recognizably undecidable contingent statements; and it will be impossible, because of the intuitionistically contentious nature of the transition involved, to argue directly that someone who accepts the validity of classical logic for non-ED statements thereby commits himself to the possibility of their possessing verification-transcendent truth values. But if it is not, and recognizably undecidable statements are a possibility, it appears that the argument may succeed and that Dummett's revisionary contraposition may have to be allowed.

In fact, it is hard to see what sort of considerations might persuade someone with general anti-realist sympathies to plump for (N). In mathematics the intuitionist can – I do not say 'should' – be seen merely as having adapted the classical conception of negation to the constraint that mathematical truth be in principle humanly recognizable truth. Classically, the negation of a well-defined mathematical statement, P, is true just in case (it is true that) no aspect of mathematical reality is so constituted as to make P true, but if mathematical truth is understood as in principle humanly recognizable truth, then the classical account collapses into the stipulation that the negation of P is provable just in case it is provable that no proof can be achieved of P – whence, since there are no assertion-grounds for the claim that P is provable save actual possession of a proof of P, precisely the intuitionistic account of the assertion-conditions of mathematical negation issues. (N), however, cannot be seen, comparably, as simply an adaptation of the classical account to an anti-realistically purified notion of truth; for, in contrast with proofs, the assertion-grounds of contingent statements tend to supply a *defeasible* warrant for the assertion of those statements and thus cannot be construed as truth-conditions.[9]

8 For further discussion of this, see Essay 14, section III.

9 We cannot in general, that is to say, attempt to construe the *truth* of a contingent statement as consisting in the availability of a total state of information which justifies its assertion; for if a state of affairs is sufficient to constitute the truth of a statement, it ought to continue to be so no matter how augmented – which is not the situation in the case of the best type of grounds we can have for asserting almost all types of contingent statement.

There is no clear sense, therefore, in which (N), in contrast with its mathematical analogue, can be seen merely as an adaptation of the realist account which it is proposed to supersede. Add to that the obvious difficulties in the way of achieving a satisfactory formulation of what (N) intends – it is not clear, for example, that the present formulation succeeds in excluding the suggestion that enrichment of our present TSI by the Four Minute Warning would entitle us to assert the negations of virtually all hitherto undecided statements! – and it is clear that the question, how best to frame a generalized anti-realist account of negation, is still open.[10]

III

Even if (N) were to fall by the wayside, however, there is a further problem with the sketched argument from Excluded Middle to realism – its outright reliance on the distributivity of truth over disjunction: the principle that in order for a disjunction to be true, it is necessary and sufficient that at least one of its disjuncts be true. For this principle is open to question in a familiar class of cases. One kind of case is where truth is consequent upon decision, or convention, of some sort; if, for example, we have the conception that fictional characters have exactly those properties which, either explicitly or implicitly, their authors give them, then it is going to be a possibility that an author assigns some disjunctive property to one of his characters yet omits to determine which of the disjuncts holds of that character, so that a disjunction will be truly assertible although none of its disjuncts is.[11] It is, likewise, acceptable English to say of an intermediate shade of colour that it is either red or orange while recognizing that it could not happily be described as either in particular.[12] And if, following, for example, Fine,[13] we take it that a (compound) colour predicate definitely applies to an object just in case it would still apply

10 If the anti-realist refuses to equate the content of the assertions 'P' and 'P is justifiably assertible' (note 9 contains the germ of an argument why he should so refuse; see section V of Essay 1 and Essay 14, passim) an apparently different tactic on negation, suggested to me by John Skorupski, would be: (N*). A TSI justifies the assertion of the negation of P just in case it leads, in conjunction with the hypothesis that P, to absurdity. I say 'apparently different' because (N*) would seem to identify the assertibility conditions of 'not-P' with those of 'if P, then Q', where Q is some absurdity; so that the effect of (N*) depends upon what account is given of the assertibility-conditions of the conditional. I cannot pursue the issue further here.

11 To see this kind of example as a genuine failure of truth to distribute over disjunction, it is, of course, necessary to see the author's fiction as constituting a kind of *truth*; otherwise, the undoubted failure of an appropriate 'in fiction' operator to distribute over disjunction is not to the point.

12 Cf. *Truth and Other Enigmas*, pp. 255–6.

13 'Vagueness, Truth and Logic'.

to it if the constituent predicates were made completely precise in such a way as to respect existing cases of their correct application, then one could correctly assert of objects of which no definitely correct *simple* colour description can be given that they are, say, definitely either red or not red.

More generally, assume any formal deductive theory, and the following constructive notion of model for it: a model will be considered to be well-determined if and only if it is decidable of an arbitrary well-formed sentence of the language of the theory whether or not it holds good in the model. Let such a sentence be considered *true* (absolutely) just in case it is true in every constructive model of the theory. Obviously, a disjunction of any statement in the language of the theory with its negation will now be absolutely *true*, since one or other of its disjuncts will be true in any particular constructive model which we happen to consider. But the theory need not, for all that we have said, be negation-complete; so some statements in the language of the theory may be true in some constructive models and false in others. Excluded Middle will thus be valid for this theory even in cases where neither of its disjuncts is absolutely *true*.

More specifically, we can envisage the following stipulations:

i 'A $\vee$ B' is *true* iff ($\forall$M) 'A' is true-in-M or 'B' is true-in-M;
ii '$\sim$A' is *true* iff ($\forall$M) it is not the case that 'A' is true-in-M;
iii 'A $\rightarrow$ B' is *true* iff ($\forall$M) if 'A' is true-in-M, 'B' is true-in-M;
iv 'A & B' is *true* iff ($\forall$M) 'A' is true-in-M and 'B' is true-in-M.

If to the above we add orthodox recursive clauses for truth-in-M (so that, for example, 'A $\vee$ B' is true-in-M if and only if either 'A' is true-in-M or 'B' is true-in-M) then it is notable that the ordinary introduction and elimination rules for disjunction will preserve absolute *truth*. This is apt to seem surprising in the case of the elimination rule, since one might have supposed that only if the *truth* of a disjunction requires the *truth* of at least one of its disjuncts would it be an adequate ground for attributing a certain consequence to a disjunction that it followed separately from each of its disjuncts. But if 'B$\vee$C' is absolutely *true*, then either 'B' or 'C' is true in any particular constructive model of the theory; so if the conditionals 'B$\rightarrow$D' and 'C$\rightarrow$D' are both absolutely *true*, (iii) above immediately yields that 'D' must be true in every constructive model, so absolutely *true*. (I leave it to the reader to verify the more general transition: $A \rightarrow (B \vee C), (E \,\&\, B) \rightarrow D, (F \,\&\, C) \rightarrow D \vdash (A \,\&\, E \,\&\, F) \rightarrow D$.)

To describe the shape of an example is not to give one. What the foregoing description shows is how it *might* be that, without any appeal to Bivalence, the use of classical logic could be validated for a particular theory in the eyes of an anti-realist, even though the sentences of that theory were not effectively decidable. 'Truth-in-M', for a particular M, is, to be sure, an effectively decidable notion – but that is precisely why the anti-realist ought to have no objection to the role it plays in (i) to (iv). And there is nowhere any assumption that absolute *truth* may transcend our capacity to recognize it. Absolute *truth*, however, need not be an effectively decidable notion; indeed, for all the constraints we have put on the shape of the example, theoremhood in the theory need not be decidable either. So it cannot be correct to suppose without further ado that the endorsement of classical logic for certain non-ED statements involves a commitment to realism; it is necessary to show in addition, at least for the particular class of statements at issue, that no semantics can be found, other than the traditional truth-conditional brand or others involving essential play with recognition-transcendent notions, which validates the application of classical logic to those statements. Our formal example shows, in general terms, how that might not be so.[14]

In fact, we can go some way toward giving a concrete example by following through a suggestion of Dummett himself in 'The Reality of the Past'.[15] Let us treat 'M' in the above clauses as ranging over *sufficiently specific presently acceptable world-histories*: where a world-history, that is, a finite enumeration of statements concerning the past, is sufficiently specific with respect to a statement A just in case it contains either A or its negation, and is presently acceptable just in case it is consistent and we presently lack any reason to doubt any of its constituent statements. Then an atomic statement is true-in-M just in case it is a member of M; a compound statement is true-in-M under the conditions specified by the orthodox recursive clauses; an atomic statement is *true* just in case it holds in every sufficiently specific presently acceptable world-history; and a compound statement is *true* under the circumstances stipulated in (i) to (iv). (It seems inapposite to talk of 'absolute' truth in this case, since the ephemeral character of present acceptability is going to generate the possibility of statements becoming, and ceasing to be, *true*.) There is now every promise of validating classical logic for statements about the past. But do we do so in an anti-realistically acceptable way? Certainly it is decidable of an ordinary statement whether or not it is a member of any sufficiently specific world-history which is *given* to us as presently acceptable. But the consistency of a world-history need not be an effectively decidable issue; and that in turn involves that it need not be effectively decidable whether our present state of information justifies doubt about any of its constituents. So whether or not a particular world-history is presently acceptable need not be an effectively decidable question. That, however, is no objection, from an anti-realist point of view, to the use being

14 See Field, 'Logic, Meaning and Conceptual Role', for a quite different validating semantics for classical logic, based not on truth but on the notion of subjective probability.
15 *Truth and Other Enigmas*, pp. 366–7.

made of the notion provided we know what it is to be entitled to claim that a particular world-history is presently acceptable, and are capable of recognizing certain world-histories as being so. If that proviso is granted, then the non-revisionary anti-realist has a strategy for making good a title to the use of classical logic for statements about the past which involves no appeal to Bivalence, respects their not being effectively decidable and makes no play with verification-transcendent assumptions.[16] How the strategy would ultimately fare we can enquire no further here.

IV

A natural reply to the foregoing is that it overlooks the positive character of much of Dummett's argument: the revisionary anti-realist has no need of the assumption that an endorsement of classical logic commits one to an unacceptable realism about a large class of statements if, as Dummett does, he can argue directly that the correct anti-realist semantics enjoins a non-classical logic. Whether or not some semantics not distributive of truth and free of verification-transcendence can be cobbled up to validate the use of classical logic in what have been taken to be anti-realistically contentious areas, no one – the reply continues – is going to be tempted to think for a moment that we shall thereby successfully characterize the notion of truth that actually governs talk in such areas, or the meanings of the logical particles. Rather, here is the place for the battery of considerations, associated by Dummett with the later Wittgenstein's slogan that meaning is use, which are intended to 'dethrone the concepts of truth and falsity' from the central place which they have traditionally occupied in the philosophical theory of meaning and supplant them with *warranted assertion* and *warranted denial*. In particular, when we embark on an assertibility-conditions account of the meanings of the logical constants, it becomes clear that once non-ED statements come within the range of the propositional variables, certain of the cardinal principles of classical logic cease to be acceptable.

In order to rehearse how this comes about, let us consider the examples of Excluded Middle, and Double Negation Elimination, in the light of

16 Bivalence, in fact, will very likely be actually counter-exemplified in a large class of cases; we have only to recognize that our present state of information provides absolutely no purchase either on A or its negation in order to be in a position to construct sufficiently specific and (plausibly) presently acceptable world-histories some of which contain A and some of which contain not-A; so that neither is *true*. That statements about the past are not effectively decidable is respected by the consideration that the effective decidability of *truth* (i.e., of the question whether A is *true* or not) would require that of 'our present state of information provides reason to doubt that...'; which, as noted, is dubious.

the generalized intuitionistic account of negation, (N), proposed earlier, and the following corresponding proposals for disjunction and the conditional:

D A total state of information (TSI) justifies the assertion of the disjunction of A with B just in case it (a) justifies the assertion of A, or (b) justifies the assertion of B, or (c) can be recognized to be capable of effective transformation into a TSI of one of the types (a) and (b).[17]

C A TSI justifies the assertion of a conditional whose antecedent is A and whose consequent is B just in case it can be recognized that its enrichment into a TSI justifying the assertion of A would *eo ipso* transform it into a TSI justifying the assertion of B.[18]

Consider any non-ED statement, A. Excluded Middle is valid for A just in case 'A ∨ ~ A' is justifiably assertible in any TSI whatever. So we have to consider whether, whatever our TSI happens to be, it is bound to be of one of the following three kinds:

i It justifies the assertion of A.
ii It justifies the assertion that no TSI justifying the assertion of A can be achieved.
iii It can be recognized to be capable of effective enlargement into a state of information of type (i) or of type (ii).

But now, bearing in mind that A is not effectively decidable, it is clear that there is no reason why any of these three cases should obtain. It is perfectly possible that we are not in a position to assert A, but that, while having no reason to expect that we cannot get into a position to assert A, we have nevertheless no effective way of turning up grounds for the assertion of A or grounds for asserting that grounds for its assertion cannot be achieved. An example of a statement in this situation would be, I suggest, 'Travel at close to the speed of light will one day be possible'; we have no grounds for asserting that statement, no grounds for denying that its assertion may one day be justified, and no way of effectively

17 Obviously 'transformation' must here be interpreted so as to exclude manipulation of the relevant aspects of the world; otherwise my present TSI will justify me in asserting any disjunction the truth of one of whose disjuncts I know it to be within my power to bring about. It is a nice question just how the needed distinction should be formulated.

18 There is nothing inevitable about either 'enrichment' or '*eo ipso*'. We could have proposed: C*. A TSI justifies the assertion of a conditional whose antecedent is A and whose consequent is B just in case it can be recognized that its *modification* into a TSI justifying the assertion of A would result in a TSI capable of effective transformation into one justifying the assertion of B. There are some complex issues here, but they are not relevant to the discussion of Double Negation Elimination in the text.

securing either type of ground. So we have no alternative but to accept that Excluded Middle is no longer unrestrictedly validly assertible (which is not, I stress, to allow that it may be validly denied).

What of Double Negation Elimination? We have to consider whether our TSI is bound to be such that, for an arbitrary non-ED statement, A, its enrichment into a TSI justifying the assertion of the double negation of A would *eo ipso* transform it into a TSI justifying the assertion of A itself. Now, to be justified in asserting the double negation of a statement is to be justified in asserting that no TSI justifying the assertion of its (single) negation can be achieved; that is, it is to have one's TSI justify one in asserting that no TSI can be achieved in which one would be justified in asserting that no TSI can be achieved in which one would be justified in asserting A. Consider, therefore, the statement, 'There exists intelligent anthropoid life outside this galaxy'. To be justified in denying that statement would be, on the present account, to be justified in asserting that no TSI can be achieved which would justify its assertion; so it is arguable that not merely are we not in a position to deny the statement but that we are in a position to deny its denial, for we surely have grounds now to reject the suggestion that we shall ever have adequate grounds for ruling out the possibility that evidence of the existence of intelligent anthropoid life outside this galaxy will come our way. But, if that is correct, then we can be in a position to assert the double negation of the statement while in no position to assert the statement itself; for our grounds for asserting the double negation are manifestly not evidence of the existence of life of the appropriate kind.

Granted, then, that (N), (D) and (C) satisfactorily capture our intuitive understanding of the relevant logical constants, it appears that our logical practices outside the domain of effectively decidable statements, in so far as they are prevailingly classical, are indeed in disharmony with our understanding and ought to be revised. But, as noted earlier in the case of (N), the assumption is a major one. In particular, since the revisionist is prepared to allow from the outset that our linguistic practice can be out of line with the correct account of the meanings of certain crucial terms, it is a particularly awkward question how the *correct* account is to be conceived as recognizable – for mere *observation* of our practice will clearly not do. The classical truth-conditional account of the logical constants is, if the anti-realist is right, incoherent when given its intended wide application; but while philosophical considerations may put us in a position to recognize that circumstance, and even, perhaps, to see that conditions of warranted assertion should play a central role in the theory of meaning, nothing has so far been done to explain how we are to know what *precise* cast to give our assertibility-conditions explanations of the logical constants. Nowhere does Dummett attempt this. Until the lacuna is filled, the idea that an assertibility-conditions approach to meaning is bound, when given its widest application, to prove revisionary of classical logic, is just an assumption.

V

An inexorable course, then, from anti-realism to revisionism has yet to be mapped out. But there is, as it seems to me, a deeper assumption operating in Dummett's thought in this area. The non-distributive approach was a suggestion about how an anti-realist might coherently attempt to *explain* his acceptance of classical logic for certain non-ED statements. Someone who explored that line would be continuing to suppose that logic needs validation in terms of a philosophically acceptable semantics. That is Dummett's deeper assumption, implicit also in the idea that our inability to validate, say, Excluded Middle in terms of a satisfactory assertibility-conditions account of the logical constants would call into question the validity of the principle.

Now, what is to prevent someone from accepting the anti-realist complaints about classical semantics while refusing to seek a *semantic validation* of logic at all? If we grant, for the sake of argument, that it is by reference to conditions of warranted assertion and denial that a satisfactory account of the understanding of declarative sentences should proceed, the fact remains that the assertion or denial of a statement may be warranted by *inference* – so why should it not simply be *classical* logic that determines this class of assertion- and denial-conditions? It is true that there is no *justification* for certain principles of classical logic in terms of the sort of generalized assertion-conditions semantics prefigured in the preceding section; but why is justification necessary?

To put the matter another way: suppose we come across a community whose language contains a binary sentential operator, ϕ, competence in whose use appears to subserve the following descriptive hypothesis:

> 'ϕ (AB)' is considered justifiably assertible just in case it is believed that there are sufficient grounds for asserting A, or for asserting B, or for believing that one can get grounds of one of the first two kinds, *or* B is the negation of A, *or* B is believed to be a consequence of the negation of A.

Evidently there could be such a practice – it is designed closely to resemble our own practice with 'or'. The pattern of use seems clear and coherent enough; so what can be wrong with it?

A natural thought is that the symbol, ϕ, so used, is merely ambiguous; whereas we do not ordinarily conceive of there being such ambiguity in the sense of 'or'. But it is only a necessary condition of ambiguity that a characterization of the assertion-conditions of sentences involving a putatively ambiguous symbol should embrace a seemingly heterogeneous variety of cases. Provided the inferential connections and, to put it loosely, pragmatic consequences of relevant statements are appropriately invariant, then, variation in their assertibility-conditions notwithstanding, we shall regard the symbol as univocal. So we can suppose that the deductive liaisons of 'ϕ (AB)' are the same irrespective of which, if any, type of ground characterized is prompting its assertion; certainly that is how it is with 'or' in our ordinary inferential practice.

In classical semantics the presupposition was that the validity of a logical schema had to be traceable to the principle of Bivalence and the truth-conditional explanations of the logical constants; and a corresponding assumption is made in intuitionistic semantics, and illustrated in the examples of the preceding section. What is now being mooted is a style of semantic theory in which the validity of certain schemata will simply be taken as *primitive*. Preference for such a style would fit nicely with the view that the validity of these schemata does not *flow from* the meanings of the logical constants – rather, their acceptance as valid contributes towards determining those meanings.

The intended distinction, whether or not ultimately coherent, is easy enough to illustrate. A training in the use of foot and yard rules, normal in all respects save that it involved no explicit definitions, would put someone in a position to recognize the falsity of '4 feet = 1 yard' – so that the truth of the negation of that statement can be seen as flowing from the meanings of 'foot' and 'yard' as explained in this operational way. But our trainee would not be in a position to recognize the truth of '3 feet = 1 yard'; it would be consistent with everything that he was in a position to determine that 3 feet should equal 0.9981 yards – or whatever. So here the role of '3 feet = 1 yard' would be to determine further the meanings of 'foot' and 'yard' as fixed operationally; that sentence would be a well-motivated but nevertheless independent explicit convention. (Likewise, to take an example of Dummett's,[19] there is nothing in the ostensive training which we give our children in the use of 'green' and 'blue' – in contrast with the situation with 'green' and 'red' – to prevent their intelligently receiving a description of some suitably intermediate shade of colour as 'green and blue all over'. So, that nothing can be correctly so described is again an independent and explicit convention.)

What is being suggested, then, is that it is open to an anti-realist to regard those aspects of classical logic which resist elucidation in terms of his favoured substitute for classical semantics as independent and explicit conventions; whose effect is further to determine the meanings of the logical

19 *Truth and Other Enigmas*, p. 169.

constants as fixed by the basic explanations – the drills whose import the recursions of an appropriate theory of meaning would aim to codify. It is proposed, in short, that whatever the philosophical defects of realism and of classical semantics, there is no need to seek an anti-realistically acceptable validation for classical logic, nor, therefore, failing to find one, to propose changes; rather, it is open to us to see certain principles of classical logic simply as implicitly definitional of the concepts which feature in them and so as immune to revision or reproach in terms of semantical considerations.

VI

What objections are there to such an approach? In particular, what objections can be elicited from Dummett's work? There are two principal ones: a worry about *soundness*, and a worry about whether the position does not involve a slide into an (incoherent?) *holism*.

Dummett's occasional remarks about holism[20] are among the least satisfying in his writings. The holist is represented as advancing theses like: there is no mastering a mere fragment of a language, there is no such thing as correct assignment of content to an individual sentence of a language.[21] The possible motivation for the holist stance is not, to my knowledge, treated in detail in any of Dummett's discussions; but it would presumably have to involve the belief that no account can be given of the correct use of a declarative sentence – the conditions under which it might legitimately be held to be true, or false – save by reference to an indefinite number of background assumptions, i.e. sentences held to be true. And to these sentences the same point would apply, so that accounting for the correct use of one sentence would rapidly become a matter of accounting for the correct use of every sentence in the language.

What truth there might be in this idea is a matter of some urgency to understand. In particular we need to be clear whether it really follows that there is no fully understanding a particular sentence outside the context of mastery of a whole language. (What, for the purposes of this point,

20 See especially pp. 134–40, 218–21, 300–5, 309 and 378–9 in *Truth and Other Enigmas*. Also pp. 363–70 of the 'Concluding Philosophical Remarks' in *Elements of Intuitionism*.

21 'On such a [holistic] view, it is illegitimate to ask after the content of any single statement, or even after that of any one theory...; the significance of each statement or of each deductively systematised body of statements is modified by the multiple connections which it has...with other statements...of our language taken as a whole, and so there is no adequate way of understanding the statements short of knowing the entire language. [A statement's] . . . meaning simply consists in the place which it occupies in the complicated network which constitutes the totality of our linguistic practices' (*Truth and Other Enigmas*, p. 218; cf. p. 382, lines 19–22).

would be a 'whole language' here? How much of the language of kinetics or the theory of Complex Numbers is part of English? With the meanings of what proportion of, or which, words in the *OED* must an English speaker be familiar?) The important point for Dummett about the purported corollary, however, is this: someone who endorses it can attach no sense to what otherwise seems a very natural constraint on acceptable systems of logic and mathematics – that they *keep faith with* correct use of the sentences among which they regulate inferences. The holist, Dummett supposes, will not allow that there is, in the relevant sense, anything for logic and mathematics to keep faith with here. For in order for there to be any issue whether or not a particular logic keeps faith with the use of a particular class of sentences, we have to suppose it a possibility that someone who has as yet no grasp of the vocabulary of the logic can nevertheless understand those sentences fully and perfectly. We have to be able to ask whether uses of those sentences regulated by correct inferences in the logic really are *correct*, so it must be possible to understand what correct use of those sentences consists in independently of a mastery of the logic. But that is just to say that it is possible to achieve a perfect understanding of no more than a fragment of the language, which is precisely what Dummett's holist denies.

For the holist, then, the question whether or not a particular system of logic, over and above being consistent, is *sound* – preserves truth or inference-independent assertibility, or whatever we take the semantically central notion to be – fails of full intelligibility. On a molecular view of language, in contrast, it has to make sense to ask whether new uses of sentences, which become possible when a fragment of a language is extended in a certain way, fit the meanings previously assigned to those sentences. A good illustration is provided by Dummett's example of the people who count as we do but have as yet no other arithmetical operations.[22] These people will possess certain observational criteria for judgements of the form, 'X miscounted'; but if we now teach them to add and subtract, there will be a new range of cases in which they will be prepared to make judgements of this type: cases where, without observing any particular error in counting, they now assert that an error has nevertheless occurred just on the basis that a pool of results does not 'total up' properly. Now, on the molecular view, the issue of soundness here arises, to take just one example, in the form of the question: is it a possibility that, notwithstanding the arithmetically discordant character of a set of results, no error in counting – nor shift in the size of the groups of objects being counted – has occurred? Only if the answer is 'no' is the set of techniques which we have taught these people sound,

22 *Truth and Other Enigmas*, pp. 173–5.

and the extension of the range of uses of judgements of the form, 'X miscounted' which they have come to accept a *conservative extension*[23] of their previous practice. (*Our* natural belief, of course, is that our arithmetic *is* in this way sound, that its necessity, and utility, both reside in its fidelity to the meaning of numerical expressions as fixed by counting and observation.)

So far as I can see, the type of holism just adumbrated would simply have to reject this example as misconceived. If our language is (in a sense that now needs explaining) richer than that of Dummett's people, it simply makes no sense to suppose that there is a coincidence in meaning between a fragment of their language and a fragment of ours. For there will be no accounting for the correct use of the relevant numerical fragment of our language save by reference to the whole language in which it is embedded; and the same will go for the relevant numerical fragment of their language. So the example cannot be used to subserve the intelligibility of the question whether our techniques of addition, etc. conservatively extend their use of sentences in the relevant fragments of their language.

Holism, then, has no motive for an interest in soundness. But a demonstration of soundness surely is the motive for seeking an interesting and philosophically respectable semantics for a logic. So holism has no motive for seeking an 'interesting and philosophically respectable' semantics. What is not clear is whether Dummett is right to assert the converse: that the stance of disavowing semantical foundations for logic – that is, foundations designed to explicate the validity of all schemata deemed to be valid – must, in the end, inflate into holism.[24] How, in particular, would the anti-realist sympathizer who proposed to regard otherwise inaccessible classical postulates, like Excluded Middle, as implicitly definitional of the relevant connectives have committed himself to a holist view?

Part of Dummett's idea here may be this: that if no semantical evaluation of a particular schema is sought, if it is simply laid down, then there is no giving any substantial account of its content; it will function purely, as it were, as an *inferential mechanism*. If we simply lay it down, for example, that 'A or not-A' is always validly assertible, we have, to be sure, done enough to enjoin a certain pattern of use; but we have done nothing to say what 'or', in this case, *means*. If disjunction is explained as in (D), then the content of the assertion of 'A or B' is seemingly clear: it is that our total state of information justifies the assertion of one of the disjuncts in particular, or that it can be recognized to be capable of effective

23 This adaptation of the technical proof-theoretic notion is Dummett's; see ibid., pp. 221–2, 302 and 315–7.
24 *Truth and Other Enigmas*, p. 218.

enlargement into such a state of information. But this is not what we are saying when we assert 'A or not-A' on the view that allows it to be a special case; and there then appears to be no prospect of an account of what we *are* saying. But, on any molecular view of language, it has to be possible to give some sort of account of the content of any particular assertion; so the proponent of the implicit-definition view must either climb down or sever links with molecularism. Only holism can supply a framework within which the impossibility of giving an account of the content of a particular assertion is not immediately sufficient for the conclusion that we do not genuinely understand it.

It needs examination, however, just what sort of *account* of the content of an assertion it is proper to request on any view, molecular or holist. First, as noted earlier, it cannot be right to think that the assertibility-conditions theorist can regard the content of an arbitrary statement as being that conditions justifying its assertion obtain. His claim is, to be sure, that grasping the content of a statement is grasping its assertibility-conditions; but this cannot be held to imply the former idea unless he is to be committed to the absurdity that no justified assertion can ever be *revised* as new information becomes available. It is true that the *sentence*, 'our present total state of information justifies the assertion that S', for example, will change in status; but that is not good enough since, on any plausible view, it expresses distinct statements at different times. It will not do, therefore, to assume that the content of 'orthodox' disjunctions, whose use is explained along the lines of (D), can be taken to be immediately unproblematical – at least, if the thought is that, by offering (D), we have directly specified what they state.

Second, we cannot expect, obviously to be able in general to state the content of a particular assertion without using the very same sentence to do so, and without recourse to another language. So there must be some sentences for whose assertoric content the best we can do by way of an account, unless we are satisfied to stop with a 'homophonic' description, is to characterize their use. It therefore needs a special argument why an account which, for example, appends to (D) the clauses:

> ...or (d) B is the negation of A, or (e) B is a consequence of the negation of A

is insufficient to confer content on assertions of the form 'A or not-A' – supposing it succeeds, of course, as a characterization of the use of disjunctive statements in general.[25] Dummett's writings contain, so far as I have been able to determine, the basis of no such argument.

25 An immediate doubt on this score is occasioned by the impredicative play made with the notion of *consequence* in clause (e). But we are justified, I think, in making no attempt to allay this particular doubt here, not because the problem is not very real but because

VII

Let us try a different approach. Reflect on the generalized anti-realist accounts of the logical constants mooted earlier and the rule of disjunction elimination. Suppose we are in a position to assert an 'orthodox' disjunction, 'A ∨ B', and to assert the conditionals, 'A → C' and 'B → C'. Then the situation will be that we either are already in, or have recognized that we can effectively achieve, a total state of information in which we are entitled to assert A, or B, in particular; and that we have recognized that such is our present total state of information that any transformation of it into one justifying the assertion of A will succeed in transforming it into one justifying the assertion of C – ditto for B. It follows that we either are already in, or can effectively achieve, a total state of information justifying the assertion of C; and that this will be a state of information whose justification of the assertion of C could be recognized by someone who overlooked its justification of the assertion of 'A ∨ B'. Of course, in a particular case such an oversight might be hugely implausible; but the important point is that such are the explanations being proposed of '∨' and '→' that inferences from assertible premises via Disjunction Elimination are constrained to lead only to conclusions whose justified assertibility is recognizable *independently of their so following*.

That is an informal illustration of how constraining a logic by a respectable semantics promotes soundness. But contrast what happens if, following the implicit-definition anti-realist, we let the constraint go. Now a disjunction, 'D ∨ E', can be justifiably assertible without our having any reason to think that our total state of information can be developed so as to justify assertion of either disjunct in particular; so even if we are in a position to assert both 'D → C' and 'E → C', we have no guarantee that a state of information can be achieved of which someone who had overlooked the possibility of the inference from 'D ∨ E' could recognize that it warranted the assertion of C. But that is just to say that certain grounds for asserting C – grounds which do not connect merely contingently, or

---

it already infects in any case both the intuitionists' explanations of the connectives inside mathematics and our generalizations of them. (C), for example, appeals to the general notion of what it is for a state of information to justify the assertion of A – where A may be a statement of *any sort*; but if that notion may be presupposed, what need of (C)? The remedy, if there is one, has to lie in the availability of a base class of atomic statements whose assertion-conditions and consequence relations may be taken as clear, and to which our explanations of the connectives may be applied, one by one and in endless rotation; so that a predicative account is always available of the assertion-conditions and consequence relations of the statements so far accumulated at any stage in the resulting hierarchy.

symptomatically, with the justified assertion of C – may not be appreciable by someone familiar with every non-inferential type of ground for asserting it.

This possibility cannot be straightforwardly seen as that of *unsoundness* unless we take it that the content of an assertion of C is that non-inferential, or other canonical, grounds for its assertion are realized. But does it involve that the content of C can no longer be accounted for by a molecular view of the language in question? What is clear is that, under these circumstances, no one can be a master of the full range of conditions which justify assertion of C who is not an explicit master of a certain amount of the vocabulary and practice of logic; otherwise he will not be aware of the conventionally acceptable status of 'D ∨ E', or of what can be done with it. So it appears that any adequate training in the use of C, and of other statements in the same situation, is going to have to advert to the relevant aspects of *inferential* practice. That, however, is a far cry from saying that the only adequate training in the use of C must be one which encompasses the use of the whole language.

The essence of the molecular view, as Dummett characterizes it,[26] is that mastery of a language can be acquired piecemeal, not just in the sense of permitting division into stages but in the sense that, at each stage, competences will be possessed which are, in a certain sense, *complete* at that stage – which continue unmodified into subsequent stages. Why should the idea that certain truths of logic have a primitive, postulational status be inconsistent with this picture? What the implicit-definition view may be inconsistent with is the capacity of any particular class of non-logical statements, among which the postulates in question mediate possible inferences, to determine a possible molecular stage *by themselves*; but that is not to say that there can be no such stages – it is merely that every molecular stage must involve a logical competence.

In essentials, all that is entailed in taking 'A or not-A' as a postulate is that every statement becomes assertible in certain circumstances in which its double negation is assertible. (For, whenever we can prove a statement, C, by means of a Disjunction Elimination on Excluded Middle, we can prove its double negation independently using just the conditional rules and Reductio ad Absurdum.) Now consider any language for which an assertibility-conditions semantics is correct whose effect is to open up, for certain statements, a possible hiatus between conditions warranting the assertion of their double negations and conditions warranting the assertion of those statements themselves. The question is: if a molecular view of such a language is possible at all, how would it be compromised if the language were altered merely so as to obliterate this hitherto recognized distinction? From now on each statement is, if necessary (that is,

26 See pp. 222–3, 302, 304–5, 317–18, 378–9 of *Truth and Other Enigmas*.

if it is not effectively decidable), to be broadened in sense in such a way as to embrace among its own assertibility-conditions those formerly of its double negation. There might be all sorts of things to be said against such a change, so all sorts of reasons why *we*, if the postulational view gives a correct account of our acceptance of classical logic, would do well to move in the direction of something more sensitive. But our present concern is only whether anti-realism makes such a move mandatory, with holism as the only saving option. And the answer, it appears, is 'no – unless a language of which a molecular view is possible can be transformed into one of which it is not, merely by stipulating that the conditions of correct use of two hitherto non-equivalent types of expression shall henceforth coincide'.[27]

VIII

Let us conclude by reflecting on the appeal which Dummett makes in this context to the notion of soundness, and to cognates like 'conservative extension'.

As noted, the motivation for the sort of semantical foundation for logic which the classical and intuitionistic approaches illustrate is to ensure that

27 As John Skorupski has pointed out to me, there is a prima facie powerful objection to the suggestion that (D), supplemented by (d) and (e), and (N) might rival their classical truth-conditional counterparts as explanations of our, apparently classical, logical practices. For in the presence of the rule of Modus Tollendo Ponens, their conjoint effect would appear to be too *permissive*: if (N) is a correct account of our understanding of negation, and if the status of Excluded Middle were simply that of explicit convention, then we ought to be prepared, in the presence of MTP, to assert any statement P *wherever* we have adequate grounds to rule out our achieving a state of information which would entitle us to rule out acquiring justification for the assertion of P. Why, then, are we not prepared to advance the claim that there exists intelligent anthropoid life outside this galaxy purely on the basis of the case for its double negation made in section IV?

Evidently the problem is not special to (N) but will arise for any anti-realist account of negation sufficient to generate a prima facie doubt about the unrestricted validity of Double Negation Elimination. Thus, if the 'straightforward clauses' anti-realist winds up revising classical logic, the 'implicit definitions' anti-realist winds up saving classical logic at the price of misdescription of our conception of the assertibility-conditions of a large class of statements not effectively decidable.

The point is well taken as far as it goes, but not decisive. The 'implicit-definitions' anti-realist can be convicted of misdescription of our linguistic practices only if our dispositions to assert are a function *purely* of the assertibility-conditions of a statement and are subject to no other (pragmatic) constraints. But that conditions obtain which *justify* assertion of a particular statement is unlikely to prove sufficient *tout court* for its assertion being deemed *appropriate*. The shift to an assertibility-conditions account of meaning does not squeeze out all space for the distinctions which Grice has taught us to draw. The topic is a large one, crucially important to the question whether realist conceptions can have a distinctive linguistic manifestation. We cannot pursue it further here.

logic is faithful to the understanding which we have of the statements to which it is to be applied; the explicit vocabulary of logical inference, and of mathematics, is always to extend conservatively any language game to which it is added. The sort of holism adverted to by Dummett cannot, we noticed, find room for such a requirement; but, if the gist of the preceding section is correct, then to waive the requirement need not involve any commitment to holism. There are, however, certain independent doubts about the status of the ideal of soundness which Dummett does not consider. And unless the ideal is in good order, there would obviously be no point in taking steps to promote its realization – the central motive for the sort of philosophically inspired revision of classical logic which the intuitionists proposed. That is not to say that there could be *no* respectable philosophical motive for wanting the sort of harmony and simplicity of semantic theory and inferential practice which the classical and intuitionistic approaches essay. But it is a development which would take us closer to the later Wittgenstein's idea that philosophy can only expose error in *philosophy* – in the pictures and lay-philosophical conceptions with which we envelop aspects of our linguistic practice. It cannot show aspects of that *practice* to be mistaken, though it may provide motives of a different kind for revision of it.

We have to put on one side, of course, the case where the ideal is clearly violated: that of systems of inference which permit the derivation of mutually inconsistent statements from a consistent pool of premises. Clearly, provided only that we have assigned a coherent meaning to the statements in question, no such system can be seen as conservatively extending their use. But the sense which the ideal gets from this case is not, of course, germane. For what is to be avoided – what a philosophically well-founded semantics is supposed to ensure avoidance of – is an unsoundness that need not be reflected in inconsistency. From the point of view of an anti-realist who espoused an assertibility-conditions conception of meaning, what was to be avoided would be this: that from warrantedly assertible premises conclusions could correctly be drawn for whose warranted assertion no other ground could be given and which deserved rather, on independent grounds, to be denied. In particular, if we are concerned with statements to which observational grounds of assertion have been assigned, what has to be avoided would be the correct derivability from observationally warranted premises of a conclusion for whose assertion no warrant in observation could be found. The question is: could we ever *recognize*, inconsistency apart, that that was the situation which we were in?

Consider again Dummett's people who count as we do but do not add. Suppose they prove poor pupils: our best efforts to teach them systematic addition, multiplication, subtraction and division among zero and the positive integers are largely unsuccessful. But they do learn a number of explicit arithmetical equalities, conformity with which they now treat as necessary if counting is to be adjudged correct. So, bad pupils though they are, they will still be, as envisaged, on occasion prepared to say, 'I must have miscounted', or 'the size of the group must have changed', not because they have any directly observational grounds for saying so – the kind of ground they respected before and which we share with them – but because arithmetical rules which they have come to accept are infringed. But suppose that, as a result of who knows what misunderstanding, these people come to accept the rule that 17 + 29 = 45. So if one of them correctly counts a mixed bag of hazelnuts and walnuts, finding 17 of the former and 29 of the latter, he will conclude, without counting, that there are 45 nuts in all – a judgement for which, in our view, no satisfactory observational warrant can be found.

In our view, the fragmentary, asystematic arithmetical rules on which these people have alighted are, in just the intuitively relevant sense, unsound. They permit the derivation from independently acceptable premises of conclusions with no independent warrant – indeed, for whose *denial* independent warrant can be found; for meticulous counting of the whole bag of nuts is going to yield, we are confident, the result 46. But what, exactly, entitles us to this point of view? For we have no *guarantee* that if all the nuts were counted – first the two separate groups and then the total – then either the results would 'add up' by our arithmetical standards or we should notice a miscount or change in the constitution of the groups. It is a possibility that what we regard as arithmetically discrepant results collectively will *seem*, individually, to have been correctly arrived at. With what right do we claim that if things seem to go contrary to our arithmetic they cannot really be as they seem, so that independent observational warrant *must* emerge, if matters are sufficiently painstakingly examined, for any arithmetical conclusion correctly drawn by the lights of our arithmetic from premises for which there is such a warrant?

We are able to recognize, as we suppose, the unsoundness of these people's fragmentary arithmetic because it is inconsistent with our own. Which – of course – we know to be sound. So, we want to say, where results seem to go against our arithmetic, it cannot be that they really do so; and some hypothesis along the lines, 'I must have miscounted', 'An extra nut must have been smuggled in', etc., serving to dissolve the appearance of conflict, must be correct. So things were not as they seemed to be observed to be: it may have seemed as if all the counts were correctly conducted, that no nuts were smuggled in or out, etc., but it was not *really* so; and sufficiently painstaking observation would have revealed how it was, in particular, not so. But Dummett's people, in contrast, will rest content with their results in situations where *we* propose such a hypothesis – and will propose such hypotheses in situations where we rest content. And because of the strict *indefeasibility* of such hypotheses, occasioned by their open existential character, there will be no decisively proving the proposers wrong; indeed they may, in any particular case, be right.

Before they had any arithmetical rules, these people will have had no criterion for the occurrence of an unnoticed error or other peculiarity in a count, save that someone else did notice it and reported as much; but now they will be in a position to say, groundlessly as it will likely seem to us, that *everyone* is overlooking something; just as we are. It is, that is to say, an aspect of the role of our logical and mathematical principles of inference to determine successful negotiation of the transition between appearance and reality, to determine when appearance must be discounted. The very idea, then, that our arithmetical rules are *sound*, whereas those of these people are not, embraces a commitment to the conception that the class of circumstances in which appearance should be discounted is in no sense a conventional notion, or one relative to a 'conceptual scheme'. Our arithmetical laws, our principles of inference in general, if sound, *get these matters right*; when inferential discord bids us reassess premises and conclusion, we can take it that our previous assessment really was mistaken; that, supposing we are concerned with, broadly speaking, statements assessable by observation, things really occurred which we overlooked. Notwithstanding the indefeasibility, case by case, of the 'saving hypotheses' which users of an unsound arithmetic, or logic, will advance, sound principles of inference enjoin the proposal of some such hypothesis only when it is really true, or independently warrantedly assertible. So Dummett's people will be in the position of taking observations as veridical which are not so; and of discounting as spurious observations which are correct.

Now, what should be borne in mind at this point is that the concern with soundness was to be an *anti-realistically* possible concern; for it was to motivate the sort of systematic non-transcendent semantics which led the intuitionists to revision. A prospective tension, therefore, opens up in the following way: the anti-realist, following Dummett, has to be able consistently both to disavow the intelligibility of verification-transcendent truth and to affirm the intelligibility of the idea that there is a determinate objective class of situations in which things are indeed as they seem; a determinate objective class of situations in which warrant for a particular assertion cannot be overturned, no matter how painstaking an investigation is carried out. For if there is no such determinate, objective class, how can the conclusion be avoided that it is only from *our* point of view that the saving hypothesis proposed by Dummett's people, or their contentment with a particular series of results, can be seen as mistaken? Whereas they are to be wrong not just from our point of view but *absolutely*. If these ideas are not to be inconsistent, the objective distinction between the two classes of states of affairs must not be a transcendent one. So we are owed an account of how we can recognize, or at least be justified in claiming, that a particular state of affairs comes on one side of it or that it comes on the other; where, to stress, what is to be accounted for is not how – by reference to what criteria – *we* are accustomed to determine a situation to be of one sort or of another, but how we are to recognize the *adequacy* of the criteria which we in fact employ. Nowhere in Dummett's writings is there an attempt at such an account.

There is, however, a natural response. If we focus once more on the example of elementary arithmetic, and ask, what *is* the source of our confidence in its soundness, the answer has to be: the susceptibility of its equalities to *proof*; if concord, or discord, with our arithmetic is one of our criteria for working the appearance/reality distinction, we recognize the adequacy of the criterion – if recognize it we do – by *proving* arithmetical equalities. This, by hypothesis, Dummett's people will not be able to do. It is the proof of 29 + 17 = 46 which brings it out that, the attitude of these people notwithstanding, their contentment with the results, 29, 17, 45, is misplaced; that if they had investigated, sufficiently carefully, they would have turned up something which *they* would have regarded as invalidating their results.

Dummett complains[28] about the 'mysteriousness' of the later Wittgenstein's conception of logical and mathematical proof, that a proof induces us to make a certain 'decision', to relate concepts in certain ways which were hitherto not so related. But the *depth*, on the present suggestion, even of what we ordinarily regard as trivial pieces of mathematics, like arithmetical sums, is really no less mysterious; for the suggestion implicitly takes it that we can confer a meaning upon signs in such a way that the question whether they are correctly used in a particular situation is settled just by that meaning and the character of the situation, and is independent of our reaction to it. Just that is what is involved in the conception that Dummett's people, on occasion, are simply, if indefeasibly, mistaken in advancing a particular saving hypothesis. The assumed depth in our arithmetic is located at this point: arithmetic puts us in a position to recognize that, however convincing a series of counts may seem to be, either they were not all correctly arrived at or there was some kind of instability in the objects being counted; arithmetic puts us in a position to apprehend aspects of the correct use of certain signs which, however operationally skilled in their use, we would, if computationally virgin like Dummett's people, have been likely to overlook.

28 *Truth and Other Enigmas*, pp. 173 and 301.

Whatever prevents our mythical people from cottoning on to arithmetic, it is hardly deniable that we too have certain limitations – if only of time, intellect and will. So how can we block the corollary that there may be certain aspects of the correct use of our signs which are opaque to us in turn, statements fidelity to the meaning of whose constituent terms requires their acknowledgement as correct, but which we shall *de facto* never be in a position to acknowledge as correct? Of course, this is an idea which we might have been inclined anyway unthinkingly to accept. But the requisite notion of objectivity of meaning gets virtually no attention in Dummett's writings. What is involved is neither more nor less than that is is fixed and predeterminate, and in no sense conditional upon our ratification, what use in a new context of an expression accords with our previous use of it, or of its constituents. It seems to me far from obvious that this idea can be satisfactorily explained without reinvocation of the transcendent objectivity whose intelligibility the anti-realist repudiates.

Where the requisite notion of objectivity does come in for critical attention is in Wittgenstein's later writings, particularly in the discussion of following a rule in the *Investigations* and in the *Remarks on the Foundations of Mathematics*. Dummett's thought on the philosophy of language is, for all its striking originality, redolent simultaneously of the influence of two very opposed sources: Frege and the later Wittgenstein. But he makes nothing of Wittgenstein's thought on this topic.[29] And the possibility seems to me still to be open that Dummett, at least when wearing his revisionary anti-realist hat, has essayed to occupy an incoherent middle position between those of his two great luminaries. This is not because his anti-realist ideas lead in the direction of a more radical revisionism than those of the intuitionists (though there is a powerful case for thinking that, if allowed to be revisionary at all, they do),[30] but because the explanation of why these ideas should be revisionary at all appears to need appeal to an objectivity of meaning to which the anti-realist's entitlement has still to be made out. If holism can make nothing of the possibility of consistent but unsound principles of inference, no more can anyone who does not believe that, in conferring meaning upon a sign, we thereby create indefinitely many potentially never-to-be-ratified facts about its correct use.[31]

29 Equally surprising, for all that he canvasses the prospect of taking conditions of warranted assertion as the central notion in the theory of the meaning of declarative sentences, Dummett makes nothing of the (later Wittgenstein's?) notion *criterion*.

30 *Truth and Other Enigmas*, pp. 248–9. See pp. 123–8 of my *Wittgenstein on the Foundations of Mathematics*; and Essay 4 in this volume.

31 I am indebted to the late Gareth Evans, and to Christopher Peacocke and John Skorupski, for helpful comments on an earlier draft of this essay.

16

Realism, Bivalence and Classical Logic

In their 'Realism and Logic', Stig Rasmussen and Jens Ravnkilde undertake a reappraisal of the relationship between semantic realism and classical logic. Their principal conclusions are

a that endorsement of the principle of Bivalence[1] for statements not known to be effectively decidable is the essential and distinctive doctrine of realism;
b that *agnosticism* about Bivalence for statements not known to be effectively decidable is the essential and distinctive doctrine of anti-realism;
c that a universally 'non-revisionary' anti-realism is indefensible, there being in particular no anti-realistically acceptable semantics which will validate classical logic for all statements not known to be effectively decidable; and
d that the anti-realist must perforce embrace some form of *idealism*.

Dummett himself has, of course, advocated (or sympathetically entertained) these theses (or close relatives of them) at various stages in his writings. Rasmussen and Ravnkilde may thus be seen as rallying to

1 'Bivalence is here, and henceforth whenever nothing is said to the contrary, to be understood as *Generalized Bivalence*: the principle that every (non-vague, non-ambiguous) statement is determinately either true or not. Generalized Bivalence (sometimes called *Determinacy*, and dubbed *DEBivalence* by Rasmussen and Ravnkilde) tolerates (determinate) truth-values other than truth and falsity, and (determinate) truth-value gaps. I shall call *Strict Bivalence* the (correspondingly intolerant) principle that every (non-vague, non-ambiguous) statement is determinately either true or *false*.

The proviso about non-vagueness is, of course, an enormous weakness, which ought to make anyone think twice about (a) as a satisfactory characterization of realism in general. A vague statement *may* be determinately true: is a realist conception of that circumstance not to be possible?

the defence of anti-realist orthodoxy against the heresies of 'non-revisionism'. Especially when arguing for (a) and (c), they are severely critical of ideas floated in sections I to III of Essay 15. So it seemed appropriate, on the occasion of a reprinting of that paper, to try to take the measure of some of their criticisms, and, more generally, to indicate how, as it seems to me, their discussion leaves matters concerning (a) to (d).

I
Does Endorsing Bivalence for Statements not Known to be Effectively Decidable Commit One to Semantic Realism Concerning Those Statements?

Semantic realism, for our purposes, may be identified with the conjunction of the second and third non-equivalent elements in realism characterized on p. 435. The semantic realist, that is, holds that our understanding of all statements, including some whose truth – if they were true – need not, or would not, be recognizable by us, is to be viewed as consisting in grasp of their truth-conditions. Rasmussen and Ravnkilde have the following argument linking Bivalence and semantic realism:

i To say that Bivalence holds for sentences not known to be effectively decidable – non-KED sentences – is to say that those sentences possess determinate truth-values (truth-status).

ii The belief that sentences not known to be effectively decidable possess determinate truth-values (truth-status) is incompatible with anti-realism.

iii Hence, applying Bivalence to sentences not known to be effectively decidable entails (semantic) realism.[2]

That this argument involves an additional assumption is the gist of the following thought:

> ...it is true that if somebody accepts Bivalence for a class of statements for whose truth-values he cannot in every case guarantee means of decision, then he is at least committed to holding that there is no guarantee that truth everywhere coincides with decidable truth. But, unless he accept the transition from 'There is no guarantee that P' to 'It is a possibility that not-P', he has not thereby committed himself to the possibility of verification-transcendent truth. This transition is intuitionistically suspect...[3]

2 Rasmussen and Ravnkilde, 'Realism and Logic', p. 389.

3 From Essay 15, p. 434.

Thus consider, say, an arithmetical intuitionist who believes – never mind why – that Bivalence holds for number-theoretic statements as a class; hence he believes that each such statement is determinately either true or not. Since he cannot guarantee that it is possible to decide the truth-value of an arbitrary number-theoretic statement, it might seem to follow that he cannot guarantee that the determinate truth-status which his belief in Bivalence bestows on such a statement is in every case determinable. That would be enough, already, to sustain Rasmussen's and Ravnkilde's (ii), specialized to number-theoretic sentences and arithmetical intuitionism. For it is of the essence of the intuitionistic outlook that there *is* a guarantee that any true, or untrue, number-theoretic statement can be recognized to be so: it is in the nature of the *concept* of arithmetical truth, intuitionistically understood, that there should be such a guarantee. Hence, it might seem – I shall re-scrutinize the matter shortly – it is at least a *blunder* on the part of the anti-realist to endorse Bivalence. But what the thought expressed in the quoted passage queries is the transition to Rasmussen's and Ravnkilde's (iii); the claim that the blunder is tantamount to a commitment to the possibility of verification-transcendent truth, i.e. to realism.

To elaborate somewhat. The semantic realist does hold, precisely, that the extensions of 'true' and 'ascertainably true' may possibly diverge. And this 'possibly' is not merely epistemic. The realist's view is not that it is consistent with everything we know, or whatever, that truth can outrun evidence; it is that it *really* can outrun evidence[4] – that the availability or otherwise of evidence is no conceptual constraint on the capacity of a statement to be true. Now obviously, to lack a guarantee that the extensions of two predicates are the same is *not* to be obliged to admit the (real) possibility that they diverge: we have, for instance, no guarantee that the extensions of the predicates 'counter-example to Goldbach's Conjecture' and 'prime number between 32 and 36' coincide, since we have no guarantee that there are no counter-examples to Goldbach's Conjecture, i.e. that it is true. But to find ourselves in this state of ignorance is, emphatically, not to have to admit that there is a possibility that the extensions of those two predicates diverge; we simply do not know whether that is a possibility or not.

Thus anyone – realist or anti-realist – should demur at the form of transition – from 'There is no guarantee that P' or 'We have no reason to suppose that P' to 'It is a possibility that not-P' – which is involved here.

4 *Ad homines*: if the epistemic reading were the strongest that the realist would admit, it would be realism, rather than anti-realism, which would best be characterized as a kind of agnosticism: agnosticism, namely, about the epistemological constraints on truth and falsity which the anti-realist wishes to impose.

What makes the transition additionally questionable from an intuitionistic point of view is the existence, intuitionistically, of actual counter-examples to it, generated by the failure of Double Negation Elimination. Wherever we have grounds for asserting not-not-P but no grounds for the assertion of P, it will be true both that we cannot guarantee that P but that we *can* rule out the possibility that not-P. The most immediate example would be to take for 'P' the law of Excluded Middle itself. However, to stress: the suspect transition does not itself amount to a Double Negation Elimination – otherwise it would be suspect *only* to the intuitionist among the present protagonists. What the intuitionist is uniquely in a position to do is to produce cases where he is actually in a position to assert both the hypothesis and the negation of the conclusion. We may conclude that, whether their reasoning is to be appraised by classical or intuitionistic standards, Rasmussen's and Ravnkilde's transition from (i) and (ii) to (iii) is a non-sequitur.[5]

5 (Warning: do not read this note unless willing to pursue diminishing marginal fleas.) The point, small as it is, is apt to seem convincing enough. Still Rasmussen and Ravnkilde find it confused. (See their 'Realism and Logic', section 3, pp. 390–1, and their footnote 21, p. 432). To begin with, they think they discern in it an equivocation between two different inferences; namely

1 There are non-KED sentences
∴ There are, or may be, non-ED – (effectively decidable) – sentences;

and

2 Bivalence applies to non-KED sentences
∴ There are or may be non-ED sentences.

(1), say Rasmussen and Ravnkilde, is indeed intuitionistically invalid; but it is (2) which is involved in explicating the commitment to semantic realism which Bivalence brings; and (2) is intuitionistically valid.

It is necessary to do a little work to bring out the relevance of their discussion here. First, it might seem unclear why it should be thought distinctive of semantic realism to accept the existence, or possible existence, of sentences which are not *effectively* decidable: clearly, if the shared conclusion of (1) and (2) is to be something anti-realistically unpalatable, then Rasmussen and Ravnkilde must be interpreted to mean *undecidable* by 'non-ED'. And so, it turns out, they do. (See their footnote 17). Second, it has then to be presupposed that the anti-realist, following the lead of mathematical intuitionism, will regard the negation of P as assertible just in case, as suggested above (pp. 436–7), we have grounds for asserting that no grounds for asserting P can be attained. Otherwise it is not clear why (recognition of) absolute undecidability should be anti-realistically problematic.

Even so qualified, however, the shared conclusion of (1) and (2) is prima facie not the conclusion of the transition with which my quoted passage was concerned. For the conclusion of the quoted passage is not 'there are or may be undecidable sentences' but 'it is a possibility that truth does not everywhere coincide with decidable truth'; and while the latter entails the former, the converse inference requires the assumption of Bivalence for the sentences in question. However, since any undecidable sentence will be non-KED, the assumption is guaranteed by the premise of (2), understood – as intended – as the hypothesis that Bivalence

Nevertheless, the quoted passage from Essay 15 *does* commit an error. Only, the error occurs one stage further back; and pointing it out should provide no comfort to a sympathizer with either of the theses, (a) and (b). Suppose our arithmetical intuitionist visits the oracle at Delphi and inquires of the Pythian Priestess, 'Who, intuitionist or platonist, has the truth of the matter as far as number-theory is concerned?' And suppose that her answer is 'Bivalence holds for all number-theoretical statements'. If Rasmussen and Ravnkilde are right, this response, uncharacteristically forthright, is tantamount to an endorsement of arithmetical realism. In fact, however, the response is in keeping with the best traditions of Delphic ambiguity, since from an intuitionist viewpoint it will equally well bear interpretation as the claim that all number-theoretic problems are resoluble. Whence the error in the quoted passage. For if the intuitionist accepts the pronouncement under the latter interpretation, it is evident that he can also continue to accept that we cannot *guarantee* the decidability of all arithmetical statements, yet still incur no commitment to 'we cannot

---

applies to *all* non-KED sentences. So (2) is, after all, acceptable enough as a version of the quoted transition.

Now, Rasmussen and Ravnkilde give no reason for supposing (2) is valid, contenting themselves with the assertion that it is 'inexorable' for realist and anti-realist alike. However, they offer a diagnostic suggestion why I might have failed to perceive its validity. The trouble, it seems, lay in an equivocation between two different senses of 'We cannot guarantee that truth everywhere coincides with decidable truth'. In its weak sense, they suggest, the claim coincides with the premise of (1); in its strong sense, it coincides with the conclusion of both (1) and (2). Neither interpretation, however, hits what I intended or – if I may say so – what I actually said. The stated premise of the quoted passage says that something is not guaranteed, viz., that every true sentence is decidably true. That this is not equivalent to Rasmussen's and Ravnkilde's 'weak' interpretation is evident from the reflection that an intuitionist who accepted the premise of (1) – on the grounds that there are, obviously, sentences for which we at present possess no means of decision – would nevertheless, given the generalizations of the intuitionistic readings of the constants suggested above, and their natural counterpart for the universal quantifier, insist that we do *know* that every true sentence is decidably true: for to be in a position to assert the truth of a sentence is to be in a position to assert that its truth has been recognized. As for the 'strong' interpretation, I claim merely that Rasmussen and Ravnkilde would not have suggested it if they had not completely missed the force of my original reservation about the quoted transition. Once again; that we do not know P is no reason to suppose that not-P depicts a real possibility, whatever proposition P may be.

Perhaps I am partly to blame for Rasmussen's and Ravnkilde's misunderstanding of my intention. For the quoted passage will bear interpretation as the suggestion that the intended lacuna is a lacuna only from an intuitionistic point of view. Yet they give no sign of any diffidence in their interpretation: 'We are reluctant to attribute to Wright the fallacy we impute; yet it seems plain in his text,' and what follows is the quoted passage (Rasmussen and Ravnkilde, 'Realism and Logic' p. 432). Evidently I succeeded in making 'plain' to Rasmussen and Ravnkilde something diametrically different to what I meant.

Rasmussen and Ravnkilde also have some hard things to say about my discussion of the Jones example (on pp. 436–7, this volume). There I remarked that if, following Dummett,

guarantee that (number-theoretic) truth everywhere coincides with decidable (number-theoretic) truth'. Hence the claim made by the first sentence of the quoted passage is false; and so is Rasmussen's and Ravnkilde's (ii).

What *would* generate commitment to 'we cannot guarantee that (number-theoretic) truth everywhere coincides with decidable (number-theoretic) truth' would be the assumption:

1 that we cannot guarantee that all (number-theoretic) statements are decidable, and
2 that we *can guarantee* that Bivalence holds for all (number-theoretic) statements.

The realist, of course, believes he has the guarantee described by (2), flowing from the nature of statement-meaning. The anti-realist, in contrast, who accepts Bivalence on the say-so of an oracle, or as an expression of his

---

we interpret 'Jones was brave' and its negation as a pair of contrary counter-factual conditionals, then – in the circumstances which Dummett describes, and assuming the distributivity of truth over disjunction – anyone who is willing to regard Excluded Middle as validly applicable to the example will commit himself to the existence of a verification-transcendent truth. I pointed out, however, that so to construe the negation of 'Jones was brave' is to 'part company' with anything resembling the intuitionistic account of negation. Rasmussen and Ravnkilde regard this observation as irrelevant:

> It does not matter whether Dummett employs notions unavailable to intuitionists: what matters is whether he employs notions unavailable to *anti-realists*. Wright's correct observation, that intuitionists cannot make sense of the Jones example, can be taken as grounds for thinking Dummett is unfair to a species of anti-realism only on the assumption that anti-realism entails IL [intuitionist logic] and by contraposition that CL entails semantical realism. Wright's observation would be to the point only if the conjecture to be explored is, not whether CL may go in tandem with anti-realism but, conversely, whether IL may go in tandem with realism. What we want to know, however, *is* whether CL is compatible with anti-realism... (pp. 391–2)

What is going on here? Dummett's example was meant to be a case where a rejection of a realist view of the meaning of the statement in question would force one to discard the belief that the law of Excluded Middle was valid for that statement, so that, contraposing, an endorsement of classical logic for that statement and its kin would involve a commitment to realism. What I did was to describe how someone who accepted an anti-realist view of 'Jones is brave' could nevertheless quite coherently retain the belief that Excluded Middle was validly applicable to that statement; his strategy will be to insist, first, that the putative counter-example misidentifies the negation of 'Jones is brave' – (which is, independently, a plausible enough claim in this particular case, since nobody thinks that one is in a position to deny a counter-factual conditional only if in a position to assert *another*, contrary counter-factual) – and, second, that when the negation is correctly identified, it will prove to be assertible in the circumstances which Dummett describes, so that no challenge to the validity of Excluded Middle is generated by the example. The presupposition of my response to the Jones example was thus not that anti-realism involves a commitment to 'IL' – (Rasmussen and Ravnkilde intend 'intuitionist semantics', I think, rather than 'intuitionistic logic') – but merely that the latter is *available*. Whether there is some more pertinent objection to be gleaned from the passage just quoted I leave it to the reader to estimate.

confidence that human ingenuity can surmount all obstacles, or whatever, will presumably only accept its interior that-clause.

It may seem, therefore, that Rasmussen and Ravnkilde should have proposed, rather than (a), something like

a′ that acceptance that Bivalence is valid for all statements, including those not known to be effectively decidable, as a consequence of the nature of their content, is the essential and distinctive doctrine of realism.

In fact, however, even this is unhappy. It retains the indifference of the original to the pervasive phenomenon of vagueness.[6] But there is another point. Everyone ought to accept that there are some declarative sentences – what Dummett calls *quasi-assertions*[7] – which are not genuinely apt to be true or false, whose utterance does not constitute the making of a genuine statement. Uncontroversial examples are provided by, for instance, commands expressed in the future indicative and indicative formulations of rules – 'On mortgaging a property, a player receives one-half of its official purchase price from the bank.' Controversial examples are provided by moral and aesthetic judgements, and (certain kinds of) theoretical-scientific statements. How should the boundary between the genuine statements and the rest be drawn? One quite appealing initial thought – if we continue to prescind from consideration of vagueness – is that genuine statements are marked off from the others by the circumstance that a rational subject who undertakes a sufficiently thoroughgoing investigation will eventually be left with no option but to recommend acceptance or agnosticism. Otherwise expressed: there is a particular response – acceptance, or agnosticism – which any genuine statement *commands* of a rational investigator, *modulo* a sufficiently thoroughgoing investigation; quasi-assertions, in contrast, leave rational investigators, qua rational, with the right to agree to differ. It would, obviously, take us a good way off track to attempt to pursue this proposal now. Yet suppose that an anti-realist is attracted to it. If we assume, in addition, that for a sufficiently extensive investigation to warrant agnosticism about a statement is for it to warrant the (defeasible) opinion that no sufficient grounds for accepting it are ultimately to be had – and that our anti-realist is working with something like a generalized intuitionistic account of negation[8] – the upshot is going to be this: for him to have reason to regard a class of statements as genuine is for him to have reason to suppose that, for any of them, a sufficient case can be made for accepting either it or its negation. That is for Bivalence to hold for all genuine statements, qua genuine statements.

6 Cf. note 1.

7 *Frege: Philosophy of Language*, pp. 352 and following.

8 See pp. 436–7.

Such an anti-realist, then, will accept that, in so far as being a genuine statement is a function of content, 'Bivalence is valid for all statements as a consequence of the nature of their content' is true. He may demur at the bit in (a′) which goes, '...including those not known to be effectively decidable', for he regards any genuine statement as (weakly) effectively decidable. Actually, however, he can accept that bit too, if 'effective decidability' requires the availability of some form of *canonical* ground, e.g. a proof, for each statement or its negation. Either way, (a′) fares not much better than (a).

One salient point is that an anti-realist who believes, for such reasons, that Bivalence is guaranteed for all genuine statements (of a certain kind) has to accept a sense of 'decidable' in which all (such) statements are decidable; and so cannot simultaneously accept (2) and (1) above, so construed. But that we knew anyway, since – to repeat – (1) and (2) generate the anti-realistically unacceptable 'we cannot guarantee that truth (for such statements) everywhere coincides with (their) decidable truth'.

That, so far, is the sole positive finding. The *anti*-realist may not consistently endorse *both* (1) and (2). We have uncovered no single, specific thesis about Bivalence which has a claim to be regarded as 'the essential and distinctive' realist doctrine. It is not even true that endorsing both (1) and (2) enjoins realism. To suppose the contrary is just to fall into the original non-sequitur – attempting to elicit modal conclusions from epistemic premises. Of course, none of this amounts to *proof* that there is no claim about Bivalence which constitutes the 'essential and distinctive' realist thought. But we have not found one; Dummett himself has recently expressed doubts;[9] there is the evident problem posed by the desirability of leaving space for a realist view of vague statements and their compounds; and less controversial characterizations are to hand.

II
Is Agnosticism about Bivalence for Statements not Known to be Effectively Decidable Mandatory for the Anti-realist?

The question is already answered negatively if the gist of the preceding section is acceptable. But suppose it is not. Or consider an anti-realist who wants no truck with Bivalence except when canonical decision procedures are to hand. Is agnosticism in other cases the only possibility? Rasmussen and Ravnkilde are, it seems to me, additionally mistaken in suggesting

9 See his *The Interpretation of Frege's Philosophy*, pp. 437–8. Dummett's second thoughts are criticized in Rasmussen's and Ravnkilde's Appendix to 'Realism and Logic'.

that anti-realism may not coherently *deny* Bivalence.[10] This claim may seem puzzling in view of the elementary proof of the double negation of the law of Excluded Middle furnished by both classical and intuitionistic rules for negation and disjunction. That reasoning, however, generates no more than the *internal* double negation of Bivalence:

> Of every statement, it is not the case that it is not the case that it is determinately either true or not.

And acceptance of that would be consistent with denial of Bivalence if the constants are interpreted in a generalized intuitionistic manner. For, generalizing the intuitionistic account of the universal quantifier in the most natural way, Bivalence will be assertible just in case we can recognize of our present state of information either that, presented with an arbitrary statement P, it will justify either the claim that P is true or the claim that it is not, or that it will admit of effective transformation into a state of information justifying one of those two claims. As a result, we will be in a position – in the presence of the relevant account of negation – to *deny* Bivalence just in case we believe we have recognized that no state of information of the type just described can be achieved. If we suppose that the suggestion has been discarded that Bivalence plays a constitutive role in the best account of what a genuine statement is, what error is committed by an anti-realist who thinks he can reasonably discount ever getting in position to assert Bivalence unrestrictedly – and so considers its intuitionistic denial justified?

Should we conclude, then, that no particular attitude towards Bivalence is 'of the essence' of anti-realism, that the essence of the view is simply a rejection of semantic realism – neither more nor less? Not yet. I have been proceeding on the assumption that what is at issue is a general *statement*, quantifying over statements. Such is, indeed, Rasmussen's and Ravnkilde's assumption also.[11] But it is not clear that it best serves their defence

10 Rasmussen and Ravnkilde, 'Realism and Logic', pp. 389–90.

11 Ibid., p. 382. To be strictly accurate: Rasmussen and Ravnkilde actually identify Bivalence with the principle that 'every meaningful, non-ambiguous, non-vague and non-indexical declarative *sentence* [my italics] is either true or false.' They are, of course, speaking of Strict Bivalence and not the more general principle which I have dubbed 'Bivalence' for most of the purposes of this paper. Taking the range of the principle's quantifier to be declarative sentences, rather than statements, would have the advantage of pre-empting the second sort of anti-realistic acceptance of Bivalence canvassed above, viz., treating its acceptability as constitutive of the notion of a genuine statement. But it has the obvious and decisive disadvantage that it need not be the presence of ambiguity, indexicality or vagueness which distinguishes a command, or rule, expressed in the indicative, or a threat or promise, or any of the multitude of possible types of quasi-assertion, from genuine statements. Since quasi-assertions, distinctively among declarative sentences, do not possess truth-values (in any relevant sense), the spirit, if not the letter of Rasmussen's and Ravnkilde's discussion is best served, it seems clear, by construing Bivalence, in both its Generalized and Strict senses, as a principle involving quantification over statements.

of (a) and (b). Nothing in the previous paragraph suggests how an anti-realist might coherently deny the result of applying Bivalence to Fermat's 'Last Theorem', for instance. What Rasmussen and Ravnkilde should contend, it may seem, is that while the differences between realism and anti-realism must after all crystallize in differing attitudes concerning Bivalence, the relevant attitudes will not be, or need not be, to a *statement* of the principle as such, but will emerge in disagreements concerning whether or not *particular applications* of the principle are justified. An anti-realist who accepts that being subject to Bivalence is constitutive of genuine statements still has to face a question, before he can allow any particular application of the principle, which his realist opponent does not: the question, namely whether there is reason to think that a sufficiently thoroughgoing investigation would have to produce either grounds for accepting the statement in question or grounds for doubting that such grounds exist. If the question is answered negatively, or just gets no definite answer, then applications of Bivalence which a realist finds straightforward will be anti-realistically problematical. A statement like Fermat's 'Last Theorem' is an obvious case. Must a sufficiently thoroughgoing investigation produce either reason to think it true or reason to think that no such reason can be given? Perhaps, if such reasons do not have to be supplied by proofs but can be furnished, e.g. by a failure to find counter-examples in a massive computer search. But that is controversial; whereas from the number-theoretic realist's point of view, the application of Bivalence to Fermat's 'Last Theorem' is not.

However, before such an appeal to differing attitudes to applications of Bivalence can turn the trick, we need to know what it *is* to accept something as an application of Bivalence. In particular, the distinction had better be clear between the expression of an application of Bivalence to a statement, P, and the expression of an application of classical logic to that statement. Suppose I assert 'Either P is true or it is not'. What will show whether I am endorsing an application of Bivalence to P, or whether I am, rather, endorsing an application of the Law of Excluded Middle? Clearly the presence, or absence, of words like 'determinately' could not be the basis of such a distinction; rather, such devices are merely markers for a distinction which needs to be made in some other way. But how?

The distinction is needed, admittedly, only if no demonstration is forthcoming of the correctness of Rasmussen's and Ravnkilde's thesis (c): the thesis that the anti-realist cannot, in the end, accept the global validity of classical logic. It is if that thesis is incorrect that 'Either Fermat's "Last Theorem" is true or it is not', while anti-realistically controversial qua application of Bivalence, may be anti-realistically acceptable qua application of Excluded Middle. If (c) is false, there is the prospect of an anti-realism which consistently both endorses a statement of the principle of Bivalence and accepts as true what the realist intends as applications of that principle to anti-realistically controversial cases. The difference in the respective positions must reside, it seems, in the fact that it is only for the realist that Bivalence constitutes the *ground* for the acceptability of the applications. That thought, however, cannot contribute towards an *explanation* of the intended distinction until we have been told how, when someone offers something which sounds like Bivalence in support of such an 'application', it really is Bivalence which he adduces and not an informal statement of the law of Excluded Middle, conceived as validated in some anti-realistically acceptable way.

I do not say that it is impossible to make that contrast out; indeed the whole project of investigating semantic validations of logic is founded on the faith that a clear distinction can be made between semantical principles and logical ones. Applied to a fully formalized object-system of logic, the distinction is no doubt as clear as is necessary. But the present problem concerns, ultimately, natural language and what should pass for the expression of distinctively realist/anti-realist convictions within it. *If* the Law of Excluded Middle, viewed as a schema, admits of anti-realistically acceptable validation for statements which are not effectively decidable, and if quantification over statements makes sense at all, then there must *be* a statement at which we can arrive by universal generalization over an instance of that schema, so validated. That statement may sound just like Bivalence; how are we to tell whether, in the mouth of a native colingual, it is or is not?

The foregoing remarks are premised, to stress, upon the supposition that the anti-realist may prove to be entitled to the unrestricted use of classical logic. Whether Rasmussen's and Ravnkilde's (c) is indeed false is the topic for the next section. The gist of this section and its predecessor has been that a good deal of argument and clarification is still wanted if it is to emerge that their (a) and (b) are so much as defensible, let alone the most helpful characterizations of what is at issue about semantic realism.

III
Does Endorsing Classical Logic for all Statements Not Known to be Effectively Decidable Necessitate a Realist Interpretation of Them?

Rasmussen and Ravnkilde believe that this question should be answered affirmatively, provided we are in the business of seeking non-trivial semantic validations for our logic. They hold that any semantics which purportedly globally validates classical logic for statements not known to be effectively decidable will prove, on examination, either not to furnish a genuinely global validation or to be anti-realistically unacceptable in one way or another. The latter, they contend, is the fate of the sort of supervaluational semantics – what they call the DWS – sketched in section III of Essay 15. I shall consider this claim in a moment, once another germane consideration has been noted.

It is notable that Rasmussen and Ravnkilde – as they are, of course, perfectly entitled to do – refrain from engaging the issue with which sections V to VIII of Essay 15 are concerned: the possibility of an anti-realism which regards the global acceptability of classical logic as *conventional*. A conventionalist would dispute that 'logic needs validation in the first place and that such validation is to be of a semantical nature'.[12] Rasmussen and Ravnkilde offer nothing on the disputed assumption except to record that they find it 'all but compelling'. No sympathizer with anti-realism should find it compelling, however, because of a worry, not noted in Essay 15, which is relatively easy to see. It concerns whether an anti-realist semantics, based on conditions of warranted assertion, can take it as sufficient for sameness of content that the assertion-conditions of all instances of a pair of utterance-types coincide. The point is well illustrated by the case of 'P' and 'It is warrantedly assertible in our present state of information that P'. Let 'P' express a statement whose assertion-conditions are all in principle *defeasible* under the addition of relevant further information to one's state of information. Then the claims made by 'P' and 'It is warrantedly assertible in our present state of information that P' will differ, in so far as the former but not the latter will be repudiated if such additional defeating information comes to light. As a result, the content of their respective *negations* must be regarded as differing. There is therefore no recovering a description of that difference by application merely of some uniform account of negation to their assertion-conditions which, to stress, 'P' and 'It is warrantedly assertible in our present state of information that P' share: *whatever* our account of negation, it will yield differing output only when fed different input. A similar point will apply to tenses: there will be a corresponding asymmetry with, e.g. 'It was the case that P' and 'It was the case that P was warrantedly assertible in our state of information than obtaining'.

The issue raised is therefore whether, once we consider utterances with assertion-conditions which are at best defeasible, a generalized anti-realist semantics, based on the notion of warranted assertion, can have the systematic character displayed by classical truth-conditional semantics and by intuitionistic semantics for mathematical statements. In particular, can there be any general account of negation: a uniform function determining

12 Rasmussen and Ravnkilde, 'Realism and Logic', p. 425.

the assertion-conditions of 'not P' from those of 'P'? If not, it will no longer be possible to regard the validity of logical schemata as consequent upon general semantical accounts of the logical constants. There will be, e.g. no sensible general question whether '$P \vee \sim P$' is invariably validly assertible; even in the presence of a uniform account of the semantics of '$\vee$', the answer will have to wait on determination of the assertion-conditions of the particular 'not-P'. And if negation, in particular, must perforce be viewed as having such an unsystematic character, what would remain to legitimate the desire to find a general semantic validation for logic? What obstacle, indeed, would there be to the idea that the validity of certain logical principles may actually play a constitutive role in determining the content of the 'logical constants'? There are matters of importance in the offing here; but I cannot pursue them now.[13]

Let us turn then to Rasmussen's and Ravnkilde's reservations about the sort of semantic validations of classical logic which are adumbrated in section III of Essay 15. Rasmussen and Ravnkilde are content to grant that such a supervaluational approach promises, wherever it can be properly developed, to validate classical logic without appeal to Strict Bivalence; what they dispute is that this sort of validation can be more than *locally* acceptable from an anti-realistic point of view.

Consider the case, sketched in Essay 15, of *sufficiently specific presently acceptable world-histories*. Such a history is a consistent, finite set of statements, no member of which there is at present any reason to doubt, and which is *sufficiently specific* with respect to P just in case it contains either P or its negation. P is absolutely *true* if it is true in (i.e. is a member of) every sufficiently specific presently acceptable world-history; it is absolutely *false* if its negation is true in every sufficiently specific presently acceptable world-history; otherwise it has no determinate absolute *truth*-value. I omit repetition of further details. Evidently the sort of semantics sketched will be anti-realistically acceptable only if two conditions are met. It must respect the fact that the statements (of the historical sort) in question are not (in general) effectively decidable *and* it must make no essential use of evidence-transcendent notions. Rasmussen's and Ravnkilde's exposition of their reservations is complicated by their conviction that agnosticism with respect to Bivalence is distinctive of anti-realism. But if we pare that disputable thesis away, what is left, if I interpret them correctly, is the suspicion that those two conditions cannot simultaneously be met, except at the cost of surrendering the prospect of an anti-realism which *globally* endorses classical logic.

13 For some further, somewhat qualified thoughts on the matter, see Essay 14, this volume, pp. 419–20.

Let P be any statement concerning, say, sixteenth-century London. If we are presently justified in believing P, then P will be a member of any sufficiently specific presently acceptable world-history, and so will be absolutely *true*. Conversely, the only way P can qualify for membership of *every* sufficiently specific presently acceptable world-history is by being justifiably assertible in our present state of information. Absolute *truth* is thus – unsurprisingly – tantamount to current warranted assertibility; accordingly, to recognize that there is at present reason neither to believe nor to doubt P is to recognize that it is *determinately* neither absolutely *true* nor absolutely *false*. This would be a decisive objection to the semantics if we were persuaded that no semantics can be anti-realistically acceptable which does not conserve agnosticism with respect to Strict Bivalence. But that is not even Rasmussen's and Ravnkilde's view. Their view concerns *Generalized* Bivalence.[14] In any case, it should be obvious that there is so far nothing anti-realistically suspect about any of the notions in play.

What, then, is their worry? Something like the following, I think.[15] Suppose the question is raised, what attitude ought the anti-realist take to the question whether statements concerning the past should be regarded as *determinate* in point of absolute *truth*-value; is it determinate of any particular statement concerning the past that it is *true*, or *false*, or neither? Then there now arises the following dilemma. To accept such determinacy is, in effect, to accept a version of Generalized Bivalence: it is to hold that every statement in the relevant class is determinately either *true* or not. So, notwithstanding the reflections above concerning ways in which an anti-realist might consistently accept Bivalence, an explanation is now owing of how, from the anti-realist point of view, admitting determinacy in *truth*-status can be reconciled with the first condition, that is, with due acknowledgement of the non-effective-decidability of statements concerning sixteenth-century London. One suggestion I made was that an anti-realist might accept Bivalence as a matter of conviction of the *de facto* decidability of all members of a problematic class of statements. But, the non-revisionary anti-realist would hardly want the conservative power of the envisaged style of semantics to *require* such a conviction of him; in any case, if he is content with faith, classical semantics will serve his purpose. But if, alternatively, the validity of Bivalence is viewed as implicitly definitional of the idea of a genuine statement, the problem becomes that of explaining what reason the anti-realist has to think that everything which we are happy to treat as a genuine statement concerning sixteenth-century London, and to apply classical logic to, may legitimately be regarded as a

14 Cf. note 1.
15 Cf. Rasmussen and Ravnkilde, 'Realism and Logic' pp. 398–9.

genuine statement in the sense which he endorses. Does not his non-revisionism still reduce to a matter of ungrounded conviction – the conviction that every historical sentence to which we would normally quite contentedly apply classical logic, is indeed determinate in respect of absolute *truth*-value, and so qualifies as a genuine statement in his sense?

That is one half of the dilemma. Suppose, on the other hand, the anti-realist proponent of this style of semantics does not endorse determinacy in absolute *truth*-status. Then the question is: what is to be his attitude to the family of disjunctions of the form 'P is absolutely *true* or not', where P is any statement in the relevant class? If his non-revisionism is indeed to be global, he must accept each of these disjunctions, qua instance of the Law of Excluded Middle, as valid. But what do they respectively assert if not determinacy in absolute *truth*-status for the relevant P? And how, in that case, can his endorsement of them be reconciled with his unwillingness to endorse a general statement of determinacy in absolute *truth*-status for such sentences?

The proper response to this dilemma depends on whether statements of the form 'P is warrantedly assertible in our present state of information' should themselves be regarded as effectively decidable. Actually, there is a question whether, unless such statements *are* effectively decidable, the anti-realist's own response to his basic negative arguments, viz., that of supplanting truth-conditions with conditions of warranted assertion, can be germane. But, beyond a remark below (see note 17), I shall not pursue that question here. What is clear is that *if* statements of this sort are effectively decidable, then so are absolute *truth*-values. Accordingly there can be no objection from an anti-realist point of view to supposing absolute *truth*-value to be determinate for every P of the relevant sort. Generalized Bivalence would thus be acceptable for these statements in the straightforward way in which, for the intuitionist, Strict Bivalence is acceptable for effectively decidable mathematical statements. So the problems which were threatened on the first horn of the dilemma, consequent on the acceptance of determinacy in *truth*-status as, in one way or another, a matter of ungrounded conviction, would be spurious.

What needs emphasis is that there would be, nevertheless, no compromise of the intuitive non-effective-decidability of historical statements. Effective decidability of absolute *truth*-value would involve such a compromise only if absolute *truth*-values corresponded to truth-values as intuitively understood. But they do not. Classical truth-values are eternal: if a historical statement is ever classically true, then it always is. Absolute *truth*-values are, by contrast, ephemeral: they are liable to change as the character of our present state of information changes. Not that recourse to talk of classical truth-values would be a happy way of expressing the intuitive non-effective-decidability of historical statements from an anti-realist point of view. For an anti-realist, the non-effective-decidability of such statements resides rather in the fact that we cannot in general guarantee to be able to come up with grounds warranting their assertion or denial; but *that* point is amply respected by the consideration that we cannot in general guarantee to be able to realize a state of information in which either P or its *negation* is absolutely *true* – something perfectly consistent with a guarantee that P is either absolutely *true* or not.

If we may assume that present warranted assertibility is an effectively decidable matter for all statements to which we attach definite sense, then, so far as I can see, Rasmussen and Ravnkilde succeed in adverting to absolutely nothing in the strategy for validating classical logic embodied in semantics of the relevant kind, which in any way prejudices the chances of a global non-revisionary anti-realism.[16]

What though if present warranted assertibility is deemed *not* to be an effectively decidable matter?[17] In that case there is no basis for asserting that everything we should customarily regard as a bona fide statement concerning sixteenth-century London is determinate in absolute *truth*-value. The second horn of the sketched dilemma therefore comes into force. What should be the response of the would-be globally non-revisionary anti-realist to applications of Excluded Middle of the form, 'P is absolutely *true* or not'?

16 To be sure, their impression to the contrary depends heavily on their belief that the anti-realist *must* be agnostic with respect to Generalized Bivalence. In fairness to them, the reader should note footnote 16 of Essay 15 on p. 441 above which betrays a similar confusion in the mind of the present author at the time of its original writing.

17 It may seem difficult to see how a non-revisionary anti-realist could so deem; for he will, presumably, insist at least that present warranted assertibility may not be evidence-transcendent – otherwise shifting to an assertion-conditions conception of meaning gains him no advantage over his classical opponent. But in the presence of classical logic – which he accepts – there is no resisting the transition from:

> It is not the case that: P is presently warrantedly assertible but there is no verifying that P is presently warrantedly assertible

to:

> If P is presently warrantedly assertible, then it is possible to verify that it is.

And a similar thought will apply, of course, to 'P is not presently warrantedly assertible'. So, with the Law of Excluded Middle on board, the effective decidability of 'P is presently warrantedly assertible' seems assured.

This, though, is incorrect. It is true that the non-revisionary anti-realist should, for just the reasons outlined, accept the disjunction, 'Either it is possible to verify that P is presently warrantedly assertible or it is possible to verify that it is not'. But when – as in the sketched reasoning – a *supervaluationally* validated disjunctive premise is used, there is a question about whether the import of the conclusion is indeed that 'P is presently warrantedly assertible' is effectively decidable.

The possibilities, evidently, are three. First, the anti-realist may reject these disjunctions, and so opt for the 'eclectic' non-revisionism which Rasmussen and Ravnkilde find so unattractive,[18] classical logic being conserved for the object-language by a semantic theory whose own underlying logic is not classical. Second, the anti-realist may essay to regard the assertibility of such disjunctions as conventional; but the obvious reply to that move, whatever its independent virtues, is that it could have been made earlier, and places the play with supervaluational semantics for historical statements in the perspective of a mere detour.

The third and, it seems to me, the appropriate response for the would-be non-revisionary anti-realist who – wisely or not – has chosen to let the dialectic run to this point, is to seek a *further* supervaluational semantics which will validate the disjunction in question without presupposition of determinacy in absolute *truth*-status for historical statements (or whatever other problematic statements the original supervaluational semantics was designed to deal with). Let me accordingly close this section by airing a suggestion about how such an ulterior semantics might run, apt for the validation of classical logic as applied to statements of every sort, including those concerning absolute *truth*-values.

The suggestion is very simple. The problem arose on the assumption that there was a doubt whether current warranted assertibility was itself a decidable notion. We therefore replace it with a notion about which there can be no such doubt: *currently verified* warranted assertibility. And the sufficiently specific presently acceptable world-histories give way to the more general *sufficiently specific non-discredited data-sets*; where a non-discredited data-set is consistent, finite set of statements none of which has actually been recognized to be currently warrantedly deniable. Now let M range over these data-sets, and let 'true-in-M' be characterized in the orthodox recursive manner as before. Finally, define *hypertruth* in a fashion exactly parallel to stipulations characterizing absolute *truth* on p. 439 above. A statement will thus be *hypertrue* just in case it is true in every sufficiently specific non-discredited data-set.

If the tactic worked before, it should work again. Hence, in particular, 'P is absolutely *true* or not' will be validated as *hypertrue* without any presupposition of determinacy in respect to absolute *truth*-value. Of course, the question will be pressed again, what of determinacy with respect to *hypertruth*-value? But this time the anti-realist need feel no hesitation about answering that *hypertruth*-values are indeed determinate: that it is determinately the case of every statement that it is *hypertrue*, or that its negation is *hypertrue*, or that neither situation obtains. For whether we have actually recognized that we are currently in a position to assert a

18 Rasmussen and Ravnkilde, 'Realism and Logic', p. 399.

particular statement, or to assert its negation, or have recognized neither circumstance is, of course, an effectively decidable matter.

At any rate, it seems unlikely that there will be any technical objections to the attempt to validate classical logic by reference to *hypertruth* which do not equally confront a semantics based on absolute *truth*.[19] That being so, there is every prospect that the anti-realist may accept classical logic, even for statements not known to be effectively decidable – that is, for which we cannot guarantee to uncover adequate grounds for their assertion or denial – as a system of inference conservative with respect to *hypertruth*; and hence, for the special case of atomic statements, as conservative with respect to the property of having been recognized to be warrantedly assertible in our present state of information. That may seem, no doubt, a rather unexciting property to conserve; valid inference from attested premises will never give us results we don't *already* consider ourselves to be in a position to assert. But, however that may be, and even allowing that Rasmussen and Ravnkilde are right to suppose that the would-be non-revisionary anti-realist *must* produce a validating semantics for classical logic if his position is to deserve credibility, no clear reason has emerged why the devising of such a semantics, both technically effective and anti-realistically acceptable, must be a doomed undertaking.

It is worth remembering, finally, that supervaluations are only one of a number of possible approaches; and that Rasmussen's and Ravnkilde's claim, that *no* semantics which validates classical logic globally can avoid utilising anti-realistically unacceptable notions, is really very strong. I would wish to claim only that the issue is open.

19 One objection is that there is no prospect of validating the orthodox recursions for the connectives, for instance

'not' $\frown$ P is T iff not: P is T

and

P $\frown$ 'or' $\frown$ Q is T iff P is T or Q is T,

if absolute *truth*, or *hypertruth*, is taken for the T-predicate. (The point is correct, I think, even if the biconditional is construed as a conjunction of non-distributive disjunctions.) But if this is an objection, it is an objection to *any* supervaluational semantics. Why is it an objection? We do have

$(\forall M)$ ('not' $\frown$ P $\in$ M) iff (not: P $\in$ M)
$(\forall M)$ (P $\frown$ 'or' $\frown$ Q $\in$ M) iff (P $\in$ M or Q $\in$ M),

and it would be a bold claim that ordinary usage intends the 'orthodox' clauses rather than these. Still, it remains that I have suggested no strategy for simultaneous anti-realist validation both of classical logic and the orthodox recursions. If Rasmussen and Ravnkilde could show that the latter must be respected by anti-realism, they would be, I think, on firmer ground.

IV
Anti-realism and Idealism

Ontological realism, for Rasmussen and Ravnkilde, is the belief that

> nearly all kinds of sentence...deal with an objective or mind-independent reality, a reality, that is, that exists irrespective of any capacity on our part to attain knowledge about it.[20]

Such a conception of the world, and of the place of our thought and language in the world, is evidently inescapable for the semantic realist; for it is precisely what is involved in allowing the possibility that statements which we perfectly well understand may be rendered true even though we can gather no grounds for affirming them to be true. The question is whether it is at least *available* to anti-realism too. For if it is not, the anti-realist must, it appears, be committed to some version of the claim that human thought and cognition *constitute* the world. What is idealism but that?

Part of the reason for the intensity of Rasmussen's and Ravnkilde's interest in the question whether classical logic is globally available to the anti-realist is that they believe that *only* if that is so can anti-realism consistently combine with ontological realism. That is, they accept the conditional

A If endorsing classical logic entails accepting semantic realism, then anti-realism entails idealism.[21]

We have, I suggest, seen reason to doubt the antecedent of (A). I wish to suggest, moreover, that, even were non-revisionary anti-realism an incoherent stance, Rasmussen and Ravnkilde offer no solid reason for believing (A).

Their thought is that the anti-realist who would be an ontological realist *needs* classical logic? Why? Because, say Rasmussen and Ravnkilde, he will have to allow that

> the world, to the extent it is mind-independent, cannot be captured in language,...that the mind-independent segments of the world are such as not to make any of our declarative sentences...either true or false.[22]

That being so, the ontologically realist anti-realist needs recourse to non-constructive existential quantifiers in the very formulation of his position; only thereby can he avoid the impossible demand to *specify* those aspects of reality which elude formulation in his language.

20 Rasmussen and Ravnkilde, 'Realism and Logic', p. 379.
21 Ibid., p. 380.
22 Ibid., p. 380.

This thought, it seems to me, is thoroughly unconvincing. Even if we accepted the assumption that to believe in a 'mind-independent' world is to believe that it must contain aspects resistant to all our means of description, what would follow is only that the anti-realist needs a non-constructive interpretation of the existential quantifier, not that he needs the whole apparatus of classical logic. (It would, for example, be quite possible for an anti-realist to introduce the existential quantifier definitionally, as is done classically, in terms of the universal quantifier, while retaining a generalized intuitionistic account of the semantics of the latter; and, consistently with that, he could repudiate Bivalence and classical propositional logic for all but effectively decidable statements. Such an anti-realist would have, so far as I can see, no difficulty with the difficulty which Rasmussen and Ravnkilde think they see for him.)

But is not the assumption, in any case, at fault? Surely belief in the 'mind-independence' of the world cannot *require* belief in the existence of the ineffable; if it did, ontological realism would not be a consequence of semantic realism, for the latter entails only that *formulable* truths may outrun our capacities for knowledge. Rasmussen and Ravnkilde might reply that it is *for the anti-realist* that there is no content to the belief in mind-independence except as a belief in the existence of the ineffable. But that reply is unconvincing too. The belief in Strict Bivalence for decidable statements is – prescinding from our earlier doubts about its distinctive manifestability – a perfectly adequate vehicle for the conviction that the world is mind-independent, for it presupposes what I have elsewhere called the *investigation-independence* of those statements[23] – the conviction that the world confers determinate truth-values upon them independently of our actually carrying out any investigation into their truth-status. We are not dealing with anything worthy of the title of idealism until this belief is discarded. Superficially, however, it is quite compatible with the kind of anti-realism which Dummett expounds and which Rasmussen and Ravnkilde invariably have in mind.

Yet that appearance is, perhaps only superficial. I have argued elsewhere that the demands which the notion of investigation-independence make on the concept of meaning cannot be sustained by one who accepts the assumptions which Dummett's arguments for anti-realism presuppose.[24] So while the reasons advanced by Rasmussen and Ravnkilde for their (A) seem to me to be unconvincing, and its antecedent false, its consequent is worth further scrutiny. The committed anti-realist may, in apparent consistency, claim to believe that the world, conceived as a totality of

23 See e.g. my *Wittgenstein on the Foundations of Mathematics* pp. 204-7; and Essay 4 of this volume, pp. 148–9.

24 See *Wittgenstein on the Foundations of Mathematics* pp. 215–27.

objects, exists independently of his investigations of it; but it is doubtful whether he may conceive of his statements concerning those objects as investigation-independent. In consequence, clear content still needs to be given, it may reasonably be urged, to his professed belief in the autonomy of the objects themselves. That is a matter for another occasion.

Bibliography

Albritton, R. 'On Wittgenstein's Use of the Term "Criterion"' in G. Pitcher (ed.), *Wittgenstein: The Philosophical Investigations*, pp. 231–50.

Alston, W. P. 'Ontological Commitments', *Philosophical Studies*, 9 (1958), pp. 8–17.

Antony, Louise M. 'Can Verificationists Make Mistakes?', *American Philosophical Quarterly*, 24 (1987), pp. 225–36.

Appiah, Anthony. 'An Argument Against Anti-Realist Semantics', *Mind*, 93 (1984), pp. 559–65.

—— 'Anti-Realism Unrealized', *Philosophical Quarterly*, 34 (1984), pp. 85–103.

—— 'Verification and the Manifestation of Meaning', *The Aristotelian Society*, Suppl. Vol. LIX (1985), pp. 17–31.

—— *Assertion and Conditionals*, Cambridge University Press, Cambridge, 1985.

—— *For Truth in Semantics*, Oxford, Blackwell, 1986.

—— 'Representations and Realism', *Philosophical Studies*, 61 (1991), pp. 65–74.

Aristotle. *De Interpretatione*, cf. *Aristotle's Categories and De Interpretatione*, translated with notes by J. L. Ackrill, Oxford, Oxford University Press, 1963.

Ascher, Nicholas. Review of Crispin Wright, *Realism: Meaning and Truth, The Philosophical Review*, 100 (1991), pp. 107–9.

Ayer, A. J. *Language, Truth and Logic*, 2nd edn, London, Victor Gollancz, 1946.

Baker, G. P. 'Criteria: a New Foundation for Semantics', *Ratio*, 16 (1974), pp. 156–89.

—— 'Defeasibility and Meaning' in P. M. S. Hacker and J. Raz (eds), *Law, Morality and Society*, Oxford, Oxford University Press, 1977, pp. 26–57.

Baker, G. P. and Hacker, P. M. S. *Language, Sense and Nonsense*, Oxford, Blackwell, 1984.

—— *Scepticism, Rules and Language*, Oxford, Blackwell, 1984.

—— *Wittgenstein: Rules, Grammar and Necessity*, Oxford, Blackwell, 1985.

Bar-Hillel, Y. (ed.) *Proceedings of the 1964 International Congress for Logic, Methodology, and Philosophy of Science*, Amsterdam, North-Holland, 1965.

Beeson, M. J. 'Problematic Principles in Constructive Mathematics' in D. van Dalen, D. Lascar, and J. Smiley (eds), *Logic Colloquium '80*, pp. 11–55.

Benacerraf, Paul. 'Tasks, Supertasks, and the Modern Eleatics', *Journal of Philosophy*, 59 (1962), pp. 765–84.

—— 'What Numbers Could not Be', *Philosophical Review*, 74 (1965), pp. 47–73; reprinted in P. Benacerraf and H. Putnam (eds), *Philosophy of Mathematics*, second edition, pp. 272–94.

—— 'God, the Devil and Gödel', *The Monist*, 51 (1967), pp. 9–32.

—— 'Mathematical Truth', *Journal of Philosophy*' 70 (1973), pp. 661–80; reprinted in P. Benacerraf and H. Putnam (eds), *Philosophy of Mathematics*, second edition, pp. 403–20.

—— 'Skolem and the Skeptic', *The Aristotelian Society*, Suppl. Vol. LIX (1985), pp. 85–115.

Benacerraf, P. and Putnam, H. (eds) *Philosophy of Mathematics*, Englewood Cliffs, New Jersey, Prentice-Hall, 1964, second edition, Cambridge, Cambridge University Press, 1983.

Bernays, Paul. 'Sur le platonisme dans les mathematiques' *L'Enseignement Mathematique*, 34 (1935), pp. 52–69; English translation in P. Benacerraf and H. Putnam (eds), *Philosophy of Mathematics*, second edition, pp. 258–71.

Bertolet, Rod. 'Realism Without Truth', *Analysis*, 48 (1988), pp. 195–8.

—— Critical Study of Michael Devitt, *Realism and Truth, Dialectica*, 42 (1988), pp. 59–71.

Beth, E. W. *Foundations of Mathematics*, Amsterdam, North-Holland, 1968.

Blackburn, Simon. 'Moral Realism' in J. Casey (ed.), *Morality and Moral Reasoning*, pp. 101–24.

—— (ed.) *Meaning, Reference and Necessity*, Cambridge, Cambridge University Press, 1975.

—— 'Reply: Rule-Following and Moral Realism' in S. H. Holtzman and C. M. Leich (eds), *Wittgenstein: to Follow a Rule*, pp. 163–87.

—— 'The Individual Strikes Back', *Synthese*, 58 (1984), pp. 281–301.

—— *Spreading the Word*, Oxford, Oxford University Press, 1984.

—— 'Errors and the Phenomenology of Value' in T. Honderich (ed.), *Morality and Objectivity*, pp. 1–22.

—— Review of Crispin Wright, *Realism, Meaning and Truth, Times Literary Supplement*, 27 February 1987.

—— 'Attitudes and Contents', *Ethics*, 98 (1988), pp. 501–17.

—— 'Manifesting Realism', *Midwest Studies in Philosophy*, 14 (1989), Notre Dame, University of Notre Dame Press, pp. 29–47.

—— 'Realism: Quasi or Queasy?', in J. Haldane and C. Wright (eds), *Reality: Representation and Projection*, forthcoming.

Block, I. (ed.) *Perspectives on the Philosophy of Wittgenstein*, Oxford, Blackwell, 1982.

Boolos, G. 'Nominalist Platonism', *Philosophical Review*, 94 (1985), pp. 327–44.

—— 'Introductory Note to #1951', in Kurt Gödel, *Collected Works*, vol. III, edited by Solomon Feferman et al., New York, Oxford University Press, 1993.

Brandom, R. 'Truth and Assertibility', *Journal of Philosophy*, 83 (1976), pp. 137–49.

Brown, R. and Watling, J. 'Amending the Verification Principle', *Analysis*, 2 (1951), pp. 87–9.

Brouwer, L. E. J. *Collected Works*, Vol. 1, ed. by A. Heyting, Amsterdam, North-Holland, 1975.

—— *Brouwer's Cambridge Lectures*, ed. by D. van Dalen, Cambridge, Cambridge University Press, 1981.

Brueckner, A. L. 'Putnam's Model-Theoretic Argument Against Metaphysical Realism', *Analysis*, 44 (1984), pp. 134–40.

—— 'The Failure of an *A Priori* Argument for Realism', *Philosophical Quarterly*, 34 (1984), pp. 491–8.

Budd, M. 'Wittgenstein on Meaning, Interpretation and Rules', *Synthese*, 58 (1984), pp. 303–23.

Bunge, M. (ed.) *The Critical Approach to Science and Philosophy*, New York, Free Press, 1964.

Burgess, J. 'Dummett's Case for Intuitionism', *History and Philosophy of Logic*, 5 (1984), pp. 177–94.

Butler, Joseph. 'On Personal Identity', first appendix in J. Butler, *The Analogy of Religion*, 1736; reprinted in J. Perry (ed.), *Personal Identity*, pp. 99–105.

Butler, R. J. (ed.) *Analytical Philosophy, Second Series*, Oxford, Blackwell, 1965.

Butterfield, J. (ed.) *Language, Mind and Logic*, Cambridge, Cambridge University Press, 1986.

Campbell, J. 'Knowledge and Understanding', *Philosophical Quarterly*, 32 (1982), pp. 17–34.

—— 'Possession of Concepts', *Proceedings of the Aristotelian Society*, LXXXV (1985), pp. 149–70.

Carruthers, P. 'Frege's Regress', *Proceedings of the Aristotelian Society*, LXXXII (1982), pp. 17–32.

—— 'Ruling Out Realism', *Philosophia*, 15 (1985), pp. 61–78.

Casey, J. (ed.) *Morality and Moral Reasoning*, London, Methuen, 1971.

Cassam, Quassim. Review of Crispin Wright, *Realism: Meaning and Truth, Philosophical Books*, 30 (1989), pp. 10–16.

Chihara, C. F. 'On the Possibility of Completing an Infinite Process', *Philosophical Review*, 74 (1965), pp. 74–87.

—— 'The Wright-Wing Defence of Wittgenstein's Philosophy of Logic', *Philosophical Review*, 91 (1982), pp. 99–108.

Chihara, C. F. and Fodor, J. A. 'Operationism and Ordinary Language: a Critique of Wittgenstein', *American Philosophical Quarterly*, 2 (1965), pp. 281–95.

Church, A. Review of *Language, Truth and Logic*, 2nd edn, *Journal of Symbolic Logic*, 14 (1949), pp. 52–3.

Clark, A. J. 'Anti-Realism and Recognitional Capacities', *Philosophical Quarterly*, 35 (1985), pp. 171–78.

Clark, Andy. 'Meaning, Publicity and Epistemology', *Theoria*, 53 (1987), pp. 19–30.

Clark, P. J. and Read, S. L. 'Hypertasks', *Synthese*, 61 (1984), pp. 387–90.

Cockburn, David. 'The Problem of the Past', *The Philosophical Quarterly*, 37 (1987), pp. 54–77.

Cohen, L.J. 'Is a Criterion of Verifiability Possible?', in P. French, T. Uehling and H. Wettstein (eds), *Midwest Studies in Philosophy V* (1980), Minneapolis, University of Minnesota Press, pp. 347–52.

Cohen, R. S. and Wartofsky, M. W. (eds) *Language, Logic, and Method*, Dordrecht, Reidel, 1983.

Collin, Finn. *Theory and Understanding*, Oxford, Blackwell, 1985.

Craig, E. J. 'Phenomenal Geometry', *British Journal for the Philosophy of Science*, 20 (1969), pp. 121–34.

—— 'Meaning, Use and Privacy', *Mind*, 91 (1982), pp. 541–64.

—— 'Privacy and Rule-Following', in J. Butterfield (ed.), *Language, Mind and Logic*, pp. 169–86.

Currie, G. and Eggenberger, P. 'Knowledge and Meaning', *Nous*, 17 (1983), pp. 267–79.

Dale, A. J. 'Hempel Revisited', *Analysis*, 44 (1984), pp. 90–2.

van Dalen, D., Lascar, D., and Smiley, J. (eds) *Logic Colloquium '80*, Amsterdam, North-Holland, 1982.

van Dantzig, D. 'Is $10^{10^{10}}$ a Finite Number?', *Dialectica*, 10 (1956), pp. 273–77.

Dauer, F. W. 'Empirical Realists and Wittgensteinians', *Journal of Philosophy*, 69 (1972), pp. 128–47.

Davidson, Donald. 'Theories of Meaning and Learnable Languages' in Y. Bar-Hillel (ed.), *Proceedings of the 1964 International Congress for Logic, Methodology, and Philosophy of Science*, pp. 383–94; reprinted in D. Davidson, *Inquiries into Truth and Interpretation*, pp. 3–15.

—— 'Truth and Meaning', *Synthese*, 17 (1967), pp. 304–23; reprinted in J. W. Davis, D. J. Hockney and W. K. Wilson (eds), *Philosophical Logic*, pp. 1–20; and in D. Davidson, *Inquiries into Truth and Interpretation*, pp. 17–36.

—— 'True to the Facts', *Journal of Philosophy*, 66 (1969), pp. 748–64; reprinted in D. Davidson, *Inquiries into Truth and Interpretation*, pp. 37–54.

—— 'Semantics for Natural Languages', *Linguaggi Nella Società e Tecnica*, Milan, Edizioni di Communità, 1970, pp. 177–88; reprinted in D. Davidson, *Inquiries into Truth and Interpretation*, pp. 55–64.

—— 'Radical Interpretation', *Dialectica*, 27 (1973), pp. 313–28; reprinted in D. Davidson, *Inquiries into Truth and Interpretation*, pp. 125–39.

—— 'On the Very Idea of a Conceptual Scheme', *Proceedings and Addresses of the American Philosophical Association*, XLII (1974), pp. 5–20; reprinted in D. Davidson, *Inquiries into Truth and Interpretation*, pp. 184–98.

—— 'Thought and Talk' in S. Guttenplan (ed.), *Mind and Language*, pp. 7–23; reprinted in D. Davidson, *Inquiries into Truth and Interpretation*, pp. 155–70.

—— 'The Method of Truth in Metaphysics' in P. A. French, T. E. Uehling, Jr., and H. K. Wettstein (eds), *Contemporary Perspectives in the Philosophy of Language*, pp. 294–304; reprinted in D. Davidson, *Inquiries into Truth and Interpretation*, pp. 199–214.

—— 'Communication and Convention' in D. Davidson, *Inquiries into Truth and Interpretation*, pp. 265–80.

—— *Inquiries into Truth and Interpretation*, Oxford, Oxford University Press, 1984.

Davidson, D. and Harman, G. (eds), *Semantics of Natural language*, Dordrecht, Reidel, 1972.

Davies, David. 'Horwich on "Semantic" and "Metaphysical" Realism', *Philosophy of Science*, 54 (1987), pp. 539–57.

Davies, David. 'How Not to Outsmart the Anti-Realist', *Analysis*, 47 (1987), pp. 1–8.

Davies, Martin. *Meaning, Quantification, Necessity*, London, Routledge and Kegan Paul, 1981.

—— 'Taylor on Meaning-Theories and Theories of Meaning', *Mind*, 93 (1984), pp. 85–90.

—— 'Tacit Knowledge, and the Structure of Thought and Language' in C. Travis (ed.), *Meaning and Interpretation*, pp. 127–58.

—— 'Tacit knowledge and Semantic Theory: Can a Five Per Cent Difference Matter?', *Mind*, 96 (1987), pp. 441–62.

Davis, J. W., Hockney, D. J., and Wilson, W. K. (eds), *Philosophical Logic*, Dordrecht, Reidel, 1969.

Devitt, Michael. 'Dummett's Anti-Realism', *Journal of Philosophy*, 80 (1983), pp. 73–99.

—— *Realism and Truth*, Oxford, Blackwell, 1984.

—— '"Realism Without Truth": A Response to Bertolet', *Analysis*, 48 (1988), pp. 198–203.

—— 'Aberrations of the Realism Debate', *Philosophical Studies*, 61 (1991), pp. 42–63.

Dummett, Michael. 'Truth', *Proceedings of the Aristotelian Society*, LIX (1959), pp. 141–62; reprinted in M. Dummett, *Truth and Other Enigmas*, pp. 1–24.

—— 'Wittgenstein's Philosophy of Mathematics', *Philosophical Review*, 68 (1959), pp. 324–48; reprinted in M. Dummett, *Truth and Other Enigmas*, pp. 166–85.

—— 'The Philosophical Significance of Gödel's Theorem', *Ratio*, 5 (1963), pp. 140–55; reprinted in M. Dummett, *Truth and Other Enigmas*, pp. 186–201.

—— 'The Reality of the Past', *Proceedings of the Aristotelian Society*, LXIX (1969), pp. 239–58; reprinted in M. Dummett, *Truth and Other Enigmas*, pp. 358–74.

—— 'The Justification of Deduction', Henriette Hertz Annual Philosophical Lecture, *Proceedings of the British Academy*, LIX (1973), pp. 3–34; reprinted in M. Dummett, *Truth and Other Enigmas*, pp. 290–318.

—— *Frege: Philosophy of Language*, London, Duckworth, 1973, second edition 1981.

—— 'What is a Theory of Meaning?' in S. Guttenplan (ed.), *Mind and Language*', pp. 97–138.

—— 'The Philosophical Basis of Intuitionistic Logic' in H. E. Rose and J. C. Shepherdson (eds), *Logic Colloquium 1973*, pp. 5–40; reprinted in M. Dummett, *Truth and Other Enigmas*, pp. 215–47.

—— 'Wang's Paradox', *Synthese*, 30 (1975), pp. 301–24; reprinted in M. Dummett, *Truth and Other Enigmas*, pp. 248–68.

—— 'What is a Theory of Meaning? (II)' in G. Evans and J. McDowell (eds), *Truth and Meaning*, pp. 67–137.

—— 'Is Logic Empirical?' in D. H. Lewis (ed.), *Contemporary British Philosophy*, fourth series, pp. 45–68.

—— *Elements of Intuitionism*, Oxford Logic Guides, Oxford, Oxford University Press, 1977.

—— *Truth and Other Enigmas*, London, Duckworth, 1978.

—— 'Realism' in M. Dummett, *Truth and Other Enigmas*, pp. 145–65.

—— 'Platonism' in M. Dummett, *Truth and Other Enigmas*, pp. 202–14.

—— 'Common Sense and Physics' in G. F. MacDonald (ed.), *Perception and Identity*, pp. 1–40; reply by A. J. Ayer, pp. 277–89 and 293–98.

—— 'What Does the Appeal to Use Do for the Theory of Meaning?' in A. Margalit (ed.), *Meaning and Use*, pp. 123–35.

—— 'Critical Notice on L. E. J. Brouwer: *Collected Works' Mind*, 89 (1980) pp. 605–16.

—— 'Comments on Professor Prawitz's Paper' in G. H. von Wright (ed.), *Logic and Philosophy*, pp. 11–18.

—— *The Interpretation of Frege's Philosphy*, London, Duckworth, 1981.

—— 'Realism', *Synthese*, 52 (1982), pp. 55–112.

—— 'Replies to Essays on Dummett', in B. Taylor (ed.), *Michael Dummett: Contributions to Philosophy*, pp. 219–330.

—— *The Logical Basis of Metaphysics*, Cambridge, Massachusetts, Harvard University Press, 1991.

Edgington, Dorothy. 'Meaning, Bivalence and Realism', *Proceedings of the Aristotelian Society*, LXXXI (1981), pp. 153–73.

—— 'The Paradox of Knowability', *Mind*, 94 (1985), pp. 557–68.

—— 'Verification and the Manifestation of Meaning', *The Aristotelian Society*, Suppl. Vol. LIX (1985), pp. 33–52.

Edwards, Jim. 'Atomic Realism, Intuitionist Logic and Tarskian Truth', *The Philosophical Quarterly*, 40 (1990), pp. 13–26.

Eldridge, Richard. 'Metaphysics and the Interpretation of Persons: Davidson on Thinking and Conceptual Systems', *Synthese*, 66 (1986), pp. 477–503.

Ellis, Brian. *Rational Belief Systems*, American Philosophical Quarterly Monograph, Oxford, Blackwell, 1979.

—— 'Internal Realism', *Synthese*, 76 (1988), pp. 409–34.

Evans, Gareth. 'Semantic Structure and Logical Form' in G. Evans and J. McDowell (eds), *Truth and Meaning*, pp. 199–222; reprinted in G. Evans, *Collected Papers*, pp. 49–75.

—— 'Reference and Contingency', *The Monist*, 62 (1979), pp. 161–89; reprinted in G. Evans, *Collected Papers*, pp. 178–213.

—— 'Reply: Semantic Theory and Tacit Knowledge' in S. H. Holtzman and C. M. Leich (eds), *Wittgenstein: to Follow a Rule*, pp. 118–37; reprinted in G. Evans, *Collected Papers*, pp. 322–42.

—— *Varieties of Reference*, ed. by J. McDowell, Oxford, Oxford University Press, 1982.

—— *Collected Papers*, Oxford, Oxford University Press, 1985.

Evans, G. and McDowell, J. (eds), *Truth and Meaning: Essays in Semantics*, Oxford, Oxford University Press, 1976.

Feyerabend, Paul. 'Realism and Instrumentalism' in M. Bunge (ed.), *The Critical Approach to Science and Philosophy*, pp. 280–308.

Field, Hartry, H. 'Quine and the Correspondence Theory', *Philosophical Review*, 83 (1974), pp. 200–28.

—— 'Logic, Meaning and Conceptual Role', *Journal of Philosophy*, 74 (1977), pp. 379–409.

—— *Science Without Numbers*, Oxford, Blackwell, 1980.

—— *Realism, Mathematics and Modality*, Oxford, Blackwell, 1989.

Fine, Kit. 'Vagueness, Truth and Logic', *Synthese*, 30 (1975), pp. 265–300.

Fitch, F. B. 'A Logical Analysis of Some Value Concepts', *Journal of Symbolic Logic*, 28 (1963), pp. 135–42.

Fogelin, R. 'Wittgenstein and Intuitionism', *American Philosophical Quarterly*, 5 (1968), pp. 267–74.

Foster, John. 'Meaning and Truth Theory' in G. Evans and J. McDowell (eds), *Truth and Meaning*, pp. 1–32.

—— *The Case for Idealism*, London, Routledge and Kegan Paul, 1982.

—— *A. J. Ayer*, in series edited by Ted Honderich, *The Arguments of the Philosophers*, London, Routledge and Kegan Paul, 1985.

van Fraassen, B. C. 'Presuppositions, Supervaluations, and Free Logic' in K. Lambert (ed.), *The Logical Way of Doing Things*, pp. 67–91.

—— 'To Save the Phenomena', *Journal of Philosophy*, 73 (1976), pp. 623–72.

—— *The Scientific Image*, Oxford, Oxford University Press, 1980.

French, P. A., Uehling, T. E., and Wettstein, H. K. (eds), *Contemporary Perspectives in the Philosophy of Language*, Minneapolis, University of Minnesota Press, 1979.

Fricker, Elizabeth. 'Semantic Structure and Speakers' Understanding', *Proceedings of the Aristotelian Society*, LXXXIII (1983), pp. 49–66.

Gandy, R. O. 'Limitations to Mathematical Knowledge' in D. van Dalen, D. Lascar, and J. Smiley (eds), *Logic Colloquium '80*, pp. 129–46.

Gentzen, Gerhard. *The Collected Papers of Gerhard Gentzen*, edited by M. Szabo, Amsterdam, North-Holland, 1969.

George, Alexander. 'Reply to Weir on Dummett and Intuitionism', *Mind*, 76 (1987), pp. 404–6.

—— 'Intuitionism, Excluded Middle and Decidability: A Response to Weir on Dummett', *Mind*, 97 (1988), pp. 597–602.

Glymour, Clark, 'Conceptual Scheming, or, Confessions of a Metaphysical Realist', *Synthese*, 51 (1982), pp. 169–80.

Gödel, Kurt. 'What is Cantor's Continuum Problem?', *American Mathematical Monthly*, 54 (1947), pp. 515–25; reprinted in P. Benacerraf and H. Putnam (eds), *Philosophy of Mathematics*, second edition, pp. 470–85.

—— 1951 Josiah Willard Gibbs Lecture, delivered to the American Mathematical Society, first printed in Kurt Gödel, *Collected Works*, vol. III, edited by Solomon Feferman et al., New York, Oxford University Press, 1993.

Goldfarb, W. 'Kripke on Wittgenstein and Rules', *Journal of Philosophy*, 82 (1985), pp. 471–88.

Goldman, Alan. 'Fanciful Arguments for Realism', *Mind*, 93 (1984), pp. 19–38.

Goldstein, I. 'Communication and Mental Events', *American Philosophical Quarterly*, 22 (1985), pp. 331–38.

Goodman, Nelson. *Ways of Worldmaking*, Sussex, Harvester Press, 1978.

Grayling, A. C. *An Introduction to Philosophical Logic*, Sussex, Harvester Press, 1982.

Green, Karen. 'Dummett's Ought from Is', *Dialectica*, 45 (1991), pp. 67–82.

Grünbaum, A. 'Can an Infinitude of Operations be Performed in a Finite Time' in A. Grünbaum, *Philosophical Problems of Space and Time*, second edition

(Boston Studies in the Philosophy of Science, XII), Dordrecht, Reidel, pp. 630–45 and 849–51.

Guttenplan, S. (ed.), *Mind and Language*, Oxford, Oxford University Press, 1974.

—— 'Meaning and Metaphysics' in C. Travis (ed.), *Meaning and Interpretation*, pp. 177–200.

Haack, Susan, *Deviant Logic*, Cambridge, Cambridge University Press, 1974.

—— '"Alternative" in "Alternative Logic"' in S. Blackburn (ed.), *Meaning, Reference and Necessity*, pp. 32–55.

—— 'Is Truth Flat or Bumpy?' in D. H. Mellor (ed.), *Prospects for Pragmatism*, pp. 1–20.

—— 'Dummett's Justification of Deduction', *Mind*, 91 (1982), pp. 216–39.

—— 'Realism', *Synthese*, 73 (1987), pp. 275–99.

Hacker, P. M. S. *Insight and Illusion*, Oxford, Oxford University Press, 1972.

Hacker, P. M. S. and Raz, J. (eds), *Law, Morality and Society*, Oxford, Oxford University Press, 1977.

Haldane, John and Wright, Crispin (eds), *Reality, Representation and Projection*, New York, Oxford University Press, forthcoming.

Hale, Bob. 'The Compleat Projectivist', *The Philosophical Quarterly*, 36 (1986), pp. 65–84.

—— 'Can There Be a Logic of Attitudes?', in J. Haldane and C. Wright (eds), *Reality, Representation and Projection*, forthcoming.

Hand, Michael. 'Anti-Realism and Holes in the World', *Philosophy*, 65 (1990), pp. 218–24.

Hare, R. M. 'Ontology in Ethics' in T. Honderich (ed.), *Morality and Objectivity*, pp. 39–53.

Harman, Gilbert. *The Nature of Morality: An Introduction to Ethics*, Oxford, Oxford University Press, 1977.

Hart, W. D. 'The Epistemology of Abstract Objects: Access and Inference', *The Aristotelian Society*, Suppl. Vol. LIII (1979), pp. 152–65.

Hart, W. D. and McGinn, C. 'Knowledge and Necessity', *Journal of Philosophical Logic*, 5 (1976), pp. 205–8.

Hazen, A. 'McGinn's Reply to Wright's Reply to Benacerraf', *Analysis*, 45 (1985), pp. 59–61.

Heal, Jane. 'On the Phrase "Theory of Meaning"', *Mind*, 87 (1978), pp. 359–75; reprinted in D. L. Boyer, P. Grim, and T. Sanders (eds), *The Philosopher's Annual*, Vol. 2, 1979, pp. 111–27.

—— *Fact and Meaning*, Oxford, Blackwell, 1989.

Healey, R. *Reduction, Time, and Reality*, Cambridge, Cambridge University Press, 1981.

Heil, John. 'Recent work on Realism and Anti-Realism', *Philosophical Books*, 30 (1989), pp. 65–73.

Hempel, C. 'Problems and Changes in the Empiricist Criterion of Meaning', *Revue International de Philosophie*, 4 (1950), pp. 41–63.

Heyting, A. *Intuitionism*, Amsterdam, North-Holland, 1956, third revised edition 1971.

Holtzman, S. H. and Leich, C. M. (eds), *Wittgenstein: to Follow a Rule*, London, Routledge and Kegan Paul, 1981.

Hookway, C. and Pettit, P. (eds), *Action and Interpretation*, Cambridge, Cambridge University Press, 1978.
Honderich, T. (ed.), *Morality and Objectivity: A Tribute to J. L. Mackie*, London, Routledge and Kegan Paul, 1985.
Hopkins, James. 'Visual Geometry', *Philosophical Review*, 82 (1973), pp. 3–34.
—— 'Wittgenstein and Physicalism', *Proceedings of the Aristotelian Society*, LXXV (1975), pp. 121–46.
Horwich, P. 'Three Forms of Realism', *Synthese*, 51 (1982), pp. 181–201.
Hunter, Geoffrey. 'Dummett's Arguments About Numbers', *Proceedings of the Aristotelian Society*, LXXX (1980), pp. 115–26.
Jacob, Pierre. 'Is There a Path Half-way Between Realism and Verification?', *Synthese*, 73 (1987), pp. 531–47.
Jardine, N. ' "Realistic" Realism and the Progress of Science' in C. Hookway and P. Pettit (eds), *Action and Interpretation*, pp. 107–25.
Johnston, Mark. 'Objectivity Refigured: Pragmatism Without Verificationism', in J. Haldane and C. Wright (eds), *Reality: Representation and Projection*, forthcoming.
Kamp, Hans. 'The Paradox of the Heap' in U. Mönnich (ed.), *Aspects of Philosophical Logic*, pp. 225–77.
Kielkopf, C. F. *Strict Finitism*, The Hague and Paris, Mouton, 1970.
Kino, A., Myhill, J. and Vesley, R. E. (eds), *Intuitionism and Proof Theory*, Amsterdam, North-Holland, 1970.
Klagge, James C. 'Moral Realism and Dummett's Challenge', *Philosophy and Phenomenological Research*, 48 (1988), pp. 545–51.
Klenk, V. H. *Wittgenstein's Philosophy of Mathematics*, The Hague, Martinus Nijhoff, 1976.
Koethe, J. 'Putnam's Argument Against Realism', *Philosophical Review*, 88 (1979), pp. 92–99.
Kreisel, G. 'Wittgenstein's *Remarks on the Foundations of Mathematics*', *British Journal for the Philosophy of Science*, 9 (1959), pp. 135–58.
Kripke, S. A. 'Naming and Necessity' in D. Davidson and G. Harman (eds), *Semantics of Natural Language*, pp. 253–355 and pp. 763–69; reprinted as S. A. Kripke, *Naming and Necessity*, Oxford, Blackwell, 1980.
—— 'Wittgenstein on Rules and Private Language' in I. Block (ed.), *Perspectives on the Philosophy of Wittgenstein*, pp. 238–312; reprinted as S. A. Kripke, *Wittgenstein on Rules and Private Language*, Oxford, Blackwell, 1982.
Lambert, K. (ed.), *The Logical Way of Doing Things*, New Haven and London, Yale University Press, 1969.
Lear, Jonathan. 'Ethics, Mathematics and Relativism', *Mind*, 92 (1983), pp. 38–60.
Leeds, S. 'Theories of Reference and Truth', *Erkenntnis*, 13 (1978), pp. 111–29.
Lewis, D. H. (ed.), *Contemporary British Philosophy*, fourth series, Muirhead Library of Philosophy, London, George Allen and Unwin, 1976.
Lewis, David. *Convention: A Philosophical Study*, Cambridge, Massachusetts, Harvard University Press, 1969.
—— 'Statements Partly about Observation', *Philosophical Papers*, 17 (1988), pp. 1–31.

Loar, Brian. 'Truth Beyond All Verification', in B. Taylor (ed.), *Michael Dummett: Contributions to Philosophy*, pp. 81–116.

Lorenzen, P. and Schwemmer, O. *Konstruktive Logik, Ethnik und Wissenschaftstheorie*, Mannheim, Bibliographisches Institut Wissenschaftsverlag, 1973, second edition, 1975. (No English translation.)

Lovibond, Sabina. *Realism and Imagination in Ethics*, Oxford, Blackwell, 1983.

Lucas, J. R. 'Minds, Machines and Gödel', *Philosophy*, 36 (1963), pp. 112–37.

—— 'Mathematical Tennis', *Proceedings of the Aristotelian Society*, LXXXV (1985), pp. 63–72.

Luntley, Michael. 'The Real Anti-Realism and Other Bare Truths', *Erkenntnis*, 23 (1985), pp. 295–317.

—— *Language, Logic and Experience*, London, Duckworth, 1988.

—— 'Aberrations of a Sledgehammer: Reply to Devitt', *Philosophical Studies*, 62 (1991), pp. 315–23.

MacDonald, C. F. (ed.), *Perception and Identity: Essays Presented to A. J. Ayer, with Replies to Them*, London, Macmillan, 1979.

MacKinnon, D. M. 'Idealism and Realism: an Old Controversy Renewed', *Proceedings of the Aristotelian Society*, LXXVII (1977), pp. 1-14.

Margalit, A. (ed.) *Meaning and Use*, Dordrecht, Reidel, 1979.

Martin, J. N. 'Epistemic Semantics for Classical and Intuitionistic Logic', *Notre Dame Journal of Formal Logic*, 25 (1984), pp. 105-16.

McDowell, John. 'Truth Conditions, Bivalence and Verificationism' in G. Evans and J. McDowell (eds), *Truth and Meaning*, pp. 42-66.

—— 'On "The Reality of the Past"' in C. Hookway and P. Pettit (eds), *Action and Interpretation*, pp. 127-44.

—— 'Anti-Realism and the Epistemology of Understanding' in H. Parret and J. Bouveresse (eds), *Meaning and Understanding*, pp. 225-48.

—— 'Anti-Realism, Truth-Value Links, and Other Minds', paper read at the 1981 University of Keele Conference on the Philosophy of Language and Logic.

—— 'Meaning, Communication, and Knowledge' in Z. van Straaten (ed.), *Philosophical Subjects*, pp. 117-39. (cf. P. Strawson's reply pp. 282-87.)

—— 'Non-Cognitivism and Rule-Following' in S. H. Holtzman and C. M. Leich (eds), *Wittgenstein: to Follow a Rule*, pp. 141-62.

—— 'Criteria, Defeasibility, and Knowledge', Henriette Hertz Trust Annual Philosophical Lecture, *Proceedings of the British Academy*, LXVIII (1982), London, Oxford University Press, pp. 455-79.

—— 'Wittgenstein on Following a Rule', *Synthese*, 58 (1984), pp. 325-63.

—— 'Values and Secondary Qualities' in T. Honderich (ed.), *Morality and Objectivity*, pp. 110-29.

—— 'In Defence of Modesty', in B. Taylor (ed.), *Michael Dummett: Contributions to Philosophy*, pp. 59–80.

—— 'Mathematical Platonism and Dummettian Anti-Realism', *Dialectica*, 43 (1989), pp. 173–92.

McFee, G. 'On the Interpretation of Wittgenstein', *Mind*, 90 (1981), pp. 592–99.

McFetridge, I. G. 'Realism and Anti-Realism in an Historical Context', in J. Haldane and C. Wright (eds), *Reality: Representation and Projection*, forthcoming.

McGinn, Colin. An *A Priori* Argument for Realism', *Journal of Philosophy*, 76 (1979), pp. 113–33.

—— 'Truth and Use' in M. Platts (ed.), *Reference, Truth and Reality*, London, Routledge and Kegan Paul, 1980, pp. 19–40.

—— 'Modal Reality' in R. Healey (ed.), *Reduction, Time and Reality*, pp. 143-87.

—— 'Reply to Tennant', *Analysis*, 41 (1981), pp. 120–22.

—— 'The Structure of Content' in A. Woodfield (ed.), *Thought and Object*, pp. 207–58.

—— 'Realist Semantics and Content-Ascription', *Synthese*, 52 (1982), pp. 113–34.

—— 'Ideal Justification: Review of H. Putnam's *Realism and Reason*', *Times Literary Supplement*, November 25 (1983), p. 307.

—— *Wittgenstein on Meaning*, Oxford, Blackwell, 1984.

McGinn, Marie. 'Wright's Reply to Benacerraf', *Analysis*, 44 (1984), pp. 69–72.

Melchert, Norman. 'Metaphysical Realism and History', *Analysis*, 46 (1986), pp. 36–38.

Mellor, D. H. (ed.), *Prospects for Pragmatism*, Cambridge, Cambridge University Press, 1980.

—— *Real Time*, Cambridge, Cambridge University Press, 1981.

Merrill, G. H. 'The Model-Theoretic Argument Against Realism', *Philosophy of Science*, 47 (1980), pp. 69–81.

—— 'Three Forms of Realism', *American Philosophical Quarterly*, 17 (1980), pp. 229–35.

Millar, A. 'Truth and Understanding', *Mind*, 86 (1977), pp. 405–16.

Mönnich, Uwe (ed.) *Aspects of Philosophical Logic*, Dordrecht, Reidel, 1981.

Moore, A. W. 'Transcendental Idealism in Wittgenstein and Theories of Meaning', *Philosophical Quarterly*, 35 (1985), pp. 135–55.

Moore, G. E. 'Wittgensteins Lectures of 1930–33' in G. E. Moore, *Philosophical Papers*, London, George Allen and Unwin, 1959, pp. 252–324.

Mostowski, A. *Infinitistic Methods*, Warsaw and Oxford, Pergamon Press, 1961.

Newton-Smith, W. H. *The Rationality of Science*, London, Routledge and Kegan Paul, 1981.

Nidditch, P. 'A Defence of Ayer's Verifiability Principle against Church's Criticisms', *Mind*, 70 (1961), pp. 88–9.

Papineau, D. *Theory and Meaning*, Oxford, Oxford University Press, 1979.

Parikh, R. 'Existence and Feasibility in Arithmetic', *Journal of Symbolic Logic*, 36 (1971), pp. 494–508.

—— 'The Problem of Vague Predicates' in R. S. Cohen and M. W. Wartofsky (eds), *Language, Logic, and Method*, pp. 241–61.

Parret, H. and Bouveresse, J. (eds) *Meaning and Understanding*, Berlin and New York, Walter de Gruyter, 1981.

Peacocke, C. 'Truth Definitions and Actual Languages' in G. Evans and J. McDowell (eds), *Truth and Meaning*, pp. 162–88.

—— 'Necessity and Truth Theories', *Journal of Philosophical Logic*, 7 (1978), pp. 473–500.

—— *Holistic Explanation*, Oxford, Oxford University Press, 1979.

—— 'Causal Modalities and Realism' in M. Platts (ed.), *Reference, Truth and Reality*, pp. 41–68.

—— 'Are Vague Predicates Incoherent?' *Synthese*, 46 (1981), pp. 121–41.

—— 'Reply: Rule-Following: the Nature of Wittgenstein's Arguments' in S. H. Holtzman and C. M. Leich (eds), *Wittgenstein: to Follow a Rule*, pp. 72–95.
—— *Sense and Content*, Oxford, Oxford University Press, 1983.
—— 'Colour Predicates and Colour Experience', *Synthese*, 58 (1984), pp. 365–81.
—— *Thoughts: an Essay on Content*, Oxford, Blackwell, 1986.
—— 'Understanding Logical Constants: A Realist's Account', in *Proceedings of the British Academy*, LXXIII (1987), pp. 153–200.
—— 'The Limits of Intelligibility: A Post-Verificationist Proposal', *The Philosophical Review*, 97 (1988), pp. 463–96.
—— 'What Determines Truth-Conditions?', in P. Pettit and J. McDowell (eds), *Subject, Thought and Context*, pp. 181–207.
—— 'Proof and Truth', in J. Haldane and C. Wright (eds), *Reality, Representation and Projection*, forthcoming.
Pearce, D. and Rantala, V. 'Realism and Formal Semantics', *Synthese*, 52 (1982), pp. 39–53.
—— 'Realism and Reference: Some Comments on Putnam', *Synthese* 52 (1982), pp. 439–47.
Penrose, Roger. *The Emperor's New Mind*, New York, Oxford University Press, 1989 (Vintage paperback edition 1990).
Percival, Philip. 'Fitch and Intuitionistic Knowability', *Analysis*, 50 (1990), pp. 182–7.
—— 'Knowability, Actuality and the Metaphysics of Context-Dependence', *Australasian Journal of Philosophy*, 69 (1991), pp. 82–97.
Perry, J. (ed.), *Personal Identity*, Berkeley, Los Angeles and London, University of California Press, 1975.
Perry, T. *Moral Reasoning and Truth*, Oxford, Oxford University Press, 1976.
Pettit, Philip and McDowell, John (eds), *Subject, Thought and Context*, Oxford, Oxford University Press, 1986.
Pitcher, G. (ed.), *Wittgenstein: The Philosophical Investigations*, New York, Macmillan, 1966 (London and Melbourne, 1968).
Plantinga, A. 'How to be an Anti-Realist', *Proceedings and Addresses of the American Philosophical Association*, LXVI (1982), pp. 47–70.
Platts, Mark. *Ways of Meaning*, London, Routledge and Kegan Paul, 1979.
—— (ed.), *Reference, Truth and Reality*, London, Routledge and Kegan Paul, 1980.
Pokriefka, M. L. 'Ayer's Definition of Empirical Significance Revisited', *Analysis*, 43 (1983), pp. 166–70.
—— 'More on Empirical Significance', *Analysis*, 44 (1984), pp. 92–3.
Popper, K. R. *Conjectures and Refutations*, London, Routledge and Kegan Paul, 1963.
Prawitz, Dag. 'Meaning and Proofs: on the Conflict Between Classical and Intuitionistic Logic', *Theoria*, 43 (1977), pp. 2–40.
—— 'Some Remarks on Verificationistic Theories of Meaning', *Synthese*, 73 (1987), pp. 471–7.
—— 'Dummett on a Theory of Meaning and its Impact on Logic', in B. Taylor (ed.), *Michael Dummett: Contributions to Philosophy*, pp. 117–65.

—— 'Intuitionistic Logic: a Philosophical Challenge' in G. H. von Wright (ed.), *Logic and Philosophy*, pp. 1–10.

Price, Huw. 'Sense, Assertion, Dummett and Denial', *Mind*, 92 (1983), pp. 161–73.

—— *Facts and the Function of Truth*, Oxford, Blackwell, 1988.

—— 'Why "Not"?', *Mind*, 99 (1990), pp. 221–38.

Putnam, H. 'Brains and Behaviour' in R. J. Butler (ed.), *Analytical Philosophy*, second series, pp. 1–19.

—— *Philosophical Papers 1: Mathematics, Matter and Method*, Cambridge, Cambridge University Press, 1975.

—— *Philosophical Papers 2: Mind, Language and Reality*, Cambridge, Cambridge University Press, 1975.

—— 'Brains and Behavior', in *Philosophical Papers 2: Language, Mind and Reality*, Cambridge, Cambridge University Press, 1975, pp. 325–41.

—— 'Minds and Machines', in *Philosophical Papers 2: Mind, Language and Reality*, Cambridge, Cambridge University Press, 1975, pp. 362–85.

—— 'What is "Realism"?', *Proceedings of the Aristotelian Society*, LXXVI (1976), pp. 177–94.

—— 'Realism and Reason' in H. Putnam, *Meaning and the Moral Sciences*, London, Routledge and Kegan Paul, 1978, pp. 123–38.

—— 'Models and Reality', *Journal of Symbolic Logic*, 45 (1980), pp. 464–82; reprinted in H. Putnam, *Philosophical Papers 3: Realism and Reason*, pp. 1–24.

—— *Reason, Truth and History*, Cambridge, Cambridge University Press, 1981.

—— *Philosophical Papers 3: Realism and Reason*, Cambridge, Cambridge University Press, 1983.

—— 'A Quick Read is a Wrong Wright', *Analysis*, 45 (1985), p. 203.

Quine, W. V. O. 'Two Dogmas of Empiricism', *Philosophical Review*, 60 (1951), pp. 20–43; reprinted in W. V. O. Quine, *From a Logical Point of View*, pp. 20–46.

—— *From a Logical Point of View*, Cambridge, Massachusetts, Harvard University Press, 1953, second revised edition, 1961.

—— *Word and Object*, Cambridge, Massachusetts, M.I.T. Press, 1960.

—— 'Ontological Relativity' in W. V. O. Quine, *Ontological Relativity and Other Essays*, New York and London, Columbia University Press, 1969, pp. 26–68.

—— *Philosophy of Logic*, Englewood-Cliffs, New Jersey, Prentice-Hall, 1970.

—— 'Use and Its Place in Meaning' in A. Margalit (ed.), *Meaning and Use*, pp. 1–8; reprinted in W. V. O. Quine, *Theories and Things*, pp. 43–54.

—— 'What Price Bivalence?', *Journal of Philosophy*, 78 (1981), pp. 90–93.; revised reprint in W. V. O. Quine, *Theories and Things*, pp. 31–37.

—— *Theories and Things*, Cambridge, Massachusetts, Harvard University Press, 1981.

Rasmussen, S. A. 'Quasi-Realism and Mind-Dependence', *Philosophical Quarterly*, 35 (1985), pp. 185–91.

Rasmussen, S. A. and Ravnkilde, J. 'Realism and Logic', *Synthese*, 52 (1982), pp. 379–437.

Ravnkilde, J. *Quine's Indeterminacy Thesis and the Foundations of Semantics*, Doctoral Thesis submitted to the University of Copenhagen on 25 May, 1979, Copenhagen 1980.

Read, S. and Wright, C. 'Hairier than Putnam Thought', *Analysis*, 45 (1985), pp. 56–8.

Rorty, R. 'Wittgenstein, Privileged Access, and Incommunicability', *American Philosophical Quarterly*, 7 (1970), pp. 192–205.

—— 'Criteria and Necessity', *Nous*, 7 (1973), pp. 313–29.

—— *Philosophy and the Mirror of Nature*, Princeton, New Jersey, Princeton University Press, 1979.

Rose, H. E. and Shepherdson, J. C. (eds), *Logic Colloquium 1973*, Amsterdam, North-Holland, 1975.

Ross, Angus. 'Why Content Must be a Matter of Truth Conditions', *Philosophical Quarterly*, 39 (1989), pp. 257–75.

Sainsbury, R. M. 'Understanding and Theories of Meaning', *Proceedings of the Aristotelian Society*, LXXX (1980), pp. 127–44.

Sanford, D. H. 'Competing Semantics of Vagueness: Many Values Versus Super-Truth', *Synthese*, 33 (1976), pp. 195–210.

Schueler, G. F. 'Modus Ponens and Moral Realism', *Ethics*, 98 (1988), pp. 492–500.

Scruton, R. 'Truth-Conditions and Criteria', *The Aristotelian Society*, Suppl. Vol. L (1976), pp. 193–216.

Shapiro, S. 'Second-Order Languages and Mathematical Practice', *Journal of Symbolic Logic*, 50 (1985), pp. 714–42.

Sheffler, I. *The Anatomy of Inquiry*, New York, Knopf, 1963.

Sintonen, M. 'Realism and Understanding', *Synthese*, 52 (1982), pp. 347–78.

Skorupski, John. 'Relativity, Realism and Consensus', *Philosophy*, 60 (1985), pp. 341–58.

—— 'Anti-realism: Cognitive Role and Semantic Content', in J. Butterfield (ed.), *Language, Mind and Logic*, pp. 151–67.

—— 'Objectivity and Convergence', *Proceedings of the Aristotelian Society*, LXXXVI (1986), pp. 235–50.

—— Critical study of Crispin Wright, *Realism, Meaning and Truth, Philosophical Quarterly*, 38 (1988), pp. 500–25.

—— 'Anti-Realism, Inference and the Logical Constraints', in J. Haldane and C. Wright (eds), *Reality, Representation and Projection*, forthcoming.

Sluga, H. 'Crispin Wright on Wittgenstein', *Inquiry*, 25 (1982), pp. 115–38.

Smart, J. J C. 'Metaphysical Realism', *Analysis*, 42 (1982), pp. 1–3.

Smith, Peter. 'Smart's Argument for Realism', *Analysis*, 43 (1983), pp. 74–78.

—— Review of Crispin Wright, *Realism, Meaning and Truth, Philosophical Investigations*, 12 (1989), pp. 70–5.

Sochor, A. 'The Alternative Set Theory and Its Approach to Cantor's Set Theory', *Proceedings of the 2nd World Conference: Mathematics at the Service of Man*, 1982, pp. 63–84.

Stevenson, Leslie. 'Meaning, Assertion and Time', *Australasian Journal of Philosophy*, 66 (1988), pp. 13–25.

van Straaten, Zak. (ed.) *Philosophical Subjects: Essays Presented to P. F. Strawson*, Oxford, Oxford University Press, 1980.

Strawson, P. F. *Individuals*, London, Methuen, 1959.

—— 'Meaning and Truth', Inaugural Lecture at the University Press, Oxford University Press, 1969; reprinted in P. F. Strawson, *Logico-Linguistic Papers*, London, Methuen, pp. 170–89.

—— 'Scruton and Wright on Anti-Realism, Etc.', *Proceedings of the Aristotelian Society*, LXXVII (1977), pp. 15–22.

—— Review of Crispin Wright, *Realism, Meaning and Truth, Mind*, 96 (1987), pp. 415–18.

Sturgeon, Nicholas. 'Moral Explanations', in D. Copp and D. Zimmerman (eds), *Morality, Reason and Truth*, New Jersey, Rowman and Allanheld, 1985, pp. 49–78.

Taylor, B. 'On the Need for a Meaning-theory', *Mind*, 91 (1982), pp. 183–200.

—— 'The Truth in Realism', *Revue Internationale de Philosophie*, 41 (1987), pp. 45–63.

—— (ed.) *Michael Dummett: Contributions to Philosophy*, Dordrecht, Martinus Nijhoff, 1987.

Tennant, Neil. 'Truth, Meaning and Decidability', *Mind*, 86 (1977), pp. 368–87.

—— *Natural Logic*, Edinburgh, Edinburgh University Press 1978.

—— 'Language Games and Intuitionism', *Synthese*, 42 (1979), pp. 297–314.

—— 'Is This a Proof I See Before Me?', *Analysis*, 41 (1981), pp. 115–19.

—— 'Were Those Disproofs I Saw Before Me?', *Analysis*, 44 (1984), pp. 97–105.

—— 'Weir and Those Disproofs I Saw Before Me', *Analysis*, 45 (1985), pp. 208–12.

—— 'Holism, Molecularity and Truth', in B. Taylor (ed.), *Michael Dummett: Contributions to Philosophy*, pp. 31–58.

—— *Anti-realism and Logic*, Oxford, Oxford University Press, 1987.

Thomson, J. F. 'Tasks and Supertasks', *Analysis*, 15 (1954), pp. 1–13.

Travis, C. (ed.) *Meaning and Interpretation*, Oxford, Blackwell, 1986.

Tuomela, R. 'Putnam's Realisms', *Theoria*, 45 (1979), pp. 114–26.

Ullian, J. 'A Note on Sheffler on Nidditch', *Journal of Philosophy*, 10 (1965), pp. 274–5.

Vesey, G. (ed.), *Idealism: Past and Present*, Royal Institute of Philosophy Lecture Series, Vol. 13, Cambridge, Cambridge University Press, 1982.

Vopěnka, Petr. *Mathematics in Alternative Set Theory*, Leipzig, Teubner, 1979.

Walker, Ralph, C. S. *The Coherence Theory of Truth: Realism, Anti-Realism, Idealism*, London, Routledge, 1989.

Wang, Hao. 'Eighty Years of Foundational Studies', *Dialectica*, 12 (1958), pp. 469–97; reprinted in H. Wang, *A Survey of Mathematical Logic*, Peking, Peking Science Press, 1964, pp. 34–66.

—— *From Mathematics to Philosophy*, London, Routledge and Kegan Paul, 1974.

Ward, Andrew. 'A "Semantic Realist" Response to Dummett's Anti-Realism', *Philosophy and Phenomenological Research*, 48 (1988), pp. 553–5.

Weir, Alan. 'Truth Conditions and Truth Values, *Analysis*, 43 (1983), pp. 176–80.

—— 'Rejoinder to Tennant', *Analysis*, 45 (1985), pp. 68–72.

—— 'Dummett on Meaning and Classical Logic', *Mind*, 95 (1986), pp. 465–77.

—— 'Realism and Behaviourism', *Dialectica*, 40 (1986), pp. 167–200.

—— 'Rejoinder to George', *Mind*, 97 (1988), pp. 110–12.

Weisberger, Andrea M. 'Haack on Dummett: A Note', *Philosophical Studies*, 55 (1989), pp. 337–43.

Wiggins, David. 'Truth, Invention, and the Meaning of Life', Henriette Hertz Trust Annual Philosophical Lecture, *Proceedings of the British Academy*, LXII (1976), pp. 331-78.

—— 'Truth and Interpretation' in *Language, Logic and Philosophy*, Proceedings of the International Wittgenstein Symposium held at Kirchberg-am-Wechsel, Austria, 1979, pp. 36–49.

—— 'What Would be a Substantial Theory of Truth?' in Z. van Straaten (ed.), *Philosophical Subjects*, pp. 189-221.

—— *Needs, Values, Truth*, Blackwell, 1987.

Williams, Bernard. 'Wittgenstein and Idealism' in *Royal Institute of Philosophy Lectures VII: Understanding Wittgenstein*, London and Basingstoke, Macmillan, 1974, pp. 76–95.

Williamson, T. 'Intuitionism Disproved?', *Analysis*, 42 (1982), pp. 203–7.

—— 'Realism and the Burden of Proof', *Irish Philosophical Journal*, 3 (1986), pp. 42–57.

—— 'On Knowledge and the Unknowable', *Analysis*, 47 (1987), pp. 154–8.

—— 'On the Paradox of Knowability', *Mind*, 96 (1987), pp. 256–61.

—— 'Bivalence and Subjunctive Conditionals', *Synthese*, 75 (1988), pp. 405–21.

—— 'Knowability and Constructivism', *Philosophical Quarterly*, 38 (1988), pp. 422–32.

—— 'On Intuitionistic Modal Epistemic Logic', *Journal of Philosophical Logic*, 21 (1992), pp. 63–89.

Wittgenstein, Ludwig. *The Blue and Brown Books*, Oxford, Blackwell, 1958, second edition 1969.

—— *Remarks on the Foundations of Mathematics*, dual-language edition, Oxford, Blackwell, 1956, third revised edition, 1978.

—— *Philosophical Investigations*, dual-language edition, Oxford, Blackwell, 1953, second edition 1958.

—— *Zettel*, dual-language edition, Oxford, Blackwell, 1967, second edition, 1981.

—— *On Certainty*, dual-language edition, Oxford, Blackwell, 1969.

Woodfield, A. *Thought and Object*, Oxford, Oxford University Press, 1982.

Woods, Michael. 'Existence and Tense' in G. Evans and J. McDowell (eds), *Truth and Meaning*, pp. 248-62.

Worrall, J. 'Scientific Realism and Scientific Change', *Philosophical Quarterly*, 32 (1982), pp. 201–31.

Wright, Crispin. 'On the Coherence of Vague Predicates', *Synthese*, 30 (1975), pp. 325-65.

—— 'Language-Mastery and the Sorites Paradox' in G. Evans and J. McDowell (eds), *Truth and Meaning*, pp. 223-47.

—— *Wittgenstein on the Foundations of Mathematics*, London, Duckworth, 1980.

—— 'Rule-Following, Objectivity and the Theory of Meaning' in S. H. Holtzman and C. M. Leich (eds), *Wittgenstein: To Follow a Rule*, pp. 99–117.

—— *Frege's Conception of Numbers as Objects*, Aberdeen, Aberdeen University Press, 1983.
—— 'Kripke's Account of the Argument against Private Language', *Journal of Philosophy* 81 (1984), pp. 759–78.
—— 'Understanding Novel Utterances', *Times Literary Supplement*, 11 January, 1985.
—— 'Skolem and the Skeptic', *The Aristotelian Society*, Suppl. Vol. LIX (1985), pp. 117–37.
—— 'Rule-following, Meaning and Constructivism' in C. Travis (ed.), *Meaning and Interpretation*, pp. 271–97.
—— 'Inventing Logical Necessity' in F. Butterfield (ed.), *Language, Mind and Logic*, pp. 187–209.
—— 'Facts and Certainty', *Proceedings of the British Academy*, LXXI (1985), pp. 429–72.
—— 'Realism, Anti-realism, Irrealism, Quasi-realism', *Midwest Studies in Philosophy*, 12 (1987), Minneapolis, University of Minnesota Press, pp. 29–47.
—— *Truth and Objectivity*, Cambridge, Massachusetts, Harvard University Press, 1992.
—— 'Anti-realism: The Contemporary Debate – W(h)ither Now?', in J. Haldane and C. Wright (eds), *Reality, Representation and Projection*, forthcoming.
Wright, John. 'Realism, Verificationism and Underdetermination', *Southern Journal of Philosophy*, 23 (1985), pp. 503–29.
von Wright G. H. (ed.), *Logic and Philosophy*, The Hague, Boston, and London, Martinus Nijhoff, 1980.
Yessenin-Volpin, A. S. 'Le programme ultra-intuitioniste des fondements des mathématiques' in A. Mostowski (ed.), *Infinitistic Methods*, pp. 201–23.
—— 'The Ultra-Intuitionistic Criticism and the Anti-Traditional Program for the Foundations of Mathematics' in A. Kino, J. Myhill, and R. E. Vesley (eds), *Intuitionism and Proof Theory*, pp. 3–45.
Zadeh, L. A. 'Fuzzy Sets', *Information and Control*, 8 (1965) pp. 338–53.
Zahar, E. 'Why did Einstein's Programme Supersede Lorentz's?', *British Journal for the Philosophy of Science*, 24 (1973), pp. 95–123, 233–62.

Index